Am-NA-c-86

Changing Canadian Cities

Changing Canadian Cities: The Next 25 Years

Leonard O. Gertler
and Ronald W. Crowley

with the assistance of Wayne K. Bond

McCLELLAND AND STEWART

in association with
the Ministry of State for Urban Affairs
and Publishing Centre, Supply and Services Canada

Copyright © Minister of Supply and Services Canada 1977
Reprinted 1979
Government Catalogue No. SU31-33/1976
All rights reserved

ISBN: 0-7710-3279-X

McClelland and Stewart Limited
The Canadian Publishers
25 Hollinger Road
Toronto Ontario
M4B 3G2

Printed and Bound in Canada.

TABLE OF CONTENTS

List of Tables 9
List of Figures 12
List of Maps 16
Acknowledgements 18
Introduction 20

CHAPTER 1 **Urban Canada: Demographic Perspectives** 35
The World Context of Canada's Urban Growth 35
Urban Growth in Canada 41
National and Provincial Population Growth:
  Components of Change 51
Urban Growth in Canada: Components
  of Change 66

CHAPTER 2 **Prospects for the Future** 83
Introduction 83
Projected Population to 2001 85
Some Issues Arising from the Projections 95

CHAPTER 3 **Growth Forces: National Pattern, Regional Diversity and the Urban System** 105
Canadian Economic Development and Regional
  Diversity 105
The Spatial Organization and Development of
  Canada's Urban Systems 121
Growth Forces within Systems of Cities 137

CHAPTER 4 **Alternative Urban Patterns: Some Regional Possibilities** 172
The Nation and the Region 172
A Strategy for Deconcentration: Regional Town
  Centres, Vancouver District 174
Saint John, New Brunswick—A Regional Growth
  Pole? 183
The Peace River Region: Prospects for Human
  Settlement 193
Policy Approaches 211

CHAPTER 5 **Urban Environment: The Quality Dynamic** 217
Environment, Settlement and Regional Diversity 217

	The Quality of Metropolitan Environments *235* The "Other Canada": Life in Canada's Resource Regions *250* Policy Approaches *260*
CHAPTER 6	**The Urban Surroundings** *267* Changing Town-Country Areas: Urban Fringe, Shadow and Field *267* The Natural Environment of the Urban Surroundings *271* The Urban Surroundings as a Production Environment *278* The Urban Surroundings as a Place to Live *282* Repercussions: Land and Social Issues *289* Policy Approaches *297*
CHAPTER 7	**The Urban Human Condition** *302* Residential Desirability: What Kind of Cities Do Canadians Prefer? *302* The City as a Moral Issue *308* The City in Literature *311* Inner City—Epitome of the Urban Experience *320* Policy Approaches *341* Perspective *342*
CHAPTER 8	**Forms of Urban Settlement: Towards the Open City** *347* What is "Settlement"? *347* The Form and Structure of Cities *348* Canadian Regions: Big, Small, and Intermediate *350* Shapers of Urban Form *353* The Open City Emerges *405* Policy Approaches *408*
CHAPTER 9	**Some Conclusions and Policy Notes** *415* Summary Perspectives *415* The Imagined Future *417* Strategies for the Imagined Future *425* Urban Settlement, Urban Policy and the Style of Governing *452*

Index 459
Credits 473

LIST OF TABLES

CHAPTER 1

1.1 Projections of Urban Growth in Major Regions of the World, 1960–85 *38*

1.2 Population of Urban Centres by Size Group, Canada, 1901–71 *49*

1.3 The Growth of Canada's Larger Cities, 1966–71 *50*

1.4 Components of Growth for the Canadian Population by Intercensal Interval, 1871–1971 *52*

1.5 Patterns of Fertility in Canada, 1871–1971 *55*

1.6 The Changing Age Structure of Canada's Population: Median Age and Dependency Ratios, 1901–71 *56*

1.7 The Changing Attributes of the Immigrant Flow into Canada, 1896 Onwards *59-60-61*

1.8 Factors Influencing the Characteristics of the Immigration to Canada *62-63*

1.9 Canada, Interprovincial and International Migration Flows, 1961–75 *65*

1.10 Streams of Internal Migration Among Urban and Rural Areas for Persons Aged Five and Over, 1956–61, 1966–71 *68-69-70*

1.11 Some Parameters of Canadian Urban Migration, Twenty-One Metropolitan Areas, 1966–71 *73*

1.12 The Changing Sex-Age Composition of Urban and Rural Canada *76*

CHAPTER 2

2.1 Canada – Selected Population Projections: Assumptions, Methodologies, Results *86-87*

2.2 Actual and Projected Population of Canada and the Provinces, 1971–2001 *89*

2.3 Actual and Projected Population for Metropolitan Areas, Canada, 1971–2001 *91*

2.4 Population of Canada's Metropolitan Areas by Size Group and Region, 1971–2001 *92*

2.5 Projected Household Increases as Compared with Population Increases, Canada's Metropolitan Areas, 1971–2001 *94*

2.6 Expansion of the Working Age Population (Aged 15–64) in Canada's Metropolitan Areas, 1971–2001 *96*

CHAPTER 3

3.1	Preference Scales as Measured by Volume of Flows Between Provinces	*113*
3.2	Average (Per Capita) Participation Income by Major Region Relative to the National Average, 1910–11 to 1970–71	*115*
3.3	Average Family Income and Family Income Distribution: Canada and the Provinces, 1971	*116*
3.4	Regional Disparities in Age Structure, Labour Force Participation and Unemployment Rates	*118*
3.5	Average Family Income by Urban Size Class and by Region as a Per Cent of the National Average, 1971	*119*
3.6	The Stability of the Canadian Urban System: The Rank of Selected Metropolitan Areas by Size of Population	*126*
3.7	Boundary Effects: Airline Passenger Flows, 1971	*130*
3.8	Canada's Urban System by Dominant Function: 1971 Labour Force Data	*134-135*
3.9	The Changing Occupational Structure of the Canadian Labour Force	*144*
3.10	Revenue and Assets Held by Canada's 150 Largest Corporations, 1971	*145*
3.11	Residence and Control of Dominant Directorship Positions, by Sector, 1972	*154*
3.12	Foreign Ownership of Manufacturing Firms by Selected Metropolitan Areas, 1970	*156*

CHAPTER 5

5.1	Eight Urban Regions – Broad Characteristics	*220*
5.2	Selected Urban Indicators, Social Development	*237*
5.3	Selected Urban Indicators, Economic Development	*238*
5.4	Selected Urban Indicators, Physical Development	*239*
5.5	Stages and Characteristics of Resource Town Development	*255*

CHAPTER 6

6.1	Distribution of Parcel Ownership by Ownership Type, 1968–74, Northeast Toronto Fringe	*292*
6.2	Selected Structural Characteristics of Land Development Firms Included in the Developer Study, Northeast Toronto Fringe, 1974	*294*

CHAPTER 7

7.1	Mean Socio-Economic Status (SES) Index by Distance from the Centre of Metropolitan Areas by Mile Zones, 1971 *321*
7.2	The Inner City: Dimensions of the Four Types *322-323*
7.3	Index of Socio-Economic Status and Juvenile Delinquency Rates, by Groups of Census Tracts, London, Ontario, 1965 *325*
7.4	Montreal Inner City – Stability and Decline, Hochelaga and Centre Sud: Similarities *331*
7.5	Montreal Inner City – Stability and Decline, Hochelaga and Centre Sud: Differences *331*

CHAPTER 8

8.1	Classification of Urban Forms by Scale, Canada *352*
8.2	National Housing Stock, by Type of Dwelling *357*

CHAPTER 9

9.1	Objectives, Strategies, Programs, by City Size Group *433*
9.2	Regional Development/Population Dispersal Policies *440*

LIST OF FIGURES

CHAPTER 1

1.1 Past and Projected Population Totals in Major Regions of the World, 1950–85 *39*
1.2 Per Cent of Population in Urban Canada, 1871–1971 *42*
1.3 Per Cent of Population in Urban Canada by Province, 1871–1971 *46*
1.4 Canada: Net International Migration, 1871–1971 *53*

CHAPTER 2

2.1 Anticipated Sources of Projected Population Increases: Canada's 22 Metropolitan Areas, 1971–81 *93*

CHAPTER 3

3.1 Inter-regional Commodity Flows in Canada *114*
3.2 The Geographical Distribution of Canadian Cities Along an East-West Axis *122*
3.3 The Geographical Distance of Canadian Cities from the United States Border *123*
3.4 The Canadian Urban Hierarchy as Determined by Air Passenger Traffic, 1971 *128*
3.5 The Broad Economic Structure of Canada's Metropolitan Areas, 1971 *132*
3.6 Density of Interlocks Between Corporate Sectors, 1972 *153*
3.7 The Composition of Foreign Investment in Canada, 1867–1970 *155*
3.8 Canada: Geographic Distribution of United States' Controlled Manufacturing – Hundred Mile Distance Bands from Toronto *158*
3.9 Urban Growth as a Circular and Cumulative Process *160*

CHAPTER 4

4.1 Illustrative Regional Town Centre Development Management Process, Vancouver *182*
4.2 Citizens' Views Regarding Population Growth in the Peace River District, Alberta *204*
4.3 Citizens' Views Regarding Environmental Quality in the Peace River District, Alberta *205*

CHAPTER 5

5.1	Vancouver – aerial view	*222*
5.2	Penticton – aerial view	*223*
5.3	Edmonton – aerial view	*225*
5.4	Regina – aerial view	*227*
5.5	Sudbury – aerial view	*228*
5.6	Hamilton – aerial view	*229*
5.7	Quebec City – aerial view	*232*
5.8	Saint John – aerial view	*233*
5.9	Voter Turnout: Percentage Voting in Municipal Elections, since 1969 *240*	
5.10	Public Library Usage: Annual per Capita Book Loans, 1971 *240*	
5.11	Number of Criminal Code Offences per 10,000 Population, 1971 *241*	
5.12	Number of Juveniles Charged with Criminal Code Offences per 10,000 Persons, 1971 *241*	
5.13	Number of Missing Persons per 10,000 Population, 1971 *242*	
5.14	Educational Level: Per Cent of 20–34 Age Group Not Presently in School and with Grade 10 Education or less, 1971 *242*	
5.15	Illegitimate Births, Number per 1,000 Births, 1973 *243*	
5.16	Average Income: Mean Income after Federal Tax, 1972 *243*	
5.17	Average Income: Adjusted for Federal Tax and Housing Costs, 1972 *244*	
5.18	Occupational Status Index: Proportion in Top Categories, 1971 *244*	
5.19	Unemployment Rate Among Active Labour Force Participants, 1971 *245*	
5.20	Female Labour Force Participation Rate for Age Group 20–64, 1971 *245*	
5.21	Annual Strike Days Lost per 100 in Labour Force, 1971 *246*	
5.22	Average Estimated Total Costs for New Single-Detached Housing Financed under NHA, 1974 *246*	
5.23	Housing Choice: Per Cent Apartment Units Vacant, 1974 *247*	
5.24	Percentage of Children Living in Apartments, 1971 *247*	
5.25	New Housing Units Constructed per Additional Household, 1970–73 *248*	

5.26   Fire and Automobile Hazard Index Adjusted for 1,000 Population, 1971   *248*

CHAPTER 6

6.1   Land in the Urban Fringe, a National Estimate, by City Size   *270*
6.2   Distribution of Urban Fringe Land, by Province   *271*
6.3   "Active" Land Use by Ownership Type, 1954 – 71, North Toronto Fringe   *291*

CHAPTER 7

7.1   Caging Effects, the Child in High-Rise   *340*

CHAPTER 8

8.1   Four Urban Forms   *348*
8.2   Form and Structure Co-ordinates   *349*
8.3   Population Growth Along the Trans-Canada Highway, 1911 – 71   *351*
8.4   Dwelling Starts, by Type of Unit, 1956 – 71   *358*
8.5   Apartment Building Completions by Size of Building, Selected Metropolitan Areas, 1970 and 1971   *358*
8.6a   North Vancouver   *369*
8.6b   Vancouver, Downtown Skyline   *370*
8.6c   Vancouver, Redevelopment   *370*
8.6d   Vancouver, Sun Tower   *371*
8.6e   Vancouver, Harbour   *371*
8.7a   Penticton, Houses Around Lake   *372*
8.7b   Penticton, Alpine Landscape   *373*
8.7c   Penticton, Main Street   *373*
8.8a   Edmonton, Downtown Skyline   *374*
8.8b   Edmonton, Recreation Space   *375*
8.8c   Edmonton, North Saskatchewan Valley, East Towards Petro-chemical Industry   *376*
8.8d   Edmonton, High-Level Bridge and University   *377*
8.9a   Regina, Saskatchewan Legislature   *378*
8.9b   Regina, Wascana Lake, Centre of the Arts   *379*
8.9c   Regina, Skyline   *379*
8.9d   Regina, Proposed Downtown Mall   *379*
8.10a Sudbury, View of the City, Water Tower   *380*
8.10b Sudbury, View of the City, Church Steeples   *381*
8.10c Sudbury, Urban-scape   *381*
8.10d Sudbury, Social Centre   *382*
8.10e Sudbury, City Hall   *382*

8.11a	Hamilton, Apartments Overlooking Niagara Escarpment *383*	
8.11b	Hamilton, Downtown and across Harbour to Burlington *384*	
8.11c	Hamilton, Downtown Street *385*	
8.12a	Quebec City, Historic Museum *386*	
8.12b	Quebec City, Steps to Lower Town *387*	
8.12c	Quebec City, Place Royale *388*	
8.12d	Quebec City, Basilica *388*	
8.12e	Quebec City, Old Town Square *389*	
8.12f	Quebec City, Harbour *390*	
8.12g	Quebec City, Dufferin Terrace *390*	
8.12h	Quebec City, Hotel on Grande-Allée *391*	
8.13a	Saint John, Champlain's Statue *393*	
8.13b	Saint John, Redevelopment *394*	
8.13c	Saint John, King Square and Cemetery *395*	
8.13d	Saint John, Market Hall, Interior *395*	
8.13e	Saint John, Skyline *396*	
8.14	Individual Systems *399*	
8.15	City and Group Systems *401*	
8.16	City Farming *406*	

CHAPTER 9

9.1	Elements of a Policy Process *427*
9.2	Actors in a Policy Process *430*

LIST OF MAPS

CHAPTER 1

1.1 Two Cartographic Faces of Canada: Its Land and Its People *44-45*

CHAPTER 3

3.1 The Evolving Geographic Pattern of Canada's Urban System, 1851–1951 *125*

CHAPTER 4

4.1 Growth Management Strategy: Lower Mainland, British Columbia *175*
4.2 Ratio of Jobs to Resident Workers in Sub-Regional Areas: Lower Mainland, British Columbia *177*
4.3 Transit and Regional Town Centres *180*
4.4 Planning Regions and Planning Districts in New Brunswick, 1974 *187*
4.5 Port Development: Saint John, New Brunswick *189*
4.6 Southern New Brunswick *191*
4.7 The Peace River Region in the Context of Western North America *194*
4.8 Watersheds of the Peace River Region *195*
4.9 The Disposition of Agricultural Land in the Peace River District, Alberta *196*
4.10 Recreational Facilities and Areas: Present and Prospective, Peace River District, Alberta *198*
4.11 Major Transportation Facilities of the Peace River–Liard: Peace River Regional Districts and the "South-Central Bowl" *200*
4.12 Summary of Structural Policy: Peace River Regional Plan, Alberta *209*

CHAPTER 5

5.1 The Canadian Ecumene *252*
5.2 Canadian Resource Towns *253*

CHAPTER 6

6.1 Distribution of Urban Centres and Good Farmland in Southern Quebec *272-273*

6.2	Distribution of Urban Centres and Good Farmland in Southern Ontario *274*	
6.3	Open Space Proposals, Greater Vancouver Regional District *277*	
6.4	Spatial Distribution of Agro-climatic Resource, Farmland and Urban Population in Southern Ontario and Quebec *280-281*	
6.5	Vancouver Region, Selected Fringe Features *284*	
6.6	Thunder Bay, Selected Fringe Features *286*	
6.7	Edmonton Region, County of Parkland, Country Residential Locations *288*	

CHAPTER 7

7.1	Calgary Response Group: Preference Patterns *304-305*
7.2	Halifax Response Group: Preference Patterns *306-307*
7.3	Socio-economic Status and Juvenile Delinquency, London, Ontario, 1965, by Census Tracts *324*
7.4	Montreal: Inner City Quartiers *330*
7.5	Study Area: Child in High-Rise, West Annex, Toronto *336*
7.6	Mental Map of Nine Year Old Girl, Low-Rise *337*
7.7	Mental Map of Nine Year Old Girl, High-Rise *338*

ACKNOWLEDGEMENTS

We are indebted to a number of people, who in a variety of ways, have made this book possible. Our wish to disinter, interpret and communicate the findings of policy research on urban issues, received encouragement at the Ministry of State for Urban Affairs — particularly from the then Secretary, Jim MacNeill, who posed a direct challenge, and from the administrator of external research, Jean Filion, who helped to launch the Ministry grant that supported this book project. Later, during the research and writing phase, John Stewart, and then David Belgue, of the Ministry's Policy and Research Wing sustained an active and most constructive liaison with the project. Peter Nicholson of the Canadian Participation Secretariat, Habitat, and Fred Schindeler, Director of Urban Institutions and Services, offered timely advice as Ministry reviewers of the manuscript. For his assistance sustained throughout the period of production we wish to thank Wayne Bond, Policy and Research Wing, who made a substantial contribution to the development of this book.

In addition to the numerous researchers on whose work we have drawn, three scholars at the Faculty of Environmental Studies, University of Waterloo, prepared background papers addressed specifically to some of the themes of the book: Larry Martin on land development; Richard Preston on alternative settlement forms; and Lorne Russwurm on the urban fringe in Canada. The substance of their work, which in each case was conceptually innovative, was greatly appreciated—as was their unsurpassed cooperation and critical interest in the project. In addition, a study was undertaken by the Montreal economist, Dian Cohen, on corporate decision-making and urban development. Ross Wilson, then a senior student in the Waterloo Man-Environment program, assembled the material which was the basis for the section on "The City in Literature." In this task, he received much help from Stan McMullin, of the English Department, University of Waterloo, who made available his extensive file on Canadian fiction and poetry. Among the many other people who generously provided information, we wish to single out Jim Simmons of the Geography Department, University of Toronto, who made available his freshly completed manuscript on *The Canadian Urban System*.

The drawings of city scenes, which appear in the book, are from the pen of Joseph Skvaril, Regina artist, architect and planner. The other illustrations, maps and figures, were produced by Gary Brannon and Norman Adam of the cartography unit, Environmental Studies, University of Waterloo.

Throughout the project the authors were assisted in the research aspects by three Master's students in the Waterloo graduate planning program: John Curry, who took a special interest in the land use issues of the urban-rural fringe; Brad Hodgins, who provided background on housing and inner city issues; and Angus Schaffenburg, whose contribution was mainly in the area of the institutional and process aspects of urban affairs. In addition, Mr. Schaffenburg assumed a general expediting role, helping to bring together the multitude of operations and details that go into the production of any complex book. Graduate assistance was also received from Harry Harker, Ph.D. candidate, who prepared a background paper on the Peace River region, and generally served as a resource person on the urban aspects of northern development.

The appointment of Harry Lash, planning consultant and former Director of Planning, Greater Vancouver Planning District, as external reviewer of the manuscript was a stroke of good luck. His stern and uncompromising critique was just the medicine we needed.

Finally, but not least, special thanks to Joanne Young who was the competent secretary of the project at its Waterloo base and to Claire O'Reilly and Mariette Lachance who performed with similar devotion at the Urban Affairs' Ministry; to Hélène Papineau, Urban Affairs Acting Chief of Publications and Editorial Services, who steered the publication gracefully through the inevitable reefs; to Peter McGuire, Claire O'Reilly and Wayne Bond who helped correct the final page proofs; and to Blair Bruce, of the Office of Research Administration, University of Waterloo, whose enlightened approach contributed to making this entire enterprise a pleasure.

Len Gertler
Ron Crowley
December, 1976.

INTRODUCTION

"A city is something more than a mass of buildings, housing, a crowd of human beings. We have defined it as an association of human beings who have a feeling that they constitute a community, and who have succeeded in translating this feeling into the terms of a practical corporate life. To call Megalopolis a city in this sense would be to beg the fateful question that has been raised by its advent. The question is whether the physical megalopolis can ever be made into a city in the social sense. During the last two centuries there has been a race between the proliferation of Megalopolis and the humanization of the conditions of life in it; and, so far, we do not know whether, in this grim race, it is brute matter or humanizing form that is going to come out the winner."

Arnold Toynbee in *Cities of Destiny*, 1967

The central issue that we address in this book is the increasing concentration of the Canadian population in a few large cities. This is a continuing process with far-reaching consequences for Canada's future. On the one hand, increasing urbanization has been associated with rising personal incomes, a full range of employment opportunities, a high intensity of social interaction, the provision of specialized services and the unfolding of a vibrant cultural life. On the other, urban expansion has appeared to exacerbate a whole array of social costs and environmental stresses—despoliation of the natural ecology, the envelopment of agricultural land, crowding, congestion, community instability, personal anomie and alienation. One interpretation suggests the bigger the city the better; the other, the bigger the worse. Further complicating the situation are the deep-rooted disparities in income and opportunity across Canada—disparities that are correlated with the national pattern of urban development.

This book is an overview aspiring to deal with salient urban issues, research insights and policy initiatives. First, there is an attempt to describe and analyse the forces that have shaped Canada's urban system on a national and regional basis, triggering it's growth, creating its distinctive patterns across the land,distributing its benefits and generating its stresses. Next, within the broad national context, various aspects of the local urban environment are studied, including the conflicting use of lands along the urban fringes, the diverse problems faced by inner city neighbourhoods, and the prospects for Canada's resource communities. To illustrate these issues, case studies of eight Canadian cities of distinctly different regional circumstances are used throughout. Finally, a synthesis of the direction in which we believe urban Canada should head is provided; "the imagined urban future" is set out together with policy alternatives. The approach then is to move from an identification of conditions, problems and trends to a definition of objectives, thence to a discussion of policy options.

An important secondary purpose of the book is to clarify, interpret and "translate" to the *non-specialist* the policy implications of the growing volume of urban research, initiated and/or sponsored by the Ministry of State for Urban Affairs.

A series of different styles and modes of presentation are employed in the book. Statistics are marshalled, scenarios drawn, subjective impressions offered, models described, figures projected and literary interpretations presented. Problems are identified and the need for action urged from a variety of perspectives – from that of the farmer on the urban fringe, the housewife in the suburbs, the resident in one of our resource towns, the child living in a big-city apartment, or the fisherman in a remote coastal village.

This diversity in presentation was prompted by several considerations. First, the study of urban Canada – the richness of experience, the complexity of forces, the depth of its problems and the intricacy of its fabric – could not be fully grasped if the manner of analysis and presentation were unidimensional. A second consideration was to reach a *wide audience* of people interested in urban affairs: political leaders, administrators, community and professional groups, teachers and students, and the interested general public, some of whom are impressed by statistical evidence, others of whom prefer more subjective material.

A brief resumé of each chapter now follows. The intent is not so much to summarize the content as it is to outline the key questions posed, point out the critical issues addressed and then hint at the findings obtained and the conclusions reached.

1. *Urban Canada: Demographic Perspectives*

Urbanization in Canada is considered in Chapter 1 – the historical patterns, the components of population growth, the root causes and the problems engendered. With regard to the natural increase and migratory movement of Canada's population, answers are sought to the questions: Who? How many? From where? To where? and, Why?

The population size, the age composition, the ethnic mix and the occupational structure of present-day towns and cities cannot be understood apart from regional and national demographic trends throughout Canada's history.

For example, the post-war "baby boom" swelled the ranks of the city and, for a time, increased the youthful dependent population. At the same time, progressively declining mortality rates have prompted a long-term ageing of city population. Meanwhile, periodic waves of heavy immigration, more and more from non-traditional sources, have created an ethnic mosaic in certain receiving cities.

Yet the real thrust of urbanization has derived in large measure from internal migration within Canada. Native Canadians and their immigrant counterparts have exhibited little inclination to remain permanently settled in one location. The seemingly inexorable growth of cities, especially the more populous and prosperous ones, has been fuelled by migration – from farmstead to urban neighbourhood, from sleepy town to bustling city, from Maritime outport to Ontario metropolis. Migrants have converged on the metropolis from rural areas, from smaller urban places, from other metropolitan areas, from out-of-province and from overseas (immigrants have demonstrated a proclivity for seeking the largest urban centres). They have come for many and diverse reasons: some driven by a lack of opportunity in the home area; others attracted by money and jobs at the destination; and still others to avail themselves of the diverse cultural pursuits that the metropolis can offer. They represent critical resources for the social and economic advancement of the city: youth, vigour, high education, professional and managerial status. But the migrants have heightened many problems in mushrooming metropolitan centres, by intensifying the demands for land, housing, transit and community services.

2. *Prospects For The Future*

Expanding upon the historical and contemporary perspective on Canada's urban population provided by Chapter 1, Chapter 2 speculates on the consequences of urban population growth anticipated in the future.

In the Canada of 2001 – how many people will there be? Where will they live? What will be the size of the labour force? Into how many households will the population be grouped? What proportion of the people will be of school age? of retirement age? Such questions form the focus of the second chapter, and answers are of immense importance to decision-makers. The change and the rate of change in the size, age composition and geographic distribution of the Canadian population can deepen regional disparities, aggravate unemployment, escalate the demand for housing, cause crowding in schools, tax the resources of health care units, and place strain on social security programs.

On the basis of expected rates of fertility, mortality and migration, the likely limits within which Canada's future population growth will occur are projected at national, provincial and metropolitan scales. The results point to urban growth of perhaps startling magnitude which must give Canadians cause to ponder the type of urban environment in which they wish to live. What are some of the issues?

Urban Size:	— How should the benefits of innovation specialization and consumer choice be balanced against the costs of density and congestion?
Urban Services:	— Can a network of interconnected centres allow for a range of specialized services while affording less stressful living conditions?
Urban Fabric and Institutions:	— Can neighbourhood government and functionally-mixed areas create community cohesiveness?
Energy:	— What settlement patterns, building types and technologies best conserve energy?
Land:	— How are the conflicting demands for land as building sites, an investment, an agricultural input, a recreational resource, and a natural habitat to be reconciled and regulated?
Regional Development:	— Given limited funds, what balance do development programs strike between areas that exhibit growth potential or places that have chronically lagged behind?

3. Growth Forces: National Pattern, Regional Diversity and the Urban System

The Canadian urban pattern is not something which has been imposed at random on the map – despite what first appearance may lead one to suspect. As documented in Chapter 3, the pattern reflects in a very real way the historical forces that have shaped our destiny. The evolution of the Canadian economy through a succession of staples—fish, furs, forests and farms—provided the pre-conditions for the transformation to a highly industrialized and urbanized nation. Equally important, however, were the institutional relationships resulting from the exploitation of staples. The sequence of staples development has been, it is suggested, largely manipulated through the control of capital and technology, to suit the major institutions – first the railways and land companies, and later the Bay Street financiers and multi-national corporations. The national policies of the federal government – high protective tariffs, the construction of railways linking East and West – profoundly affected the urban geography of the nation. Such national policies tended to sacrifice the interests of the hinterland to those of the economic heartland. Industrial advancement in Canada continues to be based on harmonious interaction between government and business, reflecting ties to powerful neighbours and partners. Today, however, the frontier of settlement is no longer one producing agricultural staples for Europe, but, rather a coterie of capital-intensive resource industries, producing raw materials mainly for the United States.

Among regions, economic disparities in income, employment and industrial structure are severe, complex in origin and naggingly persistent as Chapter 3 points out. Attention is drawn to the fundamental differences in economic structure between Canada's heartland and hinterland, as illustrated by patterns of commodity flows. Perhaps most startling, however, is the revelation that disparities in family income levels are more pronounced among cities of different size than among different regions. Hence, the extent of urbanization and the completeness of the regional urban system strongly influence the economic well-being of a region.

Another way of analysing Canada's urban and economic expansion is through the eyes of a systems theorist. From the systems perspective, the urban places of a region are viewed as tightly interconnected with one another by flows of managers and labourers, money and goods, ideas and information. This outlook suggests that the economic destinies of cities in a regional system are bound up with each other such that any significant change in economic activity, employment structure, population composition or income levels in one city will affect other cities in the system. Evidence on linkages among Canada's cities points to an identifiable Canadian urban system and illustrates some of its chief characteristics – its hierarchical nature, its independence and openness, its space-filling nature and its historical stability.

What is the range of variation in functions performed by Canadian cities? Are the economies of certain cities highly specialized while others are diversified? Does the type of work done in Canadian cities vary according to size and location? In pursuing answers to these questions the structure of economic activity emerges in Canada's urban system as one of stark contrasts between manufacturing specialization in the Windsor-Quebec City axis and orientation to transportation and distribution activities in the hinterlands; between capital-intensive industry in southern Ontario and labour-intensive production in southern Quebec; between agricultural service activity and resource-oriented manufacturing in Canada's hinterland.

Some questions are raised repeatedly by observers of the urban scene. How do cities grow? How do systems of cities evolve? Why do some cities grow while others decline? Does the spatial concentration of growth increase as control emanates from large corporations located in metropolitan areas? And most importantly, what are the policy implications and alternatives for influencing established patterns of urban size, structure, growth and prosperity?

Although the development of each city may follow a unique pathway, certain growth forces have affected all. Specialization of labour, rising industrial productivity, escalating technological change, almost instantaneous communications, the ascendancy of white collar occupations, and an increasing concentration of corporate power have formed the context within which urban growth has occurred. A potentially rich hinterland, initial advantage, economies of agglomeration, dynamic leadership from the enterpreneurial elite, and favourable investment decisions by "outside" corporations or government agencies have permitted certain cities to leap ahead.

As shown in Chapter 3, these growth forces affect Canada's urban system in a complex and cumulative manner. Hence, policies that do not pay heed to the nature of the urban growth process by operating at other than the level of the urban system will likely result in failure. And such has been the case. The history of public intervention into Canada's urban system has been marked by the best of intentions but plagued by inauspicious results.

4. *Alternative Urban Patterns: Some Regional Possibilities*

It has been suggested that the socio-economic circumstance of cities, the interlinkage of places in the regional and national network, and the broad patterns of urban settlement are strongly influenced by federal government policy: industrial incentives, transportation, housing, land and immigration. Nevertheless, in a country of stark regional contrasts such as Canada, dotted by places which are experiencing both the shocks of rapid growth as well as the trauma of stagnation, objectives and strategies that flow up from the regions have a legitimate role in provincial and national policy-making. It is in this spirit then that we turn in the fourth Chapter to the examination of three regional cases which represent different growth-related difficulties and different planned responses: one in the Vancouver district, one in Saint John, New Brunswick, and one in the Peace River region.

The Vancouver study describes the efforts to deconcentrate and restructure the runaway growth of a dynamic metropolis. A key feature of the growth management strategy is the nurturing of regional town centres which would serve to siphon off employment from the downtown to the outlying regions, thus effecting a more balanced employment pattern in suburban communities that otherwise would have remained predominantly dormitory in function. Intimately related is the concern for realigning the transportation system away from its overwhelming focus on downtown Vancouver toward the linking of outlying communities across the region. But planning strategies alone are not sufficient. Their implementation relies on broad co-ordination at the regional level and supportive action from other jurisdictions. The need for concerted action at all levels of government to attain fundamental metropolitan restructuring in the pursuit of enhanced livability is vividly demonstrated by the Vancouver case, and is applicable to all of Canada's major metropolitan areas.

The Saint John case illustrates the process of stimulating the change, renewal and sometimes orderly growth of slowly developing or stagnating places. The three-pronged development approach which seeks to create a regional growth centre stresses: (1) the improvement of the port; (2) the fostering of a metal working industrial complex; and (3) the renewal of the inner city infrastructure. The most significant aspect of the Saint John experience is the demonstration that co-ordinated public and private sector action can begin to surmount deep-seated problems. Also of importance is the way in which the Saint John strategy, with its principal manufacturing role, intermeshes with the broader development concepts for the Atlantic urban system.

To plan the resource frontiers of Canada, as exemplified by the Peace River case, is to seek ways to break the established mould of hinterland exploitation and to replace it with regional mechanisms for planning resource development and desirable social change. Unexploited resource development, shortages of investment capital, distance from the country's economically advanced areas and a paucity of community services are problems that plague the Peace River district. It is however, an area of outstanding natural and human resource potential. But the region will not throw off its shackles if development merely consists of tapping the storehouse of resources. Rather, as evidenced by the Peace River experience, the planning process must involve the rise of local institutions capable of giving sustained leadership on social, economic and ecological issues.

5. *Urban Environment: The Quality Dynamic*

An understanding of the forces fuelling demographic change and economic advance is essential for enlightened urban policy-making, but due accord must also be given to the other side of the equation: the environments of Canada's human settlements, the quality of those environments, and the quality of life that those environments accommodate. Urban environments are composed not only of air, water and soil, but also are seen to consist of a series of interacting elements, including life-support systems, landscape features, man-made structures, peoples' lifestyles and the various cultural institutions that are expressions of human values.

Three approaches to interpreting Canada's urban environment are offered in Chapter 5. The first is a broad integrated view, a *gestalt*, which pinpoints the salient elements of our urban regions – the factors that make an urban environment enjoyable or that harm it. What emerges is an image of places different from one another, shaped by distinctive geography and history, providing opportunities for different varieties of the "good life," but facing critical problems which must be overcome if their promise of a good life is to be fulfilled. In Vancouver, a scarcity of land is leading to inescapable choices between growing food or housing families. The attainment of an ecological balance between agricultural and recreational activity is the issue in Penticton. For Edmonton, the choice between metropolitan concentration and dispersal into new communities is an urgent reality. The alienated and depressed position of native peoples poses a dilemma in Regina. To achieve its potential as a diversified centre, air pollution must be overcome in Sudbury. The curbing of environmental degradation has to be the watchword in Hamilton. Though not without environmental problems, historical and cultural assets are the special "genus" of Quebec City. The development of service functions in a manner that complements the other Maritime regional centres is the task confronting Saint John. For all, the message is that government policy at municipal, provincial, and national levels should reinforce unique strengths while alleviating critical environmental difficulties.

A second view of Canada's urban environments presents a quantitative picture of metropolitan areas by means of comparing urban indicators – a new descriptive and evaluative tool that shows some promise. Most interesting were the findings that medium-sized cities exhibited strength on social development criteria while the larger places scored highly on economic measures.

The third view of urban environments draws attention to a characteristically Canadian feature of urbanization: the string of approximately 600 resource communities that stretch across the nation in the mid-Canada zone of resource exploitation. These towns are usually generated by metropolitan interests, both corporate and governmental; but as settlements, they represent the predicament of developing areas in Canada: social isolation and economic instability. Some of the difficulties inventoried for such places are limited vocational opportunities, rapid labour turnover, a lack of cultural facilities and an in-grown social sphere. Where do we go from here? Possibly the interlinkage of small communities in a regional network offers some hope for improving resource town environments.

6. *The Urban Surroundings*

The interaction of "town" and "country," the problems that interaction creates and the options available for improvement are the subjects for Chapter 6. The most critical 85,000 square miles in Canada is the land that surrounds urban places with 10,000 or more population. For this is the land that will bear the brunt of urbanization in the next quarter century and will serve many of the vital needs of Canadians: space for constructing communities, land for producing food, area for recreational pursuits, and access to ecological resources, from rare plant and wind shelter forests to major ground water storage areas. The urban surroundings are a natural resource and as a consequence an area where fundamental choices are evaded only at our peril.

Urban fringe lands are the subject not only of conflicts between resource use, but also of conflicts between people. Many groups of people are beginning to call these surroundings their home, including the advancing tide of urban dwellers, the clusters of exurbanites, weekend cottagers and hobby farmers, as well as the permanent tillers of the soil and other rural people who are engaged full-time in primary activity. The mixed occupation of the urban surroundings engenders contrasting and sometimes conflicting perspectives. The choices, the allocations, the trade-offs in resource use are inextricably bound up with patterns of thought and living. This human aspect poses the greatest opportunities as well as dilemmas to decision-makers.

The unfolding of land use and human settlement patterns on the urban fringe is inescapably an area of public policy and public concern. The Canadian quality of living in upcoming decades will be strongly affected by the way in which we manage the use of the urban fringe, both individually and collectively. Hence, policy-makers must consider difficult questions: Which areas are least costly to service for future urban development? In what areas must natural eco-systems be protected to ensure full functioning in the future? By what mechanism can prime arable lands be retained for food-producing? What institutions will ensure that farmers, ex-urbanites and cottagers better understand one another?

7. *The Urban Human Condition*

In Chapter 7, the urban human condition is viewed from four different vantage points. The first is based on perception: what images do we have of our Canadian cities? The second view is philosophical: what aspirations do we have for our Canadian cities? The third is literary: what aspects of urban life are reflected in creative literature? And the fourth is the perspective of policy research: what can we find out about urban conditions by the methods of scholarly investigation?

What kind of cities do Canadians prefer? The images, as reflected by the responses of high school students to a questionnaire, show that some consensus prevails. There are cities with highly favourable images: large and medium-sized metropolitan centres in Western Canada. And places with extremely negative images: centres of extractive and heavy industry in Ontario and Quebec. Perceptions of the "good city" also depend on where Canadians are looking from. Marked tendencies exist for (1) people to prefer their home city, (2) people from small towns to view small towns favourably, (3) francophones to prefer cities in Quebec province, (4) people from outlying regions to express their alienation from central Canada, and so on. These reported preferences provide one set of clues as to how one group of Canadians react to the urban environment.

Philosophically, it is suggested, the city may be regarded as a lifestyle, a "design for living," shaped by its institutions of work, leisure, education and family life. The pursuit of private interests or the attainment of shared social purposes is a major moral dilemma to be resolved in the "good city." The fundamental features of urban settlements — size, internal physical structuring, institutional traits, neighbourhood form — are each expressions of the balance that has been struck between the needs for individual freedom and the requirements of the larger community of societal interests.

The city in literature explores the continuum between values and attitudes, lifestyles and institutions, and bricks and mortar — the physical city. There is a tendency for the creative imagination to view the city in terms of its contradictions, its often precariously poised potential for good and evil. "Paradise lost" and "paradise regained" are recurring themes in Canada's urban literature.

Direct scholarly examination of conditions in Canadian cities, particularly the inner city, reveals the polarity of decline and renewal, of human despair and hope. Current investigation of residential areas in the inner city suggests that there are four basic types: neighbourhoods experiencing decline, stability, revitalization or massive redevelopment. Each represents a different set of problems, potentials and peoples' needs. In areas of decline, emphasis is given to the interlocking nature of physical and social problems related to poverty. In stable areas, attention is drawn to the continued existence of long established residential communities which, though not by any means affluent, have within themselves the personal and social resources for survival as attractive communities. Revitalizing areas are shown to be the "benefactors" of a family mobility cycle which will continue for some time to place such areas under pressure from new groups of people with different incomes and outlooks than the earlier blue collar inhabitants. And in those parts of the city where large-scale redevelopment is the rule, attention is drawn to the plight of children in a high-rise setting, as a symptom of the inhuman environments that have proliferated since the mid-fifties.

In sum, viewing the urban human condition from different perspectives reveals different facets of the urban experience, and thus contributes to the formulation of suitable policy alternatives.

8. *Forms of Urban Settlement: Towards the Open City*

Canadians must have a clear idea of the kind of city they should have, if they are to discover the right means for significantly improving their urban environment. Building upon previous discussions, we seek to answer certain fundamental questions in Chapter 8: What are the alternative forms and structures of urban settlement available? What are the forces shaping urban settlement form? What are the basic needs, as expressed through a range of lifestyles, which must be embraced in the concept of the "open" city? And finally, in terms of becoming an "open" city, what are the possibilities and limitations ingrained in the varying conditions of Canadian metropolitan and city regions?

The notions of urban form and structure can be associated with certain extremes—either toward dispersion or concentration in form or towards integration of urban structure on a total regional basis or integration only within the parts or sectors of urban regions. These dimensions determine the basic character of an urban place, for example, whether it is a low-density spread-out city with a weak core and scattered parts, or a compact highly centralized city with a single overpowering core. Between these extremes exists a full range of alternatives, each implying a different set of living conditions. For example, the concentration of business activity in a heavily built-up core area may imply a chronically congested transit system, yet the emergence of a network of "multi-towns," composed of functionally integrated but selectively specialized communities, may facilitate greater access through the use of a variety of transportation modes.

The form and structure of a city can be moulded by a multiplicity of forces or "policy" variables. Some of the most critical variables are: (1) the distribution of employment and services; (2) housing density and distribution; (3) the transportation system; and (4) the distribution of open space and leisure amenities. Changes in these variables can have far-reaching repercussions for the whole urban system, due to the high leverage they offer, so they are of great interest to planners and policy-makers. Yet to deploy these forces effectively requires both an understanding of how they shape settlement form and of what form of settlement is most desirable—issues that are addressed in Chapter 8.

To think constructively about desired future forms of settlement, and to work through and at the same time transcend existing circumstances, require an appeal to fundamentals. Basic human needs which **underlie observed lifestyles must be defined.** Towards this end, one approach suggests that all living systems, be they individual persons, social groups, or the city as a whole, can only "exist" and "live" in a satisfying manner if certain basic requirements are met. In the most general terms, the basic needs for a city system may be identified as follows: *resources*, the intake, use and discharge of the materials goods and energy to sustain life; *protection* of persons, physical things and institutions against both premeditated and accidental harm; *communication* of information, about rights and obligations as well as all manner of public events and issues essential to the functioning of the system; *integration* of information by individuals and groups so as to produce a high level of voluntariness and spontaneity in interpersonal and intergroup relationships and towards the polity as a whole; *culture*, the shared values that enable the system to cope with a wide range of situations; and *flexibility*, the ability of the system to adapt values and practices to changing conditions.

Knowledge of the implications of such needs, together with an understanding of the repercussions of the policy variables, provide us with a basis for suggesting some of the attributes that an optimum form of Canadian city would exhibit. We have chosen to call this optimum form the open city—"open" in the way it relates to the countryside, in its rich array of opportunities, in its information and transportation channels, in its citizens' access to government, in its cultural and administrative flexibility, and in its hospitality to differences in lifestyles, ethnic background, social status and design.

While the open city is portrayed only in broad terms, it is a concept with implications here and now for Canada's cities. Certain features of Canadian centres are not consistent with the open city (the lack of employment diversity in Regina, Sudbury's uncertain conquest of air pollution), but the seeds of the good life as prescribed by the concept are also apparent in certain places (Vancouver's high recreation potential, Hamilton's neighbourhood movement). Attaining the open city in Canada, then becomes a matter of devising planning strategies that suppress the negative and enhance the positive elements of each city. Towards the fulfilment of this goal, a series of policy suggestions are outlined in the final chapter.

9. *Some Conclusions and Policy Notes*

What type of urban Canada do Canadians want and by what means can it be attained are the questions we address in the concluding chapter. In brief, the answers are not clear-cut nor are the means for achieving a collective response readily evident. In the earlier chapters, urban Canada is viewed from a diversity of perspectives. Canadian cities are depicted as dynamic centres of growth, as the object of a full array of economic forces, as parts of highly interconnected urban regions, as the focus of decision-making power, as providers of services, as exploiters of surrounding land, as sources of environmental degradation and, of course, as places for people.

Nevertheless, if the analysis is to prove beneficial, it must be directed towards action rather than becoming an end in itself. Thus, for purposes of policy development, our diagnosis of forces and conditions, and our perception of the values and lifestyles of Canadians are integrated into a model of Canada's imagined urban future. Critical elements of the urban future include:

INTRODUCTION   33

National Urban Pattern	— Strenuous efforts by communities to pull the reins on runaway growth, to avoid the exhorbitant costs in housing, land, services and infrastructure associated with excessive expansion. — Development encouraged in small and medium-sized cities. — Isolation alleviated, choice facilitated through creating clusters of interacting communities, which are diversified and stable. — Inter-regional gaps in living standards and opportunities narrowed.
Urban Environment: Settlement Form	— Emphasis on community identity, internal mobility, communication, energy conservation, openness to the countryside, flexibility in design.
Social Justice	— A striving for social justice in the distribution of environmental goods and the control of environmental pollutants.
Diversity	— Maintenance of diversity in landscapes, lifestyles and outlook of different urban places across Canada.
Housing	— Direct provision by governments of social housing which blends with community character.
Land	— Development impacts on urban fringe lands mitigated, productive farmland and recreational landscapes preserved.
Inner City	— Stable neighbourhoods protected; decline slowed in problem areas.

This view of the urban future embodies some distinct values; opportunities for individual fulfilment through participation in community decision-making and the breadth of choice available in integrated urban networks; the expression of social justice in the distribution of housing, services and facilities between areas and groups; the emphasis on conservation in the older inner city undergoing renewal; the stress on diversity in the economic base of the regional urban system. While this viewpoint does not appear unreasonable, it may become increasingly elusive. Policy proposals may be for naught unless government structure and process are adapted to the nature of Canada's urban life. Urban places are interdependent, urban problems many-sided, and urban initiatives multi-sectoral; but in our federal state, political authority is fragmented, delivery mechanisms are uni-sectoral, and co-ordinated action fraught with difficulty.

In conclusion, therefore, we stress the urgent necessity of seeking a new style of government particularly at the "upper" levels, if urban Canada is to progress. The complexity of urban problems, the pitfalls of administration at a distance, the expanded capabilities of enlarged municipal jurisdictions, and the requirements for community participation are factors which we must build into the redesign of government processes. We argue for a basic shift in emphasis. We must concentrate more on building consensus about what should be done, on finding ways to mobilize and allocate talent and information and money for agreed purposes – and then allow a large degree of initiative and freedom of action to each sphere of responsibility. The freeing of creative community endeavour from stifling bureaucratic supervision in a multi-level administration and the releasing of provincial and federal governments to focus on issues that reverberate through the entire urban system (e.g. underlying financial allocations and socio-economic strategies) are some of the benefits foreseen.

CHAPTER 1

Urban Canada: Demographic Perspectives

The World Context of Canada's Urban Growth

Only recently has the growth of human population been viewed as startling and continuous. After the agricultural revolution of the fourth and fifth millennia B.C., civilizations grew, flourished and disintegrated; periods of good and bad weather occurred; pestilence, famine and war took their toll. Of course, there has been no accurate record of human population sizes until modern times, and even today demographic statistics for many regions of the globe are unreliable. Nevertheless, a generalized picture of ever accelerating population increase emerges. It is now commonplace to observe that the doubling time of the world population has been dramatically reduced, falling from 200 years in 1650 to eighty years in 1850 and forty-five years in 1930. Today, the globe is expected to house twice as many inhabitants a mere thirty-five years hence.[1]

The present rate of exponential population increase—over 2.0 per cent a year worldwide and approaching 3.0 per cent a year in the less developed nations—is not only unprecedented in human history; it promises further increases of an all but inconceivable kind. Each expanding generation leaves an even larger base for the next expansion. The 1.6 billion people in the less developed regions of the world as of 1950 are expected to swell to 3.7 billion by 1985—more than doubling within the span of a single generation. If there are no changes in policies and lifestyles, the peoples in the developing world cannot fail to reach 5.5. billion by the year 2000.[2] The projected growth rate for developed regions is more modest, with population doubling in seventy years, but this is more than offset by the escalating growth rates in developing regions such as Latin America where population has an anticipated doubling time of only twenty-four years. World population projections for the twenty-first century are gargantuan. No one can give a precise estimate for the ultimate number of people our planet can support. This depends, of course, upon the standards at which they want to eat, be housed, made healthy, and move about. But no one denies there is a limit: a limit that may be fast approached if present growth rates remain unchanged.

Mankind is not uniformly distributed over the face of the earth. Overpopulation is usually thought of in relation not to the absolute size of a population but rather to its density. Besides the obvious burdens placed upon the resource base and the telltale strain exerted upon the resiliency of the environment, some researchers have suggested that the phenomenon of more people in less and less space is linked to the pathologies of aggression, social disorder and group disorganization.[3] Hence, the present difficulties and, some would say, the impending calamity posed by exorbitant population increases are exacerbated by the rising tide of urbanization, in both developed and developing nations.

Viewed in relation to the whole of human history, the congregation of people in urban agglomerations is relatively recent. Pre-agricultural man, by necessity, was dispersed over the landscape. Existing in nomadic tribes, with hunting and gathering as a way of life, man could neither congregate in large groups nor form permanent settlements. But the agricultural revolution began to change that. Because more food could be produced in a smaller area, primitive communities formed. Since a farmer could feed more than his own family, a fraction of the population could be freed from their direct ties to the land. The division of labour was not the only stimulus towards urbanization. The social institutions of a city came to be necessary because of certain other developments: the development of irrigation systems and other complex activities for support of agricultural pursuits on flood plains; the collection, storage and distribution of foods; the mediation of political disputes; and the defence of prime farmland.

The first cities probably appeared along the banks of the Tigris and Euphrates Rivers between 4000 and 3000 B.C.[4] Over the next several millennia urbanization advanced slowly. During the middle ages, however, the foundations for rapid growth were being set: new lands and new trade routes, improved agriculture and transport, the rise of a highly organized hand craft industry and the migration of "surplus" population from farm to city. But mediaeval European towns still remained small, never embracing more than a minor fraction of a region's population.[5] On the eve of the industrial revolution, at the turn of the nineteenth century, Europe was still overwhelmingly agrarian with cities of 100,000 people accounting for an estimated 2.2 per cent of the total population.[6]

Rapid urbanization began with the enormous increase in productivity prompted by the harnessing of inanimate energy through use of machinery and fossil fuels. With the industrialization of Northwestern Europe, the transformation to an urbanized society was truly striking. City dwellers in nineteenth century Britain, for example, increased from 20 per cent of the total population in 1800 to nearly 80 per cent by 1900. As industrialization spread, the same thing happened in other nations. By 1970, over 64 per cent of the people inhabiting the world's developed regions lived in urban areas (see Table 1.1 and Figure 1.1).

And rapid urbanization is not confined to industrialized countries. During the short span of twenty-five years, from 1960 to 1985, the proportion of the population living in cities is expected to rise from 21.0 per cent to 34.7 per cent in the less developed regions of the world. Although the level of urbanization is still relatively low in the world's developing nations (25.9 per cent in 1970), the rate of urban growth is currently 4.5 per cent annually, far outstripping the present 1.9 per cent rate for industrialized nations. (The high rates reflect in part the relatively smaller proportion of the population – and hence base for calculating percentages – that is urban.)

The process of urbanization in developing nations has not been the same as that which occurred in industrialized nations. Since the end of World War II, impoverished rural peasants in Latin America have increasingly flooded urban areas. Yet employment opportunities have not materialized there. The result has been huge shantytowns known by different names in each country: *favelas* in Brazil, *tugurios* in Colombia, *ranchos* in Venezuela and *barriadas* in Peru.[7] The story has been the same on the African continent, with hundreds of thousands migrating annually to cities in search of a better life, and contributing to a 4.9 per cent annual rate of urbanization – the highest in the world.

To further complicate accelerating worldwide urbanization, there is a tendency to concentration in the largest metropolitan areas. From 1870 until 1975, the number of cities larger than a million inhabitants mushroomed from seven to 191. This represented more than a ten-fold increase in the share of the ever increasing world population that they comprised.[8] Within another decade, the roll call of million-plus cities may have been lengthened to 273, with Siberia's Krasnoyarsk and Madagascar's Tananarive joining Vancouver, Aleppo and Kabul. United Nations' estimates also suggest that the proportion of the world's population in "big cities" of 500,000 or more will rise from 12.7 per cent in 1960 to 21.6 per cent in 1985. Even these projections fail to dramatize the full impact. For less developed regions of the globe, the share of the population residing

Table 1.1. Projections[1] of Urban Growth in Major Regions of the World, 1960-85

Major Regions	Percent Population Urban			Percent Population in Big Cities[2]			Annual Percentage Rate of Population Growth: 1970		
	1960	1970	1985	1960	1970	1985	Total	Urban	Big City
World	33.1	37.4	44.6	12.7	15.4	21.6	2.0	3.2	4.4
More Developed Regions	57.9	64.2	72.9	24.0	27.2	33.9	1.0	1.9	2.5
Less Developed Regions	21.0	25.9	34.7	7.2	10.3	17.3	2.5	4.5	6.4
East Asia	22.6	29.6	42.3	9.7	12.7	18.7	1.7	4.2	4.2
South Asia	18.0	20.7	26.2	4.9	7.0	12.1	2.8	4.4	7.3
Europe	58.3	63.6	71.0	23.1	24.4	28.0	0.7	1.5	1.7
USSR	49.5	57.1	67.5	12.7	16.2	23.2	1.0	2.3	3.3
Africa	18.0	22.3	30.3	4.5	6.2	12.3	2.8	4.9	7.4
Oceania (incl. Australia and N.Z.)	65.2	67.5	70.5	32.3	40.7	44.0	2.1	2.5	2.7
Latin America	48.4	56.2	66.9	18.1	23.4	32.9	2.9	4.2	5.7
North America	69.7	74.3	80.2	36.2	41.0	49.5	1.3	1.9	2.7
Canada[3]	69.7	76.1	83.1	25.9	35.2	45.4	1.7		

Notes: 1 Estimates and projections are the medium variant produced by the United Nations Population Division.
2 Urban agglomerations of 500,000 or more.
3 Data for Canada are for 1961, 1971 and 1986 respectively.

Source: Adapted from: United Nations, *Study of Housing Statistics, 1971* (New York: Department of Economics and Social Affairs, Statistical Offices, 1974), Table 2: Population and Households, pp. 25–30.

URBAN CANADA 39

Figure 1.1 Past and Projected Population Totals in Major Regions of the World, 1950-85

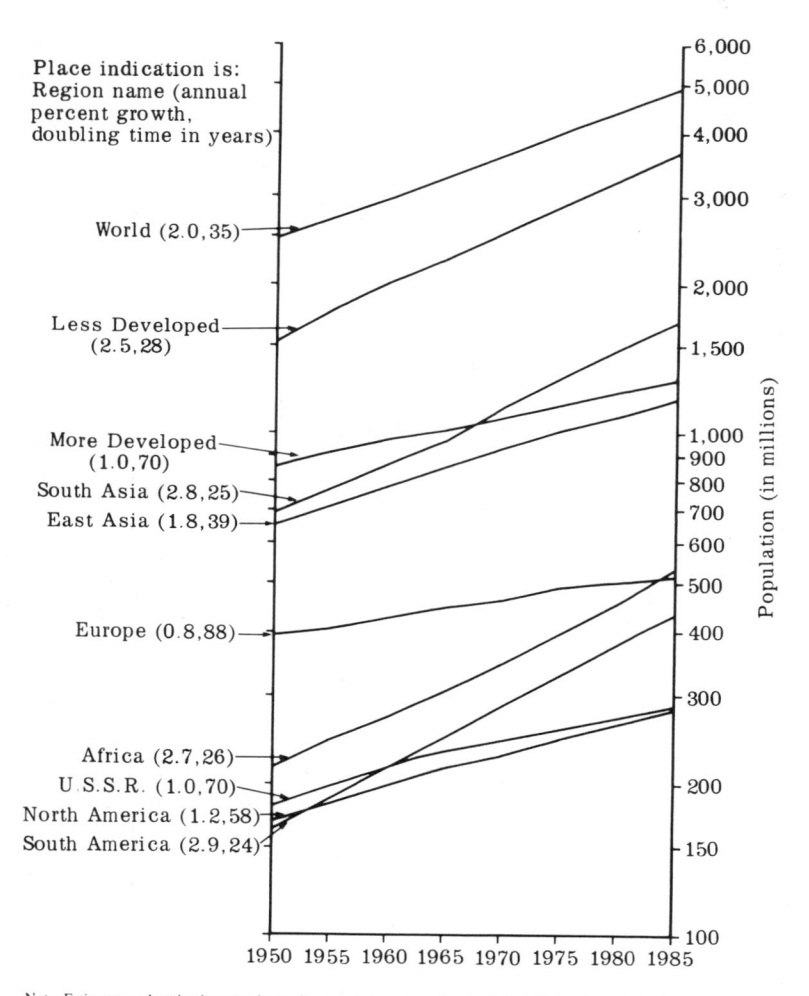

Place indication is:
Region name (annual percent growth, doubling time in years)

World (2.0, 35)
Less Developed (2.5, 28)
More Developed (1.0, 70)
South Asia (2.8, 25)
East Asia (1.8, 39)
Europe (0.8, 88)
Africa (2.7, 26)
U.S.S.R. (1.0, 70)
North America (1.2, 58)
South America (2.9, 24)

Population (in millions)

1950 1955 1960 1965 1970 1975 1980 1985

Note: Estimates and projections are the medium variant produced by the United Nations Population Division. More developed regions include Europe, U.S.S.R., North America, Japan, Temperate South America, Australia and New Zealand. Less developed regions include South Asia, East Asia (excluding Japan), Africa, Latin America (excluding Temperate South America), Melanesia, Polynesia and Micronesia.

Sources: United Nations, *Data Sheet of the Population Bureau*, 1971; United Nations, *Compendium of Housing Statistics*, 1971 (New York: United Nations, Department of Economic and Social Affairs, Statistical Office, 1974), Table 2, Population and Households, pp. 25-30; and United Nations' *Demographic Yearbook, 1973* (New York: United Nations, Department of Economic and Social Affairs, Statistical Office, 1974), Table 1, World Population Summary, p.81.

in big cities has increased incredibly quickly and current annual growth rates of large cities in Africa, South Asia and Latin America (7.4 per cent, 7.3 per cent and 5.7 per cent respectively) are extraordinarily high. On average, these cities are growing at rates which will result in a doubling of population every ten years.

For the first time in human history, man is becoming typically an urban animal. In 1960, two-thirds of the world's three billion people lived directly from the land; by the end of the century, over one-half of an estimated seven billion will be city dwellers.

Yet many futurists are hopeful, believing that urban areas may merge into a worldwide urban system – a universal city. "Ecumenopolis," C. A. Doxiadis[9] claimed, will be the inevitable future for human settlements during the next few generations: a universal city the population of which will tend to numerical stability but with increasingly more physical, social and intellectual development.

Other soothsayers have argued that man's numbers are manageable and that the urban explosion is overstated. Buckminster Fuller,[10] for example, dramatically emphasized this point:

- "man lives in scattered patches covering less than 5% of the earth's surface";
- "all cities of our planet cover sum-totally less than 1% of the earth's surface";
- "all humanity (as of 1965) could be brought indoors in the buildings of Greater New York City, each of us with as much floor room as at a cocktail party."

Many experts are less prone than Fuller to discount the grim reality posed by world demographic statistics. Meadows[11] concludes that the depletion of nonrenewable resources may bring about the end of today's civilization. Others, taking a less distant look into the future, highlight the prospects for those living in the warrens of the new multi-million-person agglomerations that now dot the developing world. Over half of the three billion bodies that will be added to the human race by the year 2000 will live in the most rapidly expanding, Asian, African and Latin American cities. "Great" city conditions cited by Ward and Dubos[12] for sanitation and sewerage are generally horrendous. To take one case, Djakarta is a vast agglomeration of rural villages; its five million residents have no sewerage, no reliable drinking water, few transport links, and no policy whatever for the location of markets or industries. Although subject to a hectic pace of growth, the world's poor cities are ill equipped to accommodate the relentless influx of newcomers from surrounding rural areas. Up to a third of the people now living in Manila, Caracas and Cairo are illegal squatters, living in tents, tin shacks or waterless, drainless hovels. So severe is the housing shortage that some experts see no alternative to unpoliced, unserviced shantytowns as the dominant form of city life for developing regions in the near future.[13]

From a global perspective, Canada's population size and growth rate may seem relatively modest. And Canada's growing pains pale in comparison to the recent experience of most undeveloped nations. But population growth and concentration have profound effects on the type of Canada in which we live and which we will bequeath to future generations.

Urban Growth in Canada

> "We know that in Canada changes will be required, rapid, continuous changes, in policy probably more than in technology. In common with many countries, we anticipate that we will have to build as much new urban area, as many new settlements, in the next 25 years as we have in our entire history." (J. W. MacNeill notes for an address to the Habitat Regional Preparatory Conference, July 1975).

Canadians, like bees, have been hiving. Since the end of the Second World War, Canada's rate of urban growth has outstripped that of any other western industrial nation. Three-quarters of the nation's population is concentrated on less than 1 per cent of its land area.[14] Population multiplied six-fold between Confederation and 1971, yet during the same period, the urban population grew by a factor of twenty-five. At the time of Confederation, 18.3 per cent of Canada's people were classified as urban. In 1971, more than three-quarters of Canadians were urban residents.[15] By the year 2001, some demographers have estimated that 90-95 per cent of Canada's population will be urban dwellers. The hiving of Canadians means that Canada's problems are becoming primarily urban ones. National problems are tending to become the problems of cities.

The degree of urbanization has advanced in every decade since Canada became a nation.[16] Less than one Canadian in five was a resident of a town or city in 1871, but the proportion had increased to one in three by the turn of the century (Figure 1.2). Fuelled by the dramatic influx of immigrants (many of whom sought to live in urban places despite the avowed government policy of favouring farmers, miners and railway labourers), the percentage of Canadians living in urban areas had reached nearly 50 per cent in 1921. Then during the interwar period, only a modest increase in the proportion of population urban was recorded. Moderated by the "quota system" placed on immigration in the late 1920s and slowed by the Great Depression of the 1930s, the level of urbanization had reached

42   CHANGING CANADIAN CITIES

Figure 1.2. Per Cent of Population in Urban Canada, 1871-1971

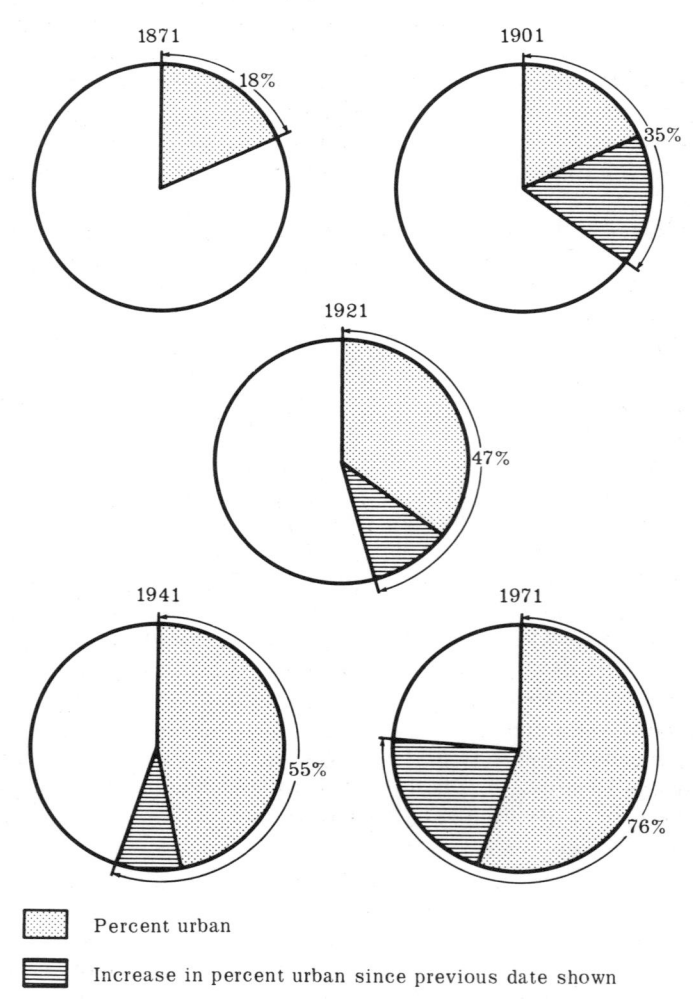

1871 — 18%

1901 — 35%

1921 — 47%

1941 — 55%

1971 — 76%

Percent urban

Increase in percent urban since previous date shown

Note: For 1871 and 1901, per cent urban refers to the population of incorporated cities, towns and villages of 1,000 and over. For 1921, 1941, the urban population figures are based on the 1961 census definition of "urban" which includes: (1) all incorporated cities, towns and villages of 1,000 and over; (2) all unincorporated towns and villages of 1,000 and over; (3) unincorporated urbanized fringes of cities of 5,000 and over. The 1971 definition of urban population is not identical, but essentially the same.

Sources: For 1871, 1901, 1921 and 1941: L.O. Stone, *Urban Development in Canada* (Ottawa: Dominion Bureau of Statistics, 1967), p.29; and for 1971: Statistics Canada, *1971 Census of Canada: Urban and Rural Distributions*, Bull. 1.1-9 (Ottawa: 1973).

only 55.7 per cent by 1941. Coincident with the robust population growth following World War II, however, urbanization had reached 76.1 per cent in 1971.

Increasing urbanization is also reflected in the transition of Canada's labour force from mainly agricultural to primarily industrial and service occupations. At the turn of the century, just prior to the major influx of homesteaders to the Canadian Prairies, four out of every ten gainfully employed workers in Canada were farmers. The actual number of agricultural workers continued to increase until the onset of the Great Depression as the Prairie sod was broken and farms began to dot the Western landscape. But the proportion of the Canadian labour force employed in agriculture declined constantly, reflecting increased mechanization, expanded farm sizes and increased productivity per worker. By 1971 fewer persons were in agricultural occupations than in 1901.

The results of the urbanization of Canadians can be dramatically portrayed in the language of the geographer. The Canada of today projects two distinct cartographic faces: one of its land, another of its people. A conventional map of Canada makes a striking contrast to an "isodemographic map," a map which displays areas proportional to population (Map 1.1). For example, the spatial concentration of Canada's population enlarges the Great Lakes – St. Lawrence Lowlands so that this region represents more than half of Canada.

Urbanization has not proceeded at the same pace by provinces across Canada. As Figure 1.3 illustrates, the provinces differ markedly both in current level of urbanization and the timing of past changes in urbanization. By 1971, population classified as urban ranged from 38.3 per cent in Prince Edward Island to 82.4 per cent in Ontario. Although three of every four residents in Canada were urban dwellers, only three of the ten provinces had surpassed this proportion: Ontario, Quebec and British Columbia. However, all provinces, except Prince Edward Island, are now 50 per cent urbanized.

At the time of Confederation, Ontario and Quebec had a larger share of inhabitants in cities and towns than was the case in British Columbia. During the ensuing decades, however, urbanization in the westernmost province leaped ahead, fuelled by the exploitation of forest and mineral resources, the completion of the Canadian Pacific Railway (CPR) and the accompanying surge of initial settlement. By 1901, British Columbia was the most urbanized province in the nation. This trend later reversed, however, as urban growth in British Columbia fell behind the central provinces, particularly during the 1911-21 period. Since 1921, the rate of urbanization in the three most urban provinces has been similar – slowing during the Great

Map 1.1. Two Cartographic Faces of Canada: Its Land and Its People

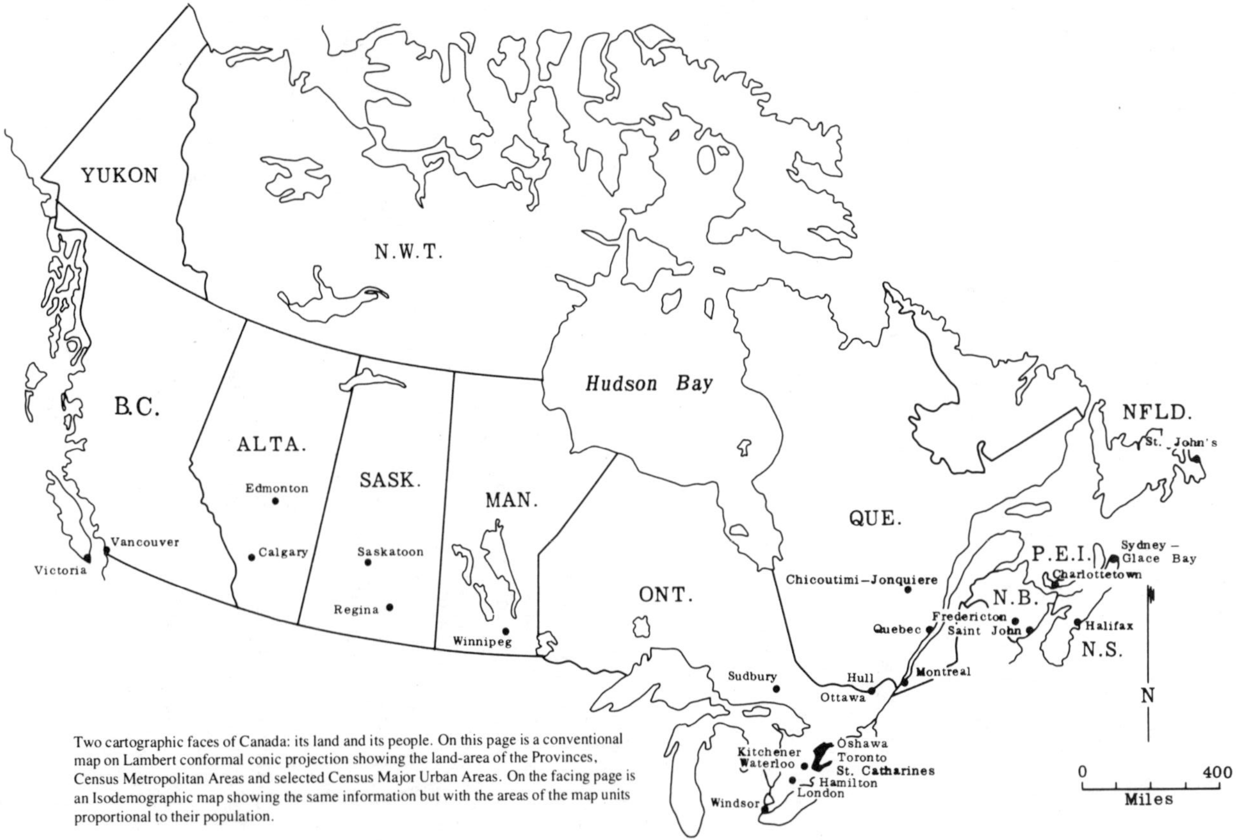

Two cartographic faces of Canada: its land and its people. On this page is a conventional map on Lambert conformal conic projection showing the land-area of the Provinces, Census Metropolitan Areas and selected Census Major Urban Areas. On the facing page is an Isodemographic map showing the same information but with the areas of the map units proportional to their population.

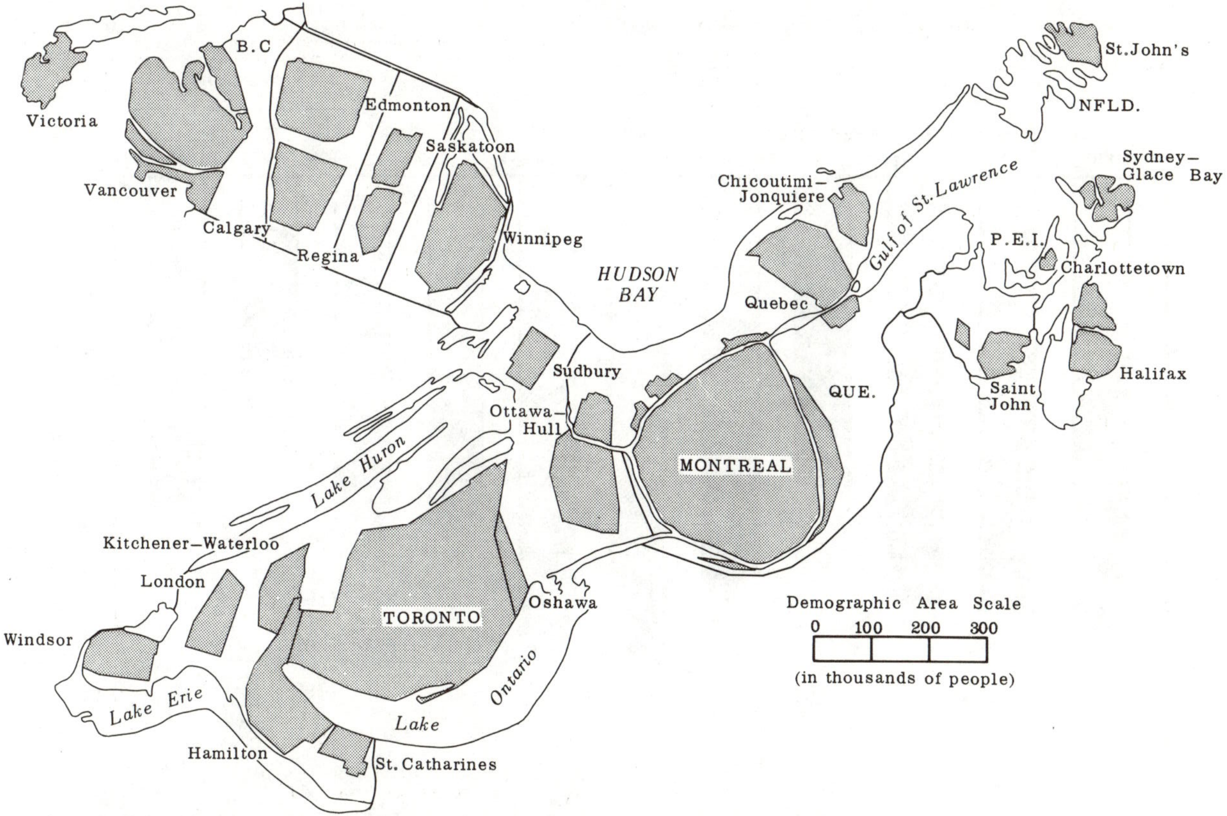

URBAN CANADA 45

Demographic Area Scale
0 100 200 300
(in thousands of people)

St. John's
NFLD.
Sydney–Glace Bay
Charlottetown
P.E.I.
Halifax
Saint John
Gulf of St. Lawrence
Chicoutimi–Jonquière
Quebec
QUE.
MONTREAL
HUDSON BAY
Sudbury
Ottawa–Hull
Oshawa
Winnipeg
Ontario
Edmonton
Saskatoon
Lake Huron
TORONTO
Lake Ontario
St. Catharines
B.C.
Regina
Calgary
Kitchener–Waterloo
Hamilton
London
Lake Erie
Vancouver
Windsor
Victoria

Sources: L. Skoda and C. I. Jackson, "A Mechanical Method of Constructing Equal Population Density Maps," Discussion Paper B.72.4 (Ottawa: Ministry of State for Urban Affairs (MSUA), 1972) and L. Skoda and J. C. Robertson, *Isodemographic Map of Canada*, Department of Environment, Geographical Paper No. 50 (Ottawa: Information Canada, 1972).

46 CHANGING CANADIAN CITIES

Figure 1.3. Per Cent of Population in Urban Canada by Province, 1871-1971

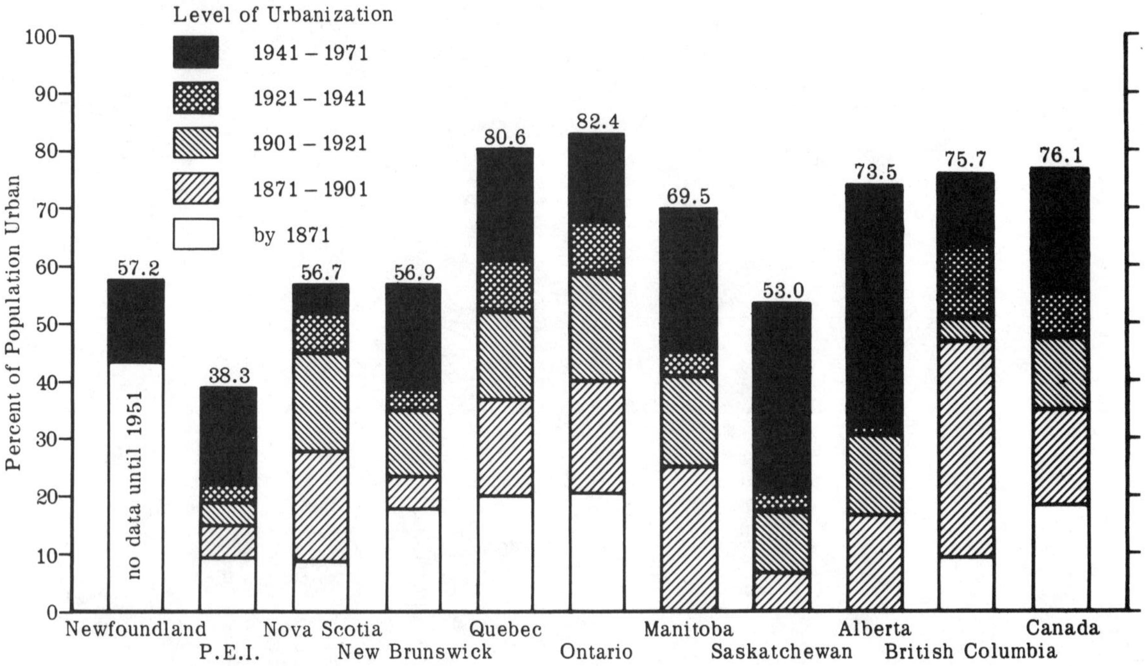

Level of Urbanization:
- 1941–1971
- 1921–1941
- 1901–1921
- 1871–1901
- by 1871

Newfoundland: 57.2 (no data until 1951)
P.E.I.: 38.3
Nova Scotia: 56.7
New Brunswick: 56.9
Quebec: 80.6
Ontario: 82.4
Manitoba: 69.5
Saskatchewan: 53.0
Alberta: 73.5
British Columbia: 75.7
Canada: 76.1

Percent of Population Urban

Note: Please see note for Figure 1.2.

Sources: For 1871, 1901, 1921 and 1941: L.O. Stone, *Urban Development in Canada* (Ottawa: Dominion Bureau of Statistics, 1967), p. 29; and for 1971: Statistics Canada, *1971 Census of Canada: Urban and Rural Distributions*, Bull. 1.1-9 (Ottawa: 1973).

Depression, accelerating rapidly after World War II and tapering off slightly during the 1960s.

The Maritime provinces were probably more highly urbanized than central Canada during the first half of the nineteenth century.[17] But the Atlantic region did not share in the commercial and industrial expansion enjoyed by southern Ontario and Quebec during the 1881-1914 period. Instead, it became largely an isolated backwater without the potential continental hinterland, without resources complementary to those of central Canada, thwarted by tariff regulations and unable to capitalize upon the technological and organizational advances that made industrialization possible. Coincident with the painfully slow rise of urban-oriented mining, manufacturing and service activities, the Maritime provinces experienced a low level of urbanization during most of Canada's first hundred years. Upsurges in urbanization were not sustained, when they occurred at all. The urban population of New Brunswick increased by less than 4 per cent from 1921-41 – half the rate of Canada as a whole during the same twenty year period. Only in very recent times has the economic base of Maritime cities showed signs of sustained expansion and the associated growth of employment and population. It is of course too soon to tell whether this economic and demographic turnabout, as documented over the 1971-74 period, is a long-term trend.

Urban growth on the Prairies has been characterized by sharp peaks and troughs. Following the great wave of western settlement prior to World War I (1896-1914), there was a period of retrenchment. Urban places which had been poorly located, over-built and over-mortgaged during the heady days of town-building that marked the period of initial settlement stagnated and, in many cases, declined, during the years that intervened between the two World Wars. The onset of the Great Depression, which struck the Prairies most severely, hastened this process. Thus, while the central provinces were urbanizing consistently from 1921 to 1941 (Ontario's level increased from 59 per cent to 68 per cent and Quebec's from 52 per cent to 61 per cent), Prairie urbanization lagged around 30 per cent. From 1941, however, the level of urbanization climbed rapidly, particularly in Alberta where increases in business activity to service the burgeoning oil and natural gas industry stimulated urban areas during the 1950s and 1960s. By 1971, the proportion of Alberta's population residing in urban areas approached that of British Columbia, while in Saskatchewan once the most rural of Canada's provinces, more than half of the people lived in a city or town.

Perhaps more significant than regional differences in the rate of urbanization is the concentration of growth in Canada's largest urban areas.[18] Although the combined population in urban centres of less than 5,000 people has trebled during the past sixty years, the proportional share of centres in the smallest size group (1,000 – 4,999) has declined from 29 per cent to 16 per cent to 10 per cent during the years 1901, 1931 and 1971 (Table 1.2). In contrast, the population of 100,000-plus places has increased twenty-fold. The largest centres have advanced more or less continuously from one-fourth of the nation's people in 1901 to nearly two-thirds by 1971 (Table 1.3).

An interesting diversion to the study of changes in the size of urban places through time and space is the so-called rank-size rule.[19] This rule is an empirical regularity obtained by ranking all urban centres in an area in descending order of population size and then plotting size against rank. For the 100 largest cities in the United States, Zipf came to the rather startling conclusion that a city was directly proportional in size to the largest city. Hence, the forty-ninth largest city was 1/49 (one-forty-ninth) the size of New York, the largest city.

Not all countries have exhibited this pattern. In contrast, some (e.g., Denmark, Thailand) have a "primate distribution" which means there is a marked gap between the population of the largest city and the population distribution of smaller cities.[20] A country like Canada has two primate cities (Toronto and Montreal) but a straight line or usual population distribution for smaller centres.

What causes a rank-size relationship such as this? Zipf claimed that the regularity expressed in the rank-size rule was characteristic of a system of cities that was "mature" in the sense that the "forces of unification" and the "forces of diversification were in equilibrium." On the basis of this, Berry[21] suggested that the rank-size rule is the steady state of the growth process in a national urban system. Nevertheless, the interpretation of the rank-size rule is still being debated.[22] We shall return, in Chapter 3, to the reasons for Canada's particular pattern and distribution of cities.

Of the one and one-half million people added to the Canadian population in the latter half of the 1960s, almost two-thirds were located in centres 400,000 or larger. Over 40 per cent were located in the three largest metropolitan areas – Montreal, Toronto and Vancouver. For Calgary, every 100 people residing there in 1966 were joined by twenty-two additional people in 1971. Only slightly lower increments were recorded for Edmonton (16.5), Vancouver (16.0), Toronto (14.8) and Ottawa-Hull (13.9) during the same five-year time span.

The problems and the potential of urban Canada in the 1970s have not arisen simply from the shift of people from farms and

Table 1.2. Population of Urban Centres by Size Group, Canada, 1901–71
(number in thousands and percentage)

Size Group	1901	1911	1921	1931	1941	1951	1961	1971
100,000 and over	476 (25.5)	1081 (35.9)	1659 (41.8)	2328 (45.1)	2645 (45.2)	5222 (59.2)	8401 (64.0)	10426 (62.4)
30,000–99,999	343 (18.4)	489 (16.3)	496 (12.5)	697 (13.5)	928 (15.9)	1231 (14.0)	1647 (11.8)	1931 (11.8)
5,000–29,999	503 (26.9)	783 (26.0)	1058 (26.6)	1305 (25.3)	1370 (23.4)	1198 (13.6)	1641 (12.7)	2593 (15.8)
1,000–4,999	545 (29.2)	655 (21.8)	765 (19.1)	831 (16.1)	910 (15.5)	1167 (13.2)	1595 (11.5)	1641 (10.0)
Total Urban	1867 (100.0)	3008 (100.0)	3977 (100.0)	5161 (100.0)	5854 (100.0)	8818 (100.0)	13972 (100.0)	16411 (100.0)

Notes: This information only gives a broad indication of the secular trend. The definition of "urban" employed in the respective census years are utilized. From 1951 onward, the smaller-sized centres included within the boundaries of census metropolitan areas, major urban areas (1961) and census agglomerations (1971) are allocated to the larger centre.

A Census Metropolitan Area (CMA) is defined as the main labour market of a continuously built-up area having a population of 100,000 or more.

Source: D. Kubat and D. Thornton. *A Statistical Profile of Canadian Society* (Toronto: McGraw-Hill, Ryerson Limited, 1974), Table P–5, p. 20.

Table 1.3. The Growth of Canada's Larger Cities, 1966–71[1,2]

Size Group[3]	Number of Cities	Absolute Growth (000's)	Per cent Growth	Growth Ratio Canada[4]	Proportion of Canada's Growth (per cent)[5]
1,000,000 and over	3	650	11.21	1.44	41.83
– Montreal		172	6.70	0.86	11.08
– Toronto		338	14.77	1.90	21.76
– Vancouver		149	16.00	2.06	9.59
400,000 – 999,999	6	333	12.39	1.60	21.44
100,000 – 399,999	14	212	9.19	1.18	13.27
30,000 – 99,999	34	114	6.94	0.89	7.35
CANADA	–	1553	7.76	1.00	100.00

Notes:
1. Calculations are based on the relatively short, five-year time span because municipal boundary changes and annexations make the reconstruction of common real units exceedingly difficult. As it stands, boundary readjustments in Brandon, Chatham, Lethbridge and Moose Jaw during the 1966–1971 period impart a very slight upward bias to the growth of the 30,000–99,999 size group.
2. Each Census Metropolitan Area and Census Agglomeration is treated as a single unit and the data for all units within each such area are aggregated.
3. According to the 1971 population figures.
4. Growth Ratio/Canada = Percentage Growth of Urban Size Group divided by Percentage Growth of Canada.
5. Proportion of Canada's Growth = Absolute Growth of Urban Size Group divided by Absolute Growth of Canada, all multiplied by 100.

Source: Derived from Statistics Canada, *1971 Census of Canada*, Vol. 1, 1-8. Reproduced by permission of the Minister of Supply and Services Canada.

hamlets to towns and cities. They are more the manifestation of mushrooming growth in a few metropolitan agglomerations: the "Lower Mainland" in British Columbia; the Calgary-Edmonton "Transportation Corridor" in Alberta; the "Golden Horseshoe" in southwestern Ontario; the "Golden Triangle" in southern Quebec; and the "Central Corridor" in the Maritimes. At the same time, the social, economic and environmental malaise experienced in some Canadian cities is undoubtedly less the product of their absolute size than it is the consequence of a phenomenal rate of expansion. A few of the ramifications of unbridled metropolitan growth are: the conversion of land from agricultural production to urban purposes; the competition for and resulting price escalation of scarce urban land resources; low-density suburbanization and associated traffic congestion generated by the excessive use of the automobile; ill conceived and poorly located development which gives little recognition to the conservation of the natural environment; rapid increases in public expenditure for certain public services; and the concentration of low income families in inner city neighbourhoods, often marked by congestion, pollution, a scarcity of recreational facilities and a deteriorating housing stock. Finally, regional disparities in income and opportunity have been accentuated as urbanization has focused upon the largest urban centres.

National and Provincial Population Growth: Components of Change

The magnitude, demographic characteristics and spatial patterns of Canada's urban growth must be analysed in the context of national and regional population growth and distribution in order to be fully appreciated. Variations in the rates of births and deaths, in the historic waves of immigration and of emigration, as well as in the internal movements of people are the stuff that make population changes. Unfortunately, much of the information on demographic processes is incomplete or inexact, particularly data relating to the period before 1921 and information on the volume of emigrants even today. Hence, parts of the analysis must, of necessity, be sketchy.[23]

Table 1.4 illustrates the overwhelming predominance of natural increase in the growth of the Canadian population. Over 85 per cent of Canada's population growth during the past century can be attributed to a surplus of births over deaths.[24] In no decade since 1871 has the contribution of *net* migration comprised more than half of the change in population.

But immigration has profoundly influenced Canada's demographic composition, creating concentrations of people in the young

Table 1.4. Components of Growth for the Canadian Population by Intercensal Interval, 1871–1971

Census Interval	Population at Beginning of The Interval 000's	Total Population Increase 000's	Natural Increase 000's	Per cent Share of Population Increase Natural	Net Migration 000's	Per cent Share of Population Change from Net Migration
1871–81	3,689	636	723	114	−87	−14
1881–91	4,325	508	714	141	−206	−41
1891–1901	4,833	538	718	133	−180	−33
1901–11	5,371	1,836	1,120	61	716	+39
1911–21	7,207	1,581	1,350	85	231	+15
1921–31	8,788	1,589	1,360	86	229	+14
1931–41	10,377	1,130	1,222	108	−92	−08
1941–51	11,507	2,141	1,971	92	170	+08
1951–61*	13,648 (14009)	4,229	3,148	74	1,081	+26
1961–71	18,238	3,330	2,592	78	738	+22
1971	21,568					
1871–1971 Total		17,518	14,917	85	2,601	+15

Definitions: Natural Increase = Total Births less Total Deaths
Net Migration = Total Immigrants less Total Emigrants

* Two population figures are given in 1951: the one including (in parentheses) and the other excluding the population of Newfoundland. The components of change calculations for 1941–51 and 1951–61 do not include the 361,000 people that Canada gained when Newfoundland entered Confederation.

Notes: There is considerable disagreement among authorities on the levels of immigration and emigration that have existed through time. Specifically, four competing estimates have been calculated, which vary according to assumptions regarding the completeness and accuracy of data on immigration and emigration, fertility and mortality (especially during the early decades), the presumed nature of the errors and the procedures used in correcting of these errors. The four competing estimates, which differ up to the 1941–51 decade are by N. Keyfitz, "The Growth of Canadian Population," *Population Studies*, Vol. 4, 1950, pp. 47–63; D. M. McDougall, "Immigration into Canada, 1851–1920" *Canadian Journal of Economics and Political Science*, Vol. 27, No. 2, 1961, pp. 162–175; N. B. Ryder, "Components of Canadian Population Growth" *Population Index*, Vol. 20, No. 2, 1954, pp. 71–80; and P. Camus, E. P. Weeks, and Z. W. Sametz, *Economic Geography of Canada* (Toronto: Macmillan, 1964), pp. 56-64.

Sources: Derived from Canada, Department of Manpower and Immigration, *Canadian Immigration and Population Study*, Vol. 3, *Immigration and Population Statistics*, (Ottawa: 1974), Table 1.4; and Daniel Kubat and David Thornton, *A Statistical Profile of Canadian Society*, (Toronto: McGraw-Hill Ryerson, 1974). Reproduced by permission of the Minister of Supply and Services Canada.

adult age groups, broadening the ethnic mix, strengthening the labour force and diversifying the mix of occupational skills. Economic development has been spurred and our culture enriched through immigrant arrivals. Given the substantial contribution of immigrants, it may seem surprising that net migration has accounted for only a small proportion of Canada's population increase. The apparent paradox is explained, however, not by a small flow of newcomers, but rather by the large numbers who left Canada, primarily for the U.S. (Figure 1.4).

Since Confederation, the total outflow of emigrants from the country has amounted to about three-quarters of the approximately 9.8 million immigrants who have come to Canada. During the final three decades of the nineteenth century, Canada was truly a demographic railway station: emigrant outflow exceeded immigrant inflow by a wide margin. Easy access to the Canadian West had not been achieved, and a relatively depressed economy made the opportunities for employment and free land in the American Mid-West attractive to domestic born Canadians as well as to recent immigrant arrivals.

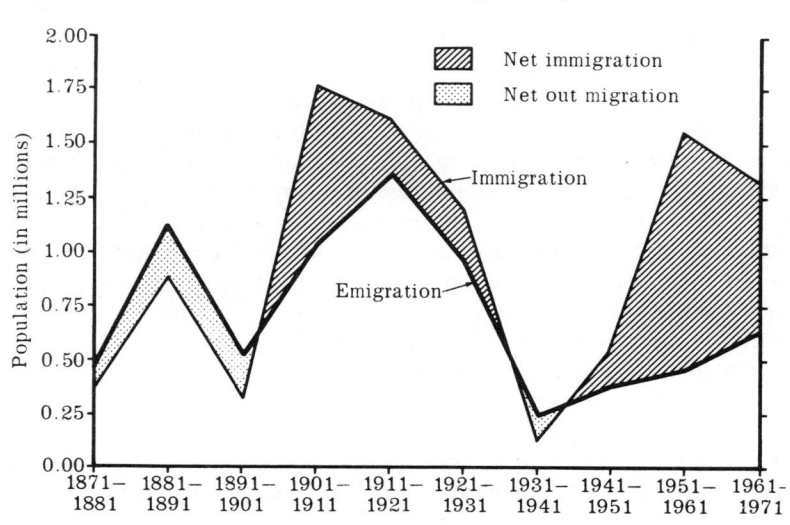

Figure 1.4. Canada: Net International Migration, 1871-1971

Source: Canada Manpower and Immigration, *Canadian Immigration and Population Study: Immigration and Populations Statistics* (Ottawa: Information Canada, 1974).

THE FERTILITY OF CANADIANS

Rates of fertility in Canada have fluctuated considerably during the past 100 years.[25] At the time of Confederation, the average woman would have borne seven children in the course of her life. During the late nineteenth century, the total fertility rate dropped dramatically as Canadians left behind pioneer life, but it evened out in the early twentieth century with the influx of immigrants. During the 1920s fertility proceeded downward, and then plummeted sharply during the depression years when young couples postponed marriage and child-bearing (Table 1.5). From a low average of 2.65 children per women in 1937, the fertility rate edged upward as depression conditions eased, only to be retarded again by the ensuing war years. Following World War II, the much talked-about baby boom occurred. Fuelled by attitudes favouring large families, generally robust economic conditions and a huge inflow of foreign immigrants, many of whom were young adults, the total fertility rate continued to rise throughout the 1950s. The 'sixties, however, was a time of precipitous decline and this trend has continued during the 1970s. The fertility rate is now slightly below what demographers call the "replacement level" (2.1 for Canada) or the rate at which population size would remain constant with zero net migration.

What has caused the substantial decline in the birth rate during the past fifteen years? Changing social attitudes towards family size is undoubtedly one prime reason. Several decades ago, Canadian society accorded unquestioning approval to large families. The church, the community and the baby bonus all encouraged couples to obey the age-old injunction: "Go forth and multiply." Fears about over-population, the environment and simple dollars and cents worries about the high cost of raising children in inflationary times have, however, helped to alter attitudes in favour of smaller families. The general re-orientation of woman's role in society, a higher level of female participation in the labour force and a greater degree of career consciousness among women, coupled with improved methods of birth control, are other factors that have militated against high fertility rates. A comparison of results from polls conducted thirty years apart shows that the majority of Canadian couples today feel that the ideal family should contain two or fewer children, whereas the majority of their counterparts in 1945 wanted four or more children.[26]

Will current trends in fertility become a permanent feature of Canadian society? Demographic analysts, in contrast to laymen, have been cautious in commenting on the decline of births. Some explain the present fertility decline by maintaining that many young couples are only delaying for the present the start of their families.[27] Recent evidence from the American experience lends some support to this contention. Although a high proportion of U.S. women under age thirty have not yet borne children, attitudinal surveys show that most childless married women still expect to have two or more children. This has prompted a team of American demographers to forecast a "bottoming out" of the birth rate and the coming of a mini baby boom.[28] Will the same occur in Canada?

Table 1.5. Patterns of Fertility in Canada, 1871-1971

Year	Crude Birth Rate	General Fertility Rate	Total Fertility Rate
1871	45.0	189	6.83
1891	35.7	144	4.92
1911	34.4	144	4.70
1921	30.5	120	3.98
1926	24.7	97	3.36
1931	23.2	94	3.20
1937	20.1	81	2.65
1941	22.4	87	2.82
1947	28.9	112	3.57
1951	27.2	109	3.48
1956	28.0	117	3.84
1959	27.4	116	3.95
1961	26.1	112	3.86
1966	19.4	82	2.82
1971	16.8	67	2.19
1974	15.4		1.90

Definitions: *Crude Birth Rate*: Annual number of births per 1000 of mid-year population.
General Fertility Rate: Annual number of births per 1000 women in their child-bearing years (aged 15 – 49).
Total Fertility Rate: Given the age-specific fertility rates for a given year, it represents the number of children the average woman would have during her child-bearing years (aged 15 – 49). It presupposes that the women are unaffected by mortality.

Sources: —Crude Birth Rate 1871 – 1921: J. Henrepin, *Trends and Factors of Fertility in Canada* 1961 Census Monograph, (Ottawa: Statistics Canada, 1972), Table B6, p. 366.
—Crude Birth Rate 1926 onward: D.B.S., *Vital Statistics*, (Ottawa: Queen's Printer, 1958, 1964, 1968 and 1974), Cat. 84,202 and 84,204.
—General Fertility Rate: Henrepin, *op. cit.*, Table 2.1, p. 21.
—Total Fertility Rate 1871 – 1921: Henrepin, *op. cit.*, Table 2.3, p. 30.
—Total Fertility Rate 1926 onward: Statistics Canada, *Population Projections for Canada and the Provinces, 1972-2001*, (Ottawa: Queen's Printer, 1974), Tables 4.2 and 4.3, Cat. 91 – 514.
—Reproduced by permission of the Minister of Supply and Services Canada.

THE MORTALITY OF CANADIANS

Although birth rates have fluctuated in response to changing attitudes, death rates in Canada have gradually, but consistently declined since accurate record-keeping began in 1921. In fact, death rates adjusted for age structure of the population halved from 1921 to 1971. This is accounted for by improvements in public health dramatically reducing levels of infant mortality, success in combatting communicable diseases lowering mortality among children and adolescents, and various improvements in health care facilities (and access to them) prolonging life. This steady downward trend in mortality has levelled in recent years; however, since accidents and chronic disorders have become the principal causes of death, a further reduction in mortality rates may be attainable.[29]

Table 1.6. The Changing Age Structure of Canada's Population: Median Age and Dependency Ratios 1901 – 1971

Year	Median age	Youth dependency ratio	Old-age dependency ratio
1901	22.7	56.8	8.3
1911	23.8	52.9	7.5
1921	23.9	56.6	7.9
1931	24.7	50.3	8.8
1941	27.0	42.4	10.2
1951	27.7	49.0	12.5
1961	26.3	58.1	13.1
1971	26.3	47.5	13.0

Definitions: Median Age: Fifty per cent of the population is below the median age.
Youth Dependency Ratio: The number of persons in their childhood years (aged 0 – 14) per 100 persons in their productive adult years (aged 15 – 64).
Old-age Dependency Ratio: The number of persons in their retired years (aged 65 +) per 100 persons in their productive adult years (aged 15 – 64).

Source: Statistics Canada, *Perspective Canada: A compendium of Social Statistics* (Ottawa: Queen's Printer, Cat. 11 – 507, 1974), Table 1 – 13, p. 12. Reproduced by permission of the Minister of Supply and Services Canada.

Decreasing fertility and mortality have led to an "ageing" of Canada's population. This has had and will continue to have, a profound influence on Canadian society. The proportion of old people in the population (Table 1.6) has moved steadily upward since 1911, although the post-war baby boom temporarily interrupted the rise in the median age of Canada's population. The future outlook in Canada is for a marked ageing of the population, as the baby boom population bulge moves through the life cycle, causing first an increase in the working age population followed by a rise in the elderly dependent population. Among the consequences of this changing age composition, which will be felt most acutely after the year 2000, are higher expenditures on social security systems, difficulties in labour force adjustment because of a higher proportion of older workers, changes in the level of demand for different forms of housing and sharp variations in the need for social services such as hospitals and schools.

THE EFFECT OF IMMIGRATION ON CANADA'S POPULATION

The flow of immigrants into Canada has fluctuated dramatically. Numbers have soared and plummeted. Alternating cycles of male and female predominance have been observed. The preponderance of British newcomers during earlier times was first challenged by a rising tide of Southern and Eastern Europeans and then, more recently, by a steady stream of peoples from Asian and Caribbean lands. Those destined to till the fields, build the railways and serve as domestic help have been largely replaced by aspiring professionals, clerical workers and manufacturing employees. Some principal changes in the character of immigration according to volume, age-sex composition, area of origin and occupational skills are outlined in Table 1.7. Factors which influenced the evolving characteristics of the immigrant inflow are many and complex, though some demographers have attempted to classify them into general categories of "push", "pull" and "intervening aids or obstacles" (Table 1.8).

Although the numerical impact of net migration upon Canada's population growth has been limited (because of periodically heavy emigration), differences in immigrants compared to emigrants in terms of age, sex, ethnicity, and the like, have helped to shape the composition and distribution of the Canadian population. For example, prior to World War I, a largely male dominated flow of young adults sought their livelihood in the fields, mines and construction labour camps. Especially in the pioneering West this resulted in a surplus of males and a concentration of people in the young, productive years of working life. A "catch-up" flow of females to Canada was particularly noticeable during the early 1920s and late 1950s. A balanced age distribution among immigrants has also appeared after periods of high immigration, once newcomers have become financially able to sponsor parents and elderly relatives. In fact, the partial balancing in immigrant age composition in recent times has prompted the authors of one recent government report to conclude that "in the absence of specific policies concerning an immigrant's age, the flow of immigrants will have virtually no impact on the age structure of the population."

Whatever the diverse views held regarding the social effects of immigrants, the long term economic consequences of immigration are clear. The energies, enthusiasms and skills of immigrants drawn from a widening number of countries have made an immense contribution to many facets of Canada's development. Although a temporary dislocation of labour resources occurs from time to time, Canada's economic advancement has been fuelled to a significant degree by immigrants who have constituted the backbone of certain sectors in Canada's labour force: farming, lumbering, mining and railway construction, and more recently, light manufacturing, small businesses and certain professional groups in the largest cities. Because they are mainly of working age, immigrants have heightened the adaptability of the labour force; because of consistently high female participation, they have contributed substantially to labour force size. Indeed, the economic contributions of immigrants, coupled with the pronounced declines in the Canadian birth rate, oblige Canadians and their government to contemplate a future in which the number of immigrants affects, not only population size, but also the rate at which economic growth occurs.[30]

Whatever the consequences of past or future immigration for the population as a whole, the consequences are doubly critical to the nation's largest cities. Despite long-standing government policies to the contrary, immigrant inflows have favoured cities since the earliest times. Hence, a higher proportion of foreign born (compared to native born) are urban dwellers. Undoubtedly, Canadian cities are commercially stronger, more culturally lively, cosmopolitan and outward-looking because of immigration. But intensifying urban demands for housing, transit facilities, community services and just plain space mean that immigrants make increasing demands on the receiving community's hospitality, or so it seems. Although a sympathetic assessment of previous immigrant contributions may be accorded, such trade-offs are the grist for the extended policy debate that is currently underway.

URBAN CANADA 59

Table 1.7. The Changing Attributes of the Immigrant Flow into Canada, 1896 Onwards

ATTRI-BUTE	WHEAT ECONOMY (1896–1914)	POST WORLD WAR ONE (1919–1930)	THE GREAT DEPRESSION (1931–1939)	POST WAR ECONOMIC BOOM (1946–1961)	REDUCING RESTRICTIONS (1961–1975)
VOLUME	—EXTREMELY HIGH — Increased steadily from 16,000 (1896) to an all time high of 400,000 (1913) as a result of "open door" policies.	—MODERATE — Gradually accelerated from 64,000 (1922) to 166,000 (1928). — Immigration policy was regulative rather than promotional.	—EXTREMELY LOW — Declined from 27,000 (1931) to 11,000 (1935) as a result of depression conditions and restrictive entrance regulations.	—HIGH — Surged upward from 64,000 (1947) to consistently 100,000 plus during 1950s. — Robust economic growth, post war refugees and occasional political upheavals in Europe were responsible.	—HIGH — A lull in the early 1960s was followed by a continuous string of 100,000-plus years from 1964 onwards. — Partly reflects easing of entrance restrictions.
AGE-SEX COMPOSITION	—MALES, YOUNG ADULTS — Predominantly young adult males (aged 25-34) suited for the hard life of frontier type society in the Canadian West.	—FEMALES, FAMILIES — Females predominated the moderate influx of the early 1920s as men sought to reunite families. — As the inflow increased in the late 1920s, the cycle reversed with males becoming the larger group.	—FEMALES, CHILDREN — Flow characterized by high preponderance of females and children as men arranged for their families to join them; restrictive policies "cut off" other forms of immigration.	—MALES, YOUNG ADULTS — Males in majority until 1958 when another cycle of excess females and elderly dependents commenced. — Average age younger during 1950s (20-24), especially for Southern Europeans.	—YOUNG ADULTS, MORE BALANCE

(cont'd.)

Table 1.7. The Changing Attributes of the Immigrant Flow into Canada, 1896 Onwards

ATTRIBUTE		WHEAT ECONOMY (1896–1914)	POST WORLD WAR ONE (1919–1930)	THE GREAT DEPRESSION (1931–1939)	POST WAR ECONOMIC BOOM (1946–1961)	REDUCING RESTRICTIONS (1961–1975)
AREA OF ORIGIN		—BRITISH, UKRAINIAN, JEWISH — British featured the largest share, though the majority decreased sharply during 1910–1914, as Jews, Italians and Ukrainians flocked to Canada. — Northern and Western Europeans were noticeably absent.	—SCANDINAVIA, EAST EUROPEAN — Over 50 per cent from British Isles in early 1920s as a result of preferred status and restrictions on aliens. — Influx from Germany, Scandinavia in late 1920s; also from Eastern Europe under special agreements.	—AMERICAN — Primarily American, and British, since with a few exceptions, only certain British subjects and American citizens could enter Canada.	—SOUTH EUROPEAN — British remained numerically largest, but proportion much reduced with strong flows of Italians, Germans and Southern Europeans. — Orientals severely restricted until late 1950s.	—THIRD WORLD — With the relaxation of restrictions a noticeable shift towards Asian, African and Caribbean immigrants. — The USA (18.3 per cent) and Britain (14.8 per cent) were leading source countries (1972).
OCCUPATIONAL STRUCTURE		—UNSKILLED, PRIMARY OCCUPATIONS — Foreign born relatively uneducated and unskilled. — Over-representation in mining, transportation, domestic service and farm labour categories.	—UNSKILLED PRIMARY OCCUPATIONS	—DEPENDENTS — Mostly dependents, very few workers, since regulations prohibited the importation of job seekers who could displace Canadian labour.	—BLUE COLLAR AND WHITE COLLAR — A duality of the skilled and unskilled. — Labourers, construction and manufacturing workers largest segment, but professional and clerical groups became increasingly important. — Few with financial, communications, commercial and managerial capacities.	—SKILLED, WHITE COLLAR — Professionals rose from 17 per cent (1961) to 32 per cent (1969) of immigrants. — Proportion of labourers declined sharply while percentage of construction workers also down. — An upsurge in semi-skilled workers, particularly in the service industries since 1970.

Sources: Information for the commentary was obtained from:
Department of Manpower and Immigration, *The Immigration Program*, A Report of the Canadian Immigration and Population Study (Ottawa: Queen's Printer, 1974), pp. 1–39.
Department of Manpower and Immigration, *Immigration and Population Statistics*, A report of the Canadian Immigration and Population Study (Ottawa: Queen's Printer, 1974).
W. Burton Hurd, *The Origins and Nativity of the Canadian People*, 1931 Census Monograph No. 7 (Ottawa, Dominion Bureau of Statistics, 1937).
Warren E. Kalbach, *The Impact of Post World War II Immigration on Canada's Population*, 1961 Census Monograph (Ottawa: Queen's Printer, 1970).
Warren E. Kalbach, and Wayne W. McVey, *The Demographic Bases of Canadian Society* (Toronto: McGraw-Hill, 1971).
Warren E. Kalbach, *The Effect of Immigration on Population* (Ottawa: Manpower and Immigration, 1974).
Daniel Kubat and David Thornton, *A Statistical Profile of Canadian Society* (Toronto: McGraw-Hill-Ryerson, 1974).

Table 1.8. Factors Influencing the Characteristics of the Immigration to Canada

TYPE	DEFINITION, DESCRIPTION	EXAMPLES PERTAINING TO CANADA
Factors *"Pushing"* Emigrants from their Homeland	– Economic deprivation, unemployment. – Political oppression, upheavals, loss of land, etc. – Institutional assistance to emigrate.	– War, persecution, provocation and political upheaval has variously motivated Jews, Poles, Ukrainians, **Hungarians**, Finns and more recently, Ugandans, Chileans and Vietnamese to seek refuge in Canada. – After World War 1, the Empire Overseas Settlement Act, the Assisted Passage Scheme and other programs were enacted to encourage emigration from Britain to Canada and other Commonwealth nations. – A substantial inflow of peoples from Greece, Portugal and southern Italy has occurred since World War II, as they sought relief from poverty imposed by a rigid societal structure and a lagging economy.
Factors *"Pulling"* Emigrants to Canada	– Economic motivation (income differentials, availability of employment). – Quality and quantity of information available (from those who immigrated previously). – Image (from media or promotional efforts).	– Canada has periodically needed immigrant labour for its robust economy – from farmers, miners and railway workers who opened the Prairie frontier in the early 1900s, to professionals who could contribute to an expanding university and scientific community during the 1960s. – Promotion of further immigration through the funnelling of information back to the homeland was assisted by sponsorship arrangements which have facilitated the transplant of Italian communities into Canada's big city neighbourhoods. – The role that images play in the process is difficult to estimate. Sifton was, for example, criticized by contemporaries for the rosy picture of the Canadian Prairies that was painted abroad.

URBAN CANADA 63

Table 1.8. Factors Influencing the Characteristics of the Immigration to Canada

TYPE	DEFINITION, DESCRIPTION	EXAMPLES PERTAINING TO CANADA
Intervening Aids or Obstacles to Migration	– Regulatory measures of the Canadian government. – Willingness of foreign governments to permit and assist emigration. – Technology: improvements in transportation and communication.	– Attempts through policy by the Canadian government to influence the incoming flow of immigrants according to characteristics, such as: (1) Size of Flow (promotional efforts when labour shortages experienced; regulatory measures as unemployment rises). (2) Ethnic Composition (though recently rescinded, a longstanding policy of favouring Northern and Western Europeans, who were considered more easily assimilable). (3) Occupational Characteristics (traditionally, agriculturalists were desired). (4) Destinations Within Country (early in the century immigrants were encouraged to settle in the Prairies and Rural Canada).

Sources: Information for examples cited obtained from: F. Hawkins; *Canada and Immigration: Public Policy and Public Concern*, (Montreal and London (McGill-Queen's University Press, 1972); W. E. Kalbach, *The Impact of Immigration on Canada's Population*, 1961 Census Monograph (Ottawa: Dominion Bureau of Statistics, 1970); G. F. Plant, *Overseas Settlement: Migration from the United Kingdom to the Dominion*, (London: Oxford University Press, 1951); A. H. Richmond, *Post-War Immigrants in Canada*, (Toronto: University of Toronto Press, 1967); and W. G. Smith, *A Study in Canadian Immigration*, (Toronto: Ryerson Press, 1920).

INTERNAL MIGRATION IN CANADA

Canadians are a mobile people. Neither immigrants nor the native born have shown any overwhelming inclination to remain permanently attached to their community of settlement or birth. During the 1966—71 period, the number of people aged five years and over who moved was 41.9 per cent of Canada's 1971 population total. However, the vast majority of moves were of relatively short distance, occurring within or between municipalities in the same province. Interprovincial migration accounted for only one out of every ten changes in residence during the 1966-71 period.

Some may find it startling that during the past fifteen years, the total of interprovincial migrants far exceeds international immigrants.[31] In the peak year 1966–67, internal migration among provinces was more than twice as large (450,000) as the total immigration from abroad to Canada of 215,000. In the trough years of 1961-62, and 1971–72 when the economy was relatively slack, the total interprovincial moves were approximately four times as high as foreign migration to Canada.[32] Hence, internal migration is generally of greater importance to urban-rural population differentials, sustained regional population imbalances and city growth.

Apart from the depression decade, interprovincial migration has become increasingly significant since the turn of the century. The percentage of persons residing outside their province of birth rose from 6.5 per cent of the Canadian-born population in 1901 to 12.3 per cent in 1961.[33] Although lifetime interprovincial migration statistics yield only a broad historical picture, some notion of changes in the levels and patterns of in-migration and out-migration by province can be surmised. Sharp reversals in the migratory patterns during the seventy-year period are evident. Heavy westward movement to the Prairie provinces during the early 1900s had lost its momentum by the 1920s and was succeeded by out-migration, which accelerated during the depression years and continued until the present time in Manitoba and Saskatchewan. Ontario, which experienced an unparallelled outflow of its native born population to the American and Canadian West prior to World War I has become a prime recipient of interprovincial migrants since the 1920s. Consistency is the keynote of the other provinces, with the Maritimes being long-term losers and British Columbia a long-term gainer.

Since the end of the World War II, only the three most economically advanced provinces – Ontario, Alberta and British Columbia – have consistently gained population through interprovincial migration. Three distinct patterns of population movement are revealed by the data in Table 1.9.

First, Ontario, Alberta and British Columbia experienced a net

Table 1.9. Canada, Interprovincial and International Migration Flows, 1961-75

Province	(1961-66)			(1966-71)			(1971-75)		
	Net Inter-provincial Migration	Net Inter-national Migration	Net Total Migration	Net Inter-provincial Migration	Net Inter-national Migration	Net Total Migration	Net Inter-provincial Migration	Net Inter-national Migration	Net Total Migration
Newfoundland	− 15,300	− 7,400	− 22,700	− 19,300	− 4,900	− 24,200	− 2,500	− 7,500	− 10,000
Prince Edward Island	− 3,000	− 1,600	− 4,600	− 2,800	− 800	− 3,600	+ 3,200	+ 200	+ 3,400
Nova Scotia	− 27,000	− 8,900	− 35,900	− 16,400	− 1,000	− 17,400	+ 7,200	+ 3,400	+ 10,600
New Brunswick	− 25,700	− 7,700	− 33,400	− 19,600	− 7,900	− 27,500	+ 10,200	+ 2,300	+ 12,500
Quebec	− 19,800	+ 13,700	− 6,100	− 122,700	+ 70,000	− 52,700	− 65,000	+ 48,900	− 16,100
Ontario	+ 85,300	+ 157,700	+ 243,000	+ 150,700	+ 353,500	+ 504,200	− 17,400	+ 295,100	+ 277,700
Manitoba	− 23,400	− 3,500	− 26,900	− 40,700	+ 25,500	− 15,200	− 22,600	+ 21,700	− 900
Saskatchewan	− 42,100	− 9,600	− 51,700	− 81,400	+ 3,700	− 77,700	− 46,600	+ 4,300	− 42,300
Alberta	− 2,300	+ 1,500	− 800	+ 32,000	+ 44,000	+ 76,000	+ 34,000	+ 40,100	+ 76,100
British Columbia	+ 77,800	+ 26,900	+ 104,700	+ 115,000	+ 90,600	+ 205,600	+ 96,700	+ 87,500	+ 184,200

Notes: Figures are rounded to the nearest hundred. Annual counts are for the period June 1 to May 31 the following year. Data for emigration and interprovincial migration are estimates. Estimates of interprovincial migration are based upon family allowance data, which is derived from the count of change of address cards received in the Department of Health and Welfare, Government of Canada.

Source: Derived from Immigration Statistics: Department of Manpower and Immigration, *Monthly Reports*. Emigration and Interprovincial Migration Statistics: Unpublished data prepared by Population Estimates and Projections Division, Census Field, Statistics Canada. Reproduced by permission of the Minister of Supply and Services Canada.

inflow of internal as well as foreign migrants leading to rapid growth in these provinces. The largest share of international immigrants (over 50 per cent) accrued to Ontario while gains from interprovincial migration were greatest in British Columbia.

Second, small net inflows of foreign migrants combined with large outflows of internal migrants were responsible for an absolute decline in Saskatchewan and the anaemic growth of populations in Manitoba and Quebec.

Third, relatively high rates of natural increase in the Atlantic provinces during the 1960s were offset by a net outflow of migrants, thus resulting in slow population growth.

The mobility of Canadians is therefore expressed through interprovincial migration towards those parts of the country where incomes are high, where the number and variety of jobs are greatest and where the range of social amenities – educational facilities, health services and recreational opportunities – is most appealing. Although variations are apparent for internal and international flows, the predominant focus of both flows on Ontario, Alberta and British Columbia gives rise to the suggestion that the forces that govern the directions of internal migration may be the same as those that influence the choices of immigrants.[34]

To conclude, natural increase, not international migration, has been primarily responsible for Canada's overall population growth since Confederation. However, internal migration has been more important than natural increase in accounting for provincial differences in population growth.[35] Data available from 1921 onwards indicate, for example, that rates of natural increase experienced in the Atlantic provinces and Saskatchewan have been consistently higher than the Canadian average, but that out-migration siphoned off population. In contrast, Ontario and British Columbia which generally have had the lowest rates of natural increase in the nation, have had to rely upon high in-migration each decade in order to fulfil labour force requirements.[36] A province's population "retaining power" would appear therefore to depend in large measure upon its rate of economic expansion.

Urban Growth in Canada: Components of Change

Although we have discussed components of national and provincial growth, we have only touched upon questions of urban growth. How does urbanization occur? Where do urbanites come from? The answers to these questions are not unfamiliar: the proportion of people in cities can rise because the excess of births over deaths is greater in the city than in the country; or because people move from the country to the city (internal migration); or because immigrant arrivals seek urban destinations more often than rural destinations (international immigration).[37]

The evidence is clearcut. During the 1921-60 period, urbanization was spurred by a combination of (1) strong rural-urban migration within the country and (2) the selection of primarily urban destinations by immigrants to Canada. The rate of natural increase in rural areas has exceeded that of urban areas at least since 1921. Not only were birth rates higher in rural than in urban areas, but death rates were also lower in hamlets and farms than in cities.[38] Because the natural increase of the rural population exceeded that of the urban population, one would have expected the rural-urban structure to have been changing in favour of the rural sector. Yet, urban growth, swelled by migration from farm to city, has far outstripped rural population increases.

NATURAL INCREASE AND NET MIGRATION

Net migration has been less important to the growth of Canadian cities than it has been for changing the balance of the rural-urban population. Figures suggest that an excess of births over deaths accounted for a far larger portion of city growth during the 1930s and 1940s than did migratory movement (though the contribution of the two components was quite similar during the 1920s.[39] Data for the 1950s are less reliable due to definitional difficulties which excluded many of the post-war suburbs from the urban population at the beginning of the decade, but they do indicate that the contribution of net migration to urban growth was somewhat larger than the contribution of natural increase. But during the 'sixties natural increase accounted for about two-thirds of overall urban growth, and was the dominant factor in all centres except Toronto, Vancouver and Victoria.[40]

However, aggregates can sometimes be misleading. Considerable variation exists in the relative contribution of factors by urban size group. The influx of migrants, both domestic and foreign, was a prime reason for the expansion of the largest (100,000 population and over) urban centres, accounting for about 50 per cent of the increase during the 1951–61 period. On the other hand, natural increase of resident population accounted for more than 80 per cent of the growth in small urban places (less than 10,000 population).

MIGRATION FLOWS AMONG URBAN AND RURAL AREAS

A common though erroneous notion is that the flow of economically and culturally deprived from isolated farms to towns and cities is still chiefly responsible for the rapid expansion of urban areas. Un-

Table 1.10. Streams of Internal Migration Among Urban and Rural Areas For Persons Aged Five and Over, 1956–61, 1966–71

(1) Interprovincial Migrants, 1956–61
(Number and Percentage)

From \ To	Urban	Rural Non-Farm	Rural Farm	Total Out Migration
Urban	341,992 (65.4)	66,662 (12.7)	10,611 (2.0)	419,265 (80.1)
Rural Non-Farm	18,894 (3.6)	5,909 (1.3)	4,250 (0.8)	30,053 (5.7)
Rural Farm	49,118 (9.4)	22,386 (4.3)	2,295 (0.4)	73,799 (14.1)
Total In-Migration	410,004 (78.4)	95,957 (18.3)	17,156 (3.3)	523,117 (100.0)
Net Migration	−9261 (−1.8)	65,904 (12.6)	−56,643 (−10.8)	

(2) Interprovincial Migrants, 1966–71
(Number and Percentage)

From \ To	Urban	Rural Non-Farm	Rural Farm	Total Out-Migration
Urban	594,245 (70.8)	83,315 (9.9)	17,440 (2.1)	695,000 (82.8)
Rural Non-Farm	84,295 (10.0)	18,925 (2.3)	5,360 (0.6)	108,575 (12.9)
Rural Farm	26,835 (3.2)	6,925 (0.8)	2,675 (0.3)	36,470 (4.3)
Total In-Migration	705,375 (84.0)	109,165 (13.0)	25,475 (13.0)	840,015 (100.0)
Net Migration	10,375 (1.2)	590 (0.1)	−10,965 (−1.3)	

(3) *Intraprovincial, Intermunicipal Migration, 1966 – 71*
(number and percentage)

From \ To	Urban	Rural Non-Farm	Rural Farm	Total Out-Migration
Urban	1,686,835 (61.5)	315,690 (11.5)	107,810 (3.9)	2,110,330 (77.0)
Rural Non-Farm	312,265 (11.4)	106,345 (3.9)	32,480 (1.2)	451,090 (16.5)
Rural Farm	126,915 (4.6)	27,895 (1.0)	25,475 (0.9)	180,290 (6.5)
Total In-Migration	2,126,015 (77.6)	449,930 (16.4)	165,765 (6.0)	2,741,710 (100.0)
Net Migration	15,685 (0.6)	−1160 (−0.1)	−14525 (−0.5)	

(4) *Total Internal Migration, 1966 – 71*

From \ To	Urban	Rural Non-Farm	Rural Farm	Total Out-Migration
Urban	2,281,080 (63.7)	399,005 (11.1)	125,250 (3.5)	2,805,325 (78.3)
Rural Non-Farm	396,560 (11.1)	125,270 (3.5)	37,840 (1.0)	559,670 (15.6)
Rural Farm	153,750 (4.3)	34,820 (1.0)	28,150 (0.8)	216,720 (6.1)
Total In-Migration	2,831,390 (79.1)	559,095 (15.6)	191,240 (5.3)	3,581,725 (100.0)
Net Migration	26,055 (0.8)	−575 (0.0)	−25480 (−0.8)	

(5) *Total Internal Migration, 1966 – 71 With distinction between metropolitan and non-metropolitan areas* (number and percentage)

To From	Urban CMA	Urban Non-CMA	Rural Non-Farm	Rural Farm	Total Out Migration
Urban CMA	1,220,055 (34.1)	296,625 (8.3)	202,060 (5.6)	63,925 (1.8)	1,782,665 (49.8)
Urban Non-CMA	416,995 (11.6)	347,405 (9.7)	196,940 (5.5)	61,320 (1.7)	1,022,665 (28.5)
Rural Non-Farm	195,775 (5.5)	200,785 (5.6)	125,270 (3.5)	37,840 (1.0)	559,670 (15.6)
Rural Farm	71,180 (2.0)	82,570 (2.3)	34,820 (1.0)	28,150 (0.8)	216,720 (6.1)
Total In- Migration	1,904,005 (53.2)	927,400 (25.9)	559,095 (15.6)	191,240 (5.3)	3,581,725 (100.0)
Net Migration	121,340 (3.4)	−95265 (−2.6)	−575 (0.0)	−25480 (−0.8)	

Sources: Raw data derived from: DBS, *1961 Census of Canada*, Vol. 4:1−9, Tables 13 and 15; and Statistics Canada, *1971 Census of Canada*, Vol. 1:2−7, Table 33−1. Reproduced by permission of Minister of Supply and Services Canada.

Definitions: *Urban*: includes the population living in (1) incorporated cities, towns and villages with a population of 1,000 or over: (2) unincorporated places of 1,000 or over having a population density of at least 1,000 per square mile: (3) the built-up fringes of (1) and (2) having a minimum population of 1,000 and a density of at least 1,000 per square mile.
Rural: includes all the remaining non-urban population.
Rural farm population includes the population living in dwellings situated on farms in rural areas. A farm for census purposes is an agricultural holding of one or more acres with sales of agricultural products of $50 or more in the previous year.
Census Metropolitan Area: The main labour market of a continuously built-up area having a population of 100,000 or more.
Internal Migrants: Individuals who move from one municipality to another. People who change their place of residence within a municipality are not considered to be internal migrants.

Notes: Additions may not yield exact totals for the 1966−71 results because of random rounding to "5" or "0".
The distinction between "rural farm" and "rural non-farm" is not totally consistent for the two census periods. Given the complications that would arise with self-enumeration, which was employed in 1971 respondents were not required to classify themselves as "rural farm" or "rural non-farm." Instead, entire municipalities were classified under one of these designations. Hence, exact comparison of the data for the two succeeding census periods is not advisable, although general trends may be distinguished.
Respondents in "the municipality not stated" and "location of residence not stated" categories have been excluded from the tabulations.

doubtedly, the lure of steady (and high) incomes, community services and the bright lights, enticed farm sons and daughters to seek their fortune in the city, and was of prime importance in the past. But, more recently, movement between urban areas has comprised by far the largest portion of total internal migration in Canada. During 1966–71, changes of residence between urban areas predominated among both long distance moves between provinces and short distance transfers between municipalities within the same province. And the proportion of internal migration arising from inter-urban moves is increasing, as one would expect with urban population increasing as a proportion of the total (Table 1.10).

There has also been an increasing "counterstream" of those moving from urban to rural-farm areas. During 1956–61, 9.4 per cent of all interprovincial migrants consisted of the traditional flow of farm people to the cities while only 2.0 per cent were a counter flow (Table 1.10). By 1966–71, the gap between the two had narrowed considerably. The rough balancing between these flows suggests that rural-urban movement is providing little present stimulus to overall urban growth.

Net migration statistics (Table 1.10) force one to conclude that internal migration was responsible for remarkably little of the change that took place during the 1960s in the distribution of population between the rural and urban sectors of Canadian society. As an example, the 3.6 million internal migrants recorded during 1966–71 resulted in a net transfer of only 26,000 people from rural to urban areas in Canada. The balance between migration streams is best illustrated by observing flows between pairs of sectors, such as the urban and the rural non-farm sectors. Of 800,000 people involved, 399,000 people took up residence along a township road or on a country estate, while an equivalent number, 396,500, sought to establish a new home in an urban community.

In recent years, internal migration resulted more in population redistribution between urban size groups than between urban and rural areas. For 1966–71, of the net gain of 121,340 persons which accrued to metropolitan areas via internal migration, in excess of three-quarters were former residents of smaller (non-metropolitan) urban centres while less than one-quarter, 25,000 were residents in the farm sector (Table 1.10).

Unfortunately there are problems. Many of the smaller "urban" groupings are rural by any reasonably intuitive definition, moreover, one should be cautious, when analysing small net differences in migration. The demographic structure of a city can change dramatically even though flows of in-migrants and out-migrants are roughly balanced in terms of numbers. Obviously this occurs when flows of arriving and departing migrants differ systematically from one another according to sex, age, ethnicity, occupational status, and so on.[41]

IMMIGRANTS AND INTERNAL MIGRANTS TO METROPOLITAN AREAS

As mentioned earlier, there is a strong tendency for immigrants to concentrate in the largest metropolitan areas (Table 1.11). For example, Montreal, Toronto and Vancouver collectively accounted for almost 70 per cent of all foreign in-migrants to the twenty-one largest cities. About one-third of all immigrants to Canada chose Toronto alone during the 1966–71 period. Indeed, Toronto's robust growth has not been due to internal migration but to immigration from abroad.

In contrast, internal migration appears less strongly related to size and growth of Canada's metropolitan areas. Indeed, a pattern of internal migration for Canada's metropolitan areas is hard to determine. Volume has been high; almost one Canadian in five arrived in and/or departed from one of Canada's largest centres during 1966–71. But rates of internal migration have varied considerably from one city to another and from one year to the next. If internal migration was the only source of population change, some of the largest cities in central Canada (e.g. Montreal, Toronto, Winnipeg) would have lost population between 1966 and 1971; at the same time, other Western centres (e.g. Calgary, Edmonton, Vancouver) would have registered healthy gains. But again a cautionary note. Many domestic out-migrants from a particular city appear to have remained in what might be termed "the urban field" of the metropolitan centre. Many of the recorded moves, particularly in the Toronto region, are to destinations in communities which are situated outside, though in proximity to the metropolitan area. Such "local" outward movement therefore may reinforce rather than detract from the population size and growth of the metropolis.

Generally speaking, the origin of in-migrants is associated with the population size of the destination city. On the basis of 1966–71 data four sources of in-migrants to Census Metropolitan Areas can be delineated: foreign, urban counties, non-urban counties in other provinces and non-urban counties in the same province.[42] Smaller urban centres (100,000 to 150,000) attract migrants primarily from non-urban counties in the same province.[43] Cities in the 300,000 range draw migrants predominantly from other urban counties. Metropolitan areas in the 500,000 range attract a sizeable number of foreign migrants, though migrants from other urban areas remain dominant. The three major metropolises, however, exhibit different

Table 1.11. Some Parameters of Canadian Urban Migration, Twenty-one Metropolitan Areas, 1966–71

Metropolitan Areas*	Population 1971	Total Net Migration	In-migrants From elsewhere in Canada	Percentage of Total In-migrants To 21 Cities	Immigrants From outside Canada	Percentage of Total Immigrants To 21 Cities
Vancouver	1,082,352	+132,900	267,200	12.4%	84,100	10.7%
Edmonton	495,702	+38,900	152,500	7.1	25,600	3.2
Calgary	403,319	+51,200	148,900	6.9	27,700	3.5
Saskatoon	126,449	−1,100	68,300	3.2	4,700	.6
Regina	140,734	−6,700	55,200	2.6	3,900	.5
Winnipeg	540,262	+9,600	109,600	5.1	30,200	3.8
Thunder Bay	112,093	−3,000	27,900	1.3	4,100	2.0
Windsor	258,643	+9,600	33,800	1.6	15,900	2.0
London	286,011	+23,200	77,000	3.6	20,000	2.5
Sudbury	155,424	+13,800	56,200	2.6	5,200	.7
Kitchener	226,846	+23,400	60,200	2.8	18,300	2.3
Hamilton	498,523	+7,900	81,100	3.8	31,600	4.0
Toronto	2,628,043	+205,600	346,900	16.1	324,600	41.1
St. Catharines	303,429	+9,300	55,600	2.6	12,600	1.6
Ottawa–Hull	602,510	+44,200	124,500	5.8	30,300	3.8
Montreal	2,743,208	+57,800	277,300	12.9	127,000	16.1
Quebec	480,502	+22,900	83,900	3.9	6,200	.8
Chicoutimi	133,703	−6,400	24,100	1.1	800	.1
Saint John	106,744	−2,900	18,400	.9	1,700	.2
Halifax	222,637	+3,000	52,900	2.5	6,700	.8
St. John's	131,185	−1,200	27,600	1.3	2,600	.3
21 City Total	11,678,319		2,149,100	100.0	783,800	100.0

* Aggregations of counties and census divisions to correspond as closely as possible to Census Metropolitan Areas: Data were unavailable for Victoria.
Source: Derived from a special tabulation by Statistics Canada based on Department of National Revenue information. Reproduced by permission of the Ministry of Supply and Services Canada.

patterns of in-migration. Toronto's flow is dominated by foreign migrants, Montreal's by migrants from non-urban counties in Quebec, and Vancouver's by migrants from other urban counties.[44]

THE CHARACTERISTICS OF MIGRANTS: THEIR EFFECT ON THE URBAN DEMOGRAPHIC STRUCTURE

We now know where migrants come from and where they go, but who are the migrants? What is characteristic of those who migrate within Canada, and more specifically those who have sought homes in urban Canada? After all, the migration process serves as an agent of change, strongly influencing the demographic structure of a region, shaping its age-sex composition, its ethnic features and its occupational characteristics. Knowing about those who move, in comparison to those who remain, is helpful in understanding urban Canada and the dynamics of its change:

Sex: For the most recent period (1966 – 71), no general pattern of sex selectivity appears. Some variation exists with distance spanned and destination sought; males dominate somewhat among both long distance (interprovincial) movers and migrants to rural areas.

Other studies have indicated a substantial female selectivity in net migration to urban areas.[45] This long standing "female dominance" in the composition of internal net flows from rural to urban areas (approximately 1881 – 1951) has tended to increase birth rates in the cities by continually adding to the size of the female urban population in the most fertile age groups.[46]

Age: During the 1966 – 71 period, a marked age selectivity existed for migrants within Canada. They tended to be younger than the population as a whole and the most numerous age group was the twenty-five to twenty-nine years age category. Female migrants tended to be slightly younger than males.

This excess of young adults among migrants is not surprising, since they are in a transition phase in the life cycle. Those aged twenty to twenty-nine years are undergoing a period of adjustment in relation to their family, the completion of education, their entry into the labour force, and their marital status.[47]

Education, Occupation: Those who migrate tend to have higher education levels than those who stay, not surprisingly since younger adults have higher average education levels than those who are older. Moreover, the mean level of educational achievement is greater for those moving longer distances. The trend is readily interpretable since facilities for higher education, jobs requiring specialized skills, and career positions which are nationally advertised are concentrated in a few large urban centres to which the skilled and educated must move if they are to take advantage of the opportunities presented.[48]

Demographic structure invariably reflects overall demographic processes. Table 1.12 indicates that Canada's urban population has consistently had an excess of females, largely because of relatively abundant female employment opportunities in cities and a concomitant scarcity of jobs usually filled by females in rural areas.

The relatively stable long run sex composition of urban Canada has occasionally been jolted. Most noticeable was the sudden rise of the male to female sex ratio to an all-time high in 1911 (both urban and rural Canada). This was largely the result of the highest ever flow of immigrants, predominantly males, who entered Canada under the encouragement of the Laurier government's "open door" immigration policy. Later, wartime mortality among males was reflected in the sharp drop of both the urban and rural sex ratios in 1921. In recent decades, the proportion of males to females in all parts of the country has become relatively equal.

There are also proportionately more women in large cities than in smaller settlements. This probably reflects, if only crudely, systematic variations in occupational structure between cities of different sizes. Women have found most of their jobs in personal services, clerical and sales positions and the professions, all of which tend to be located in urban areas. On the other hand, employment opportunities for men in manufacturing, mining and transportation usually constitute a larger share of the job market in smaller urban places.

Differences between urban and rural areas have been observed in the proportions of young, mature and aged persons. Although the age composition of farm and city has been similarly affected by fluctuating levels of fertility and the long term decline of mortality, the population of urban areas has consistently had larger proportions of people in the productive age groups (15 – 64 years) and fewer in the dependent age groups (0 – 14 years, 65 years and over). As well, larger centres have even more people in the productive age groups and less in the dependent groups. Although partly a reflection of lower birth rates, smaller family sizes and slighter higher death rates in cities, these age structure differences have been caused largely by the propensity of young adults to leave non-metropolitan areas.

WHY PEOPLE HAVE MOVED TO URBAN CENTRES

Now the most difficult question: Why do people migrate?

The conclusion of most migration studies is that the "economic" motive explains a substantial proportion of migratory movement. The observation that migration is induced by man's desire "to better

Table 1.12. The Changing Sex-Age Composition of Urban and Rural Canada

Year	Sex Ratio – All Ages			Sex Ratio – Aged 20–34		Dependency Ratio	
	Urban Canada	Rural Canada	Toronto	Urban Canada	Rural Canada	Urban Canada	Rural Canada
1871	94.9	104.7	96.5				
1881	93.9	105.6	94.2				
1891	95.5	107.8	94.3				
1901	96.0	110.9	87.7				
1911	105.7	118.5	98.1	112.7	137.3	50.6	68.7
1921	97.4	115.9	92.6	89.7	121.4	56.7	73.1
1931	98.8	118.2	93.8	92.8	128.3	50.6	68.8
1941	96.7	116.0	93.9	90.6	120.3	44.2	62.5
1951	95.8	114.1	94.9	88.9	113.0	53.8	74.5
1961	98.1	112.1	98.	97.2	114.0	65.8	83.5
1971	98.	109.	98.	99.1	109.9	57.1	71.9

Definitions: The *sex ratio* is obtained by dividing the total number of males by the number of females. The unit of measurement is males per 100 females.
The *dependency ratio* is the number of persons not in the labour force (aged 0–14 and 65 or over) divided by the number of persons who potentially can be members of the labour force (aged 15–64). This ratio is multiplied by 100.
Toronto: The City of Toronto (1871–1931); the boundaries of Metropolitan Toronto (1941–1951); the boundaries of the Toronto Census Metropolitan Area (1961–1971).

Sources: Derived from Leroy O. Stone, *Urban Development in Canada*, 1961 Census Monograph, (Ottawa: Dominion Bureau of Statistics, 1967); Dominion Bureau of Statistics, *Census*, Vol. 1, t, 16, 1951; Bull. 1:1–7, t, 12–1, 1961; and Statistics Canada, *Census*, Bull. 1:2 –2, t, 2, 1971; Bull. 1:2–3, t, 8, 1971. Reproduced by permission of the Minister of Supply and Services Canada.

himself in material respects"[49] has been incorporated into virtually all treatises and models of migration. Technological change and the exploitation of new resources, some have contended, inevitably create imbalances between the distribution of the population and the location of economic opportunities. These require a continuing redistribution of labour in order to capture the benefits of economic growth. As Lowry[50] says: "People migrate in search of jobs from low wage areas to high wage areas, from areas of labour surplus to those with labour shortages." The long-term redistribution of Canada's population during this century, from rural farm to urban community, from stagnant hinterland to bustling metropolis or, in step-wise fashion, from dormant village to enterprising town to thriving city has been interpreted largely from an economic perspective.[51] Courchene's (1970) study of income tax returns for Canadian men from 1965 to 1968[52] showed that migrants did, on average, obtain higher percentage increases in their incomes than non-migrants. Another analysis by Vanderkamp (1968)[53] indicated that the mobility rate for the unemployed far exceeded that of employed individuals.

All the evidence suggests reciprocal relationships between migration and economic development. The expansion of a city is fuelled by migrants who serve both as necessary increments to the labour force and welcome additions to the local market of consumers. At the same time, potential movers are attracted by an abundance of opportunities. This description is highly oversimplified, but it does draw attention to the self-sustaining nature of growth in urban areas.

Nevertheless, forces that "push" migrants away from their origins and "pull" them towards specific destinations should not be interpreted totally in economic terms. In his studies of internal migration among U.S. urban areas, Lowry[54] concluded that out-migration from metropolitan areas was insensitive to local economic conditions but that other factors act to "select" those who migrate. These life cycle factors tend to be associated with demographic characteristics such as the proportion of young people in the city's population. Both prosperous and depressed communities experience a substantial outflow of educated, vigorous and ambitious young adults. However, given their propensity to move they choose their destinations on the basis of available employment opportunities.[55]

Some researchers have also emphasized the role played by "information."[56] "The pattern of migration conforms closely to the pattern of information flows, although still moving generally in the direction of improved earnings."[57] Information regarding employment alternatives, wage levels and living conditions at a particular place does not flow freely, but is impeded by distance, filtered down the urban hierarchy and channelled through relatives and acquaintances who migrated previously. People generally wish to minimize uncertainty and risk. Thus, a migrant is likely to take advantage of employment opportunities about which he knows, rather than risk migrating to an "unknown" destination. The image of "metropolitan culture" projected by the media and, more importantly, by word of mouth, undoubtedly has a strong influence on the flow of migrants.

Individual perceptions and evaluation of alternative destinations "colour" and filter the objective facts.[58] Migration streams are composed of a vast diversity of people—Italian and British, poor and rich, trained professional and illiterate labourer—each of whom made an individual decision to move under a wide variety of circumstances—some upon a whim, others under duress. This is an important perspective to remember, since too often, the people and their actual motives become lost under the weight of aggregate statistics and migrations are viewed as mechanical responses to economic attractions.

Man does not move for bread alone. Though economic concerns are demonstrably important, cities, in their pull upon migrants, offer more than the clear-cut job opportunities and diversified labour market which appear in times of plenty. They offer specialization—in educational facilities, research institutes, and medical centres. They offer choice—in homes, theatres, restaurants and retail outlets. They offer freedom—from small town social control as occurs openly in company towns but also more covertly in other centres through gossip and social sanctions. And for some in-migrants, such as Newfoundlanders who have moved to Toronto, the city offers a receiving area, a neighbourhood of former migrants in which new arrivals can gradually become acclimatized to the ways of big city dwellers.[59]

Lest the wrong impression be left, Canadian cities are not a mecca. There are many aspects of urban life that do not appeal to in-migrants. Higher housing prices, pollution, noise, lengthy commuting times and anonymity all have to be tolerated by the migrant seeking economic and other gains. Such are the trade-offs that Canadians have had to make. Clearly many have opted for the city, though many may, in fact, have had little real choice.[60]

Notes

1. P. R. Ehrlich and A. H. Ehrlich, *Population, Resources and Environment* (San Francisco: W. H. Freeman, 1972), p. 6.
2. B. Ward and R. Dubos, *Only One Earth* (New York: W. W. Norton, 1972), p. 149.
3. K. Lorenz, *On Aggression* (New York: Harcourt, Brace Jovanovich, 1974, second edition); and J. C. Calhoun, "Population Density and Social Pathology," *Scientific American*, Vol. 206, No. 2, 1962, pp. 139-148.
4. E. E. Lampard, "Historical Aspects of Urbanization," in P. M. Hauser and L. F. Schnore, (eds.), *The Study of Urbanization* (New York: Wiley, 1965), p. 25.
5. K. Davis, "The Origin and Growth of Urbanization in the Western World," *American Journal of Sociology*, Vol. 60, March, 1955, pp. 429-437.
6. K. Davis, "The Urbanization of the Human Population," *Cities* (New York: Alfred A. Knopf, A Scientific American Book, 1967), p. 8.
7. Ehrlich and Ehrlich, *op. cit.*, p. 45.
8. R. L. Forstall and V. Jones, "Selected Demographic, Economic and Governmental Aspects of the Contemporary Metropolis," in S. Miles, (ed.), *Metropolitan Problems* (Toronto: Methuen, 1970), pp. 10-18, 63-69; P. Wilsher and R. Righter, *The Exploding Cities* (New York: Quadrangle/The New York Times Book Co., 1975).
9. C. A. Doxiadis, *Ecumenopolis: The Settlement of the Future*, Research Report No. 1 (Athens, Greece: Athens Centre of Ekistics, 1967).
10. R. Buckminster Fuller, *Utopia or Oblivion? The Prospects for Humanity* (New York: Bantam Books, 1969).
11. D. L. Meadows, D. H. Meadows, J. Randers, and W. W. Behrens, *The Limits To Growth* (New York: New American Library, 1972).
12. Ward and Dubos, *op. cit.*, pp. 181-190.
13. Wilsher and Righter, *op. cit.*
14. D. M. Ray, "Canada: The Urban Challenge of Growth and Change," Discussion Paper B.74.3 (Ottawa: Ministry of State for Urban Affairs, 1974), p. 37.
15. For the 1971 Census of Canada, "urban" population included those living in (1) incorporated cities, towns or villages with a population of a 1,000 or over; (2) unincorporated places of 1,000 or over having a population density of at least 1,000 per square mile; (3) the built-up fringes of such centres having density of 1,000 per square mile.

    Nevertheless, the urban influence in Canadian communities is only partially indicated by the 76 per cent level of urbanization in 1971. Although census definitions of "urban" were revised in 1951, 1956 and again in 1961 to include population living in densely built-up areas outside municipal corporate boundaries, a portion of the population classified as rural consisted of persons who commuted to work within recognized urban centres. Still more people classified as rural in 1971 had occupations and lifestyles far removed from those typical of rural society. Similarly, since the definition of "urban" includes those living in towns of 1,000, some of these might more appropriately be considered "rural," or at least not characteristic of our largest cities.
16. The term "urbanization" requires clarification. It does not refer only to growth of cities, but to increases in the proportion of the total population concentrated in urban settlements. For an elaboration of this distinction, see Kingsley Davis, "The Urbanization of the Human Population," in *Cities* (New York: Alfred A. Knopf, 1967).
17. S. A. Cudmore and H. G. Caldwell, *Rural and Urban Composition of the Canadian Population*, 1931 Census Monograph No. 6 (Ottawa: King's Printer, 1938).

18. Urban growth is primarily due to increasing size of existing cities rather than new incorporations. New incorporations usually take place in urban centres housing less than 5,000 inhabitants. From 1871 to 1971, only fourteen of 192 new urban places in the 5,000-plus size group occurred by incorporation. For a more detailed review, see L. O. Stone, *Urban Development in Canada*, 1961 Census Monograph (Ottawa: Dominion Bureau of Statistics, 1967), p. 270.
19. G. K. Zipf, *Human Behaviour and the Principles of Least Effort* (Cambridge: Addison-Wesley Press, 1949), Chapter 9.
20. B. J. L. Berry, "City Size Distributions and Economic Development," *Economic Development and Cultural Change*, Vol. 9, 1961, pp. 573-588.
21. B. J. L. Berry, *The Geography of Market Centres and Retail Distribution* (Englewood Cliffs: Prentice-Hall, 1967), p. 76.
22. J. U. Marshall, *The Location of Service Towns* (Toronto: University of Toronto Press, 1969), p. 50.
23. Registration of births and deaths on a uniform and relatively complete basis has existed in Canada only since 1921, with Quebec data integrated in 1926. Information on vital events can be derived from parish records in Quebec back to the earliest times, but otherwise only the decennial census provides reliable fertility and mortality information prior to 1921. The extent and nature of emigration from Canada even today is a subject of considerable conjecture, since data for persons leaving Canada to establish residence elsewhere are not systematically collected. See: J. Henrepin, *Trends and Factors of Fertility in Canada*, 1961 Census Monograph (Ottawa: Statistics Canada, 1972); and D. M. McDougall, "Immigration into Canada, 1851-1920," *Canadian Journal of Economics and Political Science*, Vol. 27, No. 2, 1961, pp. 162-175.
24. The full impact of immigrants is underestimated since children born to immigrant families are counted as part of the natural increase of the domestic population.
25. See Table 1.5 for definitions of these terms.
26. Toronto *Star*, August 23, 1975.
27. D. Kubat and D. Thornton, *A Statistical Profile of Canadian Society* (Toronto: McGraw-Hill, 1974), p. 35.
28. B. Berkov and J. Sklar, "The American Birth Rate: Evidence of a Coming Rise," *Science*, Vol. 189, No. 4205, August 29, 1975.
29. Statistics Canada, *Population Projections for Canada and the Provinces, 1972*, 2 vols. (Ottawa: Information Canada, 1974), pp. 15-26.
30. Manpower and Immigration, Canada, *Canadian Immigration and Population Study*, Vol. 1, *Immigration Policy Perspectives* (Ottawa: Information Canada, 1974), p. 3.
31. Additional indirect evidence suggests that over the period from 1921 to 1960 internal net migration was more than twice as large as the net movement into Canada. It should be noted, however, that from one period to another, many of the same people may be interprovincial migrants; hence, over the long term, these relative proportions are less. For a further elaboration on the estimates, see I. Anderson, *Internal Migration in Canada 1921-1961*, Economic Council of Canada, Staff Study No. 13 (Ottawa: Queen's Printer, 1966), p. 15.
32. Manpower and Immigration, *op. cit.*, Volume 3, *Immigration and Population Statistics*.
33. M. V. George, *Internal Migration in Canada: Demographic Analyses*, 1961 Census Monograph (Ottawa: Dominion Bureau of Statistics, 1970), p. 90.
34. S. T. Nielsen, *Immigrants and the Indigenous Population* (Ottawa: Manpower and Immigration, 1973).
35. Anderson, *op. cit.*, p. 25.
36. W. E. Kalbach and W. W. McVey, *The Demographic Bases of Canadian Society* (Toronto: McGraw-Hill, 1971), pp. 75-89.
37. The proportion of people living in cities can also rise because of re-classification by census takers.

38. Anderson, *op. cit.*, p. 23.
39. *Ibid.*, pp. 21-26.
40. R. W. Crowley, "Population Distribution: Perspectives and Policies," in *Internal Migration: A Comparative Perspective*, A. Brown and E. Neuberger, (eds.) (New York: Academic Press, forthcoming).
41. L. O. Stone, *Migration in Canada: Regional Aspects*, 1961 Census Monograph (Ottawa: Dominion Bureau of Statistics, 1969), p. 7; and Kalbach and McVey, *op. cit.*, p. 32.
42. Manpower and Immigration, Canada, *Internal Migration and Immigrant Settlement*, in collaboration with Ministry of State for Urban Affairs (Ottawa: Information Canada, 1975), pp. 53-60.
43. Urban counties are aggregations of counties and census divisions that correspond as closely as possible to the boundaries of Census Metropolitan Areas. The remainder are classified as non-urban counties.
44. If we classify the twenty-two urban centres by the four stages, we obtain the following list:
    First stage
    Chicoutimi, Regina, Saskatoon, St. John's, Saint John, Quebec City, Thunder Bay, Sudbury, Montreal.
    Second stage
    Halifax, Kitchener, London, Windsor.
    Third stage
    Calgary, Edmonton, Hamilton, St. Catharines, Ottawa, Winnipeg.
    Fourth stage
    Toronto, Vancouver.
45. J. Cameron and W. B. Hurd, "Population Movement in Canada, 1921-1931," *Canadian Journal of Economics and Political Science*, Vol. 1, 1935, pp. 222-245; George, *op. cit.*, pp. 149-153; and L. O. Stone, *Urban Development in Canada*, 1961 Census Monograph (Ottawa: Dominion Bureau of Statistics, 1967), p. 64.
46. E. Charles, *The Changing Size of Family in Canada*, 1941 Census Monograph (Ottawa: King's Printer, 1948); and L. O. Stone, 1967, *op. cit.*, pp. 64-66.
47. H. S. Shyrock, *Population Mobility Within the United States* (Chicago: Community and Family Study Centre, 1964); George, *op. cit.*, pp. 153-154; and E. S. Lee, "A Theory of Migration," *Demography*, Vol. 3, No. 1, 1966, p. 57.
48. Stone, 1969, *op. cit.*, pp. 116-120.
49. E. G. Ravenstein, "The Laws of Migration," *Journal of the Royal Statistical Society*, Vol. 48, 1889, pp. 167-227.
50. I. S. Lowry, *Migration and Metropolitan Growth, Two Analytic Models* (San Francisco: Chandler, 1966), p. 13.
51. Anderson, *op. cit.*, pp. 29-42; and R. M. McInnis, "Provincial Migration and Differential Economic Opportunity," in L. O. Stone, (ed.), *Migration in Canada: Regional Aspects*, 1961 Census Monograph (Ottawa: Dominion Bureau of Statistics), pp. 131-202.
52. T. J. Courchene, "Interprovincial Migration and Economic Adjustment," *Canadian Journal of Economics*, Vol. 3, 1970, pp. 550-576.
53. J. Vanderkamp, *Mobility Behaviour in the Canadian Labour Force*, Economic Council of Canada, Special Study No. 16 (Ottawa: Information Canada, 1973).
54. Lowry, *op. cit.*, pp. 24-32.
55. J. B. Lansing and E. Mueller, *The Geographic Mobility of Labour*, Survey Research Centre (Ann Arbor, Michigan: Institute for Social Research, 1967); W. Alonso, *The System of Intermetropolitan Population Flows*, Working Paper No. 155, Centre for Planning and Development Research (Berkeley: University of California, 1971); and P. A. Morrison and D. A. Relles, *Recent Research Insights into Local Migration Flows* (Santa Monica: The Rand Corporation, Rand Paper Series, P-5379, 1975).
56. A. R. Pred, *Behaviour and Location: Foundations for a Geographic and Dynamic*

Location Theory, Part I, Lund Studies Geography Series, B, Human Geography, No. 27 (Sweden: University of Lund, 1969), pp. 19-52.
57. P. Nelson, "Migration, Real Income and Information," *Journal of Regional Science*, Vol. 1, 1959, pp. 43-74.
58. J. Wolpert, "Behavioural Aspects of the Decision to Migrate," *Papers and Proceedings of the Regional Science Association*, Vol. 15, 1965, pp. 159-169; and "Migration as an Adjustment to Environmental Stress," *Journal of Social Issues*, Vol. 22, No. 4, 1966, pp. 92-102; L. Brown and E. Moore, "The Intra-Urban Migration Process: A Perspective," *Geografiska Annaler*, Series B., Vol. 52B, No. 1, 1970; and S. Gale, "Explanatory Theory and Models of Migration," *Economic Geography*, Vol. 49, 1973, pp. 257-274.
59. Ministry of State for Urban Affairs, "Spatial Demographic Trends," MUPIM Group, mimeographed, 1974, pp. 14-16.
60. A key argument of *Guideline for the Seventies* (Government of Manitoba, 1973) is that Canadians from farms and villages are "forced" by social and economic circumstances to move to large cities even though they prefer the small town atmosphere and way of life. The choice of staying in rural Canada, is a choice of staying behind which for most people isn't a choice at all. Hence, the government policies aimed at enhancing this choice have been labelled the "Stay Option."

CHAPTER 2

Prospects for the Future

Introduction

> "It seems necessary... to reiterate a caution concerning any enterprise which aims to project the social future. There are two essential aspects to this caution: the one which says that to use past experience to predict future structures and processes is a dubious activity; and the other why it is a dubious activity – because the emergence of new conditions may make past experience obsolete."

> (G.F.N. Fearn in *Canadian Social Organizations*, 1973, p. 198).

In the Canada of 2000: How many people will there be? Where will they live? What will be the size of the labour force? Into how many households will the population be grouped? What proportion of the people will be of school age? of retirement age? Such questions are of immense importance to those who must take tough, long-term decisions: politicians, policy-makers, community planners, and corporate executives. The change and rate of change in population strongly influence economic development. They also set the requirements for physical and social infrastructure (such as schools, hospitals, transit systems and the like).

Demographic processes have many ramifications. If the shift of population from the "have not" to the "have " provinces continues, regional disparity may be aggravated and political relationships among provinces imbalanced. If people settle on the fringes of metropolitan centres, prime agricultural land may be swallowed up. If household formation rises substantially, housing shortages may be exacerbated. If the work force ages, there may be problems in supplying the necessary public services. If the number of people of retirement age increases dramatically, the costs of social security will escalate. It may be surprising to some that all of these "Ifs" are likely to become reality in Canada during the next few decades.

If current rates of natural increase and net migration remain as they are, Canada's population will number approximately thirty million by 2001 – an increase of over eight million from 1971. Thirty years from now, nine out of every ten Canadians will reside in urban communities. This implies that the ranks of the urbanites will swell by some eleven millions. Much of the growth will occur on the fringe of metropolitan areas, with centres of 400,000 to 1,000,000 expanding most rapidly. Western cities, such as Calgary, Edmonton and Vancouver, will likely continue to lead the nation in rates of growth; some important centres will attract a decreasing share of population growth – Montreal, Saint John, Winnipeg and Regina. A substantial relative shift of population will occur in favour of the provinces of Ontario, Alberta and British Columbia. Trends, in sum, suggest an increased clustering of Canadians into large cities and prosperous provinces.

Profound changes in demographic structure have also been projected. The number of households in Canada's three largest metropolitan areas is expected to increase 35 per cent during the 1971 – 81 decade. Although the number of births will increase as "baby boom" children themselves become parents, Canadians under the age of fifteen will become a smaller proportion of the Canadian population. The numbers of middle aged and elderly Canadians will increase considerably.

But projections, and the assumptions that underlie them, have their limitations. Let us digress for a moment and discuss some of these. Any projection is no more nor no less than a calculated exaggeration to dramatize the effect of current tendencies. They are not indications of what will be, but of what might be, and usually show a future that is "out-of-balance." They cannot account for the homeostatic or self-adjusting forces that usually come into play. But one reason for preparing projections is to see what balancing forces should be brought into play.

Fairly presented, population projections define the likely limits within which future population growth will occur. Needless to say, they are based on assumptions concerning the rate of natural increase, mortality, net migration as well as on base figures for the age-sex structure and geographic distribution of the population. Although every effort is made to ensure that assumptions are as reasonable as possible, a certain element of arbitrariness is unavoidable because an intricate web of socio-economic circumstances is at work. Fertility rates, for example, are influenced by levels of employment and income, rates of female participation in the labour force, the

PROSPECTS FOR THE FUTURE 85

role played by women in society and attitudes toward family size. None of these is entirely predictable. As one means of taking some of these uncertainties into account, projections are generally calculated according to alternative assumptions.

Projections can become outdated with alarming speed if population trends change. For example, the projections provided in *Canada 2000* and later cited in *Urban Canada: Problems and Prospects* today appear far too high. The population as a whole and the population in metropolitan areas each have grown more slowly than anticipated. Table 2.1 illustrates how some projections of Canada's future population size have been revised downward over the past twenty years.

Projected Population to 2001

For purposes of discussion here, we have adopted a method of projection generated by the Statistics Canada Population Model (SCPM). The model operates in two stages. In the first, detailed population projections are generated for each province; in the second, the model aggregates these sub-national projections to obtain population totals for Canada as a whole.[1] The assumptions of the model are as follows:

Mortality is assumed to be slightly declining. There has been a consistent pattern of declining death rates from specific diseases in Canada. Hence, life expectancy at birth is assumed to increase to 70.2 years for males and 78.4 years for females by 1986. Historically, the three Prairie provinces have had the lowest mortality rates in Canada while Quebec has had the lowest life expectancy.

Fertility trends in the past have fluctuated widely. From a low during the depression, the number of births per woman rose rapidly following World War II, only to plummet during the 1960s. A conservative fertility rate of 1.8 children per woman by 1986 was adopted.[2]

International Migration is difficult to estimate. During the 1960s, three-year moving averages of annual immigration gave flows ranging from 80,000 to 200,000 per year. Much less volatile than immigration, the emigrant outflow varied from 60,000 to 64,000 annually over the same period. We have assumed net gain through immigration to be 100,000 persons per year. Within Canada, Ontario and British Columbia are the main beneficiaries of net migration. For purposes of projection, the interprovincial distribution of immigrants is assumed to be the same as the 1972–75 pattern.

Interprovincial Migration showed no consistent upward or downward

Table 2.1. Canada – Selected Population Projections: Assumptions, Methodologies, Results

Stated Assumptions (rates per year)

Source and Year	Time Span covered	Projected Population 1981 2001 (millions)		Crude Birth Rate or total fertility rate[1]
System Dimension Ltd. *Urban Canada: The Challenge of 2001.* (1976). – Preferred (Medium)	1971 – 2006	24.0	28.5	Crude Birth Rate 14.5 per 1000
Statistics Canada. *Population Projections for Canada and the Provinces* (1974) – Series A	1972 – 2001	25.3	34.6	High – 2.6 (by 1985)
– Series B		24.5	30.7	Medium – 2.2 (by 1985)
– Series C		24.0	28.4	Low – 1.8 (by 1985)
– Series D		24.0	28.4	Low – 1.8 (by 1985)
Manpower and Immigration *Canadian Immigration and Population Study* (1973) – High	1972 – 2001	27.0	43.7	High – 2.4 (by 2001)
– Medium		25.2	36.2	Medium – 2.0 (by 1985)
– Low		24.0	30.6	Low – 1.8 (by 1985)
Economic Council of Canada (1967) – High	1966 – 1980	27.0	–	Crude Birth Rate 22.2 per 1000 (1970) to 24.3 per 1000 (1980)
– Low		24.0	–	Crude Birth Rate 20.1 per 1000 (1970) 18.8 per 1000 (1980)

Notes: [1]Total Fertility Rate is the number of children born per woman during her fertile years.

Sources: Derived from Economic Council of Canada. *Fourth Annual Review: The Canadian Economy from the 1960s to the 1970s.* (Ottawa: Queen's Printer, 1967; W. M. Illing. Y. Kasahara. F. T. Denton, and M. V. George. *Population, Family, Household and Labour Force Growth to 1980.* Economic Council of Canada, Staff Study No. 19 (Ottawa: Queen's Printer, 1967); W. E. Kalbach, *The Effect of Immigration on Population,* A Study com-

Net International Migration	Interprovincial Migration	Technique Employed	Purpose of Study
80,000	50,000 net (declines 10% every 5 years)	Cohort Survival method with age specific projections for fertility, mortality and net migration	– To provide benchmark data for urban and regional planners. – To contribute to an understanding of the forces which cause change in urban areas.
100,000 60,000 60,000 60,000	450,000 gross 73,000 net (1969–71 average) 435,000 gross 59,000 net (1966–71 average) 435,000 gross 29,000 net (50% of 1966–71 average for net) 218,000 gross 22,000 net (1961–71 data)	Regional components method with projection of fertility, mortality and migration rates by province – calculation of ratios for rates of growth between regions.	– To provide a basis for social and economic planning and policy decisions.
170,000 (1971) to 380,000 (2001) 105,000 (1971) to 183,000 (2001) 42,000 (1971) to 64,000 (2001)	371,000 gross (1951–56 average) 371,000 gross (1951–56 average) 412,000 gross (1956–61 average)	Regional components method	– To show the relative importance of immigration to the future Canadian population.
120,000 20,000		Components method	To provide a basis for various quantitative estimates for future economic growth.

missioned for the Canadian Immigration and Population Study. (Ottawa: Manpower and Immigration, 1974); Statistics Canada. *Population Projections for Canada and the Provinces, 1972–2001*, Cat. 91–514. (Ottawa: Information Canada, 1974); and T. Zaharchuk, et. al., "Urban Canada: The Challenge of 2001" (A study prepared for the Ministry of State for Urban Affairs by Systems Dimensions Ltd., 1976) (mimeographed). Reproduced by permission of the Ministry of Supply and Services Canada.

88 CHANGING CANADIAN CITIES

trend from 1951 to 1971, fluctuating between 371,000 and 435,000 per year. We have therefore assumed a constant proportion of the population and this results in 450,000 migrants per year. However, there is considerable variation in interprovincial flows and some preliminary evidence that traditional processes may be changing. These assumptions must therefore be considered a bit "shaky."

SOME DETAILS OF THE PROJECTIONS

(1) *Population Growth*: What are the prospects for future growth? Considerable potential for growth is inherent in the youthful age structure of the Canadian population. Consequently, the depressing effect of the current decline in fertility will be offset to some extent by the relatively large numbers of women of child-bearing ages during the late 1970s and early 1980s.

Even with zero net immigration and fertility rates below replacement levels (1.9 births per woman), Canada's population would continue to expand, reaching 24.5 million by 1986, and 26.5 million by the turn of the century.[3] However, net immigration is highly unlikely to be zero and, at whatever level, will have a significant effect on population growth.

On the basis of the above assumptions, Canada's population would increase by some 4.5 million people to reach a total 26 million by 1985. For the longer term, the projections suggest a population of some 29,735,000 by the year 2001 (Table 2.2).

(2) *Geographical Distribution*: Higher than average population increases would occur in Ontario, Alberta and British Columbia largely as a result of their proportionately greater numbers of in-migrants. British Columbia can anticipate the fastest growth: its population would double to 4,257,000 by 2001 and its percentage share of the national population would rise to 14.3 per cent. Ontario would have the largest absolute population increase while Newfoundland, Nova Scotia, Quebec and Manitoba would have moderate increases, but a slight relative decline in their percentage share of the nation's people. For Saskatchewan, the projections suggest an absolute decrease, if the outflow of migrants were to continue at the same pace.

(3) *Age Structure*: A prime demographic feature of Canada is the progressive ageing of population. Between 1972 and 2001 a shift will occur from the youthful dependent to the elderly dependent population. Those under age fourteen will decline from 28.8 per cent to 19.8 per cent of the population while the retired age group will increase from 8.2 per cent to 11.4 per cent. At the same time, the working age population will progressively become older. The group

Table 2.2. Actual and Projected Population of Canada and the Provinces, 1971–2001

Province or Territory	Actual Enumerated Population 1971	Projected Population 1986	2001
	Population in thousands		
Canada	21,568.3	25,989.6	29,734.6
Newfoundland	522.1	613.9	694.4
Prince Edward Island	111.6	144.4	181.6
Nova Scotia	789.0	920.2	1,035.9
New Brunswick	634.6	794.5	954.9
Quebec	6,027.8	6,572.8	6,751.5
Ontario	7,703.1	9,487.2	11,038.9
Manitoba	988.2	1,093.7	1,167.6
Saskatchewan	926.2	916.9	866.1
Alberta	1,627.9	2,174.0	2,709.9
British Columbia	2,184.6	3,205.8	4,257.4
Yukon	18.4	27.3	36.9
Northwest Territories	34.8	39.0	39.5
	Per cent of Total Population		
Canada	100.00	100.00	100.00
Newfoundland	2.42	2.36	2.34
Prince Edward Island	0.52	0.56	0.61
Nova Scotia	3.66	3.54	3.48
New Brunswick	2.94	3.06	3.21
Quebec	27.95	25.29	22.71
Ontario	35.71	36.50	37.13
Manitoba	4.58	4.21	3.93
Saskatchewan	4.29	3.53	2.91
Alberta	7.55	8.36	9.11
British Columbia	10.13	12.33	14.32
Yukon	0.09	0.11	0.12
Northwest Territories	0.16	0.15	0.13

Source: K. S. Gnansekeran and J. Perrault, "Special Projections of Population for Canada and the Provinces, 1972–2001." Prepared by the Population Estimates and Projections Division, Census Field, Statistics Canada under contract for the Ministry of State for Urban Affairs, September 1975 (Mimeographed). Reproduced by permission of the Minister of Supply and Services Canada.

from which the labour force primarily draws for new workers (age 15–24) will decline from 18.9 per cent to 14.1 per cent.

PROJECTED POPULATION GROWTH AND CHANGE IN CANADA'S METROPOLITAN AREAS

The projected uneven distribution of population growth among provinces is cause for concern: so, too, is population distribution among urban centres. Projections for the nation's twenty-two metropolitan areas[4] suggest a continuing expansion of Canada's metropolitan areas, from 11.9 million in 1971 to perhaps as many as 21.5 million people in 2001. However, the most plausible assumptions, similar to those for the national and provincial projections outlined above, give a mid-range figure of 17.4 million in 2001. The individual metropolitan projections making up this total are the ones on which we focus attention.

The most rapidly growing metropolitan areas are likely to be in Western Canada: Calgary and Edmonton, Victoria and Vancouver (Table 2.3). By 2001, Calgary would more than double and Edmonton almost double to become cities of close to one million people. Similarly, Vancouver and Victoria would increase to 2.1 million and 400,000 respectively. Ontario centres would grow at about the national average: the increases for Windsor, Toronto and London, for example are projected to be 39 per cent, 40 per cent and 58 per cent respectively. Sudbury and Ottawa could anticipate growth of 70 per cent to 80 per cent. But on the other end of the scale, cities such as Chicoutimi, Regina and Thunder Bay would not increase at all.

Distinctive patterns emerge when metropolitan centres are grouped by region and size group (Table 2.4). The fastest growing places are on the Prairies and in British Columbia, and these are the medium-sized Canadian cities of 400,000 to 1,000,000. Atlantic and Quebec centres are the slowest growing as are centres of less than 200,000 people. All this suggests that the centre of gravity in urban Canada might be displaced westward, perhaps slightly away from Ontario.

The three largest metropolitan areas would grow differently if the projections are correct. Toronto would become the largest city in Canada. Vancouver would increase its *share* of the national population from 5 per cent to 7.4 per cent. Montreal, however, would decrease slightly its share of the nation's population.

Figure 2.1 shows how the relative importance of migration and natural increase varies with growth rates. Net in-migration would account for a significant proportion of growth in the fastest growing centres of Victoria, Vancouver, Calgary, Ottawa–Hull and London. For others with about average growth, such as Toronto and Wind-

Table 2.3. Actual and Projected Population for Metropolitan Areas, Canada, 1971–2001 ("Low Moderate Projections")

Metropolitan Area	Population (thousands) 1971	Projected Population (thousands) 1986	Projected Population (thousands) 2001	Projected Population as Percentage of 1971 Population 1986	Projected Population as Percentage of 1971 Population 2001
Calgary	403.3	642.5	955.9	159%	237%
Vancouver	1,082.3	1,542.8	2,101.5	143	194
Sudbury	155.4	219.6	289.7	141	186
Edmonton	495.7	688.5	898.8	139	181
Victoria	195.8	262.8	351.1	134	179
Ottawa – Hull	602.5	807.7	1,031.5	134	171
Kitchener	226.8	301.8	379.9	133	167
London	286.0	368.9	454.4	129	158
Quebec	480.5	611.1	746.0	127	155
Toronto	2,628.0	3,229.7	3,688.6	123	140
Windsor	258.6	312.1	360.5	121	139
St. Catharines – Niagara	303.4	352.9	393.5	116	129
Halifax	222.6	258.2	285.2	116	128
Hamilton	498.5	576.7	637.0	116	127
St. John's	131.8	150.4	163.4	114	123
Montreal	2,743.2	3,095.9	3,355.3	113	122
Saskatoon	126.4	141.7	153.0	112	121
Winnipeg	540.3	597.9	636.6	111	117
Chicoutimi – Jonquière	133.7	137.6	135.4	103	101
Regina	140.7	144.6	142.0	103	100
Thunder Bay	112.0	113.2	110.4	101	98
Saint John	106.7	105.6	101.2	99	94
Total CMA's[1]	11,874.2	14,662.2	17,370.9	123	146

Note: [1] Census Metropolitan Areas.

Source: Data derived from: T. H. Yoo et. al., 1975B. "Interim Population Projections of 22 Census Metropolitan Areas (1971–2001)," Discussion Paper B. 75.10. (Ottawa: Ministry of State for Urban Affairs, 1975). Reproduced by permission of the Ministry of Supply and Services Canada.

Table 2.4. Population of Canada's Metropolitan Areas by Size Group and Region, 1971–2001

	Population (thousands) 1971	Projected Population (thousands) 1986	Projected Population (thousands) 2001	Projected Population as Percentage of 1971 Population 1986	Projected Population as Percentage of 1971 Population 2001
1. BY REGION					
Atlantic – 3CMAs	461.1	514.2	549.8	112	119
Quebec – 3CMAs[1]	3,357.4	3,844.6	4,236.7	115	126
Ontario – 9CMAs	5,071.2	6,282.6	7,345.5	124	145
Prairies – 5CMAs	1,706.4	2,215.2	2,786.3	130	163
B.C. – 2CMAs	1,278.1	1,805.6	2,452.6	141	192
2. BY SIZE GROUP (AS OF 1971)					
Over 1,000,000 – 3CMAs	6,453.5	7,868.4	9,145.4	122	142
400,000 – 999,999 – 6CMAs	3,020.8	3,924.4	4,905.8	130	162
200,000 – 399,999 – 6CMAs[2]	1,493.2	1,856.7	2,224.6	124	149
100,000 – 199,999 – 7CMAs	906.7	1,012.7	1,095.1	112	121
Total – 22CMAs	11,874.2	14,662.2	17,370.9	123	146

Notes: 1. Ottawa–Hull is included with Ontario.
2. Victoria is grouped in the 200,000–399,999 class
Source: Data derived from T. H. Yoo et al., 1975B. "Interim Population Projections of 22 Census Metropolitan Areas (1971–2001)," Discussion Paper B.75.10, (Ottawa: Ministry of State for Urban Affairs, 1975). Reproduced by permission of the Minister of Supply and Services Canada.

sor, natural increase and net in-migration would play nearly equal roles. For Montreal, Halifax, Winnipeg and other centres of comparatively slow growth, natural increase would be the dominant factor. Zero growth may occur in centres such as Saint John and Thunder Bay if population losses through out-migration balance the gains from natural increase.

SOME IMPLICATIONS OF METROPOLITAN POPULATION GROWTH

Perhaps as important as aggregate population growth are the levels of household formation and the expansion rates of the working age population.[5]

(1) *Household Formation*:[6] In determining future housing needs, what happens to household formation is obviously important. Those who use the old rule of thumb that one new household is created for

PROSPECTS FOR THE FUTURE 93

Figure 2.1. Anticipated Sources of Projected Population Increases: Canada's 22 Metropolitan Areas, 1971-81

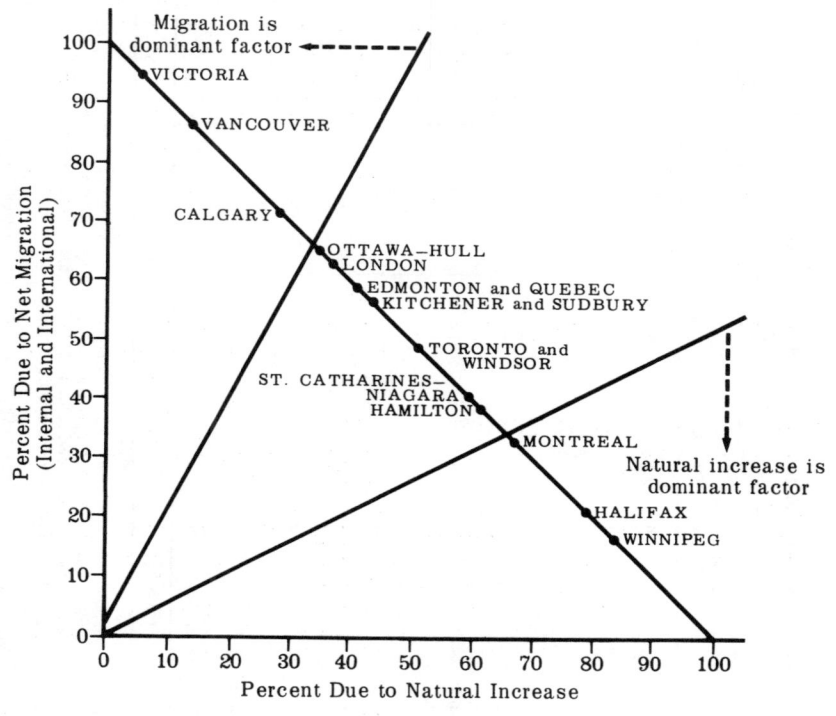

```
Percent Due to Net Migration (Internal and International)

100 — Migration is dominant factor ◄------
      ● VICTORIA
 90 —
      ● VANCOUVER
 80 —
 70 — CALGARY ●
 60 — ● OTTAWA–HULL
      ● LONDON
      ● EDMONTON and QUEBEC
      ● KITCHENER and SUDBURY
 50 —
      ● TORONTO and WINDSOR
      ● ST. CATHARINES–
 40 —   NIAGARA
      ● HAMILTON
 30 —
      ● MONTREAL
                    Natural increase is dominant factor
 20 —              ● HALIFAX
                   ● WINNIPEG
 10 —
  0 —
     0  10  20  30  40  50  60  70  80  90  100
          Percent Due to Natural Increase
```

Note: The dominant factor has been defined as more than two-thirds of the total growth.

Source: Demographic Research Group, "Interim Population Projections of 22 census Metropolitan Areas 1971-2001" (Ottawa: MSUA, March, 1975) (mimeographed).

every three people added to the population are certain to err. Analysis and projections suggest not only deviation from this rule but considerable variation among metropolitan areas. In Vancouver and Victoria, the new "rule of thumb" should be "one new household for every 2.07 people added to the population" for instance, while for Windsor and Winnipeg the figures will be 2.25 and 2.58 (Table 2.5).

The high rate of household formation is associated with an expected decline in the average size of the Canadian family (from 3.5 in 1971 to 3.2 persons by 2001). At the same time, the size of non-family households is expected to drop from 2.6 to 2.4 persons. But perhaps most important, non-family households are expected to in-

Table 2.5. Projected Household Increases as Compared with Population Increases, Canada's Metropolitan Areas, 1971–2001

Metropolitan Areas	Absolute Population Growth (000's) 1971–86	Absolute Population Growth (000's) 1971–2001	Absolute Household Growth (000's) 1971–86	Absolute Household Growth (000's) 1971–2001	Ratio: Popn Growth/Hshld Growth 1971–86	Ratio: Popn Growth/Hshld Growth 1971–2001	Average Family Size 2001	Average Non-Family Household Size 2001
St. John's	106.7	179.2	29.9	48.7	3.57	3.68	3.9	3.7
Halifax	47.8	79.2	12.3	21.2	3.89	3.74	3.6	4.0
Saint John	11.0	20.9	2.3	5.2	4.78	4.02	3.7	3.9
Chicoutimi-Jonquière	3.4	0.9	12.1	15.2	0.28	0.06	3.6	1.6
Quebec	120.6	188.2	58.2	98.4	2.07	1.91	3.2	2.4
Montreal	381.9	543.8	267.5	428.6	1.43	1.27	2.9	2.6
Ottawa-Hull	236.2	442.4	92.7	161.1	2.54	2.75	3.3	2.6
Toronto	988.9	1,872.7	443.1	756.9	2.23	2.47	3.0	2.6
St. Catharines-Niagara	41.6	67.1	25.6	35.3	1.63	1.90	3.2	2.2
Hamilton	108.8	196.2	59.3	91.1	1.83	2.15	3.1	2.3
Kitchener-Waterloo	107.5	208.6	46.2	81.9	2.33	2.55	3.1	2.3
London	94.8	178.4	38.8	66.8	2.44	2.67	3.1	2.6
Windsor	52.4	96.7	27.2	42.9	1.93	2.25	3.2	2.4
Sudbury	63.0	120.1	28.4	47.1	2.22	2.55	3.5	2.2
Thunder Bay	5.6	5.8	5.9	6.4	0.95	0.91	3.2	2.5
Winnipeg	105.9	190.6	42.7	74.0	2.48	2.58	3.2	2.4
Regina	28.9	54.9	11.0	20.3	2.63	2.70	3.3	2.5
Saskatoon	30.1	52.0	10.6	21.7	2.84	2.40	3.3	2.5
Calgary	213.9	409.8	76.1	143.0	2.81	2.87	3.3	2.3
Edmonton	211.2	394.7	81.3	144.7	2.60	2.73	3.3	2.3
Vancouver	285.2	579.5	162.7	287.4	1.75	2.02	3.0	1.7
Victoria	34.6	64.2	17.8	31.0	1.94	2.07	2.9	2.0
Canada	3,804.6	6,903.4	2,068.4	3,368.1	1.84	1.81	3.2	2.4

Note: Assumptions upon which population projections were made are as follows: Mortality – 1971 level throughout; Fertility – crude rate of 14.5 per thousand; net international immigration – 80,000 per year; Net internal migration – 50,000 per year declining by 10 per cent every five years. Trends in family size and non-family household size are to a slight but noticeable decline from 1971–2001. Exceptions to the rule are Chicoutimi-Jonquière, Quebec and Montreal, all of which experienced a dramatic decrease in family and non-family size.

Source: T. Zaharchuk, et al., "Urban Canada: The Challenge of 2001." A study prepared for the Ministry of State for Urban Affairs by Systems Division Ltd. 1976 (Mimeographed). Reproduced by permission of the Minister of Supply and Services Canada.

crease from 18.8 per cent to 26.6 per cent of all households in Canada by the turn of the century.

What are the reasons? Smaller family size can be directly attributed to low fertility rates. The decreasing size and increasing number of non-family units result from higher standards of living and changed mores. The increased economic well-being of young, single adults has permitted many of them to leave homes earlier than heretofore and to establish their own households. The elderly too, are often economically independent—the death of a spouse no longer automatically means moving in with children or relatives as it once did. Changing social mores as reflected in attitudes towards marriage, children and working women, also favour the establishment of non-family households.

Differences in economic circumstances and social attitudes across the country add up to considerable regional variations. By the turn of the century, cities in Quebec and British Columbia would have the highest proportion of non-family households. Centres in the Atlantic provinces, which already have the largest sized households, will continue to do so. In Quebec, household formation is likely to increase reflecting the continuing de-emphasis of traditionally strong family ties. Faster growing places such as Calgary, Edmonton, Kitchener-Waterloo and Ottawa-Hull are expected to have relatively lower rates of household formation than slower growing centres such as Windsor, Winnipeg and Thunder Bay.

An overall lack of population growth therefore does *not* necessarily imply that few new households will be established or that no new housing units will be required. Changes in the age structure of the population and the evolution of social mores may more than offset other factors.

(2) *Labour Force*: In the near future, there will be a substantial increase in the proportion of Canada's population that is of working age (Table 2.6). The proportion of Canada's population aged 15 – 64 is projected to rise from 62 per cent in 1971 to 69 per cent by 1986, and then level out until the turn of the century. This increase probably will be distributed relatively evenly across Canada.

Some Issues Arising from the Projections

Urban growth of this magnitude poses tough policy questions that force Canadians to consider what kind of society they want and what type of urban environment they wish to live in.

Satellite city or suburban fringe, new communities or patchwork sprawl, decentralized nodes or centralized core, dispersed network or all-enveloping metropolis—what form of settlement would best accommodate Canada's future urban growth?

Table 2.6. Expansion of the Working Age Population (Aged 15–64) in Canada's Metropolitan Areas, 1971–2001

Metropolitan Areas	Total Working Age Population (000's)			Working Age Popn as % Total Popn		
	1971	1986	2001	1971	1986	2001
St. John's	80.1	154.8	209.1	60.8	64.9	67.2
Halifax	143.1	182.2	207.2	64.3	67.4	68.7
Saint John	65.0	76.4	85.6	60.9	64.9	67.1
Chicoutimi-Jonquière	84.7	99.0	96.6	63.4	72.2	71.8
Quebec	315.5	425.8	473.1	65.7	70.8	70.8
Montreal	1800.4	2218.3	2296.0	65.6	71.0	69.9
Ottawa-Hull	387.3	579.5	728.6	64.3	69.1	69.7
Toronto	1722.5	2513.9	3298.7	65.5	69.5	73.3
St. Catharines-Niagara	190.0	233.2	250.4	62.6	67.6	67.6
Hamilton	316.3	417.4	473.9	63.5	68.7	68.2
Kitchener-Waterloo	144.5	232.4	304.3	63.7	69.8	69.9
London	182.0	259.9	322.4	63.6	68.3	69.4
Windsor	159.0	212.5	244.6	61.5	68.3	68.8
Sudbury	97.8	154.2	192.9	62.9	70.6	70.0
Thunder Bay	70.5	78.9	79.5	62.9	67.1	67.5
Winnipeg	345.9	416.3	486.7	64.0	64.4	66.6
Regina	87.7	109.6	129.0	62.3	64.6	66.0
Saskatoon	78.3	102.1	126.8	61.9	65.2	67.3
Calgary	254.8	421.3	552.8	63.2	68.3	68.0
Edmonton	313.7	479.2	606.0	63.3	67.8	68.3
Vancouver	698.6	915.3	1179.7	64.5	66.9	68.1
Victoria	119.1	150.7	178.2	60.8	65.4	68.5
Canada	13458.6	17444.4	19671.4	62.4	68.8	69.1

Note: Assumptions upon which population projections were made are as follows: Mortality – 1971 level throughout; Fertility – crude rate of 14.5 per thousand; Net international immigration – 80,000 per year; Net internal migration – 50,000 per year declining by 10 per cent every five years.

Sources: T. Zaharchuk, et al., "Urban Canada: The Challenge of 2001." A Study prepared for the Ministry of State for Urban Affairs by Systems Dimensions Ltd., 1976 (mimeographed). Reproduced by permission of the Minister of Supply and Services Canada.

The past is an inadequate guide to the future. As Carver has said:

> We have to admit that though our motives are not regretted and our opportunities have been privileged, the results are only middling fair—and sometimes terrible. We have a sense of guilt because we have had the opportunity to build great cities in a way of our own choosing, but we have settled for compromises and not really cared enough... And we are frustrated because we possess no clear image of what we should be striving to accomplish.[7]

Still, some notion of desired forms of urban settlement is necessary. What are the issues?

URBAN SIZE: BALANCING BENEFITS WITH FINANCIAL AND HUMAN COSTS

Are our cities too big? What is the best size for a city? There are many benefits from large cities. Cities support specialized services and cultural organizations that fulfil the most esoteric tastes, and they possess the concentration of population which fosters an intensity of social and intellectual interaction. At the same time, however, cities exert pressure on their natural resource base, leading sometimes to water shortages, air pollution, and a lack of open space. Costs of some services increase disproportionately. Congestion is a feature of urban life. Some writers, such as Louis Wirth,[8] have observed that cultural roots and community stability are lost in cities, thus producing a sense of anomie and alienation. Higher density may increase tensions, reduce residential satisfaction and exacerbate social ills.[9]

Small town living, at first blush, seems to provide respite from the continuous pace of urban life. But life in smaller places may be far from idyllic. There may be a lack of public services, limited consumer choice, a dearth of interesting employment opportunities, inherent economic instability and a smothering, intolerant social web.

Given this sort of ambivalence for both large and small centres, what policy approach can be taken? Finding an optimum city size has proven elusive. Cessation of development or uninhibited expansion of an urban area is a clear-cut but none too useful choice.[10]

However, there are some guidelines. It has been suggested that there is some fairly wide range of city sizes (e.g. 200,000 to 750,000) which are not markedly superior or inferior to one another for supporting industry, supplying services and accommodating diverse lifestyles.[11] As well, some theorists have suggested a minimum city size (e.g. 100,000 to 250,000) as a prerequisite for adequate consumer choice, efficient provision of public services and the formation of a diversified industrial base.[12] Others have suggested that it is the rate of growth rather than absolute size that should be the root of concern.

All of this suggests a policy approach that would better manage rates of growth and at the same time foster the growth of medium-sized cities. Because individuals differ greatly, the policy must also ensure that people are given a realistic choice in the size and nature of communities where they may want to live.

SOCIAL AND ECONOMIC SERVICES

It may be that many of the difficulties of large cities are not so much inherent in their size as in their structure. What is required is a type of urban form that can fulfil the need for specialized services while also affording less stressful living conditions than often is the case now. To accomplish this, perhaps the concept of a "regional city" encompassing a number of centres connected with a central city by high speed communication could be developed. Mumford argued long ago that the modern city has upset the human ecological balance by both cramping and overwhelming the individual.[13] The regional city, he suggested, is necessary for the extensive exchange of ideas, the elaborate division of labour and for the formation of local community institutions that can provide individuals with a sense of belonging. It is also interesting to note that the policies recommended in one of Canada's first major planning documents[14] included the encouragement of industrial decentralization and stressed the promotion of industrial town centres.

URBAN FABRIC AND INSTITUTIONS

To call for a redistribution of future growth among regional cities would mean a substantial re-moulding of urban landscape. But what of life in existing cities? Can it be improved? Some, who have less antipathy for the modern metropolis than Mumford have offered alternative approaches. Bunge,[15] for example, has argued that the impersonality of city life and the sense of personal powerlessness that he thinks is felt by urbanites can be alleviated, "not by utopian schemes to build new towns at astronomical cost in the midst of pastoral greenery," but by establishing smaller neighbourhood governments and administrative units which approximate the scale of delivery for most functions. Government units, he contends, could be set out in a hierarchy, with policies made as much as possible by those directly affected. Jacobs[16] has advocated a re-thinking of present tendencies to separate the urban functions performed by cities. In her view, places of work and places of living should be more intimately related in order to enhance the social and economic cohesiveness of communities. Perhaps, for instance, small commercial establishments could be situated in the same block as residential units.

URBAN FORM: URBAN INFRASTRUCTURE AND ENERGY

Reflecting upon human society, Kenneth Boulding[17] argued a number of years ago that human society is passing through one of its great transitions, a transition powered by extravagant use of physical resources, and including within it the seeds for its collapse through an energy crisis. Impending energy shortages may have been overstated by some, but the problems in Canada are real, and in the face of increasing urban growth solutions will have to be sought.

Questions such as the following must be considered:
—What type of built environment will best conserve energy stocks and allow for the most judicious use of energy (high-rise apartments, town housing, or single detached dwellings)?
—What pattern of regional urban settlement tends to lower the level of existing energy use (a regional network of densely developed urban nodes or a metropolitan quiltwork of suburbs)?
—What modes of transport and technologies best fulfil the goal of energy conservation (private auto and the expressway, the bus and the urban arterial, a form of light rapid transit)?

Obviously the selection of alternative settlement forms or different transportation technologies is not an either/or situation but rather a case of opting for a little more of one and a little less of another. Nor can the goal of energy conservation be pursued to the exclusion of other goals. Given that high-rise apartments are energy efficient, should all new Canadian families become apartment dwellers? If a greater density of development results in the use of less energy, should the allotment of urban open space be dramatically reduced? Should the use of the private automobile and the time-saving convenience it affords be largely forgone? Clearly the goal of conserving energy in the planning of cities must be traded off against other social, pyschological and economic objectives. Nevertheless, Canadians likely will not be able to develop their cities, build their transportation systems and design their dwelling units without first considering energy requirements.

LAND: A COMMODITY, A RESOURCE, AN ENVIRONMENT

Nine of every ten acres of Canadian land are still in public hands. Of the 3,800,000 square miles of land in Canada, only 400,000 square miles are privately owned,[18] but most are in high value urban and agricultural uses and hence of considerable importance

In the past, Canadians have viewed their land largely as a commodity, and because of the seeming large amounts of easily available land, have been unconcerned with the rate at which land was consumed for development. Low-density suburbs, complete with single-family homes, shopping centres, arterials and expressways have relentlessly encroached on farmsteads. The future of prime agricultural areas, wetlands, woodlots, escarpments and other fragile ecosystems has been decided by the vagaries of the real estate market, the need for larger municipal tax bases, the profit margins of quarry operators, or the desires of the cottage owner, to cite but a few examples. Only in the past few years have attitudes towards land begun to change. That the allocation of land to the highest bidder through market competition does not always result in the best social use has been slowly recognized.[19] Increasing concern with environmental and ecological systems has led to a sharpened awareness of the inter-relatedness of land uses. Some merging of the conflicting views is necessary:

> The idea that land is a resource as well as a commodity may appear self-evident, but in the context of our traditions of land use regulation it is a highly novel concept. Our existing systems of land use regulation were created by dealers in real estate interested in maximizing the value of land as a commodity.... A realization is growing that important social and environmental goals require more specific controls on the use that may be made of scarce land resources.[20]

In the jargon of economists, the price of land on which decisions are taken must reflect social as well as private costs. Increasingly, Canadians are finding it possible to devote more time to personal concerns such as leisure and recreational activities.[21] Yet this very phenomenon has posed a threat to the conservation of "natural environments." Nowhere is the use and abuse of land more prominent than in the recreational areas surrounding Canada's major metropolitan areas.

It is a paradox that North Americans live in large cities but often prefer rural and natural environments. Those who are financially able often have demonstrated their desire to live in a semi-rural environment by building country estates in exclusive suburbs, or near small towns. As well, there has been of late a substantial increase in the number of hobby farms owned by city dwellers[22] and in the development of cottages in environmentally sensitive lands (e.g. the Muskoka area near Toronto).

Recently, governments have been prompted to increase their efforts to inventory, classify, regulate and assess land and land use. Many initiatives, however, are still in a preliminary stage.

AGRICULTURAL LAND: PRESERVATION FOR FOOD PRODUCTION

The supply of land is limited. As population, urbanization and recreation increase, competition for land increases, even in countries as geographically vast as Canada.

The Federal Department of Environment, through the Canada Land Inventory, has concluded that only about 8.3 per cent of Canada's land area is usable, with no serious limitations for crop production; another 8.5 per cent of the land is marginally usable. If only the acreage devoted to food production (about 5 per cent) is considered, then the ratio of agricultural land to people is about 5.4 acres of producing farmland per capita or, 119 people per square mile of farmland in production.[23]

More problematic, however, is the fact that many of Canada's principal agricultural regions—the St. Lawrence valley, southern Ontario and the Lower Fraser valley—are under the greatest pressure from urban expansion. Reliable figures on the loss of agricultural land are not easy to come by. In a now somewhat dated study, Crerar[24] estimated that for every 1,000 increase in urban population within the Windsor-Quebec City corridor, 130 acres of land are consumed for buildings and supporting infrastructure. However, the direct conversion of land from agricultural to urban purposes is only the tip of the proverbial iceberg. The encroachment of cities on the countryside is also manifest in the rise of hobby farms, non-agricultural occupancy of farm houses, the development of rural residential estates, the construction of recreational facilities and perhaps most importantly, the abandonment of farming on lands that are the object of holding actions by land speculators.[25] Research suggests that the "urban shadow" of the city extends far beyond the built-up portion, encompassing much of the prime agricultural land.[26] Moreover, much of this land is irreplaceable, for example, the tender fruit acreages lost in the Niagara Peninsula.[27]

It is evident that continued urbanization will cause increasing dependency on marginally productive lands or foreign food supplies. Some government initiatives to stay this trend, such as the establishment of the British Columbia Land Commission and the advent of the land speculation taxes and of land banking in various provinces, have taken place. But some fundamental propositions require consideration:

—Are the presumed social and psychological benefits of low density housing worth the large acreages of land consumed?
—Is the freedom of an individual to enjoy his private property more fundamental than the need of the public for food supplies and/or open space?

— Is the private land market relatively more efficient than public intervention in looking after community and housing needs?
— Is national ownership of land such an unreasonable proposal?

THE DISTRIBUTION OF URBAN GROWTH: EQUITY VERSUS EFFICIENCY

A fundamental dilemma in many public policy decisions is the trade-off between the objectives of equity and efficiency. Equity considerations have led some analysts to conclude that development aid (i.e., manpower training, industrial incentives, equalization payments) should be regarded largely as charity and that priority target regions should be selected according to the "worst first" rule of priority. Conversely, the efficiency approach which is directed towards achieving the maximum amount of additional income and employment opportunities per dollar expended for regional development, has led others to conclude that assistance should be focused primarily on the most promising of the nation's relatively disadvantaged areas. Closely associated is the question of whether to try to make people more prosperous where they now live regardless of the economic position of their community or instead to try to make more prosperous places which demonstrate growth potential. Should the emphasis be on moving jobs to people or moving people to jobs? Should growth centres (i.e. Toronto, Vancouver) be subjected to restrictive development controls?

Reconciliation of these objectives is nearly impossible. Areas of abject poverty and consequent high economic distress generally suffer from a low level of productivity and an essentially non-competitive economic position. This means that development efforts will be costly, often ineffectual, and likely required to be more-or-less permanent. Alternatively, areas of relative stagnation and out-migration, but where development potential appears highest, usually tend to have income levels and employment rates closely approximating the national average. Since the total resources available for regional development are limited, hard choices must be made between regional programs emphasizing relief of distress and more judicious programs stressing regional transformation and self-sustaining growth. As well, the efficacy of the policy options available must be considered. Attempts to entice industry to locations outside the economic mainstream may produce inauspicious results, but programs intended to move unemployables to other communities are also likely to meet with failure. At the same time, attempts to regulate the level of new development in large centres such as Toronto may not necessarily stem the influx of migrants.

PROSPECTS FOR THE FUTURE 103

Ultimately, determining the policy emphasis must be a political process. Imbedded within the chain of decisions is an implicit balancing between economic efficiency in one region and the level of short-term human welfare attained in another region. The implications for national unity of pursuing or not pursuing a balanced population distribution policy must also be considered.

This chapter has portrayed some of the dimensions of the huge problems that face Canadians in deciding what type of urban Canada they want. Perhaps we have painted a picture favourable to a different population distribution than now exists—and that is our bias. Biases aside, however, serious issues are involved that require national debate. The impression should not be left that these issues can be easily resolved. It is often an arrogant illusion to suppose that twentieth century man can chart the dynamics of societies. We cannot even chart the precise orbits of three billiard balls moving under mutual gravitation—though we can do it for *two*! But, at the same time, in "following our noses" we must try to ensure that decisions are taken in full view of all the available information.

Some of these issues are treated in greater depth in the chapters that follow, and in Chapter 9 we explore some of the policy options that are available for changing the urban pattern in Canada.

Notes

1. For a detailed description of the model, see Statistics Canada, 1974B, *Technical Report on Population Projections for Canada and the Provinces, 1972-2001*, Cat. 91–516, Chapter 1. A discussion of the projection methods is found in Statistics Canada, 1974A, *Population Projections for Canada and the Provinces, 1972–2001* (Ottawa: Information Canada, Cat. 91–514, Chapters 3, 4 and 5.
2. A fertility rate of 1.8 may prove an unreasonably low assumption. A substantial reduction in total fertility can occur for a short period because child bearing is postponed, but in the long term low fertility can be achieved only with a corresponding reduction in family size. A family size of only 1.8 children implies that about 25 per cent of women remain childless. Measured against historical precedence, this would be a rather high level of childlessness.
3. Statistics Canada, 1974A, *op. cit.*, p. 84.
4. T. H. Yoo, *et al.*, 1975A, "Interim Population Projections of 22 Census Metropolitan Areas 1971–2001" (Ottawa: Ministry of State for Urban Affairs, March 1975, mimeographed); and 1975B, "Interim Population Projections of 22 Census Metropolitan Areas (1971–2001)," Discussion Paper B.75.10 (Ottawa: Ministry of State for Urban Affairs).
5. Household and labour force projections for Canada's metropolitan areas are based on the work of T. Zaharchuk *et al.*, "Urban Canada: The Challenge of 2001," (A study prepared for Urban Affairs by Systems Dimensions Limited, 1976, mimeographed), rather than on the study completed directly by the Ministry of State for Urban Affairs, by T. H. Yoo *et al.*, 1975A, 1975B, *op. cit.*

Fertility, mortality and international immigration hypotheses are similar but differences occur regarding the volume and direction of internal migration.
6. A *household* consists of a person or group of persons occupying one dwelling. It usually consists of a family, but may consist of two or more families or a group of unrelated persons sharing a dwelling. A *non-family household* refers to one person or group of persons, occupying one dwelling, who do not constitute a census family. A *census family* consists of a husband and wife (with or without children) or a parent with one or more children never married.
7. H. Carver, *Cities in the Suburbs* (Toronto: University of Toronto Press, 1962), p. 4.
8. Louis Wirth, "Urbanism as a Way of Life," in R. L. Warren, (ed.), *Perspective on the American Community* (Chicago: Rand McNally, 1966), pp. 44-53.
9. The bulk of the evidence suggests that population density is a far less important variable affecting human behaviour than some would have us believe. H.P. Homenuck, J. P. Morgenstern, and R. Keeble, "An Analysis of Social and Psychological Effects of High-Rise," Discussion Paper B.75.9 (Ottawa: Ministry of State for Urban Affairs, 1975), pp. 2-3.
10. The Task Force on Urbanization and the Future, *Choices for Metropolitan Growth* (The Province of Alberta, 1972).
11. W. R. Thompson, "Urban Economics" in H. W. Eldredge, (ed.), *Taming Megalopolis, Vol. 1* (New York: Praeger, 1967), pp. 156–190.
12. N. M. Hansen, "Criteria for a Growth Center Policy" in A. Kuklinski, (ed.), *Growth Poles and Growth Centres* (The Hague: Mouton, 1972), pp. 103–124.
13. L. O. Gertler, *Regional Planning in Canada: A Planner's Testament* (Montreal: Harvest House, 1972).
14. Thomas Adams, *Rural Planning and Development: A Study of Rural Conditions and Problems in Canada* (Ottawa: Commission of Conservation, 1917).
15. W. Bunge, "Urban Nationalism," Discussion Paper B.72.18 (Ottawa: Ministry of State for Urban Affairs, 1972).
16. J. Jacobs, *The Death and Life of Great American Cities* (New York: Random House, Vintage Books, 1961).
17. K. Boulding, *The Meaning of the Twentieth Century* (New York: Harper and Row, 1965), pp. 121–136.
18. A. J. Greiner, "Land Policy in Canada," Discussion Paper B.74.10 (Ottawa: Ministry of State for Urban Affairs, 1974), pp. 1–4.
19. L. H. Russwurm, "The Urban Fringe as Regional Development," (University of Waterloo: Department of Geography, 1975, mimeographed).
20. F. Bosselman and D. Callies, *The Quiet Revolution in Land Use Control: Summary Report* (Washington: U.S. Government Printing Office, 1971), pp. 43–45.
21. R. S. Clark, J. Ewers, and K. R. Balmer, "A Planning Response to Post-Industrialism," Discussion Paper B.73.25 (Ottawa: Ministry of State for Urban Affairs, 1973).
22. Toronto *Star*, "The Fallow Farm: Hobby Farmers Use Thousands of Acres," September 29, 1973.
23. Juan F. Scott, "Relationships Between Land and Population: A Note on Canada's Carrying Capacity," (Environment Canada: Lands Directorate, October 1974, mimeographed).
24. A. D. Crerar, "The Loss of Farmland and the Growth of Metropolitan Regions of Canada," in R. R. Krueger *et al.*, (eds.), *Regional and Resource Planning in Canada* (Toronto: Holt, Rinehart and Winston, 1962; (rev. ed.), 1970).
25. Agricultural and Rural Development Act (ARDA), *Planning for Agriculture in Southern Ontario*, prepared by the Centre for Resource Development (University of Guelph: ARDA Report No. 7, 1972).
26. Gertler, *op. cit.*
27. R. R. Krueger, "The Disappearing Niagara Fruit Belt," in Krueger, *et al., op. cit.*

CHAPTER 3

Growth Forces: National Pattern, Regional Diversity and the Urban System

> It is still possible nowadays to pick up a book portraying Canada to foreigners – including some books written by Canadians – and get the impression, from scanning the subject headings and illustrations, that this is a country dominated by such industries as agriculture, mining, forestry, hydro-electric power and fishing. (Economic Council of Canada, *Seventh Annual Review*, 1970: p. 14).

Canadian Economic Development and Regional Diversity

The course of regional economic development and population growth in Canada has depended largely upon the exploitation of physical resources. Canadian economic historians have described the process within a framework which has been called the "staples" theory of economic development. And it is true that past growth cannot be understood without reference to the role of staples in Canada's economic development and to the resulting legacy of regional differences. But future, so-called post-industrial economic growth will focus increasingly on metropolitan centres with their skilled labour pools and their management and financial resources. It is likely, as well, that government will play a greater role in future than in past development, attempting to direct it toward national objectives.

STAPLES, ECONOMIC GROWTH AND URBAN ECONOMIES

In an uniquely Canadian contribution to economic history, Harold Innis and his disciples since the 1930s have elaborated a staples theory of economic development.[1] Innis characterized the early growth of Canada's economy as a process by which "hinterland" Canada supplied "heartland" Europe with a succession of staple exports, which in turn bolstered one regional economy after another: first fish and fur, then timber and wheat, and finally, minerals and fuel oil. Differences in the sequencing of resource development and the types of economic linkages forged had a fundamental effect on the regional nature of Canada's economy and on the form of the urban system.

Staples are distinguished typically by ease of production resulting from relative abundance, low capital and labour requirements, cheap transportation, and non-competitiveness with heartland products.[2] The deployment of modern technology from abroad, dependence on foreign financing, and an infusion of entrepreneurship from other nations are also characteristics of a staples oriented economy.[3]

Canada's first staples were Atlantic salt cod fish and St. Lawrence valley furs which were exported as early as the sixteenth century. Lumber, potash, pork, beef and wheat from across eastern Canada were the major staples exports by the mid-nineteenth century. Wheat from the Prairies was added by the turn of the century, while minerals from the Canadian Shield and fuel oils from the West came into prominence somewhat later. An east-to-west progression of staple production usually occurred with a growing demand for staples in Europe, their depletion in the most accessible regions of Canada, the development of continental transportation facilities and the introduction of new staple products. Important east-to-west differences, first created by the pattern of staples exploitation, have remained as a naggingly persistent feature of Canadian regionalism. For example, the low incomes, lagging population and moderate growth of the Atlantic region have been attributable, in part, to the region's difficulty in coping with its declining staples base.

Staple exports stimulate the domestic economy through so-called spread effects which promote growth of secondary and tertiary activity.[4] These economic linkages are three-fold: backward linkages causing increased production among suppliers to the export staple industry; forward linkages causing domestic processing of staple outputs before exporting; and final demand linkages causing consumer goods to be produced for domestic consumption by workers in staple export industries.[5]

The magnitude and regional incidence of these stimuli have varied considerably, depending on the characteristics of the staple. Few backward linkages were necessary for instance, to support the cod fishery. Permanent fishing villages were not established in North America until the industry was several centuries old. By contrast, many inputs from other industrial sectors were required for producing and marketing wheat, including fertilizer and farm implements, wagons and grain elevators, rail lines and rolling stock. To the extent that backward linked products replaced imports, the domestic economy grew.

Forward linkages from staples initially were few and far between. The drying and salting of cod, the square-cutting of timber and the curing of furs could hardly compare, in terms of additional employment, to the boats and beaver hats manufactured abroad from Canadian raw materials. The situation has changed somewhat, although the recurring image of Canucks as "hewers of wood and drawers of water" still raises the ire of many a Canadian. The industrial Canada of today features pulp and paper mills, chemical plants, petroleum refineries and steel blast furnaces, but subsequent processing of Canadian resources still occurs frequently outside the country as largely foreign-owned subsidiaries export staple products to parent companies.

Similarly, the extensiveness of final demand linkages has differed markedly by type of staple. Fishermen who landed only long enough to dry their catch, or fur trappers who were constantly on the move and mainly self-sufficient demanded few supplies that would support domestic manufacturers. Agriculturalists, on the other hand, soon established a permanent farmstead and commanded a broad range of goods and services. Farming on the Canadian frontier was primarily of a commercial nature, tied from the outset to an import/export distribution network. Seldom was subsistence farming practised, and then only until transportation was improved.[6]

The varying influence of spread effects created a diversity of urban sub-systems across Canada. With exports of fish and timber, Maritime port cities developed, particularly Halifax. As furs grew in importance, continental penetration by the voyageurs led to a focusing of international trade on Montreal as the single large entrepôt. During this early period, centres such as Montreal and Quebec City, Halifax and Saint John functioned as parasitic cities, as mercantile outposts of a resource area whose exploitation was organized by the metropolitan system of western Europe. Mutual interdependence in the form of two-way trading linkages between the city and its hinterland was almost non-existent. The parasitic centre served only as a collection point for raw materials from its hinterland, which were then forwarded directly to the mother country for further processing.

Wheat, however, had a different impact. In contrast to the shifting base of operation for earlier staples, wheat production required residential settlement.[7] Hence, fledgling urban systems, consisting of a hierarchy of central places to serve the farm population, began to take shape in the wheat-growing areas, first in southwestern Ontario and then on the Prairies. Inputs required by the central places for backward linkages and final demand linkages were imported at early stages of development, but as agricultural exports grew, domestic incomes rose, markets reached adequate scale, and domestic production began to replace imports, first concentrating in Montreal and then increasingly, because of its more advantageous location, in Toronto.[8]

Thus, final demand linkages arising from the spread effects of staples production particularly favoured Ontario and Quebec, thereby helping to establish a national heartland-hinterland relationship which has become a pervasive element of Canada's economic geography.

National heartland-hinterland differences have persisted and in certain cases, intensified in twentieth century Canada. By way of example, manufacturing activity has always been concentrated in Ontario and Quebec. Although the proportion of the labour force employed in manufacturing in the Prairies and Maritimes briefly increased in the late nineteenth century, it later declined substantially.[9] Perhaps most telling are the many socio-economic characteristics which vary directly with distance from Toronto. Average family income levels tend to decline with increasing distance from Toronto, as do per cent of male labour force employed in manufacturing, and the numbers of post-World War II immigrants. Economic disparities rise with distance from Toronto.[10]

The staples theory of economic development may be criticized easily for its narrow scope. It is not a comprehensive growth theory. Many forces that fuel growth are neglected, including technological change, autonomous investment, government budgeting and consumer spending. Nevertheless, the staples theory provides a useful interpretation of resource-oriented growth in the frontier economy of early Canada when there was an abundance of resources but a scarcity of labour and capital. It has been suggested that the history of Canadian economic growth over the past 150 years indicates that a viable economy and society is possible (though not necessarily preferable) through reliance on primary resources.[11] To this day, staples remain as a fundamental basis for spatial linkages in the Canadian economy.[12]

But many economists would maintain that sustained growth requires a diversity of resources, flexibility in their deployment through invention and innovation, and ultimately, shifts to new lines of more labour-intensive and technologically-sophisticated production. And such an evolution of development has occurred in the Canadian economy. The proportion of Canada's economic activity accounted for by the primary sector fell from one-half in 1870, to one-quarter by the 1920s, and currently stands at just over one-tenth.[13] The process of exploiting and exporting staples gave rise to the basic pre-conditions for an urban-focused economy: incomes rose, markets expanded, capital and labour accumulated, appropriate structural changes were forthcoming. The success of staples, especially wheat, as engines of growth in Canada's resource-oriented economy permitted the transformation to an advanced industrial and highly urbanized nation, no longer so dependent on staple exports. Of the "five F's" by which Griffith Taylor described the Canadian economy – fish, furs, forests, farms and factories – Canada's urbanized economy has gradually focused more and more on "the final F" and gone beyond to a service-oriented economy.

Furthermore, it may be suggested that Canadian cities are no longer mere commercial outposts trans-shipping resources to a foreign nation. Formerly "parasitic" cities have either been eclipsed, or evolved into "generative" centres, centres which provide a full range of functions and stimulate development rather than merely draw resources away. This does not mean that the Canadian economy simply "takes in its own laundry"; foreign trade accounts for approximately one-quarter of the Canadian Gross National Product (GNP). But this trade, increasingly based on industrial manufacturers rather than exclusively upon primary products, emanates largely from the nation's urban system.[14]

As a result, the earlier heartland-hinterland, or metropolis-periphery relationship that existed at the international scale, has gradually come into being at the national level, within Canada. The trend toward domestic production of a wide range of goods and services has accentuated contrasts between Canada's industrial heartland, partly an extension of the United States manufacturing belt, and the nation's raw material producing hinterlands. In effect, therefore, the staple export continues to drive the growth of most cities and regions that are outside of the Windsor-Quebec City corridor,[15] with these hinterland areas diversifying from intensive resource specialization only as local markets achieve sufficient size to support profitable local enterprise.

NATIONAL POLICIES FOR ECONOMIC DEVELOPMENT

> The only firm conclusion we may draw is that the process of national development and spatial integration is an eminently political one, involving fundamental relations of power and exchange and the resolution of resulting conflicts. Planning which fails to recognize this basic truth and proceeds as though the spatial allocation of resources were merely an exercise in applied rationality is bound to be disappointing in its results.[16]

Staples production has played a key role in the evolution of regional economies in Canada. Perhaps equally important have been institutional relationships resulting from the exploitation of staples. For instance, Simmons has contended that "there is a long history of intimate connections between monopolistic staple capitalism and policy-making agents."[17] The space-time sequence of staples development has been manipulated, through the controls of capital and technology, to suit the major institutions based in large cities in Canada or abroad – first the railways and land companies, and later the Bay Street financiers and multi-national corporations.

Even today, Canada's economic structure owes much to "three basic national decisions" taken by the new Dominion in the decade following Confederation: (1) acquisition and subsequent settlement of Rupert's Land and the North-West Territory as a Canadian frontier region; (2) construction of a railway spanning the continent; and (3) rapid industrialization of the Great Lakes-St. Lawrence Lowland through protective tariffs and other policies.[18] The policy package, which in various guises predominated the Canadian scene for the four decades preceding World War I clearly represented the subordination of "laissez-faire" economic forces to the political end of providing a material base for Confederation.[19] In the words of one economic historian, "Sir John A. Macdonald gave us our first national policy and our first lesson in the irrelevance of economics... Macdonald was the first great Canadian non-economist."[20]

The national policies of the federal government profoundly affected geographic ties, economic structure and institutional relationships in the country. The national policy – to the extent that it was successful – steadily enhanced the interdependence of the scattered provinces and regions of Canada, thus transforming the British North American Territories of the mid-nineteenth century into a political and economic unit.[21] But at the same time, divergent mercantilist relations were formed between the Canadian heartland and the Western hinterland. There were many ways in which the national policy differentiated between the nation's hinterland and its metropolitan areas, largely to the benefit of the latter. Among them:

– High tariff barriers protected "infant" Canadian manufacturing industries and artificially accelerated the rate at which imports were replaced by domestically produced goods. This reinforced the industrial dominance of cities, and particularly those which were extensions of the American manufacturing belt, the Quebec to Windsor axis.

– A transportation network, founded on the epic building of the CPR under Macdonald and filled out by the construction of the

National Trans-continental and the Grand Trunk Pacific under Laurier (later consolidated as the CNR), connected heartland and hinterland. Characteristically, this network facilitated the outflow of resources from the frontier and the inflow of finished goods from the metropolitan centre.

– Policies effectively restricted the hinterland to producing a small number of staples, while buying machinery and consumer goods manufactured in the Great Lakes-St. Lawrence heartland.[22]

– Internationally, the interests of the hinterland were usually sacrificed to those of the heartland.[23]

The Macdonald-Laurier national policy was implemented with a strong reliance on large business interests. This has led some to charge that the national policy did not arise from people seeking a distinctive national identity, but that it stemmed from "certain business, political, religious and cultural interests seeking the establishment of a monopolistic system of control."[24] Whatever the case, public companies grew through British indirect investment in bonds, and American direct investment in stocks and equity ownership.

The period following World War I saw some shifting of economic ties and policy directions within Canada. "The new industrialism based on minerals, pulp and paper, and hydro-electricity turned the emphasis on economic development away from the Western provinces to the Canadian Shield, with emphasis on the integration between it and contiguous parts of the United States."[25] But old economic policies never die; they are only muted. Vestiges of the Macdonald-Laurier national policy still remain (e.g., the Crow's Nest Pass Agreement), and development of east-west infrastructure, an essential element of the policy, has continued. Since World War II, the Trans-Canada highway, the Trans-Canada pipeline, two national television networks, two national airlines and a system of airport facilities have linked Canada's heartland and hinterland ever more closely together and helped maintain a certain dominance of centre over periphery.

Today, most of the threads of past national (and regional) development policies are still evident. Policies for a mid-1970's Canadian economy prescribe, among other things, (1) the development of innovative capacity within Canadian industry,[26] (2) the need for balanced and diversified regional growth throughout the country,[27] and (3) the reservation of key, technologically-advanced sectors for Canadian ownership and control.

Although these policy orientations appear to signify a departure from previous directions, they are in many respects congruent with past Canadian experience and serve to perpetuate existing economic relationships among regions.[28] Like construction of railways and opening of mines, the enhancement of industrial performance and innovative capacity is based on the harmonious interaction of government, business and now, university elites. The production and distribution of staples continue as important means of developing and linking regions, but the east-west orientation with staples produced mainly for European markets has changed.

> The frontier of settlement is no longer a frontier of settlement producing agricultural staples for Europe; it is a frontier of capital-intensive resource industries producing raw materials for the United States. Development therefore to the extent that it is based on those staples [is] in the direction of continental integration along north-south lines.[29]

As provincial premiers complained at the Western Economic Opportunities Conference (July, 1973), industrial assistance programs for innovative research and enhancement of productivity accrue disproportionately to large firms situated in central Canada. Regional development programs, they contended, have to be very effective merely to offset the longstanding bias of industrial assistance programs towards the manufacturing belt of southern Ontario and Quebec. Call them what you will, heartland-hinterland, centre-periphery or east-west, contrasts in economic development persist, and they reflect, no doubt, government policies. It is to these economic contrasts that we now turn.

REGIONAL DISPARITIES: BETWEEN PROVINCES, BETWEEN URBAN AREAS

> The economic history of Canada has been dominated by the disparity between the centre and margin of western civilization.[30]

It is true that "regional disparities in Canada are to be expected given the sheer size of the country and regional differences in resource endowment."[31] But the nation-wide disparities in income, employment and economic structure which Canada faces, are severe, complex in origin and persistent. What follows in this section is an outline of the situation, in order to provide a sense of the enormity of economic contrasts.

National heartland-hinterland differences in Canada of the 1960s and 1970s can be sketched in rough fashion from a variety of perspectives. Preference scales, as devised by Lycan[32] and Simmons[33] suggest spatial biases in the flows of people and messages (Table 3.1). Population has shifted westward to British Columbia and Alberta and also migrated, on balance, to the urban centres of Ontario and Quebec. In the case of business telephone calls, messages begin at peripheral points and are directed towards the commercial core of the nation, Ontario and Quebec.

Interprovincial patterns of commodity flow also reflect fundamental differences in the economic structure of Canada's heartland and hinterland. The pattern of production and consumption is markedly biased (Figure 3.1). The vast bulk of primary products are exported directly outside the country, while industry in Ontario is a net recipient of a small portion of Western Canadian resources. However, only the heartland provinces, Ontario and Quebec, are net exporters of manufactured goods, both to foreign countries as well to the rest of Canada. Structural differences within the Great Lakes-St. Lawrence Lowlands also emerge: the manufacture of industrial products (particularly metal products) is located in southern Ontario, but the fabrication of consumer products is concentrated (particularly textiles and clothing) in southern Quebec.

Table 3.1. Preference Scales as Measured by Volume of Flows Between Provinces

Migration	Business Telephone Calls
British Columbia	Ontario
Alberta	Quebec
Ontario	New Brunswick
Quebec	Prince Edward Island
New Brunswick	Manitoba
Prince Edward Island	Nova Scotia
Nova Scotia	Newfoundland
Manitoba	Alberta
Saskatchewan	British Columbia
Newfoundland	Saskatchewan

Notes: The ranking is obtained by observing the net flow of migrants (or business calls) for each pair of provinces (dyad) and then shuffling the provinces around until net flows towards a given province are positive from provinces below it in the list and negative for those above. Thus, for migration, provinces are ranked such that there is net migration from the lower ranked province to the higher one.

Sources: R. Lycan, "Interprovincial Migration in Canada: The Role of Spatial and Economic Factors" *The Canadian Geographer*, Vol. 13, (1969) 237–254. J. W. Simmons, *Interprovincial Interaction Patterns in Canada*, Centre for Urban and Community Studies, Research Paper, No. 24. (Toronto: University of Toronto, 1970).

Figure 3.1 Inter-regional Commodity Flows in Canada

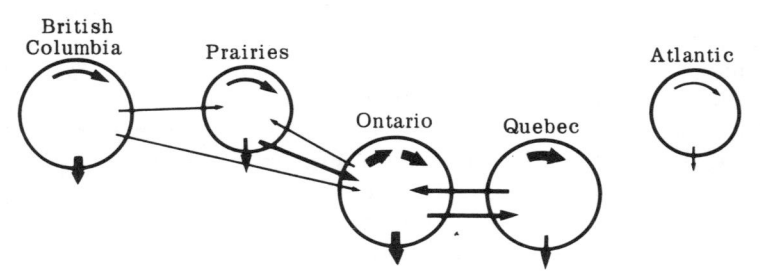

(a) Primary products (wood, paper, primary metals, non—metals, petroleum)

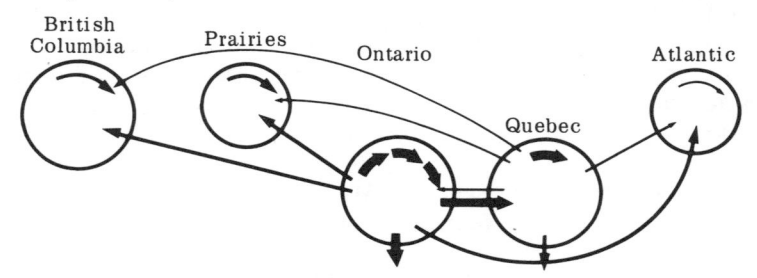

(b) Secondary products (leather, textiles, knitting, metal fabrication, machinery, electrical, chemical, transportation)

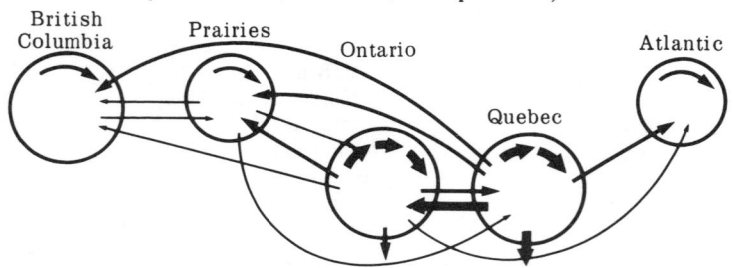

(c) Consumer products (food, tobacco, rubber, clothing, printing, furniture)

➡ less than 1 billion dollars
→ less than 300 million dollars
— less than 100 million dollars

Note: Derived from Statistics Canada, *Destination of Shipments of Manufactures* (1967).

Source: J.W. Simmons, *The Canadian Urban System* (Toronto: University of Toronto Press, forthcoming).

Sophisticated quantitative analyses, summarizing patterns of social, cultural and economic characteristics have painted Canada's regional dimensions in broad brushstrokes.[34] East-to-west contrasts can be highlighted by the variations in the foreign-born population, newcomers from other provinces, and family income. Fundamental, but immensely complicating factors, are the cultural differences and geographic separation of English and French. They may be contrasted not only on the basis of language and religion but also by other characteristics such as age structure, family size, education and occupation. Distinct variations in economic activity across Canada can also be identified with secondary manufacturing, U.S. subsidiaries and corporate head offices being concentrated in the heartland. The emergence of a Northern hinterland as a separate economic entity appeared as a result of the relatively increasing importance of resource extraction, particularly mining. Finally, a metropolitan gradient can be detected: People earning high incomes, possessing university educations, pursuing careers in finance and employed in head offices are more likely to be found residing in metropolitan areas. There is, therefore, a complex array of regional contrasts, some stemming directly from early colonization and staples exports, and some from subsequent industrialization.

Table 3.2. Average (Per Capita) Participation Income by Major Region Relative to the National Average 1910-11 to 1970-71

Period	Canada	British Columbia	Prairie Region	Ontario	Quebec	Atlantic Region
1910-11	100	186	127	105	77	64
1920-21	100	121	117	108	84	69
1930-32	100	137	75	123	94	72
1940-42	100	127	87	122	88	69
1950-52	100	117	107	118	82	65
1960-62	100	115	99	118	88	67
1970-71	100	108	92	119	89	66

Note: Participation or employment income, is income from wages and salaries and the net incomes of farm and non-farm unincorporated business. It differs from personal income by the exclusion of investment income and government transfer payments.
Source: D. M. Ray, "Canada: The Urban Challenge of Growth and Change," Discussion Paper B.74.3, (Ottawa: Ministry of State for Urban Affairs, 1974), p. 18. Reproduced by permission of the Minister of Supply and Services Canada.

Economic disparities, measured by personal income differences between provinces are substantial and continuous. Per capita incomes of the wealthiest provinces have been nearly twice as high as those in the four Atlantic provinces (Table 3.2). These marked and persistent differences are corroborated by other measures. Average *family* income (Table 3.3) – perhaps a better measure of financial well-being – varied from a low of $6,680 in Newfoundland to a high of $10,661 in Ontario as of 1971. Yet averages only partially show the extent of prosperity and poverty. The actual distribution shows that those families reporting earnings of less than $5,000 in 1971 comprised respectively 44 per cent and 39 per cent of all families in New-

Table 3.3. Average Family Income and Family Income Distribution: Canada and the Provinces, 1971

Province	Average Income $	Per cent families in income groups			
		Below $5,000	$5,000 – $9,999	$10,000 – 14,999	$15,000 +
Canada	9,600	23.0	38.3	24.8	13.9
Atlantic					
Newfoundland	6,680	44.3	37.1	13.2	5.3
Prince Edward Island	6,989	41.7	39.2	13.0	6.1
Nova Scotia	7,858	32.1	42.6	17.6	7.6
New Brunswick	7,479	34.4	42.9	16.4	6.4
Quebec	9,260	23.8	41.3	22.2	12.7
Ontario	10,661	17.1	36.4	29.2	17.4
Prairies					
Manitoba	8,646	28.4	38.9	22.3	10.4
Saskatchewan	7,328	39.1	36.3	17.1	7.5
Alberta	9,475	24.9	36.3	25.1	13.7
British Columbia	10,019	20.2	37.3	27.8	14.8

Note: A census family consists of a husband and wife (with or without children) or one parent with one or more children never married, living in the same dwelling. A family may also consist of a man or woman living with a guardianship child or ward under 21 years of age for whom no pay was received. Family income refers to the sum of incomes received by all members of the family 15 years and over, from all sources, during the calendar year 1970. Included are wages and salaries, net income from business and professional practice, net income from farm operations, transfer payments, retirement pensions, investment income and other miscellaneous sources.

Source: Statistics Canada, *1971 Census of Canada: Families: Incomes of Families, Family Head and Non-Family Persons*, Bulletin 2.2 – 12 (Ottawa: Information Canada, 1975). Reproduced by permission of Minister of Supply and Services Canada.

foundland and Saskatchewan, but only 17 per cent and 20 per cent of Ontario and British Columbia families. It is worth noting that these persistent interprovincial income disparities are in sharp contrast to the U.S. experience, where there has been a steady and significant lessening in the inter-regional spread of incomes since the early 1930s.[35]

Income differences reflect interprovincial disparities in human resources and levels of productivity. The Atlantic region, compared to the Canadian average, has a low proportion of population in the working age groups, a low labour force participation rate and a higher level of unemployment (Table 3.4). Moreover, the situation may be worse than perceived at first glance. Cyclical unemployment, which most affects the unskilled manual worker who is least equipped to weather a prolonged loss of earnings, is invariably higher in peripheral regions. As the Canadian unemployment experience of the early 1970s suggests, the Atlantic provinces were the last to show signs of recovery from the economic downturn of 1971 and the first to feel the pinch of impending recession in 1974. An unprecedented wheat boom accounts for the recent unemployment trend in the Prairie region.

More permanent unemployment also exists; much of Canadian unemployment appears to be structural and long-term. The nonworking population consists mostly of the involuntarily excluded: the old, the young, and the handicapped. But the persistently poor employment opportunities and limited job variety may eventually cause job seekers to drop out of the labour force altogether. Low labour force participation rates are thus a symptom of class unemployment which is "made up primarily of those individuals whom our society, with its technical and cultural changes has either displaced or never placed".[36] This situation is still comparatively more frequent in Canada's peripheral regions as attested by a participation rate of 55.7 per cent for Maritime residents of working age (15 – 64 years) compared to 67.3 per cent for those in Ontario. The dearth of economic activity on the periphery is further reflected in the proportionately smaller number of young adults in the population, since many have migrated in search of their fortune elsewhere. By 1971, only 55 per cent of the people in the Atlantic region were aged 15 – 64 versus nearly 63 per cent in Ontario and 67 per cent in British Columbia.

Provincial data permit a sketch of regional disparities, but to appreciate the detail, disaggregation is necessary. Disparities in Canada may be attributed, in part, to differences in the development of the urban system among regions.[37] It has been observed in many countries that incomes in larger cities generally are higher than in smaller towns and villages. Canada is no exception.[38] Table 3.5

Table 3.4. Regional Disparities in Age Structure, Labour Force Participation and Unemployment Rates

Region	Population of Working Age (%15-64 years of total) - 1971 -	Labour Force Participation (% of working ages) - 1971 -	Average Annual Unemployment Rates			
			1971	1972	1973	1974
Canada	62.0	64.2	6.4	6.3	5.6	5.4
Atlantic Region	55.4	55.7	8.6	9.0	8.9	9.7
Quebec	63.5	62.5	8.2	8.3	7.4	7.3
Ontario	62.6	67.3	5.2	4.8	4.0	4.1
Prairie Region	60.6	65.9	4.5	4.5	3.9	2.8
British Columbia	66.5	66.5	7.0	7.6	6.5	6.0

Sources: Statistics Canada, *1971 Census of Canada, Population: Age Groups*, Bull. 1.2–3, (Ottawa: Information Canada, 1973); Statistics Canada, *The Labour Force*, Cat. 71–001, (Ottawa: Information Canada, 1975), and Statistics Canada, *Historical Labour Force Statistics, Actual Data, Seasonal Factors, Seasonally Adjusted Data*, Cat. 71–201, (Ottawa: Information Canada, 1975). Reproduced by permission of Minister of Supply and Services Canada.

Table 3.5. Average Family Income by Urban Size Class and by Region as a Per Cent of the National Average, 1971

Size Class	Average Income $	Canada Per cent	Atlantic	Quebec	Ontario	Prairies	British Columbia
Total	9,600	100	77	96	111	90	104
Metropolitan							
1,000,000 +	11,001	115	na	107	123	na	111
250,000 – 999,999	10,750	112	na	106	115	109	na
100,000 – 249,999	9,996	104	98	95	112	100	103
Non-metropolitan							
50,000 – 99,999	9,732	101	85	93	111	na	na
30,000 – 49,999	9,282	97	89	91	101	97	102
20,000 – 29,999	9,323	97	89	100	99	94	106
10,000 – 19,999	9,209	96	91	85	100	96	103
Non-urban areas	7,342	76	64	77	86	69	92
AVERAGE INCOME $	9,600		7,414	9,260	10,661	8,684	10,019

Source: D. M. Ray and T. N. Brewis, "The Geography of Income and its Correlates," *The Canadian Geographer*, Vol. 20, No. 1, 1976, Table IV.

shows income levels progressively increasing with city size, from the intermediate size classes upwards. The average family income for smaller Canadian cities (10,000 to 20,000) was $9,209 in 1971 compared with $11,001 for the three metropolitan areas of a million-plus people.

Furthermore, inter-regional disparities in average family income for cities of the same size class are generally less than income disparities between cities of different size classes. Hence, the extent of urbanization and the completeness of the regional urban system strongly influence the economic well-being of a region. The lowest average incomes are found in the Atlantic region (where only one person in five resides in a metropolitan area) while the highest levels are found in Ontario (with two out of three residents in cities).

Why do income levels increase with city size? Ray and Brewis[39] suggest that part of the answer rests in differences in the industrial (occupational) mix of the labour force for cities of different sizes. Income levels vary substantially among occupations. High paying positions (corporate managers, professionals, government administrators) are located disproportionately in larger urban places while occupations of modest income (sales positions, textiles manufacture, food and beverage processing) tend to be over-represented in smaller-sized centres. Of course, the relationship is far from "perfect." Some of the highest average family incomes in Canada are enjoyed by small mining communities such as Labrador City. At the same time, in 1971, Montreal ranked thirty-third among cities in terms of average income. Nevertheless, the generalization holds for most places.

Are income disparities among provinces and cities really significant? The answer is far less clear than seems at first blush. Perhaps, as Poetschke suggested,[40] too much has been made of inter-regional disparities in income and insufficient attention accorded to regional variations in the quality of life. As well, low income and poverty are relative. Many of today's "necessities" were unavailable to half of Canada's households as recently as twenty-five years ago.[41] The real question is whether those who reside in cities are better off than those who do not. And it is difficult to know whether higher incomes sufficiently offset higher costs of living and other net disadvantages of city life. "Certainly, differences in the cost of living with city size must substantially reduce inter-regional disparities in real income."[42]

Poverty, in whatever form, is not something any society wants to tolerate. Balanced regional growth and an equitable sharing in economic development have been prominent national policy objectives. But poverty has become to a large extent an urban phenomenon.[43] Low incomes are associated with low rates of regional development and city growth. Perspective on all these issues requires an understanding of cities within the system of cities and it is to this task that we now turn.

The Spatial Organization and Development of Canada's Urban Systems

The concept of a "system" has become an important tool for analysis, first used by natural scientists, then by social scientists and most recently by planners and policy-makers. The idea of a system of cities is also relatively new.[44] From the systems perspective, the urban places of a region are viewed as tightly interconnected with one another by flows of managers and labourers, money and goods, ideas and information. The systems outlook suggests that cities are interdependent, so that any significant change in economic activities, employment structure, population composition or income levels of one city will affect other cities in the system.

Seldom have Canadian cities been regarded as constituent parts of a national urban system. Although urbanization is a fact of Canadian life, Simmons[45] and others have concluded that our consciousness of the urban environment as a whole remains largely undeveloped. For whatever reasons, Canadians see the nation as rural or urban, or as provinces or regions, instead of as a highly interconnected network of urban nodes. Yet to understand Canadian growth and development, it is misleading to rely exclusively on the province or the region as the unit of analysis.[46] Since the province rarely coincides with the boundaries of the urban system, the study of growth and decline among urban places must be examined on the basis of urban regions or urban fields.[47]

THE SPATIAL PATTERN OF CANADA'S URBAN SYSTEM

Aside from the bulge associated with the Prairie breadbasket, Canada's "ecumene" or "inhabited land" is a linear strip 4,000 miles long and from 50 to 100 miles wide. It encompasses about one-tenth of Canada's total land area, but contains over nine-tenths of the nation's population. The "useful Canada" or "populous zone" as Griffith Taylor has called it, is discontinuous and uneven. It parallels the American border to such an extent that Hamelin[48] has likened the Canadian ecumene to "the second floor of a North American building, of which the United States is the foundation."[49]

Within the ecumene, most Canadian cities of 10,000 or over are situated in two major clusters around Toronto and Montreal; the rest are strung out thinly across the country (Figure 3.2). Regional breakpoints distinguishing the Canadian heartland from the hinter-

Figure 3.2. The Geographical Distribution of Canadian Cities Along an East-West Axis

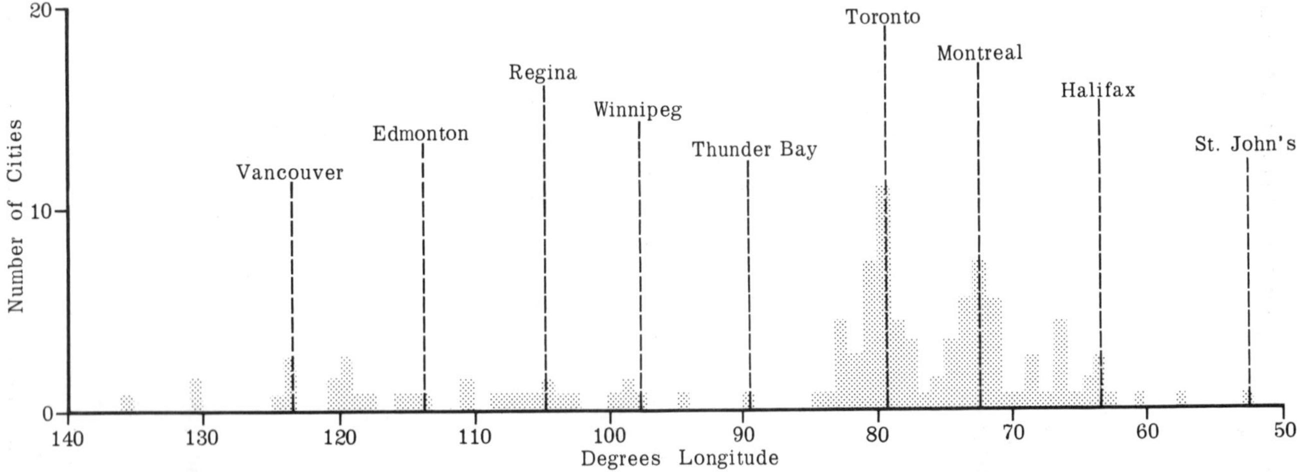

Note: All census metropolitan, major urban areas and cities over 10,000 as of 1971 are included: a total of 124 points. Each urban place is a single unit on the graph. The centres were considered separately from their hinterlands so as to enable the determination of precise locational co-ordinates.

Source: J.W. Simmons, *The Canadian Urban System* (Toronto: University of Toronto Press, forthcoming).

Figure 3.3. The Geographic Distance of Canadian Cities from the United States Border

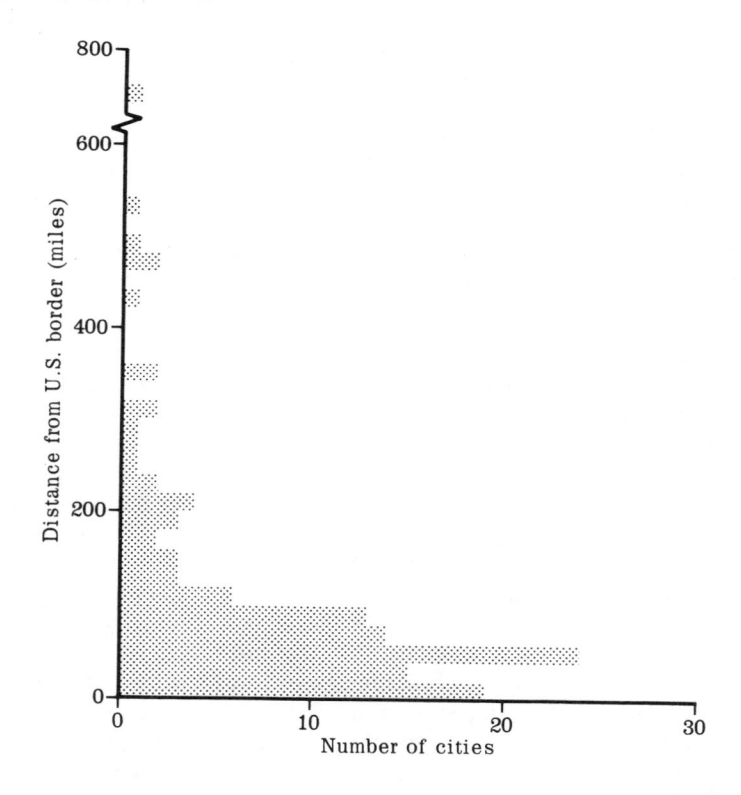

Note: Please see note for Figure 3.2.

Source: J.W. Simmons, *The Canadian Urban System* (Toronto: University of Toronto Press, forthcoming).

land are easily discernible and suggest that there are two different spatial sub-systems of cities in Canada. The one runs east and west across the nation at an evenly spaced but relatively low density of one major city every 100 to 300 miles. The other, stretching in a line from Windsor to Quebec City and alternatively called "the Ontario-Quebec Urban System"[50] or "Canada's *Main Street*"[51] has a fundamentally different economic structure and linkage pattern, and operates at a density about ten times higher than the first sub-system. The contrasts in structure and linkages between the urban sub-system of the heartland and hinterland have been emphasized by Preston who observed:

The state of development of the Canadian urban system is such that an integrated and well developed space economy exists only in the heartland, while beyond, the space economy is fragmented and comparatively unintegrated.[52]

Another prominent feature of the locational patterns of Canadian cities is their proximity to the American border. Although the north-south dimension of Canada extends some 2000 miles, 102 of Canada's 124 cities of 10,000 plus population are situated within 200 miles of the United States boundary, with most located 40 to 60 miles from the border (Figure 3.3). The 49th parallel, in fact, appears to be the only thing preventing Canada's urban system from edging southward.[53]

(1) The Evolution of the Urban System: A Brief Historical Sketch
Map 3.1 documents the emergence of places with 10,000 people or more during the 1851–1951 period. First, the east-west sequence of the growth is apparent: Toronto passed the 10,000 population mark by 1851, and Winnipeg by 1891, but other westerly Prairie cities not until 1911 when the surge of Prairie settlement permanently altered the overall distribution in Canada's urban system. It is also possible to observe the unchanging nature of the settlement pattern which first appeared in Eastern Canada. The system of cities which was laid out by 1851, including Halifax and Saint John, Montreal and Quebec, Toronto and Hamilton are the most prominent places in their region to this day. Only Kingston is an exception. The distribution of cities within the system has remained relatively unaltered among larger centres, although the system has become more dense through the emergence of once-smaller centres, such as London and St. Catharines near the Toronto-Hamilton area.

Despite the unparallelled growth in Canada's urban system since the opening of the West, there have been relatively few changes since 1921 in the rank by population size among the largest urban places. For instance, Montreal, Toronto and Vancouver have not varied in rank despite substantial population growth over the fifty-year period (Table 3.6). Only a few systematic changes are evident. Those most prominent are the rise of Calgary and Edmonton at the apex of the Western resource economy, and the relative decline of Halifax and Saint John as the kingpins in a persistently lagging Maritime economy. The stability of the size ordering among the largest places reflects, if only crudely, the self-reinforcing growth process that occurs in metropolitan areas which feature a diversified industrial base, a populous local market and a multitude of connections with other major centres. Smaller cities, however, have not exhibited the same stability and this suggests, perhaps, that steady

GROWTH FORCES 125

Map 3.1 The Evolving Geographic Pattern of Canada's Urban System, 1851-1951

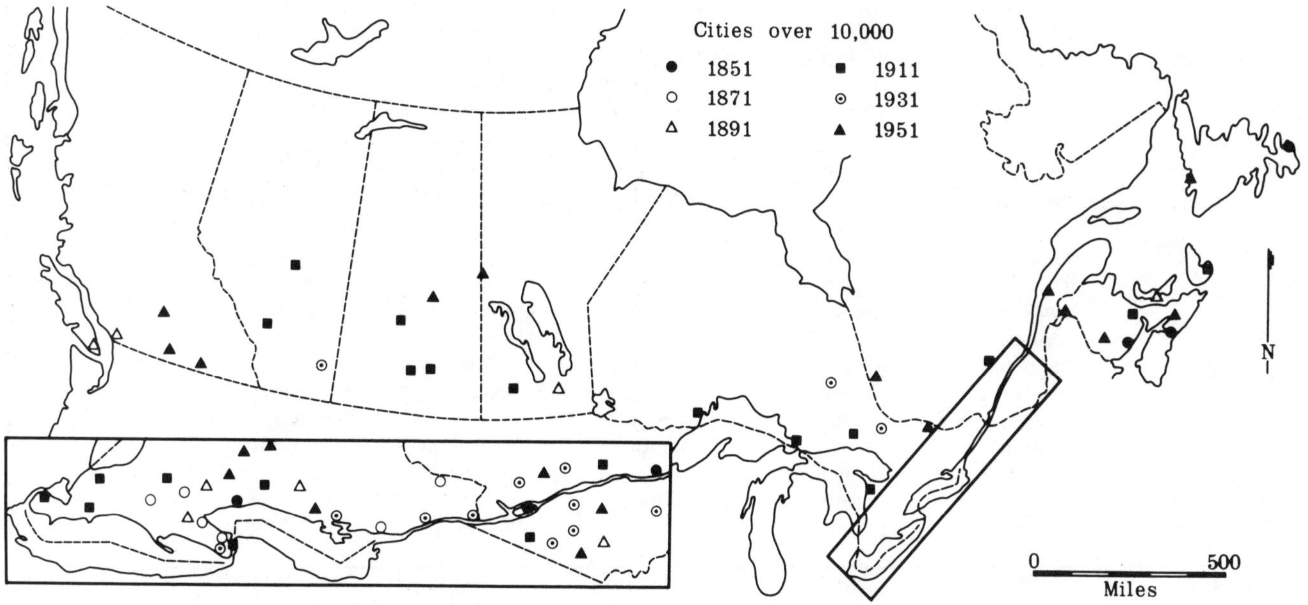

Cities over 10,000
- ● 1851
- ○ 1871
- △ 1891
- ■ 1911
- ⊙ 1931
- ▲ 1951

Source: J.W. Simmons, *The Canadian Urban System* (Toronto: University of Toronto Press, forthcoming).

Table 3.6. The Stability of the Canadian Urban System: The Rank of Selected Metropolitan Areas by Size of Population

Rank	1921	1931	1941	1951	1961	1971
1	Montreal	Montreal	Montreal	Montreal	Montreal	Montreal
2	Toronto	Toronto	Toronto	Toronto	Toronto	Toronto
3	Vancouver	Vancouver	Vancouver	Vancouver	Vancouver	Vancouver
4	Winnipeg	Winnipeg	Winnipeg	Winnipeg	Winnipeg	Ottawa
5	Ottawa	Ottawa	Ottawa	Ottawa	Ottawa	Winnipeg
6	Quebec	Quebec	Quebec	Quebec	Hamilton	Hamilton
7	Hamilton	Hamilton	Hamilton	Hamilton	Quebec	*Edmonton*
8	*Halifax*	Windsor	Windsor	*Edmonton*	*Edmonton*	Quebec
9	London	London	*Edmonton*	Windsor	*Calgary*	*Calgary*
10	Windsor	*Calgary*	*Halifax*	London	London	London
11	*Calgary*	*Edmonton*	London	*Calgary*	Windsor	Windsor
12	*Edmonton*	*Halifax*	*Calgary*	*Halifax*	*Halifax*	Kitchener
13	Victoria	Kitchener	Kitchener	Victoria	Victoria	*Halifax*
14	*Saint John*	Victoria	Victoria	Kitchener	Kitchener	Victoria
15	Kitchener	*Saint John*	*Saint John*	*Saint John*	Sudbury	Sudbury
16	Thunder Bay	Thunder Bay	Thunder Bay	Sudbury	Regina	Regina
17	Regina	Regina	Regina	Thunder Bay	Thunder Bay	Saskatoon
18	Saskatoon	Saskatoon	Sudbury	Regina	*Saint John*	Thunder Bay
19	Sudbury	Sudbury	Saskatoon	Saskatoon	Saskatoon	*Saint John*

Note: Boundaries of the census metropolitan areas were defined according to 1971 limits.

Source: George A. Nader, *Cities of Canada; Volume One: Theoretical, Historical and Planning Perspectives*, (Toronto: Macmillan of Canada, 1975), p. 212.

growth is less assured with small local markets and narrow economic bases.

The intensity and complexity of connections among cities of the urban system have also increased. Rapid escalations have taken place in the mobility of people, the movement of commodities, the flow of information and the transfer of capital as new modes of transport have been introduced, travel time and costs decreased, and communications become generally better. Yet the greatest improvements in accessibility and the most rapid upswing in contacts occurred between the more populous metropolitan areas from which the early transportation network fanned out, and perhaps more important, from which the decisions to build or expand routes and facilities emanated. This self-reinforcing process of strengthening linkages more between larger places than among smaller places is an important aspect of growth to which we will return.

(2) *Defining the Urban System of Today*
If data on movements of people, goods and information within the urban system are available, it is possible to delimit a system on the basis of such movements.[54] Various measures of flow between origin and destination cities have been used, including mail flows,[55] telephone calls,[56] rail freight movement[57] and automobile traffic.[58] In terms of delineating the broad hierarchy of metropolitan areas at the national level, however, airline passenger flows are probably the most defensible and readily accessible source of data.[59]

As an indication of the strength of connections among large corporations, and hence metropolitan areas, the Air Passenger Origin and Destination data of Statistics Canada are useful since approximately 75 per cent of all airline trips are made for business purposes.[60] Since comparable data exist for United States' destinations, it is possible to measure the extent to which Canada's urban areas are linked to the American system of cities. However, caution is in order since 25 per cent of all trips are of a social or recreational nature, and travel patterns reflect routes selected, the scheduling in effect, and the cost and quality of service given relative to other modes of transport.[61]

Figure 3.4 depicts the strength of linkages among large Canadian cities talked about above. Toronto is perched on top of Canada's urban system, having the highest volume of passenger flows to New York, and experiencing a high degree of interaction with other Canadian metropolitan centres.[62] Next in line are Montreal which oversees the city system in Quebec province, and rapidly rising Vancouver which heads a far Western system. The Prairie subsystem dominated by Winnipeg and the Maritime sub-system dominated by Halifax are primarily oriented toward Toronto's financial

Figure 3.4. The Canadian Urban Hierarchy as Determined by Air Passenger Traffic, 1971

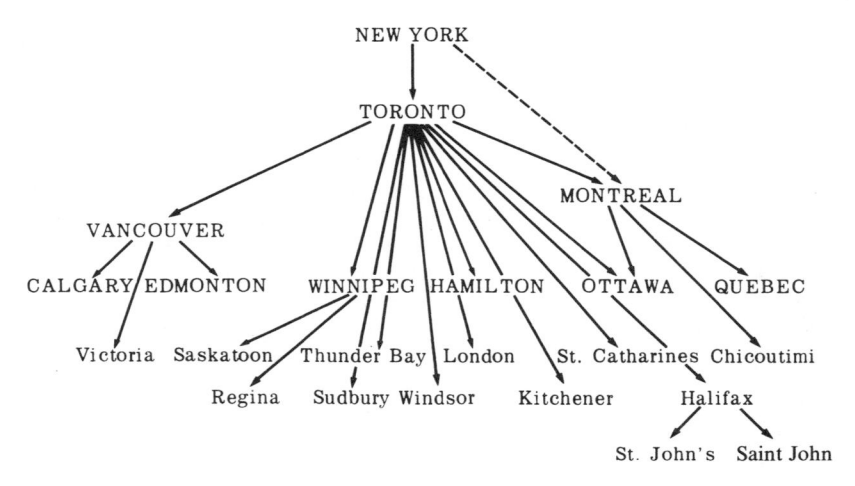

```
                        NEW YORK
                           |
                        TORONTO
                       /   |   \
                      /    |    \
                            MONTREAL
   VANCOUVER
   /     \
CALGARY/EDMONTON   WINNIPEG  HAMILTON   OTTAWA   QUEBEC

Victoria  Saskatoon  Thunder Bay  London  St. Catharines  Chicoutimi
           Regina    Sudbury Windsor   Kitchener    Halifax
                                                 St. John's  Saint John
```

Source: R. Muncaster, "The Contemporary Canadian System of Cities" prepared for the Urbanization Theme, The Canada Studies Foundation - Canadian Association of Geographers, (1975) (mimeographed).

and business community. All metropolitan centres in southern Ontario fall under Toronto's influence, except for Ottawa which, as the nation's capital, appropriately divides its allegiance between both Toronto and Montreal.

(3) *The Character of Canada's Urban System as Shown by Linkages Between Cities*

Systems exhibit various types of properties. Canada's urban system is no exception. A few properties, such as its *identifiability* and its *stability*, have already been discussed. Another, its *controllability* through policy is considered in a later chapter. Several other attributes of Canada's system of cities are sketched below:

Space-Filling Nature: Do the market areas served by Canada's census metropolitan areas fully occupy the nation-space? On the basis of daily newspaper circulation data, Muncaster[63] concluded that this was the case. With few exceptions, the dominant market areas for newspapers distributed from the twenty-two metropolitan centres cover all counties and census divisions in Canada.[64] Thus the large, high order urban places distribute goods and services to smaller cities, towns and villages throughout the country. Consumer goods such as mass circulation newspapers are not, however, exclusively disseminated from the top of the hierarchy since only a relatively small market area is dominated by the dailies from Toronto, Montreal and Vancouver. On the other hand, specialized information for a national professional clientele may be quite centralized. The distribution of the Toronto *Globe and Mail* to a small cadre of influential businessmen and professionals across the country suggests that this is the case, as does the fact that other financial/business publications tend to be centred in Toronto.

Hierarchy and Dominance: Geographers have coined the notion of a hierarchy of urban centres, in which each succeeding level of larger and more populous places holds influence over smaller places.[65] In terms of communication flows, the existence of a hierarchy of urban centres would be supported by the following patterns of interaction: a high proportion of messages from centres of similar size all being directed toward a place of larger size; the inflow of messages to a smaller city from a metropolitan area far exceeding the opposite outflow; and/or a high volume of communications between distant metropolitan areas, but a relatively small flow of messages between smaller centres at a distance.

All three of these patterns were found when communications linkages among cities and towns of the Windsor-Quebec axis were analysed. Based on an analysis of long distance business telephone calls in Ontario and Quebec, Simmons[66] concluded that there are two hierarchies of urban settlement, one dominated by Toronto, the other by Montreal. For instance, the messages for many places in southwestern Ontario flow into London which in turn communicates primarily with Toronto. The provincial capital is also the recipient of large inflows from the St. Clair area (Windsor), the Niagara Peninsula (St. Catharines), the Georgian Bay area (Owen Sound) and as well, the Kingston, Peterborough and Muskoka areas. Further to the east, Ottawa, the principal destination of business messages from eastern Ontario centres, subsequently forwards information to Montreal, as do Quebec City, Sherbrooke and Trois-Rivières. Only in the business messages exchanged between Montreal and Toronto are the two systems interlinked to any extent. The existence of an urban hierarchy in southern Ontario has also been corroborated by Russwurm[67] through his investigation of patterns of postal communications.

Independence: Despite the size and wealth of the United States urban system (about ten times that of Canada) investigations using air passenger data suggest that the Canadian urban system remains independent within the North American continent. Of the 20.3 million passenger trips that arrived or departed from Canadian cities in 1971, roughly 36 per cent began or ended south of the border. But,

Table 3.7. Boundary Effects: Airline Passenger Flows, 1971

	No. of Trips		No. of Trips
Toronto – New York	450,100	Toronto – Montreal	685,800
(500 miles, 15 million)		(350 miles, 3 million)	
Toronto – Los Angeles	66,200	Toronto – Vancouver	182,800
(2800 miles, 10 million)		(2800 miles, 1.5 million)	
Toronto – Chicago	147,700	Toronto – Winnipeg	163,100
(550 miles, 7 million)		(1300 miles, 0.5 million)	
Toronto – Minneapolis	19,700	Toronto – Thunder Bay	96,500
(900 miles, 2 million)		(900 miles, 0.1 million)	
Toronto – Boston	62,100	Toronto – Halifax	103,100
(600 miles, 3 million)		(1200 miles, 0.3 million)	
Vancouver – Seattle	32,600	Vancouver – Victoria	57,700
(150 miles, 1.5 million)		(60 miles, 0.2 million)	

Note: Data in brackets are distance in miles and approximate metropolitan population at destination.

Source: J. W. Simmons, *The Canadian Urban System* (Toronto: University of Toronto Press, forthcoming), C.4, p. 14.

as Table 3.7 shows, cross-border flights from a given centre equalled only one-tenth of the magnitude of flights to Canadian destinations of the same population and distance from the origin. Hence, the Canadian-American boundary appears to be more than an "imaginary line." However, it is important to note that the degree of independence from the American economy varies for different commodities and media: "Newspapers are less permeable than T.V. shows; fiction moves more easily than non fiction; academics are less place-based than politicians, lemons are more likely to be imported than butter."[68]

Openness: How open or closed is the Canadian urban system, at what points do external contacts occur, and in what sectors, with what impacts? Interaction is more intense among Canadian cities than it is with urban areas in the "outside" world. However, flows of migrants, money and messages across the Canadian-U.S. boundary result in such openness that urban growth and development can only be understood in the context of continental growth and development.[69] At the same time linkages with the United States are highly channelled, largely as an extension of Canada's urban hierarchy. Despite the large number of alternative destinations in the United States, over one-fifth of all trans-border flights are Toronto-New York or Montreal-New York runs, while an additional one-third of cross-border excursions connect Toronto or Montreal to major regional centres such as Boston, Chicago, Washington and Philadelphia. A relatively small proportion of flights link smaller centres on opposite sides of the border.

What is revealed by this examination of interconnections within the Canadian urban system? Briefly, airline origin-destination data suggest an urban system in which flows between metropolitan areas tie the far-flung country together. Although the Canadian urban system is open, the same data suggest a system which is distinct. Long distance business telephone and mail flows similarly define a hierarchy of relationships among cities. Finally, newspaper circulation data show the space-filling nature of the system such that newspapers for twenty-two metropolitan areas reach a majority of the Canadian people. Identifiable, somewhat integrated and independent but open, are the attributes that describe Canada's system of cities.

(4) *The Functions Performed by Canada's Urban System*

Cities vary in size and range of economic activities. None is entirely self-sufficient; each interacts with others within the overall system. Canada provides no exception. "The Canadian urban system is characterized by consistent spatial variations in the economic role of cities, variations which shape the occupations and attitudes of the inhabitants and determine the flows of commodities and influence within the system."[70] Hence, the *structure* of economic activities is simply the other side of the coin from the *process* of transactions and flows among places which link them together within the system.

To provide focus for the abbreviated analysis of *structure* within Canada's system of cities, several questions can be posed. What is the range of variation in functions performed by cities? Are the economies of certain cities specialized almost solely in the production of one type of good or service while other cities are highly diversified? Does the type and range of "work" done in Canadian cities vary according to their relative location in urban Canada (e.g. central as opposed to peripheral) or in association with city size?

Distinct regional groupings emerge when the labour force in Canada's metropolitan areas is classified according to three broad industrial categories: (1) primary extraction and manufacturing, (2) trade, service and finance, and (3) transportation, public administration and defence. Figure 3.5 shows that many centres situated along the Windsor-Quebec City axis (including Windsor, Hamilton, St. Catharines, Kitchener, Sudbury and Chicoutimi-Jonquière) are clustered towards the Resource Extraction and Manufacturing segment of the graph, highlighting the concentration of manufacturing in the central Canada heartland. Towards the Trade, Service and Finance segment of the graph, the regional service centres of the peripheral hinterland appear: Saskatoon, Regina, St. John's and Quebec City. Met-

132 CHANGING CANADIAN CITIES

Figure 3.5. The Broad Economic Structure of Canada's Metropolitan Areas, 1971

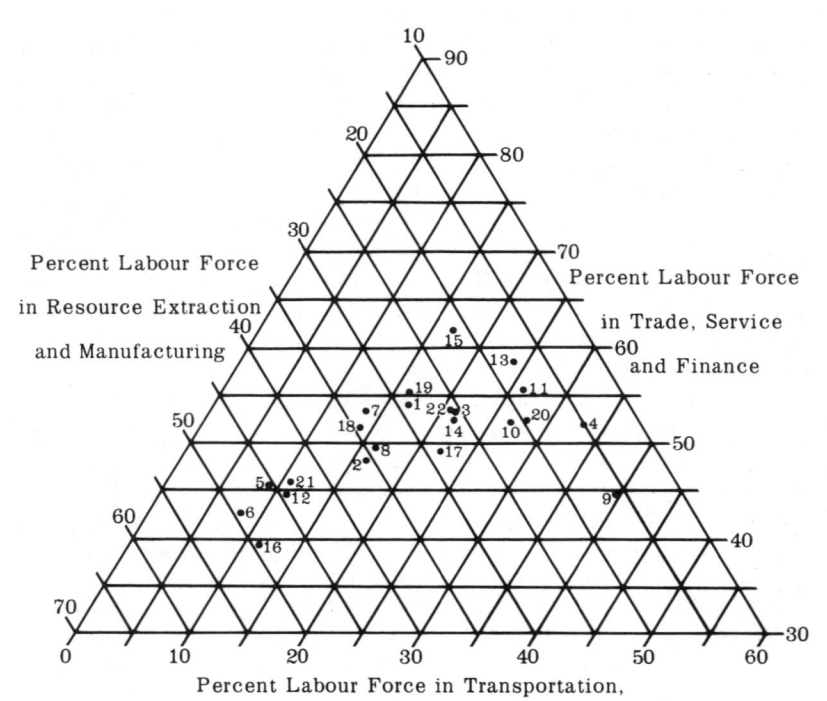

Percent Labour Force in Resource Extraction and Manufacturing

Percent Labour Force in Trade, Service and Finance

Percent Labour Force in Transportation, Public Administration, and Defence

1.	Calgary	12.	St. Catharines–Niagara
2.	Chicoutimi–Jonquiere	13.	St. John's
3.	Edmonton	14.	Saint John
4.	Halifax	15.	Saskatoon
5.	Hamilton	16.	Sudbury
6.	Kitchener	17.	Thunder Bay
7.	London	18.	Toronto
8.	Montreal	19.	Vancouver
9.	Ottawa–Hull	20.	Victoria
10.	Quebec	21.	Windsor
11.	Regina	22.	Winnipeg

Note: The table is similar to that found in R. Muncaster, "The Contemporary Canadian System of Cities". The axes represent percentage of the labour force in a category.

Source: Statistics Canada, *1971 Census of Canada: Industries*, Bull. 3.4-5, T.5-1 to 5-28 (Ottawa: 1975).

ropolitan centres which offer a high proportion of jobs in Transportation, Public Administration and Defence are seats of government (Ottawa, St. John's, Halifax, Regina and Victoria), defence bases (Halifax) and transportation nodes or ports of entry (St. John's, Halifax, Regina). Finally, situated in the middle of the graph are metropolitan areas which feature a diversified labour force and a balanced economic base. Toronto, London, Winnipeg, Calgary and Vancouver are examples of this type of city.

If we look at labour force data in more detail, additional distinctions appear. For example, Sudbury, noted for its nickel mining and processing as the home of INCO and Falconbrige, is the only metropolitan centre founded on resource extractive activity, though Calgary is also prominent because of its oil and gas interests. Or "finance" is an important function for Toronto, Vancouver, Montreal and London! Why London? Because it serves as a base for several large insurance companies.

On average, over one job in five is a service job, but in a few centres, including Saskatoon, Victoria, Quebec and St. John's, the figure is nearly one job in three. However, the specific service role differs substantially, with Saskatoon specializing in higher education, Quebec City in education and religious organizations, St. John's in the provision of health and welfare services and Victoria, sometimes called the retirement capital of Canada, in personal services.

Employment in so-called city-forming activities can differ sharply from one city to another, reflecting the comparative advantages of the regional economy and the position that each city holds within the urban system. Manufacturing specialization apparently exists for metropolitan centres in the Windsor-Quebec axis while hinterland cities must devote more of their labour force to transportation and wholesaling in order to overcome considerable distances among a thinly spread population engaged in primary activities. A natural resource orientation may also be the *raison d'être* for a city, although it is rare to find a mining community even half the size of Sudbury. Finally, government fiat in rare cases has helped lay the economic foundation of a city, as in the decision to designate Halifax as Canada's major naval base.

Despite difficulties of trying to classify cities according to economic activities, the exercise does throw light upon broad regional patterns within the urban system. The use of simple, but crude measures can help to put functions in context. Table 3.8 shows that the regional pattern of economic structure for metropolitan areas is reflected for the most part in the functional profiles of Canada's smaller cities. Of the twenty-one cities sized 30,000 to 100,000 whose dominant economic activity is manufacturing, nineteen are located

Table 3.8. Canada's Urban System by Dominant Function: 1971 Labour Force Data

City Size		Extraction	Manufacturing	Construction	Transportation
1,000,000 +	Heartland	–	2	–	–
	Hinterland	–	–	–	1
	Total	–	2	–	1
400,000 – 1,000,000	Heartland	–	1	–	–
	Hinterland	1	1	–	–
	Total	1	2	–	–
100,000 – 400,000	Heartland	–	5	–	–
	Hinterland	1	1	–	2
	Total	1	6	–	2
30,000 – 100,000	Heartland	–	19	–	–
	Hinterland	2	2	–	2
	Total	2	21	–	2
10,000 – 30,000	Heartland	2	22	–	–
	Hinterland	9	19	2	4
	Total	11	41	2	4
TOTAL	Heartland	2	49	–	–
	Hinterland	13	23	2	9
	Total	15	72	2	9

Source: Compiled from data assembled by Shiu-Yeu Li, "Labour force statistics and a functional classification of Canadian cities," in D. Michael Ray (ed.), *Canadian Urban Trends: National Perspective*, Vol. 1 (Toronto:

in the central Canadian heartland. The data are not as conclusive, but the general tendency is repeated for places in the 10,000 to 30,000 size group. On the other hand, those cities of 10,000-plus population whose dominant function is extraction, distribution, transportation or government administration and defence, are located to an overwhelming extent in the hinterland areas of Canada.

The distinction between heartland and hinterland cities was also drawn by Maxwell based on his analysis of 1961 labour force data. Manufacturing cities of the heartland, Maxwell suggested, "form basic units in fully integrated manufacturing regions where interaction among cities is very significant."[71] High degrees of industrial linkage have developed between cities, and all types of manufacturing occur, from blast furnace activity to electronics manufacturing and food processing. In contrast, cities of the hinterland which specialize in manufacturing are few in number, isolated in location and tend to stand apart from other periphery cities, since they are not primarily concerned with servicing surrounding rural areas. Extremely specialized, these centres are usually one-industry towns

Wholesale, Retail Trade	Community & business Services	Personal Service	Public Administration & Defence	Total
–	–	–	–	2
–	–	–	–	1
–	–	–	–	3
–	–	–	2	3
–	–	–	1	3
–	–	–	3	6
–	–	–	–	5
–	2	–	3	9
–	2	–	3	14
–	1	–	–	20
–	1	–	3	10
–	2	–	3	30
–	1	–	3	28
5	12	1	4	56
5	13	1	7	84
–	2	–	5	58
5	15	1	11	79
5	17	1	16	137

Copp Clark Publishing, 1976); originally from the Ministry of State for Urban Affairs.

involved in resource processing as exemplified by ore smelting in Kitimat or Trail, and pulp and paper mills in Powell River, Kapuskasing or Port Alberni. However, manufacturing activity in the vast majority of Maritime and Western cities has arisen from and continues to support transportation and wholesaling functions.[72] Prince Rupert is a classic case of a city that has built up a manufacturing sector on a transport break-in-bulk point.

Using more disaggregated data, Marshall[73] observed several further contrasts. He found, for example, that the structure of manufacturing industries differs quite sharply between the urban areas located in the Ontario and Quebec portions of the Windsor-Quebec axis. "Manufacturing in the cities of southern Ontario is typically diversified and capital intensive, but in southern Quebec there is much less variety and much greater dependence on labour intensive production, notably in the textile and clothing industries."

Contrasts between peripheral cities revolve around the types of primary activities serviced or exploited. Compared to the economies of Prairie cities which are still primarily supported by an agricultural base, the functional orientation of cities in the remainder of Canada's hinterland tends to be based more on mineral and forest resources. Indeed, the wheat-growing areas of the Prairies stand out as areas almost devoid of the primary activities—fishing, forestry, mining, hydro-electric power—which would give rise to the "one industry town" or the resource-oriented manufacturing centre.

Diversification and Specialization in Canada's Urban System
The functional diversification or "balance" of economic activities within cities and regions has been studied fairly intensively in many countries since the Great Depression, when it was discovered that towns highly specialized in a single industry were most vulnerable to acute seasonal and cyclical unemployment.[74] A considerable literature developed regarding the measurement of functional diversification, but methodological difficulties unfortunately remain' unresolved and results are sometimes even contradictory.[75] Nonetheless, the functional diversification of a community has been considered by some planners as an important goal which may help alleviate economic problems.

Many have agreed with Thompson's assertion: "Clearly increased city size brings greater industrial diversification."[76]

For Canada, Crowley[77] concluded, on the basis of six different measures of diversification that larger Canadian cities did indeed tend to be more diversified than smaller ones. The results were qualified, however, by reference to severe data and statistical constraints. Using another approach, Marshall[78] also found that there is a weak, but definite association between city size and the degree of industrial diversification in Canadian centres of 10,000 people or more.

The evidence[79] suggests that the most specialized centres are those dominated by mining, a single manufacturing activity, a military installation, or general manufacturing with no dominance by a single industry. The reasons are not hard to understand. Mining and resource centres must be located near bodies of ore which are frequently isolated on the Canadian Shield, and hence without large local markets for goods and services. Many manufacturing centres in southern Ontario and southern Quebec are highly specialized because the interconnectedness among centres makes it possible for one city to rely on others. Single industry and military installations are obvious.

With respect to various regions of the country, it has been observed that diversification is greatest in the Prairies. Cities such as Portage-La-Prairie, North Battleford and Red Deer all serve a surrounding agricultural area.[80] On the whole, the most specialized region of the country is southern Quebec where a limited variety of manufacturing, notably textiles and clothing, gives rise to towns which are markedly specialized compared to elsewhere.

Both the structure of economic activity and the process of intercity linkages in Canada's urban system have now been described. Each gives rise to issues and questions about patterns of change that have occurred or will occur in Canada's urban system. To what extent is the development of the urban system biased towards established patterns of urban size, growth, income and intercity relationships? Does this bias benefit or harm places which are small, peripheral, poor or otherwise disadvantaged? Does the spatial concentration of growth increase as control increasingly emanates from large corporations and institutions located in metropolitan areas? What are the policy implications and alternatives? These and other issues are the focus of the next section.

Growth Forces Within Systems of Cities

Some questions are repeatedly raised by observers of the urban scene: How do cities grow? How do systems of cities evolve? And, perhaps most importantly, why do some cities grow while others stagnate or decline?

In the final analysis the development of each city is unique. However, certain elements are common denominators for change. Rising industrial productivity, escalating technological change, almost instantaneous communications, the ascendancy of white collar occupations, and an increasing concentration of corporate power have formed the context within which urban growth has occurred. A potentially rich hinterland, initial advantage, dynamic leadership from the entrepreneurial elite, and favourable investment decisions by "outside" business corporations or government institutions have permitted certain cities to grow and prosper. The relative weight of some of these elements is illustrated in the early rivalry of Montreal and Quebec, Toronto and Kingston, and Vancouver and Victoria. "Surprisingly, the relative losers in each case had the initial advantage and two of these had the further benefit of being provincial capitals."[81]

How then, do these basic factors operate in fuelling urban development?

SPECIALIZATION: THE DIVISION OF LABOUR AND MARKET EXCHANGE

Specialization by various members of society has been basic to the formation of cities. Indeed, the division of labour formerly performed by one person or plant in order to achieve an economy of time, effort, and resources is the prime source of higher productivity and material well-being. Without specialization, each family would be a Swiss Family Robinson, raising its own food, weaving its own cloth, building its own house and providing its own amusement. And the poverty of such a world would be beyond the comprehension of modern Canadians.

Could this division of tasks be accomplished by a population dispersed throughout the countryside? The answer is largely no. Increasing specialization imposes a certain measure of interdependence and demands a higher level of spatial interaction. The work of the specialist, who by definition provides a narrow range of goods and services, only achieves economic significance as it is integrated with the work of others, whether the task is the production of an auto, a theatrical performance, or a magazine. Hence, the growth of the modern city and the march of the industrial revolution have been, among westernized nations, the joint products of a single cultural strand: specialization. E. E. Lampard elaborates:

> If specialization makes for higher productivity over time, it also tends to concentrate productive activities over space. It is a dynamic process which transforms the spatial order of production and distribution. In pre-industrial societies, where factors are relatively unspecialized, economic functions and organizations tend to be uniform, simple, and scattered – very much according to circumstances of geography. The small urban nuclei which often develop in such societies are essentially service centres of an agrarian way of life.... To be sure, towns are sometimes centres for craftsmen, but the bulk of so-called primary and secondary activities remain undifferentiated in space and are tied to the self-sufficient hinterland where the mass of population perforce resides. Specialization revolutionizes the spatial pattern of economic activity.... [82]

The city is not only the product of specialization; it is a pre-condition of specialization. As Adam Smith realized long ago, it is only in cities "where people are agglomerated or separated by distances associated with relatively low transportation costs that markets become large and a division of labour and exchange becomes developed."[83]

THE DEVELOPMENT OF A PROSPEROUS HINTERLAND

The exchange of goods and services with the surrounding tributary area is the *raison d'être* for many urban places, particularly during their formative years. Under most circumstances, a city can only survive and prosper if a symbiotic trading relationship evolves between the city and its hinterland. As N. S. B. Gras, an early analyst of urban growth, stated: "the metropolitan economy is the organization of producers and consumers mutually dependent for goods and services wherein their wants are supplied by a system of exchange concentrated in the largest city, which is the focus of local trade and the centre through which normal economic relations with the outside are maintained."[84] The relationship is most crucial to the growth of an urban centre during the period of initial settlement, but it lessens in importance with the growth of large internal markets within the metropolis itself. The survival of small centres which exist as central places, providing goods and services to persons engaged largely in primary activities, is directly dependent upon the economic health of the hinterland.

The salutary influence of city-hinterland trading relations on Toronto's early advancement illustrates the process.[85] The history of Toronto in mid-nineteenth century is a story of growth and transition from an administrative village to a "vast commercial emporium." Development as a commercial-wholesale complex stemmed largely from its proximity to the rich agricultural hinterland of southwestern and central Ontario, which was rapidly filled by succeeding waves of British immigrants. Changes in the occupational structure favouring merchants and craftsmen over the professionals marked Toronto's transformation into a fledgling mercantile capital during the 1830s and 1840s.[86] In contrast, Kingston, which was larger and more commercially robust initially, stagnated in part, because its rocky hinterland could support only a handful of settlers.

Careless has suggested that the stage of hinterland development exerted considerable influence on the growth and form of cities and city systems. "As the hinterland evinced new complexity and scope, so did the urban side of the equation – though this does not infer any constant state of harmony between them."[87] For example, fisheries, fur trading outposts, timber cutting operations and cattle ranches produced a few colonial garrison towns but not significant urban growth. Later, as activities requiring residential settlement came to the fore (e.g. agriculture, saw milling, shaft mining), small communities blossomed and older, well situated towns ascended. With the spread of primary processing (e.g., flour milling, tanning, canning, cabinet making and mineral smelting), manufacturing centres began to appear and towns moved towards a real dominance. Finally, hinterland economies broadened from their original resource exploitation to include local service activities and, in some cases, industrial production. This description undoubtedly simplifies a highly diverse chain of historical events, but it serves to emphasize the inter-relationship between city and hinterland in the development process.

Arising from the notion of trade as a prime stimulus of urban growth is the concept of *economic base*.[88] Economic base theory is premised on the proposition that the regional economy can be subdivided into two components—the basic (city-building) activity, e.g., automobile production, which is "exported" outside the region allowing the city system to derive dollars from the national economy, and the non-basic (city-serving) activity, e.g., convenience retailing, which is consumed internally. The money obtained from the export of basic production, in the short run, drives the non-basic functions by means of its continued circulation throughout the urban economy during succeeding rounds of expenditure. Whether non-basic activities actually provide a significant long run impetus to urban growth is a moot point.[89]

TECHNICAL CHANGE

Closely related to economic advancement through specialization is economic growth induced by higher labour productivity.[90] With the enlarged markets of a city, opportunities for *industrial* specialization emerge. Increasingly, firms become suppliers to other firms, permitting a more efficient inter-industry division of labour.

For Canada, the pre-World War I rise of large scale manufacturing and the concomitant decline of artisan workshops may be attributed, in part, to technological advances. The introduction of new machinery and techniques increased the optimum scale of operations. As scales increased, the size of market was enlarged; new technologies permitted firms to substitute higher shipping costs (i.e., over long distances) with reduced labour costs through higher productivity. Another effect of technological progress was increased interdependencies among firms. Inter-industry linkages generally assured that firms forming successive stages in a production process would locate near one another. This also weakened the natural resource orientation of many industries by reducing the importance of any one raw material in the locational decision of the firm.

For example, the changes wrought by technological improvements upon the urban network of late nineteenth century Ontario have been documented.[91] Higher productivity tended to centralize industry in larger centres and, at the same time, cause the disintegration of trade, the decline of manufacturing and ultimately, the demise of many small nucleated settlements in rural Ontario. Of the sixty hamlets that once flourished in Peel County (adjacent to Toronto), only three retained the status of a rural village by 1911; the remainder featured only a few houses and a small store, if they continued to exist at all.[92] Toronto was one of the chief beneficiaries from the process of industrial concentration in the province:

With the use of steam power and later electric power, mass production techniques were introduced; and the manufacturing industry changed from one comprised of large numbers of artisans and small craft industries [scattered throughout the province] to one comprised of a small number of plants with large numbers of employees [situated in larger centres].[93]

The more efficient, large scale producers in Toronto, such as the breweries, generally were able to eliminate less efficient producers in smaller towns. Many firms first established in small Ontario towns began to move en masse to Toronto by the 1870s. These included woollen mills from Streetsville, a carpet factory from Elora, the Massey farm implements plant from Newcastle and the Harris firm from Beamsville.[94] Consequently, Toronto's share of manufacturing in south central Ontario rose from 10 per cent in 1871 to 25 per cent in 1891, and to 34 per cent by 1901. By the turn of the century, the industrial sector had become the single most important source of employment and income in the City of Toronto.[95] The Toronto of today has proportionately fewer manufacturing jobs than many other urban centres in southern Ontario, but the turn-of-the-century growth spurt that confirmed Toronto's metropolitan dominance was marked by the transition from primarily a commercial-wholesale complex to an industrial economy.

TRANSPORTATION ECONOMIES

Given the vast geographical domain of Canada, perhaps the most significant technological changes have been the improvements in transportation which have rapidly whittled down the effective distance between urban places. This "shrinking" of the nation has tended to support the emergence of large metropolitan areas which have extended their economic dominance over broad regions.[96]

Since the late nineteenth century, firms have located increasingly in large cities where road, rail and water routes converge, in order to minimize costs of collecting materials and distributing finished products. Although the advent of widespread auto and truck use during the 1940s permitted many producers to relocate from the congested central city to outlying areas, most firms sought sites in the adjacent suburbs rather than distant isolated communities, because they wished to minimize their total transportation bill.[97]

The importance of transportation was not lost upon the city fathers cum "town boosters" of nineteenth century Ontario. It seemed that every town wished to invest in railway construction to ensure a link to the regional transportation network. Frequent overbuilding resulted. The map of turn-of-the-century Ontario was, in effect, a set of criss-crossing rail lines unrelated to potential growth.

The result of all this frenetic activity was to affirm the position of Toronto. As the rail transportation network in southern Ontario grew, the rationale for a single producing and marketing area emerged. Increasingly, as railway building accelerated during the 1870s and 1880s, lines were constructed to focus on Toronto and acted as a means for "hinterland piracy." More and more feeder lines to Lake Ontario ports were cut off or partly absorbed by lines radiating from Toronto. "On the eve of the First World War, eleven railways converged upon the capital, giving it undisputed hegemony as the trade and service centre for a major part of the province."[98]

The later development of the highway network in the 1940s and 1950s served only to further concentrate activity in larger urban places. The influence of the automobile upon the thinning out of small trading villages was probably most pervasive in the Prairie community system.[99] In general, the higher level of access accorded to certain centres by changes in transportation technology encouraged an urban hierarchy and favoured the redistribution of certain economic activity up the urban hierarchy to larger places.

A corollary to transportation economies as a stimulus to urban development is the influence of *market accessibility* and the achievement of *market thresholds*. According to location theory, new firms appear as a city grows and achieves a minimum concentration of population (or market threshold) needed to support a larger unit of production or distribution. Such considerations help to explain the centre-periphery contrasts in the location of manufacturing firms within the Canadian urban system. Ray[100] (1969) has shown the great advantage of the Toronto-Montreal axis in providing access to the Canadian market, both in terms of population and, even more, of income. The disadvantages of the periphery are also evident:

> The growth of markets in the West has not yet been sufficient to generate any independent industrial complexes. The advantages of access to the national market from Central Canada still outweigh the access to local market. In part, this occurs because there is no single local market in the West.... [101]

On a more local scale, the constraining influence of large cities on the growth of smaller communities has intensified as (1) the transportation system improved access to the larger urban places, (2) organizational changes (e.g., supermarkets) increased the market threshold for goods, and (3) the dispersed rural population declined. One way by which a city can grow within an urban system is by expanding its share of the income received from "lower order" places or retained from "higher order" places.[102] By and large, this form of growth has benefited larger cities and tolled the death knell for the smallest agricultural communities.[103]

Providing market access, and tying together Canada's far-flung urban system has been a long standing priority of the Canadian government. Many have stressed the importance to the urban system of federal policies which have attempted to integrate regional economies – the building of the CPR, freight rates, Air Canada, the Trans-Canada highway and the St. Lawrence Seaway. Yet regional policy dilemmas remain. Greater access through transportation improvements has had ambivalent effects, some good, some bad. Experience suggests that mere provision of improved transport links from urban places in lagging areas to cities in prospering regions will not suffice as a development policy. On the contrary: "In many depressed areas better connections have proved that roads lead out as well as in, by opening their markets to competition from more efficient producers and by encouragement of shipment of primary products without local elaboration."[104]

CHANGES IN OCCUPATIONAL STRUCTURE AND CORPORATE ORGANIZATION

> The degree of economic dominance presently attained by large private and public organizations in advanced economies is such that any particular highly industrialized society may be described basically as an aggregation of organizations, each normally consisting of spatially separated units linked together by formal and informal channels for exchanging information, goods, and capital[105]

In recent decades, the controlling force exerted by production methods and transportation technologies has been complemented by structural changes in employment and corporate organization. Occupational composition has shifted increasingly from blue collar to white collar employment; firms once small and independent have been integrated into huge multi-functional corporations. Both have tended to confirm the ascendancy of a few cities.

Most advanced economies, including Canada, have left the "industrial" age to enter the "post-industrial" era. As Table 3.9 indicates, the proportion of primary production jobs in the Canadian economy has decreased precipitously since the turn of the century. At the same time, employment in the service sector has increased dramatically. Hence, most employment growth has occurred in the so-called white collar occupations. And many jobs, especially those controlled by the largest organizations, have become increasingly associated with the exchange and processing of specialized information rather than the transportation and processing of resources. Moreover,

Table 3.9. The Changing Occupational Structure of the Canadian Labour Force

Occupational Categories	1881	1921	1951	1971
Primary	51.3	36.6	19.8	8.3
Manufacturing	24.3	20.8	25.1	22.2
Construction	4.5	5.8	6.2	6.0
Transportation	2.9	7.8	9.5	8.8
Trade & Finance	5.3	9.4	10.1	16.9
Service	11.6	19.2	28.2	37.6
TOTAL	100.0	100.0	100.0	100.0

Note: The labour force is composed of non-institutional population, 10 years of age and over in 1881 and 1921, but 14 years of age and over in 1951 and 1971.

Source: D. Michael Ray, "Canada: The Urban Challenge of Growth and Change." Discussion Paper B.74.3. (Ottawa: The Ministry of State for Urban Affairs, 1974. pp. 4-11. Reproduced by permission of Minister of Supply and Services Canada.

"the expanding consumption and production of specialized information by job-providing organizations tends to favour the growth of already large metropolitan areas...."[106]

Economies of scale, the expansion of incomes and markets, changes in management techniques and improvements in communications have led to an expansion of firm sizes in virtually every business sector. This has occurred in many ways. Mergers, spurred in some measure by a desire to eliminate competition, have resulted in oligopolistic corporate structures, or the *horizontal* consolidation of a number of suppliers of similar goods or services (e.g., the Canadian banking system). *Vertical* integration also has occurred where suppliers, intermediate processors and distributors in a production sequence have merged into a single corporate entity (e.g., most of the major oil companies). More recently, diversified *conglomerates* and holding companies have been assembled to control a broad range of largely unrelated activities (e.g., the CPR, the George Weston empire, the Power Corporation). All of these corporate combinations nourish the growth of a centralized staff.

Clement has suggested that the Canadian economy and its development are now dominated by fewer than 150 corporations.[107] As of 1971, a substantial proportion of all assets and revenue in many industrial sectors were possessed by these dominant corporations (Table 3.10). A prime illustration of this concentration of corporate power and the stimulus that it provides to metropolitan growth, is the Cana-

Table 3.10. Revenue and Assets Held by Canada's 150 Largest Corporations, 1971

Sector	% Assets	% Revenue
Finance		
Banks	90	91
Life Insurance	86	81
Sales Finance	90	—
Mortgage and Trust	80	—
Trade		
Retail	39	45
Wholesale	15	11
Transportation and Utilities		
Utilities	66	81
Railways	89	87
Transportation (incl. pipelines)	90	31
Communications	97	93
Mining		
Metal Mining	56	64
Mineral Fuels	48	40
Manufacturing		
Paper Products	52	57
Food and Beverages	66	56
Petroleum	90	94
Non-Metallic Minerals	44	30
Primary Metals	55	57
Transportation Equipment	59	59
Machinery	66	58
Electrical Products	35	31
Other Manufacturing	29	43

"—"—not available

Source: Wallace Clement, *The Canadian Corporate Elite* (Toronto: McClelland and Stewart, 1975), p. 129.

dian banking system.[108] At the centre of the financial power bloc in Canada are five dominant banks, which account for 90 per cent of the assets and 91 per cent of the income of all banks. This is one of the most concentrated banking structures in the world. All were founded before or just after Confederation; and no bank has failed in Canada since 1923. Three of the five dominant banks have their head offices in Toronto, two in Montreal. The situation is similar for life insurance, consumer loans and finance, and trust and mortgage companies. For example, the thirteen dominant life insurance companies accounted for 86 per cent of assets and 81 per cent of income earned by their sector. Nearly all of their head offices are located in southern Ontario or Montreal. The financial stranglehold exerted by Toronto and Montreal interests is such that many contend that regional disparities have been exacerbated and regional development policies frustrated by the concentration of economic power (see, for example, the proceedings of the Western Economic Opportunities Conference, July, 1973). Indeed, the Bank of British Columbia was founded with the intention of offsetting the influence of central Canadian financial interests.

The emergence of large, multi-functional, multi-locational firms has enhanced the influence of the metropolis on the urban system. The process by which this took place has been described by Pred:

> As organizations merge and enlarge, thereby controlling units at an increasing number of places, the need for coordination among a greater number of specialized units under more complex circumstances and the ability of modern communications equipment to cheaply transmit routine or programmed commands to distant units combine to encourage decision-making activities and related administrative employment to become more highly concentrated at a limited number of headquarters centers.[109]

With the growing complexity of enterprise, there has developed a spatial separation of management and production. "The controlling headquarters unit, which devotes much of its time to planning... or nonroutine decisions, sits atop the [urban] hierarchy and in the vast majority of instances is located in a metropolitan complex of national importance."[110] Power has become concentrated both organizationally and spatially. For instance, in 1972, Canada's five largest banks with head offices in Toronto and Montreal directly controlled 94,900 jobs while twenty of Canada's largest manufacturing corporations were responsible directly for another 364,900 jobs.[111] And the prospects for further concentration are almost assured, if corporate size is any indication. The many multi-locational firms which today have more than 10,000 employees are expected to grow larger and more functionally complex, partly as a result of attitudes held by corporate administrators who identify their prestige, security and advancement with an organization's size and growth.[112]

A complicating factor in Canada has been the rapid rise of multinational corporations headquartered in the United States.[113] The power wielded by the multi-nationals for instance, has introduced a demonstrable bias into the locational decisions of American subsidiaries. Ray[114] has shown that they tend to locate along a vector between their home office and Toronto, or simply as close to Toronto as possible. More on this later.

The rise of multi-locational firms with their concomitant concentration of corporate power has profound policy implications for urban and regional growth strategies. Drawing upon the British experience with regional development, Parson[115] has argued that government industrial decentralization policies have been blunted since local profits are often returned to distant head offices rather than being invested locally. After reviewing development policy in a number of countries, Friedmann[116] also suggested that government efforts to industrialize traditionally backward regions had succeeded in enticing production units to the periphery, but failed to attract corporate management. Hence, "decapitated" production units in smaller urban places find themselves dependent on the "outside" decisions of management centred in metropolitan areas. As a result, Pred has concluded: "Unless some accurate insights into city-system development in advanced economies are established, there is a great danger that... policies designed either to discourage metropolitan concentration or to aid lagging and depressed regions will continue to prove counterproductive...."[117]

ECONOMIES OF AGGLOMERATION: LOCALIZATION ECONOMIES

More and more, labour is devoted to intermediate production; that is, to the manufacture of products for subsequent use by other firms in their production process. And the necessity for a high degree of interaction among firms producing intermediate inputs has caused the progressively greater clustering of economic activity in urban centres. Benefits to individual businesses, known as economies of localization, may be derived from the clustering of firms or industries into mutually supporting, tightly-knit complexes.[118] Examples of "external" economies of localization include the availability of a large and skilled labour pool, the establishment of firms which supply specialized parts (e.g. auto glass, auto bumpers) at a lower cost, the forming of auxiliary firms which perform particularized tasks such as the maintenance of sophisticated equipment for the large industrial grouping, and the development of easily accessible markets by the attraction of firms wishing to use the finished products of the industry.

Reproducing economies of localization in lagging regions through public policy has proved exceedingly difficult. Providing basic infrastructure—sewerage, roads and utilities—in an industrial park is relatively straight-forward, but attracting many interlinked firms away from the metropolis to peripheral areas is another thing. One heroic attempt is the New Brunswick Multiplex Corporation,[119] but their inauspicious results have demonstrated how formidable a task the redirecting of growth forces really is.

ECONOMIES OF AGGLOMERATION: URBANIZATION ECONOMIES

Urbanization economies result from the broad array of services generated externally to the firm. Firms agglomerate in large urban areas so as (1) to enjoy the benefits of "public goods," (2) to minimize uncertainty and (3) to facilitate communication.

There exists a range of goods – public goods – which can be provided at lower cost when provided collectively. Whereas an isolated firm could not normally afford the expense of a road system, a number of firms together could make the facility viable. Hence, the concentration of people and industries in large urban centres favours the provision of a high quality of public services such as police and fire protection, water, hydro power, sewerage, computer networks and huge shipping terminals, all of which permit firms to operate more efficiently than they could in smaller centres.

What applies to firms applies equally to individuals. The metropolis, in contrast to the small city, provides a rich and varied environment of boutiques, cinema and theatres, fine restaurants and professional sports, which make it an attractive place of residence for management and professionals. These "joint consumption goods" are what many people see as the major advantage of large cities.

Large cities are likely to attract a disproportionate share of new and innovative industries. "Thus, the frequent claim that cities encourage innovation can be turned about to suggest that innovative industries migrate to cities because it is cheaper to operate there."[120] Large cities, especially in their inner areas, act as a common pool for space, materials, and labour, meeting the inherent uncertainties for small new businesses' operations and allowing them to operate according to Hoover's principle of "massing of reserves,"[121] thus spurring their formation and proliferation.

In contrast, the "company town," with its limited range of occupations and narrow base of job skills, is not a hospitable place for the entrepreneur to initiate a new business activity. In fact, the remote, one-plant resource town has an inherently unstable economy, which runs the triple risk of a fading product, an obsolete facility and incompetent management.[122]

Urban strategists who attempt to generate growth in lagging regions ignore, only at their peril, infrastructure investment, including public utilities, roads and aid to local business services for organizational and manpower development. Blumenfeld[123] and others have argued that the tertiary sector, the community and business services, constitute the real economic base of a place.

Large cities long have been a haven for corporate headquarters requiring face-to-face contacts and rapid access to substantial amounts of specialized information.[124] Managers may find that their jobs require frequent short-notice meetings with representatives from other businesses. Hence other specialized services—legal, financial, advertising, data processing, consulting—tend also to be disproportionately concentrated in large metropolitan areas.[125] Further compounding the advantages of the metropolis for head office personnel is the pressence of efficient and high speed transportation to other centres.

Although it is fair to conclude that up to a point the overall efficiency of an urban system is enhanced by increased concentration of economic activity, it is also true that increased concentration yields certain diseconomies. These include congestion, pollution and the like. This disparity between public and private benefits is a chief rationale for public intervention. But as the policy-makers set to work, difficult questions arise: What size of centre is sufficient for particular functions (e.g., headquarters' units) to reap agglomeration economies? Or alternatively, when is a centre too large to yield additional benefits?

In Toronto, from 1962 to 1973, the growth of office space accelerated sharply in the core area from an average annual increase of 1.0 million square feet before 1970 to over 2.6 million square feet per annum after 1970.[126] Yet it has been suggested that only about 27 per cent of the office employment located in Toronto's central core requires face-to-face contact and spatial proximity, at least as indicated by either a relatively high frequency of meetings or a concentration of business partners.[127] Based on these sorts of statistics, City of Toronto planners have proposed to deconcentrate core area business activity throughout the Toronto metropolitan area.[128] Efforts to counteract the forces of growth and agglomeration by decentralizing corporate administration and ancillary services, however, have not been made. And the attempts of other governments to decentralize white collar employment have shown the task to be formidable.[129]

CAPITAL AND CORPORATION INERTIA

For a long period in history, communication was synonymous with transportation. However, the telegraph and electronic media have changed that and communication in many respects now is instantaneous. But for corporations, the system of information dissemination is structured by networks, channels and complex institutions. The spatial interdependencies generated by large organizations include flows of goods, capital and specialized information among suppliers', purchasers' and headquarters' decision-makers. These interdependencies are significant for the growth and development of the urban system since they influence locational decisions regarding suppliers, market outlets and production facilities. The location of information sources can strongly affect site selection since most corporations generally conduct only a limited search of alternatives.[130] At the same time, corporate inertia – the incentive for a firm to remain in its initial location and to augment existing plant rather than to incur the huge capital expenditure of abandoning usable facilities in favour of relocation is often strong enough to cause firms to remain when the initial advantages of a location have disappeared. For example, "up to 80 per cent of all new manufacturing investment in advanced industrial countries is allocated to the expansion of existing plant."[131]

The accumulated investment in the physical infrastructure of the city itself (roads, houses, sewers, public buildings, etc.) in conjunction with the social institutions is also a major source of inertia. Hence, whichever city has the "jump" on others and achieves early economic dominance usually maintains it. Success breeds success. The stability over time of the size-rankings for large cities in the Canadian urban system provides some indirect evidence in support of this proposition.

INVENTION AND INNOVATION

> It is in the cities where new work has been created, or where new forms of economic activity have been developed as the numbers of people on the face of the earth grow.[132]

Innovations, whether they take the form of providing new products, involving the use of new production processes or the restructuring of an organization, all stimulate city growth. Jobs are provided; enhanced productivity frees resources for investment elsewhere; one innovation paves the way for subsequent ones. Friedmann has even argued that "the larger the city in the size of its effective population, the greater will be the probability of innovation."[133] What features have contributed to this role?

– Institutions with sufficient financial, technical and organizational resources for invention/innovation are found in greater numbers in large cities.
– Entrepreneurial creativity, aggressiveness and managerial skills tend to focus in the city.
– Large cities are information-saturated environments with higher potential for interaction than smaller communities.
– As the innovation experience is repeated, attitudes and expectations receptive to further innovation are fostered; the process becomes institutionalized.
– Certain innovations are feasible only with large markets available in a metropolis.

But to speak of large cities as the most promising environment for the conception and subsequent spread of innovations is to tell only half the story. Large corporations are usually the instruments of innovation. The spatial bias in the circulation of specialized information also means that firms situated in larger places are more likely to know of new innovations than firms in smaller towns. Hence, innovation serves to reinforce the pattern of mushrooming expansion in the metropolis and continual decline within lagging regions. Metropolis-hinterland differences in levels of per capita income and other indices of socio-economic development are therefore exacerbated by the innovation diffusion process.[134]

Among others, Thompson,[135] Hoover[136] and Thomas[137] have suggested that firms and the products they produce pass through several phases of growth, often in different locations. New and small "growth" industries generally undergo an incubating period within a large centre, where community and business services are available. With maturity, and a wider market, the advantages of the metropolis begin to wane. The firm may then seek small-city locations that feature lower input costs, particularly lower land costs and wage rates. But the relative stimulus to small-city development provided by mature industries producing a standardized product for a saturated market by a routine process may not be that great. If growth of an industry is fastest in the early stages, then presumably, larger centres which host the newest "growth" industries can be expected to grow proportionately faster than peripheral places which are the recipients of "mature" industries. In sum, the industrial mix of a local urban economy, as it is affected by the diffusion process, has implications for the growth potential of the urban area.

From a policy standpoint, it may appear that regional development efforts in Canada have paid little attention to the effects of innovation, adoption and diffusion on the urban growth process. Department of Regional Economic Expansion (DREE) programs, for example, have focused on persuading industry to relocate production facilities to peripheral regions, but firms that acquiesce are usually those producing a standardized product and seeking low wage areas. National programs designed to assist research and development, and hence to improve productivity and growth, largely fall under the jurisdiction of the Department of Industry, Trade and Commerce. As a consequence, they have rarely been viewed as having urban and regional development implications. And David Lewis[138] has argued that most of the development "seed" money has been allocated to the nation's largest corporations whose head offices are situated in the cities of central Canada. Clearly a rethinking may be necessary. Friedmann appears to be correct when he asserts that "only a concerted governmental effort to establish conditions favourable to accelerated innovation at selected points in the periphery is likely to produce a marked reorganization of an urban growth pattern that, under normal conditions, displays a remarkable stability."[139]

GIVING "FACES" TO GROWTH FORCES

"Tell me your industries and I'll tell your future" asserts Thompson.[140] Perhaps he is a bit overconfident. Industrial structure tells part of the story, but not all of it. The shift-share analysis of growth for fifty-six industries in Canadian cities conducted by Crowley and Hartwick[141] revealed that, on average, only about 50 per cent of the labour force growth rate for each city could be explained by national growth rates. Forces unique to individual cities are undoubtedly at work.

The account of growth forces that has been presented in this chapter would be incomplete if it dealt with the process only in impersonal and mechanistic terms. The forces described represent prevailing trends within which cities work out their destiny, but they are not ironclad. Growth is the result not only of these forces but also of the manifold actions of many people – migrant and stayer, entrepreneur and employee, elite and common folk.

In accounting for urban growth, the initiative of elites, both public and private must be recognized. Some historians, for example, have credited Winnipeg's early ascendancy in the West, and the relative decline of some Maritime cities to their commercial elites.[142] Similarly, the transformation of Toronto from an administrative outpost to a commercial emporium occurred, in part, because of the expansionist outlook and business acumen of its commercial and political elite, who first survived a rivalry with nearby Kingston and later withstood keen competition from Montreal. Their decision to form the Bank of Upper Canada in 1822 as an alternative to financial dealings with the larger and more prosperous commercial community in Montreal, the later transactions of trade with England via New York rather than their arch-rival, Montreal (after the corn laws were repealed), and the incorporation of numerous building and loan associations to serve the local farm population are only a few events to illustrate the entrepreneurial and risk-taking abilities of Toronto's merchant princes.[143] But the instances cited are merely illustrative. Probably many more examples can be found of how specific decisions encouraged the growth of a town and thereby helped shape Canada's urban system. All the ingredients for urban growth may be present, but the skill and initiative of the entrepreneur is needed before development can take place.

As a student of nineteenth century urban Canada, one can extol the virtues of a cunning entrepreneur or ridicule the blatant opportunism of a "town booster." But, as a present-day urbanist, one must be aware of the real concentration of economic power in fewer and fewer hands within larger and larger organizations. The corporate decision-making elites today in Canada are first, those "descendants" of the Montreal-centred, British-backed merchants-cum-financiers who evolved into the financial community, with control over banks, trust and insurance companies, public utilities and transportation corporations; second, the senior managers and directors of foreign-controlled branch plants, mainly in manufacturing and resource industries; and third, the senior management of multi-national corporations who make their decisions for branch plants on the basis of a world view of their particular company. Both Porter[144] (1965) and Clement[145] (1975) have shown that the corporate elite is a tightly interwoven group. One measure of this is the extent to which the directorships of the 100 largest corporations are interlocked (Figure 3.6).

This concentration of power has profound implications for the growth of the urban system. Some of these are loss of community control and ownership of regional branch plants; the second-class priorities given to the economic, social and cultural needs of the region over the needs of the corporation; the increasing concentration of management functions in the metropolis.

Figure 3.6 Density of Interlocks Between Corporate Sectors, 1972

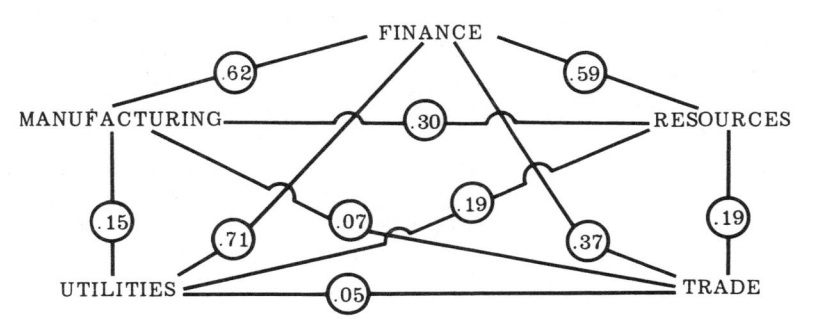

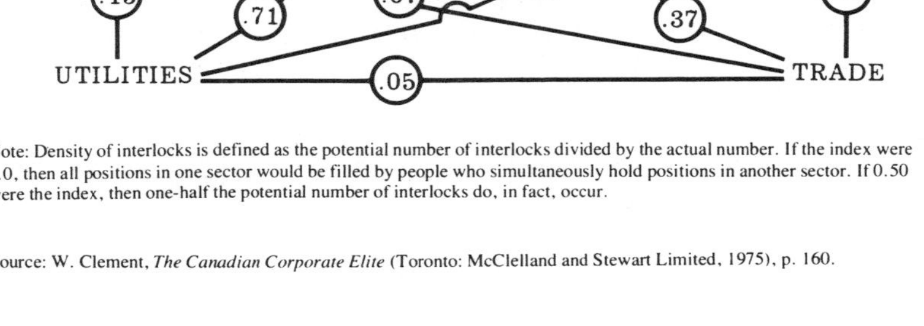

Note: Density of interlocks is defined as the potential number of interlocks divided by the actual number. If the index were 1.0, then all positions in one sector would be filled by people who simultaneously hold positions in another sector. If 0.50 were the index, then one-half the potential number of interlocks do, in fact, occur.

Source: W. Clement, *The Canadian Corporate Elite* (Toronto: McClelland and Stewart Limited, 1975), p. 160.

THE IMPACT OF FOREIGN INVESTMENT AND OWNERSHIP

We have argued that large organizations and their corporate elite have a profound effect on the extent and nature of urban growth. Since one-quarter of the directors in the largest corporations in Canada are Americans (with the primary resource, trade and manufacturing sectors leading the way with 52 per cent, 37 per cent and 32 per cent), the perspective of American managers is critical (Table 3.11). Certain questions follow: Do foreign investors blindly attempt to gain the highest rate of return? Are they conscious of the Canadian urban system? Are local managers co-opted? Are decisions made from the viewpoint of Timmins or Toronto or New York? In effect, how different are the decisions of foreigners from those of Canadians?

The United States has more foreign capital invested in Canada than in any other foreign country. By 1970, about one-half of manufacturing industry in Canada was controlled by residents of the United States and only one-third by Canadians. This represents a considerable increase since 1926, the first year for which official data are available, when almost two-thirds of manufacturing was controlled by Canadians. In addition, this increase in foreign ownership has been associated with a long-term shift away from United Kingdom portfolio investment to United States direct investment (Figure 3.7). Most of this direct investment is in the subsidiaries of multinational corporations. Of the 100 largest Canadian corporations listed in the *Financial Post* (August 1974),[146] fully fifty-nine of them were foreign controlled.

Some of the problems of foreign direct investment have been studied through a succession of government commissions and task forces, starting with the Gordon Commission in the 1950s. However,

Table 3.11. Residence and Control of Dominant Directorship Positions, by Sector, 1972

Residence & Control	Finance %	Utilities %	Trade %	Mfg. %	Resource %	Total %
Canada	79.6	75.3	51.7	44.7	24.0	60.0
United States	12.1	22.4	37.9	32.3	52.6	26.0
United Kingdom	7.0	1.2	10.4	12.0	8.4	7.7
Other	4.0	1.2	—	11.1	15.0	6.3
Total	100.0	100.0	100.0	100.0	100.0	100.0
Number	(852)	(170)	(174)	(226)	(333)	(1755)

Source: Wallace Clement, *The Canadian Corporate Elite* (Toronto: McClelland and Stewart, 1975), p. 154.

GROWTH FORCES 155

Figure 3.7. The Composition of Foreign Investment in Canada, 1867-1970

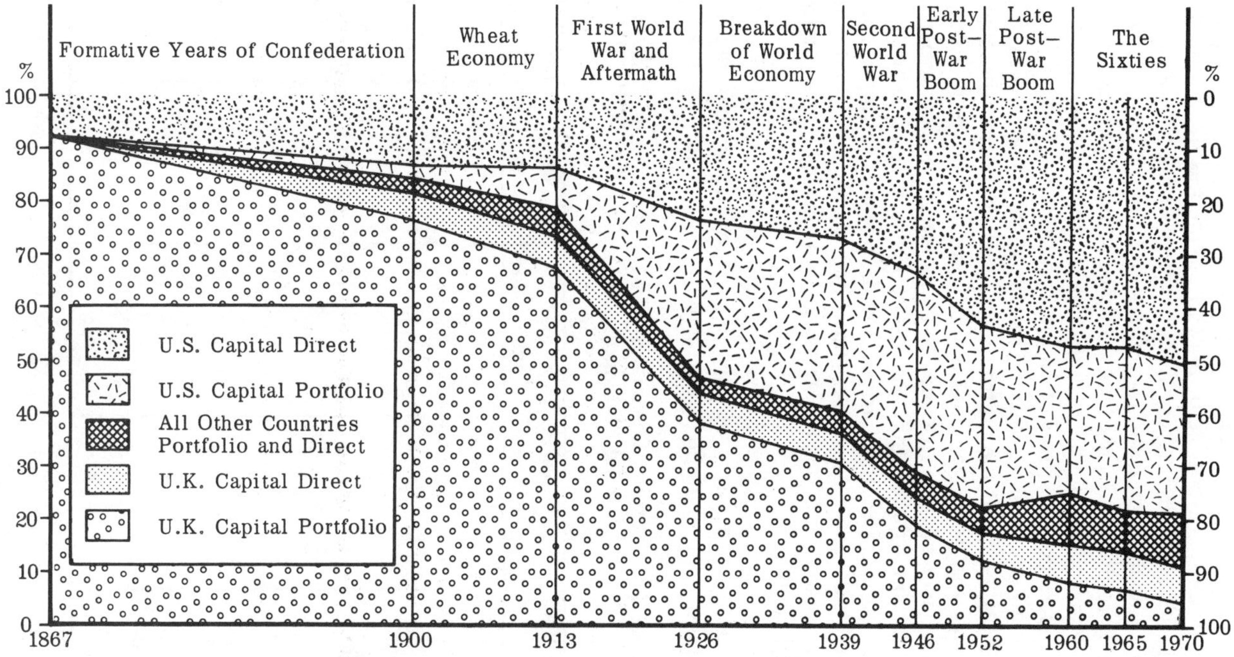

Sources: Kari Levitt, *Silent Surrender: The Multinational Corporation in Canada* (Toronto: MacMillan, 1970), p. 66; and Statistics Canada, *Canada's International Investment Position, 1968-1970*, cat. 67-202, (Ottawa: 1975), p. 44.

these studies have paid little attention to the impact of foreign investment on industrial location, regional disparities and urban development. Only the outline of the full picture has been discerned.

Of the 1724 manufacturing establishments under American ownership in Canada's metropolitan areas in 1970, 1,023 or 59 per cent were in Toronto and four other southern Ontario centres.[147] United States-controlled employment and share of dollar value added represent a much greater proportion of manufacturing activity in the metropolitan areas of southern Ontario than elsewhere in Canada (Table 3.12). None of the metropolitan centres outside the heartland approaches the extent of control in Toronto, and only Edmonton and Vancouver have even come close to the 25 per cent mark. It is also important to note that the boost given to city growth by an influx of American subsidiaries extends beyond a simple count of new establishments. American-controlled firms tend to be highly capital-intensive and technologically-sophisticated, and hence the most productive.

The clustering of American investment in the heartland of Canada's urban system has prompted Ray[148] to argue that the United States control of manufacturing activity in Canada casts an "eco-

Table 3.12. Foreign Ownership of Manufacturing Firms by Selected Metropolitan Areas, 1970

Metropolitan Area	United States Firms		Other Foreign Firms	
	% Employment	% Value Added	% Employment	% Value Added
Halifax	17.4	33.7	23.3	18.0
Saint John	10.3	10.7	4.1	6.2
Quebec City	10.9	13.0	13.8	25.1
Montreal	24.8	31.2	9.0	12.1
Ottawa-Hull	35.1	35.9	14.6	19.4
Toronto	40.1	50.0	10.5	11.5
Hamilton	31.3	30.6	5.7	5.3
Kitchener	40.9	44.6	2.7	6.0
London	38.5	42.8	11.2	6.5
Winnipeg	16.4	20.5	8.5	11.7
Regina	11.4	24.7	10.0	8.4
Saskatoon	12.1	23.5	4.0	5.5
Edmonton	24.3	35.3	8.2	12.7
Calgary	14.9	22.2	10.8	12.6
Vancouver	25.4	28.9	8.2	10.5

Source: Douglas A. Scorrar, and Michael H. Williams, "Manufacturing activity and the urban hierarchy" in D. M. Ray (ed.). *Canadian Urban Trends: National Perspective*, Vol. 1 (Toronto: Copp Clark Publishing, 1976).

nomic shadow" over the country. He suggests that "the number of subsidiaries and the amount of manufacturing employment in a Canadian city that are controlled [from head offices] within a United States metropolitan area are directly proportional to the market accessible from the Canadian city and the number of head offices in the United States metropolitan area, and are inversely proportional to the distance of the Canadian city from the U.S. metropolitan area."[149] More specifically, the corporate heads have tended to locate their subsidiaries in the "axes" that link Toronto to the location of the parent company situated in the United States.[150] The close proximity of southern Ontario to the American manufacturing belt, is such that it is sometimes described as a mere extension of America's industrial northeast. This also contributes to some heartland-hinterland differences in manufacturing activity (Figure 3.8).

The decisions of foreign investors have helped to shape more than the broad contours of Canada's urban system. Through real estate holdings, absentee owners have been creating their own vision of what a Canadian city should be. Foreign developers and property owners are now firmly entrenched on the Canadian scene and have played a significant role in altering the face of Canadian cities. Many Canadians seem unaware that major decisions affecting their way of life are now taken by non-Canadians who apply their particular concept of "good" development to Canada's cities. This includes residential land, shopping malls as well as commercial office complexes. Indeed, the extent of foreign-controlled holdings in Canada is startling. One conservative estimate places the current figure at $10 billion; this investment has its sources in a host of countries including Britain, Germany, Hong Kong, Switzerland, the U.S.A., Italy and Japan.[151] In the Toronto region, as an example, nearly one-half of recent commercial development has a foreign component while a large percentage of the prime developable land ringing the metropolis is in the hands of foreign firms. And this situation is reflected in different ways in other Canadian cities from downtown redevelopment by Trizec in St. John's to the purchase of Vancouver landmarks by Hong Kong money. Perhaps more worrisome than the extent of foreign real estate ownership in this country is the restructuring of the development industry through mergers into fewer and larger corporations, dominated for the most part by foreign interests. To effectively redirect growth and plan development in Canada's cities, government officials must therefore negotiate with foreign-owned conglomerates.

Real estate transactions stemming from foreign initiatives have a pervasive influence on Canada's urban growth and form. First, metropolitan areas are heavily favoured. Non-Canadian real estate

158   CHANGING CANADIAN CITIES

Figure 3.8. Canada: Geographic Distribution of United States' Controlled Manufacturing - Hundred Mile Distance Bands from Toronto

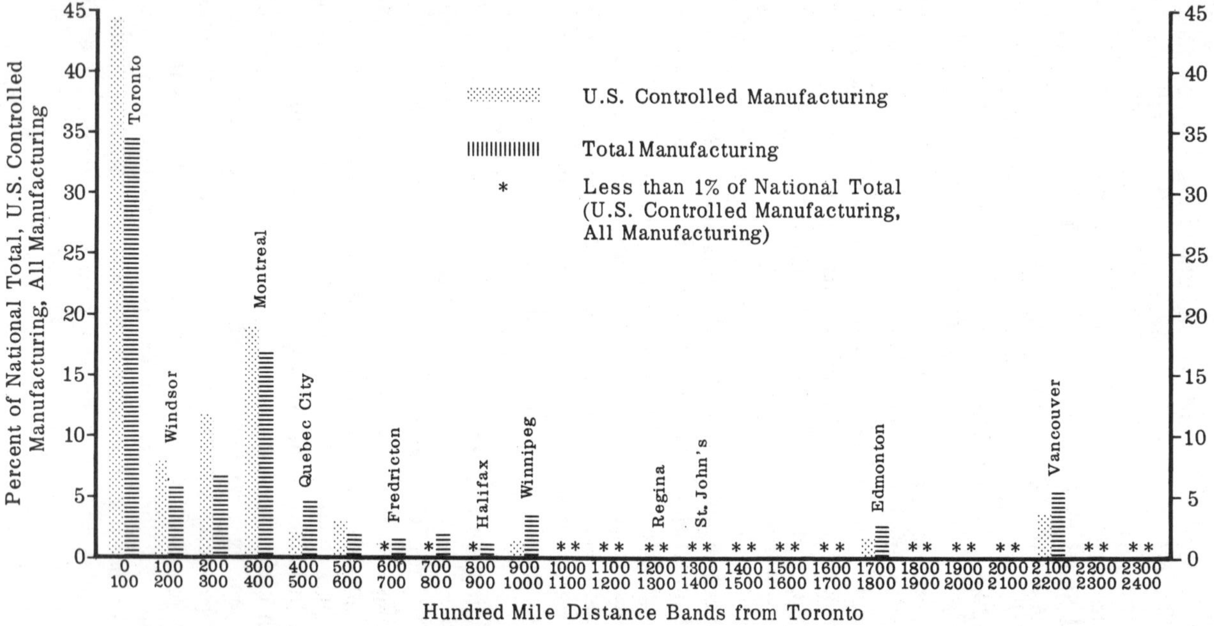

Note: Manufacturing employment data were collected by county and census division and arranged in distance bands of one hundred miles width, forming a series of concentric rings according to distance away from the centre point, Toronto. For example, Regina in the west and St. John's in the east are located adjacent to one another in the figure, being approximately the same distance from Toronto.

Source: D.M. Ray, *Regional Aspects of Foreign Ownership of Manufacturing in Canada* (Ottawa: Queen's Printer, 1967), p.76.

investors "show a marked preference for major urban centres, being in many cases reluctant to even venture outside the major cities to look at property."[152] Second, the prestige, profits and apparent security of commercial projects have lured away foreign money perhaps to the detriment of the residential housing industry. The allocation of resources to office complexes and other commercial ventures, has undoubtedly contributed to the escalating costs of building homes. Third, by tying up sizeable blocks of residential land near the largest Canadian cities, non-Canadian investors have helped create a scarcity of building sites, and thus aggravated the shortage of housing experienced in these centres.

Despite these negative effects, conventional wisdom says that Canada must endure them because the country lacks sufficient funds to make the necessary investment. But the Ontario Legislature's Select Committee on Cultural and Economic Nationalism offered a different point of view:

> To the contrary, the committee is advised that...on an overall basis, both Canada and Ontario are substantially capital self-sufficient. While there may be specific capital needs which at any given time cannot necessarily be met from Canadian sources and institutions, it is increasingly accepted that the Canadian financial markets are largely able to meet the range of financial requirements for the province and the country.[153]

> With particular reference to the real estate industries, available evidence and prevailing concern suggest that there is too much rather than too little capital seeking real estate investment in Canada[154]

Clearly Canada's corporate elite as well as the executives of foreign multi-nationals have influenced Canada's pattern of urban growth. Urban development policy in Canada that is not cognizant of growth stimuli emanating from decisions in the boardrooms of corporations at home and abroad is almost certainly doomed to failure.

THE BEGINNING OF A SYNTHESIS

How does a city grow? "Specialization" and "division of labour," improved transportation technology, economies of scale, localization and urbanization economies, large scale organizations, entrepreneurship, foreign ownership, the need for specialized information networks, and other factors all play a role. But what is required is a comprehensive way of explaining the mechanisms by which a city's economy grows.

One method of synthesis is to portray urban growth as a circular

Figure 3.9. Urban Growth as a Circular and Cumulative Process

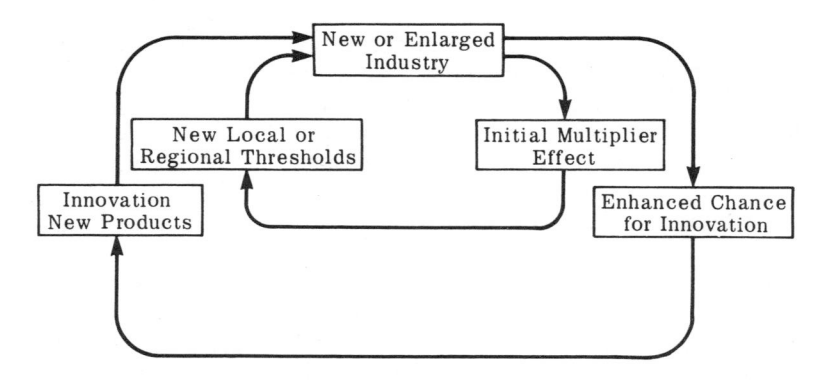

```
                    ┌──────────────────┐
          ┌────────▶│ New or Enlarged  │─────────┐
          │         │     Industry     │         │
          │         └──────────────────┘         ▼
   ┌──────────────┐                      ┌──────────────┐
   │  New Local or│                      │   Initial    │
   │Regional Thresholds│                 │  Multiplier  │
   └──────────────┘                      │    Effect    │
┌──────────────┐                         └──────────────┘
│  Innovation  │                              ┌──────────────────┐
│ New Products │                              │ Enhanced Chance  │
└──────────────┘                              │  for Innovation  │
       ▲                                      └──────────────────┘
       │                                              │
       └──────────────────────────────────────────────┘
```

Source: A.R. Pred, *The Spatial Dynamics of U.S. Urban Industrial Growth, 1800-1920* (Cambridge: Massachusetts Institute of Technology Press, 1966), p.25.

and cumulative process, as Myrdal first expounded (Figure 3.9). In this scheme, successive rounds of expenditure and investment (multiplier effects) filter through the urban economy, promote the fulfilment of successive market thresholds for industry, and enhance the possibility for invention and innovation through a network of communications.

This notion implies that growth begets further growth. Employment generated by the introduction of new industry attracts additional workers, thus increasing the city's population; wages paid out augment the aggregate purchasing power of the urban population, thereby permitting the city to attain higher market thresholds; all of which in turn support further industry. With the establishment of the second set of industries, another round of growth is triggered, yielding still higher market thresholds, more additions of skilled labour and increasing prosperity. This in turn sets the stage for further successive rounds.

The initial multiplier from the introduction of industry into the urban economy also serves to stimulate secondary multiplier effects, as the enlarged payroll in the community and the increased personal income of households raise the demand in the "consumer-oriented" service, government and construction sectors. Business services expand and transportation and other public infrastructure improves. These, in turn, provide the climate for self-generating growth which is further accelerated by (1) technological interdependencies of firms, (2) organizational decision-making which favours expansion in known locations and (3) specialized information exchange which leads to concentration of headquarters' functions.

Although the notion of "cumulative causation" or the "growth spiral" has an intuitive appeal, many questions remain unanswered: Is there a critical size at which a city's growth becomes self-sustaining? Does growth occur in bursts as a city achieves a certain size threshold? And finally, is there an optimum city size beyond which further growth is undesirable? The answers to all of these questions are less than fully clear.

There is some evidence to suggest that large cities reach a threshold size or size range beyond which growth is largely fuelled by internal forces in a cumulative manner. Drawing on the American experience, Thomson[155] has found that metropolitan areas of 250,000 or more seldom show actual declines in population from one census to the next; his "urban size ratchet" hypothesis is based on the advantages of agglomeration, industrial diversification, and the rich local market attained as a centre approaches the critical population size. Mixed empirical support for the notion of an "economic take-off" has also been compiled by Hansen.[156] Hansen argues that most American metropolitan areas experienced a substantial growth spurt within the 150,000 – 200,000 size range, though no evidence of automatic self-sustaining growth followed the spurt.

The question of an optimum city size continues to pose a conundrum. Spengler[157] is probably correct when he suggests that there is a range of city sizes that will satisfy the socio-economic well-being of urban dwellers equally well, and that this range varies with technological change and environmental circumstances. And possibly Thompson[158] provides a more appropriate focus for urban growth policy when he argues that the well-being of urbanites is more immediately sensitive to the rate of growth than the size of city. Suggested optima have ranged from the 5,040 recommended by Plato for ancient Athens to the 3,000,000 prescribed by Le Corbusier. But where they have been offered, optima favoured by most researchers as providing a reasonable balance between agglomeration economies and dis-economies generally fall within the 200,000 to 750,000 size group. We return in Chapter 9 to this concern.

SPECIALIZATION AND INTERDEPENDENCE WITHIN THE URBAN SYSTEM

Although much of the growth in large urban areas may be induced from within, a city does not stand alone. It is part of an urban system interconnected with other cities by the exchange of commodities, the flow of information, the diffusion of innovations and the dissemination of policy directives from private and public decision makers. The fate of a particular centre, therefore, is intimately tied to the development of the urban system as a whole.

Growth throughout the urban system occurs, in large part, as it does within the city. To the extent that the inputs required by a firm and the products that it sells are purchased or distributed outside the city, the expansion of individual firms tends to stimulate growth throughout the urban system. However, the influence of such forces is not evenly distributed: "The multiplier effects of rapid system growth... accrue primarily to the largest centres."[159] The metropolis as a transportation hub, an enlarged labour pool, a lucrative market, an information saturated environment, a rich source of business services, and a home of many corporate head offices, is the main beneficiary. Over the years, mineral discoveries in Northern Ontario probably have generated directly and indirectly as many jobs in Toronto as they have in the mines of the north. Savings in bank branches across the Prairies have augmented the investment portfolios of Toronto-based banks, perhaps to the detriment of the Western provinces as many Westerners suspect. Direct employment in Alberta's petroleum industry has always been small, but has contributed substantially to the development of Calgary and Edmonton.[160]

The plight of "slow growth" peripheral cities is perhaps best understood through the "short-circuiting" of local multipliers – the loss of income and jobs to other units in the hierarchy. The unenviable position of these centres derives, in part, from a narrow industrial base and a paucity of agglomeration economies. Local expenditures tend to be quickly siphoned off to other places. Few headquarters, regional offices or other white collar units of large job-providing organizations are located in lagging regions.[161] Hence, successive rounds of expenditures within the organizations are lost to the small city.

Growth stimuli within the urban system are transmitted not only up and down the urban hierarchy. Increasingly, they move horizontally as the interdependencies among metropolitan areas are strengthened by flows of investments, information and resources. The modern metropolis relates not only to its immediate hinterland, but typically acquires its inputs and establishes its markets both near and far. As well, the dense information networks and subsequent diffusion of innovation among metropolises cause even greater concentrations of corporate administrative units in the largest metropolitan centres.

PERFORMANCE AND FUTURE PROSPECTS

Growth forces in the Canadian urban system are diverse, complex and cumulative. Policies that do not acknowledge the nature of the urban growth process, by operating at the level of the urban system, will almost certainly result in failures. Selectivity in development assistance provided by governments is needed, since benefits or incentives awarded alike to all centres and regions tend to accumulate in the metropolis.

On balance, government policies have reinforced the tendencies for robust growth in the larger metropolitan areas. Seldom, however, have they been evaluated in terms of their growth stimulus. For example, the Canada-U.S.A. Auto Agreement, though some might disagree, undoubtedly has benefited in Canada mainly the manufacturing centres of the Windsor-Quebec City corridor. In the field of transportation, the construction of freeways and airports both increased the accessibility to Toronto and Montreal, while rail and air policy helped create and later partially destroy the economic viability of Winnipeg as a transportation centre. Through manpower training and mobility programs, some government agencies have encouraged people to move to major centres; at the same time, infrastructure and industrial relocation assistance has been aimed at keeping people where they were. Similarly, other programs, such as unemployment insurance and central banking, have had distinct though unintentional impacts on the distribution of population. More locally, the location of government institutions such as post offices, medical centres, universities, community colleges, hospitals and defence bases, often can ensure the survival or spell the demise of a community. But perhaps change is in the wind. It was after all a recognition of these effects that helped lead to the creation of a federal Department of Regional Economic Expansion in 1969 and a Ministry of State for Urban Affairs in 1971.

There is also a large and growing deficit in federal expenditures relative to income generated in the poorer provinces. According to Palmer[162] who documented federal revenues and expenditures in the province of Nova Scotia for the 1950–65 period, a large part of the net flow of federal funds into less well-off regions has not been the result of measures expressly designed to assist lagging areas. The increased reliance placed on the personal income tax by the federal government has benefited low income provinces because of the progressive nature of the tax. At the same time, these provinces have received a greater share of the institutional transfer payments (e.g., equalization payments to provincial governments) and personal transfer payments (e.g., unemployment insurance and welfare benefits). The higher per capita expenditures and lower per capita federal taxes have resulted in a massive injection of federal funds into provinces such as Nova Scotia.

Though these funds have undoubtedly contributed to regional growth, difficulties have resulted from this largesse. Aside from the overdependence created, the effectiveness of the expenditures for engendering development is in doubt. If it were possible to trace the successive rounds of spending generated from the initial transfer, it is likely that one would find that a substantial portion of the benefits accrue to central Canada, where many of the required goods and services are produced.

The history of public intervention into Canada's urban system, which has been marked by good intentions but cursed by inauspicious or contradictory results, has shown the need for comprehensive and consistent regional development policies that recognize the various growth forces influencing urban areas. The ingredients of such a policy package could comprise among other things:

– improved transportation and communication not only between small cities and the regional metropolis, but among the small cities in the outlying region;
– public infrastructure and industrial incentives;
– amenity provision so as to make small city lifestyles more attractive to professionals and managers;
– appropriate mechanisms to offset the centralizing influence of Canada's financial structure, including particularly the funding of research and development and the bankrolling of innovative approaches in smaller cities;
– the development of incentives and regulatory measures to encourage the location of white collar jobs in places other than metropolitan cores;
– a co-ordinated, region-wide or system-wide approach to the location of public facilities so as to stimulate growth where it is possible; and
– recognition of the regional incidence of development at stake during the negotiation of trade agreements or the conduct of foreign investment reviews.

We shall return to this question of appropriate policies in Chapter 9.

Notes

1. For an explanation of the staples theory of economic development, using the Canadian context, the reader is referred to: H. A. Innis, "The Importance of Staple Products," in W. T. Easterbrook and M. H. Watkins, *Approaches to Canadian Economic History*, Carleton Library No. 31 (Toronto: McClelland and Stewart, 1967; and M. H. Watkins, "A Staple Theory of Economic Growth," in Easterbrook and Watkins, *Ibid*.
2. D. M. Ray, "Canada: The Urban Challenge of Growth and Change," Discussion Paper B.74.3 (Ottawa: Ministry of State for Urban Affairs, 1974), p. 24.
3. Watkins, in Easterbrook and Watkins, *op. cit.* (Originally in *Canadian Journal of Economics and Political Science*, Vol. 29, May 1963).
4. J. W. Simmons, *The Canadian Urban System* (Toronto: University of Toronto Press, (forthcoming 1977), C. 3, p. 23.
5. A lucid explanation of backward linkages, forward linkages and final demand linkages is provided by E. M. Hoover, *An Introduction to Regional Economics* (New York: Alfred A. Knopf, 1971), pp. 215–216.
6. W. T. Easterbrook and M. C. J. Aitken, *Canadian Economic History* (Toronto: Macmillan, 1956).
7. D. C. North, *The Economic Growth of the United States, 1790–1860* (Englewood Cliffs, N.J.: Prentice-Hall, 1961).
8. N. H. Lithwick, *Urban Canada: Problems and Prospects* (Ottawa: Central Mortgage and Housing Corporation, 1970), p. 72.
9. Ray, *op. cit.*, pp. 4–12; and E. F. Koenig, J. S. Lewis, and D. M. Ray, "Allometry and Manufacturing Hierarchy: A General System Theory Approach to Manufacturing Employment and Industry Incidence," Discussion Paper B. 73.19 (Ottawa: Ministry of State for Urban Affairs, 1973).
10. R. W. Crowley and J. M. Hartwick, *Urban Economic Growth: The Canadian Case*, Working Paper. A.73.5 (Ottawa: Ministry of State for Urban Affairs, 1973).
11. Simmons, *op. cit.*, C. 1, p. 23.
12. *Ibid.*, C. 1, p. 21.
13. N. H. Lithwick and G. Pacquet, *Urban Studies: A Canadian Perspective* (Toronto: Methuen, 1968), p. 29.
14. Economic Council of Canada, *Sixth Annual Review: Perspective 1975* (Ottawa: Queen's Printer, 1969), T5–5, p. 89.
15. Simmons, *op. cit.*, 1977, C.1, p. 28.
16. J. Friedmann, "The Spatial Organization of Power in the Development of Urban Systems," *Development and Change*, Vol. 4, No. 3, 1973, p. 17.
17. J. W. Simmons, *Canada: Choices in a National Urban Strategy*, Research Paper No. 70 (Toronto: University of Toronto, Centre for Urban and Community Studies, 1975), p. 9.
18. W. A. Mackintosh, *The Economic Background of Dominion-Provincial Relations*, prepared for the Royal Commission on Dominion-Provincial Relations (Ottawa: King's Printer, 1939). Also (Toronto: McClelland and Stewart, 1964).
19. A. Rotstein, *The Precarious Homestead: Essays on Economics, Technology and Nationalism* (Toronto: New Press, 1973), p. 14.
20. J. Dales, "Canada's National Policies," in J. Dales, (ed.), *The Protective Tariff in Canada's Development* (Toronto: University of Toronto Press, 1966), p. 144.
21. Mackintosh, *op. cit.*; and V. C. Fowke, "The National Policy—Old and New," *Canadian Journal of Economics and Political Science*, Vol. 18, 1952, pp. 271–286.
22. D. V. Smiley, "Canada and the Quest for a National Policy," *Canadian Journal of Political Science*, Vol. 8, No. 1, 1975, p. 43.
23. *Ibid.*, p. 43.
24. S. D. Clark, "Canada and the American Value System," in S. D. Clark, (ed.),

The Developing Canadian Community, Second Edition, (Toronto: University of Toronto Press, 1968), p. 232.
25. Smiley, *op. cit.*, p. 45.
26. The most authoritative statements of the prescription for developing innovative capacity for indigenous industry are: *The Report of the Senate Special Committee on Science Policy*, Vol. 2 (Ottawa: Information Canada, 1972); and *The Gray Report on Foreign Direct Investment in Canada* (Ottawa: Information Canada, 1972).
27. A goal emphasized by Prime Minister Trudeau at the Western Economic Opportunities Conference held in Calgary, July 24 – 26, 1973.
28. Smiley, *op. cit.*, pp. 59 – 62.
29. H. J. C. Aitken, *American Capital and Canadian Resources* (Cambridge, Massachusetts: Harvard University Press, 1961), p. 136.
30. Innis in Easterbrook and Watkins, *op. cit.*, p. 18.
31. Economic Council of Canada, *Second Annual Review: Toward Sustained and Balanced Economic Growth* (Ottawa: Queen's Printer, 1965), p. 97.
32. R. Lycan, "Interprovincial Migration in Canada: The Role of Spatial and Economic Factors," *The Canadian Geographer*, Vol. 13, 1969, pp. 237 – 254.
33. J. W. Simmons, *Interprovincial Interaction Patterns in Canada*, Centre for Urban and Community Studies, Research Paper, No. 24 (Toronto: University of Toronto Press, 1970).
34. The analyses involved defining composite dimensions summarizing the variation inherent in about sixty social, cultural and economic attributes derived largely from the decennial census returns. Cf. D. M. Ray, *Dimensions of Canadian Regionalism*, Department of Energy, Mines and Resources, Geography Paper No. 49 (Ottawa: Information Canada, 1971); E. E. D. Day, *The Spatial Structure of Canadian Economic Development* (Ottawa: Department of Finance, Economic Development Division, Working Paper 7201, 1972); D. M. Ray and P. Y. Villeneuve, *Population Growth and Distribution in Canada: Problems, Process and Policies,* prepared for "The Management of Land for Urban Development," a conference sponsored by the Canadian Council on Urban and Regional Research, 1974; and D. M. Ray and T. N. Brewis, "The Geography of Income and Its Correlates," *The Canadian Geographer,* Vol. 20, No. 1, 1976, pp. 41 – 71.
35. Economic Council of Canada, *Second Annual Review, op. cit.*, p. 102.
36. Oscar Ornati, *Poverty and Affluence*, (New York: New School for Social Research, 1966).
37. Economic Council of Canada *Fourth Annual Review: The Canadian Economy from the 1960's to the 1970's* (Ottawa: Queen's Printer, 1967), pp. 182, 187.
38. Ray and Brewis, *op. cit.*
39. *Ibid.*
40. L. E. Poetschke, "Regional Planning in a Dynamic Planning Process," *Plan Canada*, Vol. 12, No. 1, 1972.
41. J. Podoluk, *Incomes of Canadians*, 1961 Census Monograph (Ottawa: Dominion Bureau of Statistics, 1968), p. 184.
42. Ray and Brewis, *op. cit.*
43. Lithwick, *Urban Canada: Problems and Prospects*, Research Monograph No. 1, (Ottawa: Central Mortgage and Housing Corporation, 1971).
44. B. J. L. Berry, "Cities as Systems within Systems of Cities, "*Economic Development and Cultural Change*, Vol. 9, 1961, pp. 573 – 587.
45. Simmons, 1977, *op. cit.*, C.1, p. 1.
46. J. H. Chung and M. Meunier, "Urban System and Regional Growth in Canada: Some Preliminary Findings," Economic Council of Canada (first draft, mimeographed, 1975), p. 2.
47. The urban field is defined as the total area linked to a metropolitan centre for economic, social and recreational purposes. The concept allows one to

GROWTH FORCES 167

emphasize the changing scale of area over which city development now has a significant impact, pointing out that the so-called "fringe" of urban areas must be considered more than an incidental part of overall urban development. For a full discussion of the urban field concept, see: G. Hodge, "The Emergence of the Urban Field," in L. S. Bourne and R. D. MacKinnon, (eds.), *Urban Systems in Central Canada: Selected Papers* (Toronto: University of Toronto, Department of Geography Research Publications, University of Toronto Press, 1972); and J. Friedmann and J. Miller, "The Urban Field," *Journal of American Institute of Planners*, Vol. 31, No. 4, 1965, pp. 312–320.

48. Louis-Edmond Hamelin, "Types of Canadian Ecumene," in R. M. Irving, (ed.), *Readings in Canadian Geography* (Toronto: Holt, Rinehart and Winston, 1968), p. 25.
49. Although the use of resource exploitation in the North and the decline in the relative importance of agriculture in Canada have made less relevant the ecumene as defined by Hamelin (i.e., areas where commercial farming is feasible), the majority of cities are by definition situated within the ecumene. The maximum size of city outside the ecumene is 20,000 (Whitehorse, Thompson, Timmins, Sept-Iles) and this has changed very little in the last twenty years. Simmons, 1975, *op. cit.*, C. 2, p. 32.
50. Bourne and MacKinnon, *op. cit.*, p. 35.
51. M. Yeates, *Main Street: Windsor to Quebec City* (Toronto and Ottawa: Macmillan and Information Canada, 1975).
52. R. E. Preston, "A Perspective on Alternate Settlement Forms," (Waterloo: Department of Geography, University of Waterloo, mimeographed, 1975), p. 37.
53. Simmons, 1977, *op. cit.*, C. 2. pp. 32 and 35.
54. Although linkages among cities are an important aspect of the city system, they are not easily studied. There are few compilations of origin-destination measures and most of them differ according to geographic unit (i.e., city, county, province, telephone exchange district, postal zones) and have been collected for varying time spans in different years, and thus are not comparable.
55. L H. Russwurm, *Development of an Urban Corridor System: Toronto to Stratford Area 1941 – 1966* (Toronto: Regional Development Branch, Department of Treasury, Economics and Intergovernmental Affairs, Province of Ontario, 1970).
56. J. W. Simmons, *Patterns of Interaction Within Ontario and Quebec*, Research Paper No. 41 (Toronto: University of Toronto, Centre for Urban and Community Studies, 1970B).
57. *Ibid.*
58. Chung and Meunier, *op. cit.*, pp. 25 – 29.
59. R. Muncaster, "The Contemporary Canadian System of Cities," prepared for the Urbanization Theme, Canada Studies Foundation – Canadian Association of Geographers, mimeographed, 1975.
60. Data from the Air Passenger Origin and Destination report of Statistics Canada include origin and destination of passengers for all domestic scheduled flights of Air Canada, CP Air, Eastern Provincial Airways, Nordair, Pacific Western Airlines, Quebecair, Transair and Norcanair.
61. Care must also be taken in assessing the intensity of interaction between places proximate to one another when using airline passenger data, since sometimes a local airport falls in the "air traffic shadow" of a larger airport (e.g. Hamilton and Toronto) or air is not the primary mode of transit (e.g. Calgary and Edmonton, Ottawa and Montreal).
62. Muncaster, *op. cit.*, p. 11.
63. *Ibid.*, pp. 6 – 9.
64. Counties near Kingston, Three Rivers, Sherbrooke, Moncton, Cornerbrook, and Charlottetown are not dominated by a metropolitan daily. Publications originating within these areas dominate the local market which lies at the interstices between the market areas of the more distant metropolitan centres. See Muncaster, *op. cit.*, p. 9.

65. This process is, in part, described by central place theory, for which lucid summaries are available in: B. J. L. Berry, *The Geography of Market Centres and Retail Distribution* (Englewood Cliffs, N.J.: Prentice-Hall 1967); and J. U. Marshall, *The Location of Service Towns* (Toronto: University of Toronto Press, 1969), C.2.
66. Simmons, 1970B, *op. cit.*
67. Russwurm, *op. cit.*, pp. 145–154.
68. Simmons, 1977, *op. cit.*, C. 4, p. 12.
69. K. Levitt, *Silent Surrender: The Multination Corporation in Canada* (Toronto: Macmillan, 1970).
70. Simmons, 1977, *op. cit.*, C. 3, p. 6.
71. J. W. Maxwell, *The Functional Structure of Canadian Cities: A Classification of Cities* (Ottawa: Ministry of State for Urban Affairs, 1973), pp. 21–22. (Also in R. M. Irving, (ed.), *Readings in Canadian Geography*, Second Edition (Toronto: Holt, Rinehart and Winston, 1972).
72. *Ibid.*, pp. 26–27.
73. J. U. Marshall, "City Size, Economic Diversity, and Functional Type: The Canadian Case," *Economic Geography*, Vol. 51, No. 1, 1975, pp. 47–48.
74. A. E. Smailes, 'Ill Balanced Communities—A Problem in Planning," in E. A. Gutkind, (ed.), *Creative Demobilization*, Vol. 2, *Case Studies in Rational Planning* (London: Regan, Paul, Trench, Trubner and Co., 1943), p. 227.
75. The relationship between city size and functional diversification has received little empirical verification. A. Rodgers, "Some Aspects of Industrial Diversification in the United States," *Economic Geography*, Vol. 33, 1957, pp. 16–33, and F. Clemente and R. B. Sturgis, "Population Size and Industrial Diversification," *Urban Studies*, Vol. 8, 1971, pp. 65–68, have concluded that the clarity of the relationship is questionable. Population size does not emerge as a strong predictor of industrial diversification. On the other hand, R. W. Bahl, R. Firestine, and D. Phares, "Industrial Diversification in Urban Areas: Alternative Measures and Intermetropolitan Comparisons," *Economic Geography*, Vol. 47, 1971, pp. 414–425, have argued for a significant parabolic relationship between city size and functional diversification. The inconclusive results may arise, R. W. Crowley, "Reflections and Further Evidence on Population Size and Industrial Diversification," *Urban Studies*, Vol. 10, 1973, pp. 91–94, suggested, because of (1) data constraints, (2) the method of sampling or selecting cities and (3) the chosen index of diversification among the many available.
76. Wilbur R. Thompson, *A Preface to Urban Economics*, published for Resources for the Future, Inc. (Baltimore: John Hopkins Press, 1965), p. 147.
77. R. W. Crowley, *Labour Force Growth and Specialization in Canadian Cities*, Working Paper, A.71.1 (Ottawa: Ministry of State for Urban Affairs, 1971); and "Reflections and Further Evidence etc.," *op. cit.*
78. Marshall, 1975, *op. cit.*, p. 41.
79. *Ibid.*, pp. 42–46; and Maxwell, *op. cit.*, pp. 27–29.
80. Maxwell, *op. cit.*, pp. 29–30; and Marshall, 1975, *op. cit.*, pp. 46–47.
81. G. A. Stelter, *Urban History Review* (Ottawa: National Museum of Man, National Museums of Canada, No. 1–75, 1975, p. 1.
82. E. E. Lampard, "The History of Cities in Economic Advanced Regions," *Economic Development and Social Change*, Vol. 3, No. 2, 1955, p. 90.
83. Quoted in J. M. Hartwick and R. W. Crowley, "The Economics of Urban Growth," *Canadian Perspectives in Economics*, K5 (Toronto: Collier Macmillan, Canada Ltd., 1972).
84. N. S. B. Gras, *An Introduction to Economic History* (New York: Harper and Row, 1922).
85. J. Spelt, *Urban Development in South-Central Ontario* (Toronto: McClelland and Stewart, Carleton Library No. 57, 1955); and *Toronto* (Don Mills: Collier-Macmillan, Canada Ltd., 1973).

GROWTH FORCES 169

86. P. G. Goheen, *Victorian Toronto 1850 to 1900: Pattern and Process of Growth*, Research Paper No. 127 (Chicago: University of Chicago, Department of Geography, 1970), p. 5.
87. J. M. S. Careless, "Urban Development in Canada," *Urban History Review*, (Ottawa: National Museum of Man, No. 1—74, 1974), pp. 9—14.
88. C. M. Tiebout, *The Community Economic Base Study*, Supplementary Paper No. 16 (New York: Community for Economic Development, 1962); W. Isard, *Methods of Regional Analysis* (Cambridge, Massachusetts: Massachusetts Institute of Technology Press, 1960), pp. 189—204; and Thompson, 1965, *op. cit.*, pp. 27—33.
89. H. Blumenfeld, "The Economic Base of the Metropolis, Critical Remarks on the 'Basic Nonbasic' Concept," *Journal of the American Institute of Planners*, Vol. 21, 1955, pp. 114—132.
90. Cf., e.g., M. D. Thomas, "Structural Change and Regional Industrial Development," Discussion Paper B.73.13 (Ottawa: Ministry of State for Urban Affairs, 1973).
91. For those interested in a more complete discussion of commercial and industrial growth forces at work in late nineteenth century Ontario, especially as pertains to Toronto's advancement, reference should be made to Goheen, *op. cit.*, pp. 51—68; Spelt, 1955, *op. cit.*, pp. 123—130, 166—173, and 183—186; Spelt 1973, *op. cit.*, pp. 28—36, and 58—59; and the City of Toronto Planning Board, Core Area Task Force, *Technical Appendix*, September 1974, pp. 15—20, and 33—35.
92. Spelt, 1955, *op. cit.*, p. 182.
93. City of Toronto Planning Board etc., 1974, *op. cit.*, p. 18.
94. Spelt, 1955, *op. cit.*, p. 171.
95. Goheen, *op. cit.*, pp. 65—66.
96. Simmons, 1977, *op. cit.*, C. 8, p. 20.
97. N. C. Field and D. P. Kerr, *Geographical Aspects of Industrial Growth in the Metropolitan Toronto Region* (Toronto: Ministry of Treasury, Economics and Intergovernmental Affairs, Province of Ontario, 1968), pp. 30—37.
98. Spelt, 1973, *op. cit.*, p. 32.
99. C. C. Zimmerman and G. W. Moneo, *The Prairie Community System* (Ottawa: Agricultural Economics Research Council of Canada, 1971), pp. 3—15, and 35—55.
100. Ray, 1971, *op. cit.*
101. Simmons, 1977, *op. cit.*, C. 8, p. 11.
102. *Ibid.*, pp. 1—2.
103. Zimmerman and Moneo, *op. cit.*
104. W. Alonso, "Problems, Purposes and Implicit Policies for a National Strategy of Urbanization," in S. M. Mazie, (ed.), *Population Distribution and Policy* (Washington, D.C.: U.S. Commission on Population Growth and the American Future, Commission Research Reports, Vol. V, 1972).
105. A. R. Pred, *Major Job Providing Organizations and Systems of Cities* (Washington: Association of American Geographers, Commission on College Geography Resource Paper No. 27, 1974), p. 1.
106. *Ibid.*
107. Wallace Clement, *The Canadian Corporate Elite: An Analysis of Economic Power* (Toronto: McClelland and Stewart, Carleton Library No. 89, 1975).
108. The discussion is based upon Clement, *ibid.*, pp. 129—150.
109. A. R. Pred, "Diffusion, Organizational Spatial Structure and City System Development," *Economic Geography*, Vol. 51, No. 3, 1975), p. 254.
110. Pred, 1974, *op. cit.*, p. 8.
111. *Fortune*, September 1973 and September 1974.
112. J. K. Galbraith, *Economics and the Public Purpose* (Boston: Houghton Mifflin, 1973).
113. W. Gordon, *Storm Signals: New Economic Policies for Canada* (Toronto: McClelland and Stewart, 1975).

114. D. M. Ray, "The Location of United States Manufacturing Subsidiaries in Canada," *Economic Geography*, Vol. 47, No. 3, 1971, pp. 389–400.
115. G. F. Parson, "The Giant Manufacturing Corporations and Balanced Regional Growth in Britain," in J. Blunden, C. Brock, G. Edge, and A. Hay, (eds.), *Regional Analysis and Development* (London: The Open University Press by Harper and Row, 1972), pp. 220–223. Also in *Area*, Vol. 4, pp. 99–103.
116. Friedmann, 1973, *op. cit.*
117. Pred, 1975, *op. cit.*, p. 267.
118. Thompson, 1965, *op. cit.*, p. 33.
119. W. F. Luttrell, "Industrial Complexes and Regional Economic Development in Canada," in A. Kuklinski, (ed.), *Growth Poles and Growth Centres* (The Hague: Mouton, 1972), pp. 243–262.
120. Hartwick and Crowley, 1972, *op. cit.*
121. E. M. Hoover, *Location Theory and the Shoe and Leather Industries*, Harvard Economic Studies, Vol. 55 (Cambridge, Massachusetts: Harvard University Press, 1937), p. 121.
122. Wilbur R. Thompson, "The National System of Cities as an Object of Public Policy," *Urban Studies*, Vol. 9, No. 1, 1972).
123. Blumenfeld, *op. cit.*
124. Pred, 1974, *op. cit.*, p. 25.
125. E. M. Hoover and R. Vernon, *Anatomy of a Metropolis* (New York: Doubleday, 1962).
126. City of Toronto Planning Board etc., 1974, *op. cit.*, pp. 391–401.
127. G. Gad, *Central Toronto Offices: Observations on Location Patterns and Linkages*, a report prepared for the City of Toronto Planning Board (Toronto: City of Toronto Planning Board, 1975).
128. City of Toronto Planning Board, *Proposals: Central Area Plan Review; Part I, General Plan*, October 1975, B1–1–B1–59.
129. J. L. Sundquist, *Dispersing Population: What America Can Learn from Europe* (Washington, D.C.: The Brookings Institute, 1975), pp. 143–144.
130. I. M. Cyert and J. G. Marsh, *A Behavioural Theory of the Firm* (Englewood Cliffs, N.J.: Prentice-Hall, 1963), p. 86.
131. Pred, 1974, *op. cit.*, p. 54, quoting R. C. Estall, "Some Observations on the Internal Mobility of Investment Capital," *Area* Vol. 4, 1972.
132. J. Jacobs, *The Economy of Cities* (New York: Random House, Vintage Edition, 1970), p. 150.
133. Friedmann, 1973, *op. cit.*, p. 27.
134. Pred, 1974, *op. cit.*, pp. 44–45, and 50–51; and 1975, *op. cit.*, pp. 256–264, has been careful to emphasize that information exchange and innovation diffusion do not necessarily flow in a strictly hierarchical fashion from large to small places. His view is a reaction to earlier studies, such as that of B. J. L. Berry, "Hierarchical Diffusion: The Basis of Development Filtering and Spread in a System of Growth Centres," in N. M. Hansen, (ed.), *Growth Centres in Regional Economic Development*, (New York: The Free Press, 1972), pp. 108–138, which suggested the opposite.
135. Wilbur R. Thompson, "The Economic Base of Urban Problems," in N. W. Chamberlain, (ed.), *Contemporary Economic Issues* (Homewood, Illinois: Irwin, 1969), pp. 6–9.
136. Hoover, 1971, *op. cit.*, pp. 149–151.
137. Thomas, *op. cit.*
138. David Lewis, *Louder Voices: The Corporate Welfare Bums* (Toronto: James Lewis and Samuel, 1972).
139. Friedmann, 1973, *op. cit.*, p. 24.
140. Thompson, 1965, *op. cit.*, p. 46.
141. R. W. Crowley and J. M. Hartwick, *Urban Economic Growth: The Canadian Case*, Working Paper A.73.5 (Ottawa: Ministry of State for Urban Affairs, 1973).

142. Stelter, *op. cit.*
143. Spelt, 1955 and 1973, *op. cit.*
144. J. Porter, *The Vertical Mosaic: An Analysis of Social Class and Power in Canada* (Toronto: University of Toronto Press, 1965).
145. Clement, *op. cit.*
146. *Financial Post*, August 1974.
147. The southern Ontario centres are Hamilton, Kitchener, London and Windsor.
148. D. M. Ray, *Regional Aspects of Foreign Ownership of Manufacturing in Canada* (Ottawa: Queen's Printer, 1967), p. 81; and Ray, 1971, *op. cit.*, p. 36.
149. Ray, 1967, *op. cit.*, p. 81.
150. Ray, 1974, *op. cit.*, pp. 53 – 56.
151. M. Cutler, "How Foreigner Owners Shape Our Cities," *Canadian Geographical Journal*, June, 1975.
152. J. Donald, "Evaluation Criteria, Financing Method and Purchasing Techniques," a paper presented at a seminar on *The Effects Foreign Investment are Having on the Real Estate Markets of our Countries*, jointly sponsored by the American Institute of Real Estate Appraisers and the Appraisal Institute of Canada, Montreal, March 14, 1975, p. 13.
153. Cutler, *op. cit.* pp. 42 – 43.
154. *Ibid.*, p. 42.
155. Thompson, 1965, *op. cit.*, p. 24.
156. N. Hansen, "Criteria for a Growth Centre Policy," in A. Kuklinski, *op. cit.*, pp. 103 – 124.
157. J. Spengler, "The Arguments Against New Towns," Discussion Paper B.73.29, (Rev.) (Ottawa: Ministry of State for Urban Affairs, 1973).
158. Thompson, 1972, *op. cit.*, p. 106.
159. Simmons, 1975b, *op. cit.*, C. 6, p. 8.
160. *Ibid.*, C. 8, p. 7.
161. Pred, 1974, *op. cit.*, p. 62.
162. J. R. Palmer, *The Role of the Federal Deficit in the Economic Growth of the Depressed Regions: A Case Study of Nova Scotia, 1950 – 1965*, Discussion Paper 74 – 02 (Halifax: The Institute of Public Affairs, Dalhousie University, 1974).

CHAPTER 4

Alternative Urban Patterns: Some Regional Possibilities

The Nation and the Region

Canada's national and regional growth patterns draw attention to the importance of national population distribution as an issue of public policy. It is not a black and white issue—of concentration is bad and decentralization is good or *vice versa*—but a very complex question of finding the degree of concentration, consistent with national well-being. Certain persistent conditions and relationships stand out. Economic growth, the concentration of economic decision-making and economic opportunities are associated with urbanization. Regional economic disparities at the national level reflect interprovincial disparities in urban and metropolitan growth. The concentration of urban growth in a few large metropolitan areas experiencing high rates and volumes of growth shows a number of symptoms of strain: steeply rising land and housing costs, low housing vacancy rates, escalating municipal costs, and functional disorders in critical systems like transportation, sewage disposal and pollution control. In addition, as will become more specifically evident in the chapter that follows, Canada's biggest cities are located in sensitive environments containing some of the country's most productive land.

These are some of the circumstances that underlie concern with the size of cities and the way cities and towns are distributed across the Canadian landscape, on the part of both governments and various "publics."[1] For example, an opinion survey of a random sample of 2,500 Vancouverites reports the predominant view that "the city is becoming too big, and that a no-growth situation has to be imposed quickly, while simultaneously inducing growth in other areas of the province."[2]

Population trends and projections are, however, no respecters of

ALTERNATIVE URBAN PATTERNS 173

such prescriptions. Chapter 2, viewing the urban future through the lens of the Statistics Canada Population Model revealed a population pattern much like today's, albeit with some important nuances. Juggling of the key variables—mortality, fertility and migration—produces a range of distributions by province, but none fundamentally alters the dominance of central Canada nationally, and of the largest metropolitan areas, both regionally and nationally. Looking at Canada from its centre, the national urban pattern appears to be glacially immovable.

Chapter 3 has drawn attention to the depth and persistence of centre-periphery forces in Canada—the forces that spatially centralize people, places of work and cities. "Regions are not unique entities," observes D. Michael Ray. "Rather they are distinctive blendings of common ingredients progressing along independent pathways of growth."[3] Various patterns of domination: east over west; heartland over hinterland; urban over rural; and metropolitan over nonmetropolitan—are entrenched and not easily transformed. "Policies in Canada to cope with the problems of poverty, of immigration and of urban and metropolitan growth, of lagging regional development and of foreign investment cannot work unless the inter-dependencies between all these dimensions of regionalism are considered, and a comprehensive programme of compatible, self-reinforcing policies is evolved."[4]

While this perspective points towards a grand strategy to implement a national consensus, we think it is important to emphasize the dynamics of the relationship between the centre and the periphery—in broad social, political and institutional terms. Once certain favoured areas obtain an advantage, their controlling elites tend to perpetuate the established relationships (through both political and economic mechanisms), either because they have it so good, or because they genuinely don't appreciate the potentials of the hinterland.

> Private investors consistently overestimate the profitability of investments at the centre relative to the periphery... [because of]... a lack of objective knowledge about production opportunities on the periphery, the relative ease of making new investments at the centre, the strong preferences of enterprises for a metropolitan environment, and an absence of a spontaneous interest in the periphery, except for relaxation from the rigors of a harried city life.[5]

It follows from this that basic alterations in urban and economic patterns usually require a determined challenge to the established order by the affected regions. Indeed, centre-periphery relationships, which are often have/have not relationships are said to inspire just such challenges, and to become, in this way, the mainspring of social change. From this point-of-view, a legitimate goal of policy is to support a process whereby the objectives and strategies that flow up from the regions are allowed to influence both provincial- and national-scale policies, as well as to deploy certain master levers: industrial incentives; land, housing and transportation programs; immigration and so on. In a country like Canada, with all its variety of regional conditions, this approach has reference to both places which are experiencing the shocks of rapid growth as well as the trauma of stagnation, and various shades in-between.[6]

It is in this spirit that we will now turn to three regional initiatives: in the Vancouver district, in Saint John, New Brunswick, and in the Peace River region. The first initiative is an effort to deconcentrate and restructure the growth of a metropolis; the second to create a major regional growth pole; and the third to plan the future of a large diversified region in the resource frontier. Each in a different way is a constructive response to the growth issues resulting from the prevailing national growth pattern.

A Strategy for Deconcentration: Regional Town Centres, Vancouver District

In the two decades, 1951–71, the Vancouver metropolitan area experienced a very high rate of growth (averaging about 4 per cent annually), and in the process acquired a population of over a million. While currently the population increase has moderated a little, projections of growth indicate an annual rate from 2.5 per cent to 3.5 per cent which in either case would produce a metropolitan population well over two million by 2001. Much of the growth is attributable to Vancouver's attraction for people moving in from other parts of the country or other countries. With about 9.5 per cent of the total population of the twenty-two census metropolitan areas, Vancouver attracted over 26 per cent of those immigrants destined for metropolitan places outside Ontario in the five years 1966–71, and about 21 per cent of total net domestic migration. Internal migration in that period accounted for over half of Vancouver's growth and close to one-third of those originated in rural counties within British Columbia. Vancouver is a strong magnet for people and it is not very likely that the "tap" can be turned off very quickly, nor very much.[7]

This situation has been recently reviewed by the planners of the Greater Vancouver Regional District (GVRD) and they put forward

Map 4.1. Growth Management Strategy: Lower Mainland, British Columbia

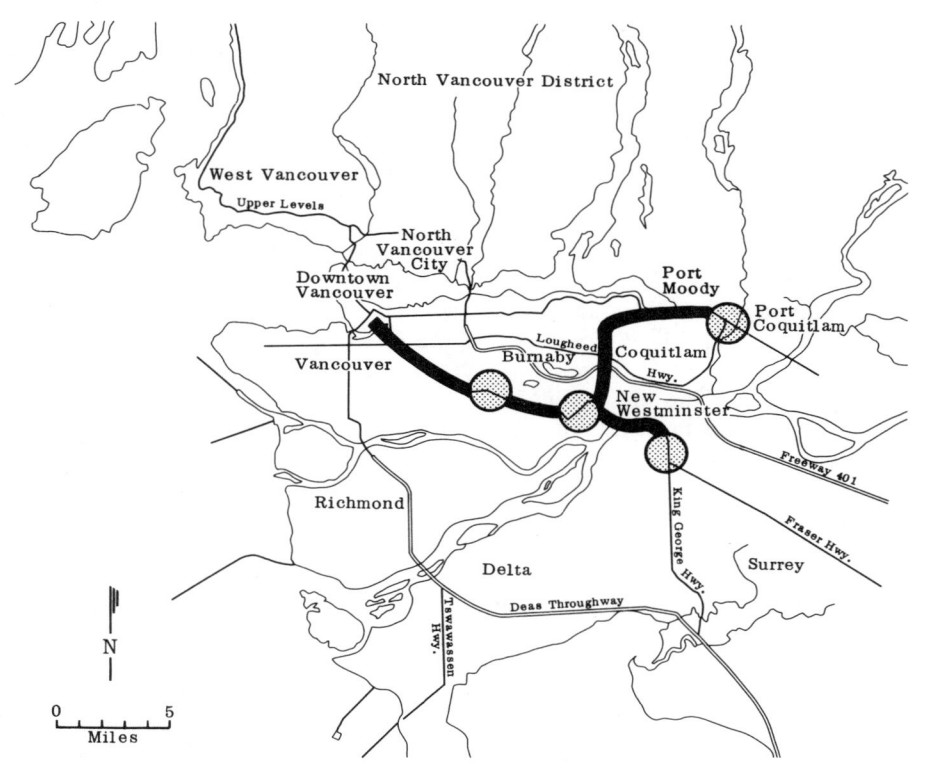

Note: The growth management strategy proposes starting four Regional Town Centres by 1986.

Source: *The Livable Region 1976/1986 Proposals to Manage the Growth of Greater Vancouver* (Vancouver: Greater Vancouver Regional District, 1975), p. 18.

(March, 1975) a set of "proposals to manage the growth of Greater Vancouver" (see Map 4.1). These represent a double-barrelled strategy (1) to work with federal and provincial governments to influence immigration and other factors which affect population growth, and (2) to direct and channel new growth "so as to maintain or enhance the livability of the Region." One of the key features of that strategy is the concept of regional town centres. This tactic is of general interest for two main reasons. It is central to achieving a radical change in the balance of employment between Vancouver, particularly the downtown, and outlying areas, which otherwise will be predominantly dormitory in function. And the concept has matured

176 CHANGING CANADIAN CITIES

to the point where a specific method of implementation—an "action program"—has been spelled out. These aspects will be of interest to other metropolitan areas like Toronto, Montreal and Edmonton, which are equally preoccupied with the management of growth.[8]

BASIS OF THE CONCEPT

A number of considerations have come together to produce the concept of the regional town centre. One consideration is the pressure on downtown Vancouver. This arises from the persisting build-up of jobs and structures in the small peninsula that contains the downtown. Behind the city's mushrooming Manhattan image are such indices of concentration as 62 per cent of the region's total employment (1971) in the downtown; 60 per cent of the rentable office space (1973); 65 per cent of the office space under construction (1973) and 50–60 per cent of the office space in the planning stage (1973). The area is also the setting for some of the region's major cultural facilities: theatres, museums, art galleries, as well as interesting restaurants and fashionable shopping.[9]

The critical evaluation of this trend raises concern about the impact on the physical environment and metropolitan transportation movements. About 40 per cent of downtown Vancouver would have to be torn down and rebuilt to accommodate this proportion of growth to 1996; and development would have to assume an increasingly concentrated high-rise form. Access to the downtown core, which is feasible only by means of a relatively few arteries and bridges, would become progressively aggravated because of the regional distribution of jobs and houses associated with the pattern of centre dominance. The balance of residential growth has shifted decidedly towards suburban locations north, south and east of the City of Vancouver. Ratios of jobs to resident workers of 1 to 1.7 for the North Shore, and 1 to 1.8 for the North-East sector and Northern Delta Surrey (Map 4.2) mean heavy cross-town journey-to-work traffic and mounting pressures on the downtown itself for car space —particularly as only 10 per cent of daily trips in the region are made on public transit. Neighbourhoods along the major transportation channels will also experience increased environmental disruption.[10]

A second consideration underlying the "regional town centres" proposal arises from the desire to improve existing town centres in the outlying municipalities. These vary in size from under 50,000 square feet of commercial floor space in Port Moody (White Rock South Surrey) to huge centres with 800,000 to 1,000,000 square feet in the facilities at Lougheed (Burnaby), and Park Royal (North Shore).[11] Some of these are very big developments considering that

ALTERNATIVE URBAN PATTERNS 177

Map 4.2. Ratio of Jobs to Resident Workers in Sub-Regional Areas: Lower Mainland, British Columbia

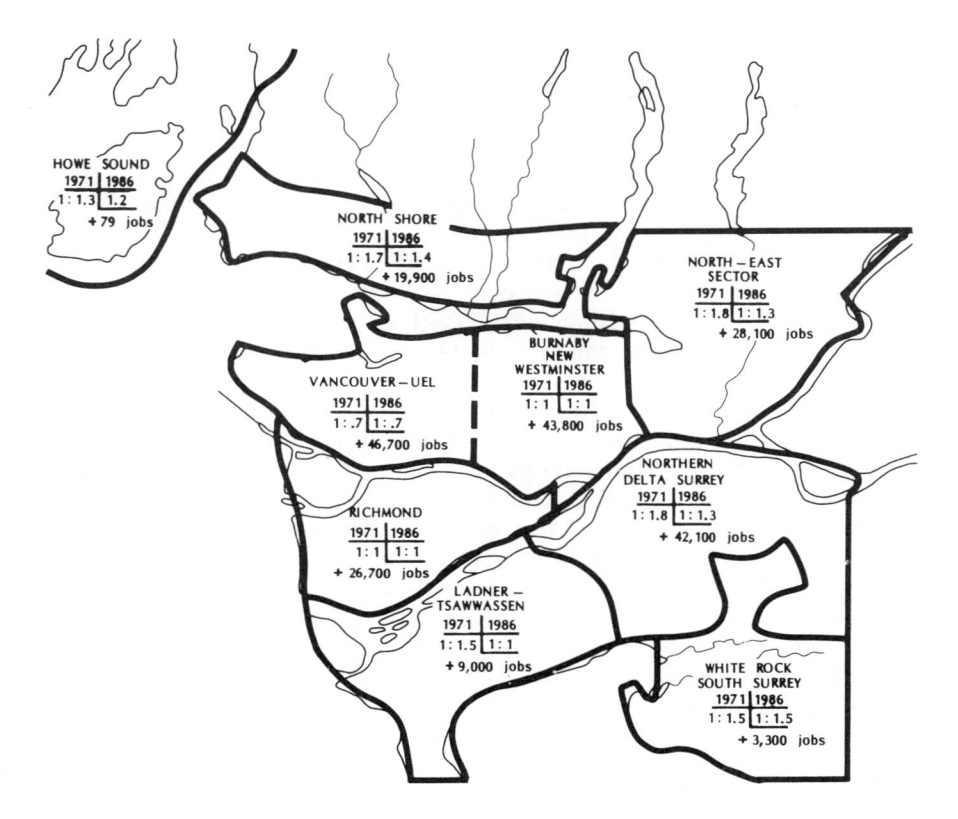

Note: A ratio of 1:1 means the number of jobs in the area is equal to the number of workers living there. A ratio of 1:2 means there is an imbalance: only one job available locally for every two workers living in the area. (The North Shore at 1:1.7 is close to this.) Comparing the 1971 and 1986 ratios for each area shows how much they propose to improve this balance by 1986. Also shown is the actual number of new jobs to be created by 1986.

Source: *The Livable Region 1976/1986 Proposals to Manage the Growth of Greater Vancouver* (Vancouver: Greater Vancouver Regional District, 1975), p. 15.

typically the central business district of a medium-sized Ontario city of 100,000+ population has about 500,000 square feet. But size apart, all of these are essentially shopping centres, and not town centres in the sense of focal points that provide the range of services required by most communities. As such, they have some serious limitations. They may offer a choice of half a dozen shoe stores but no library or medical clinic or good hotel. There may be a lot of relatively unskilled service jobs in retail establishments, but very little professional and administrative employment in offices. Both of these conditions spell heavy dependence of the city's residents on one or two more fully developed centres such as the downtowns in Vancouver and New Westminster, and all that implies in the way of the costs and stresses of cross-town urban traffic.

FEATURES OF REGIONAL TOWN CENTRES

The response to these circumstances that has emerged from the Livable Region program is a proposal to transform some of the existing centres into the focal points of communities that each serve a minimum of 100,000 to 150,000 people. These centres would be sufficiently large and diversified to play a "specific role in bringing jobs, leisure and education nearer to home by attracting activities that would otherwise continue to locate in Vancouver."[12] Certain minimum size requirements are suggested: 7,000 to 10,000 jobs; 700,000 square feet of retail space; 1,000,000 square feet of office space; theatres for stage performances with seating capacity up to 500; and up to 3,000 dwellings mixed into each centre. The critical transformation as far as activities are concerned is in the arithmetic of the three basic components: shopping, offices, and other commercial and leisure activities. The ratios of shopping to offices to leisure and other commercial activities have to be changed from the typical mix in existing centres of 4, 3, 1 to a future ratio of 4, 6, 2. The balance must shift from shopping to personal and professional services, to offices, and to such leisure facilities as swimming pools and theatres.[13]

Turning shopping centres into regional town centres requires the right mix and balance of activities—but much more than that. The concept implies certain design features: an intimate human scale; pedestrian orientation; separation of cars and people, consumer and delivery/maintenance circulation; effective public transportation access; and the expression of the unique attributes of each location.[14]

These are elements which in themselves do not assure success. They are important for the principle they suggest: attraction to people. The alchemy of design links the local and regional roles of such centres. Only by giving intrinsic satisfaction to residents in the surrounding communities can regional town centres help relieve the pressure on downtown Vancouver and attain a better regional balance of jobs to population.

PRIORITY LOCATIONS, TRANSPORTATION LINKS AND CENTRE FUNCTIONS

Applying the tests of need and feasibility the planners of the Vancouver district identified four priority locations: in New Westminster, Burnaby, the North-East sector and Surrey (see Map 4.1). In the latter two areas there will be a large gap between planned residential growth and local employment unless strong regional town centres are created. And the policy statement anticipates that beyond 1986 such centres will be crucial to sustain a pattern of decentralized metropolitan growth[15] within an arc of about twenty-five miles from downtown Vancouver.

The creation of regional town centres is strongly linked in the regional growth strategy with a certain approach to urban transportation. The basic policy asserted is that the transportation system has to be moved from its overwhelming focus on downtown Vancouver to a system which satisfies two other requirements: the access of employees and clientele to regional town centres, and the linking of centre to centre. "A transportation plan that improves the local accessibility of centres to the communities they serve, and links them with each other across the region, can encourage centre development." The way in which this transportation policy would be built into the centre concept is illustrated in Map 4.3. It shows a station for light rapid transit service (light-weight, high performance, high capacity electric railcars) to other regional centres and downtown Vancouver, as well as feeder routes from residential and industrial areas to the centre and its station.[16]

While the rationale for a program of regional town centres is compelling, the inescapable question arises: Can it be done? The regional planners in Vancouver have taken a hard look at this question. They have studied the locational preferences and tendencies of centre-oriented activities. It was discovered, through a survey of corporations, that particular functions depend strongly on the milieu of the major urban core, while others have a weaker affinity. In the first category are head office administration, marketing and finance functions. And in the second are such activities as research and development; some computer-related operations such as credit accounting, airline reservation systems and forest resource inventorying; and certain businesses with marketing operations that are not highly dependent on downtown promotion such as utility and resource companies, liquor and food processors; as well as new companies not yet enmeshed in a web of downtown contacts.[17]

In addition, some kinds of public sector and community functions can play a critical role in the process of centre development as well as providing the necessary balance and variety of facilities. Federal and provincial government offices are both comparatively flexible in locational requirements and in the decade to 1986 could be a substantial decentralizing force. They will account for about one-quarter of the total new office space. And developments related to government offices—private projects following government, and supporting

Map 4.3. Transit and Regional Town Centres

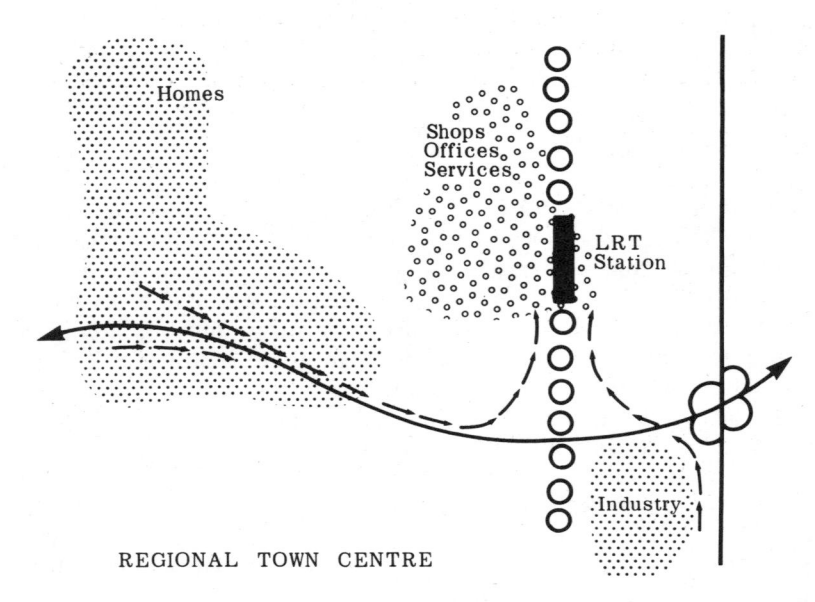

REGIONAL TOWN CENTRE

Convient to local jobs, shopping, and services

Local transit also is feeder to rapid transit

People drive, walk, or ride local transit to LRT station

Source: *Regional Town Centres: a Policy Report* (Vancouver: Greater Vancouver Regional District, November, 1975, draft), p. 12.

businesses and services—could constitute an important indirect employment and development stimulus. Similarly, recreational and cultural functions, ranging from sports arenas to arts and crafts studios, are presently underdeveloped and provide a lot of scope for centre development. Per capita public expenditure on such activities, which show a range in existing municipalities of $10 (West Vancouver) to $1 (Coquitlam), indicate that most of the areas's potential regional centres have nowhere to go but up.[18]

THE ACTION PROGRAM

While the GVRD regional studies have indicated the conditions favourable to the attainment of regional town centres, such places will not develop without a regional strategy to coax and push the identified prospects into reality. The strategy assumes the form of an "action program" with four major features: joint planning, the reservation of sites, land assembly, and a development management process. While these are expressed in terms that apply to the conditions and institutions of Vancouver and British Columbia, there are certain general features that can be identified. The program is of interest as a demonstration of how municipalities and regional agencies can play a constructive role in the urban development process.

The *planning* aspects involve both a number of formal steps to establish the concept of regional town centres as official policy, and certain processes to ensure the effective implementation of that policy. Thus, under British Columbia legislation, a plan for each proposed centre would be incorporated in the appropriate municipal by-laws as an Official Community Plan, and the entire set of centres would be incorporated in the Official Regional Plan.

The Greater Vancouver Regional District would serve as the agency for the broad direction of a regional program, evolved through the interplay of local, regional and provincial interests. For each regional town centre, joint planning and administration would be assumed by a Development Corporation. The regional planning functions would include (1) a co-ordinated servicing program which identified the government agencies responsible for roads, public transportation, parking, utilities and community facilities, as well as the costs and schedule for construction; and (2) a five-year program, updated annually, which would combine the servicing program for each regional town centre with the region-wide program – including costs, schedules and revenue allocations – for urban service and utility improvements and public land acquisition.[19]

In the period before the planning mechanisms are fully effective steps would be taken to *reserve* sites for the priority centres and linking transportation corridors. The instruments used would be a combination of official plan and zoning amendments, and public purchase of land at market value less speculative increases. The latter would require new legislation.[20]

Total land requirements would be substantial and beyond the normal capacity of municipal budgets. Some extraordinary measures would have to be taken to ensure the required scale of public *land assembly*. One possibility is the establishment of a revolving fund, supported by the municipalities and the province. The operative principle would be to generate revenues from the initial capital outlays (through the sale or preferably lease of centre lands) and to plough gains back into the development of successive centres.[21]

The Development Corporation set up for each centre would be mainly responsible for the *development management process*, including site reservation, land assembly, the staged planning of the centre, and the co-ordination of public and private inputs. The Corporation,

Figure 4.1. Illustrative Regional Town Centre Development Management Process, Vancouver

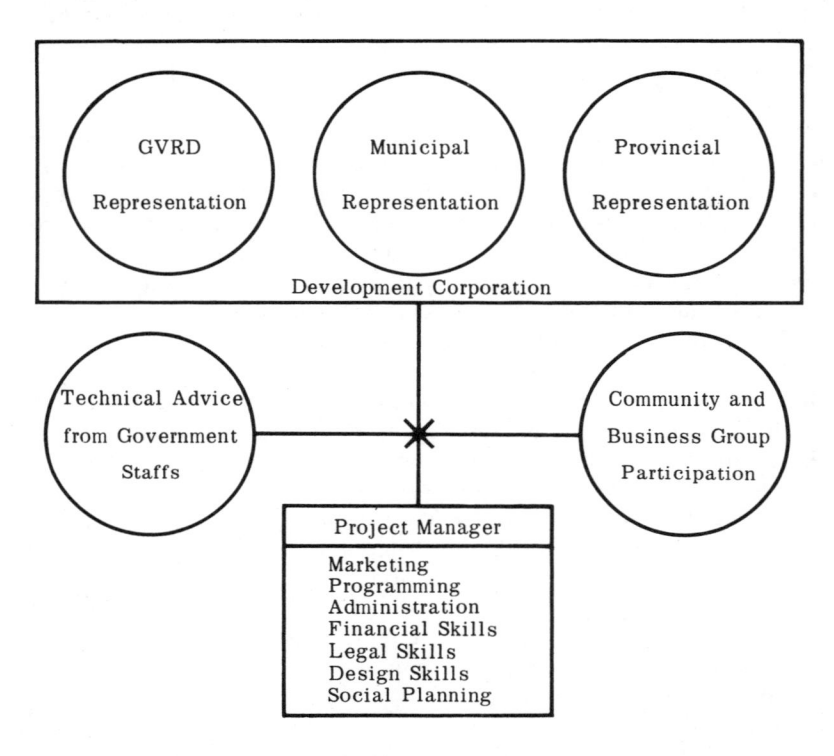

```
┌─────────────────────────────────────────────────────────────┐
│   ( GVRD          )   ( Municipal      )   ( Provincial     )│
│   ( Representation)   ( Representation )   ( Representation )│
│                                                             │
│                   Development Corporation                   │
└─────────────────────────────────────────────────────────────┘

( Technical Advice )                      ( Community and    )
( from Government  ) ─────── ✕ ────────── ( Business Group   )
( Staffs           )                      ( Participation    )

                    ┌─────────────────────┐
                    │   Project Manager   │
                    ├─────────────────────┤
                    │ Marketing           │
                    │ Programming         │
                    │ Administration      │
                    │ Financial Skills    │
                    │ Legal Skills        │
                    │ Design Skills       │
                    │ Social Planning     │
                    └─────────────────────┘
```

Source: *Regional Town Centres: a Policy Report* (Vancouver: Greater Vancouver Regional District, November, 1975, draft), p.37.

financed by the revolving fund, would include provincial, municipal and GVRD representation on its Board of Directors; it would also have an advisory community and business group (Figure 4.1). To be effective the Corporation would have to be backed up by regional city policies and programs that actively support regional decentralization of office employment. Some of the mechanisms for achieving this would include agreed targets, development control, and programs of monitoring and information to assure that targets are met and not exceeded in the downtown, and developers are made aware of opportunities in the regional town centres.[22]

The concept of regional town centres is of interest in itself as a development feature, but it has greatest significance in a discussion of urban patterns as a tactic in a broad strategy to create a decentralized form of metropolitan growth. It is a solidly developed, creative response to some of the characteristic problems of metropolitan growth. Its full demonstration will be eagerly awaited and observed.

Saint John, New Brunswick – A Regional Growth Pole?

REGIONAL POLICY

When a new federal regional economic policy was unfolded in 1969 it brought with it a certain new gospel of economic development. That dispensation had three books: the books of planning, urban growth poles, and strategic investment. The first made the formulation of plans for economic expansion and social adjustment central to the process of providing stimulus to "special areas," regions that clearly did not provide adequate opportunities for "productive employment." This was to be a cooperative federal-provincial process, financially lubricated from federal coffers. The second provided a priorities principle for allocating scarce resources. Within special areas all forms of federal assistance would be directed mainly to the points of strength in regional economies: to the towns and cities which possessed some structural capability for responding positively to the injection of aid.[23]

The theme of the third book was tantamount to a new proverb: "blessed are the strong." It was argued that the key to successful public intervention was to find the strategic activities which would unlock the development of an entire socio-industrial system. In some areas this might be a secondary industry ripe for accelerated growth; in others, a particular form of social capital like housing which if improved would overcome a barrier to the development process. The policy allowed for assistance to both, as appropriate—either through federal-provincial agreements which made specific commitments or through "regional development incentives," providing capital for establishing, expanding or modernizing secondary industries in "designated areas."

SAINT JOHN, CREEPING CRISIS

There has been a lot of water under the bridge since the new regional policy was announced in 1969. And it has been difficult to believe government intentions—to keep the faith. At times there has appeared to be an extremely thin line between supporting "development opportunities" wherever they may arise, and political expediency and opportunism. Perhaps that is because the mythology of the pork barrel is so strong in North American politics, and a program which must encompass the selective allocation of quite large funds must swim against and overcome a strong current of public disbelief.

In the veil of skepticism which has surrounded Canada's regional economic programs, both federal and provincial, it may not generally have been observed that events in at least one urban region in Canada have unfolded very much along the lines of declared policy. Since the late 'sixties, Saint John, New Brunswick, as an organized community has demonstrated an extraordinary determination to improve its economic and social prospects.

Generally the fact and image of twentieth century Saint John is well known. It was a city which seemed to express all too clearly the malaise of the Atlantic region after the collapse of the sailing ship economy in the 1880s. Only a certain faded glory remained. It was the biggest city in New Brunswick and the third largest in the Atlantic region. It attained a general plateau of development based on the processing of forest and agricultural products from the hinterlands of the Saint John valley, and on its function as a winter port for central Canada. But its manufacturing base remained extremely limited, its shipbuilding function survived only through Navy contracts and even its role as a winter port was curtailed by an improved icebreaking service on the St. Lawrence and by freight rate competition from New York to central Canada. The city retained a retail and wholesale marketing role for its immediate region, but was losing overall predominance in wholesaling to Moncton, and was dominated culturally by Fredericton. Much of the inner city, which was rebuilt with somewhat ramshackle wooden structures after a major fire in 1877, was in poor physical shape. Not surprisingly, all of this was reflected in its rate of growth, which right up to the recent past was extremely low, even by the standards of other Atlantic cities. In the two decades, 1951 to 1971, when the average annual growth rate of Halifax and St. John's (the other metropolitan areas having population in excess of 100,000) was over 3 per cent, the rate for Saint John was about 1.5 per cent. In the last decade of that period it had suffered decline to 0.8 per cent. This rate which was below the population replacement level, meant that the young and energetic, the more able and better educated were moving on to greener pastures—and deepening the crisis of the city.[24]

SAINT JOHN, CREDENTIALS AS A GROWTH POLE

This was the situation that prevailed when a number of forces began to converge in the late 'sixties around the concept of Saint John as a regional growth pole—although the city did not conform to the ideal theoretical model. In spite of hard times it was a natural choice once

ALTERNATIVE URBAN PATTERNS 185

national policy was committed, as it was, to reducing the chronic disparities between the Atlantic region and the rest of Canada. There were assets—potential more than realized—which in any strategy of regional development could not be ignored. In spite of all vicissitudes, it retained a strong marine tradition, backed up materially by a deep water port, by large dry dock facilities, as well as the financial, insurance and marketing services for shopping and international trade. The city was the home of credit institutions for some of the Atlantic fisheries, and the Atlantic coast terminus of the Canadian Pacific Railway. Politically, the area was strengthened by the 1967 amalgamation of the Cities of Saint John and Lancaster and the Parishes of Simonds and Lancaster. This not only made possible the more efficient organization of regional services for what is in fact a physically and socially unified area; as it turned out the amalgamation also created conditions favourable to provincial and federal assistance for the improvement of the urban services structure. And (perhaps not at all least) Saint John was the home of K. C. Irving, entrepreneur extraordinaire, who from his elegant estate overlooking Saint John Harbour, had already begun to elaborate his schemes for dramatic expansion in shipbuilding and port facilities.[25]

Saint John's aspirations were confirmed when it was designated in 1969 as one of twenty-two Canadian growth centres eligible for the federal-provincial program of industrial incentives. This was in addition to the assistance that generally became available within the province under a General Development Agreement. New Brunswick became a "special area" eligible for grants and loans for quite a wide range of public purposes, including major roads and services for land development.[26]

PLANNING

The development of Saint John has come to read like a script for the federal gospel of regional development. Certain provincial initiatives of the 'sixties began to take shape in the late 'sixties and early 'seventies. Through the "Program for Equal Opportunity" the province assumed financial and administrative responsibility for services to people: education, justice, health and welfare, and set up twelve (later eleven) Administrative Regions for that purpose. Apart from the intrinsic benefits for people, these arrangements served to provide much-needed financial relief for the enlarged City of Saint John.

Through a new *Community Planning Act*, passed in 1972, the province established a planning system which by design or otherwise was tailored to the requirements of the development process. The system provides for Regional and District or City plans. The first, prepared by the province, is a strategic concept concerned with the definition of provincial policies, reflecting social and economic change, which acting together build a framework for co-ordinated municipal planning and development. The second, prepared at the District or City Level, is a statement of how the regional strategy may be translated into the physical environment of the city (or town) and its surroundings.[27] A network of seven Planning Regions was established (Map 4.4), including one focused on Saint John and its associated area in the lower Saint John valley, along the Fundy coast and the valley of the Kennebecasis.

As far as the City of Saint John is concerned the planning process anticipated rather than followed the provincial system. Regional and local concepts were presented in the Saint John Urban Region Impact Study and the Comprehensive Community Plan respectively, which were completed before 1972—although the latter was not adopted by the Common Council of the city until May, 1973.

THE STRATEGY FOR RENEWAL

The development approach which emerged from this planning process placed emphasis on a relatively few but crucial objectives: to improve the port, to foster a metal working industrial complex, and to renew the essentially nineteenth century shell of the inner city.

(1) The Port

The basis for the first objective lies in a major shift in the technology of shipping and of harbours. The key to it is containers and big ships. The commercial interests of Saint John were quick to respond to the factors that no longer favoured inland ports like Toronto and Montreal. The economics of containerization which in effect is an application of mass production techniques to freight shipment, are biased towards huge bulk carriers, deep water ports, special terminal container facilities, the integration of marine and inland transportation, and a system enjoying the economies of uninterrupted year-round operation. The port development of Saint John has capitalized on these factors. The Port Development Commission has managed a two-phase construction program: first, a single berth container-based terminal (Brunterm) opened in 1971; and then a fully-outfitted facility, the Rodney terminal which opened in January, 1975 with the docking of an auto carrying ship transporting 750 Datsun cars and trucks, named appropriately, *World Finance*. The first-phase terminal was converted to specialization in paper products.[28]

There are two other features of the port development program—

ALTERNATIVE URBAN PATTERNS 187

Map 4.4 Planning Regions and Planning Districts in New Brunswick, 1974

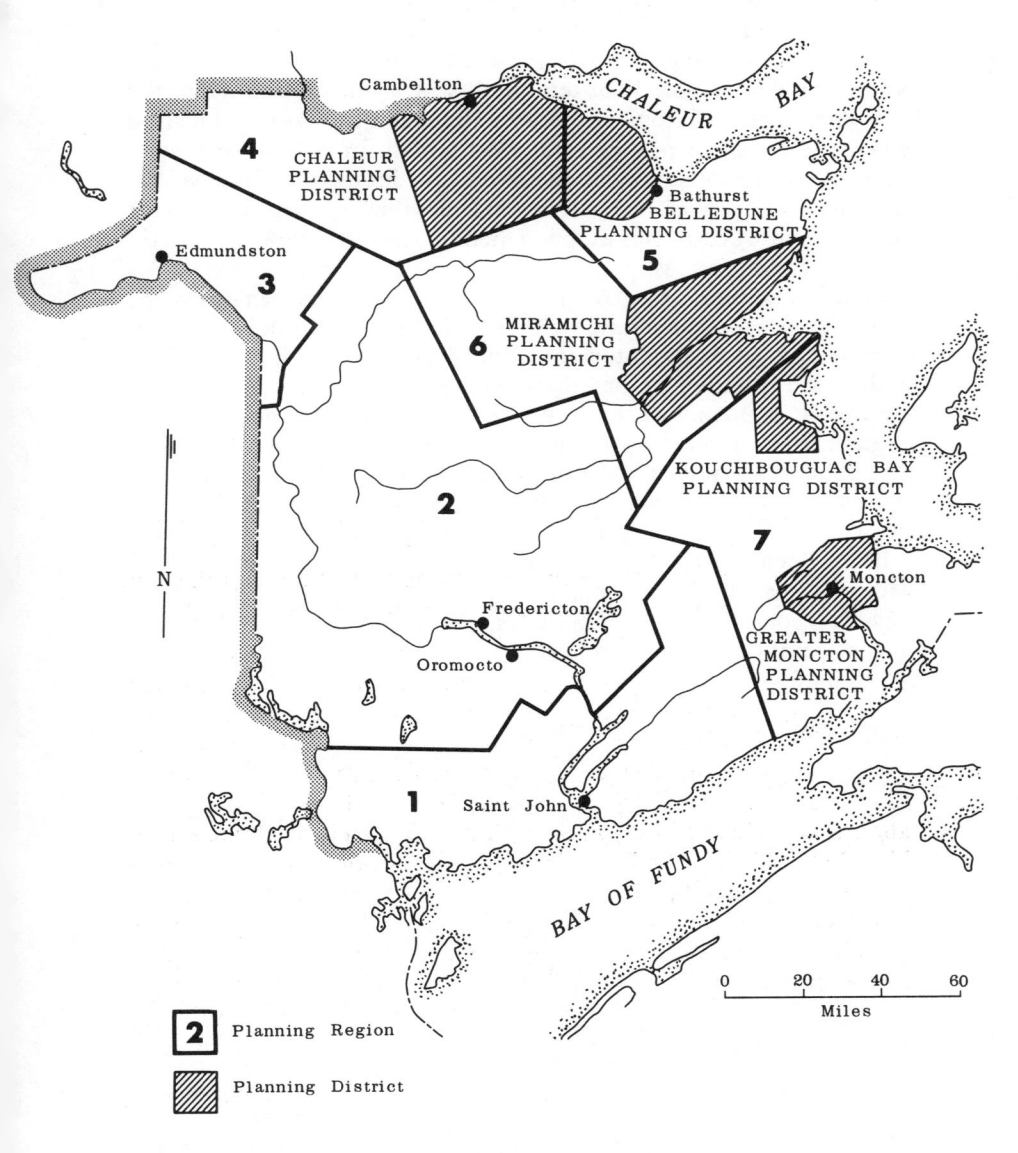

Source: R.R. Krueger, "Changes in the Political Geography of New Brunswick," *Canadian Geographer*, vol. 19, No. 2, 1975, p. 132.

one realized, and the other, still uncertain. The first is "Canaport," developed by the Irving interests, one mile off Mispec, just east of the city. This is designed for the offshore accommodation of petroleum super tankers in the 200–300 thousand ton category. It is the first facility of its type in North America. The other is a deep water terminal, at Lorneville about ten miles west of Saint John. Here the New Brunswick Development Corporation, the province's industrial promotion agency, is putting into effect a plan for an effective land/sea transportation interchange to serve heavy industry and the largest bulk carriers in service. After some considerable investment in wharf facilities, construction has stopped pending more favourable world economic conditions (Map 4.5).

These are projects that require large capital sums, which to the present time have been raised either privately (Irving development) or by the province. Intergovernmental negotiations will most likely result in the federal government assuming a share of these costs.

While it is premature to assess the impact of the new harbour program, basic indicators are positive. In the period 1969 to 1974, before the Rodney terminal was in operation, Saint John's share of the Eastern Canadian container traffic increased from 7.3 per cent to 9.4 per cent for containers, and for general cargo from 15.5 per cent to 19.7 per cent. Saint John seems to be well on its way to re-establishment as a port of international stature, served by numerous shipping lines, with routes to the United States, England, Europe, the Mediterranean, Caribbean, South America, Australia, New Zealand, Japan and China.[29]

(2) The Multiple Industry Complex
The second objective of the strategy for renewal, an industrial complex based on metals, is an innovative attempt to create an entirely new set of activities. Its origins go back to the late 'sixties when the Federal Department of Regional Economic Expansion (DREE) contracted with a firm of economic analysts to explore the potentials for rooting in the Saint John region, not one or two new firms, but a whole network of related industries. This was foreseen as an application of the growth pole concept that basic and enduring economic change depends on the creation of a cluster of related activities — with backward and forward linkages — which together provide sufficient size, specialization and integration for survival in a competitive world. Prospects identified by the investigation were sufficiently promising to establish an implementing agency, a federal-provincial Crown corporation, known as Multiplex Limited. By late 1975 the complex began to take shape with several new industries in Saint John, including pipe fabrication, industrial fastenings, forgings, and a number of other metal-related firms in centres west (St. Stephen)

ALTERNATIVE URBAN PATTERNS 189

Map 4.5. Port Development: Saint John, New Brunswick

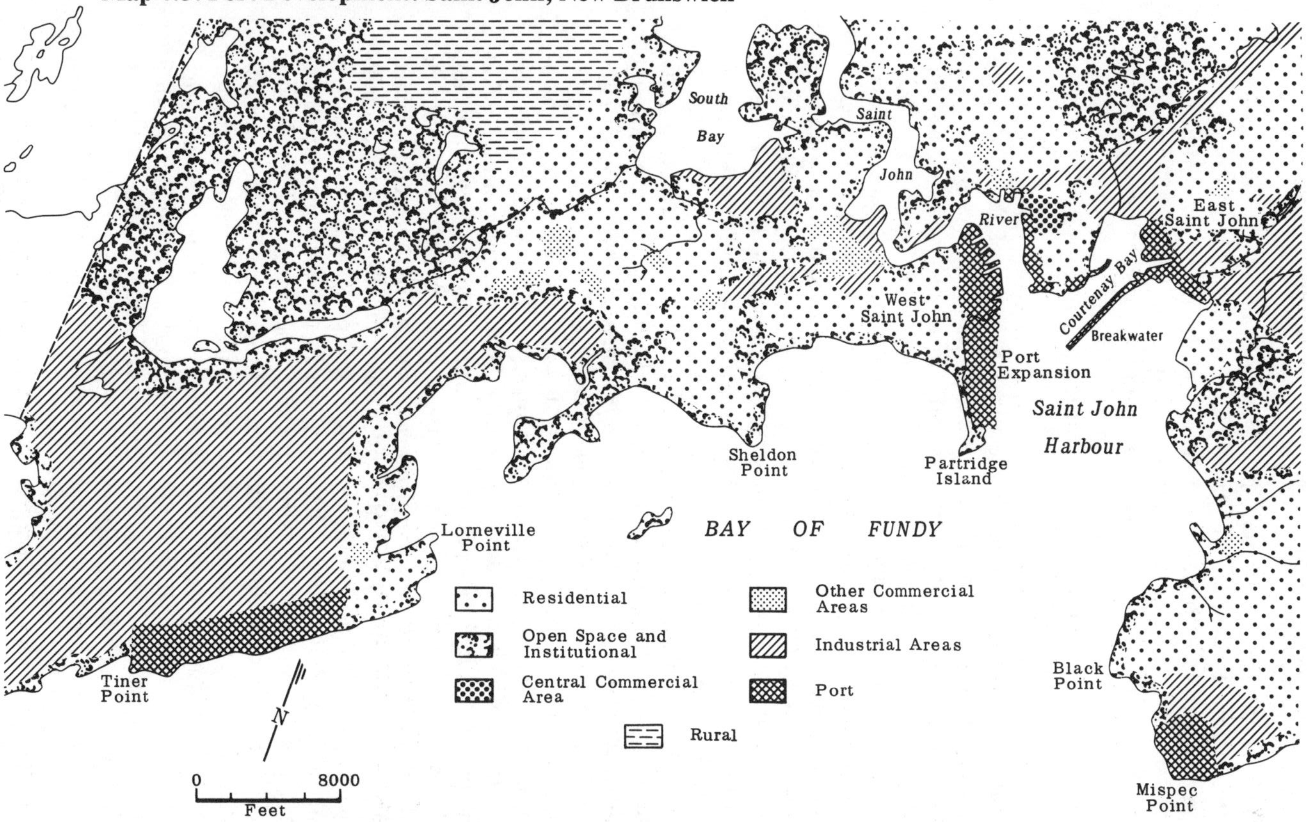

Source: *Comprehensive Community Plan, Saint John, N.B.* (Saint John: City of Saint John Planning Department, 1972), pp. 2-28.

and east (Sussex) of Saint John, within the planning region of the lower Saint John valley.[30]

This feature of the strategy has been a major determinant of the planned future form of the city. The Comprehensive Community Plan has opted for concentrated growth in the Saint John Metropolitan Area because "the operational requirements of the multiple industry complex preclude the possibility of a sizeable segment... being removed to a satellite community more remote from other related complex industries than about ten to fifteen miles."[31]

(3) Renewal of the City Core

Priorities for improvements in the physical plant of the city's core, the third area of emphasis, are stated in the Comprehensive Community Plan. The harbour bridge and Throughway, which are features of the freeway system, have knit together Central Peninsula and West Saint John and Lancaster, have improved accessibility to the city core, and have begun to foster a ribbon form of settlement northeastward in the attractive landscape of Kennebecasis Bay and River, as far as Sussex (Map 4.6). Depending on how this trend is managed, it could result in unattractive, uneconomic, land-wasting development, or in a unique clustered settlement form featuring the closeness of city and country.[32]

Another objective of the Plan is to renew the centre of the city, removing the most blighted properties, rehabilitating others (through federal-provincial *Neighbourhood Improvement Programme* (NIP) and *Residential Rehabilitation Assistance Programme* (RRAP)), and making room for new civil and commercial functions. This effort is concentrated on two comprehensive schemes: the Brunswick Square development, which includes a new City Hall complex, and Market Square, which features downtown housing and cultural facilities. From a city-building point-of-view these projects have a number of features, both of substance and process, which are of special interest. They involve a mix of private and public functions. Unlike many schemes of this type around the world, key civic facilities—the City Hall and Regional Library—have priority in the development schedule. The scale and mix of community and civic features, together with back-up private development like hotels, shopping, off-street parking, restaurants and other personal services, make this an all-out effort to consolidate Saint John as the cultural centre for southern New Brunswick. The facilities to be included in the Market Square are, in addition to the Regional Library, a 1,000 seat civic theatre, a museum and art gallery, a convention centre and meeting facilities for labour organizations. A federal government building is planned as an integral part of the development.[33]

The planning and development process involves the three levels of

ALTERNATIVE URBAN PATTERNS 191

Map 4.6. Southern New Brunswick

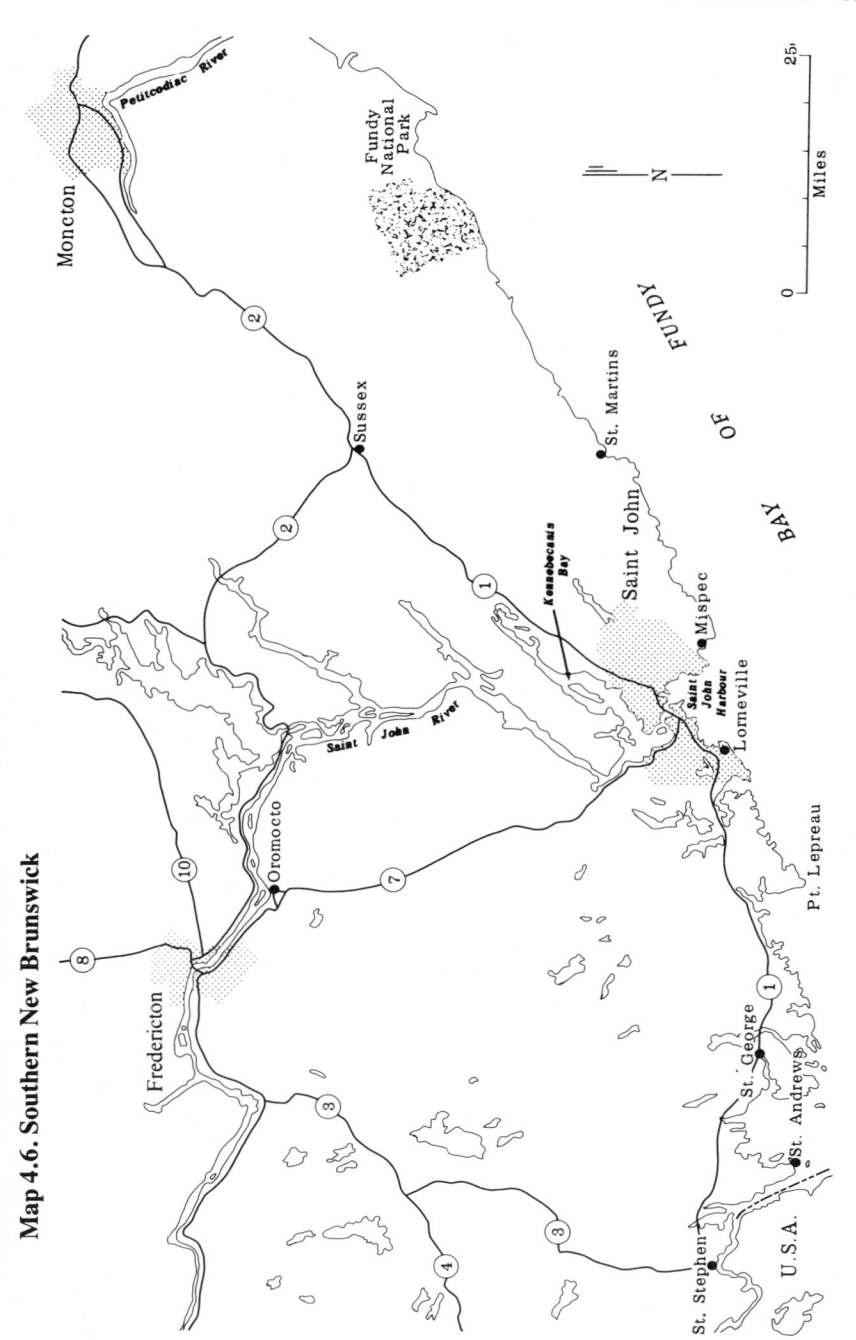

Source: New Brunswick Department of Tourism, *New Brunswick Highway Map* (1975).

government and a private corporation. Some of the capital for land acquisition is expected to come from a federal-provincial DREE agreement (1972). A tri-level committee for Saint John, which includes representation from the provincial Department of Municipal Affairs and the federal Ministry of State for Urban Affairs has taken an active part in co-ordinating the interests of the various public agencies. At the time of writing (December, 1975) its agenda included the review of proposals submitted by the development corporation, *Rocca Group Limited*. The city is proceeding under enabling provincial legislation to assemble the necessary property.[34]

(4) Other Elements
In addition to the three basic objectives of the Saint John initiatives, port improvement, a metal working complex and core renewal, there are two other major categories of development that play a part in the city's resurgence: shipbuilding and power facilities. Saint John Shipbuilding and Drydock is operating at full capacity with 1,700 workers, and its facilities are being expanded to increase construction capability from vessels of 100,000 to vessels of 200,000 tons. Power developments include an oil fired thermal plant at Lorneville (west of Saint John), which is part of a large industrial park established by the New Brunswick Development Corporation; and the initial phase of the provincial Power Commission's first nuclear plant at Point Lepreau, twenty miles southwest of the city.[35]

THE TURN-AROUND AND SOME IMPLICATIONS

These recent changes in metropolitan Saint John have been presented uncritically (some urban environment implications are indicated in Chapters 5 and 8), as elements in an economic-urban development strategy that underlie the city's improved economic prospects. There are a number of symptoms of a turn-around. Large establishments' employment (firms with twenty or more employees) increased by 18.2 per cent between 1970 and 1974 (from 24,061 to 28,450), but over half of the increase, an increase of 2,500 in employment, occurred between 1973 and 1974. Between August, 1970 and August, 1974, average weekly earnings increased by 62.1 per cent which was high compared to other major Atlantic cities (Moncton, 49.9 per cent; Fredericton, 55 per cent; Halifax, 45.3 per cent). At $162.77 metropolitan Saint John enjoyed the highest absolute level of weekly wages amongst Atlantic cities. Generally, the city is experiencing a construction boom, resulting in selective labour shortages and the influx of some 2,000 workers from Bathurst and northeastern New Brunswick.[36]

These signs of economic improvement are not yet an established trend, but there are some general circumstances in the Atlantic region that reinforce the Saint John-based developments. An intriguing thesis has been advanced on "growth centres in Atlantic Canada" by two senior development economists, C. D. Burke of the Nova Scotia Department of Development and D. J. Ireland, of the Canada Department of Regional Economic Expansion, Moncton office. In a paper prepared for the Conference on Growth Centres and Development Policy held in Halifax, April 10 and 11, 1975, they mobilize convincing evidence that an urban-industrial core has emerged, extending from Saint John, Fredericton and Moncton, N.B., through Amherst, Truro, New Glasgow and Bridgewater to Halifax-Dartmouth. This central corridor contains two-fifths of the Atlantic region population (1971) and approximates the economic characteristics of "Central Canada." Differences have dramatically narrowed in level of urbanization, labour participation, economic structure and income. While personal income per capita for the Atlantic region as a whole is 28 per cent below the Canadian average, the gap for the urban/industrial core is only 14 per cent. It is concluded that "when account is taken of the diversity of lifestyles, the easy access to recreational areas and the lack of pollution offered by most parts of the urban core, the overall 'quality of life' there is probably not significantly below the 'more prosperous' parts of Canada."[37]

The importance of this broader regional perspective for Saint John is that it suggests a development strategy in which each centre develops along unique lines to the advantage of the entire subsystem: Halifax as the multi-functional centre of the network; Saint John, with the principal manufacturing role; Moncton and some of the small centres, concentrating on distribution and light manufacturing; Fredericton, with a services emphasis, and so on. Attainment of the full potentials of this network will require that the public policy of the two provinces directly concerned and of the federal government be sensitively attuned to the different prospects of the component centres. In the meantime, the Saint John approach, with its triple-barrelled policy of broad planning, building growth centre potential and strategic investment appears to be consistent with the "central corridor" concept.

The Peace River Region: Prospects for Human Settlement

Most Canadians, living as they do in the larger cities and towns south of the 50th parallel, may find it difficult to stretch their imagination to the conditions of the Peace River Region. It is an area conceived on a grand scale (Map 4.7). It straddles two prov-

Map 4.7. The Peace River Region in the Context of Western North America

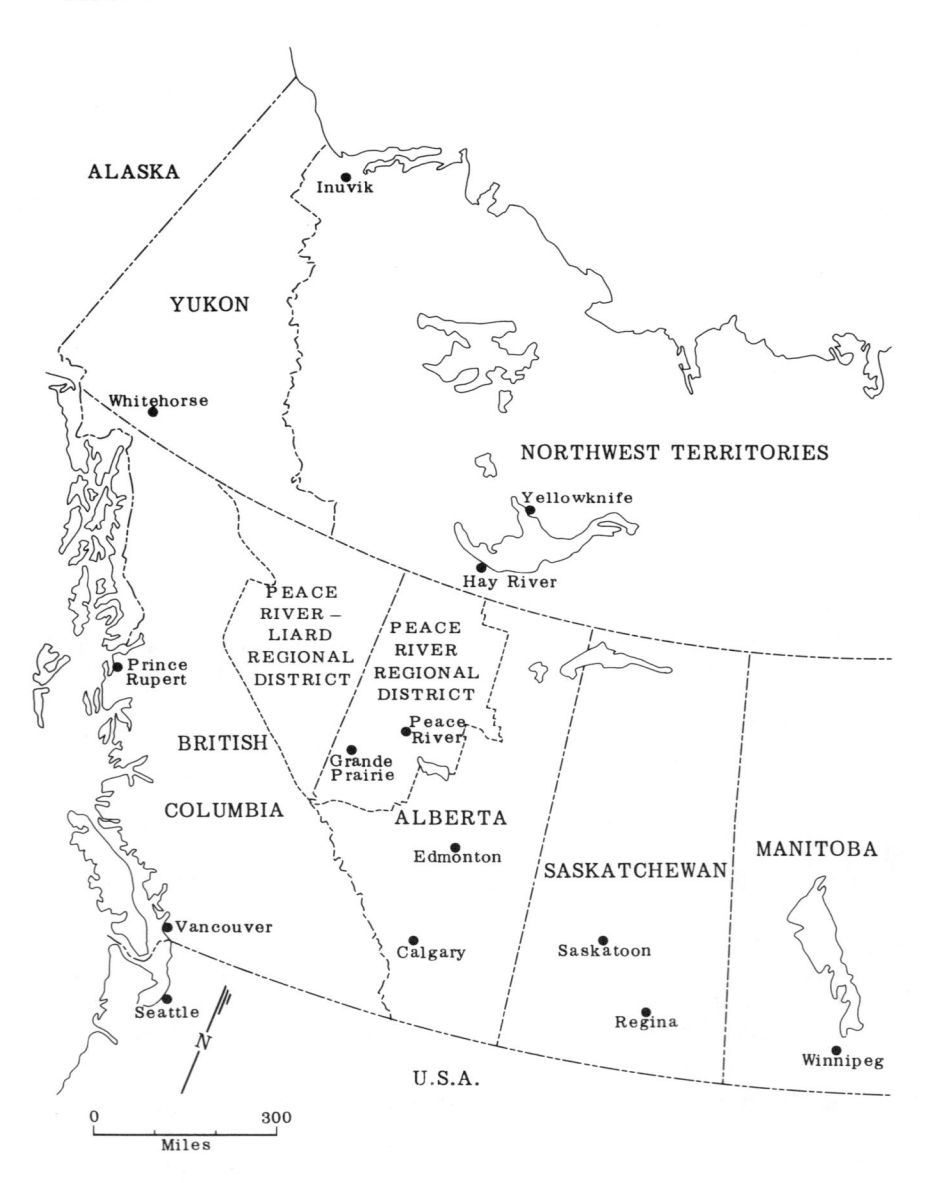

Sources: *Development and Planning Concepts* (Dawson Creek: Planning Department, Peace River - Liard Regional District, 1972); and *The Preliminary Regional Plan* (Grande Prairie: Peace River Regional Planning Commission, 1973).

ALTERNATIVE URBAN PATTERNS 195

inces and is larger than the State of California. It acquires its name from a river system that has a drainage basin extending 600 miles southwest-northeast to Great Slave Lake (Map 4.8). While the Peace is over 200 miles northwest of Edmonton, most of its agricultural area has a comparable frost-free season—the isotherms play tricks, showing an average annual reading of eighty days for both. Its landscape, from the Rockies to the Prairies, is highly dramatic, deserving in full measure its historic characterization by the explorer Alexander Mackenzie as "this magnificent theatre of nature."[38]

The Peace is unique among northern regions in that it has a large supply of arable land. The major agricultural area forms a triangle, with its base around Grande Prairie, extending along the valley of the Peace and its tributaries to a point near Manning (Map 4.9).

Map 4.8. Watersheds of the Peace River Region

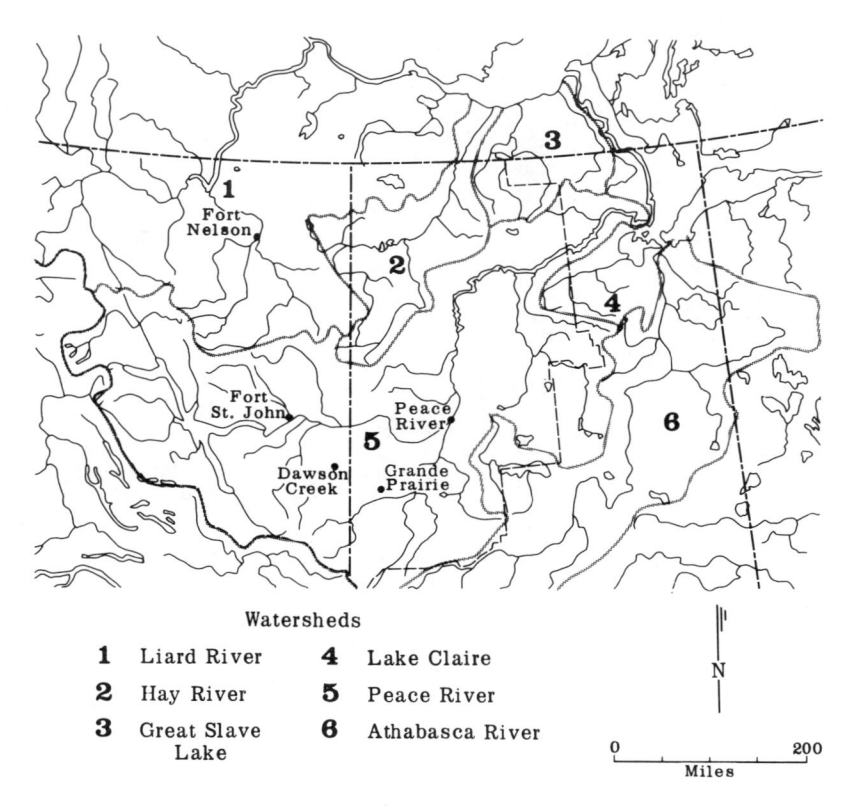

Watersheds

1 Liard River   4 Lake Claire
2 Hay River   5 Peace River
3 Great Slave   6 Athabasca River
   Lake

0   200
        Miles

Source: *The Preliminary Regional Plan* (Grande Prairie: Peace River Regional Planning Commission, 1973), map 3A.

196 CHANGING CANADIAN CITIES

Map 4.9. The Disposition of Agricultural Land in the Peace River District, Alberta

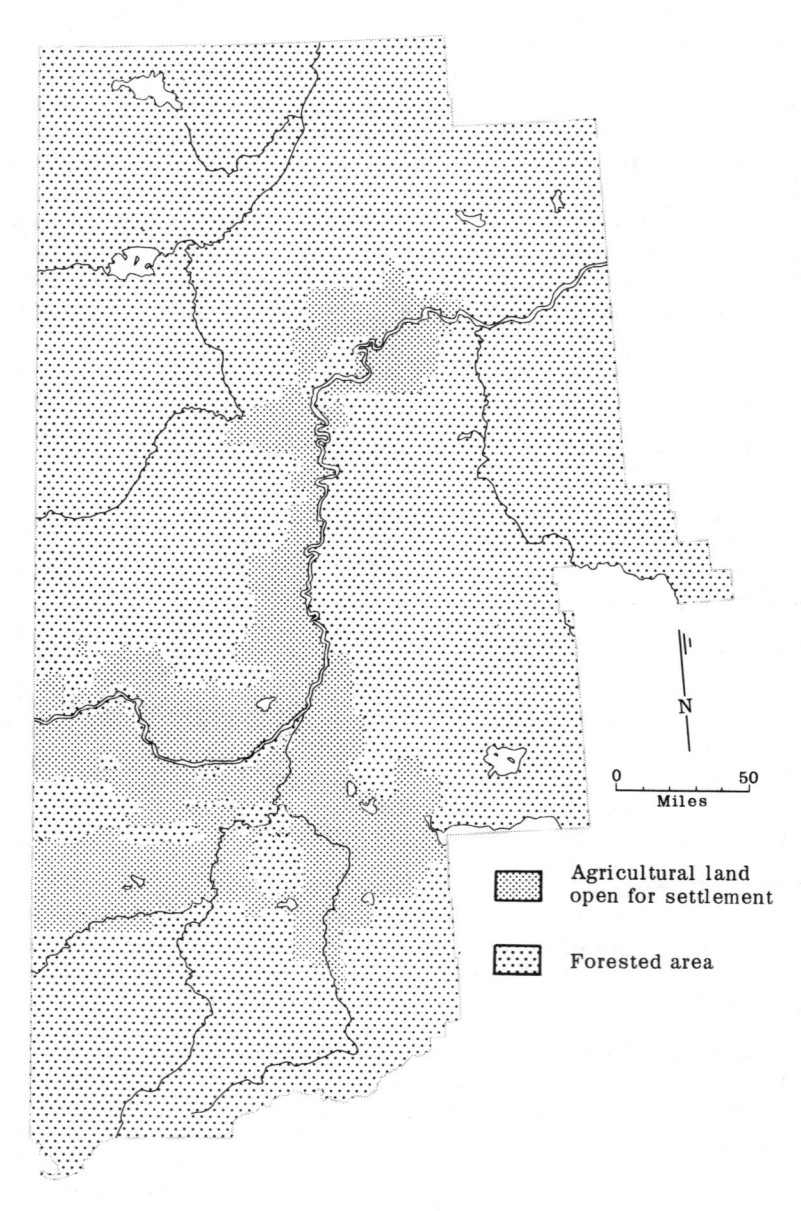

Agricultural land open for settlement

Forested area

Source: *The Preliminary Regional Plan* (Grande Prairie: Peace River Regional Planning Commission, 1973), map 9.

ALTERNATIVE URBAN PATTERNS 197

There is an additional pocket north around Fort Vermilion, and south and west in British Columbia around Dawson Creek. The core of these lands which are in Alberta consists of 16,000,000 acres of arable land (dark grey soil), about as much as southern Ontario, but only five million acres are in farmland (1973). Production is mainly in staple crops for national and international markets (wheat, barley and rapeseed), with an increasing tendency towards product diversification including beef and dairy cattle, and honey which is a specialty of the region.

This agricultural foundation has shaped the basic network of urban service centres: at the base of the triangle along the transportation spine parallelling the Peace: Grande Prairie, 12,100 (1971), Peace River, 5,300 (1971), High Prairie, 1,756 (1961), Manning, 896 (1961), etc.; and west towards the headwaters in B.C.: Dawson Creek, 11,500 (1971), Fort St. John, 8,500 (1971), Chetwynd, 1,253 (1971), and so on.

RESOURCES, LOCATION AND TRANSPORTATION

In addition to having a farm sector that provides some insurance against cycles of frontier boom and bust, the region also has the benefit of a highly diversified resource pattern. Some of the other economic resources are:

Oil: 3,000,000,000 barrels, recoverable reserves of conventional crude (Alberta); and fields in B.C., north and east of Dawson Creek, and northwest of Fort St. John. 20,000,000,000 barrels of recoverable oil in oil-bearing sands (Alberta).

Gas: 500 billion cubic feet, notably Dunvegan-Belloy area north of Grande Prairie, and natural gas fields around Dawson Creek, Fort St. John and Fort Nelson.

Coal: 250 to 500 million tons of coking coal in the Smoky River area, southeast of Grande Prairie; 349 million tons of ordinary coal (Alberta); large deposits in eastern Rocky Mountains, British Columbia. Peace River coal is used for thermal power generation at the 140,000 Kw. H. R. Milner station near Grande Cache, Alberta.

Hydro Power: Major complex in B.C.: Williston Lake hydro power reservoir, W.A.C. Bennett Dam, and, most recently developed, the Gordon M. Shrum generating station on the Peace with a capacity of 227,000 Kw.

Forest resources: 40 million board feet of coniferous sawtimber (10" diameter and up) and 100 million cords of coniferous pulp-

Map 4.10. Recreational Facilities and Areas: Present and Prospective, Peace River District, Alberta

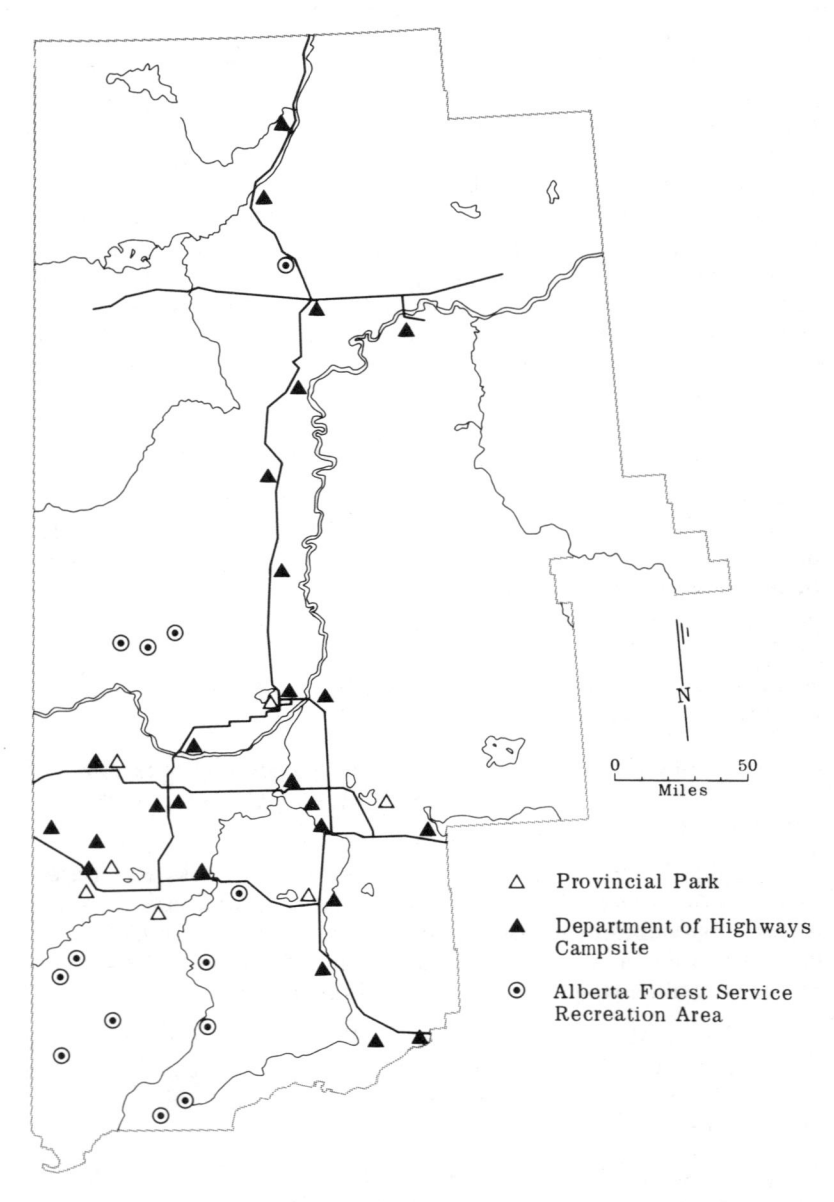

△ Provincial Park

▲ Department of Highways Campsite

⊙ Alberta Forest Service Recreation Area

Source: *The Preliminary Regional Plan* (Grande Prairie: Peace River Regional Planning Commission, 1973), map 6.

wood (4" to 9" diameter) (Alberta). Substantial reserves in B.C. part, as well; resources for larger pulp mill development have been indicated in the Liard region.

Iron: Estimated 250 million to one billion tons of low-grade sedimentary ore in the Clear Hills area near Hines Creek, in east-central part of the Alberta region; and large deposits in the Halfway River-Aiken Creek area on the B.C. side, northwest of Dawson Creek.

Fresh water: 32 million acre-feet leaving the region each year in the Peace River alone.

Some base metals: copper, lead, zinc, molybdenum, near Fort St. John, B.C.

Recreation and tourism resources: Greatest and most unique assets are wilderness environments such as the thirteen Alberta Forest areas (Map 4.9), and wildlife sanctuaries—some 87,000 acres of high-carrying capacity land has been set aside (Alberta); Peace River-Liard Region, B.C. encompasses a large part of the Canadian Rocky Mountain area, with its unparallelled possibilities to experience wildlife, and generally enjoy outdoor recreation in a wilderness setting (Map 4.10 for present recreation facilities and prospective areas).

Also important locally and as a tourist attraction are the landmarks that document the region's colourful history. It is possible to trace a path along the Peace that represents a transection of the area's past (commencing about 175 years ago) from native peoples to explorers to fur traders to missionaries to gold rushers to pioneer settlers.[39]

Like all northern development regions the Peace is preoccupied with transportation connections to the "outside." Its location, the geo-economics of its resource development and a number of government initiatives have caused the continuing and progressive improvement of its major transportation facilities (Map 4.11). Policies of land settlement and staple grain production early in the century led to railway lines from Peace River and Grande Prairie to Edmonton, and from Dawson Creek to Prince George, Prince Rupert, and Vancouver. The Alaska Highway, built as a supply route for war material in 1942, has become a major regional road, a well-travelled international tourist path, and a route for long distance commercial trucking, linking major Canadian and American centres with the far north. Today regular bus schedules are maintained from Whitehorse, Yukon, through local centres en route to Prince George and Edmonton. And places like Fort Nelson, Dawson Creek and Grande Prairie are important servicing centres for the trucking industry. In the 'fifties and 'sixties railways were pushed north to resource development: along the Peace

200 CHANGING CANADIAN CITIES

River to Great Slave Lake (1966), connecting the lead-zinc ore at Pine Point, Northwest Territories to British Columbia smelters; and from Fort St. John to Fort Nelson to serve oil and gas and mineral development in that region. A highway was also built along the railroad to Pine Point giving the area access by road to the Mackenzie valley. Other important transportation links are the scheduled airline service

Map 4.11. Major Transportation Facilities of the Peace River - Liard: Peace River Regional Districts and the "South-Central Bowl"

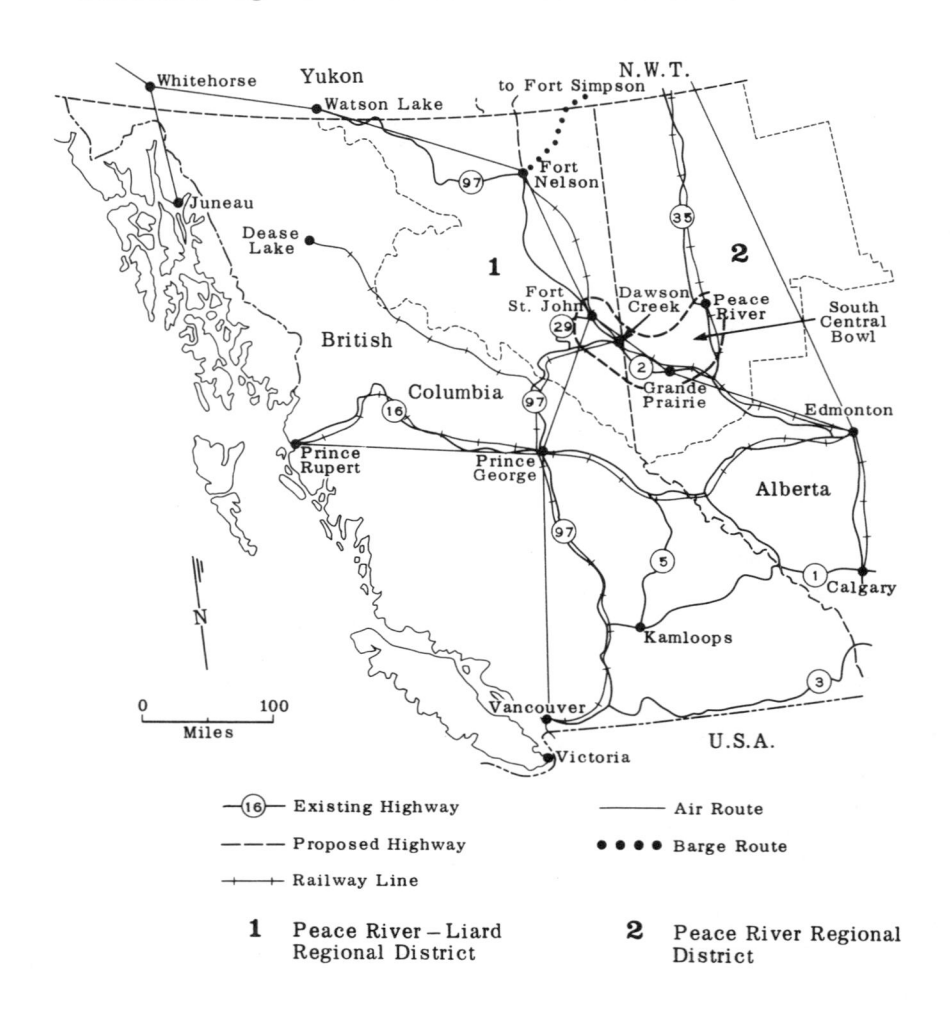

Legend:
- Existing Highway
- Proposed Highway
- Railway Line
- Air Route
- Barge Route

1 Peace River – Liard Regional District
2 Peace River Regional District

Sources: *The Preliminary Regional Plan* (Grande Prairie: Peace River Regional Planning Commission, 1973); and *Development and Planning Concepts* (Dawson Creek: Planning Department, Peace River - Liard Regional District, 1972).

connecting the region through the terminals at Fort St. John, Grande Prairie, High Level and Fort Nelson with the Yukon, Alaska, Edmonton and Vancouver; barge service to the Mackenzie valley and the Arctic coast from the railhead at Fort Nelson; and the oil and gas pipelines that converge on the region from the Mackenzie valley, northern Alberta, and northern B.C. and then link up southwards with provincial and interprovincial networks.[40]

AN UNDERDEVELOPED REGION—WITH A DIFFERENCE

This review of the Peace River in terms of its resources, locational and access patterns, serves to identify it as a region with some of the ingredients for balanced economic and social development. Given the history of frontier resource regions, this is a prospect of some consequence. In Canada we are still locked into a metropolitan-frontier relationship in which hinterland resources are extracted and shipped out, with negligible or no processing, to the southern urban/industrial belt. Under this arrangement most of the benefits flow one way: towards the metropolitan investor, and the resource region experiences just enough development to facilitate its prescribed economic function, and no more. The regions of human settlement and life opportunities that result are often, as will be shown in some detail in the chapter that follows, socially bleak and limited. Such areas experience a very halting evolution towards a mature industrial structure with primary resource, manufacturing and service components that can support a high level of community facilities. And they are sparsely settled by a chronically mobile and unstable population.

In terms of economic performance the Peace appears to conform to the predominant stereotype. The gross value of its output has the following components: primary industries—oil and gas, agriculture and forestry, 65 per cent; manufacturing, 5 per cent; commercial activities, 20 per cent; and government expenditures, 10 per cent. Oil and gas constitute more than 80 per cent of the product values in the primary sector, and forest products, 85 per cent of the secondary manufacturing sector. As for the population of the region, its single city and all of its towns, villages and farming communities together have about as many inhabitants as the City of Regina.[41]

And yet the Peace River is a northern resource region with some uncommon conditions. It has the kind of diversified resource pattern that has been the historic basis of economic development: agriculture, energy, wood, industrial metals and fresh water. And it is beginning to overcome its handicap of distance to the country's major development path, although high transportation costs are still a problem, both for supplies and marketing.

Another factor which distinguishes the Peace is its strong regional identity. "The Peace River Region is one of Canada's unique areas. Its original isolated nature gave its inhabitants a great feeling of attachment, identity and solidarity with the Region."[42] This attachment to place has been a factor in the long-term trend of net population in-migration, although there is concern about too many young people leaving to seek jobs outside the region.

Perhaps most important for the region's future is the rise of institutions capable of giving sustained leadership on the development issues facing the Peace. "To what extent," asks a recent planning statement, "will people be able to enjoy the quality of life afforded by the natural aspects of the region, and the friendliness of its people, and at the same time participate in mainstream twentieth century economic life?"[43]

In both parts of the region, this question and its many ramifications is the current concern of highly active regional planning organizations. On the B.C. side it is the planning department of the Peace River-Liard Regional District, representing seven incorporated municipalities and the unorganized portion of the District. This is an authority established under provincial legislation as an agency for regional planning, hospital development and administration, and other municipal functions delegated to the regional level. On the Alberta side, the organization is the Peace River Regional Planning Commission, also set up in accordance with provincial policy, and representing twelve rural units, twenty-three urban muncipalities and four provincial departments.[44]

These organizations play a critical role in the development of a region like the Peace. Regional development theory increasingly emphasizes the role of institutional factors—not simply the existence of a storehouse of resources but the ability to put these together in ways that are productive and that advance well-being. "Development" is defined as an innovative process leading to structural transformations. In the Peace this would not be accomplished by increasing the volume of oil production, which would be mere "growth." It would involve a change like increasing import substitution through more agricultural processing which would shift the economic structure towards more secondary activities. In developed economies, sometimes called core areas, the innovative agents for such structural change are built into the system: in private industry, in universities and research institutes, in utility companies and various public bodies. Underdeveloped or peripheral regions are by definition areas where innovative agents are scarce. The rise of effective regional planning institutions in the Peace River Region may be seen as an attempt to overcome to a degree this endemic handicap.[45]

This is demonstrated in the character of the leadership assumed by these organizations. In the British Columbia area, the regional planning department, in addition to formulating an official regional plan, has prepared a proposal for the upgrading and paving of the Alaska Highway, has made the case for the location of a steel plant within the region, and has prepared a submission to the federal government for designation under the Regional Incentives Act.

In the Alberta section of the region, the Planning Commission is playing a role as change agent in a very explicit way through both the process and substance of its planning. The documentation of its work which is quite comprehensive provides a valuable opportunity to understand the Peace and its prospects from the viewpoint of the region looking out.

PATTERNS FOR THE FUTURE: THE ALBERTA CASE

One of the more important aspects of the planning process in Alberta has been the attempt to give voice to the attitudes and preferences of "the people of the Peace" on the future course of the region's development. These citizens views that emerged, reported in August, 1972, assume a special significance in a peripheral region as they denote a shift from a passive attitude, a colonial type stance, that accepts core investments unquestioningly, to a condition of active involvement in the shaping of the region. This can best be appreciated by noting some of the findings.[46]

Most of the people favoured major population growth while having a decided preference for small towns and rural settlement (Figure 4.2). Approximately three-quarters of the respondents felt that industry should be encouraged. One in four were unfavourable to increased Eastern Canadian investment, and most of the people in the region did not favour any additional American investment. Tourism rated high as a development activity. Contradictory attitudes showed up here which were later reflected in the compromises of the regional policy plan.

The population displayed a strong concern with the quality of their environment. In all settlement types, over 90 per cent of the sample were unwilling to trade off more pollution for more income (Figure 4.3). There is generally a worry about job opportunities for youth, particularly amongst those in Grande Prairie and Peace River and in rural areas. On attitudes to planning, citizen participation, and politics, the residents of the Peace demonstrated a high level of awareness and approval of the Peace River Regional Planning Commission; were strongly supportive of the concept of city and regional planning; were skeptical (about half of them) about being able to influence the "economic development and appearance of the community"; and were decidedly not prepared to leave planning and community policy decisions to the "politicians and civil servants."

Figure 4.2. Citizens' Views Regarding Population Growth in the Peace River District, Alberta

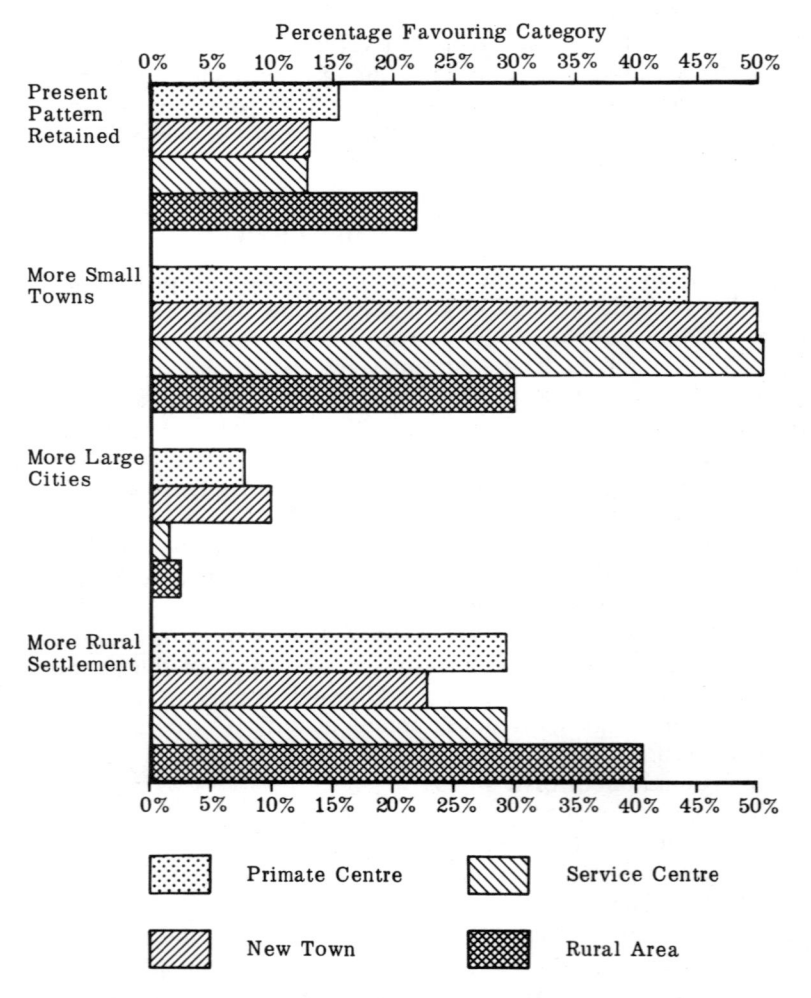

Source: *People of the Peace: their Goals and Objectives* (Grande Prairie: Peace River Regional Planning Commission, 1972), p. 39.

ALTERNATIVE URBAN PATTERNS 205

Figure 4.3. Citizens' Views Regarding Environmental Quality in the Peace River District, Alberta

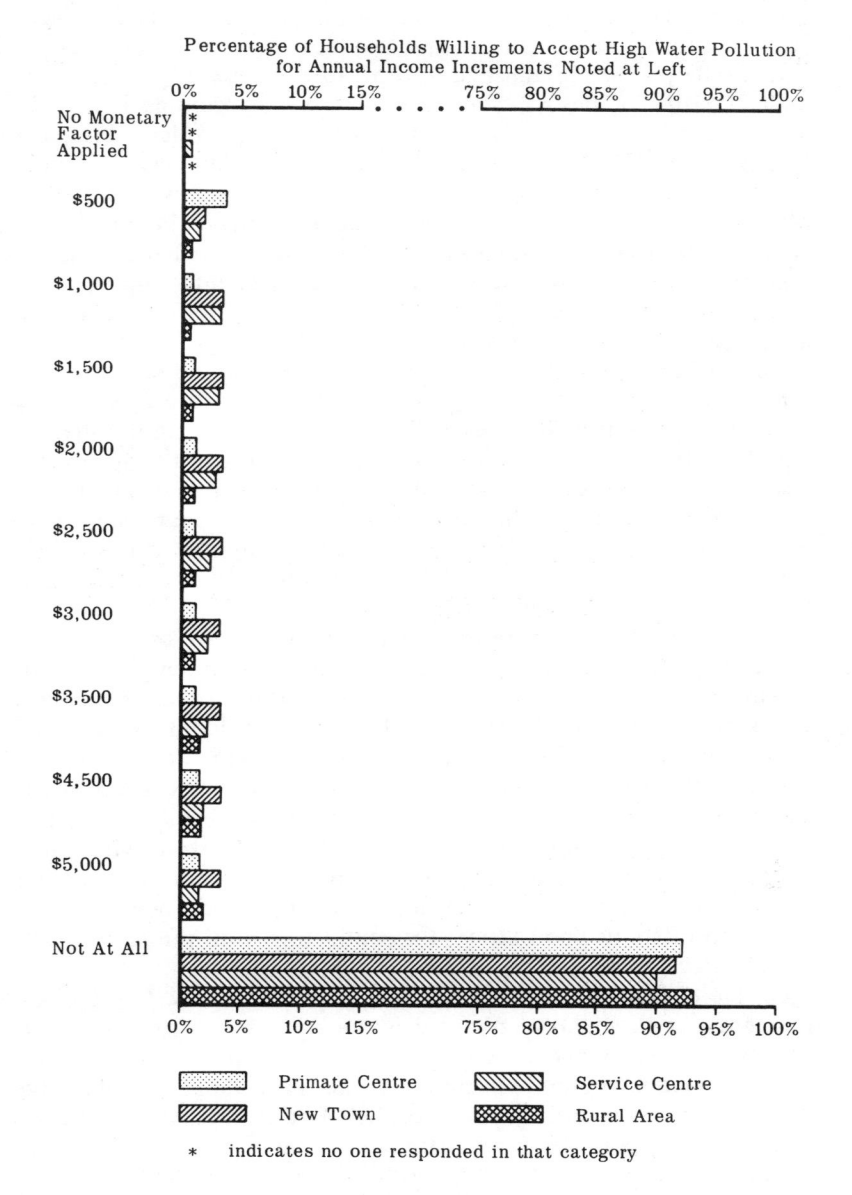

Percentage of Households Willing to Accept High Water Pollution for Annual Income Increments Noted at Left

Legend:
- Primate Centre
- New Town
- Service Centre
- Rural Area
- * indicates no one responded in that category

Source: *People of the Peace: their Goals and Objectives* (Grande Prairie: Peace River Regional Planning Commission, 1972), p .46.

This report on the objectives and attitudes of communities in the Peace was one of a number of studies leading to the formulation of a regional plan. These studies were on the themes of central places (1971), economic base (1973), and outdoor recreation and tourism (1974). The plan was published in draft form in the summer of 1973 under the title of *Patterns for the Future*, was distributed in tabloid form to each household in the region and was widely discussed amongst community and municipal groups. Provision was also made for return mailing of comments on the plan. The plan was revised in March, 1974 to reflect the views of residents, municipal councils and various provincial government departments. After further consideration by Commission members and the governments concerned, it was adopted by the Commission in May, 1974, and subsequently approved by the Provincial Planning Board.[47]

The regional policy plan that emerged strongly reflects the citizens' views, expressed in the goals and objectives study, as well as the issues presented by the 1973 statement which quite sharply posed the development choices in terms related to rates of growth, resource and industrial development, patterns of settlement and environmental quality. While the policy statement bears the marks of agonizing compromise between contending forces, it is interesting and important as an approach to one of Canada's underdeveloped but high potential regions.[48]

In philosophy the plan represents a significant step away from an exclusively *adaptive* concept, which it perceives as an exercise in picking up the pieces—making the secondary decisions about land use, services and settlement—after the basic development decisions have been made in Edmonton, Toronto or New York. Instead the declared focus of the regional policy plan is on "the problem of directing the process of development to meet the needs and achieve the goals of the region's people." To assume this role with some effectiveness the Commission asks the province for a "seat at the table" when major resource development projects are being considered; and offers its good offices for conducting local public hearings on such developments.[49]

On the basic issues of economic and population growth and environmental quality, the plan's goal is quality through growth. "The expansion of economic activity," it is asserted, "increases residents' choice of employment opportunities and may make possible the enhancement of community services."[50] And it goes on to observe that increased population will strengthen the fiscal base for community services and "increase opportunities for social interaction."[51]

While growth is to be encouraged, it is to be subject to a set of policy guidelines which will invoke other objectives: the maintenance of high standards in biosphere quality, the protection of the best farmland and of the finest landscapes for recreational enjoyment, the preservation of historic resources and so on.

The approach to the growth issue illustrates the style of the plan. It does not attempt to forecast growth nor to allocate land among competing uses. Instead it attempts to apply a set of guiding policies, and establish a process which will give significant leverage on the big structural decisions to the Commission and the municipalities involved.

To assist discussion of alternatives and to make the choices vivid, the Commission has presented a number of views of scenarios of possible futures. While no firm population projections are offered in the plan, scenario discussion is in terms of an end-of-century regional population (in the Alberta Peace) in the range of 174,000 to 250,000. The first represents a rate of growth equal to the current rate for the province as a whole (about 3 per cent per year), while the second is similar to the level of growth that prevailed in the south and centre of the province in the two decades after the discovery of major oil and gas resources.[52]

The options are presented in terms of three development models: wholesale exploitation, conservation, and the middle-road. The first is the path towards high rates of increase in resource development, population growth and gross regional product. Generally, short-run gains are offset by the rapid depletion of resources in favour of multi-national corporations; by regional price inflation; housing and services shortages; damage to the ecology; disruption of some social groups, particularly Indians and Métis; and the hazards of a boom and bust economy. At the other pole, the conservation model represents a somewhat static condition in which the environment and the existing social structure suffer little disturbance, but which involves serious social costs of another variety, such as unemployment and the steady out-migration of young people.

The preferred model lies between these extremes, and with good management, holds out the promise of the best of both worlds. There will be resource development, but only if such development is ecologically sound and returns substantial economic benefits to the region by re-investment in processing and by the improvement of the basic services structure. Because all forms of growth will be moderate, development will not be so dependent on readily available outside capital. The option will be left open for building "resource-processing complexes with Canadian capital at a later date yielding much higher returns to the region than currently are occurring or would occur with the wholesale exploitive model." Nevertheless the region will be set on the path of greater economic diversification, of growth in the regional market for goods and services, and of improvements in major infrastructure—roads, railways, power installations, and health and educational facilities. Public agencies will have to face up to some of the social and environmental hazards of growth. But these will be minimized by a decision-making process which will feature public hearings on major development proposals, environmental and social impact assessments, and consultation between the Commission and its members with the provincial and federal governments on policies and programs that have an impact on the region. In the final analysis, the consistent application of the policies of the regional plan, through the mechansims of the Provincial Planning Act, will move the region's development in the desired direction.

A map of "structural policy" that was part of the background statement of 1973, is included here because it may assist those unfamiliar with the Peace River Region to better appreciate the effect of the guiding principles of the plan (Map 4.12).[53]

Many problems will arise and will have to be overcome in the course of implementing the preferred policy. Some are mainly within the purview of local and regional action, but others have provincial and federal implications. Some of the more important of these that are anticipated and identified are indicated below.[54]

Problem Areas	*Provincial & Federal Agencies Concerned*
Investment capital for selected purposes: secondary industry, and improved facilities and services	Alberta Opportunity Fund Department of Regional Economic Expansion Canada Development Corporation
Retraining programs for farm population leaving the land due to farm consolidation	Department of Labour, Alberta Canada Manpower
Water Quality: Peace River Drainage Basin	British Columbia, Alberta, Government of Canada (Note: The policy plan proposes that "the provincial government should attempt to establish an interprovincial planning authority, which includes the Federal government, to oversee the management of the Peace River drainage basin."
Land banking for future urban development	Central Mortgage and Housing Corporation
Mortgage funds for housing in small towns	Central Mortgage and Housing Corporation

Map 4.12. Summary of Structural Policy: Peace River Regional Plan, Alberta

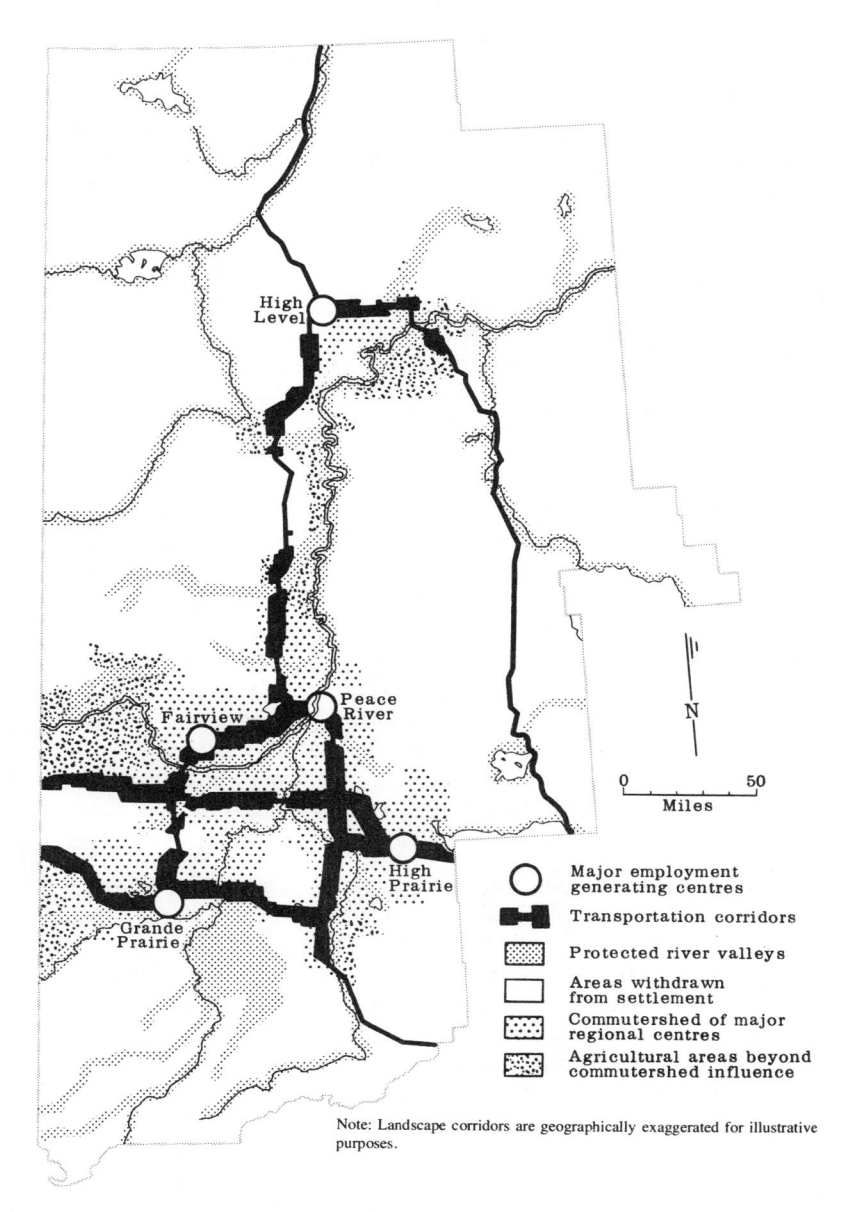

○ Major employment generating centres
■■ Transportation corridors
▨ Protected river valleys
☐ Areas withdrawn from settlement
⋯ Commutershed of major regional centres
▩ Agricultural areas beyond commutershed influence

Note: Landscape corridors are geographically exaggerated for illustrative purposes.

Source: *The Preliminary Regional Plan* (Grande Prairie: Peace River Regional Planning Commission, 1973), map 12.

THE INTERPROVINCIAL AND NATIONAL PERSPECTIVE

Planning in the Peace River Region has been constrained by two limitations in perspective: the relationships between the Alberta and British Columbia parts of the region have not been fully considered; and the national implications of the region's development have had scant attention. There is a structural fault in the Canadian government system. The fact that a natural region falls within two provincial jurisdictions should not prevent unified resource inventories, economic studies and policy development and action. But it does— and we can only guess at its consequences. Even a cursory examination of the facts suggests certain possibilities that may arise from a more comprehensive view. For example, the south-central portion of the region, extending from Fort St. John and Dawson Creek, B.C. across to Peace River, Alberta and down to Grande Prairie is rather uniquely situated at this time. It contains the major urban centres, much of the best farmland, the most favourable climate, about 70 per cent of the combined population of the region, and it is at the crossroads of the major regional and international transportation routes (Map 4.11). As such there is a very strong presumption that the full and co-ordinated development of this south-central bowl is the key to releasing the potentials of the region. But at present there is no mechanism for that kind of joint planning.[55]

The prospects of the Peace have been discussed mainly from the point-of-view of the region looking out. While this is a perspective which rarely comes to the surface in a national forum and has an integrity that cannot be faulted, a region of the size and significance of the Peace must surely have a place in the broad strategy of this country's development. In fact, this national aspect has been raised by the Peace River-Liard District (B.C.) in its request for designation under the Regional Incentives Act. The issue was stated as follows:

> In submitting our petition to be granted designation under the Regional Incentives Act we cannot pass over the deep concern caused by the study of the Federal Department of Urban Affairs (sic) published recently under the title "The Urban Future." According to this report 95 per cent of all Canadians will live in urban centres by the year 2001, with 73 per cent concentrated in twelve cities or metropolitan centres and of those approximately fifteen million people in Montreal, Toronto, and Vancouver.
>
> It is not our prerogative as a Regional District to deal with the staggering implications of such a development in the dialogue about a new Canadian constitution. However we feel that the social implications attached to such a course of events are the con-

cern of every Canadian. It is our considered opinion that the trend to the amassing of the vast majority of Canadians in a few urban centres must be stopped if we want to retain our capability to control the social issues of our society. In the light of these considerations we feel that the Regional Incentives Act can be forged into a most useful tool to maintain the vitality of semi-urban and rural Canada.[56]

The national implications of this approach—the fostering of the development of regions like the Peace to take the heat off areas of urban pressure—has hardly begun to be addressed in urban and regional economic policies.

Policy Approaches

Each of the three regional cases that have been discussed represent different aspects of Canada's urban growth pattern. The first, the *Vancouver* case, typifies the concerns of the largest metropolitan areas with the form of their future growth. The west coast metropolis has been forced into this earlier in its development cycle than Montreal and Toronto by the quite severe limitations of its land base. Ironically, but very significantly, the strategy which it has evolved dramatizes the issues and policy choices faced by cities twice its size —and already anticipated by rapidly growing metropolitan areas like Edmonton and Calgary.

Policy issues are raised at two levels: at the level of the nation or the province, and at the level of the regional district. Inasmuch as Vancouver's growth is substantially based on immigration and on domestic migration, the Province of British Columbia, other provinces and the federal government are deeply involved in dealing with the conditions that influence both "push" and "pull" factors: the motives underlying the many personal decisions to uproot from town and rural communities, and move to the big city. The responsibility of the federal government with respect to the *distribution* aspects of immigration policy has been pointed out by the Board of the Greater Vancouver Regional District. In a brief (June, 1974) to the Federal Ministry of Manpower and Immigration the Board called upon the federal government to collaborate with provincial and regional governments to create a country-wide settlement policy; to foster, as an aspect of that policy, a number of growth centres located outside the fast-growing metropolitan areas; and to co-ordinate national settlement policy with immigration policy, particularly in its distributional aspects.[57]

At the regional level, the deconcentration strategy must rely on the broad co-ordination of the Regional District, but what is important about this kind of regional strategy is that its implementation depends no less on certain kinds of supportive action from the other jurisdictions. For the city, the crucial role is in the attuning of downtown development to overall livability goals, distinguishing between the decision and service functions that are critical to the downtown's sound evolution, and the other activities, such as many office functions which could operate as well or better in regional town centres. For the province, its most important function is in establishing the right financial, legislative and institutional conditions for an effective planning and development process. Much of this is already in place in British Columbia. But the need for two kinds of legislation is indicated by the formulated action program: to acquire land for regional town centres at prices which are not speculatively inflated; and to establish development corporations, with powers and responsibilities and budgetary capacity tailored to the very exacting demands of large scale urban development.

The federal government can play its part mainly by the sympathetic and imaginative deployment of existing programs. For example, certain provisions of the National Housing Act—land assembly and new communities—should be interpreted in the light of Vancouver conditions and needs and administered accordingly. A case in point is the definition of "new community" in the Act. It could be understood as having application only to free standing communities, some distance from large urban centres.[58] Limited development land in the Vancouver case, however, dictates a tighter settlement structure with the nodes of decentralized communities closer to the metropolitan downtown than they could be in, say, a metropolitan region in southern Ontario or on the Prairies. This should be recognized and the Act administered to achieve its *intent* rather than to fit the mould of a preconceived development scale and form. This approach takes leadership at the head office as well as flexibility and intelligence in administrative field offices.

In addition, both the federal government and the province have an important role in directing the location of public sector employment; and the province can influence the structure of regional growth through its various programs, particularly housing and transportation.

This need for concerted action by all levels of government to attain basic metropolitan restructuring in the interests of greater livability is vividly demonstrated by the Vancouver case, but it applies to all of Canada's major metropolitan areas.

The Saint John case illustrates the process of stimulating the change, renewal and sometimes orderly growth of slowly developing or static centres. With due allowances for local conditions, there are aspects of the Saint John strategy which relate to such places as

Trois-Rivières, Quebec; Thunder Bay, Ontario; Brandon, Manitoba; Prince Alberta, Saskatchewan or Prince Rupert, B.C. There is national significance in the demonstration that co-ordinated intergovernmental and private sector action, working within a jointly committed strategy, can begin to affect and overcome deep-seated problems.

It is, however, important to observe the set of conditions that affect the Saint John case. One is the relationship between that city and a network of cities in an urban/industrial core. The fate of the city is linked up with the fate of a maturing urban system. A second condition is that planning studies must attempt to identify the major problems and the *keys* to basic change and improvement. This is imposed by the need to allocate scarce resources with the greatest efficiency—getting the greatest possible bang for the buck. And it is consistent with the nature of the urban social system: many forces interact but some are more *strategic* than others. It is the particular genius of a good plan that it discovers the factors that are salient in the special circumstances of the study area and builds a program on that basis. A final condition that should be noted in the Saint John experience is how in the life of the city, economic and general urban factors are intertwined and mutually dependent. This, however, is in contrast with the policy development and program delivery structures of government, which provide separate legislative and institutional channels for economic development and urban planning. The hazards in this situation should be noted.

The study of *Growth Centres in Atlantic Canada*, accords Saint John two primary functions in the Atlantic system of cities: a pivotal role in manufacturing, and predominance as a growth centre in New Brunswick with specialization in finance.[59] If it is to fulfil this destiny, certain aspects of its development pattern require emphasis—to a degree not yet expressed in current policies and programs.

> The city must move into white collar areas, with downtown as the focal point, establishing itself more firmly as the commercial centre of New Brunswick. However, just building the downtown is not enough. The external links must be looked after, and ... air service is critically important.... If Saint John is to serve as the major growth centre ... it must be recognized that a large proportion of the new residents will be francophones. It is important that the city be consciously designed to accommodate such an infusion, especially in cultural and entertainment facilities, retail trade, public administration, etc.[60]

A final question arises from the Saint John case: Who benefits? It is known that the city has a backlog of poverty and serious social problems, but it is not known how these have been affected by the economic turn-around. If equity is to be a goal of public policy then this question must be pursued in depth. The planning system should monitor social conditions, reporting changes in income distribution, housing conditions and indicators of stress and well-being. The very process of development will be questioned unless it operates in a way that improves the lot of the majority of the city's residents.

The *Peace River Region* shares with other regions in Canada's mid-North the problems of unrealized resource development, shortage in investment capital, distance from the country's more economically advanced areas, and inadequate social and community services. It is, however, a region of outstanding economic and social potential. And it is an area that has generated an impressive capacity, through its regional planning institutions, to assume leadership in directing the process of development.

One over-riding impression remains from the Peace River case study. There is a policy vacuum at the federal level with respect to the development of such regions. Here is a region that is still a significant frontier for the expansion of output in many vital resources; and which because of the depth and variety of its economic base can play a part in a national strategy to attain a greater degree of decentralized growth. And yet there are no broadly conceived national level programs or mechanisms that can relate a region like the Peace to such national issues and purposes.

In this light, the federal-provincial programs for "regional economic expansion" commonly known as the DREE programs, are shown to be unfortunately limited in their scope. All the fine apparatus and high finance of those arrangements are confined to "special areas" which lack opportunities for productive employment. Parts of the Peace River Region—Grande Prairie and a section of northeast British Columbia—have been made eligible, by designation, for industrial incentives. But the other more fundamental and far-reaching aspects of regional policy have not been applied. A region like the Peace could benefit immensely from the full application of the DREE regional development model. There are three aspects of the model which are particularly useful: (1) the federal-provincial nature of the policy/program processes; (2) the scope of development studies and plans which encompass economic, social and environmental aspects; and (3) the stress of federal-provincial agreements on implementation and the application of federal, as well as provincial funds, towards carrying out a systematically staged development program. What is now required is a creative adaptation of this approach to regions like the Peace, which provides both for the participation of region-based planning institutions, and greater private sector responsibility for the social costs of development.

Notes

1. Reference here is to the issue of "distribution and urbanization" raised by the Minister of State for Urban Affairs, and by the Green Paper on Immigration. Note the following: Honourable Barney Danson, Minister of State for Urban Affairs, "An Urban Strategy for Canada," Notes for an Address to The Conference Board in Canada, Winnipeg, April 2, 1975; and *1. Immigration Policy Perspectives*, A report of the Canadian Immigration and Policy Study, Manpower and Immigration Canada (Ottawa: Information Canada, 1974), pp. 8 – 13.
2. Robert S. Ratner, "Citizens' views on urban problems in Vancouver: Report on Phase III of the Vancouver Urban Futures project," External Research Paper C.73.2 (Ottawa: Ministry of State for Urban Affairs, 1973), p. 29.
3. D. Michael Ray and Thomas N. Brewis, "The Geography of Income and Its Correlates," *Canadian Geographer*, Vol. 20, No. 1, 1976, p. 69.
4. *Ibid.*, p. 69.
5. John Friedmann, *Regional Development Policy* (Cambridge, Massachusetts: Massachusetts Institute of Technology Press, 1966), p. 15.
6. John Friedmann, *Urbanization, Planning and National Development* (Beverly Hills: Sage Publications, 1973), p. 50.
7. Table 1.11 in Chapter 1 in this text; and Ronald W. Crowley, "Population distribution: perspectives and policies," Discussion Paper B.74.25 (Ottawa: Ministry of State for Urban Affairs, 1974), p. 6.
8. *The Livable Region 1976/1986: Proposals to Manage the Growth of Greater Vancouver* (Vancouver: Greater Vancouver Regional District, 1975), pp. 5, 8, 18.
9. *Regional Town Centres: a Policy Report* (Vancouver: Greater Vancouver Regional District, November 1975 draft), pp. 44 – 51.
10. *Ibid.*, pp. 15, 23.
11. *Ibid.*, p. 47. Reference to the medium-sized Canadian city that follows is St. Catharines, Ontario, as reported in the following: John N. Jackson, *The Canadian City, Space, Form, Quality* (Toronto: McGraw Hill Ryerson Limited, 1973), p. 164.
12. *Ibid.*, p. 3.
13. *Ibid.*, pp. 4, 9, 11.
14. *Ibid.*, pp. 12 – 17.
15. *Ibid.*, pp. 25 – 32.
16. *Ibid.*, p. 12.
17. *Ibid.*, Appendix 1, "Corporations Survey," p. 13.
18. *Ibid.*, pp. 48, 50, 54, 55 and Appendix 2, "Cultural Inventory," p. 9.
19. *Ibid.*, p. 35.
20. *Ibid.*, p. 34.
21. *Ibid.*, p. 36.
22. *Ibid.*, pp. 38, 39 and 41.
23. L. O. Gertler, *Regional Planning in Canada* (Montreal: Harvest House, 1972), pp. 71 – 85.
24. C. D. Burke and D. J. Ireland, "Growth Centres in Atlantic Canada," (Paper presented at the Conference on Growth Centres and Development Policy in Halifax, Nova Scotia, April 10 and 11, 1975), Table 1; and *Canada Year Book, 1973* (Ottawa: Information Canada, 1973), pp. 211, 219.
25. John Curry, "Saint John: A Port 100 Years Ago – A Future Today," briefing paper (Waterloo: University of Waterloo, School of Urban and Regional Planning, 1975), p. 6.
26. *Comprehensive Community Plan, Saint John, N.B.* (Saint John: City of Saint John, Planning Department, 1972), pp. 1-5.
27. *Ibid.*, 1 – 1, 1 – 2.
28. Curry, *op. cit.*, pp. 1 – 3; and John Porteous. ' "Why its new container terminal means so much to Saint John," *Financial Post*, February 8, 1975.

216   CHANGING CANADIAN CITIES

29. Letter from David A. Carter, Co-ordinator, Atlantic Region, Ministry of State for Urban Affairs, November 6, 1975.
30. Gertler, *op. cit.*, pp. 84, 85; and letter from Carter.
31. *Comprehensive Community Plan, op. cit.*, p. 2 – 1.
32. *Ibid.*, pp. 4 – 2, 3, 5 – 5, 5 – 11, 6 – 2, 6 – 5, 8 – 1; and Curry, *op. cit.*, p. 7.
33. Curry, *op. cit.*, pp. 5 – 7, 8; and John Porteous, "Saint John approves new waterfront development," *Financial Post*, February 22, 1975.
34. Curry, *op. cit.*, p. 6; and Porteous, "Saint John approves new waterfront development," *op. cit.*
35. Curry, *op. cit.*
36. Burke and Ireland, *op. cit.*, pp. 6, 7, 13, 14, Tables V, X; and letter from Carter, pp. 2 and 3.
37. Burke and Ireland, *op. cit.*, pp. 14, 28 and 29.
38. Ralph R. Krueger and Raymond G. Corder, *Canada: A New Geography* (Toronto and Montreal: Holt, Rinehart and Winston of Canada, Limited, 1968), p. 150; and *Patterns for the Future: A regional policy plan for the Peace River region of Alberta* (Grande Prairie: Peace River Regional Planning Commission, 1974), Preface.
    These introductory remarks on the Peace draw, in addition to the above, on the following: *The Preliminary Regional Plan* (Grande Prairie: Peace River Regional Planning Commission, 1973), Map 9 and p. 63; *Development and Planning Concepts* (Dawson Creek: Peace River-Liard Regional District, Planning Department, 1972), pp. 27 and 28; and Harry Harker, "The Peace River Region," briefing paper (Waterloo: University of Waterloo, School of Urban and Regional Planning, 1975), p. 2.
39. *The Preliminary Regional Plan, op. cit.*, pp. 28, 29, 35, 36 and 41; *Development and Planning Concepts, op. cit.*, pp. 30, 37, 53, 54 and Map 12; Harker, p. 9; *Location of a Steel Plant in the Peace River-Liard Region* (Dawson Creek: Peace River-Liard Regional District, Planning Department, 1973); and *Canada Year Book, 1973*, pp. 334 and 587.
40. *Development and Planning Concepts, op. cit.*, pp. 15 – 18; *The Preliminary Regional Plan, op. cit.*, pp. 71 and 79; and *Patterns for the Future, op. cit.*, pp. 17 and 22.
41. Harker, *op. cit.*, pp. 2 and 3.
42. *The Preliminary Regional Plan, op. cit.*, p. 15.
43. *Patterns for the Future, op. cit.*, p. 4.
44. Harker, *op. cit.*, pp. 5 – 7.
45. Friedmann, *Urbanization, Planning and National Development, op. cit.*, pp. 43 – 46; and *The Preliminary Regional Plan, op. cit.*, p. 2.
46. *People of the Peace, Their Goals and Objectives* (Grande Prairie: Peace River Regional Planning Commission, 1972), pp. 31, 32, 38, 41, 47 – 49, 60 and 63.
47. *The Preliminary Regional Plan*, Introduction, *op. cit.*
48. *Ibid.*, pp. 34 – 75.
49. *Patterns for the Future, op. cit.*, pp. 2, 13, and 14.
50. *Ibid.*, p. 16.
51. *Ibid.*, p. 15.
52. *Ibid.*, p. 15; and *The Preliminary Regional Plan, op. cit.*
53. *The Preliminary Regional Plan, op. cit.*, Map 12.
54. *Ibid.*, pp. 37, 57, 62 and 68; and *Patterns for the Future, op. cit.*, p. 29.
55. Harker, *op. cit.*, "The Peace River Region," pp. 8 and 9.
56. *Economic Incentives for the Peace River-Liard Region* (Dawson Creek: Peace River-Liard Regional District, January 1972), pp. 6 and 7.
57. *The Livable Region 1976/1986, op. cit.*, p. 5.
58. *National Housing Act*, Part VI.1, New Communities (Ottawa: Information Canada, 1973).
59. Burke and Ireland, *op. cit.*, p. 22.
60. *Ibid.*, pp. 5 and 6.

CHAPTER 5

Urban Environment: The Quality Dynamic

Environment, Settlement, and Regional Diversity

PERSPECTIVES

Moshe Safdie, the creator of Habitat, one of the enduring artifacts and ideas associated with Expo '67, has recently (December, 1974) spoken about the link between national policy and the quality of urban life. He said:

> The decisions that most profoundly affect the quality of life of the individual habitat, are made at the highest levels, such as those policies that determine the national and regional patterns of human settlement, the relationship and location of industry and agriculture, and the availability of transportation networks at all levels. Put in other terms, the decisions that determine whether families will be housed at densities of one or one hundred to the acre, or whether they will live in a city of a hundred thousand people, one million people, or ten million people, are the decisions which most profoundly affect the quality of their life and the economic framework surrounding it... We must therefore first give attention to the policies and decisions that affect the number, size and shape of cities, their distribution in the regional and national network, and the very broad patterns of settlement which are the very basic framework of a national economy.[1]

Safdie's remarks serve the purpose of summarizing in a few well chosen words the national level policy issues that have been the preoccupation of this book up to this point. Of particular importance is the light he sheds on the reciprocal nature of national and regional environments and policies. Speaking from his knowledge of Israel's attempt to restrain the growth of the coastal megalopolis, he points out that economic measures alone have not been sufficient to achieve the desired dispersal into new centres. The policy has foundered on a crucial element: the limitations of the cultural and social life of new settlements like Be'er Sheva, Dismona and Elat. He concludes: "Dispersal cannot be achieved as long as the qualities of life offered are not comparable to the metropolitan city."[2] National settlement policies may be prescribed, but in a free society realization of change depends on the response of people to the options offered.

We must give attention to the other side of the equation: the environments of Canada's human settlements, the quality of those environments and the quality of life that those environments accommodate. While recognizing that these terms are often used interchangeably in popular discussion, a distinction is made between quality of environment and quality of life. The difference is between the setting for life, and how that setting is experienced by individuals and groups. As one environmentalist has expressed it: "The texture, the intimacy, and the integration of contact between inner reality, the subject, and the outer reality, the environment, predicates the quality of life."[3] An inclusive view of the quality of cities and towns may include both aspects – the setting and the response – as long as the distinction between the two related components is understood.

We see the urban environments of Canada consisting of several interacting elements: (1) life-support systems of air, water and soil; (2) distinctive endowments of natural resources and landscape features, which include the relationship of city to broad land form, vegetation, climatic and soil regions; (3) man-made features expressed in structures, in the occupation and use of land and in the form of human settlement; and (4) the cultural environment, which constitutes the living human forces – peoples' values, wants, lifestyles and the various political, economic and other institutions and the technologies that they employ to attain satisfaction. The perspective must be systemic in the sense that these elements interact and affect each other, either to the detriment or benefit of the total environment (and interact with external systems). And it must be dynamic in the sense that we must recognize a process of almost continuous change. All of these elements together comprise the habitat within which people live, work and raise their children, and seek fulfilment of their aspirations.[4]

It follows from our concept of environment that the urban regions

URBAN ENVIRONMENT 219

of Canada need to be understood in terms of their distinctive physical, constructed and cultural components. This is not merely a convenient tactic for explaining the urban regions of a big country. It is a search for the philosophical insight—a way of viewing the world—that will reveal the conditions that may be important to the "good life." This is placed in perspective by the eminent biologist, Dr. René Dubos:

> To realize the multifarious biological and spiritual potentialities of mankind requires an immense diversity of environments. The real problem therefore is to learn how environmental forces can be best managed to foster the various manifestations of happiness and creativity in mankind. Technology should have as its most important goal the creation of environments in which the widest range of human potentialities can unfold.[5]

From this viewpoint a look at the different types of urban regions in Canada is an exploration of the features which, in each case, contribute to the diversity and the stimulation of the Canadian urban experience, which is the basis of a high quality life. Only salient environmental elements will be identified – some of the positive features that indicate the very special regional potentials, as well as the weak links, the vulnerable elements which if not overcome threaten to disrupt the whole system.

EIGHT URBAN REGIONS

A feeling for the diversity of Canada's urban environments can be conveyed by examining some of the characteristics of eight selected regions. These places extend from the west coast to the east coast (Table 5.1). They represent every type of physical region except those associated with the Arctic and Sub-Arctic. Each has a different function (assuming there are some very real differences between a west and east coast port, and between a Prairie capital and the capital city of Quebec province which also has important ecclesiastical and cultural functions). The cities encompass a size range from 20,000 to over 1,000,000, with medium: around 150,000, to near-big: 500,000, in between. And they include settlements as old as Quebec, 1608, and as new as Penticton, 1908. The contrasting conditions in these places are presented in two phases: first, in this chapter which focuses on broad regional characteristics, and then in Chapter 8, concerned with the form of settlement, in which the personalities of the cities are brought into sharper focus. In each case, we seek out those salient features that illustrate critical difficulties as well as the special "genius" of each place.

Table 5.1. Eight Urban Regions – Broad Characteristics

Urban area	Land Form	Climatic	Natural Vegetation	Soils	Date of Establishment	Population 1971	Function
Vancouver	Western Cordillera Coast Mountains	West Coast	West Coast Forest	Mountain	1886	1,082,350	Port, West Coast
Penticton	Western Cordillera Interior Plateau and mountains	Mountain	Mountain	Mountain	1908	18,146	Agriculture, Tourism
Edmonton	Interior Plains Alberta Plains	Prairie	The Parklands	Black Grassland	1880	495,702	Regional Service Petrochemical
Regina	Interior Plains Saskatchewan Plains	Prairie	The Grassland	Brown Grassland	1883	140,734	Government
Hamilton	Great Lakes-St. Lawrence Lowlands [Lakes]	Lower Lakes	Deciduous Forest	Mixed Forest	1813	498,523	Manufacturing, Heavy
Sudbury	Canadian Shield	South Laurentian/ Cold Continental	Mixed Forest	Mixed Forest Coniferous Forest	1893	155,400	Mining, Manufacturing
Quebec City	Great Lakes-St. Lawrence Lowlands [River]	South Laurentian	Mixed Forest	Mixed Forest	1608	480,405	Government, Cultural
Saint John, N.B.	Appalachian	East Coast	Mixed Forest	Mixed Forest	1783	106,695	Port, East Coast

(1) Vancouver

The dominant environmental factor of Greater *Vancouver* is, by far, the Coast Mountains. While providing one of the most dramatic sites for a city anywhere in the world, the peaks of the north shore as well as the rugged slopes all along the Lower Fraser valley have the effect of confining the metropolis to a tenuous foothold along the coast (Fig. 5.1). These mountains provide protection from Arctic air during winter and are critical in the weather dynamics that produce heavy precipitation, which in turn produce the conditions of warmth and moisture for highly productive horticulture. But as a tangible "fence" they dramatize the increasingly inescapable choice that has to be made between growing food or housing families. Land is a critical issue.[6]

In these circumstances, planning for the region of Vancouver has a long and embattled history. What is most interesting is the emergence of a style of planning which holds promise of becoming a major cultural force. Under the banner of "livable region" a vivid image of a humane urban civilization is beginning to crystallize: moderate growth, a wider housing and transportation choice, open space conservancies, a preserved biosphere, and the opportunity to enjoy a town life, with cultural, business and personal services closer to home. Canadians have good reason to watch this closely for at least two reasons: people – the people of the region through community groups and citizens' policy committees have had much to do in shaping the philosophy of the plan; and the ideal of the good regional life is linked to a regional district with power to implement and act.[7]

(2) Penticton

Cactus is not a plant usually associated with Canada. Its occurrence alongside the lush peach, apricot, cherry, plum and apple orchards around *Penticton* is a clue to the transformation over a period of fifty years of the near-desert conditions of the arid climatic zone in the southern Okanagan valley. Viewing the city from a plane on its descent from Kelowna (Figure 5.2) brings several regional factors into focus: urban settlement and farming confined to the valley – bottom and lower terraces in the few square miles between Okanagan Lake and Skaha Lake, and the slopes of the dominating Cascade Mountains; the omnipresent irrigation sprinklers; the highways converging from the west (Vancouver) and south (the State of Washington); the approaching airport runway; and, not least, the stunning beauty of the scene.[8]

While this setting has proved congenial to both fruit trees and tourists, the area now faces a serious dilemma. The orchard culture

Figure 5.1. Vancouver – aerial view

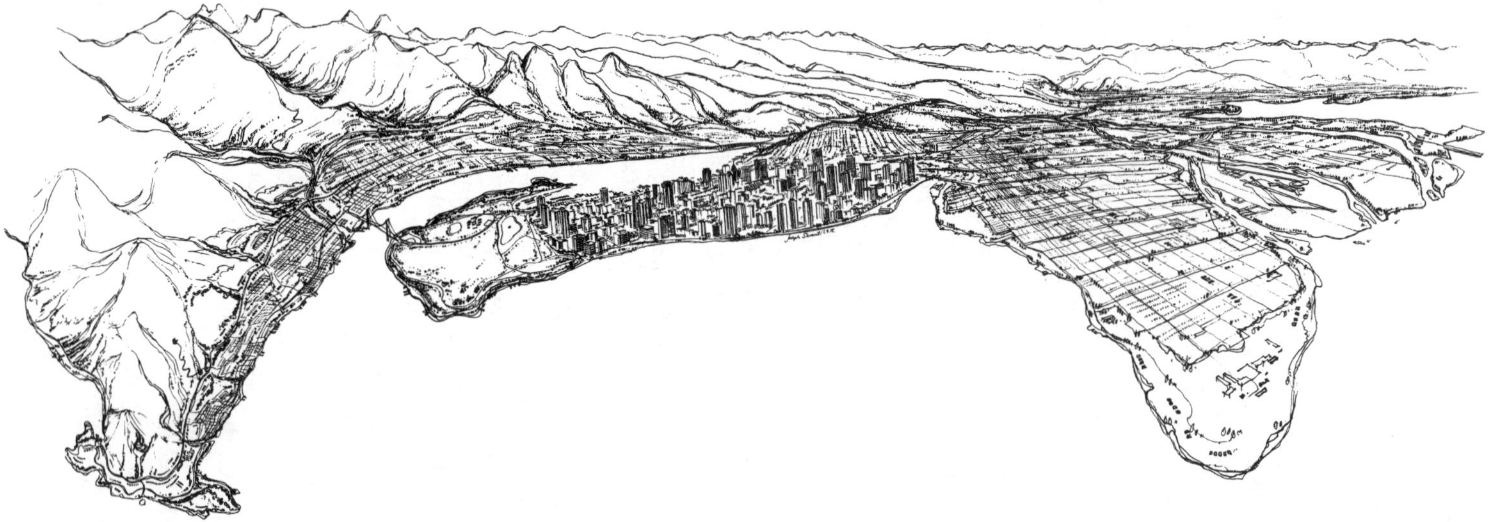

Figure 5.2. Penticton – aerial view

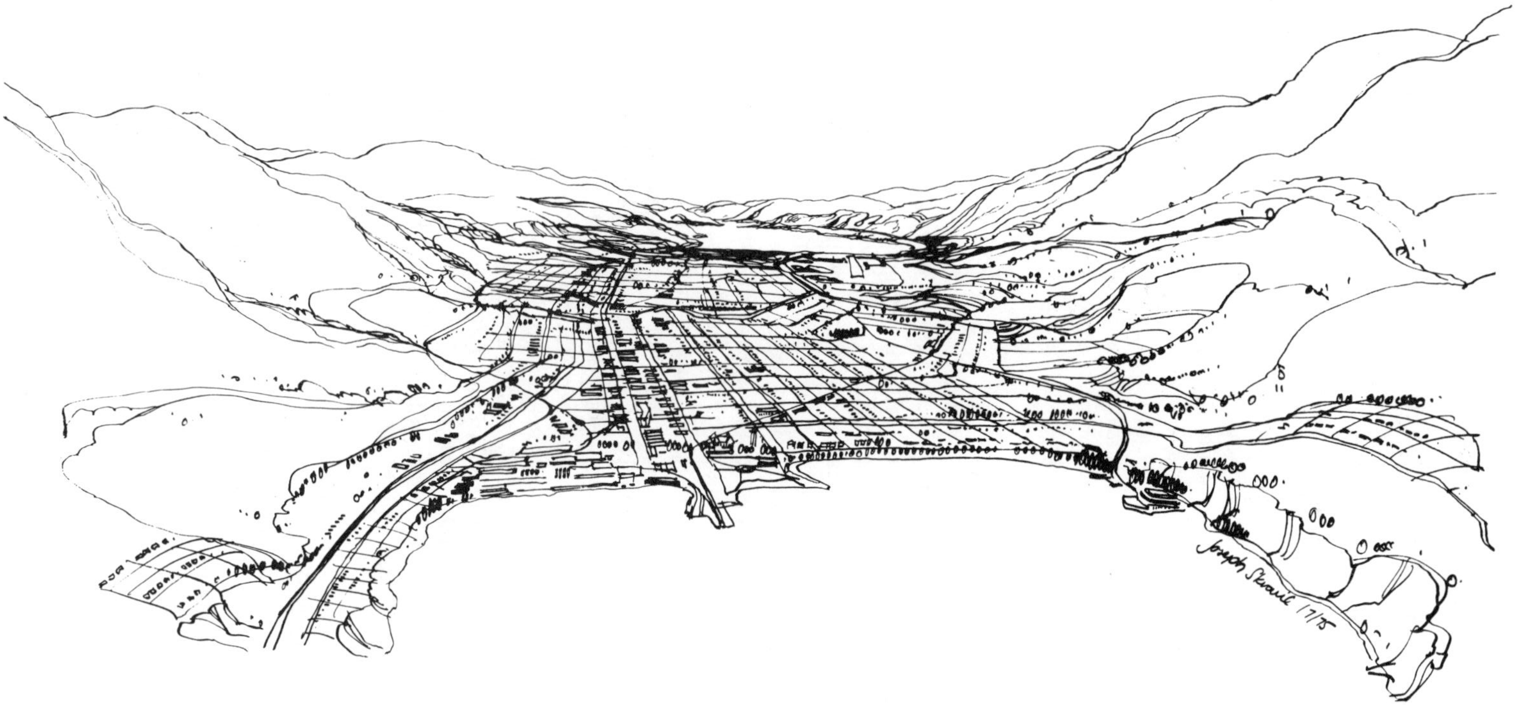

is characterized by high capital investment, a long waiting period for new plantings, and the most precise management, soil and microclimate requirements. It will flourish only where there is a high degree of stability in the use of land, where land prices are moderate, where orchards are not disrupted by intruding developments (spraying and maintenance of insect control, and homes do not always happily co-exist), and where there is not too much concentration of carbon monoxide fumes. By contrast, the tourist culture means pressure on land use and land prices and on the lakes (which teeter on the verge of pollution); an annual invasion of cars, and a general push for urbanization and commercialization. The constraints of site and environment make the attainment of ecological balance between these two sustaining activities an inescapable concern of public policy.

(3) *Edmonton*
Edmonton's location in the black belt soil zone of Alberta provides few physical barriers to growth – although downstream (east) sewage disposal and a petro-chemical industry give a Western orientation to urban development (Figure 5.3). The growth push in the region, if it persists at its twenty-year average rate, will produce a metropolis of a million people before the end of the century. The management of growth has become the central issue.

Much of the dynamic and appeal of Edmonton during its major development phase has been the city's capacity to temper the ideology of growth and money-making with a struggle for a humane city. This has been expressed in its inner life through the arts and education and the maintenance of vigorous folk cultures, and in its outer life through community associations, action to preserve some of the city's history (for example, by the Strathcona Historical Group), through neighbourhood design, public land management and the sustaining of a regional planning process. Edmonton now faces several challenges, not new in kind, but in intensity. One is the creation of a land bank to draw off some of the speculative steam of the land market – the effectiveness in this regard of Mill Woods, the southeast "major land assembly project," is yet to be demonstrated. Another is to extend the valley and ravine-based parkland network in keeping with the expansion of settlement. Still another is to set a clear course for future regional growth. The choices between metropolitan concentration or dispersal into new communities, or some mix of these options, which have been debated since the mid-fifties now constitute an urgent reality. Perhaps more than in any other area of public decision-making these choices will affect the quality and cost of living.[9]

Figure 5.3. Edmonton – aerial view

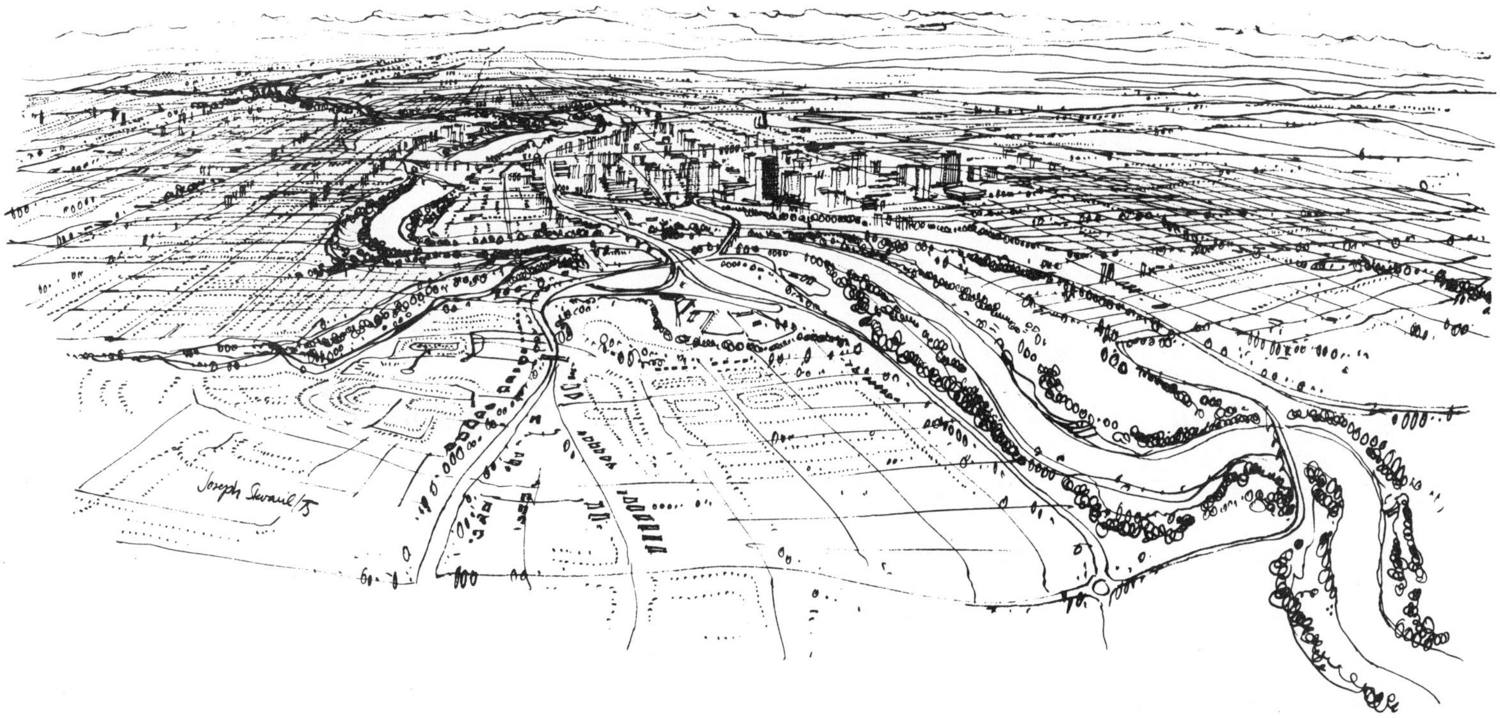

Regina

Regina has developed in defiance of the comments that greeted its birth, such as the "good wishes" of the Manitoba *Free Press, circa* 1883: "The place is no more suited for a townsite than any other flat, dry, barren section of the line of the railway." The long arm of the past is still observed in the predominant grid established by its original survey, nested in the larger square mile farmland grid (Figure 5.4). The constructive, pioneering pragmatic spirit remains as the city's greatest asset—an intangible with substantial reverberations. This is expressed not only in the city's multi-purpose Wascana Centre but in ambitious, complex schemes like the relocation of the central railway marshalling yards, through the mechanisms of the federal Railway Relocation Act (1974). In this respect, Regina will become an edifying demonstration of the potentials or pitfalls, of three-level policy formation and program delivery.[10]

In one aspect of its life, Regina reflects a problem which is a Prairie phenomenon and a Canadian concern of the 'seventies. And this is the alienated and depressed position of the native peoples who have been drifting in from the reserves and other rural areas to the inner city. As the president of the Métis Society of Saskatchewan has stated about this category of the urban poor: "There is almost no hope for the expression of individual potential. Instead, disease, insecurity, hunger, cold, injustice, harassment and oppression prevail."[11] As long as conditions like these exist anywhere in Canada then cities cannot in any intrinsic sense be called communities.

(5) *Sudbury*

The artist's conception of *Sudbury* highlights the dominance of its craggy landscape (Figure 5.5). It shows the city perched on the southern rim of the rocky nickel-bearing ridge, which is both the basis of its economic life, and barrier, on its north side, to its physical expansion.[12]

Sudbury represents an interesting case in the annals of regional development: while thirty years ago it was just a slightly larger than average dual enterprise resource town of about 30,000 souls, today it is well on its way to becoming a regional metropolis with a population five times larger. This is more than a statistical entry in the Census of Canada. There are important qualitative developments: Laurentian University, the Cambrian College of Applied Arts and Technology, Sudbury Theatre Centre, and generally a rapidly growing service sector. But the city will not attain its potentials, until it overcomes its problem of air pollution. The repercussions are both regional and local. One recent observer writes: "In summer, winds

Figure 5.4. Regina – aerial view

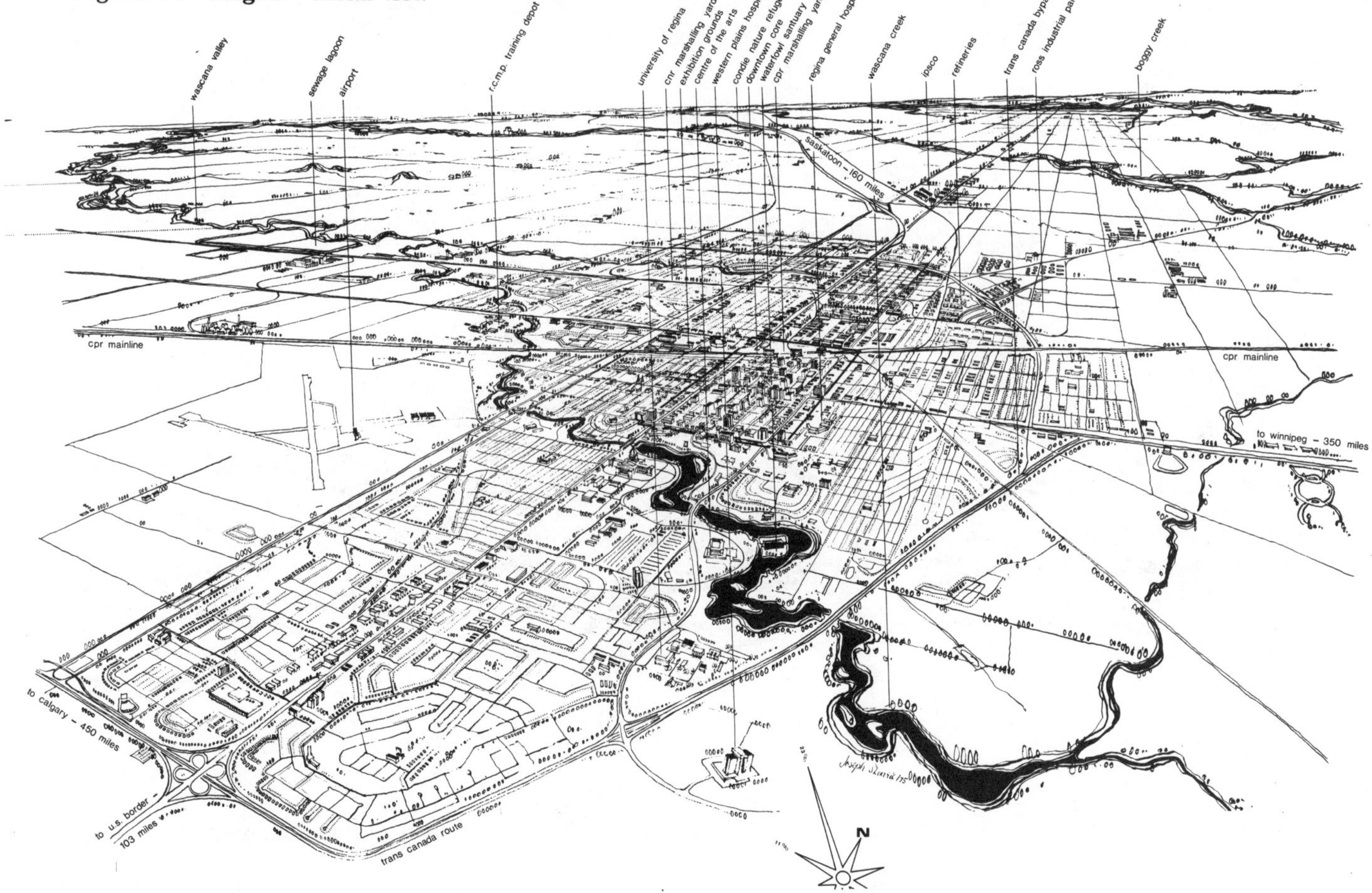

Figure 5.5. Sudbury – aerial view

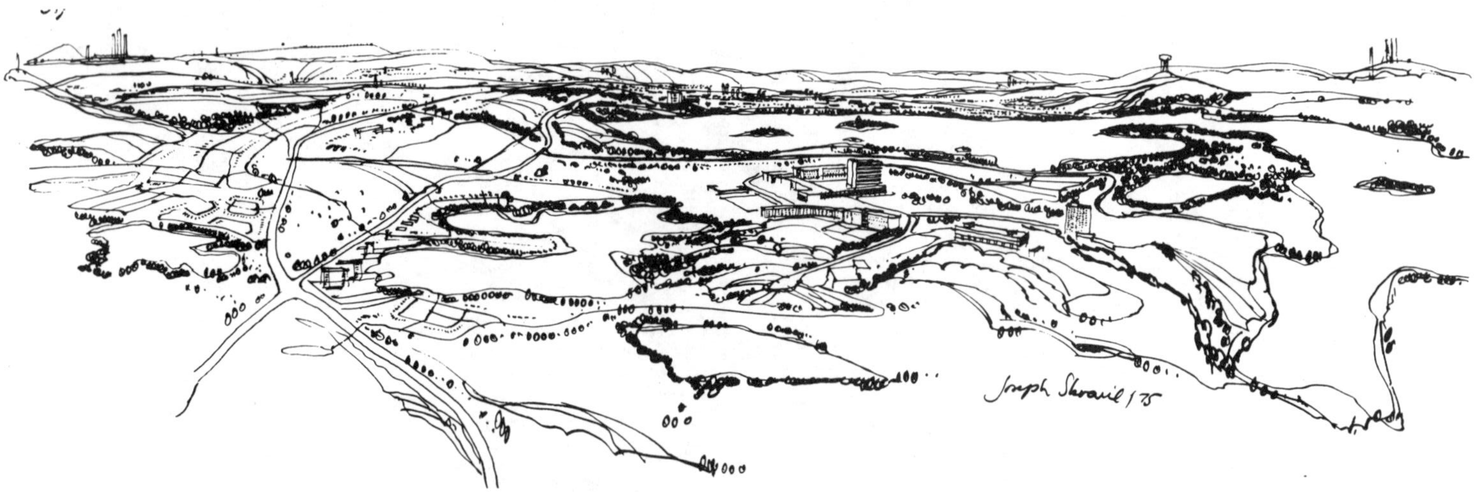

Figure 5.6. Hamilton – aerial view

originate from the southwest and this proves to be very detrimental to farming activities in the interior basin because the southerly winds spread sulphur fumes from the smelters throughout the limited farm areas."[13] And there are disquieting reports (November, 1975), not officially acknowledged, of an abnormally high incidence of lung cancer caused by excessive concentrations of sulphur dioxide.[14]

(6) *Hamilton*

At Clappison's Corners where Ontario Highway 6 crosses the crest of the Niagara Escarpment, the towers of *Hamilton* come suddenly into view (Figure 5.6). Here it is possible to capture an immediate sense of a major motif in Hamilton's development, the interplay and at times conflict between its industrial and environmental base. Powerful regional factors make Hamilton the steel centre of Canada: a sheltered deep water port on the St. Lawrence-Great Lakes systems; proximity to rail and major highways, and to the major market focused at Toronto; and until recently enough expansion space to attain the threshold of scale economies in steel.[15]

Hamilton's success has meant much to the economy of Canada, but the balance sheet of regional benefits and costs has still to be submitted. The rise of Canada's "environmental conscience" in the late 'sixties has made the steel companies good corporate citizens, but improvements are lamentably slow. And provincial data show that Hamilton air has, by a substantial margin, the highest concentration of suspended particulate matter among twenty Census Metropolitan Areas.[16]

The environmental theme in Hamilton's development has been closely associated with the Niagara Escarpment. Rising 250 feet parallel to the lakeshore, two to three miles inland, this mountain has tended to direct growth in an east-west direction. The escarpment is part of a continuous network of green space broadening out into the richly wooded Dundas valley, a natural setting that inspired one writer to say that "Hamilton was able to develop its industrial potential without sacrificing the beauty of its setting."[17]

But the region's environmental integrity remains precarious. Since the early 'fifties, development has spread to the top of the mountain and has expanded to Dundas. In late 1974, the Hamilton-Wentworth Regional Council faced a sharp growth/conservation issue. By a majority of one vote, the Council decided on a major expansion of a sewage treatment plant, discharging into the low wetland marsh of Cootes Paradise, a unique ecological sanctuary in the Dundas Valley. The move was opposed by the Hamilton Harbour Commission, the Hamilton Regional Conservation Authority and the Royal Botanical Gardens, owner of the Paradise.[18]

(7) Quebec City

The stamp of geography on city is powerfully expressed at *Quebec City* (Figure 5.7). The broad, deep estuary of the St. Lawrence encouraged a port; the high cliffs provided a site for strategic fortifications at the gateway to the interior; and the rock ledge at their base formed a large natural berthing space for ships. The fertile Ile d'Orléans and the Quebec Plain gave an agricultural base, and the Shield to the north provided a recreational hinterland, as well as the forests and hydro power for a pulp and paper industry. With these materials, history through an evolution of about 370 years produced a vibrant metropolis of half a million people.[19]

This metropolis, however, has not been immune from the perverse tendency of urban-industrial man to foul his own nest. Reflecting on the conditions of the early 'seventies, one study observes that "there are no longer any public bathing beaches to accommodate the 500,000 inhabitants of the Quebec metropolitan area."[20] There appear to be three major factors at work which limit the public use of the vast mainly crown-owned Parc des Laurentides. One is the practice of clear-cutting, by owners of timber concessions, which induces soil erosion and stream pollution. Another is the policy of leasing lake shores and ski slopes to companies, clubs and associations which enforce exclusive use of their "properties." And a third is the spread of city-based pollution to the St. Lawrence and its tributaries. As long as such conditions (one and three) prevail, the eco-system on which the human community depends is in jeopardy.

Notwithstanding these regional concerns, the city has one great asset on which to build: its historical and cultural depth. This is the magic which accounts for Quebec's perennial appeal to the North American tourist, thirsting for an experience that is not just another replica of standardized urban America. Concern for the continuity of the city's unique environment (sketched in Chapter 8) finds expression in concepts which may hold the key to creative renewal, like Jean Cimon's proposal to turn Old Quebec into a car-free zone, with underground parking outside its walls, and minibuses for internal circulation. It is not inconceivable that the same pride of place and heritage will produce the dynamic for curbing environmental degradation.[21]

(8) Saint John

At a time when *Saint John, New Brunswick* may be at a turning point in its growth cycle (Chapter 4), some words of the novelist, Hugh MacLennan, come to mind: "Not only is New Brunswick a geographical offshoot of New England: the people inhabiting the Saint John valley from Woodstock to the Reversible Falls are nearly

Figure 5.7. Quebec City – aerial view

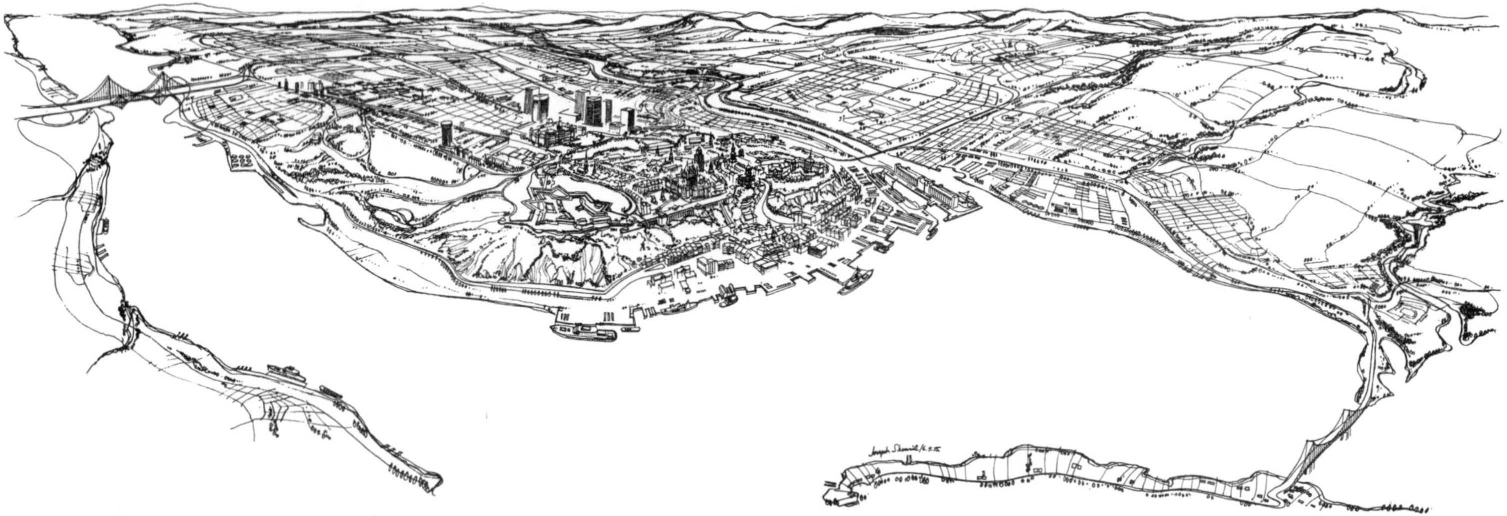

Figure 5.8. Saint John – aerial view

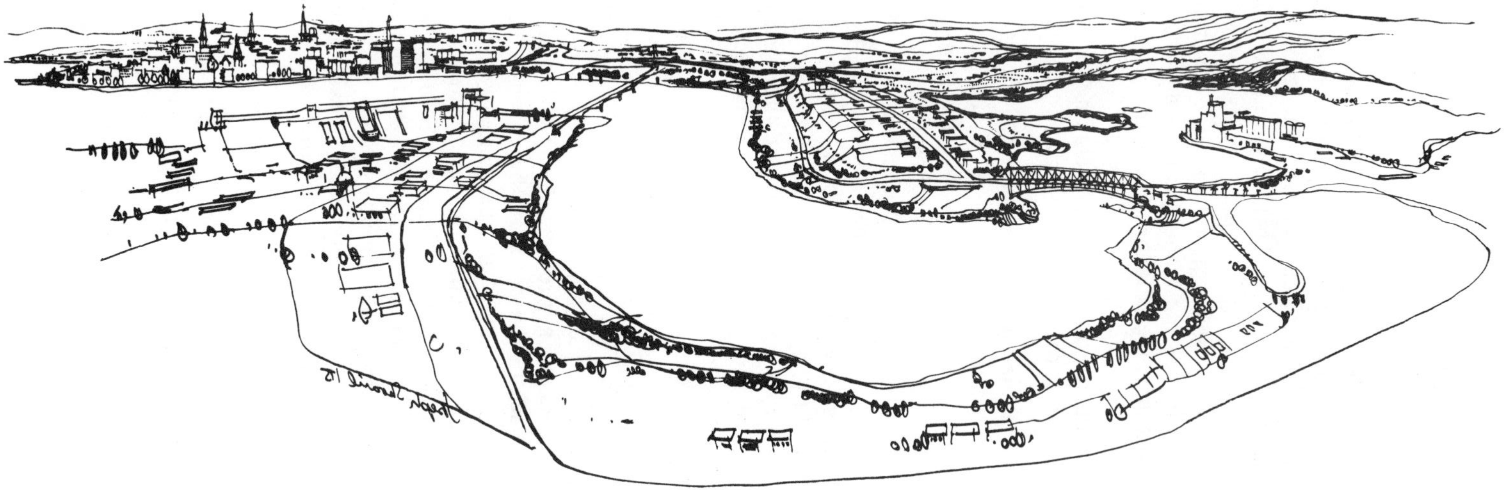

all descended from the original Anglo-Saxon stock which pioneered the United States.... The Saint John River people along the lower reaches are such staunch retainers of the past that 'conservative' is too weak a word to apply to them."[22] This background, which is by no means universal in Canada, makes one curious concerning the way metropolitan Saint John will respond to the growth prospects arising out of such initiatives as the modernization of the deep water port (Figure 5.8). Must it travel the urbanization path of central Canada?

Great expectations notwithstanding, some commentators remain skeptical about Saint John's prospects:

> Saint John has continued to be handicapped by its political, institutional and cultural subservience to Fredericton, and its non-central location with respect to both its own provincial population and that of the Atlantic region. Its metropolitan functions within New Brunswick are in fact shared with Fredericton, the provincial capital, and with Moncton, the most important railway centre in the Maritimes. It was only in 1964, for example, that the University of New Brunswick in Saint John was established as a two-year institution; and the third year of a degree program must still be completed at Fredericton. Moncton has replaced Saint John as a major wholesale-distribution centre for much of the province, and has established itself as the supply centre for Prince Edward Island, much of Nova Scotia and even for Newfoundland.[23]

An interesting question raised by this kind of diagnosis is whether intercity rivalry, perceived as a problem for Saint John, can be turned into a virtue. If each of the cities can be developed as unique parts of an internally complementary and integrated whole – a development triangle – then the communities of New Brunswick may become places in which a cherished way of life can be preserved, while the province as a whole experiences expanded social and economic horizons. And the lower Saint John could remain, as MacLennan says, "a wonderful country for growing boys...[who can]...live close to nature and at the same time see an integrated society reduced to a boy's scale."[24]

This brief kaleidoscope of Canadian urban conditions conveys some sense of the diversity of the Canadian urban environment. A substantial opportunity remains to attain Dubos' criterion of environments which through the "variety of stimulating experiences" they offer will encourage human potentialities to unfold.[25] The very richness of the national mosaic, however, means that the urge for environmental betterment must be realized through sets of regional conditions that are distinctive in their physical and cultural characteristics. Appreciation of this, both in terms of the possibilities and problems that each area offers, must be the beginning of policy wisdom.

We hope that the eight city sketches have provided some perspective on the regional factors that shape our urban environments. Efforts to influence human settlement through public policy or private action must, as well, be informed by a comparative and hopefully systematic view of conditions as we find them in Canada's major cities. That exploration will now commence.

The Quality of Metropolitan Environments

The urge for an improved quality of urban life has led to a search for effective ways of recording and monitoring existing conditions. Sometime during the late 'fifties these efforts began to be dignified in both technical and popular literature by the term "social indicators." The underlying rationale goes something like this: if we can find ways of showing on a consistent and regular basis how we are doing, say in providing housing or education or controlling pollution, then we could identify needs and gaps, and *do something about it*. In this sense indicators would be *descriptive* and *normative*. They would enable the comparison of performance with some agreed standard or objective, and they would record changes in performance from one period to another. As such, they would provide a basis for remedial action.[26]

While the interest in this kind of measure of Canadian urban conditions has valid roots in social change and social outlook, producing a set of useful indicators poses a number of difficult problems, both of concept and technique. Of particular concern, are the questions: What measures are true expressions of the quality of urban life? Is it possible to obtain consistent, comparable data at regular intervals for the urban areas of Canada? Can indicators be defined that are independent, that is, measure different aspects of the quality of life?

A response to these questions posed by a research team of the federal Urban Affairs Ministry in the fall of 1975 has produced a comprehensive look at an array of conditions in the twenty-two Census Metropolitan Areas: the urban places with populations of 100,000 or more (in 1971). Thirty-two indicators are presented, reflecting "major societal concerns" and measuring "key characteristics of the quality of urban life," and grouped under three broad headings: social development, economic development and physical development (Tables 5.2, 3, and 4 list and describe eighteen of these).[27]

This list represents the most sophisticated statistics that the state of the art can now produce on the basis of existing information and the indicators included have been validated as statistically independent, with only "minimal overlap in the urban patterns 'explained'." Figures 5.9 to 5.26 present graphs of eighteen selected indicators for metropolitan areas, plotted from west to east, Victoria to St. John's. The five metropolitan areas with the "best" environments are identified on the graph. The original study list has been reduced to exclude measures which are ambiguous – there is little agreement on how they are to be interpreted; which reflect inputs rather than output or performance-oriented measures; and for which comparable data is not available for the whole group of metropolitan areas. Examples of the first are various indicators on population like the index of "population turnover" or migration; for some, low turnover represents desirable stability, for others a stultifying lack of dynamism. The second excluded type are such measures of facilities as "amount of floor space in commercial meeting establishments per 100 population" and "number of hospital beds per 1,000 population." Three important indicators which meet the performance criteria are not shown because the data for several cities are missing; these are "air quality: suspended particulate matter," "air quality: sulphur dioxide concentration" and "public transportation ridership: fare passengers carried per capita."

A first look at the indicators suggests somewhat random and surprising results. Quebec City, Canada's most venerable urban community, and the seat of French culture in Canada, has the lowest level of public library patronage in the country, while the highest level is in the upstart Prairie city of Saskatoon. Another Western city, Regina, has close to three times the per capita criminal code offences of the metropolis of Montreal. Victoria, renowned for its image of the sedate, safe life, has proportionately six times more juvenile offenders than Windsor on the doorstep of Detroit. When average income of taxpayers is adjusted for housing costs the richest metropolitan area in the country is the principal regional centre of the resource frontier Saguenay system, Chicoutimi-Jonquière, which enjoys at well over sixty-five hundred dollars a level which is respectively a full 8 and 9 per cent higher than that of Toronto and Vancouver. The people of Halifax enjoy (1970 – 73) a rate of new housing construction in relation to new households which is two and a half times that of Vancouver. And the safest place in the country, from the viewpoint of fire and automobile hazards is, believe it or not, Toronto.[28]

Table 5.2. Selected Urban Indicators, Social Development

Indicator	Aspect Measured	Source
1. Voter Turnout for Municipal Elections, Since 1969	State of civic participation	Survey, Institute for Local Government, Queen's University
2. Public Library Usage: Annual Per Capita Book Loans, 1971	Availability and use of books; interest in reading	Recreation Canada, for municipal and regional libraries
3. Number of Criminal Offences Per 10,000 Population, 1971	Crimes committed against person and property	From police departments to Statistics Canada Catalogue 85 – 205)
4. Number of Juveniles Charged with Criminal Code Offences, 1971	Juvenile criminality: indirectly, family problems	From police departments for population 7 to 15 (or 17 and 18) depending on the province; published by Statistics Canada (Catalogue 85 – 205)
5. Number of Missing Persons per 10,000 Population, 1971	Social and family disorganization; social problems	From police departments to Statistics Canada (Catalogue 85 – 205)
6. Educational Achievement: Per cent of 20 – 34 age group not presently in school and with Grade 10 education or less, 1971	Proportion of people under-educated in relation to prevailing employment qualifications	**Statistics Canada (Special Tabulation)**
7. Illegitimate Births per 1,000 Births, 1973	Social disorder, due to family structure	From local registrars to Statistics Canada (Catalogue 84 – 204)

Table 5.3. Selected Urban Indicators, Economic Development

Indicator	Aspect Measured	Source
8. Average (Mean) Income After Federal Tax for Tax Filers, 1972	Economic well-being	National Revenue Taxation Statistics, 1974 Edition (Annual)
9. Average Adjusted Income of Tax Filers (After Federal Tax and Adjusted for Comparative Housing Costs)	Economic well-being	National Revenue Taxation Statistics, 1974 Edition (Annual) *Canadian Housing Statistics, 1974*, CMHC
10. Occupational Status Index (Per Cent labour force in three highest skilled categories)	Labour market drawing power for skilled people	Statistics Canada, Census of Canada, 1971, Catalogue 94 – 719
11. Unemployment Rates Among Active Labour Force Participants, 1971	Employment stability/instability	Statistics Canada, Census of Canada 1971, Catalogue 94 – 703. Data for "active" labour force, employed within the previous 18 months
12. Female Labour Force Participation Rates for Age Group 20 – 64, 1971	Availability and taking of job opportunities by women	Statistics Canada, Census of Canada, 1971, Catalogue 94 – 706
13. Annual Strike Days Lost Per 100 Persons in the Labour Force	Job dissatisfaction or insecurity. Union strength Incipient social breakdown	Unpublished Department of Labour data for strike days and Statistics Canada – 1971 labour force data (1971 Census, Catalogue 94 – 705)

Table 5.4. Selected Urban Indicators, Physical Development

Indicator	Aspect Measured	Source
14. Average Estimated Total Costs for New Single-Detached Dwellings Financed under NHA, 4th Quarter 1974	Purchase price of available housing	CMHC Statistical Handbook, 1974
15. Housing Choice: Vacancy Rates in Apartment Structures of Six Units and Over, December, 1974	Choice of housing for movers to or within a city Indirectly, a symptom of price competition	Canadian Housing Statistics, 1974, CMHC
16. Percentage of Children Living in Apartment Units, 1971	Problems related to physical environment of young families	Statistics Canada, 1971 Census of Canada, Special Tabulation
17. New Housing Units Constructed Per Additional Household, 1970–73	Balance between housing demand and supply	Statistics Canada, Catalogue 91–207 (annual) and Canadian Housing Statistics, 1974, CMHC
18. Fire and Automobile Hazard Index, Adjusted per Thousand Population, 1971	Probability of property loss due to fire or traffic accident. Indirect measure of safety	"Traffic Enforcement Statistics 1971," Statistics Canada, Catalogue 85–206 (annual) "Fire losses in Canada 1971," Report of the Dominion Fire Commissioner

240 CHANGING CANADIAN CITIES

Figure 5.9. Voter Turnout: Percentage Voting in Municipal Elections, since 1969

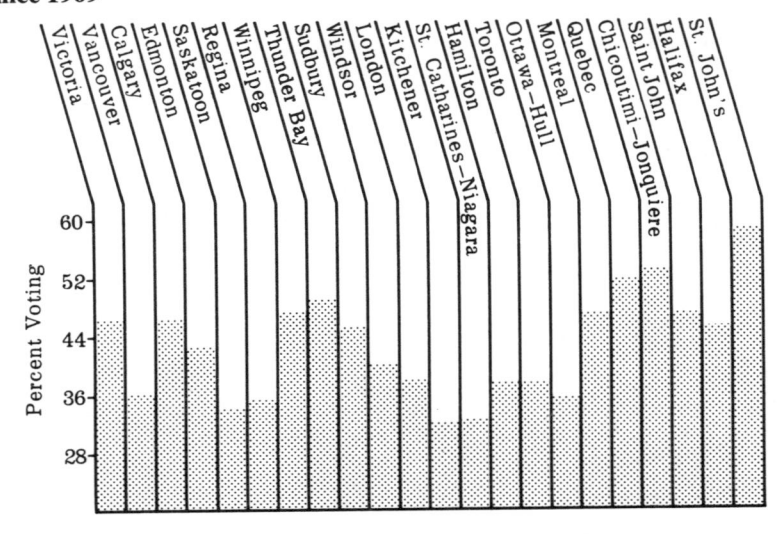

Figure 5.10. Public Library Usage: Annual per Capita Book Loans, 1971

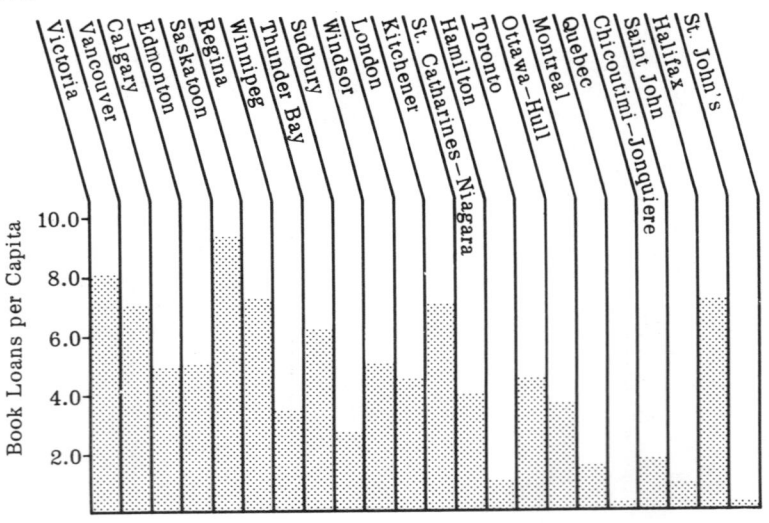

Source: John N. Stewart, D. Belgue, W. Bond, et. al., *Urban Indicators: Quality of Life Comparisons for Canadian Cities* (Ottawa: Information Canada, 1976), pp. 41 and 25.

URBAN ENVIRONMENT 241

Figure 5.11. Number of Criminal Code Offences per 10,000 Population, 1971

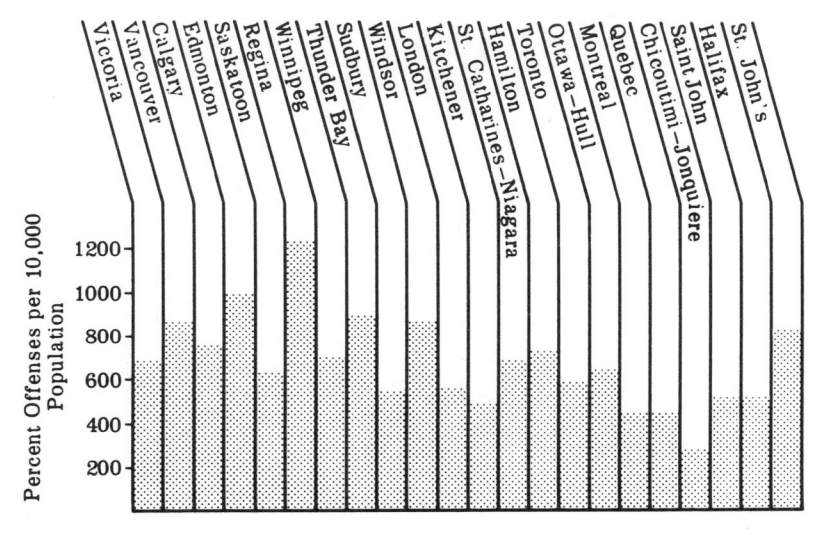

Figure 5.12. Number of Juveniles Charged with Criminal Code Offences per 10,000 Persons, 1971

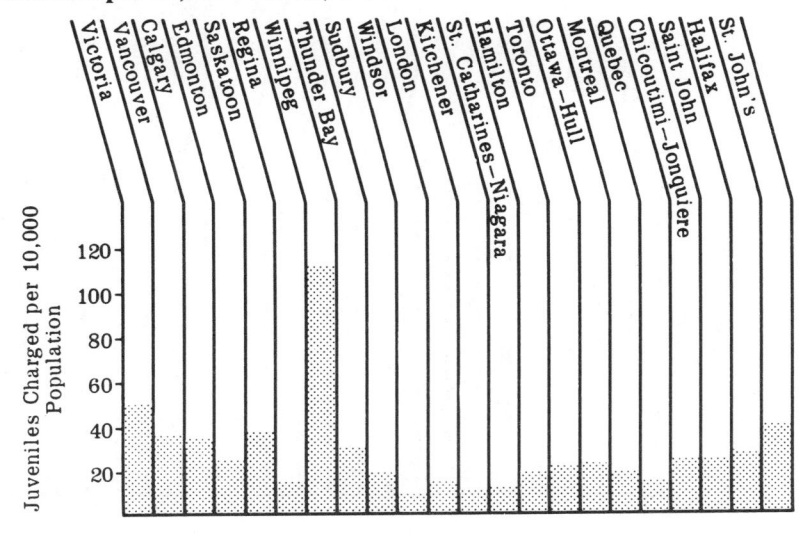

Source: John N. Stewart, *et. al, Urban Indicators: Quality of Life Comparisons for Canadian Cities* (Ottawa: Information Canada, 1976), pp. 13 and 11.

242 CHANGING CANADIAN CITIES

Figure 5.13. Number of Missing Persons per 10,000 Population, 1971

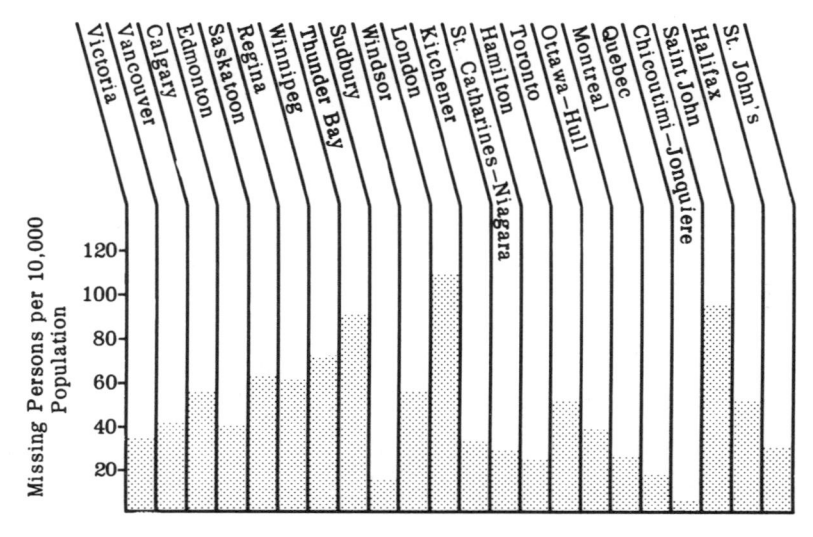

Figure 5.14. Educational Level: Per Cent of 20-34 Age Group Not Presently in School and with Grade 10 Education or less, 1971

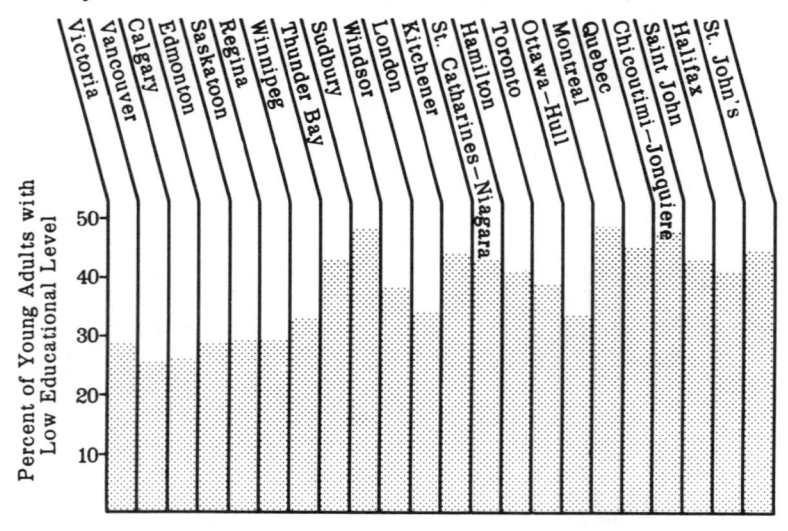

Source: John N. Stewart, *et. al, Urban Indicators: Quality of Life Comparisons for Canadian Cities* (Ottawa: Information Canada, 1976), pp, 17 and 21.

URBAN ENVIRONMENT 243

Figure 5.15. Illegitimate Births, Number per 1,000 Births, 1973

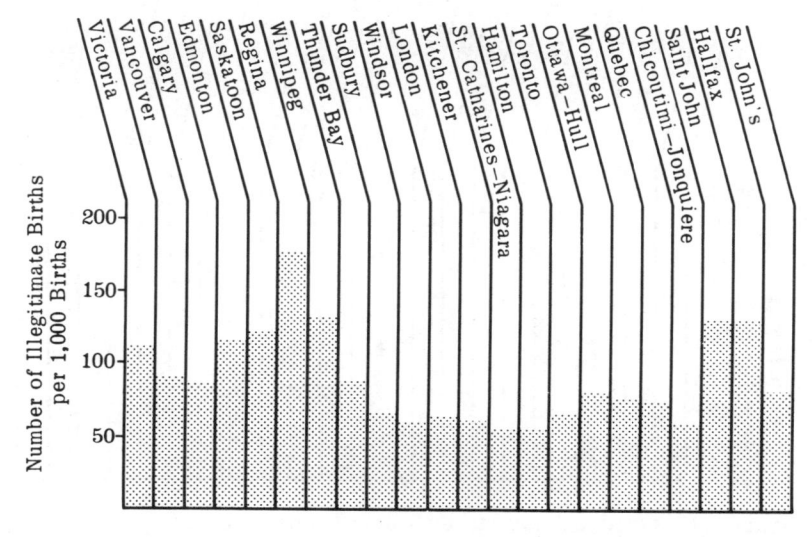

Figure 5.16. Average Income: Mean Income after Federal Tax, 1972

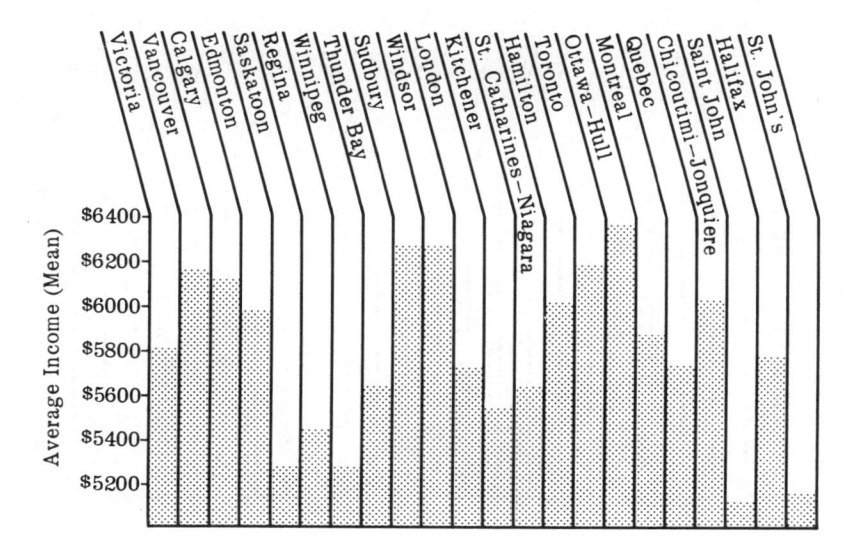

Source: John N. Stewart, *et. al, Urban Indicators: Quality of Life Comparisons for Canadian Cities* (Ottawa: Information Canada, 1976), pp. 19 and 45.

244 CHANGING CANADIAN CITIES

Figure 5.17. Average Income: Adjusted for Federal Tax and Housing Costs, 1972

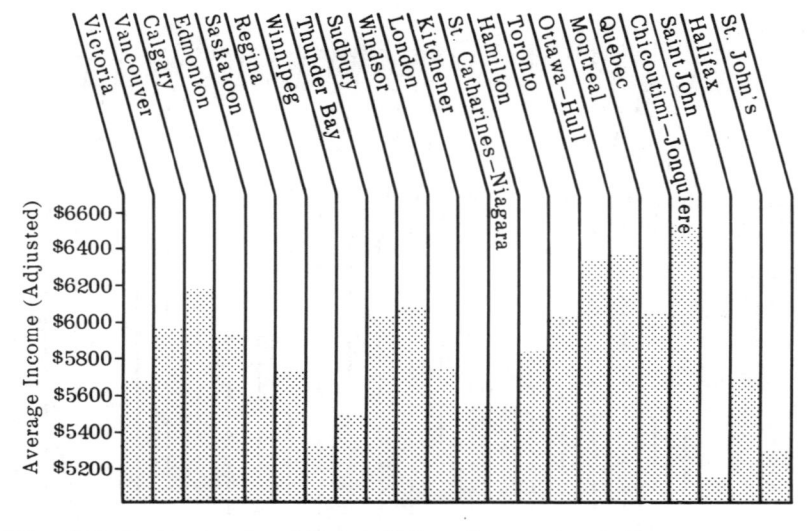

Figure 5.18. Occupational Status Index: Proportion in Top Categories, 1971

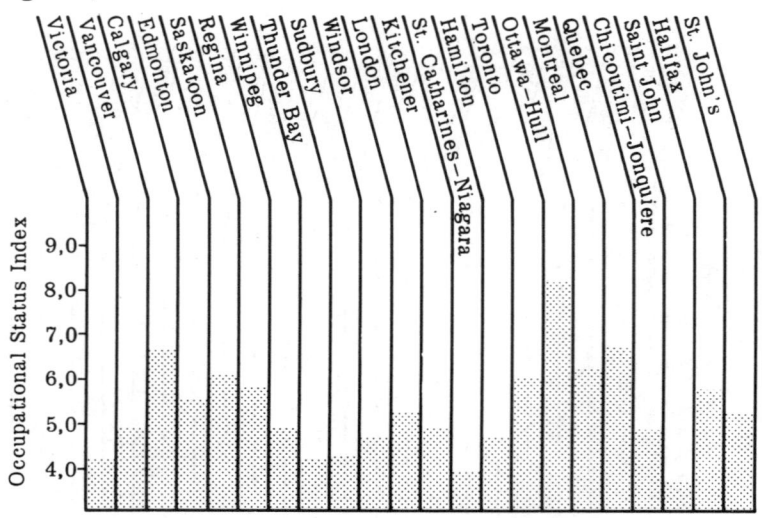

Source: John N. Stewart, *et. al, Urban Indicators: Quality of Life Comparisons for Canadian Cities* (Ottawa: Information Canada, 1976), 47 and 49.

URBAN ENVIRONMENT 245

Figure 5.19. Unemployment Rate Among Active Labour Force Participants, 1971

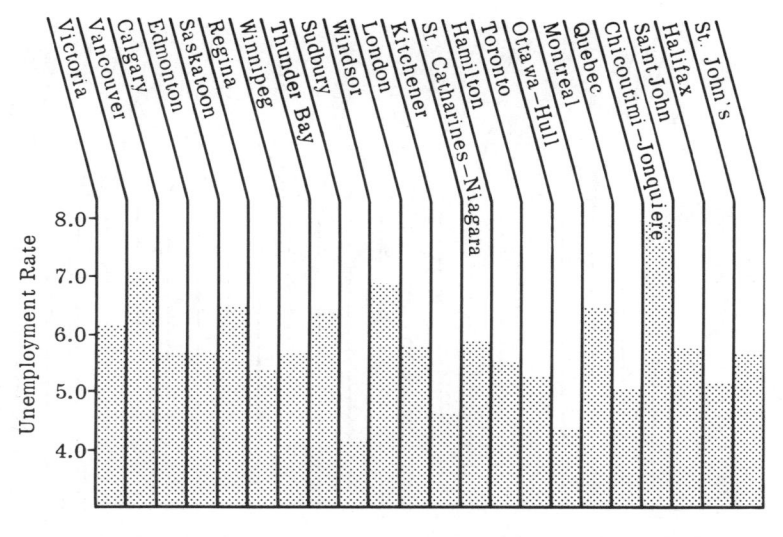

Figure 5.20. Female Labour Force Participation Rate for Age Group 20-64, 1971

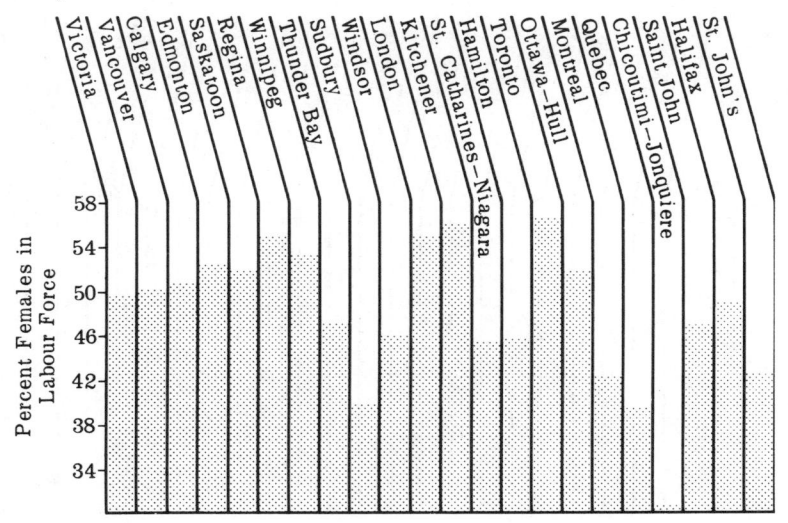

Source: John N. Stewart, *et. al, Urban Indicators: Quality of Life Comparisons for Canadian Cities* (Ottawa: Information Canada, 1976), pp. 53 and 51.

246 CHANGING CANADIAN CITIES

Figure 5.21. Annual Strike Days Lost per 100 in Labour Force, 1971

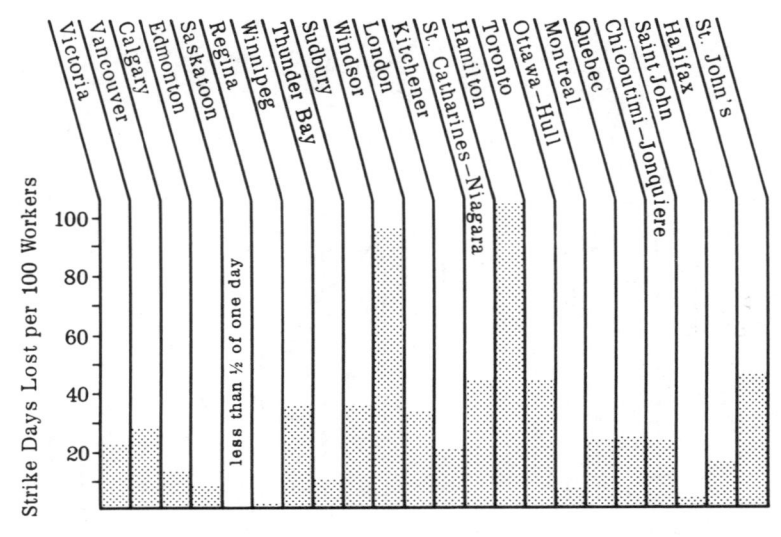

Figure 5.22. Average Estimated Total Costs for New Single-Detached Housing Financed under NHA, 1974

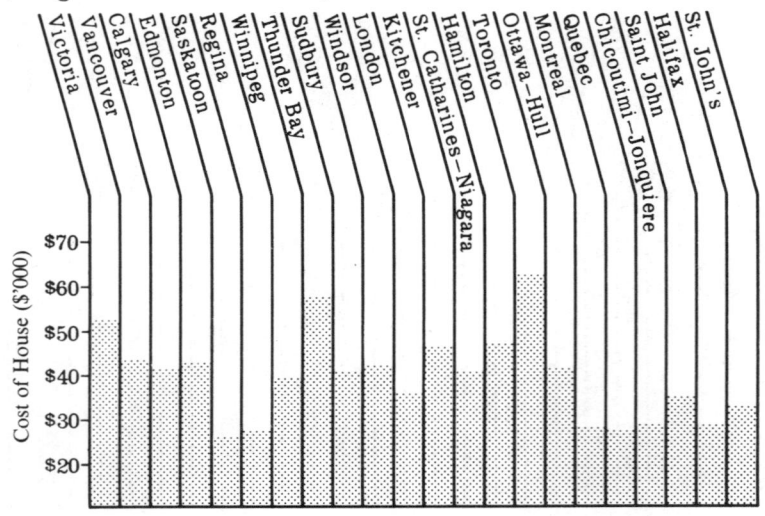

Source: John N. Stewart, et. al., Urban Indicators: Quality of Life Comparisons for Canadian Cities (Ottawa: Information Canada, 1976), pp. 55 and 59.

URBAN ENVIRONMENT 247

Figure 5.23. Housing Choice: Per Cent Apartment Units Vacant, 1974

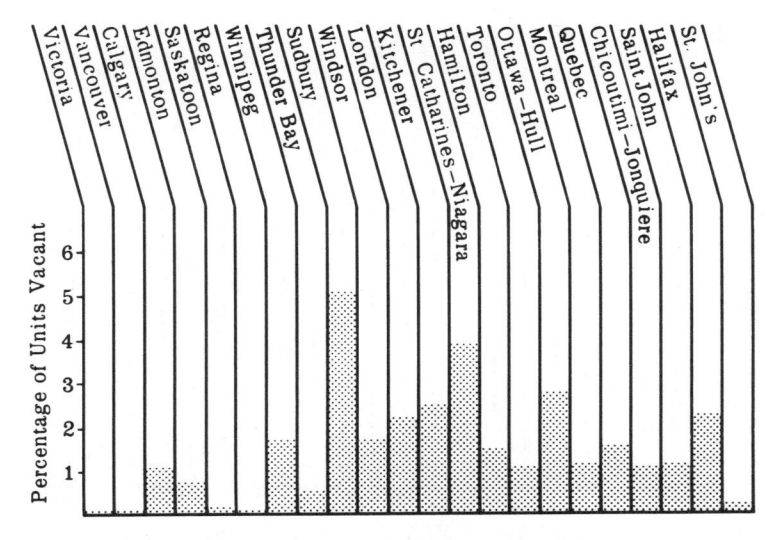

Figure 5.24. Percentage of Children Living in Apartments, 1971

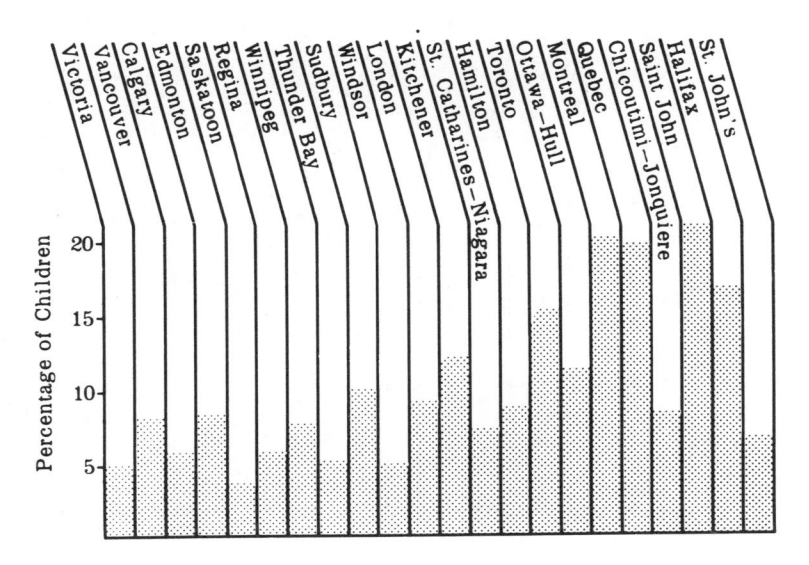

Source: John N. Stewart, *et. al, Urban Indicators: Quality of Life Comparisons for Canadian Cities* (Ottawa: Information Canada, 1976), pp. 67 and 69.

248　CHANGING CANADIAN CITIES

Figure 5.25. New Housing Units Constructed per Additional Household, 1970-73

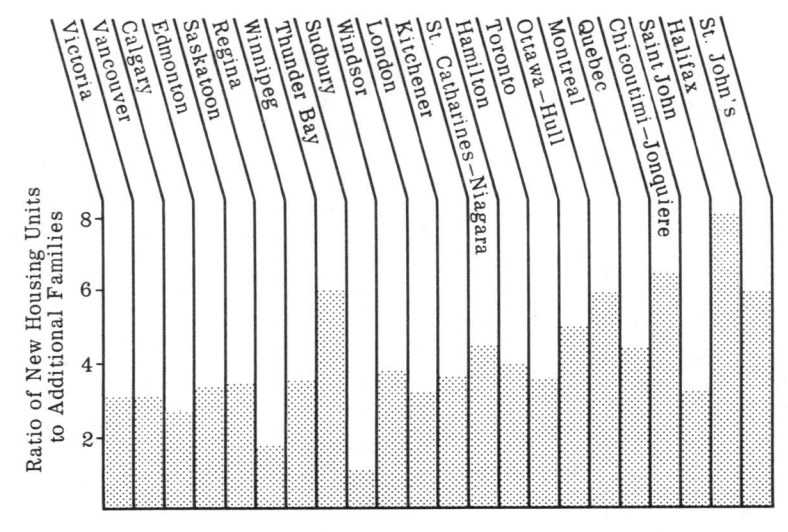

Figure 5.26. Fire and Automobile Hazard Index Adjusted for 1,000 Population, 1971

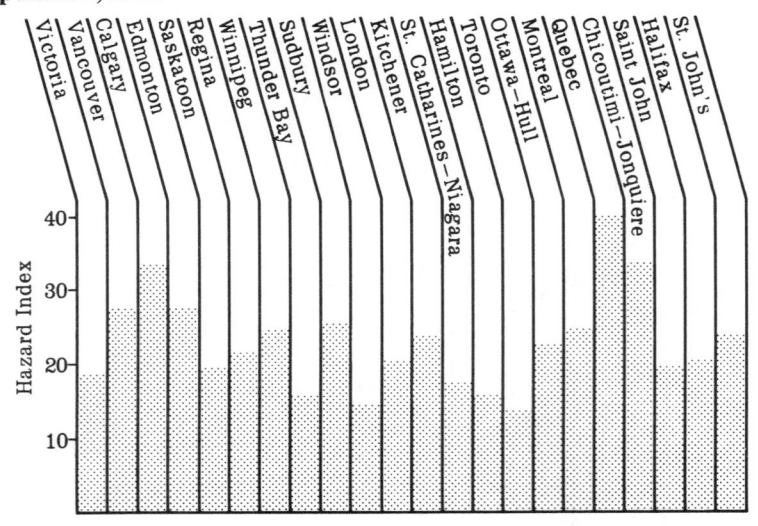

Source: John N. Stewart, *et. al, Urban Indicators: Quality of Life Comparisons for Canadian Cities* (Ottawa: Information Canada, 1976), pp. 63 and 77.

URBAN ENVIRONMENT   249

The overall haphazard impression appears to be confirmed by a correlation analysis between perceived urban problems, as reflected in the indicators, and the population size and growth rate of the metropolitan areas. Of the thirty-two original indicators only four show a significant association with city size: number of major ethnic groups, income, air quality (particulate matter) and public transit ridership. Only two – per cent living in province of birth and costs of new single detached dwellings – demonstrate an association with growth rates.[29]

Beyond these impressions a closer look at the selected indicators does yield certain patterns. In the "social development" group the highest ranking places are eastern metropolitan areas (in Ontario and Quebec) in the 150,000 to 300,000 population range. This is based on a high ranking (low incidence) for the measures of crime, and social and family disorder. An exception to this pattern is in education in which five Western cities rank highest: Vancouver, Calgary, Edmonton, Victoria and Saskatoon. Generally, the three largest metropolitan areas do not emerge strongly in the social area.

Entirely different from the places with a high social rating, the top five places for those measures reflecting economic conditions are Ottawa, Calgary, Toronto, Edmonton and Regina. Correlates appear to be *size, government functions*, and *westernism*. Four of the five cities are, in Canadian terms, large cities ranging in population from half a million to two and a half million. Four are major government centres which score high on the kind of measures that emphasize income and employment level and stability, attraction to skilled and professional people, and job opportunities for women. Three of the places are Prairie cities.

An interesting comparison emerges in the ranking of the Atlantic cities for the economic and physical criteria. Two of the three, Saint John and St. John's, are in the bottom five of the rank list for the first; and two of the three are at the top of the "physical development" list: Halifax and St. John's. Generally the largest cities fare poorly for a set of measures that emphasize the cost and availability of housing and the virtues of family type accommodation.

While the "urban affairs" indicators bring us a little closer to discovering that elusive holy grail, the quality of urban life, they must be regarded with a healthy dose of skepticism. Their limitations are not obscure. They are measures of metropolitan areas which contain a great variety of conditions within themselves: between old and new areas, inner city and suburb, rich and poor districts and so on. The selection of indicators is greatly influenced by the arbitrary factor of the information available. Inevitably, important aspects of life will be excluded. And perhaps, most fundamentally, the process of determining the validity of individual and sets of indicators has hardly begun.

On this last point, a useful approach has been suggested in a Manitoba study. Operating on the premise that "reality is in the eyes of the beholder," T. S. Palys suggests that researchers should go to the people to determine what is important. "Representative population samples" should be "interviewed regarding their perception of the reality in which they live."[30] When we discuss this for the geo-population units of interest – a city, system of cities, the nation – then we will have a significant yardstick for both the weighting and selection of social statistics. Those which most closely approximate the discovered reality will deserve the attribution of "indicator."

The importance of the Palys approach becomes clear when measures of *objective* conditions of the type described above are compared with *subjective* perceptions of cities. An examination of "residential desirability" as perceived by Canadians across the country, and reported in Chapter 7, indicates a scale of preferred cities which is dramatically different.

The "Other Canada": Life in Canada's Resource Regions

While the metropolitan areas contain a large and increasing share of national population (from one-fourth of the country's population in 1901 to over one-half in 1971), there are other Canadas, less populated, but nevertheless vital in our national life. Canada may be thought of in terms of four types of inhabited areas or "ecumene," each distinctive in population, settlement pattern and economic base.[31]

The metropolitan areas and other major urban areas constitute a core ecumene, with dense population, towns and cities offering a great variety of employment and occupational choice, and an extensive agricultural landscape. Just beyond the core is a zone of resource exploitation (zone 2), sometimes referred to as the "Mid-Canada Corridor," with a settlement pattern shaped by the distribution of resource-based urban places and widely dispersed pockets of arable land; the mine, the forest, the power site dominate economic life. Further north there is a "sporadic ecumene" (zone 3): resource-based, sparsely settled and with virtually no agricultural potential. And finally there is a remote zone in the high Arctic, important strategically, containing the path through its archipelago of the northern sea route, the home of some of the Inuit people, and with some reported potential for petroleum resources (Map 5.1).

Urban centres in zones 2 and 3 require some special attention because they represent a distinctively Canadian phenomenon. Together they constitute a steady extension of settlement into the resource frontier; individually they are small, isolated and sometimes precarious. Economically they provide much of the material for Canadian industry as well as some of the most valuable items on Canada's export list.

It is difficult to achieve a consensus on the definition and identity of these communities. One study, with a social viewpoint, mentions 600 "single enterprise" towns with populations less than thirty thousand and accommodating altogether over a million people (1970).[32] Another, applying more exacting criteria, includes ninety-three resource towns housing about half a million people (1971) (see Map 5.2). These are "permanently established communities which have been built to house and service the workers engaged in the extraction, development or primary processing of a forest, mineral or power resource," and having "the majority of its inhabitants depend upon one major industry for employment."

For the purpose of observing the quality of environment and quality of life in resource towns the numbers game is not important. What is important is to appreciate that such places are a continuing motif in Canadian development, and form a very special kind of environment, with certain attractions as well as hazards for the residents. The somewhat cautious forays into the resource hinterlands which began at the turn of the century have become progressively more extensive. Since 1945 in particular, development has "leap-frogged" to widely dispersed sites: asbestos at Cassiar in northwestern British Columbia; oil and gas at Drayton Valley and tar sands at Fort McMurray in Alberta; nickel at Thompson and Lynn Lake in north-central and northwestern Manitoba; uranium at Elliot Lake in northwestern Ontario; copper at Chibougamau in northwestern Quebec; iron ore at Schefferville and Labrador City on the Quebec-Labrador border; and so on. This centrifugal tendency continues to be fostered by the discovery of valuable ores, by advances in mining and forest technology, new rail lines and government-sponsored regional development programs. This shift in spatial patterns has also been accompanied, coincidentally, by a shift in sponsorship from the private company to government, and from site development to comprehensive town planning. The role of the metropolitan-based corporation is still very important, but increasingly provincial governments take an active role in the choice of locations, in physical planning and the provision of services and in the creation of government institutions. Leaf Rapids, Manitoba, and Fremont, Quebec, are representative examples of the new style resource communities.

Map 5.1. The Canadian Ecumene

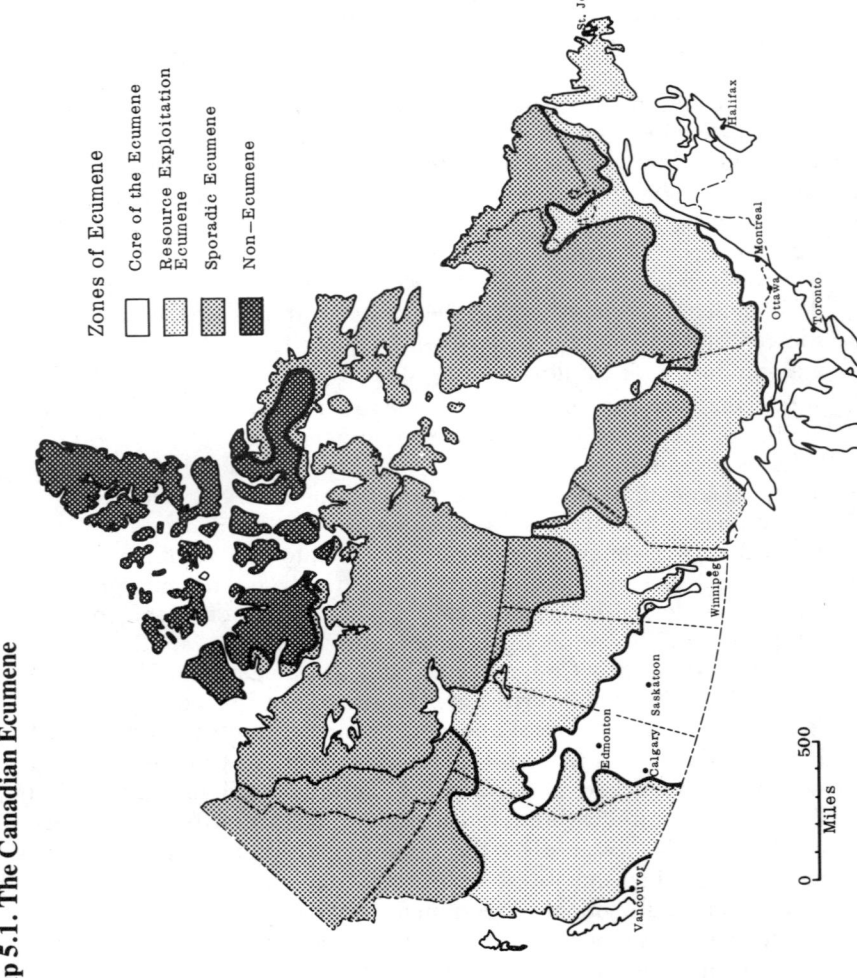

Zones of Ecumene
- Core of the Ecumene
- Resource Exploitation Ecumene
- Sporadic Ecumene
- Non–Ecumene

Source: L.D.McCann, *Canadian Resource Towns: A Geographical Perspective* (Vancouver: University of British Columbia, 1974), p.15.

Map 5.2 Canadian Resource Towns

Source: L.D. McCann, *Canadian Resource Towns: A Geographical Perspective* (Vancouver: University of British Columbia, 1974), p. 4.

The quality of life issue in resource communities is a very basic concern – a "gut issue." People will apparently not commit themselves to the Gold Rivers, Lynn Lakes and Matagamis of this country. Labour turnover as a result is very high and the disruption of production a major worry. The reasons for labour instability are generally believed to reside in conditions like inadequate housing and community services, and certain attributes of the society, such as the fact that there are usually many more men than women, and the wives lack interesting job and social opportunities. Almost a century's experience now conveys a compelling message: if resource towns are important to Canada then they must be made livable communities.[33]

The search for a better quality of life in resource towns must begin with understanding the components of their environment and their population. In making this kind of assessment it is important to visualize resource settlements not as static fixtures on the landscape but as a process evolving through several stages from the natural state to maturity. Anthony Riffel of the Centre for Settlement Studies, University of Manitoba, identifies seven stages: natural or pre-discovery, prospecting to survey, industrial and community construction, industrial operation and community improvement, industrial and community operation and consolidation, community diversification, and community maturity. Each stage will experience a different set of circumstances (Table 5.5). *Economically*, the evolution is from opening up the resource and construction of plant and community to the stabilization of industry and of community services. In *demographic* terms, the change is from a population consisting overwhelmingly of young male workmen to a population more balanced in terms of age groups and sex. And *socially* the evolution is from a construction camp/trailer town with a lot of social turbulence to a place with an array of basic urban services and amenities and a highly structured, stratified society.[34]

While Canadian resource towns are widely dispersed, and vary in age, size and specific economic base, they have certain general attributes that assume a number of broad patterns. The physical conditions of resource towns compare tolerably well with places of similar size elsewhere. But there are some differences and nuances that should be noted. These arise from their economic functions, size and distributional pattern, isolation, comparative instability, and sponsorship.

Resource towns are often located in areas of great natural beauty and outdoor recreation potential. The simple pleasures of fishing and winter sports provide incentives for migration to northern environments. But economic development and the preservation of nature

Table 5.5. Stages and Characteristics of Resource Town Development

	Economic Characteristics	Demographic Characteristics	Social Characteristics
Natural or prediscovery	No economic activity or only hunting and fishing by native peoples.	No population or only small bands of native peoples.	Unpopulated or small, isolated native communities in limited contact with white society.
Prospecting to survey	Short-term activity. Money spent "outside." Traditional native economy persists, with some trade with whites.	Short-term, summer residents. Young men, no women. If there originally, native people in the majority.	Isolated. Usually, access by air only. Shack towns without amenities. Some contact with native peoples.
Industrial and town construction	The first boom period. Mushrooming economic activity. Natives may be employed.	Mostly single men. Some young workers with families. Very high turnover rates. Native in minority; only stable group in population.	Isolated, but easier access to outside. Trailer towns with basic amenities, and "pub." Signs of social problems among native peoples.
Industrial operation and community improvement	Shift in construction from industrial to residential and commercial. More money spent in town. Falling off in employment of natives.	Slowing rate of turnover. Increasing number of married workers. Native peoples a small minority.	Improvement of housing and community facilities. Completion of roads and communications services. Reduced social problems among whites; increased among natives.
Industrial and community operation	Construction over. Services established. Much of labour skilled. Few natives employed.	Turnover rates reduced to 60%. Young married workers in majority.	Amenities well developed. Few social problems among whites, but boredom among wives. Natives on welfare. Marked stratification.
Community diversification	Stabilization of industry. Expansion of other services, especially government. Small manufacturing.	Labour turnover stablizes at 35%. Young married in majority.	Employment for wives available. Special programs, created, largely for native people.
Community maturity	Diversified economic base. Limited opportunities for expansion.	Balanced population structure in terms of age and sex. Low rates of turnover.	Sense of community and belongingness. Whites and natives on welfare. Less racial tension.

Source: J. A. Riffel, *Quality of life in resource towns* (Ottawa: Information Canada, 1975). Cat. No. SU31–19 1975, pp. 12–13. Reproduced by permission of the Minister of Supply and Services Canada.

and a salubrious biosphere are not always compatible. Pollution rears its head.

> The odour that hangs over a pulp and paper town is apparent to all who drive through; waste and tailings from a mining activity are often obvious; the fluorine given off by many smelting processes conspicuously affects foliage. Other damage, such as the raising and lowering of lake levels in power projects and log drives, or the pollution of lakes with the accumulations of bark which falls from thousands of logs on the drive, is not so apparent. Many industries emit black smoke or hydrogen dioxide or fluorine, some pour chemicals into streams and create other environmental changes.[35]

Responses of residents to such conditions vary from deep concern— "the wife... she worries quite a bit; she figures if it does that to trees and flowers, what is it going to do to the kids?"[36]; to a feeling of social impotence in the face of the industry-created environment[37]; to a cavalier acceptance of pollution as part of a resource town way of life— "the day that the air doesn't smell will be a sad one for this town."[38]

Townsite planning in resource communities displays a curious contradiction. Both corporate and government initiators have for a quarter of a century now attempted to bring to the rock and forest of the Shield the best that the art of town planning can offer. But as all good "colonialists" they have done so in a somewhat formal and unfeeling manner. At Granisle, a copper mining settlement of the late 'sixties, just off the Prince Rupert-Prince George road in northern British Columbia "a forested setting has been almost completely denuded of trees, to be replaced by standard, identical suburban houses laid out in an unimaginative grid format."[39] Even the great Clarence Stein, who extolled organic planning and humane design in America, when invited by the Aluminum Company of Canada to produce a design for Kitimat, northwestern British Columbia, produced a variant of the Radburn concept—the low density, car-defensive layout that he had pioneered in the suburbs of New York City in the late 'twenties.[40]

Not surprisingly this situation produces a mixed reaction from residents—some love it, some hate it. But most seem to agree that the plan in three dimensions is monotonous, and is generally a too literal expression in its residential patterns of local corporate hierarchies—the big lots and the best ones, with woods and commanding views, are reserved for the managerial group—and the other echelons of workers sort themselves out accordingly.[41]

One of the less appealing traits of the resource town is the squatter settlement on its edge. Typically, these ramshackle residential clusters of dubious hygiene will include concentrations of Métis and Indian population – and as such stand as an incriminating symbol of the native peoples' limbo between the reserve and white society. The general difficulty of transforming "settlement" into "community" which is an affliction of such places, assumes amongst these people a particularly poignant, and sometimes tragic, character.[42]

Residents of resource towns come to learn that there is a difference between "community" and "familiarity." Too much "social observability" in small isolated settlements results in pressures, and one way people react is in their *housing* preferences. A social study observes that "planners in the Arctic find that individuals insist upon self-contained houses despite the difficulties of heating, weather, distance and cost. The self-contained home permits family life with minimal observations from outside."[43] This preference has its consequences. The single detached house is the most expensive to build in a remote economy where housing costs generally run about 80 per cent higher than in southern communities. As a result of this combination of factors two characteristic housing patterns emerge. People move into good housing heavily subsidized or allocated by their employers – rental and/or purchase arrangements are used as incentives to attract and hold employees; or they build substandard housing. High costs, the unavailability of mortgage funds and a sense of impermanence tend to depress housing quality. In boom towns like Fort McMurray in the region of the Athabasca tar sands the housing ideal is approximated by the mobile home, which constitutes over a quarter of the housing stock in that community. As far as housing is concerned, people in resource towns must choose paternalism, poverty, or impermanence.[44]

Recreation in resource towns is characterized by a certain mystifying dilemma: it is both over-organized and apparently not wholly satisfying. This is explained by the sociologist Alex Lucas:

> From the point of view of the volunteer leaders, and those who attempt to participate in a wide range of activities, the community is over-organized because many calls are made upon the time of the keenest participants. A community can be characterized as over-organized or apathetic at the same time, depending upon the point of view ... In what sense is there 'nothing to do'? The short answer is that there is nothing *new* to do. The same old faces and the same old activities are fine, but there are occasions when it would be pleasant to 'have a change of scene', or see a play, or perhaps, just for once, go to a night club. In other words, despite the high ... level of activity in the community, there are a number of activities that are not there and never will be.[45]

Generally, residents of resource communities suffered from the lack of variety and depth in their recreational opportunities, notwithstanding the large numbers of clubs, associations and groups. This is both a function of size and isolation. In no other aspect of life is the effect of a scattered settlement pattern more keenly felt. The dominant tendency has been to locate close to the exploited resource, and even where a large mineral reserve is being developed, the towns tend to be localized – they are on their own. An interlinked urban system giving a regional population the services it needs for a full life develops painfully and slowly, if at all.[46]

Because of the fact and feeling of isolation, residents of resource towns place great emphasis on improving *access* to cities in the south, and improving *communications*, particularly broadcasting and the press. High costs associated with travel distance are to some degree buffered by various forms of company subsidy. But the very conditions of small size, isolation, and instability due to the possibility of resource depletion and erratic world markets, frustrate the desired improvements. The dynamics of the weekly newspaper – its association with and dependence on a local printery and on main street advertising – give it an introspective boosterish quality, reinforcing rather than serving to break out of parochialism. The "fighting editor" of fourth estate legend is admired because he/she is so rare. Radio and television are limited in their variety. And the cost of major improvements in long distance transportation is prohibitive for a highly dispersed population. Structural changes in the settlement pattern may have to come first.[47]

It is possible to represent the kind of life that people lead in resource communities in terms of "an average family" – perhaps more than in other places. An overwhelming percentage (75 to 90 per cent) of the employed, mainly men, work for the predominant resource industry. The majority of the population is made up of young married couples, between twenty and forty years of age with young families. And because of the intense albeit at times involuntary interaction both at work and play they come eventually to share common values and outlooks.[48] So if you are living in Uranium City, Saskatchewan, or Chibougamau, Quebec or almost any small mining or pulp and paper town you are likely to have been attracted there by a job that pays better money than most factory jobs in the south. Besides the company is leasing you a house with a fixed rent for three years, and it is big enough for the wife and three kids. After two years in town you're getting quite used to the routine of the mine and are next in line for a foreman's position. But you are not sure you will wait around that long because very few of the guys get beyond that – and you're ambitious. The really high-paying jobs in management are filled by those smart asses parachuted in from Montreal or Toronto and sometimes even New York or Chicago. And then there is Mary's problem. All the kids are at school, she wants to work – she's a legal secretary but this town cannot support more than one law office and openings are scarce. She's bored stiff and not strong on the I.O.D.E.

You have made some very close friends in town – you need them in a place where you have no other family. A bunch of you who are interested in fooling around with musical instruments – you play the trumpet – formed a band, but just when you got it going the band leader, an accountant at the plant, was called back to head office. That's how it goes.

Altogether, though, you don't find it a bad place to live. The kids are happy at school, and *they* seem to have plenty to do – they can always go fishing and the Cubs keep them busy. There's practically no delinquency in town; the kids are not on the streets. You live comfortably. You should be satisfied, but you're not. Somehow it is hard to feel that you belong. Maybe because, rightly or wrongly, you believe that whatever goes on in town is controlled by someone sitting in a big office at the top of Place Ville Marie, by the price of copper or some other damn thing over which you have no control. Local council is a farce. You wonder if you should try harder to get involved. You feel you have to or you may end up like some of those guys who have been around a little too long and have hit the bottle. What's it called – "a life of quiet desperation?"[49]

While for most people in resource settlements the stresses are, as indicated, social and psychological, an account of living conditions in the resource ecumene would not be complete, nor true to reality, without acknowledgement of those who endure an even more desperate form of existence. We refer to the victims of industrial diseases. Unfortunately, as the press reports with increasing frequency, extreme hazard to human health, and even death, due to working conditions, are not phenomena of our barbarous past.

The human devastation which can be wrought by silica dust and other hazards of mining has been chronicled (1975) with compassion by Elliott Leyton, an anthropologist at Memorial University.[50] His book shows the effects of fluorspar mining on the health of the workers in the communities of St. Lawrence and Lawn on the south coast of the Burin Peninsula, Newfoundland. Ten personal histories are given by men, or their surviving widows, about their struggles resulting from the loss of health in the mines of the St. Lawrence Corporation before Alcan took it over in 1960 and installed ventilation. The roll call, representing 100 dead men and another 100 dying, is grim. The human suffering is only faintly conveyed by the individual medical diagnoses: Silicosis and associated heart failure; Silicosis; Tuberculosis, Chronic Bronchitis, and associated heart failure; Lung Cancer, and so on. What is difficult to erase from the mind is the double burden of crushing illness and economic anxiety: "I started to cough. I had a cigarette in my hand. It was one of those long drawn out things where you can't get your breath back. I remember somebody coming in the door and that's the last thing I remember. When I came to, the wife was pulling me out from under the table. My head dropped on my hand with the cigarette, burned my eye.... I get $113 every two weeks from Welfare and a hundred dollars and thirty-three cents from Compensation. I was getting that in 1953.... Seven kids we got going to school. Hard to live boy, I'll tell you." (From the life history of Alphonse Reilly: "At 44, all you see of 'Phonse are his gigantic eyes, his face's struggle not to reveal his hurt and his tiny emaciated body".)[51]

This Newfoundland experience reflects an important aspect of the Canadian urban reality. The fluorspar mines in two quiet fishing villages were initiated, from New York for New York and other far away metropolitan centres. Fluorine and its compounds, derived from fluorspar, enter into industrial processes that manufacture many of the products, particularly of aluminum and plastics, that end up on our kitchen shelves. We cannot ignore Leyton's concluding assertion: that a humane society will not tolerate such suffering as a valid cost of its industrial advance and metropolitan comforts.

Policy Approaches

We have presented three broad views of urban Canada. The first offers perspective on the diversity of our urban regions. Together, there is an image of places different from each other, shaped by distinctive geography and history, providing opportunities for different varieties of the "good urban life," but facing critical problems which must be overcome if their promise of providing a good life is to be fulfilled. We identified these problems as the preservation of agricultural and recreational resources in Vancouver; the reconciliation of tourism and orchard farming in Penticton; the management of growth in Edmonton; the decent integration of native peoples in Regina; the control of air pollution in Sudbury; prevention of environmental degradation in Hamilton; the cleaning up of the recreational waters of Quebec City's recreational hinterland; and the finding of the right development policy in Saint John.

The message that emerges is that public policy at all levels of government should concentrate on reinforcing the unique strengths and on dealing with the critical difficulties in each place. For provincial and federal governments the need for regionally-sensitive, flexible approaches is imperative.

The findings of this cursory regional diagnosis should be taken as indicative only of problems and possible solutions. What is more important is the approach as a demonstration of policy enquiry, as a way of thinking which strives for a *gestalt*, a broad integrated view, and which seeks out the *salient elements* in a situation—the factors that make or break the environment. We suggest that the search for the right mode of policy research is critical to creative policy-making, just as the wrong mode, data grubbing without perspective or expedient response to yesterday's problems, is a drag on the policy process. The key point is that the regional diagnosis should address itself to the question: What is important? A conscientious response should yield insights that will lead to wise decisions in terms that are both *allocative*—what? where? and *distributive*—how much? and for whom?

The second view of Canada's urban environments presented a comparative picture of the major metropolitan areas through the medium of urban indicators. The results are not conclusive, but are important as an unveiling in Canada of a new descriptive tool with some promise of attaining a more inclusive view of Canadian cities. Some of the findings, tentatively stated, bear further investigation because of their policy implications: middle-sized cities are strongest in social criteria; big cities are low ranking in that dimension but at the top in economic criteria. Cities may rank low in social and economic measures, but be among the best performers as far as "physical development" is concerned. In addition to this kind of comparative view, the indicators permit a comprehensive statement for most metropolitan areas in terms of a wide assortment of measures. The maintenance of that kind of record over time will enable residents, administrators and politicians to observe changes—and draw the conclusions suggested by the moral and political judgements of the particular time. For example, a high "percentage of children living in apartment units" may be viewed with alarm in 1971, but in 1991 certain changes—the critical importance of conserving good farmland or improvements in apartments for family accommodation—may result in quite a different consensual judgement. In any case, if comprehensive information is consistently maintained and *made available to the public*, the indicator can, in an increasingly complex society, contribute to the effective participation of citizen groups in decision-making.

A sound assessment of the role of urban indicators in policy-making requires some historical perspective. In the decades of the 'sixties and 'seventies, some fundamental shifts in attitude are observable, typified, for example, by Prime Minister Trudeau's memorable definition of GNP: "gross national pollution." The rise of interest in indicators is a symptom of change in values. Many people are no longer content to measure well-being in exclusively economic terms. W. W. Rostow has depicted the evolution of Canadian society through four stages, each characterized by a predominant ethic or guiding moral principle, as follows:[52]

Stage of Growth	*Predominant Ethic*
Pre-industrial	Subsistence
Industrial	Production
Mass Consumption	Consumption and Growth
Post-Industrial	Quality of Life

We suggest that the staggering side-effects of a mass consumption society in the form of a deteriorating environment and declining stocks of energy are propelling us towards a new ethic. We are living the fact etched so vividly by the ecologist, Barry Commoner, that for every per cent increase in the gross national product, the levels of environmental pollution increase ten-fold. And we are learning the hard way. Quality replaces growth as the new dynamic, both personal and political.[53]

In this light, the struggle for more inclusive measures of well-being will go on, and genuine efforts to improve our grasp of the *urban reality* will deserve the endorsement of policy agencies. At the same time, the use of any given set of measurements of societal conditions as input to public policy, should heed three dangers that have been recently signalled: the dangers of elitism, mechanicalism and managerialism. Spelled out, these are the *hazards* of (1) selecting measures and designing them in a way that reflects the values of traditional elites and excludes the viewpoints and interests of minorities and disadvantaged groups, (2) defining problems by statistical surrogates that misrepresent the human reality and lead to insensitive solutions, and (3) using indicators as a means of monitoring and direction by a centralized bureaucracy.[54]

The third view of urban conditions draws attention to a characteristically Canadian feature of urbanization: the string of about 600 resource towns that stretch across the country in the mid-Canada zone of resource exploitation. These are usually generated by metropolitan interests, corporate or governmental, but as settlements they represent the predicaments of developing areas in Canada: isolation, small size, and instability. Many of the difficulties inventoried in this chapter are attributable to some combination of these factors. Jobs are good for the men, but chances for advancement are poor and wives have few vocational opportunities and become bored. People don't remain for long. The mobility and rapid turnover of labour plagues production. The children have to leave their home town for post-secondary education. Social and recreational life is both over-organized and desperately limited, ingrown and tedious. The high overhead costs of better transportation to the outside cannot be borne by such places. The extractive base and therefore the limited life span of many resource towns, together with the dominance of a few or even a single employer create a sense of alienation, and work against a feeling of community, and so on.

Canadian resource towns have not, however, remained static. There has been an evolution in the last quarter century from sponsor ship by private corporations to government or corporation-government partnerships, and from elementary site development to comprehensive town planning. It may now be opportune to nudge this evolutionary process toward its next logical stage: the creation of regional complexes. The central concept is the building of new economic and social structures on a regional scale, each consisting of the broadest possible economic base, for example, joining base metals, power, pulp and paper and research and development; each supporting a major regional centre containing an array of business, personal, professional and cultural services, related to a cluster of smaller centres; and each complex served by good transportation and communications, linking community to community, community to work place and the entire complex to southern cities. This strategy represents a public policy challenge on a par with Canada's historic nation-building ventures. It is an approach, however, which has a substantial basis in the needs and potentials of the resource belt. Major public/private initiative and investment will be required to start and guide the process of regional restructuring. But the payoffs that are in prospect are greater economic stability, a more committed and productive labour force, stimulus to the national economy and the overcoming of the congenital difficulties of resource towns. The evolution from bunkhouse, to settlement, to community and humanized region would be completed.

While this particular policy path requires a long range perspective, it could have very immediate consequences for the ongoing decisions of resource companies and provincial and federal governments. The location of new enterprises and settlements, or the expansion of existing ones, the scale, type and precise timing of investments in roads and power lines, communications, water supply and community services and many other things will be very much affected by the variety of development model adopted. We can travel established paths and perpetuate the isolation/instability syndrome. Or we can build solidly towards viable patterns that hold the promise of moving across two critical thresholds, from economic exploitation to stable, self-sustaining development, and from settlement to community.

In this way a strategy which begins with a search for more livable environments on the resource frontier, links up with several other strategies. One is a shift from a growth model to a model for development—"the unfolding of the creative possibilities" of regions. And another is a national population and settlement strategy concerned with putting the brakes on population concentration in a few metropolitan areas. The new development model for Canada's resource regions by working towards stable urban communities, contains the seeds of one valid alternative.[55]

Notes

1. Moshe Safdie, "Making an Environmental Code for Habitat," *Contact*, Vol. 7, Nos. 3 and 4, 1975, p. 2.
2. *Ibid.*, p. 4.
3. Kiyo Izumi, "Some Thoughts about the Environment and Telecommunications," *Plan Canada*, Vol. II, No. 1 1970, p. 36. Professor Izumi cites Shashi Pande on the relationship between quality of environment and quality of life.
4. This concept of "urban environment" is a summary, a synoptic one, which draws inspiration from a number of sources such as: J. W. MacNeill, *Environmental Management* (Ottawa: Information Canada, 1971), p. 4; René Dubos, *So Human an Animal* (New York: Charles Scribner's Sons, 1968), pp. 165 and 236; and Paul B. Sears, *The Ecology of Man* (Eugene: University of Oregon Press, 1957), p. 40.
5. *Dubos, op. cit.*, p. 164.
6. Kenneth F. Harry and John B. Wright, *The Climate of Vancouver*, Reprint of Circular -2985, TEC-258 (Ottawa: Department of Transport, Meteorological Branch, 1967), pp. 6 – 8; and *The Livable Region 1976/1986: Proposals to Manage the Growth of Greater Vancouver* (Vancouver: Greater Vancouver Regional District, 1975), pp. 7 and 12.
7. *The Livable Region 1976/1986, ibid.*, p. 7 – 90.
8. *The Okanagan Bulletin Area*, Land Service, Department of Lands and Forests, Province of British Columbia (Victoria: Queen's Printer, 1964), pp. 12, 13 and

23; and A. L. Farley, ed., *Trans-Canada Field Excursions, Guide Book*, International Geographical Congress, Montreal, August, 1972 (Vancouver: University of British Columbia, 1972), p. 175.
9. S. C. Rodgers, "Edmonton," *Urbanism and Environment*, Georges Le Pape (ed.), (Montreal: Federal Publications Service, 1974), pp. 100, 102, 112, 118 and 124; and *A Statement on the Future of This City*, Submission to the Ministry of Municipal Affairs (Edmonton: Council of the City of Edmonton, 1973), pp. 8-11.
10. Harry Heimark, "Regina," *Urbanism and Environment*, Georges Le Pape (ed.), (Montreal: Federal Publications Service, 1974), p. 236.
11. *Poverty in Canada*, A Report of the Special Senate Committee on Poverty (Ottawa: Information Canada, 1971), p. 37.
12. Farley, *op. cit.*, p. 22.
13. F. Wu, "Regional Economic Study of Sudbury" (Senior Honours Essay, School of Urban and Regional Planning, University of Waterloo, 1973), pp. 31 and 32; and Farley, *op. cit.*, p. 23.
14. "Report on Sudbury health 'suppressed'," *Kitchener-Waterloo Record*, Thursday, November 13, 1975, p. 54.
15. Ontario, Department of Municipal Affairs, *Choices For a Growing Region*, Metropolitan Toronto and Region Transportation Study (Toronto: 1967), p. 28.
16. Thomas L. Burton, *Natural Resource Policy in Canada* (Toronto: McClelland and Stewart Limited, 1972), Chapter 6; John N. Stewart *et al.*, *Urban Indicators: Quality of Life Comparisons for Canadian Cities* (Ottawa: Information Canada, 1976), p. 73. This report was prepared by the Urban Economy and Environment Directorate of the Ministry of State for Urban Affairs.
17. L. C. Evans, *Story of Hamilton* (Toronto: Ryerson Press, 1970), p. 204.
18. *Ibid.*, p. 205; and "Hamilton, Paradise Lost," *City Magazine*, Vol. 1, No. 2 (December 1974 and January 1975), p. 8.
19. *Quebec City and Environs* (Quebec: Quebec, Ministry of Tourism, 1972), pp. 27 and 28; and G. G. Tomkins and T. L. Hills, *Canada: A Regional Geography* (Toronto: W. J. Gage Limited, 1962), p. 140.
20. Peter Brooke Clibbon, "Evolution and present patterns of the ecumene of southern Quebec," in *Quebec: studies in Canadian geography*, Louis Trotier (ed.), (Toronto: University of Toronto Press, 1972), p. 26.
21. Jean Cimon, "Old Québec and Town Planning," *Urbanism and Environment*, Georges Le Pape (ed.), (Montreal: Federal Publications Service, 1974), p. 216.
22. Hugh MacLennan, *Seven Rivers of Canada* (Toronto: Macmillan of Canada, 1969), pp. 156 and 157.
23. George A. Nader, *Cities of Canada*, Vol. 1 (Toronto: Macmillan of Canada, 1975), p. 242.
24. MacLennan, *op. cit.*, p. 159.
25. Dubos, *So Human an Animal, op. cit.*, p. 173.
26. Brad Hodgins, "An Assessment of Social Indicators" (Waterloo: University of Waterloo, School of Urban and Regional Planning. 1975) (mimeographed), p.3.
27. Stewart *et al., op. cit.*, p. 3.
28. *Ibid.*, pp. 7, 11, 13, 25, 47, 63 and 77.
29. *Ibid.*, Technical Appendix, Table 6, p. 84.
30. T. S. Palys, *Social Indicators of Quality of Life in Canada: A Practical/Theoretical Report* (Winnipeg: Manitoba, Department of Urban Affairs, 1973), pp. 114 and 115.
31. L. D. McCann, *Canadian Resource Towns: A Geographical Perspective* (Vancouver: University of British Columbia, 1974), pp. 12-14.
32. Rex A. Lucas, *Minetown Milltown Railtown* (Toronto: University of Toronto Press, 1971), pp. 17 and 18.
33. McCann, *op. cit.*, pp. 2, 17, 18 and 76; and J. A. Riffel, *Quality of life in*

resource towns (Ottawa: Information Canada, 1975), pp. 3, 5, 8 and 9.
34. Riffel, *ibid.*, pp. 6 – 16; and McCann, *op. cit.*, p. 54.
35. Lucas, *Minetown Milltown Railtown*, *op. cit.*, p. 98.
36. *Ibid.*, p. 100.
37. *Ibid.*, p. 103.
38. *Ibid.*, p. 98.
39. J. Douglas Porteous, "Quality of Life in British Columbia Company Towns: Residents' Attitudes," *Contact*, Vol. 7, No. 5, October 1975, p. 32.
40. Nigel H. Richardson, "A Tale of Two Cities," *Planning The Canadian Environment*, ed. L. O. Gertler (Montreal: Harvest House, 1972), pp. 275 and 276.
41. Porteous, *op. cit.*, p. 32; and McCann, *op. cit.*, pp. 60 and 65.
42. Riffel, *op. cit.*, pp. 19 and 20; and Richard Bucksar, "The Squatter on the Resource Frontier," *The People Outside*, Jim Lotz (ed.), (Ottawa: Saint Paul University, Canadian Research Centre for Anthropology, 1971), p. 93.
43. Lucas, *op. cit.*, p. 185.
44. Lucas, *op. cit.*, pp. 37, 62 – 65; Riffel, *op. cit.*, p. 17; McCann, *op. cit.*, p. 48; and Porteous, *op. cit.*, p. 35.
45. Lucas, *op. cit.*, pp. 198 and 199.
46. *Ibid.*, p. 330; McCann, *op. cit.*, p. 9; and Riffel, *op. cit.*, p. 2.
47. Riffel, *op. cit.*, pp. 28 and 29; and Lucas, *op. cit.*, p. 234.
48. McCann, *op. cit.*, p. 58; Riffel, *op. cit.*, p. 9; Lucas, *op. cit.*, pp. 329 and 230; and Porteous, *op. cit.*, p. 28.
49. Riffel, *op. cit.*, pp. 16, 25, 31, 38, 39, 42, 45 and 46; and Lucas, *op. cit.*, pp. 235, 236, 169, 205, 206, 72, 73, 335 – 337, and 339.
50. Marci McDonald, "Massacre at Grassy Narrows," *Maclean's*, , Vol. 88, No. 11 (October 20, 1975), pp. 26 – 36; and Elliott Leyton, *Dying Hard* (Toronto: McClelland and Stewart Limited, 1975).
51. Leyton, *ibid.*, pp. 51, 52, 138 and 139.
52. Burton, *Natural Resource Policy in Canada, op. cit.*, p. 68.
53. Barry Commoner, *The Closing Circle* (New York: Bantam Books, 1971), p. 144.
54. Peter J. Henriot, "Public Policy Implications of Social Indicators Research and Development" (Ottawa: Paper presented at the Symposium on Social Indicators Research in an Urban Context, Ministry of State for Urban Affairs, July 12, 1973), pp. 15 and 16.
55. John Friedmann, *Urbanization, Planning and National Development* (Beverly Hills: Sage Publications, 1973), p. 45.

CHAPTER 6

The Urban Surroundings

Changing Town-Country Areas: Urban Fringe, Shadow and Field

Canadians are forming settlements which express strongly their increasingly mobile life style. As a result the *interaction of "town" and "country"* extends over quite a large area; limited only by the practical daily round trip driving time from the inner city. This area is sometimes called the "urban field." Its boundaries, which are more an idea than a line on a map, are defined mainly by two things: by the daily life spaces of people related to an urban centre, that is where they habitually travel to work, to friends, to recreation, to shop, to schools of all kinds, to conferences or just to get away from it all. And it is defined by the location of facilities – houses, riding stables, factories, country clubs, and the like – which for various reasons, seek an out-of-city environment but depend on convenient access to the city. Fields so defined may vary in radius from the centre of a city. Considerations of topography, climate, population size, transportation, land prices and planning controls intervene, but generally such fields will not extend less than fifty miles nor more than one hundred miles.[1] In general, this entire area of urban influence in a physical sense may be called the surroundings of the city.

What has in fact been happening during the last quarter century is the emergence of an area beyond the suburban ring of most Canadian cities which is a mix of the characteristics of both country and city, and undergoing almost continuous change. This mix can be observed by driving out-of-town on one of the main highways – be it on Highway 16 going south from Ottawa along the Rideau, or out of Edmonton along the St. Albert or Calgary Trail.[2]

Within the first few miles of such an urban field the farmland will be punctuated by some of the landmarks of the "inner urban fringe": new residential subdivisions as well as pioneer mansions converted to contemporary homes, restaurants and some say less decorous uses; country residences and other activities that depend strongly on being not too far from the city such as drive-in theatres trailer parks, motels and microwave and radio towers. If you pass a small town you will probably notice an over-size public school because the surrounding area may have quite a large ex-urbanite population (people living in the country but dependent on the city), perhaps five times greater than the farm-related residents.

Then, around a turn in the road or beyond a level crossing the landscape begins to change noticeably. There are nurseries and market gardens and golf courses and an "old folks" home, and you observe that the new city type housing does not intrude so much into the open country but is added to the edges of towns and villages. Here and there you will see a sign to a sand and gravel pit or to a snow-mobiling area and you may not be able to resist the antique places that pop up with distressing frequency. This "outer urban fringe" may continue for about fifteen miles or more, perhaps as far as the closest provincial park.

Beyond that distance you may discover if your gas is low that you may have a little trouble finding a service station of the company you patronize. The scenery is much more rural, but somehow not quite yet the real country. You may be mystified by the good dairy farm followed by what appears to be an abandoned farmstead, and wonder about the barley field that sports a sign from your friendly realtor marked "commercial property."

It is with some relief that after driving for about another ten to fifteen miles you leave this somewhat shadowy area behind and drive through deep woods or through grain fields that extend to the horizon. You are now between forty and fifty miles from the city in a thoroughly rural area. Ex-urbanite establishments – an isolated residential site carved out of a woodlot, or a group of secluded estate homes – will not turn up more often than once in five miles, although if you drive on you will continue to find for up to about seventy-five miles occasional evidence of the expanded life space of urban man in the form of a game farm, a summer lake colony or a rural retreat.

This kind of pattern: inner urban fringe, outer urban fringe, urban shadow, urban field and rural area, may be found with variations in detail in the surroundings of any Canadian city. Underlying this occurrence are certain basic development forces that leave their mark on all urban regions.[3]

There is a continuing outward push of urban population. An estimated eleven million people will be added to cities and towns by the end of the century, requiring at the current land consumption rate (about 150 acres per 1,000 people) about 1,650,000 acres.[4] The average Canadian is still highly mobile – increases in gasoline prices notwithstanding; and he is almost constantly besieged and beguiled by a battery of new space-expanding machines, from trail bikes and snow-mobiles (from 10,000 in 1965 to over 300,000 in 1975) to all-terrain vehicles, dune buggies and hydrofoils.[5] The "competition for land accelerates the thrust" into the urban field. It is estimated that the indirect urban intrusion effects, such as the promotion and sometimes speculative holding of rural land for urban purposes, consume about as much rural land as urban building itself. Behind the brisk market for fringe land is the individual Canadian's preoccupation with private property, both as economic security and as a means towards a preferred lifestyle. And with ownership go certain assumed rights which themselves become influencing forces, such as the implicit right to a speculative gain in land value, and to urban type municipal services in the country. While the need for selective expansion into the urban field is not at issue, the *form* of expansion is a matter of increasing concern, as it could have far-reaching effects on the use of land and the quality of the urban surroundings. From this viewpoint the calibre of planning policy and controls is crucial.[6]

Since the surroundings of all cities exhibit the foregoing fringe-shadow-field characteristics it is important for people and governments to get some sense of the amount of land involved. That kind of general estimate has been made by the geographer, Lorne Russwurm (Figure 6.1).[7] It includes estimates of land in the urban fringe by five urban size groups, from populations of 10,000 up to the big three – Montreal, Toronto and Vancouver – with over a million. This includes the surroundings of 136 cities, of which sixty-five are in the 10,000–25,000 size range. Although the estimate is only approximate, it demonstrates just how crucial this part of our land resource may be in national terms.

Of a total of about 85,000 square miles of fringe land, the three largest metropolitan areas alone account for about 16 per cent while the nineteen other metropolitan areas with populations ranging from just over 100,000 (Saint John, N.B.) to well over half a million (Ottawa-Hull) contain approximately 40 per cent of the estimated fringe land. This leaves more than two-fifths distributed amongst the remaining 113 urban regions. An estimate was also made of the distribution of urban fringe land by province (Figure 6.2). About three-quarters of the fringe area is in Quebec, Ontario and British Columbia – the provinces which are most heavily urbanized and where the people of the cities press on quite limited regional farm land of good quality.

Figure 6.1. Land in the Urban Fringe, a National Estimate, by City Size

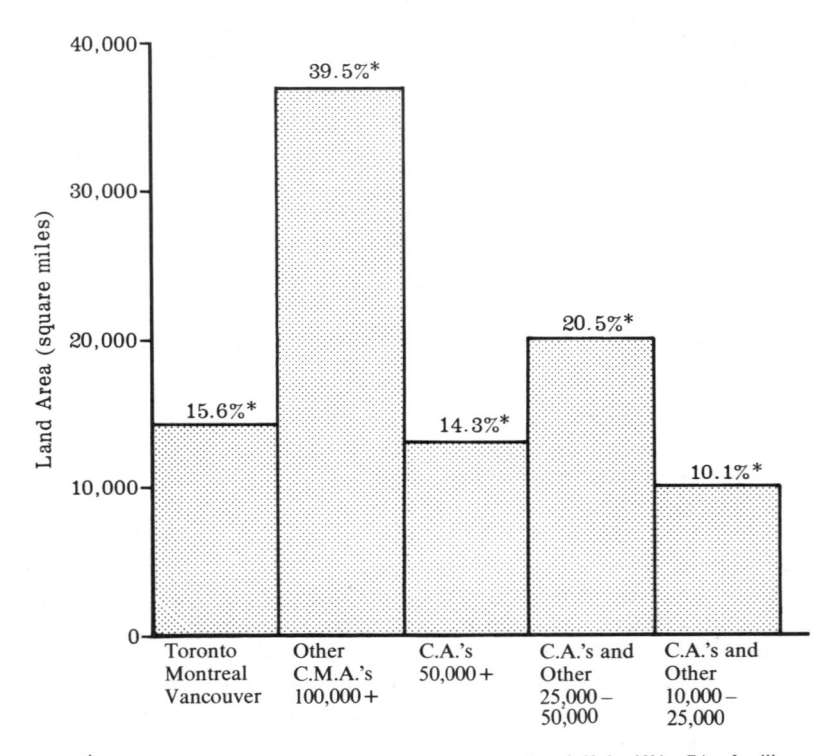

```
40,000 ┐
                39.5%*
30,000 ┤

                                        20.5%*
20,000 ┤
        15.6%*          14.3%*
                                                10.1%*
10,000 ┤

     0 ┴─────────────────────────────────────────────────
       Toronto    Other    C.A.'s   C.A.'s and  C.A.'s and
       Montreal   C.M.A.'s 50,000+  Other       Other
       Vancouver  100,000+          25,000–     10,000–
                                    50,000      25,000
```

Land Area (square miles)

*Expressed as a percentage of total (approximately 85,000 square miles) of "National Urban Fringe Land".

Source: L.H. Russwurm, "The Urban Fringe as a Regional Environment" (Waterloo: Department of Geography, University of Waterloo, June, 1975) (mimeographed).

Much of the three highest classes of farmland in Quebec and Ontario fall within the hypothetical fringe land radii of urban centres (Maps 6.1 and 6.2). (Note, the radii for the five categories of urban areas, from the big three to places as low as 10,000 in population were thirty, twenty, fifteen, ten and five miles).[8]

The area of the fringe includes some of Canada's most important natural resources. In addition to farmland, there are *recreational lands* such as Grouse Mountain, Vancouver, Qu'Appelle Valley, Regina, Gatineau Hills, Ottawa; *sand and gravel deposits* critical because of the tight constraints of transportation costs; and city *water supply* areas, like the ground water recharge areas in Wilmot Township, Waterloo Region, Pocknock Lake, Halifax and Loch Lomond,

Figure 6.2. Distribution of Urban Fringe Land, by Province

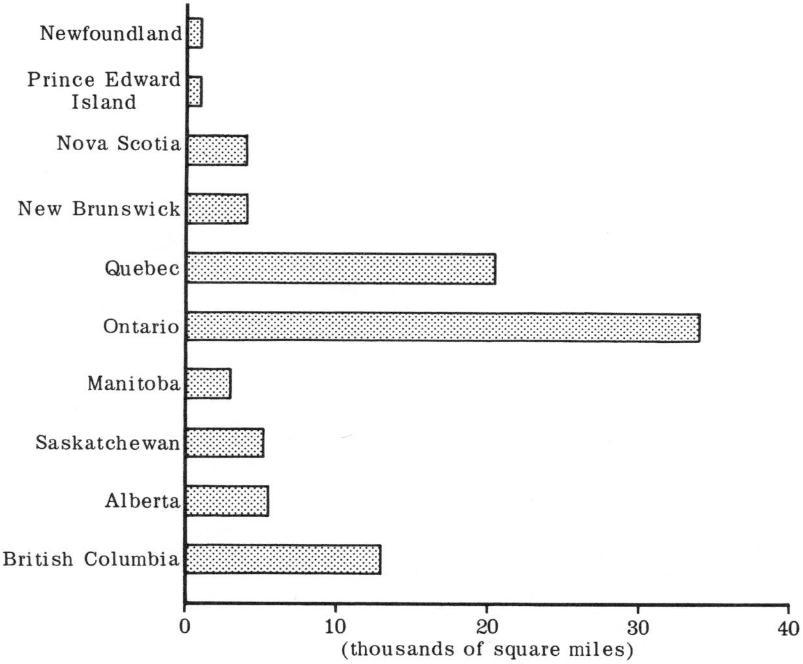

```
Newfoundland          |
Prince Edward Island  |
Nova Scotia           |
New Brunswick         |
Quebec                |
Ontario               |
Manitoba              |
Saskatchewan          |
Alberta               |
British Columbia      |
                      0    10    20    30    40
                        (thousands of square miles)
```

Source: L.H. Russwurm, "The Urban Fringe as a Regional Environment" (Waterloo: Department of Geography, University of Waterloo, June, 1975) (mimeographed).

Saint John. In fact, it has been stated that much of our land needs in the next quarter century will have to be met in the urban fringe – for urban building, for recreation, for producing food (apart from grain staples on the Prairies) and for the ecological resources on which human life – most especially urbanized man, technologically-buffered and hence vulnerable – so desperately depends.[9]

The Natural Environment of the Urban Surroundings

You are twelve years old. You live in a suburb of a large city. You can't wait for spring to come because then you can start moving around on your ten-speed. In May almost the whole gang from your street cycle three miles out to the edge of town for "spring training" where one of your friend's uncles has a farm. The hay, cut in the fall, leaves a field of short stubble that is perfect for soft ball.

Map 6.1. Distribution of Urban Centres and Good Farmland in Southern Quebec

Data Unavailable

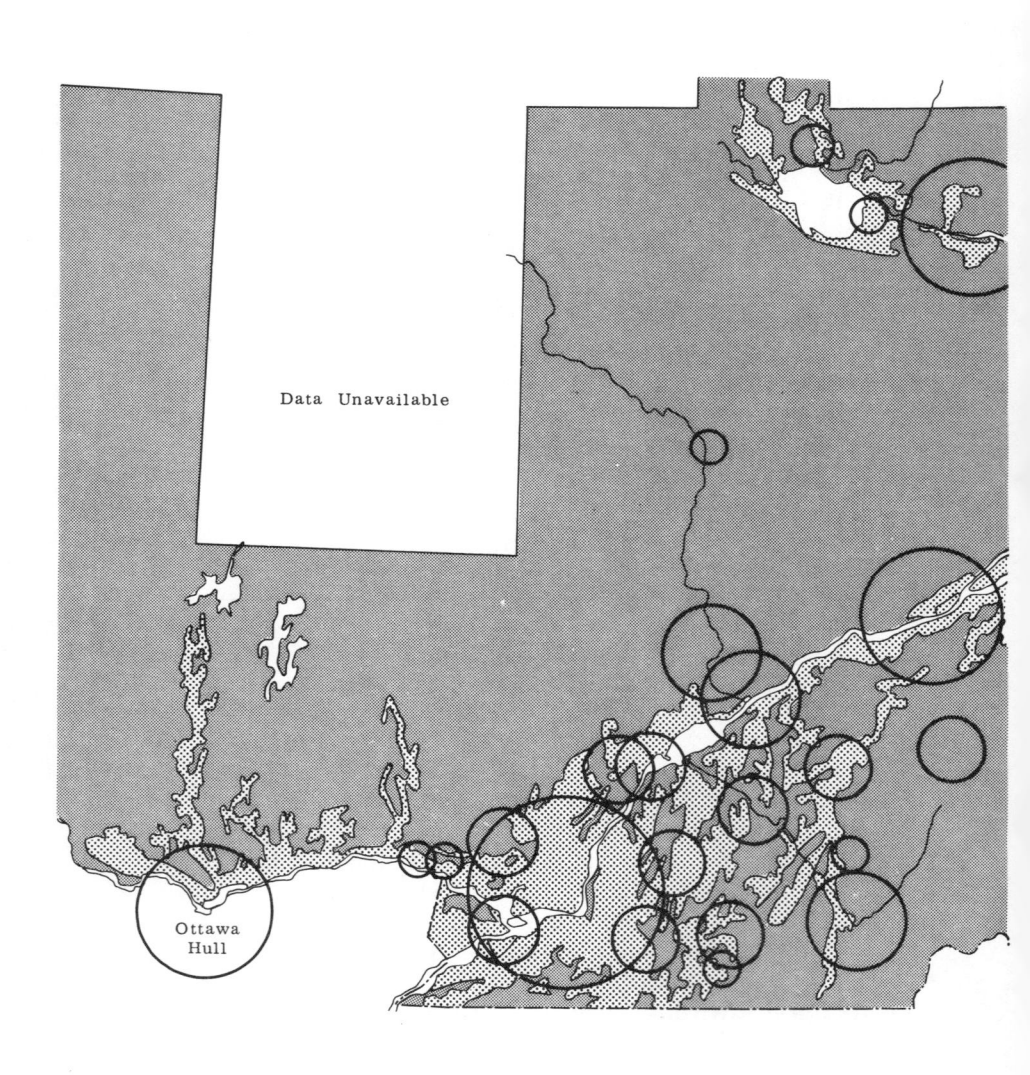

Ottawa
Hull

THE URBAN SURROUNDINGS 273

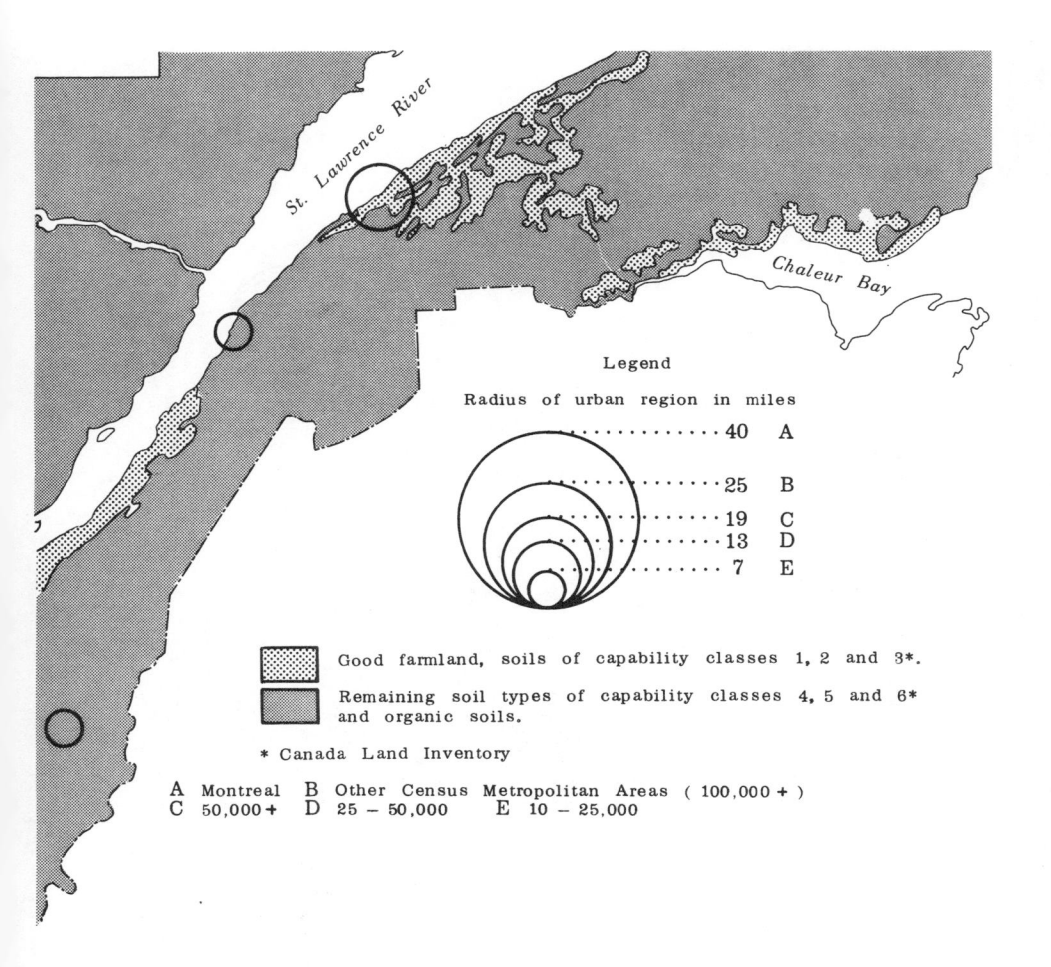

Legend

Radius of urban region in miles

40 A
25 B
19 C
13 D
7 E

Good farmland, soils of capability classes 1, 2 and 3*.

Remaining soil types of capability classes 4, 5 and 6* and organic soils.

* Canada Land Inventory

A Montreal   B Other Census Metropolitan Areas (100,000 +)
C 50,000 +   D 25 – 50,000   E 10 – 25,000

Source: J.L. Nowland, *The Agricultural Productivity of the Soils of Ontario and Quebec*, monograph No. 13 (Ottawa: Research Branch Canada Department of Agriculture, 1975).

274　CHANGING CANADIAN CITIES

Map 6.2. Distribution of Urban Centres and Good Farmland in Southern Ontario

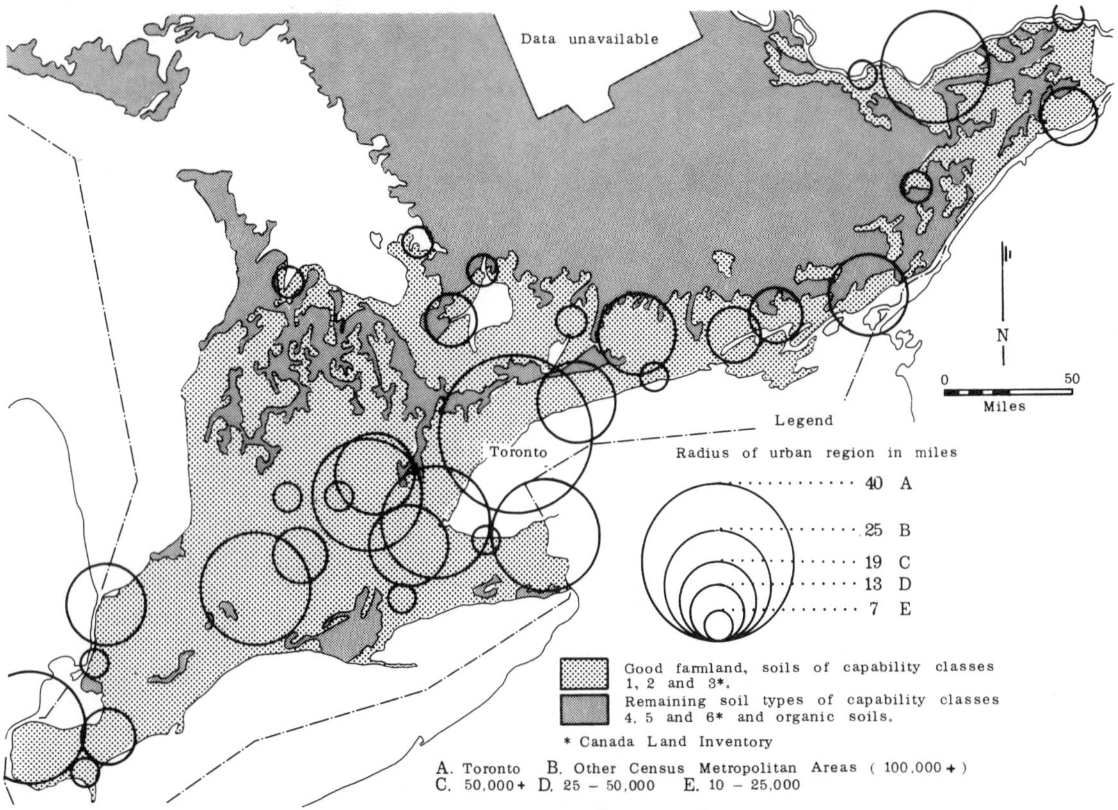

Source: J.L. Nowland, *The Agricultural Productivity of the Soils of Ontario and Quebec*, monograph No. 13 (Ottawa: Research Branch Canada Department of Agriculture,

Later in the summer you and some of your pals make the "big trip," a fifteen mile ride through ravines and along country roads to a really neat area where you camp for the day, sometimes overnight on the edge of a forest of big trees: tall sugar maples and some white pine. It is one of your favourite places because there is so much to see and do. There is a kind of mountain with some exposed limestone cliffs. One day about half-way up you spotted a white-tailed deer munching on some birch leaves. Another time in the very early morning when you were camping you saw a red fox trying to catch a rabbit for breakfast. There are trout to be caught in the creek that runs through the woods, raspberries to pick and green-headed mallards and other ducks to watch skimming along a marsh pond. And there is an abandoned quarry filled with cool clean water which feels so good after a day in the sun.

One spot you will always remember is a high point in the landscape, a hump where you can see the countryside for miles around, with the different colours and patterns of the woods, cultivated fields, farm houses, barns and silos making it look like some kind of story book paradise. Your father once said that the hump was a "glacial deposit" with lots of gravel that someone wants to dig up and take away. And you hope not.[10]

It is difficult to put into words the importance of the city's natural surroundings to personal development and well-being. The recollections, somewhat rose coloured, that we retain from our youth, express in the final analysis a sound instinct. Even in the age of communications, when it is fashionable to speak of the global village, the immediate natural environment of air, water, landforms, soils, plants and animals forms a critical part of the human ecosystem: the total network of inter-related conditions – cultural, economic and natural – required for personal and communal health.

The over-riding fact about the natural environment of the urban fringe, is that it is both highly perishable and under pressure. The spread of human settlement into the urban field has not been sufficiently selective. The view of land as a commodity has predominated over the concept of land as a resource. Consequently, the toll in terms of irretrievable environmental losses has been heavy.

This has been true even in our most favoured and dramatic landscapes. "Open space," for example, emerges as one of the worries in the Greater Vancouver region in the 1975 report on *The Livable Region 1976/1986*. Taking stock of the past, the following "entries" appear on the wrong side of the ledger: twelve of seventeen "sizeable creeks and streams" partially destroyed by pollution and/or damming; many smaller creeks obliterated and turned into flood and drainage channels; serious deterioration of riverbank quality along the Fraser; pollution of the Boundary Bay shellfish industry; waterfront bird feeding and nesting grounds destroyed; residential developments "which totally scrape plant and soil cover from treed hillsides," and so on. And the threat of environmental degradation is unfortunately a continuing one: housing projects are proposed for Burnaby Mountain; on the North Shore there is steady pressure to push urban development further up the mountain slopes (even beyond the 1,200 foot contour).[11]

In responding to the open space challenge, the Greater Vancouver Regional District has evolved an approach out of its own conditions and needs which has interesting implications for many other urban regions in Canada. Its expressed philosophy is "to retain the character of our wilderness and open land resources, and to open up many of these areas for public use."[12] And its chosen instrument is the concept of the *Open Space Conservancy*, a broadly defined land use district that would encompass all significant regional recreation and landscape features, whether publicly or privately owned. Conservancy resources would be of two types: (1) parks and conservation areas, exclusive recreation areas which must be publicly purchased, and (2) multi-use areas, such as scenic and waterfront areas in which "controlled development" is acceptable along with the guarantee of public access. This would call for various innovative forms of control to assure the public interest in the land, including easement-type agreements with private owners, landscape guidelines, and the cooperative use and development of open space held by other public agencies, at any government level.

The accompanying map of *Open Space Proposals* (Map 6.3) illustrates that the proposed conservancy would be very extensive: in fact a system of mountains, ocean shorelines, rivers and streams, tidal lands and bogs, ravines and wooded slopes, rights-of-way for various purposes, parks and institutional reserves that would permeate the District of Greater Vancouver. To implement a program of such dimensions (along with certain bold measures in other sectors), the report logically concludes that more than local and regional levels of administration will have to be involved. "Commitment and cooperation will be required from all levels of government."[13]

The Vancouver concept is symptomatic of an important change in societal attitudes towards the natural environment that surrounds urban settlement. It is expressed in a number of recent planning studies and proposals, notably in the regions of Edmonton, Waterloo, Toronto and Halifax-Dartmouth.[14] Three questions posed by the Nova Scotia study express most succinctly the emerging philosophy: Which areas are least costly to service for future urban development? In what areas must natural eco-systems be protected to

THE URBAN SURROUNDINGS 277

Map 6.3. Open Space Proposals, Greater Vancouver Regional District

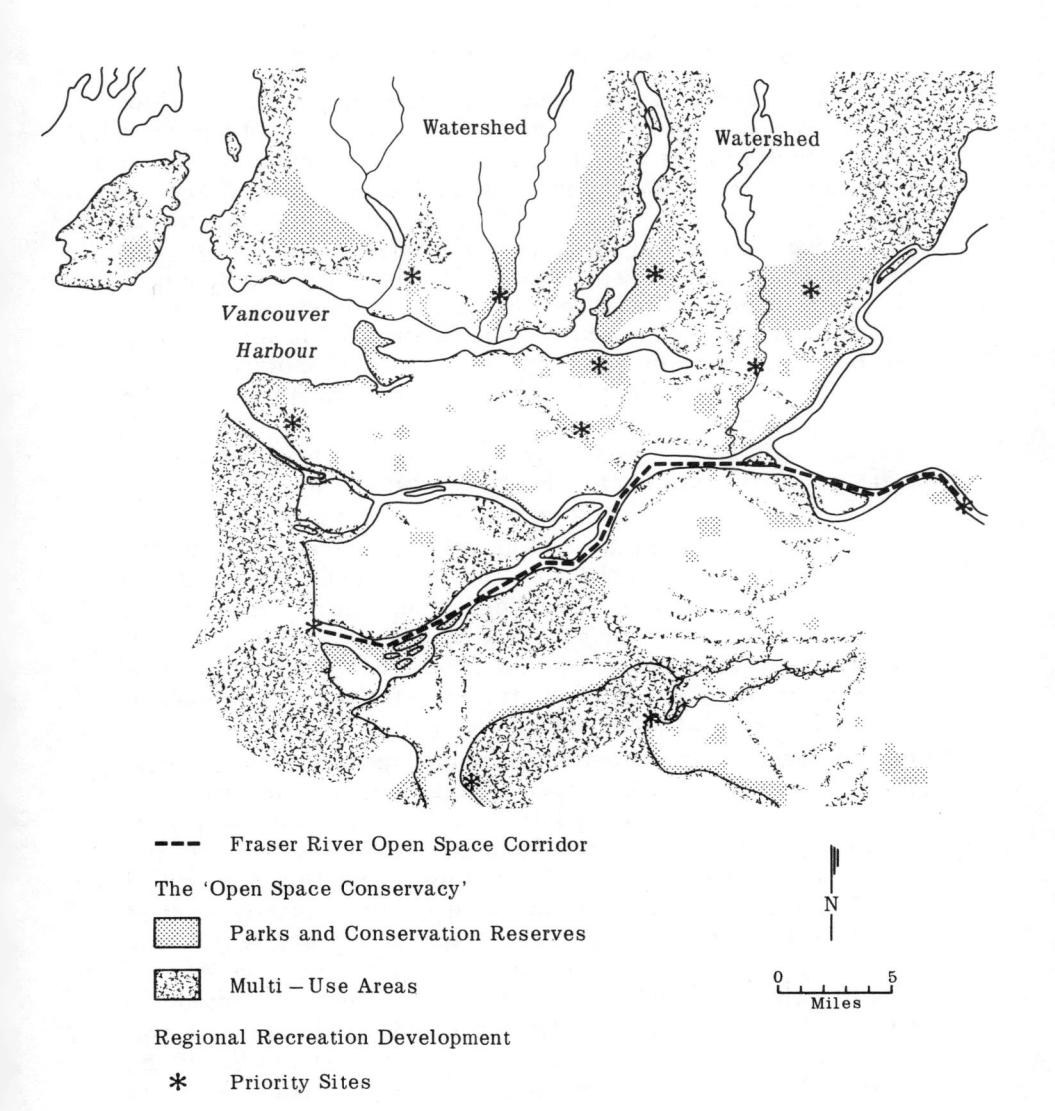

- - - Fraser River Open Space Corridor

The 'Open Space Conservacy'

▨ Parks and Conservation Reserves

▨ Multi – Use Areas

Regional Recreation Development

✷ Priority Sites

Source: *The Livable Region 1976/1986 Proposals to Manage the Growth of Greater Vancouver* (Vancouver: Greater Vancouver Regional District, 1975), p. 26.

continue functioning fully? Which high quality sites must be preserved lest urban development destroy them permanently? Canadians at last appear to be reaching for a better trade-off between the commodity and resource views of land.[15]

The Urban Surroundings as A Production Environment

In Canada, good land and homes seem to go together. The cities are found mainly in the regions of best farmland and the most favourable climate for growing things. Canada's farming areas have been rated, *agroclimatically*, in terms of the estimated number of days from ripening of an early barley variety to first fall freeze. This is illustrated on Map 6.4, which relates for each census division in Southern Ontario and Quebec three things: climate, farmland acreage and urban population. The statistical results are quite revealing. Half of Canada's urban population lives in areas having the best 5 per cent of our farmland and three-quarters in areas having the best 20 per cent. Urban growth in Canada consumes the best farmland.[16]

The human meaning of the agricultural land around our cities is many-sided. As one authority has expressed it:

> The countryside is seen as an area which embodies two particular sets of functions, those of an *economic nature* including the basic functions of employment and the production of food and timber, and *amenities*, including social, visual, aesthetic and ecological values. Farming, while having as its prime function that of food production and the livelihood of the farm population, can contribute greatly to the amenity functions in terms of management and conservation.[17]

In its agricultural role the urban surroundings contribute much to the quality of life—just *how much* is suggested by thinking of your city without its regional dairy farms, its egg and poultry supply, its local apiaries, its source of fresh vegetables, its farmers' market. At a time of intensifying global imbalance between food production and population growth, the good land around our cities also assumes provincial and national, if not international, importance. A 1974 task force report on the *Central Ontario Lakeshore Urban Complex* very bluntly spells out what is at stake in the continuing conversion of farm land to other uses. The region (Hamilton-Toronto-Oshawa-Lake Simcoe) makes up about 0.8 per cent of the area of the province, has 8 per cent of Ontario's improved farm land and 11 per cent of its best soils—Class 1 and 2. The 900,000 acres of good land has a food-producing potential for about one million people at present levels of consumption. Future growth in the region (to 2000) will consume directly and indirectly 300,000 acres of the best soils. Growth in the other urban regions of the province will have similar repercussions. With a limited land base and a growing population, something will have to give. By the year 2000 Ontario may have to import 60 per cent of its food requirements from a world which may face even more critical food shortages. At the very best the relative cost of food will go up and real standards of living, down.[18]

The urban surroundings will be under steady pressure from spreading urban development. Relating future urban population (11,000,000 additional to year 2000) and current direct and indirect consumption of farm land (200 acres per 1,000 urban population) indicates an absorption of 2.2 million acres of land for the last quarter of the century. If one-half of this urban growth continues to locate on the best 5 per cent of Canada's farmland (5 per cent of 170 million acres or 8.5 million acres) then 1.1 million acres would be lost from the urban surroundings, or approximately 13 per cent of our best farm land. This is a conservative estimate, as there are parts of Canada – Quebec City, Montreal, the Quebec-Windsor axis – where substantially higher land absorption rates have been recorded.[19]

The importance of agriculture and the constraints of land and climate that affect it, are factors that make land use decisions in the urban surroundings so critical – and difficult. There is a great deal at stake in the quality of land that is irreversibly committed to urban uses. For example, corn under optimum conditions, which yields 136 bushels to the acre when sown on Class 1 land, would yield 105 bushels on Class 2, 80 on Class 3, and 60 on Class 4. Convert this to dollar values and you can begin to get a glimpse of the economic and social costs incurred when, say, a new community site of 10,000 acres is placed primarily on Class 1 rather than Class 3 or 4 land.[20]

In response to this broad view of the present and future use of productive fringe land, certain policy principles are important. We stand to gain, regionally and nationally (1) if good land is not permitted to stand idle while awaiting scheduled development; (2) if the best land is reserved indefinitely for agricultural use; and (3) if new growth is steered away entirely from Class 1 and 2 lands. The *regional form* of growth – the way the surroundings are used as a lived-in environment – may cumulatively have far-reaching national repercussions.

This section has dealt with only one aspect of the production environment. Extractive minerals, forest products and water are three additional productive resources in the urban surroundings. While they differ in many ways, their use and development are very much affected by the presence of the advancing city. The location of

280 CHANGING CANADIAN CITIES

Map 6.4 Spatial Distribution of Agro-climatic Resource, Farmland and Urban Population in Southern Ontario and Quebec

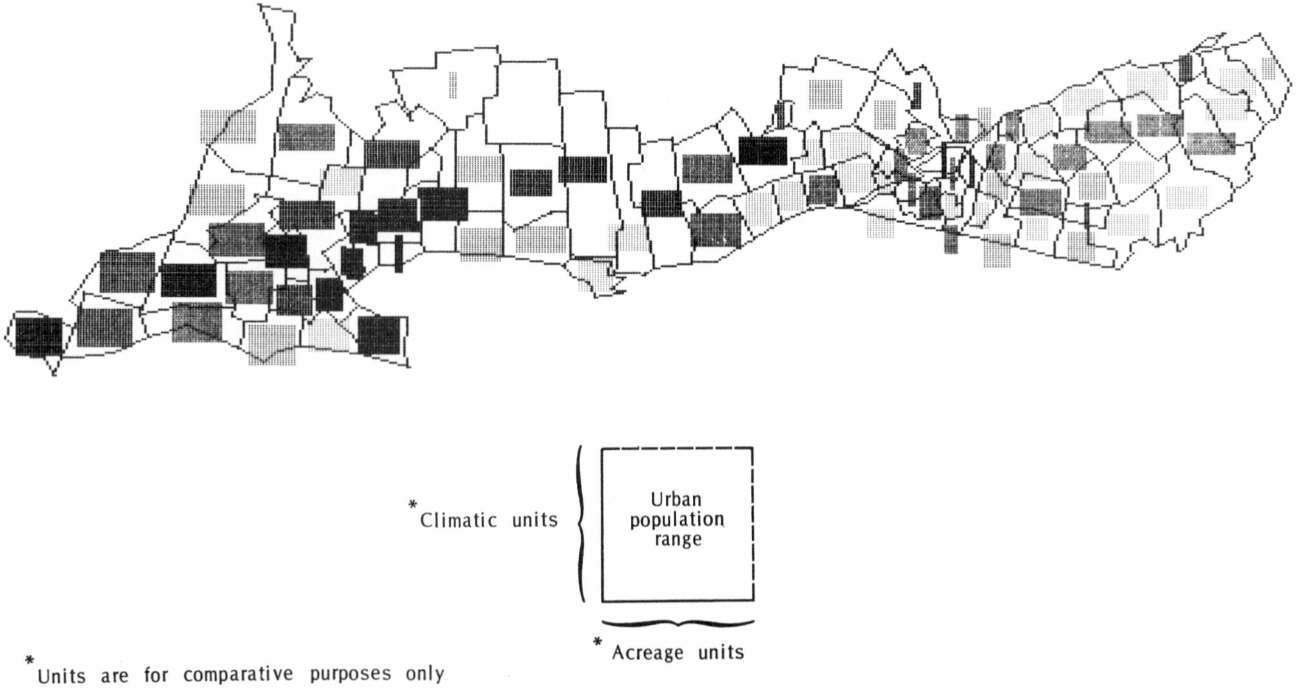

* Units are for comparative purposes only

* Climatic units
* Acreage units

Urban population range

Note: For each census division which reported at least some farmland and some urban population in 1971, a rectangle is shown in which the height represents the duration from barley ripening until first fall freeze, the width represents the census-farm acreage, and the darkness of the shading represents the magnitude of the urban population. Note particularly the concentration around the west end of Lake Ontario of divisions where the farmland is particularly subject to urban expansion pressures, as indicated by the dark rectangles.

Legend

Climatic resources		Farmland acreage		Urban population	
Height units	Range in days	Width units	Range in acres	Shading (light to dark)	Range
1	0 to 29	1	0 to 60,000	1	1,100 to 13,643
2	30 to 44	2	60,001 to 100,000	2	13,644 to 25,812
3	45 to 59	3	100,001 to 140,000	3	25,813 to 54,684
4	60 to 74	4	140,001 to 190,000	4	54,685 to 127,567
5	75 to 89	5	190,001 to 230,000	5	127,568 to 2,184,000
6	90 or more	6	230,001 to 300,000		
		7	300,001 to 500,000		
		8	500,001 to 2,000,000		
		9	2,000,001 or more		

Note: Class intervals used are based on analysis of each distribution by Census Division

Source: G.D.V. Williams, N. Pocock, L.H. Russwurm, "The Distribution of Agro-climatic Resources in Relation to Canada's Urban Population." (Waterloo: Department of Geography, University of Waterloo, 1975) (mimeographed).

sand and gravel pits is affected by the vexing fact that at about fifty miles hauling distance, overland transportation to the urban market costs more than the value of the product itself. City dwellers want a regional water supply and good summer stream-flow, but in pursuing the first from ground water sources they sometimes place the second in jeopardy; and so on. The urban surroundings are an arena where fundamental social and political choices must be faced.

The Urban Surroundings as a Place to Live

The expansion of urban growth in Canada, associated with a moderate end-of-century increase in total population, will make heavy demands on the land of our urban fields. To the degree that past settlement trends persist, the pressure will be greatest on the inner fringe. The search for more satisfactory settlement forms, particularly in the largest metropolitan areas, will tend to push elements of urban settlement much more deeply into the urban field—as regions experiment with corridor, new community or other forms of dispersed, rather than accretionary, growth.

The advancing tide of *urban dwellers* represents only one of several groups of people who call the urban surroundings their home. Others are the *ex-urbanites*, country residents living on small acreages on isolated sites or in clusters who work and retain social ties in the city; various *part-time dwellers* such as summer weekenders and owners of cottages, second homes or hobby farms; *part-time farmers*, individuals who live on and operate a farm but hold another job in a town or city or in other resource industries such as lumbering, mining and fishing; *full-time farmers*, the permanent tillers of the soil, including families that continue from the days of pioneer settlement; and other *ruralites*, employed full-time in the other primary industries or providing services in a network of hamlets and villages.[21]

As urban uses and influences advanced, the past quarter century has seen the accelerated retreat of farms and farmers from the most heavily urbanized regions of the country—for example, southern Ontario. In the two decades, 1951-71, there was a decline in improved farm land of over 1.5 million acres, or about 13 per cent of the close to 12 million acres in 1951; and that part of the provincial region called the "Urban Arc," stretching in a thirty-mile depth back from Lake Ontario, and extending from Port Hope-Cobourg on the west to the Niagara Peninsula on the east, experienced a decline in improved land at a rate which was more than double the southern Ontario rate—27 per cent, or 437,000 acres out of 1,611,000 acres in 1951.[22]

The mixed occupation of the urban surroundings, from full-time farmer to part-time urbanite, is a phenomenon occurring around most of the cities of this country. The tendency can be observed in places of different size and dramatically different landscapes, functions and regional locations.

In the Vancouver area the striking thing about the use of the surroundings is its diversity. There are small hobby farms in the Fraser valley penetrating as far as Chilliwack, seventy miles from downtown Vancouver, and forming in some areas, such as Surrey in the inner fringe and Langley in the outer fringe, almost a continuous frontage of country residents. The Gulf Islands across Georgia Strait, the Sunshine Coast across Howe Sound and other coastal lands provide a congenial environment for water-oriented weekenders and vacationists—over 60,000 boats, one for every twenty persons, are registered in and around Vancouver (Map 6.5). And others go up to the ski and alpine recreational areas in the Squamish/Garibaldi region, just about an hour's drive north of Vancouver – "cottages, ski cabins, hotels, condominiums, and hostels are mushrooming in once-isolated mountain valleys." Farmers continue to hold on with some tenacity to the highly productive valley bottoms, coastal plains and river floodplains, but there is a steady erosion of prime agricultural land in the Fraser valley – at a twenty-year rate of 2,850 acres per annum – and it is estimated that approximately 20 per cent of the Lower Fraser valley has gone out of farm production.[23] These are some of the conditions that precipitated the provincial initiative of 1973, which empowered a Land Commission to establish agricultural reserves.

An overview of rural subdivision in Alberta is provided in a study of the *Alberta Land Use Forum* for the five-year period 1969 to 1973. The investigation is based mainly on the experience within the seven Regional Planning Commission Areas, which are focused respectively on the following urban places: Grande Prairie/Peace River, Edmonton, Camrose/Westaskwin, Red Deer, Calgary, Lethbridge and Medicine Hat. Within the study period the number of applications received nearly doubled and the amount of acreage approved or conditionally approved each year for country resident purposes was approximately 1.25 townships (township = 36 square miles). Overall, the majority of the applications (54+ per cent) were for country residential purposes, on parcels less than twenty acres. The other reasons for subdivision were proportionately, agriculture 34+ per cent; resort 4 per cent; public/institutional 1 per cent; commercial less than 1 per cent; industrial 2.5 per cent, and so on. Three broad patterns characterize this Alberta experience. There is a substantial amount of country-residential acreage in the region of

Map 6.5. Vancouver Region, Selected Fringe Features

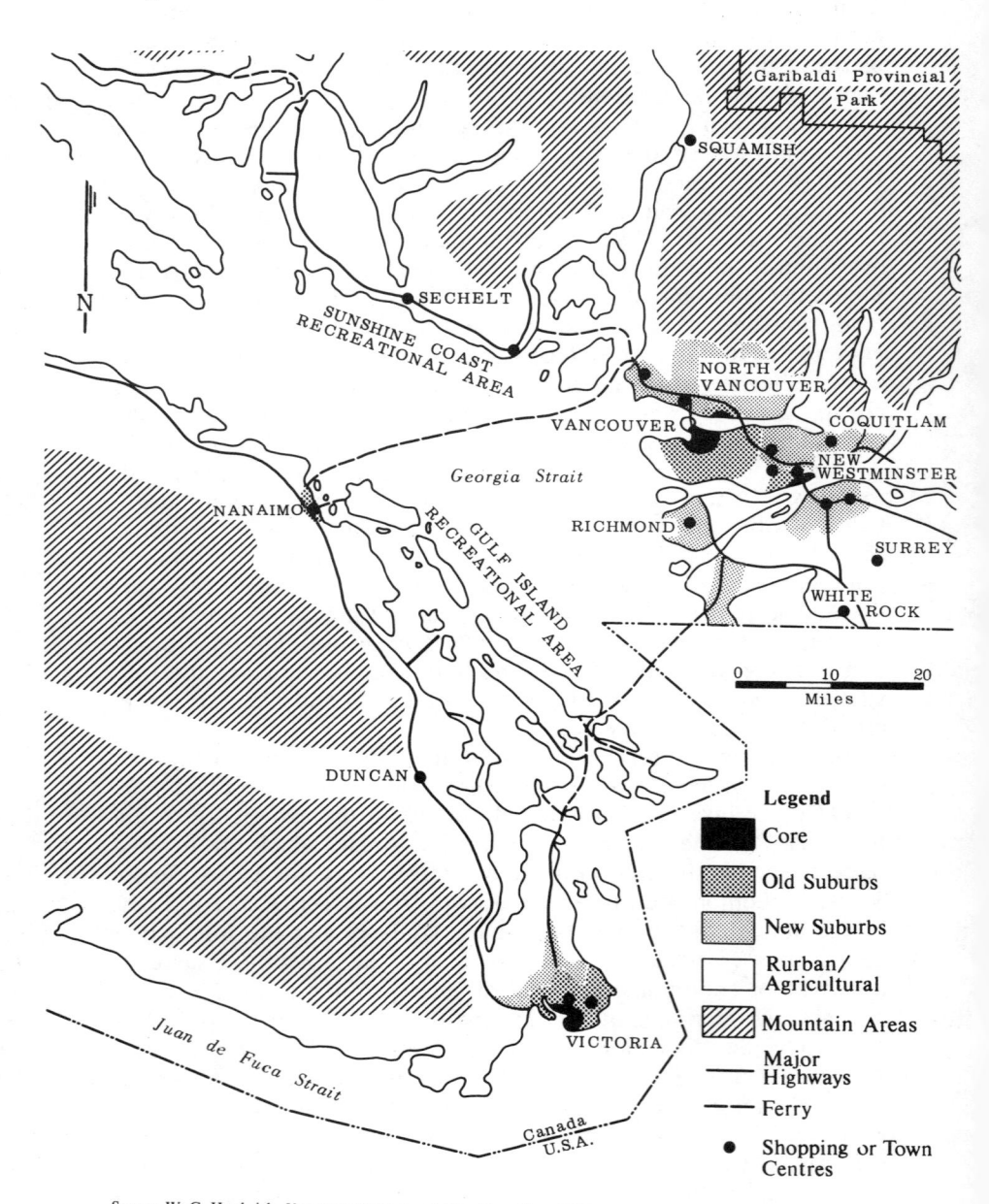

Source: W. G. Hardwick, *Vancouver* (Toronto: Collier Macmillan, 1974), p. 54.

the bigger centres, Edmonton and Calgary (48.5 per cent and 47.7 per cent of the approved acreage). Agricultural uses (75 per cent) predominate in the southerly regions around Lethbridge and Medicine Hat. There is relatively greater subdivision activity in the Edmonton region – one half of the parcels approved are located within that area.[24]

Not all provinces have had the benefit of this kind of comprehensive look at the location of the homes of city people in the country, but wherever studies have been undertaken some features of the fringe-field pattern are discovered. Around the small city of Brandon, Manitoba (31,000, 1971), the inner fringe contained (1971) six hundred non-farm households representing 8 per cent of all the households in the urban area. Most of these were along highways radiating from the city, some in association with ribbon development forming "corridors of urban sprawl."[25] In a still different environment, the rugged rock and forest terrain of northern Ontario, fringe settlement around Thunder Bay (108,000, 1971) assumes a strongly linear form (Map 6.6). One of its most conspicuous features is a belt of residences, some seasonal and some permanent, scattered along the north shoreline of Lake Superior for about twenty-five miles from the city. Another characteristic is the strings of very mixed non-residential uses, along the major connecting highways categorized as "traffic-attracted, resident-serving, zoned-out – needing large blocks of land – specialty and amenity agriculture." The Thunder Bay fringe also contains an Indian reservation along the south shoreline and five mobile home parks, a residential type which is often associated with primary resource regions having seasonal employment.[26] In southern Ontario, Lorne Russwurm has documented the steady rise of scattered non-farm population in the "urban fringe-urban shadow landscape" of the Toronto-Stratford corridor – from 2.7 per cent in 1941 to 6.7 per cent in 1966 and 8.2 per cent in 1971.[27] In Quebec a two million acre decline in farm land within the five years, 1966-71, led to an expressed concern with the large number of farms purchased by urban dwellers, about half of which are permitted to lie idle.[28] And in Halifax-Dartmouth, the Metropolitan Area Planning Committee (MAPC), has responded to the strong exurbanite pressure on the many lakes and woods, and on the attractive ocean shoreline of the region. It has recommended an "Open Landscape Conservation District" for the protection and wise management of the natural resource system.[29]

This look at the different aspects of the urban field has drawn attention to both its links with the city and its own special charac-

Map 6.6. Thunder Bay, Selected Fringe Features

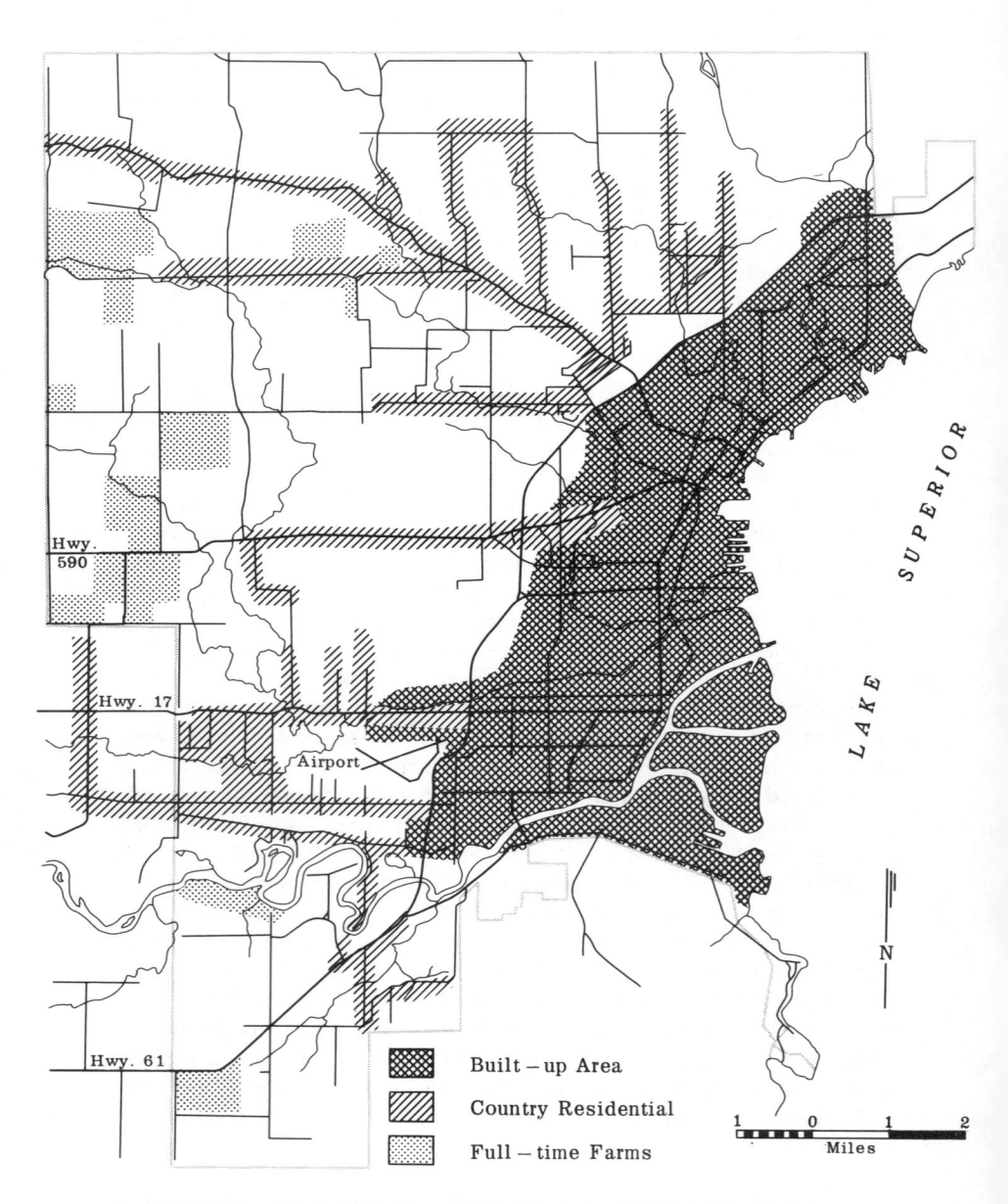

Source: B.E. Tamminen, "The Rural-Urban Fringe of the City of Thunder Bay, 1972," B.A. Thesis (Thunder Bay: Lakehead University, 1973), p.29.

teristics as a natural, production and lived-in environment. It is a sub-system within a larger system. To understand it in those essential terms an examination of one country residence settlement in a reasonably thorough way is necessary. A recent study of the County of Parkland in the Edmonton planning region affords that opportunity.[30]

The County of Parkland is adjacent to the western boundary of the City of Edmonton and extends due west for a distance close to sixty miles, through black loam, transitional and grey-wooded soil zones. It is the area within the Edmonton planning region which currently attracts the greatest number of country residential subdivisions – 1,159 parcels approved and registered from 1969 to 1972 – which is a little more than the total for the other three counties of the region. In all, there are 2,155 country residential sites in the county (with a median size of 3.8 acres) of which about a third are developed and together accommodate over three thousand people. As indicated in Map 6.7 almost all of these are located in a clustered pattern in the eastern third of the County, between Edmonton and the town of Stony Plain. By a combination of careful observation and sample surveys of the population, the study explored the relationship of subdivisions to locational factors and natural resources, the characteristics of the population and their reasons for moving to the country, and the impact of country residences on the municipal budget. In other words: Where? Who? Why? And How Much?[31]

The country residents of Parkland were mainly former residents of Edmonton (over 80 per cent) who continued to work in the city (over 78 per cent) and who chose locations mainly within thirty to fifty minutes automobile travel time from the centre of the city, and generally within two miles of a paved road. Although accessibility to the city is unquestionably a major locational factor, country residence sites are not simply an expression of free market choices. The present pattern was shaped as early as the mid-fifties when the Regional Planning Commission laid down guidelines for smallholding development. As a result the major concentrations do not intrude on good agricultural land, they have a good ground water supply, they are located mainly in areas of moderate recreation capability and they have the amenities of undulating terrain and small lakes which attract waterfowl in abundance.[32]

The people of the country residence areas gave their main reasons for living in the country as privacy, the quality of the environment, open space for the kids and dissatisfaction with the city. Such economic factors as the search for low cost living or supplementary income from farming ranked very low. People come from a variety

288 CHANGING CANADIAN CITIES

Map 6.7. Edmonton Region, County of Parkland, Country Residential Locations

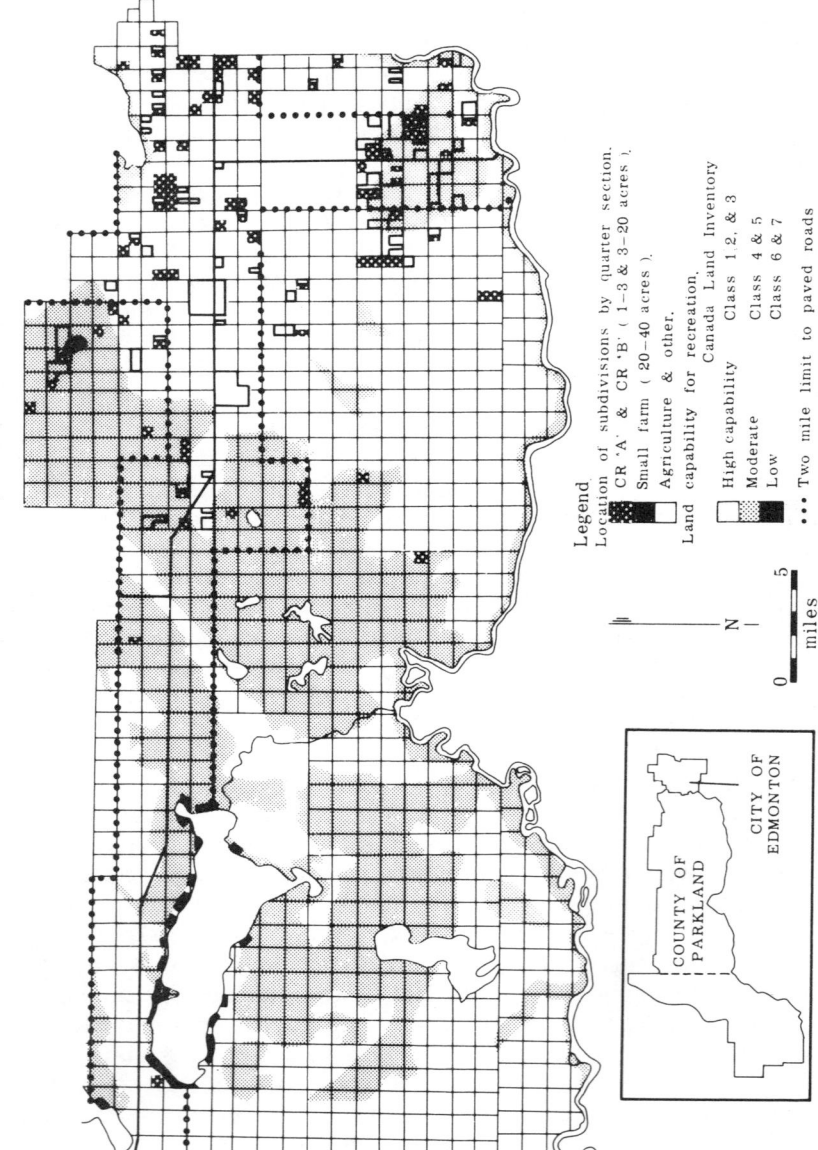

Legend

Location of subdivisions by quarter section.
  CR 'A' & CR 'B' (1–3 & 3–20 acres).
  Small farm (20–40 acres).
  Agriculture & other.
Land capability for recreation.
  Canada Land Inventory
  High capability   Class 1, 2, & 3
  Moderate   Class 4 & 5
  Low   Class 6 & 7
  ••• Two mile limit to paved roads

Source: H.L. Diemer, Parkland County, Country Residential Survey, report No. 4A (Edmonton, Alberta Land Use Forum, 1974), p. 34.

of economic/occupational groups. Forty per cent are classified as "professional, technical," but close to 14 per cent are in the unskilled labour category, and "craftsmen, production process and related workers," those in "service and recreational" and "clerical" occupations constitute close to one-third of the total.[33]

Generally the country residential families are larger and younger than their Edmonton counterparts, are highly dependent on car travel, and, while strongly oriented to the big city for work and shopping and social life, are beginning to establish some rural links, as indicated by a just emerging trend to travel on a weekly basis to the nearest country town. While some dissatisfaction was expressed with the quality of roads, with water supply, the school bus and other country services, the great majority of residents indicated that they were happy about their decision to move to the country. The low turnover rate of lots after purchase indicates very decidedly that the country residents of Parkland are not land speculators, but seekers of a preferred lifestyle. Although it is difficult to isolate the municipal "balance sheet" for this group alone, there is a strong presumption that taxation and other revenues from country residence properties do not cover the major cost items: road maintenance, schools and general servicing costs, such as police and fire protection. The distance of country residences from municipal service centres exacerbates the financial gap.[34]

Repercussions: Land and Social Issues

With so many and such different activities impinging on the urban field it has become from a land use and human settlement point-of-view one of the most complex environments in the country. It is also one of the most critical. It is the area where much of our directly experienced environmental future will be determined. The Canadian quality of living in the last quarter of this century will be strongly affected by the way, individually and communally, we manage its use. It is inescapably an area of public concern and public policy.

In moving towards *action* in the urban surroundings – the deliberate shaping of the environment – we must be very much aware of certain prevailing conditions and forces. Land use, ownership and price, as well as the nature of the development industry, are some of the factors that will have substantial impact on future settlement patterns. While we do not have in Canada a comprehensive data system providing an ongoing inventory, there are certain trends which can (must) be noted.

There is a tendency towards a substantial increase in the diversity of uses to which the land is put as well as in the forms of ownership. The most complete study available on these aspects was completed in 1974 by Professor John V. Punter, of York University. His case studies in the townships of Caledon, King, Pickering and Whitby (places within forty miles of downtown Toronto) compare active land use by ownership type in 1954 and 1971 (Figure 6.3). Active areas, land used for a definite purpose such as a house or a farm, are distinguished from passive uses, which are open and woodland areas, such as idle farmland and land subdivided and awaiting construction or being held speculatively. The "active" category has dropped from about 52 per cent of the study area to 43 per cent within the seventeen year period. The tendency towards complexity shows up quite dramatically, both with regard to land use and type of ownership. Active agricultural use substantially decreased, by about 35 per cent, and in the farming area remaining, about 80 per cent of the total active acreage, much less is owner-occupied – about 30 per cent in 1971 compared to over 75 per cent in 1954. Recreation uses increased about seven-fold, and active residential uses in these particular townships, while not constituting much more than 3 per cent of the total area, more than doubled.[35]

Punter's study records two striking changes in the ownership patterns. Absentee ownership by individuals increased from less than 5 per cent of the total area to about 20 per cent; and corporate ownership of the land which was negligible in 1954 increased to more than 20 per cent in 1971, with increases occurring particularly in the investment-developer category.[36]

Land prices showed some dramatic changes. The prices of small acreage lots increased on the average seven-fold (in constant dollars). Unserviced ex-urban lots, which were about half the cost of a comparable but fully-serviced suburban lot in 1961, were 20 per cent more expensive than such lots in 1971 (despite a 250 per cent increase in the price of the latter). This kind of price inflation was parallelled in large properties – between 1945 and 1972 the real value of parcels of seventy-five acres and above increased ten times.[37]

These trends, which are local to the surroundings of Metropolitan Toronto, are broadly representative, with some exceptions, of national trends. Land development has changed from an activity carried out by a large number of small builder/developers in the 1950s to a process in the 'seventies which is increasingly shaped by large public companies. These firms are vertically integrated, that is, organized to handle the entire development package from land assembly to servicing to planning and design, construction, property management and marketing.

THE URBAN SURROUNDINGS 291

Figure 6.3. "Active" Land Use by Ownership Type, 1954-71, North Toronto Fringe

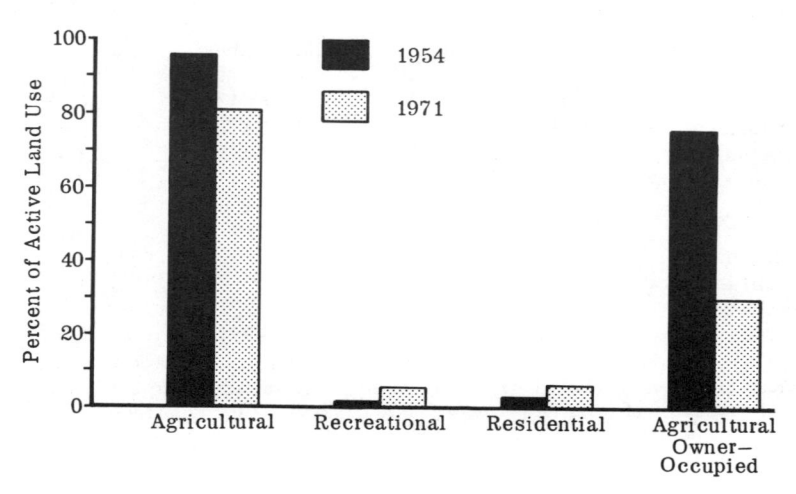

Note: Active Land Use - 52% of total acreage in 1954, and 43% of total acreage in 1971.

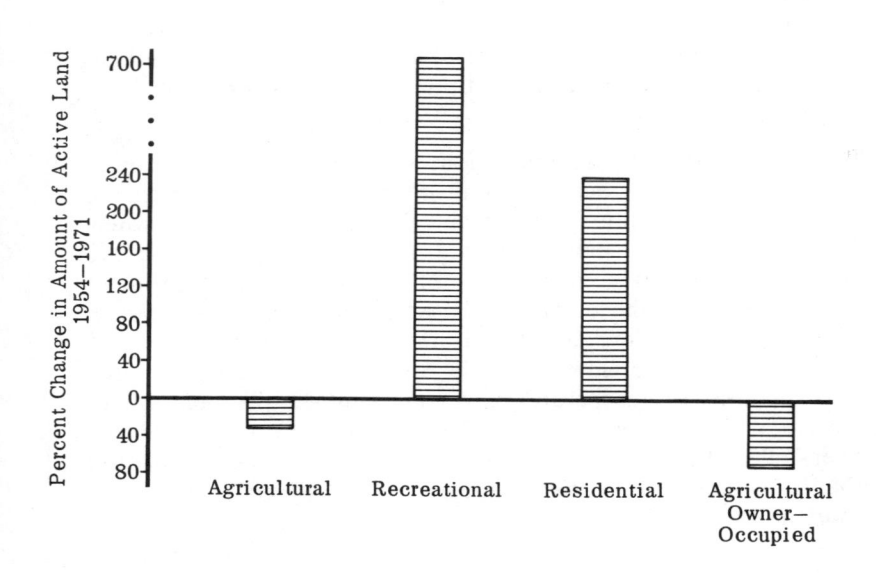

Source: J.V. Punter, *The Impact of Exurban Development on Land and Landscape in the Toronto-Centred Region 1954-71* (Ottawa: Central Mortgage and Housing Corporation, 1974), Table 23.

Table 6.1. Distribution of Parcel Ownership by Ownership Type, 1968 – 74, North east Toronto Fringe

Ownership Type	Sellers		Buyers	
	Number	Percentage of Total	Number	Percentage of Total
Joint Tenants	2,038	40.8	1,842	36.9
Individuals	1,619	32.4	1,527	30.6
Corporations	781	15.6	1,092	21.9
Executors	155	3.1	5	0.1
In Trust	144	2.9	156	3.1
Government	100	2.0	197	3.9
Partnerships	81	1.6	106	2.1
Tenants-in-Common	73	1.5	68	1.4
Unknown	3	0.1	1	0.0
Total	4,994	100.0	4,994	100.0

Source: Land Dealer Study. Larry R. G. Martin, "Structure Conduct and Performance of Land Dealers and Land Developers in the Land Development Industry," (Waterloo: School of Urban and Regional Planning, University of Waterloo, May, 1975) (mimeographed).

Currently, forty-seven firms averaging about six subsidiary companies each, hold 120,000 acres in twenty-one cities and sixteen of these [together] have plans to house one million people by 1990. In the Census Metropolitan Areas of Ontario, Manitoba, and Alberta, large firms produce 80 per cent of the detached housing.[38]

In each of the other major regions of Canada, the ownership/development pattern assumes certain distinctive features which are shaped by local conditions, needs and traditions. The land ownership and development patterns in the urban fringe of Toronto are complex and defy easy characterization. Studies in some depth of the northeast inner and outer fringes show that land transactions in the period 1968-74 were distributed amongst quite a large array of corporations and individuals (Table 6.1). At the same time, the group identified as corporations, representing 22 per cent of all buyers and 16 per cent of all sellers, is seen to "represent the nucleus of land dealer activities in the study area between 1968 and 1974."[39] A summary of the characteristics of fifteen of the more important of the land development corporations – of which five are highly active throughout the Toronto urban fringe, is presented in Table 6.2. Generally they are Canadian-controlled, well-established (not fly-by-night operations), have substantial land banks (thirteen of the fifteen) and tend to be quite considerably diversified. Their activities including site preparation, residential/commercial/industrial development and property management. The market in which they function is described as "highly competitive" and increasingly sensitive to "public opinion and political pressure." Their corporate personalities are depicted in these terms: "imaginative, highly individualistic entrepreneurs," "a large number of shares were concentrated in a few hands" amongst many of the public firms, and they "have not yet acquired any real sense of social responsibility."[40]

While some of the development conglomerates, such as the Trizec Corporation, are active in Halifax and Dartmouth, the land development industry in the Atlantic region is carried on mainly by small, general contractors and operative builders. A feature, more common in this region than others, is the individual owner-builder who constructs his own house and exchanges his labour with neighbouring owner-builders. Montreal developers appear to be less interested than their Toronto counterparts in extending their control over the entire land development process. The generally lower level of land prices and the municipal practice of assuming the initial capital cost of land services (in contrast to the Toronto area), result in less pressure to generate monumental investment capital, and in typically smaller, less diversified firms.[41]

Land ownership and development in the largest metropolitan areas of the Prairies are increasingly dominated by large conglomerates encompassing land development, construction, building materials, financing, transportation and communications. This has been documented in a recent report on Winnipeg, and a report prepared for the City of Calgary highlights the role of a single corporation, Genstar, which has "succeeded in achieving market dominance," and which through its subsidiary B.A.C.M. (and together with another conglomerate Nu West) produced about 36 per cent of the 1973 housing starts in Calgary. An exception to this pattern is Saskatoon, where the city as land assembler/developer predominates and Edmonton and Red Deer where there is mixed private/public sharing of the market, thanks to the strategic use of formerly tax delinquent lands, and to a program of public land acquisition. In the latter three cities there is some evidence that the public influence has moderated the price level of residential land; as well as some debate about "who benefits?" and "who pays?"[42]

A distinctive feature of land development in the Vancouver area is the prominent role of the real estate brokerage firms. Although some conglomerates are active in the area, the house building industry is typified by small and medium-sized developers, producing under fifty units per year, and often "paternalistically" associated with real estate interests. In the period ahead the land market

Table 6.2. Selected Structural Characteristics of Land Development Firms Included in the Developer Study, Northeast Toronto Fringe, 1974

Corporation	Public or Private	Nationality of Control	Independent Subsidiary	Assets (to Nearest $10 Million)	Years of Operation	Number of Employees	Range of Activities[a]	Land Inventory (acres) Toronto Region	Land Inventory (acres) Beyond Toronto Region	Production of Dwelling Units or Lots per Year
A	Pu	Cdn	Ind	170	18	60	all	6,000	—	3,000
B	Pu	Cdn	Ind	150	18	200	all	5,600	900	600
C	Pu	Cdn	Sub	110	10	100	P,C,I,M.	4,000	3,000	200
D	Pu	For	Sub	100	65	300	all	1,200	—	700
E	Pu	Cdn	Ind	80	14	—	all	6,200	1,400	—
F	Pu	Cdn	Ind	70	13	—	all	5,600	600	500
G	Pu	For	Ind	70	15	125	P,R	2,000+	500	—
H	Pu	Cdn	Sub	60	50	80	all	1,400	1,500	400
I	Pu	Cdn	Sub	40	21	90	all	3,000	200	1,200
J	Pu	Cdn	Sub	80	7	25	all	7,000	—	—
K	Pr	Cdn	Ind	—	5	25	all	5,000+	—	200
L	Pr	Cdn	Ind	—	25	10	P,R,C,I	3,000	—	1,000
M	Pr	Cdn	Ind	—	18	50	P,R	—	—	500
N	Pr	Cdn	Ind	—	40	—	all	2,000	—	800
O	Pr	Cdn	Ind	—	28	30	P,R,C,M	—	—	300

[a]Site preparation – P, residential – R, commercial – C, industrial I, property management – M.

Source: Larry G. Martin. "Structure, Conduct and Performance of Land Dealers and Land Developers in the Land Industry." (Waterloo: School of Urban and Regional Planning, University of Waterloo, May, 1975) (mimeographed).

and the development of the fringe will be very much affected by the establishment of Agricultural Land Reserves (75,000 acres have been designated in the Greater Vancouver area). Its immediate effect, apart from protecting crucially important farmland, has been to put a price pressure on already subdivided five to twenty acre parcels (which sell between $15,000 and $20,000 per acre), and to restrict the supply of land for country estates, amenity agriculture and hobby farms.[43]

Concerning the national trend in land prices in the urban fringe, there has been in the last two decades a sharp upward trend, with some regional variations. The most comprehensive data available are for single detached dwellings, financed under the National Housing Act. "Land Cost" in this data would represent the cost to the purchaser of buying a serviced lot in a new suburb on inner fringe land recently converted to urban uses. The ratio of land to total cost of the house was 9.6 per cent in 1951 ($1,048 to $10,948) and 20.8 per cent ($4,487 to $23,475) in 1972. Taking 1951 as the base year, land costs rose by 466 per cent to 1972, while building costs increased by 214 per cent.[44]

Attention has been given to some of the economic and institutional forces related to fringe land because these are some of the conditions that either facilitate or place obstacles in the way of obtaining the greatest benefit from the urban surroundings. For example, the emergence of the diversified integrated development firm may provide precisely the kind of management skill and sophistication for the larger-scale community building that Canada will need in the next quarter century. But, where this is associated with a near-monopoly position in regional markets then there is a strong possibility that development (its location, character, cost), will be on the terms allowed by certain predominant corporations. The developer becomes in part a speculator pressing his advantage for maximum gain, and comes to earn all the epithets reserved for such in Canadian mythology.

Again it is good that the urbanite is enjoying a wider range of recreational resources in the urban surroundings from swimming ponds (personal) to fishing clubs and nudist colonies (private); from ski clubs (semi-public) to conservation areas and walking trails (public). But the peculiarities of the "urban clock" are expressed periodically in massive pressure, as in the weekend exodus, on sensitive environments; and the single-minded pursuit of recreation technologies, such as downhill skiing, can cause, for example, excessive forest cutting, erosion, abnormal runoff and stream silting.[45]

The opportunity for alternative lifestyles, which is one of the motives behind country residential development, must be counted as a social gain, but it carries with it, usually unwittingly, the hazard of disrupting the rural economy. This may take the form of certain physical effects, such as the spreading of diseases from neglected ex-urbanite orchards in Niagara or the Okanagan, or the impact may be directly economic through a land market heated up by ex-urbanite demand. Beyond certain price thresholds, for example in Ontario $500 per acre on land used for field crops, farming becomes uneconomic.[46]

The urban surroundings as an area undergoing change can also be an area of social conflict and stress. This has something to do with the way different groups of people experience that environment. The world looks very different, depending on whether you are a middle-aged farmer, trying to make a living for your family by raising corn and cattle thirty miles from a city; or whether you are a freelance professional, satisfying a yen for the great outdoors and the simple life by living (and raising a few horses) on a small acreage within the same thirty miles of the same city.

The main thing about you as an ex-urbanite is that you have deliberately chosen your living environment. The move to the country represents a conscious rejection of certain aspects of city life—the congestion or the bad air or both—and you are willing to put up with certain inconveniences, such as distance from work and shopping, in exchange for ten acres of hardwood forest, the good honest and spacious qualities of your converted saltbox farm house and space for unwinding. You're glad that you've made the change but there are certain things about rural life that bother you. You can't understand why your farmer-neighbour dumps old cars and other junk on his back woodlot. You wonder whether all the crop spraying that goes on is good for the ecology—what does it do to bird life? And there are times when minor irritations, like being caught behind tortoise-moving farm machinery when you are rushing to keep an appointment in the city, don't seem so minor. You have made a few friends among the "natives" but wish some of the neighbours and the lady at the general store weren't so insistent on knowing what church you go to. Property taxes keep going up but you don't seem to get much for them. But these things have not made you sour on life in the country. The kids in particular love it and make friends through their school much easier than you do; and you are close enough to keep in touch with the people you enjoy seeing—the best of both worlds. Some rapport with your neighbours is building up, particularly since you and your wife got heavily involved in stopping that cement plant which would have blown dust over half the crops in the township. You can see a bright future....[47]

As a farmer, you have quite a different outlook. You wouldn't live in the city if they paid you, simply because you were born in the country, the son of a farmer who was the son of a farmer. Things have been going very well since you built the silo and switched to corn, and you're good at guessing at the beef market. But times are changing and you're not sure it is all for the better. You have had complaints about the smells. Those fancy people from the city like a good steak but don't seem to understand that cattle and manure go together and you have got to spread the stuff around sometimes. And there has been some damage lately. You don't say it is your new neighbour but you found several fences this spring cut by snow-mobilers—who will pay you for fixing them? You're on council but you don't enjoy it anymore because there is so much bickering with those hobby farmer types who have big spending ideas. And those professors' and salesmen's wives who have moved into town are always turning up and making a fuss. You don't know what the end of it all will be. You probably could get a nice price for your land and move further away from the city, but it would be a shame — it's not so easy to get good land these days, and a man should live where he feels at home.... [48]

These contrasting and sometimes conflicting perspectives and lifestyles are part of the reality of the urban surroundings. Reconciling these two dimensions: its lived-in and production environment, is not simply a physical resource problem, something to be solved by a land use plan — essential as that might be. The choices, the allocations, the trade-offs in resource use are inescapably bound up with patterns of thought and living. It is the ultimate human compatabilities and incompatibilities that pose the greatest opportunities as well as dilemmas to the decision-makers.

Policy Approaches

This look at the land around our cities has demonstrated four sets of conditions. One, there are broad areas around our cities, extending for fifty to one hundred miles that provide critical land for urban building, for recreation, for food and for ecological well-being. Nationally, these represent an area of some fifty (urban fringe) to one hundred (fringe and urban shadow) thousand square miles that contain a high proportion of Canada's best farmland. Two, the natural, production and lived-in environments of the urban surroundings have regional, provincial and national significance. Three, these areas will feel the brunt of Canadian urbanization in the next quarter century. There will be conflicts between resource uses and conflicts between people. The urban surroundings are areas where personal and corporate fortunes are made and lost, and in the scramble for private advantage it is not at all certain that the best interests of the public will be served. Four, the nature of the change processes are such that initially minor disturbances to the ecology or to the settlement patterns can have far-reaching repercussions. If Canadians are to continue to enjoy the benefits of their urban surroundings, new policy approaches and mechanisms will have to be devised.

The essential principle on which a sound foundation of policy and planning can be built is the interlocking of a set of objectives, instruments and institutions developed at each level of concern with the urban surroundings – national provincial, regional/local. These varied approaches would reflect the differences at each of these scales in experienced need, in capability: technical, financial, jurisdictional, and in viewpoint – the particular truth arising from an agency's position in the government system. For example, the urban surroundings as a place to live will be a need which is most keenly appreciated at the local/regional level, while the strategic role of fringe lands in the production of sand, gravel and stone is more likely to be of concern at the industry-wide, provincial level. A province can devise certain mechanisms, such as authorization to prepare and enforce a regional plan, but such concepts and their implementing by-laws are best applied close to the scene of the action, that is, in the affected urban region. Similarly, a regional planning authority's concern with land use may relate to the quality of environment – to avoid ribbon development and unsightly disorder – while the federal government's interest in land use may be focused on food production and its relationship to cost of living, cost of production and international balance of payments.

Each of these points-of-view are important and quite valid. They have perverse effects only when considered in isolation. What is needed is the bringing of these varying perceptions and capabilities together in an ongoing system struggling towards the optimum development of our urban surroundings. This approach is tantamount to saying that we need to plan, within the realities of a federal system, on a national scale. It is time that Canadians put aside their hesitations, and begin to apply their knowledge and best talents and management skills to the task of shaping the kind of Canadian environment that we want – applying along the way whatever tests of *excellence* and human *welfare* that we can devise. To move effectively in this direction, Canada's governments, at all levels, must find a way to co-ordinate both their objectives and strategies for the precious land around our cities.

An integral part of this concept would be a process of selective public acquisition of fringe land designed to moderate the level of prices for housing and to ensure the availability of the best natural amenities for recreation. There is increasing evidence from Canadian experience that the public purchase of about 15 per cent of the land in a five-mile zone adjoining the built-up area would have the desired restraining effect on the land market. It has been suggested that "such purchases would have to be in a checkerboard or non-contiguous pattern and would have to be strategically linked in with approved development plans backed by control and provision of services."[49] Can we afford to do this? Can we afford not to?

Notes

1. Lorne H. Russwurm, "The Urban Fringe in Canada: Problems, Research Needs, Policy Implications," Discussion Paper B.74.4 (Ottawa: Ministry of State for Urban Affairs, 1974). For an account of the concept of urban field based on some observations in the Toronto region, see: Gerald Hodge, "The City in the Periphery," in Larry S. Bourne, Ross D. MacKinnon, Jay Siegel and James W. Simmons (eds.), *Urban Futures for Central Canada: Perspectives on Forecasting Urban Growth and Form* (Toronto: University of Toronto Press, 1974).
2. Lorne H. Russwurm, "The Urban Fringe as a Regional Environment," (Waterloo: University of Waterloo, Department of Geography, June 1975) (Mimeographed); to be published in L. G. R. Martin, R. E. Preston and L. H. Russwurm, *Essays on the Urban Process and Form*, Geography Publication Series No. 7 (Waterloo: University of Waterloo, Department of Geography, forthcoming).
3. *Ibid.*, pp. 16–23.
4. Maurice Yeates, *Main Street: Windsor to Quebec City* (Toronto: Macmillan Company of Canada in association with the Ministry of State for Urban Affairs and Information Canada, 1975), pp. 343 and 344. Yeates found that the average macro-urban land consumption rate for the entire axis was 139 acres per 1,000 people in 1971; and that the trend was towards an increasing rate to about 160 acres per 1,000 in the year 2001.
5. Hodge, *op. cit.*, pp. 293 and 294.
6. Russwurm, *op. cit.* pp. 18–24, for development forces shaping the urban surroundings; and Yeates, *op. cit.*, pp. 344 and 345.
   Yeates reports "'that apart from the 266 square miles which are estimated to have

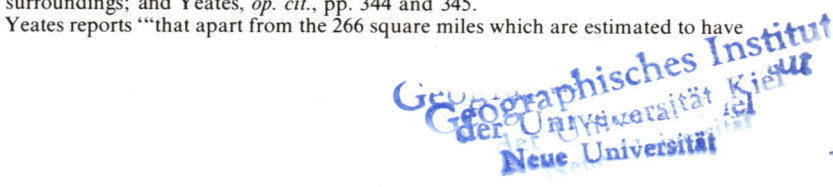

been transferred from agricultural to urban use in the 1966—71 period, 252 square miles have probably been consumed by indirect urban intrusion effects". This conforms with the findings of earlier studies by Crerar, Russwurm, and Gertler and Hindsmith which indicate a range of indirect (urban shadow) to direct (urban development) land consumption, ranging from 2 to 1 (in areas of good soils) to as high as 5 to 1 (in areas of less productive agricultural land).

7. Russwurm, *ibid.*, p. 27.
8. *Ibid.*, p. 28; and *Selected Agricultural Statistics for Canada* (Ottawa: Agriculture Canada, April 1973), Table 3, pp. 6 and 7.
9. Russwurm, *op. cit.*, p. 28; and Lorne H. Russwurm, "Land Policies Across Canada: Thoughts and Viewpoints," *Battle for Land*, Proceedings of the National Conference, September 30, 1974 (Ottawa: Community Planning Association of Canada, 1975), pp. 8 and 9.
10. The "big trip" is based on the observation of a student group, University of Waterloo, supervised by Professor Len Gertler. The area in question was part of the Niagara Escarpment corridor, from Milton Heights to Rattlesnake Point. The student group reported in December 1967.
11. *The Livable Region 1976/1986: Proposals to Manage the Growth of Greater Vancouver* (Vancouver: Greater Vancouver Regional District, 1975), pp. 27, 34 and 38.
12. *Ibid.*, p. 27.
13. *Ibid.*, p. 49.
14. *The Regional Official Policies Plan* (Waterloo: The Regional Municipality of Waterloo, 1975); *Oak Ridges Moraine Study: An Interim Policy Approach to Development* (Newmarket: Regional Municipality of York, Planning Department, 1974); M. D. Simmons, *Natural Land Capability* (Halifax: Metropolitan Area Planning Committee, 1973); P. B. Dean and D. B. Lister, *Natural Environment Survey: Description of the Intrinsic Values of the Natural Environment Around Greater Halifax – Dartmouth* (Halifax: Metropolitan Area Planning Committee, 1971); and H. L. Diemer, *Parkland County, Country Residential Survey*, Report No. 4A (Edmonton Alberta Land Use Forum, 1974).
15. Dean and Lister, *op. cit.*
16. Russwurm, "The Urban Fringe as a Regional Environment," *op. cit.* This data on the relationship between urban settlement and agricultural land is based on G. D. V. Williams, N. Pocock and L. H. Russwurm, "The Distribution of Agroclimatic Resources in Relation to Canada's Urban Population" (Waterloo: University of Waterloo, Department of Geography, 1975) (mimeographed).
17. Michael J. Troughton, "Agriculture and the Countryside," in M. J. Troughton, J. G. Nelson and S. Brown, *The Countryside in Ontario* (London: University of Western Ontario, Department of Geography, 1975).
18. *Central Ontario Lakeshore Urban Complex, Task Force*, Report to the Advisory Committee on Urban and Regional Planning (Toronto: Government of Ontario, December 1974), pp. 35, 36 and 42.
19. Yeates, *op. cit.*, pp. 343 and 344; P. Spurr, *Land and Urban Development: A Preliminary Study* (Toronto: James Lorimer and Company, 1976), pp. 433 and 434.
20. Russwurm, "The Urban Fringe as a Regional Environment," *op. cit.*, p. 47; Douglas Hoffman, "Crop Yields of Soil Capability Classes and their Uses for Planning in Agriculture," (Ph.D. thesis, University of Waterloo, School of Urban and Regional Planning, 1972), Table 15, p. 89, Tables 16 and 17, p. 96.
21. Russwurm, "The Urban Fringe as a Regional Environment," *op. cit.*, p. 49.
22. *Selected Agricultural Statistics*, Table 1, p. 4; S. Stephen Rodd, "A Remarkable Change in the Rural Land Market," *Notes on Agriculture* (Guelph: University of Guelph, April 1974), p. 22; and Douglas W. Hoffman, "The Disappearing Farmland of Ontario," The Bulletin, Vol. 22, No. 4 (October 1975), pp. 9 – 12.
23. W. G. Hardwick, *Vancouver* (Toronto: Collier Macmillan, 1974), p. 146; and

David Baxter, "British Columbia Land Commission Act, a Review," *The Management of Land for Urban Development* (Ottawa: Canadian Council on Urban and Regional Research, 1974), pp. 3 and 4.
24. R. J. Miller and G. R. McArthur, *Rural Sub-Division in Alberta*, Report No. 4B (Edmonton: Alberta Land Use Forum, 1974), pp. 6, 14 – 17 and 24.
25. Russwurm, "The Urban Fringe as a Regional Environment," *op. cit.*, citing C. Stadel and L. R. Clark, "Urban Fringe of Brandon: Land Use, Population Mobility," Brief submitted to Brandon Boundaries Commission (Brandon: University of Brandon, Department of Geography, 1971) (mimeographed).
26. Russwurm, *ibid.* citing B. E. Tamminen, "The Rural-Urban Fringe of the City of Thunder Bay, 1972" (B. A. Thesis, Lakehead University, 1973), p. 29.
27. *Ibid.*, pp. 50 and 51.
28. Tony Burman, "Urbanization Steadily Absorbing Best Farmland," *Montreal Star*.
29. "Halifax-Dartmouth Region: Urban/Regional Growth Plans and Strategies in Canada," Research Report (Ottawa: Ministry of State for Urban Affairs, 1974); and Russwurm, "The Urban Fringe as a Regional Environment," *op. cit.*, p. 31.
30. Diemer, *Parkland County, Country Residential Survey*.
31. *Ibid.*, pp. 13, 17, 24 and 68.
32. *Ibid.*, pp. 24, 25, 32, 33, and 47.
33. *Ibid.*, p. 58.
34. *Ibid.*, pp. 55, 56, 67, 68, 72 – 74, 93 – 94.
35. J. V. Punter, "The Impact of Exurban Development on Land and Landscape in the Toronto-Centred Region 1954 – 71," Report to Central Mortgage and Housing Corporation (Ottawa: Central Mortgage and Housing Corporation, Policy Planning Division, 1974), pp. 61 – 68 and Appendix, Tables 23 and 28.
36. *Ibid.*, pp. 50 – 53.
37. *Ibid.*, p. 2.
38. Russwurm, "The Urban Fringe as a Regional Environment," *op. cit.*, p. 37.
39. Larry R. G. Martin, "Structure, Conduct and Performance of Land Dealers and Land Developers in the Land Development Industry" (Waterloo: University of Waterloo, School of Urban and Regional Planning, May 1975) (mimeographed), pp. 21 and 27; to be published in L. G. R. Martin, R. E. Preston and L. H. Russwurm, *Essays on Urban Process and Form*.
40. *Ibid.*, pp. 34, 37, 39, 42, 49 – 51.
41. *Ibid.*, pp. 54 and 56; and Graham Barker *et al.*, *Highrise and Superprofits* (Kitchener: Dumont Press Graphix, 1973), p. 41.
42. Martin, *op. cit.*, pp. 57 and 58; and Russwurm, "The Urban Fringe as a Regional Environment," *op. cit.*, p. 62.
43. *The Livable Region 1976/1986*, *op. cit.*, p. 28; and Baxter, "The British Columbia Land Commission Act, A Review," p. 31.
44. Gopal K. Sarda, "The Logic of Investment Planning for Urban Land Banking in Canada," Research Report (Ottawa: Ministry of State for Urban Affairs, 1973) (mimeographed), pp. 1 and 1a.
45. Punter, *op. cit.*, p. 63.
46. L. O. Gertler, *Niagara Escarpment Study: Fruit Belt Report* (Toronto: Department of Treasury and Economics, Regional Development Branch, 1968), p. 50; and Douglas W. Hoffman, "Land Requirements for Ontario Agriculture," *Notes on Agriculture* (Guelph: University of Guelph, April 1974), p. 16.
47. Russwurm, "The Urban Fringe as a Regional Environment," *op. cit.*, pp. 64 – 73.
48. *Ibid*.
49. Russwurm, "The Urban Fringe in Canada: Problems, Research Needs, Policy Implications," pp. 84 – 88; reference to public land acquisition in Russwurm, "The Urban Fringe as a Regional Environment," *op. cit.*, pp. 86 and 87.

CHAPTER 7

The Urban Human Condition

"Beauty is in the eye of the beholder." The places where people live in Canada are surprisingly varied. We enjoy a common, industrial-based culture, but there are differences in region, size of place, history, language, the way people make a living. Even our three largest cities have strikingly unique personalities, which are the source of mystification and wonder and a staple of after supper talk.

Residential Desirability: What Kind of Cities Do Canadians Prefer?

If you had to choose between living in Medicine Hat, Rimouski and Corner Brook, which would you select? Just such a question was recently asked of a number of students, in different parts of the country, who were about to leave high school. And some of the results, as reported by a geography study at the University of Toronto, were surprising.[1]

For each of sixty cities, the following question was posed to 157 groups (all located in cities above 10,000 people): "As a place to live on leaving school, would you consider this city highly desirable, highly undesirable or somewhere between these points?" The answers that were given priority reflected the location of each of the response groups as well as certain related factors, such as size of city and the predominant language spoken. One would not expect the view of Toronto, a big metropolis in Canada's industrial heartland, to be the same from any two cities, say from Calgary in the ranching/oil economy of southern Alberta, and also Halifax, the strongly maritime and, by comparison, historically venerable capital of Nova Scotia. Responses will be influenced by the content and volume of *information* flows on Toronto, the object city, and by the *values* held by the response group which act as a kind of filter converting information into characteristic attitudes towards or images of other places.[2]

In fact, the young people of Calgary thoroughly reject Toronto while showing an apparent romantic attachment to Niagara Falls which is rated as highly desirable. Otherwise the larger Western cities are preferred; places in the Atlantic provinces are acceptable but Quebec cities are generally not preferred. By contrast, the Halifax group showed a strong preference for major cities in Ontario, including Toronto – "going down the road" dies hard – as well as for six major cities in the West; while the home city was highly regarded, all other cities in the Maritimes, with the exception of Charlottetown, were viewed as undesirable. These comparative preference patterns are illustrated in the accompanying maps (Maps 7.1 and 7.2) showing the Calgary and Halifax preferences in terms of five types of object cities – highly desirable, desirable, indifferent, undesirable and highly undesirable.

The response groups noted their preferences on a seven point scale, so it was possible to get the total score for each city and to obtain a measure of the overall desirability of the object cities.[3] It is interesting to note the cities that emerged at each end of the list. The most highly preferred city in the country was Vancouver, British Columbia; the least preferred was the asbestos centre, Thetford Mines, Quebec. The next four at the top are Victoria, Calgary, Edmonton and Winnipeg. Thus the first five, which account for about 45 per cent of all scores in the highest class, were all major cities in Western Canada.

As the list is extended downwards, other interesting preferences emerge, the next five in the highest class are Ottawa-Hull, Niagara Falls, London, Toronto and Montreal. These are all places that are strong in services: government, tourism, finance, education and the mixed array of facilities of our two largest cities; added to the top five places, 70 per cent of the students' choices are accounted for. At the other end of the scale, the ten least preferred cities represent about 55 per cent of the choices. The five at the bottom in order of least preference: Thetford Mines, Sudbury, Timmins, Chicoutimi-Jonquière and Rimouski also account for a substantial part of the scores in their class – 33.5 per cent, and are all Quebec or Ontario cities based on primary or heavy industry, such as mining, forestry, hydro power and aluminum refining. The second group of least preferred five cities are: Drummondville, Quebec; Noranda-Rouyn, Quebec; Moose Jaw, Saskatchewan; Medicine Hat, Alberta and St. Jean, Quebec, all places with a primary industry base – for this group predominantly agriculture with the exception of Noranda which is a base metal mining centre. These are all places with populations under 50,000.[4]

If beauty is in the eye of the beholder, it seems that our perceptions of "beauty" or the "good city" depend very much on our

Map 7.1. Calgary Response Group: Preference Patterns

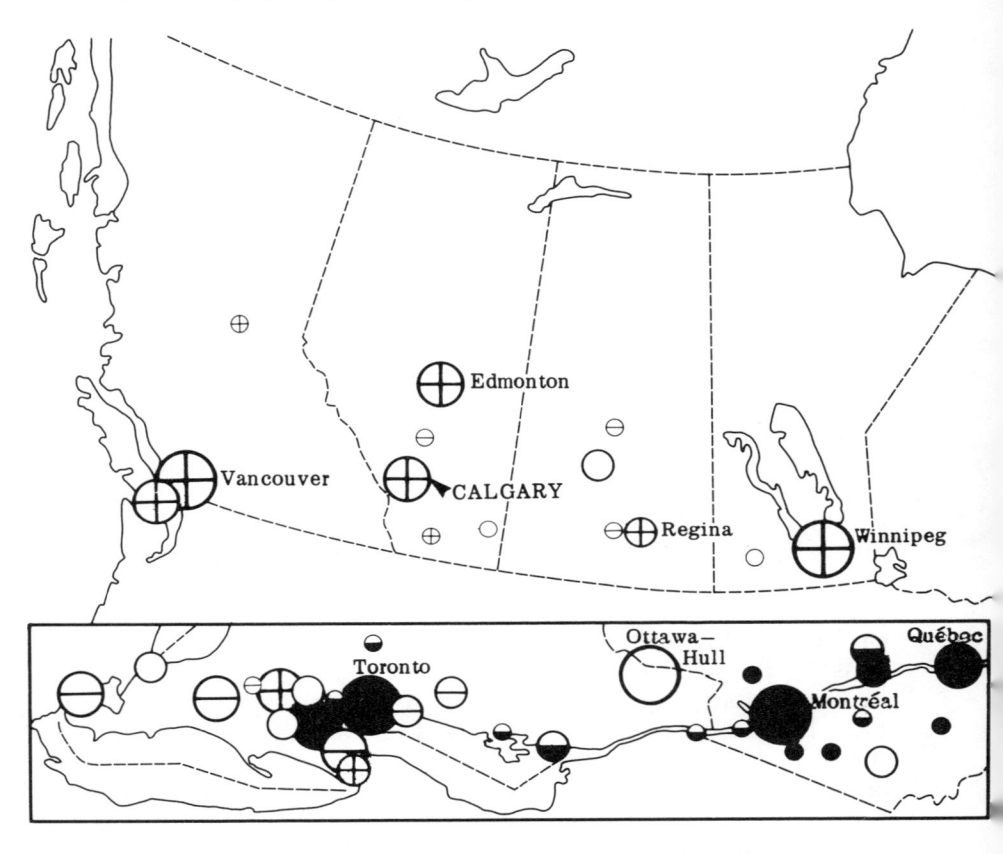

vantage point – not only on what we are looking at but where we are looking from. The Toronto study related the expressed preferences of the student response groups to the characteristics of both object cities and response places, and some of the additional findings were these:[5]

Preferences are related to region, size of city, employment growth rate and the mix of employment, e.g. service, manufacturing or extractive, and language, but not to income of object cities.

The regions considered most desirable are British Columbia and the Prairies; and the least desirable Quebec and Newfoundland.

Metropolitan areas are the most preferred class of city, but the small town is generally preferred over other major urban areas.

Cities with declining employment are considered highly undesirable.

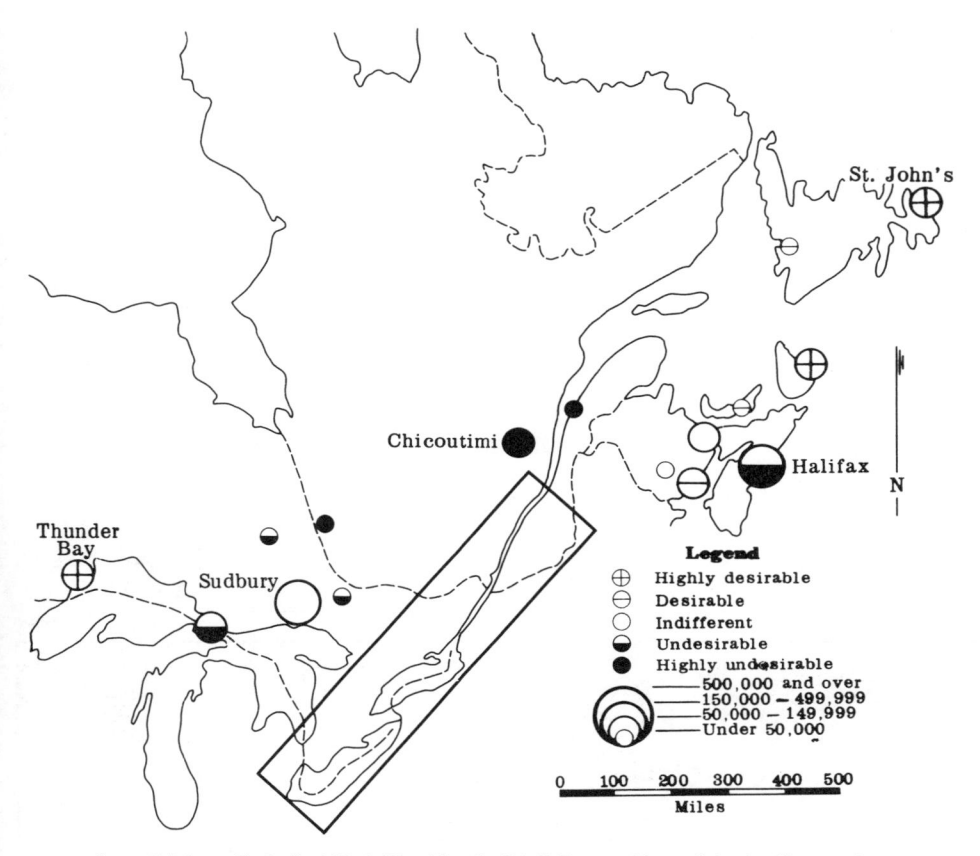

Source: E. Roberts, "The Residential Desirability of Canadian Cities" (Toronto and Ottawa: University of Toronto and MSUA, 1974) (mimeographed).

Large cities are preferred in most regions but in the Maritime provinces small cities are more desirable than larger ones in that region.

Most students express a strong preference for their home city, even when its characteristics do not correspond with what they would choose in other cities.

Students in all sizes of cities prefer Western metropolitan areas to Eastern ones, but are less concerned with the regional location of small cities.

As far as preferences for small towns are concerned, only students who live in small towns prefer small towns in the West, while students in large cities prefer small towns in the East.

Map 7.2. Halifax Response Group: Preference Patterns

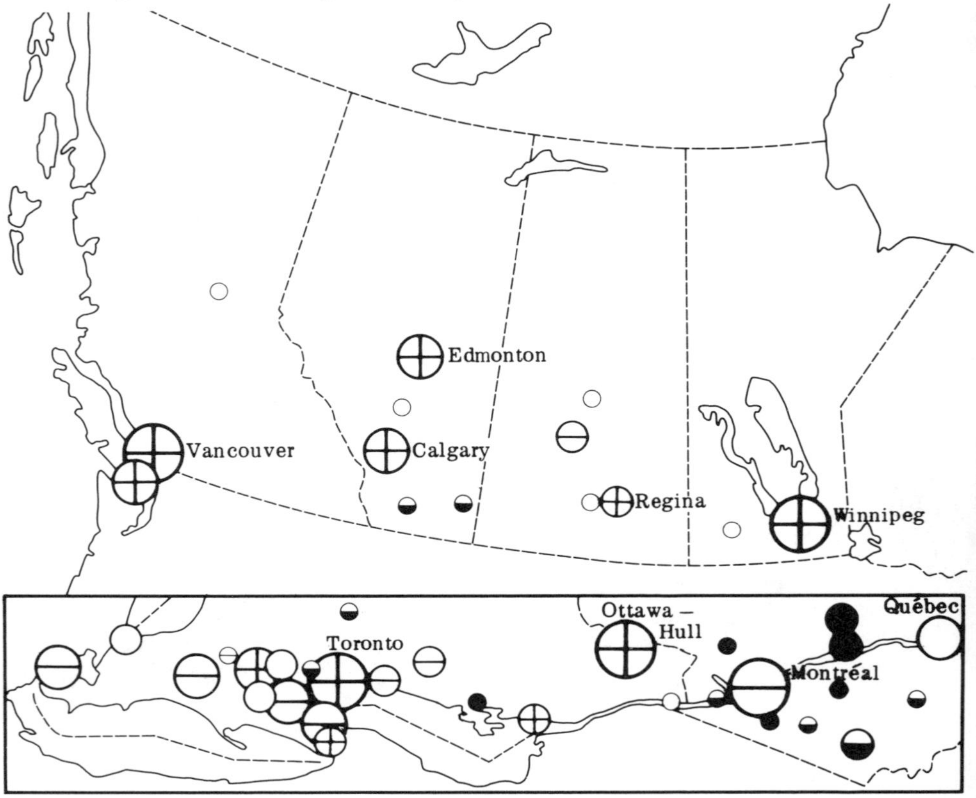

French-speaking response groups have a greater preference for cities in Quebec and English-speaking groups for places in British Columbia and Ontario.

There are signs of alienation between certain sets of regions, but these are less cultural—neither from Quebec nor towards Quebec—than the outlying regions against the centre, that is, from the West and Atlantic provinces towards Ontario and Quebec together.

These reported preferences provide some clues as to how one group of Canadians react to the urban environment, and by implication the kind of urban future aspired to by young adult Canadians. It is important to know about these things—just as important as it may be to inventory the condition of bricks and mortar or the incidence of disease or traffic accidents. But the reported results should be taken with a grain of the proverbial salt. The study itself concludes

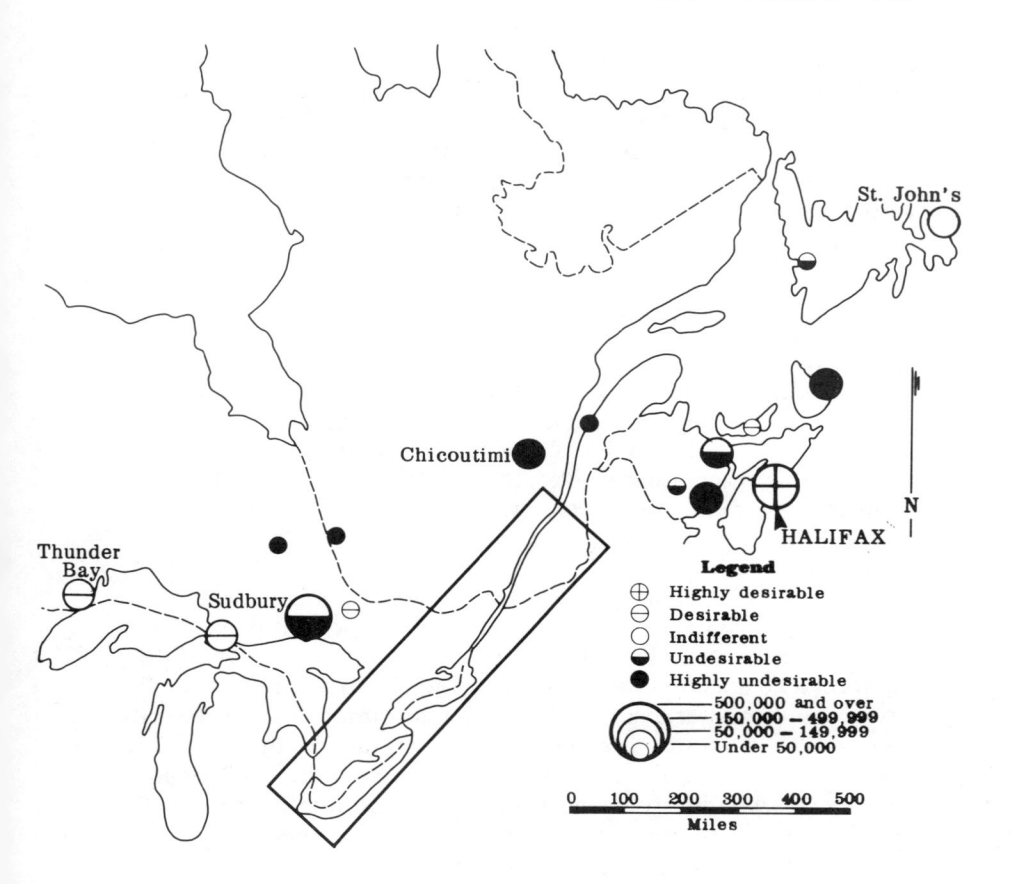

Source: E. Roberts, "The Residential Desirability of Canadian Cities" (Toronto and Ottawa: University of Toronto and MSUA, 1974 (mimeographed).

that "from the findings on the nature of preference patterns in Canada it appears that two relations existing in preference formation, through the interaction of information and values, are particularly crucial. These may be summarized as *valued misunderstanding* and *metropolitan dominance*."[6] The first refers to attitudes that may become fixed and are relatively unaffected by reality. For example, the response groups in Ontario rated Niagara Falls as only moderately desirable, while so many response places in other provinces scored that city as "highly desirable" that it emerged as the eighth most preferred place in the entire country. The romantic image persists – the city of the fabled horseshoe falls, honeymooners and the pictures on the Shredded Wheat box!

Metropolitan dominance refers to the origin and control of information in a few big cities – the centres where news is "manufactured," where the mass circulation dailies and magazines are created, which are the base of media production and broadcasting and national book publishing. In these circumstances one wonders whether population flows into metropolitan areas, and the underlying preferences, are "not a cause but a consequence of the cultural dominance of those few cities."[7]

The City as a Moral Issue

The survey of residential desirability presents a very broad judgement of Canadian cities, but it begs certain questions: What are people really looking for? What are the conditions in our cities that make the difference between good and bad? desirable and undesirable? It is necessary to consider these questions because the facts themselves – the circumstances in which Canadians live in cities – are neutral. They are given meaning and significance by how we judge them and by our aspirations.

From this point-of-view, one of the Canadian seminars leading up to the Habitat conference was offered a very important perspective.[8] Lawrence Haworth, who writes about the philosophy of urban life, put forth a compelling case for viewing the city as a moral issue. The city is people and artefacts – all kinds of constructions – but the city also embodies various lifestyles, which are shaped by its institutions of work, leisure, education, religion, family life and politics. Altogether urban lifestyles and institutions constitute the urban milieu, the "structured environment" that defines the opportunities and constraints of individuals and groups in the city. A good city is a place where the lifestyles and institutions are conducive to "self-development, self-realization and self-fulfilment." Because man is a social creature he requires identification with a community, "a condition in which the fragmentation and divisiveness of present urban life are replaced by a setting made cohesive by the presence of shared purposes."[9] This is the source of moral power. On the other hand, the expression of an individual's personal capacities, requires a significant degree of freedom to choose among the opportunities offered by the social environment.

Haworth argues that the attainment of these two requirements of the good city – moral power and freedom, community and opportunity – depends on certain objective conditions or institutional traits: the institutional traits of moral power are *richness, openness* and *person-centredness*; opportunities should be extensive, available to all on a non-discriminatory basis, and lifestyles should respect the individual's personal integrity and intrinsic dignity. The institutional traits of individual freedom are *voluntariness, flexibility* and *controllability*: they should lead to lifestyles that allow a significant degree of discretion in individual roles – when and how will he participate? As a member of his community he should enjoy the rights of social democracy: the opportunity to control the critical conditions that surround one's life.

If Haworth's argument stopped here it would, as a basis for interpreting and evaluating the contemporary city, be merely interesting and suggestive. But he goes further. He identifies the *communal* and the *individual* with two contrasting and competing lifestyles or models of the good life: the first centred on work, and the other on leisure. Each of these has its focal values, validating experiences and idealized character-traits – its heroes. In the first, these are craftsmanship and humanized work, participation in a small community through acknowledged socially useful work, and disciplined devotion to duty. In the second, these are the unfettered pursuit of pleasure along with the expansion and humanizing of technology so that work might decrease and become more tolerable; personal creativity and communication with others; and the capacity for an open, spontaneous expression of the self.[10]

Each of these "world views" shapes the character of human settlements. "The town, to use one term to cover the full range of settlements from market towns to megalopolises, is, in view of fundamental features of the lifestyles it settles, the historic embodiment and objectification of individualism," i.e. the leisure-oriented model. While the village, characterized by its insularity and self-contained settlement form is "the historic home and expression of wholism,"[11] i.e., the work-oriented model. Either of these carried to extreme has flaws as a social ideal. Individualism may lead to a shallow consumerism and the gross privatization of life. The communal existence may become excessively circumscribed and foreclose the personal and social benefits of self-realization. Better to strive for a new positive ideal in which the best features of both models are approximated in a lifestyle that combines the concepts of responsibility, professionalism and leisureliness. Briefly, responsibility means recognizing and behaving with a full awareness of the community and ecological constraints on personal needs and wants. Professionalism is the joining of competence and advanced technology – and pride in personal mastery – to the ideals of social service and social justice. And leisureliness is the savouring of experience – work or leisure, for its intrinsic rewards, for its own sake. These singly and together, would influence the form and substance of human settlement.

Haworth believes that one of the more important consequences of the new ethic would be found in the internal physical organization of the city. At present the compartmentalization of our lives into work and free time is expressed in the specialization of space into rigid, single-use districts. To the degree that work and leisure increasingly become merely phases of a single experience, our environments of work, residence and leisure would become increasingly interlaced. The resulting lifestyle would find its natural locale in the neighbourhood. This would not be "neighbourhood" as we know it: a fixed place with clearly defined boundaries, but a habitat with the openness and flexibility which are the natural counterpoint to the discipline of work. "To build 'neighborhood' is to transform the settings in which we live in ways that discourage busyness and distraction and that prompt people to come alive to and become active in their immediate surrounds."[12]

Parallelling this change in urban form there would develop reinforcing changes in social and political patterns. An environment which is flexible and open to the unfolding of an unprogrammed and creatively expanding lifestyle cannot be subject to the arbitrary whim of a centralized administration. Decentralization in certain spheres of decision-making would be the necessary accompaniment of a true "neighbourhood." Control is the issue. An institutional form would have to be discovered that strikes an appropriate balance between the small community strongly identified with the individual, and the larger community of transcending work and societal interests. Such are the moral roots of the good city, as seen by Haworth.

The City in Literature

The philosophical view of urban life suggests that the city both shapes and gives expression to our most deeply cherished values, ideas and ideals. It also suggests a certain way of viewing reality. There is a continuum between values and attitudes, lifestyles, institutions and the bricks and mortar of the physical city. Can we grasp such a complex reality?

As one way of knowing the urban human condition we can learn from those media that by their very nature strive for the synoptic view. We can turn to those whom Ottawa economist, Gail Stewart, has called the "still unsurpassed experts in the use of social indicators – the artists, poets, dramatists and writers."[13] The appeal to creative literature is rewarding in many ways:

IN THE FLASH OF DESCRIPTIVE INSIGHT –

>*Calgary is not a city*
>*It is a hammock*
>*slung between the hills*
>from Mick Burrs, "Walking the Streets of Calgary"
>*Canadian Forum*, January, 1976.

IN THE VIVID KALEIDOSCOPE OF A BIG CITY'S ETHNIC VITALITY –

>*The Main, with something for all our appetites*
>*was dedicated to pinching pennies from the poor, but*
>*it was there to entertain, educate and comfort us, too.*
>*Across the street from the synagogue you could see*
>*THE PICTURE THEY CLAIMED NEVER COULD*
>*BE MADE. A little further down the street was*
>*the Workman's Circle and, if you liked, a strip*
>*show. Peaches, Margo, Lili St. Cyr... Old*
>*men gave us snuff, at the delicatessens we were*
>*allowed salami butts, card players pushed candies*
>*on us for luck, and everywhere we were poked*
>*and pinched by the mothers. Absolutely the best*
>*that could be said of us was "He eats well knock*
>*wood," and later, as we went off to school, "He's*
>*a rank-one boy."*
>From Mordecai Richler, *The Street*, (Toronto: McClelland and Stewart Ltd., 1969), pp. 53-54.

IN DESCRIBING THE GENTEEL DECAY OF SOME OF OUR OLDER SMALL TOWNS –

These semi-ghost towns of a colonial past – we have several of them in that part of the country, and when you see them now it is hard to believe that once upon a time British officers in swallow tailcoats stepped ashore onto their wooden jetties from corvettes, frigates and sloops-of-war. I remember the town's main street was a hundred yards of battered macadam containing two wooden churches, half a dozen shops, a sad red brick bank, a sadder red brick post-office, with a four-faced clock on the roof. I can't remember the street's name, but I would lay even money it was either Wellington Street or King Street.... The only thing that seemed to matter in that town, except for the sawmills, was the railway station.

From Hugh McLennan, *The Watch that Ends the Night*, (Toronto: New American Library of Canada Limited, 1969), p. 182.

AND IN THE BROAD PANORAMA OF CANADIAN SETTLEMENT –

Civilization in Canada, as elsewhere, has advanced geometrically across the country, throwing down the long parallel lines of the railways, dividing up the farm lands into chessboards of square-mile sections and concession-line roads. There is little adaption to nature: in both architecture and arrangement, Canadian cities and villages express rather an arrogant abstraction, the conquest of nature by an intelligence that does not love it.

From Northrop Frye, in the Conclusion of *Literary History of Canada*, (Toronto: University of Toronto Press, 1965).

Apart from the expanded awareness that is the by-product of this kind of material, the search for the city in literature is obligatory because two of the major traditions in Canadian letters are preoccupied with the urban fact. This is as true for the "school," identified with Professor Northrop Frye, that sees literature as myth, as it is for the new realists, the imagists like poets John Newlove and Al Purdy who tell it as it is. The first interprets Canadian art as a symptom of the universal human story that unfolds through the four principal ages of man: birth, quest, maturity and decay. It is an archetypal tradition, and the archetype of maturity is the city. The second is a deliberate urge to break out of what has been called the "garrison mentality" in Canadian creative life, associated with colonialism, and to find a plain, unembellished truth in the "wilderness of everyday life."[14]

Literary approaches also share a tendency to view the city in terms of its contradictions, its often precariously poised potentials for good or evil. "Our world of the city and of modern technology is either becoming a hell, an infernal place of mechanism and inhumanity," writes the Montreal poet, Louis Dudek, "or it can be visualized as the perfect city of the future, the ultimate paradise of our imagination."[15] And these demonic or paradisal dimensions of the city are motifs that run through much of our contemporary literature. The particular terms in which they are expressed – the evil and the good – hold a special fascination for the student or policymaker in urban affairs.

While this polarity is expressed in the novels of Callaghan, McLennan, Roy, Moore, Laurence and Richler, it will in this book be identified through various works of poetry because of the more summary, concise nature of that medium. It would be an understatement to say that our poets have been not unimpressed with the negative aspects of Canadian cities. Taken together their critique expresses an unmistakeable lament of compassion, irony and concern:

THE CITY IS INDIFFERENT TO HUMAN SUFFERING –

A freak of the city,
little man with big head,
shrivelled body, stumps of legs
clamped to a block of wood
running on roller skate wheels.

steering through familiar waters
of spit, old butts, chewed gum,
flotsam among the jetsam of your world.

From "Roller Skate Man" by Raymond Souster, in *Colour of the Times/Ten Elephants on Yonge Street* by Raymond Souster, Ryerson Press.

IN THE CITY HUMAN RELATIONSHIPS ARE DISTORTED
BY ECONOMIC RELATIONSHIPS –

I cross the Pie IX Bridge
A cat with nine lives
And die each time I see
The city puking in my eyes

Watch your pockets my hands are in them
I can help the city stink
And then I run – escape to peaceful greenery
No competition here...

... Peaceful as a successful orgasm
Peaceful as suicide.

From "Economics" by Gertrude Katz, in *The Fiddlehead*, Winter, 1961, p. 50.

AND SOME, TRAPPED IN SUBURBAN LIFESTYLES; ARE
NUMBED INTO LIVES WITHOUT REAL FULFILMENT –

You also my week-end neighbours
Your existence must at last be acknowledged
As an item in the landscape,
You, career men, whose business it is
To pull a good oar in the galley of percentage
But whose real life consists, I am afraid,
In waiting for other people to die...

From "O Executives, O Commuters" by John Glassco, in *Canadian Forum*, August 1964, p. 107.

FOR OTHERS, THE BAR IS A KIND OF CHURCH AND THE
BARTENDER, ITS MINISTER –

Singly they come, the lonely women;
hoist on the tall stools, careless of rear spread;
greet the barman by name, pleased if he answers.
order their double whiskies or martinis...
'George' competent, professional, pours, mixes
serves drinks with sympathy or joke as called for.
Host to a deeper thirst, the brief euphoria
of being part of life, of being wanted.

From "City Bar: 5 p.m." by Amy Groesbeck, in *The Fiddlehead*, Summer, 1961, p. 30.

THE CITY IS A PLACE OF INEQUALITY AND FELT INJUSTICE –

Shop to shop they loll
  destroying time, trying on their feet
    the newest shoes, their hands dishless
      discontent, so smoothly gloved
        and swathed amid erotic furs
          the idle pampered backs that I
            would love O how...

stranger at their perfumed ears
  whispering how

for them whole factories
steam, how servants beck and call
  and slums rear slums, how harried clerks
  suffocate with ire and husbands on
their pedestals lay down no less
  than Aztec tribes their fast hold
    hearts to them...

From "Three Women Shopping" by Malcolm Miller, in *Canadian Forum*, October, 1963, p. 153.

THE CITY FEARS NON-CONFORMITY –

Somewhere in this suburban monoscope
there is, of necessity, a poem.
The uniform files of roofless cottages
pose like a graduation photograph...

No poem here – only the need.

But wait there is a god
(perhaps behind the paint-by-numbers sky)
who with a wink upsets
the careful skittles of convention
for now a flick wind
betrays my tidy picture and
blaring outrageously against the sky
a splatter of colour defies the builder's pattern.
As deliberately disturbing as an extra nose
or Miro's sun
fly, innocent and unconcerned,
the red and white polka-dots
of my father's underpants.

*The planning committee are throwing themselves
to the rush-hour traffic
in the morning, the contractor
will be found dead by his own hand,
and already, on either side, my neighbours
are packing their valuables
and selling at a loss.*

From "A Cultured Community" by Ken Livingstone, in *Quarry*, November, 1965.

AND IT IS A PLACE OF MANY SOLITUDES –

*We grow our hair very long.
We grow beards and trim them
Into mephistophelian shapes.
We live alone or in crowded rooms
With whoever catches the eye,
Talks the language, the simple tongue.*

*Mostly we are spurned.
Delinquent I suppose. We neither
Work regularly nor do we rob or love
According to the code. The faces we see
Are cruel and bluntly curious. Especially
The women's faces in the street...*

*They never pause to send a greeting
Of the eyes across the dark...*

*They don't know us.
They don't recognize the uniform.*

From "Across the Dark" by R. D. Mathews, in *Canadian Forum*, January, 1966, p. 239.

IN THE CITY, TECHNOLOGY IN THE FORM OF THE CAR GONE AMUCK, PROVOKES A SARDONIC REBELLION –

*All day cars moved and shrieked,
Hollered and bellowed and wept
Upon   the road...*

Murderous cars and manslaughter cars

*And with headlights full of tears
Begged for a master...*

THE URBAN HUMAN CONDITION 317

Limousines covered with pink slime
Of children's blood
Turned into the open fields
And fell over into ditches

The wheels kicking helplessly.
Taxis begged trees to step inside
Automobiles begged of posts
The whereabouts of their mother.
But no one wished to own them any more,
Everyone wished to walk.

From "Klaxon" by James Reany, in Karl F. Klinck and Reginald E. Watters, eds., *Canadian Anthology*, (Toronto: W. J. Gage, Rev. ed., 1966), p. 472.

THERE IS LATENT TERROR IN A TOO MECHANIZED CITY

"The Whole City" is another version
of the same painting by the same artist
Max Ernst
which hangs in the Tate
where it is called "The Citadel"
a title more in keeping
with this artist's callous conception
of man's civilization
as his concentration camp
of the world as a citified country
a metallic spiral of battlements
terrain on terrain
terrace on terrace
turning into an iron acropolis...

From "A City That Looks Like Punched Metal Strips" by John Robert Colombo, from *Abracadabra* (Toronto: McClelland and Stewart Limited, 1967).

AND FOR SOME ALL OF THE CITY'S ILLS COME TOGETHER IN THE CRESCENDO OF AN APOCALYPTIC NIGHTMARE –

Below me the city was in flames:
the firemen were the first to save
themselves. I saw steeples fall on their knees.

*I saw an agent kick the charred bodies
from an orphanage to one side, marking
the site carefully for a future speculation.*

*Lovers stopped short of the final spasm
And went off angrily in opposite directions,
their elbows held by giant escorts of fire.*

*Then the dignitaries rode across the bridges
under an auricle of light which delighted them
noting for later punishment those that went before.*

*And the rest of the populace, their mouths
distorted by an unusual gladness, bawled thanks
to this comely and ravaging ally, asking*

*Only for more light with which to see
their neighbour's destruction.*

All this I saw through my improved binoculars.

From "The Improved Binoculars" by Irving Layton, in *Selected Poems*, ed. Wynne Francis (Toronto: McClelland and Stewart, Ltd., 1969).

The creative imagination shows a greater propensity for "paradise lost" than "paradise regained." The "city of light" does find its place in Canadian literature, but it lacks the concreteness and vividness of the demonic image. It takes the form of Dennis Lee's cautious anticipation of the redemption of urban man:

*Among the tangle of
hydro, hydrants, second mortgages, amid
the itch for new debentures, greater expressways,
in sober alarm they jam their works of progress, asking where in truth
they come from and to whom they must belong.
And thus they clear a space in which
the full desires of those that begot them, great animating desires
that shrank and grew hectic as the land pre-empted their lives
might still take root, which eddy now and
drift in the square being neither alive nor dead.
And the people accept a flawed inheritance
and they give it a place in their midst forfeiting progress, forfeiting
dollars, forfeiting yankee visions of cities that in time it might grow
whole at last in their lives, they might
belong once more to their forbears, becoming their own man.*

From *Civil Elegies and Other Poems* by Dennis Lee, (Toronto: House of Anansi, 1972), p. 35.

Or the celebration of the city takes the form of the sentimental or utopian affirmations that go back to the turn of the century to Archibald Lampman's "The Land of Pallas," to A. M. Klein's "Autobiographical" (1951) that glorifies the streets of Montreal,[16] and to Earle Birney's "Vancouver Lights" (1948) and "Like an Eddy my Words Turn About Your Bright Rock" (1965) in which a city is equated with desirable woman –

"Woman you are miles
of boulevards with supple trees
unpruned and full of winding
honesties"

From "Like an Eddy my Words Turn About your Bright Rock" by
Earle Birney.

One of the strongest expressions of love of city in Canadian creative experience was in the work of the painter, Albert Franck (1899-1972). Writes Harold Town,

> To Albert Franck the grubby street world of Toronto was as impressive as the pyramids at sunset or Durham Castle in the rain. He vigorously excluded quaint details or picaresque touches that might lead to the sentimentalization of his subjects. Franck's houses were cathedrals of the ordinary, cocoons of the humdrum, painted as seriously as if they were primal structures, essential to a full understanding of man.[17]

Franck has earned a tribute from David Crombie, Mayor of Toronto, which demonstrates the link between art and urban politics:

> Even though his paintings do not show people, you have certainty that these are homes not units in some potential urban renewal scheme. Franck seems to have known before the rest of us that a livable city depends more on the serenity and security of where we live, more than the glossiness or dizzying height of super blocks. He never tried to glamorize his houses or his streets and although I'm no art critic, what he is saying to me is that there can be something fascinating and warm in the way time treats wood and brick and paint and plaster – a fascination and warmth we can't recreate in wide new roads and shiny steel boxes.[18]

The dominant voice of the Canadian writer on the city remains, however, the voice of the skeptic. It seems fitting to end this section on a conjecture:

You from the viewpoint of the chronic
window-shopper will apprise
whether or not the cause for panic
is more present than I can realize
you, unclogged by speculations, can
answer the question that I dread.
Yes, the city is broken, but the man, the man...
does he lie there sleeping, or is he dead?

From "Dancers Over the City" by Edith Weaver, in *The Fiddlehead*,
March, 1957, p. 18.

Inner City – Epitome of the Urban Experience

We come now to a more direct examination of conditions in Canadian cities, from a human point-of-view. The results of research, initiated in the early 'seventies by the federal urban agency and conducted in various centres across the country, are beginning to unfold.

The inner city—those residential and mixed use areas surrounding the central business and civic core of the city – is the most intensely urban part of the city. Here, the polarity of urban conditions, good human environments and bad, is often most acute.[19]

Recent studies indicate that generally the inner city is a place where one of the key attributes of the "good city" – openness, or non-discriminate access to opportunities for the individual – is least enjoyed. The accompanying Table (7.1) gives the index of socio-economic status (which is a composite of income, educational and occupational levels) by distance zones, at mile intervals from the centre of a number of metropolitan areas, grouped by size. The higher the index the higher the status. The index increases consistently from the centre to the suburbs for the largest urban areas: Montreal, Toronto, Vancouver, Winnipeg, Ottawa-Hull, Hamilton, Quebec City, Edmonton and Calgary. The pattern is less consistent for smaller cities. Generally, the lower-status groups concentrate in the inner city.[20]

But another study emphasizes a very different facet of the inner city. "... [T]he poor are not culturally deprived," write the directors of The Toronto Geographical Expedition.

> The Globe Theatre was in the South End of London, the definitely wrong side of the river from Shakespearean days till now. Artists colonies do not locate in the suburbs but in the slums. . . . It is the inner city or cities where progress is made. If the inner city is crushed, oppressed, destroyed – then so is that nation's progress. So the geography of progress is to articulate the city core and let its example and power extend to the nation.[21]

Table 7.1. Mean Socio-Economic Status (SES) Index by Distance from the Centre of Metropolitan Areas by Mile Zones, 1971

Metropolitan Areas	Less than 1 mile	1 to 2 miles	2 to 3 miles	3 to 5 miles	5 to 9 miles	10 or more miles
Population Size						
500,000 or more						
Montreal	38.8	41.1	45.3	47.2	49.4	49.6
Toronto	46.3	47.8	49.1	50.8	54.5	54.8
Vancouver	49.5	51.1	52.2	53.2	54.2	49.5
TOTAL	43.0	45.0	47.5	49.1	52.6	51.9
200,000 – 499,999						
Winnipeg	41.0	45.4	49.0	53.3	53.2	51.4
Ottawa-Hull	47.1	50.7	51.5	58.4	59.0	50.4
Hamilton	43.3	47.4	48.5	49.7	54.2	54.3
Quebec City	44.5	44.3	49.4	52.4	50.0	42.8
Edmonton	46.0	50.8	52.5	51.7	56.0	44.8
Calgary	47.2	52.5	50.7	53.8	55.4	—
St. Catharines-Niagara	49.1	46.9	48.8	52.3	50.9	46.4
TOTAL	44.7	47.8	50.1	53.2	54.5	47.9
100,000 – 199,999						
Windsor	44.2	47.9	48.3	53.3	52.6	49.0
Halifax	49.0	48.1	52.7	50.5	54.0	45.2
London	47.3	51.1	53.2	56.5	47.9	47.3
Victoria	46.5	48.7	54.1	57.7	52.0	47.6
Kitchener-Waterloo	44.9	49.3	53.2	53.8	46.0	47.0
Regina	44.5	45.8	43.6	49.8	54.8	—
Sudbury	50.9	47.7	49.9	53.3	49.3	49.9
Thunder Bay	47.5	48.0	46.6	48.6	46.4	42.1
TOTAL	46.9	49.3	52.0	51.7	50.9	47.9
Less Than 100,000						
Saskatoon	54.3	47.5	46.8	47.0	51.3	—
Saint John, N.B.	42.7	43.1	44.8	47.5	53.8	44.3
Sherbrooke	42.4	46.5	51.9	62.1	—	—
St. John's, Nfld.	46.8	47.1	45.3	48.5	39.0	—
Kingston	48.8	48.1	54.4	54.7	54.3	55.3
Oshawa	46.3	50.8	47.1	50.0	—	—
Trois-Rivières	44.2	44.8	47.5	52.1	—	—
Brantford	42.8	48.6	49.6	—	49.8	—
Peterborough	49.1	47.0	58.2	—	45.8	46.9
Sarnia	47.6	50.0	48.9	57.3	50.0	—
Sault Ste. Marie	51.9	48.9	48.0	46.8	48.4	—
Guelph	46.4	52.9	56.2	46.9	—	—
TOTAL	45.9	47.7	49.7	49.9	49.7	45.7

Source: T. R. Balakrishnan and G. K. Jarvis, "Changing Patterns of Spatial Differentiation in Urban Canada 1951 – 1971." (Ottawa: prepared for Ministry of State for Urban Affairs, September, 1975). Reproduced by permission of the Minister of Supply and Services Canada.

The inner parts of Canadian cities, whether viewed broadly or in detail at close range, are not monolithic. Current investigations strongly suggest that there are four basic types of inner city: Areas of decline, stability, revitalization, and massive redevelopment. Each of these will vary in terms of the essential urban attributes: the satisfaction of individual needs and wants, in its *richness* – the accommodation of a variety of group needs and lifestyles, and in *controllability*, the capacity through community organization to influence decisions that have an impact on sub-areas. The social, economic and physical dimensions of these four types are presented, in summary form, in Table 7.2.[22] These represent predominant pat-

Table 7.2. The Inner City: Dimensions of the Four Types

	Decline	**Stability**
Population	Continuing loss of population	No significant losses or gains
Socio-Economic Status	Decreasing	Stable
Family Status	Increasing proportion of non-family units and elderly	Maintenance of population mix
Ethnicity	Varies – can be influx of deprived ethnic group or breaking down of traditional community	Sometimes strong ethnic community
Community Organization	Poorly organized, unstable	Varies
Physical Conditions	Worsening	Stable
Housing/Land Costs	Stable or decreasing	Stable
Tenure	Increasing tenancy	Varies, but often high ownership
Functions	Loss of CBD functions with no replacement	Maintaining a mix of functions
Pressure for redevelopment	Low	Low

THE URBAN HUMAN CONDITION 323

terns. Within a given city, the inner city sub-areas will often embody dimensions of two or more types.

While this typology is based on a broad inventory of Canadian urban conditions, the more specific study of inner city areas is still underway in the program of the Urban Affairs Ministry. This program takes the form of a series of probes of neighbourhood change: in population, social-economic circumstances and physical quality; a comparative ten city statistical review of basic Census (1971) indices; and the selective examination of the social characteristics of inner city residents and communities. As each of the four types are interpreted below, illustrative reference will be made to the findings of this and other research.

	Revitalization	Massive Redevelopment
Population	Little change	Gain in population
Socio-economic Status	Increasing	Increasing
Family Status	Maintenance of population mix	Loss of families, gain of singles, young couples
Ethnicity	Sometimes loss of ethnic groups	Seldom important
Community Organization	Increasingly well organized	Usually unorganized
Physical Conditions	Improving	Improved housing, possible environment problems
Housing/land Costs	Increasing rapidly	Increasing
Tenure	Little change	Tenancy
Functions	Maintaining a mix of functions	Losing some CBD functions, but gaining many others
Pressure for redevelopment	Strong, but controlled	High

DECLINING AREAS

Declining areas are those inner city districts which may be found in any of our largest cities which show the symptoms of a "culture of poverty." Old and deteriorating and uncared for housing; serious social problems; signs of human despair and suffering; and pockets of crowding (too many people for the rooms available) – these are frequently the most conspicuous traits of such troubled areas.[23]

Map 7.3. Socio-Economic Status and Juvenile Delinquency, London, Ontario, 1965, by Census Tracts

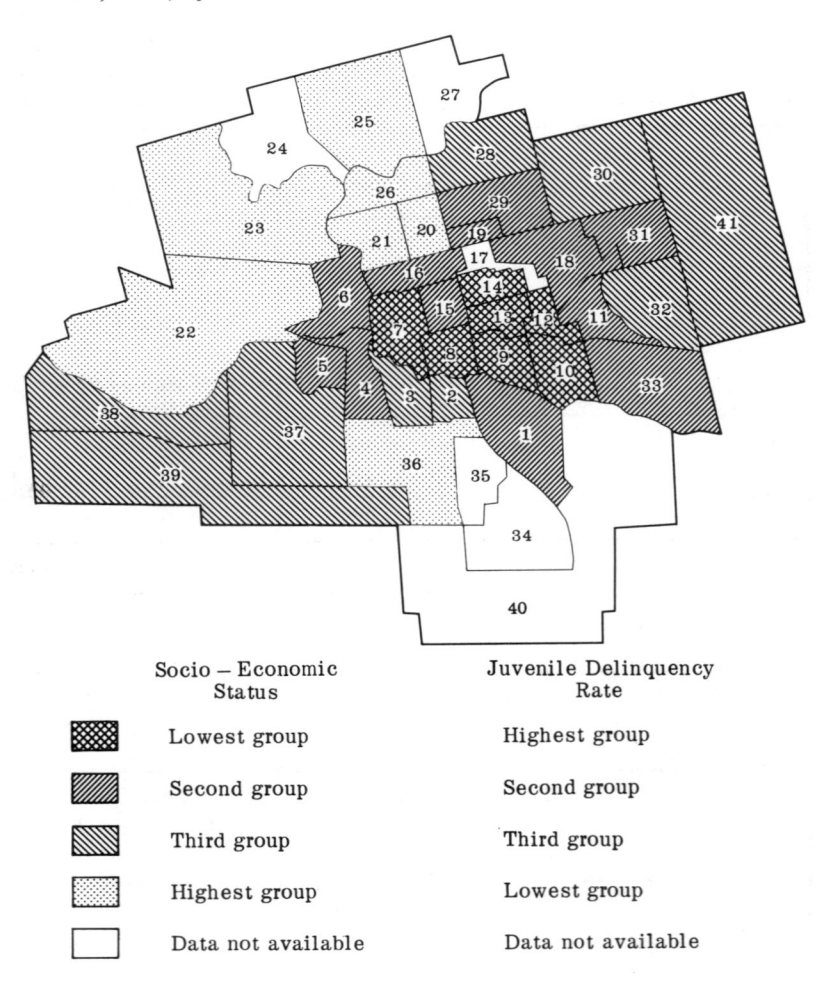

Socio – Economic Status	Juvenile Delinquency Rate
Lowest group	Highest group
Second group	Second group
Third group	Third group
Highest group	Lowest group
Data not available	Data not available

Source: *1961 Census of Canada Population* Vol. 1 (Pt. 1) (Ottawa: Dominion Bureau of Statistics, 1962), A-21. Juvenile delinquency data provided by Professor George K. Jarvis, University of Alberta.

Some of these conditions are intensified when they occur within urban regions having relatively weak economies. For example, one of Winnipeg's poorest areas, a neighbourhood called South Point Douglas, had a significantly lower average income (the size of the pay cheque brought home by its men, 1971) than its counterpart in the other metropolitan areas, such as Centre-Ville in Montreal, Strathcona in Vancouver, and the north central area of Halifax.[24]

(1) Poverty and Delinquency in Declining Areas

It is not surprising that the repercussions of decline are experienced most acutely by the vulnerable part of their population: the young. A sociologist and a medical researcher, George K. Jarvis and Harley B. Messinger, have conducted a careful analysis of the relationship between rates of juvenile delinquency and a number of basic urban conditions in London, Ontario. "Delinquency" was defined functionally on the basis of court appearances or unofficial occurrences known to the police, of the population aged ten to fifteen years, in the year 1965. There were more than five hundred cases, which were allocated to the parts of the city (census tracts) where the young people lived. Rates of delinquency related to population were computed.[25]

The conditions in the areas of occurrence were described in terms

Table 7.3. Index of Socio-Economic Status and Juvenile Delinquency Rates, by Groups of Census Tracts, London, Ontario, 1965

Index of Socio-economic Status		Rate of Delinquency per 1,000 boys and girls, aged 10 – 15	
Groups	Census Tracts	Range	Average
Lowest Group 40.8 to 44.2	Tracts 7, 8, 9, 10, 12, 13, 14	42 – 145	69.5
Second Group 44.4 to 50.1	Tracts 1, 4, 5, 6, 11, 15, 16, 18, 19, 29, 31, 33,	11 – 62	26.1
Third Group 50.3 to 59.7	Tracts, 2, 3, 28, 30, 32, 37, 38, 39, 41,	4 – 39	16.1
Highest Group 60.6 to 70.8	Tracts 20, 21, 22, 23, 25, 26, 30	0 – 22	10.5

Source: Juvenile Delinquency Data, London Ontario, 1965, provided by Professor George K. Jarvis, University of Alberta.

of four major factors which were built up from quite a comprehensive list of variables. The factors were *socio-economic status*, a poverty/affluence indicator represented mainly by income, education and rent; *blue collar familism*, designed to identify factory workers through such variables as occupational status, fertility rates for women, marital status and relative numbers of men in the population; *stability*, reflecting "relatively rooted, declining populations," in such variables as years of occupancy, and age of populations; and *density-living arrangements*, which express the density of both population and dwellings, that is of people or units to the acre; the factor was designed to include the variable of distance from the centre of the city.[26]

The comparison of rates and factors shows an overwhelming correlation between delinquency and poverty. Generally the areas with the lowest indices of socio-economic status (census tracts 7, 8, 9, 10, 12, 13, 14, Table 7.3 – Map 7.3) had the highest delinquency rates in the city. These were all inner city areas. The researchers cross-checked their general results by an analysis of housing variables in which the analogue to poverty was the per cent of housing built before 1920. Again a strong correlation with poverty emerged, as well as an important secondary correlation: delinquency and *crowding*, the average of people to rooms per dwelling.[27]

(2) *Poverty and Crowding in Declining Areas*

The link between the inner city, poverty and crowding has been convincingly demonstrated in Toronto by a 1974 study of the *Social Determinants of Human Crowding* by D. R. Johnson, Alan Booth and Donna Duvall. They had an impressive information base: a random sample of 4,889 households from a total of more than 15,000 in thirteen inner city Census tracts. They examined several determinants of crowding and concluded that "young foreign born heads of households with low socio-economic status and recent residential mobility have the greatest rooms deficit, while the high occupational status head, born in Canada or the United States, residentially stable, and age 45 through 75 has the greatest excess of rooms."[28]

In Canada, the concern with crowding in our cities is a long-standing one. It figured prominently in the annual reports of the Commission of Conservation (1911-21), which were given to comments in this vein:

> Is it really necessary in Canada, that thousands of houses, built for one family and with one set of sanitary conveniences only, should house two, three or four and even six families? Dr.

Hastings, Medical Health Officer of Toronto (1914) has estimated, that in Toronto there are still three thousand houses occupied by from two to five families each. Do we expect permanent progress and decent family life to continue under these conditions? Only those faced with it, know of the distressing and degrading effects of overcrowding.[29]

While this kind of worry has entered into our urban mythology, it has not been until quite recently that we have had the benefit of systematic enquiry into the effects of crowding on human well-being.[30] One of the most important of these is a study (1972-1974) of inner city Toronto families by a team of physicians, and social researchers under the direction of the urban sociologist, Alan Booth.[31] The study had the following features:

A sample of 560 households was selected from a large number of screening interviews in central Toronto. This population had the following characteristics: intact, white families; European or North American descent; one or more children; wife, under forty-five years of age; at least three months in their "present" dwelling. These households included both crowded and uncrowded neighbourhood conditions, as measured by number of dwelling units per residential acre; and approximately half of the household units were crowded – residents exceeded the number of rooms.

The information base for the study was obtained (1) through a series of voluntary in-depth interviews (two hour) with 522 wives, and a shorter one with 332 husbands; and (2) physical examinations of 294 women, 213 men and 900 children, conducted at a nearby health centre.

The objective of the investigation was to discover the effects of household and neighbourhood crowding on health, family relations, aggression, neighbouring and other basic aspects of domestic life.[32]

This emphasis on the *individual and the family* as the unit of analysis, rather than communities or other areal unit, gives the results of the study special interest and significance.

Four dimensions of crowding were used: *household objective*: the number of people exceed the number of rooms and other criteria related to occupancy and physical arrangements; *household subjective*, determined by eliciting a response from residents to a number of questions, such as "Does your child have a place to play at home without getting in anyone's way?"; *objective neighbourhood*: type of dwelling unit, number of dwelling units in the respondent's block and on the block face opposite, etc.; and *subjective neighbourhood*, determined by responses to such questions as "Are the neighbourhood stores in which you shop too crowded?"[33]

Noting two of the study's methods is important for an appreciation of its results: (1) related factors such as education and income were screened out statistically so that the effect of crowding could be isolated, e.g. crowded and uncrowded low income families could be validly compared; and (2) the basic analyses were re-run taking into account various measures of adversity or stress. "Comparisons on each of the health and social factors studied were made between crowded and uncrowded persons in high and low socio-economic categories in order to determine whether stress intensified the effect of crowding."[34]

By January 1975 tentative analysis was completed on the relationship between crowding and health, aggression, family relations, political behaviour and human sexual behaviour.

The preliminary report on this study concludes that in general crowding has only minor adverse effects on the residents; that such adverse effects are generally attributable to household rather than neighbourhood conditions; and that men are more adversely affected than women.[35] Bearing in mind this predominant outcome, some of the more significant findings are the following:

Discounting for all qualifying factors, 54 per cent of the men who lived in crowded households were diagnosed to have a *stress disease* (such as high blood pressure, hypertension, heart ailments and peptic ulcers) compared to 34 per cent for those living in uncrowded homes.

Women were not affected by objective household and neighbourhood crowding, but their *perception* of being crowded was reflected in a greater incidence of severe psychiatric impairment and uterine dysfunction, which are considered stress related disorders.[36]

While generally *family relations* were not dramatically affected by crowding the high incidence of some of the selected indicators would seem to reveal something about the quality of life in the inner city. For example, mothers in crowded dwellings struck their children an average of 7.6 times in the week preceding the interview compared to 5.1 times for their uncrowded sisters. The rod apparently is not being spared.

Over 50 per cent of the men and 42 per cent of women who felt crowded reported their mates were less affectionate, while among those not feeling crowded 38 per cent of the men and 30 per cent of the women reported love decrements.

THE URBAN HUMAN CONDITION 329

In contrast to the medical data, in the realm of family relationships (husband/wife, parent/children and children/children) all of the effects of objective and subjective household crowding are intensified by other sources of stress, such as poor relations with neighbours or poverty.

The Booth studies, in their unstated as well as stated assumptions, give emphasis to the importance of viewing the phenomenon of crowding in context. It is a phenomenon that occurs in a particular setting: a particular city, part of a city and a specific social environment. And within this setting its effects are differentially experienced by the inhabitants: young and old, men and women, rich and poor. What is important to bear in mind is that the conditions of the inner city may either ease or intensify the dissatisfaction with crowding or the high-rise housing form with which it is often associated.

The introduction by Booth of the concept of subjective crowding draws attention to the all-round impact of environment on the person. Crowding, physically and psychologically, may be simply the most conspicuous expression of a severely restricted lifestyle. This is emphasized by Peter Homenuck who completed at the end of 1974 a review of the major studies, 269 in all, on the social and psychological effects of high-rise. He writes: "If, through economic circumstances, persons are forced to high-rise complexes, there is a much stronger likelihood of dissastisfaction than if it is selected through exercising some choice. The lack of income coupled with the lack of choice forces persons in similar disadvantaged circumstances together in some high-rise projects, and the resulting obvious concentration of low status families and individuals further aggravate the feelings of being trapped."[37] Inasmuch as "areas of decline" remain areas with a complex of social, economic and environmental problems crowding and whatever adverse effects it may cause is not likely to respond to policies that deal with peoples' housing in isolation from their neighbourhoods.

STABLE AREAS

In contrast to declining areas, Canadian inner cities contain a number of stable residential districts which have maintained their functions as blue collar communities or immigrant receiving areas, such as Hochelaga in Montreal, or Kensington Market in Toronto.

The characteristics of stable areas may be set in relief by the comparison in a single city, Montreal, of two inner city "quartiers" – one maintaining a stable pattern, and the other tending towards decline. Hochelaga, on the east side of the inner city along the St. Lawrence is stable. Centre Sud, a district immediately to the west of

330 CHANGING CANADIAN CITIES

and bordering on downtown Montreal is declining. Their position in the city and relationship to other inner city districts are shown in Map 7.4. They both are inhabited by a French-speaking, native-born population living as tenants in various forms of multiple housing. But there the resemblances end. The accompanying tables 7.4 and 7.5 highlight some of the similarities and differences between the districts.

While Centre Sud has lost almost half of its population in the thirty years 1941-71, Hochelaga's loss was well below 10 per cent, and about half of its population demonstrates very stable tenure, having lived in the same dwelling for more than six years, compared to 46 per cent of those who remain in Centre Sud. The people who live in these districts have very modest incomes, well below the metropolitan average, but the gap between the two has been widening – from a difference of 8 per cent in average male employment

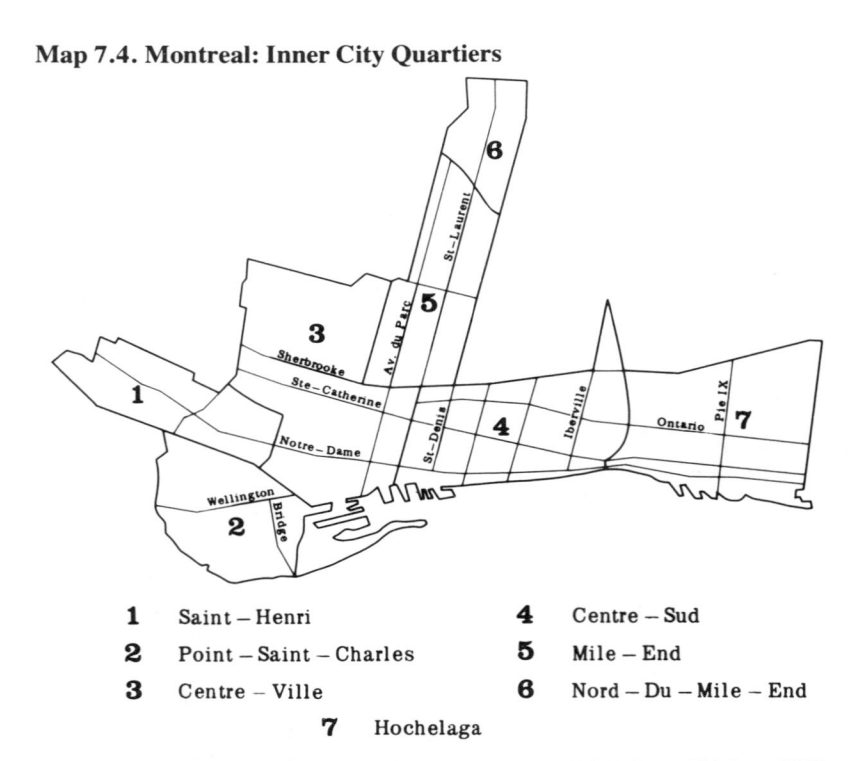

Map 7.4. Montreal: Inner City Quartiers

1	Saint – Henri	4	Centre – Sud
2	Point – Saint – Charles	5	Mile – End
3	Centre – Ville	6	Nord – Du – Mile – End
		7	Hochelaga

Source: R. McLemore, C. Aass and P. Keilhofer, *The Changing Canadian Inner City* Urban Paper A.75.3 (Ottawa: MSUA, 1975), p. 40.

Table 7.4. Montreal Inner City – Stability and Decline, Hochelaga and Centre Sud: Similarities

District	Hochelaga	Centre Sud	Metro
Population – Canadian Born			
1961	95%	96%	
1971	96%	100%	85%
Tenant Occupied Dwellings			
1951	72%	93%	
1961	88	92	
1971	90	94	
Single Detached Dwellings			
1951	1%	0%	
1961	1	0	
1971	3	3	

Table 7.5. Montreal Inner City – Stability and Decline, Hochelaga and Centre Sud: Differences

District	Hochelaga	Centre Sud	Metro
Population			
1941	78,759	96,646	
1951	80,148	90,851	
1961	82,470	76,427	
1971	72,975	50,691	
% change, 1941 – 71	7.6%	47.5%	
Avg. Male Employment Income			
1951	2138	1966	
1961	3271	2876	
1971	5448	4702	$7082
% change, 1951 – 71	155%	139%	
Persons per Household			
1951	4.5	4.3	
1961	3.9	3.7	
1971	3.3	2.9	
Rooms per Dwelling			
1951	4.9	4.9	
1961	4.7	4.5	
1971	4.6	4.4	
More than 6 years Occupancy			
1951	65	26	
1961	40	40	
1971	49	46	44%

Sources: Census of Canada, 1971; and Reg McLemore, Carl Aass and Peter Keilhofer, *The Changing Canadian Inner City*, Urban Paper A.75.3 (Ottawa: Ministry of State for Urban Affairs, 1975), Tables 14 and 16. Reproduced by permission of the Minister of Supply and Services Canada.

income in 1941 to a level in 1971 which is 15 per cent higher in Hochelaga. The decline in the average household size in Centre Sud of about one-third reflects a substantial loss of family units, while the comparatively small decrease in "rooms per dwelling" in Hochelaga suggests that dwellings for families are being maintained.[38]

Some insight on the differences in attitudes and lifestyles between these two kinds of inner city is provided in a report by SORECOM, a Montreal group of urban researchers. The varying perceptions of the residents in the eighteen districts of the Montreal Urban Community are explored through their responses to questions about their concept of their own districts, their views on the advantages and disadvantages of their areas, and about their aspirations for the districts in which they live.

The image of self reflected by Centre Sud is of a people who value and seek reinforcement from others of their own kind, with whom they are at ease, and who are worried about the quality of their housing, the noise in their neighbourhood, the dirt, and lack of green spaces. Hochelaga, by contrast, presents itself as a place that celebrates the solid domestic virtues of church, school and shopping; an attractive environment and neighbourhood peace figure strongly in its vision of civic utopia.

Not even the more stable inner city areas are impervious to change and sometimes deteriorating influences. One of the most striking examples of this is the neighbourhood of Sandy Hill in Ottawa. For over a century, Sandy Hill's low and medium density, modest middle-class existence was sheltered between the Rideau River and Rideau Canal, blocking the east and west, and a railway line blocking access from the south. Beginning in the 'fifties, however, the neighbourhood has had to absorb the repercussions of a series of traffic improvements – bridges across the Canal, the Queensway with exits and feeders into the district – and the explosion of the University of Ottawa, whose enrolment doubled between 1958 and 1964. In response the area has seen the rise of citizens groups, Action Sandy Hill and The Citizens Planning Committee, which have played a constructive role in accommodating the neighbourhood to change while preserving the best of its medium density residential core.[39]

REVITALIZING AREAS

This third inner city is in flux. It is on the receiving end of in-city migrations drawn by its central location and a housing stock that has potential for attractive rehabilitation. As a result the rich tend to drive out the poor. The kinds of pressures which have earned the epithet of "white-painting" in the Glebe of Ottawa, Don Vale in

Toronto or the south-central area of Halifax are increasingly built into Canadian social patterns. According to William Michelson of the University of Toronto the demand for central single family homes is built into what he calls the "family mobility cycle." This conclusion was based on interviews with approximately seven hundred married couples within the child-bearing years – over a period of eighteen months.[40]

This cycle has three stages: (1) baseline; (2) incremental change; and (3) approximation of the ideal. The first stage represents a young couple's first major housing choice, either at the time of family formation or of arrival in a given urban area. Their choice is necessarily not greatly affected by previous housing experience. Utilitarian considerations predominate, particularly the location of work place, and this may lead them to anywhere on the city map. The second stage is one in which housing moves begin to be affected by the North American desire for the self-contained single family house in an open low-density neighbourhood. But practical limitations intervene. An actual housing choice, in the second stage, for example, a high-rise apartment instead of the suburban bungalow, may represent a compromise which is perceived by the resident as temporary, in both housing form and location. In the third stage, which is of particular interest for "revitalizing areas," the housing consumer is in hot pursuit of his (her?) ideal and is prepared to trade off travel time and cost to approximate his ideal, which is usually a self-contained house in the suburbs or, single family or low-density multiple, downtown.

The place of the individual's choice on the suburban-downtown continuum is strongly influenced by certain conspicuous sub-cultural forces. Michelson's study identifies a group of families with a strong affinity to downtown residential locations and with the following characteristics:

- generally more highly educated than suburbanites
- both husband and wife are likely to have a profession
- interested in downtown cultural activities: plays, music, art
- the husband is generally older and more professionally advanced than his suburban counterpart
- about three-quarters of the wives do not work
- the couple is concerned with easing the husband's travel to work
- value is placed on the special attributes of the chosen neighbourhood: its environmental qualities, prestige, or "flavour."[41]

Michelson makes two observations on this group of housing consumers that have implications for the inner city. The first is that they tend to become strongly attached to their neighbourhoods – there is a permanency about the third stage housing decision. The second is that the urban forces now at play will increase the housing demand which is focused on inner city neighbourhoods. Michelson makes the point in this way:

> With an increase in the general educational and occupational level in society, and particularly large cities, one should expect the number of people seeking such units to increase. Hence the necessity to take seriously the cause for preservation of existing downtown housing... Only preservation and rehabilitation of the older stock offers any hope of a reasonable number of units available to that subsegment of the population placing a strong value on both low-rise housing and on central location.[42]

This places in perspective the forces that reverberate on those inner city areas identified as "revitalizing." Both the accommodation of the newcomers as well as the interests of their sometimes hard-pressed, lower income and involuntary hosts will become increasingly a concern of urban policy.

AREAS OF MASSIVE REDEVELOPMENT

The dynamics of city growth and change place parts of the inner city under severe pressure. Pressure comes from the business/civic core, from the suburbs, and from certain area-wide processes. Business functions invade from the centre as in the case of three monumental schemes east of the historic business district in Montreal: Place Desjardins, Place Fédérale and Place Dupuis. Transportation arteries traverse the inner city giving suburbanites access to the facilities and jobs of the central business district as illustrated by the relationship of the Queensway in Ottawa to Sandy Hill and Centretown. And the economics of land and location, in which accessibility to the centre is a major motive force, causes land values to peak toward the centre. The result is characterized by the waves of apartment "cliff building," that have moved progressively north since 1950 along the path of the Yonge subway in Toronto, from College to Bloor to St. Clair to Eglinton.[43] This kind of change has far-reaching repercussions. It may provide occasionally a welcome opportunity for renewal because the oldest housing stock of urban regions is in the inner city. At the same time rapid and capricious change, arising only from the whims of the real estate market, can be socially and environmentally disruptive. Peoples' lives are involved. And the new high-rise living forms, while sought after by people in smaller household units who place a premium on being close to downtown work, constitute *en masse* an environment which often does not meet elementary human needs very well. So the issues that arise in areas of massive redevelopment encompass these two dimensions: buffering the impact on the old neighbourhoods and preserving some of their best features, and struggling to make a humane environment out of the projects that aggressively intrude on the established "landscape."

A child is a sensitive barometer of environmental quality. A study by an urban geographer, Douglas Smith, working with the Toronto Geographical Expedition, has raised some important speculations concerning the impact of high-rise apartments on child development.[44] At the base of the study is a certain view of the relationship between children's play, learning and personal development. This perspective draws on social, psychological and design concepts associated with such names as W. D. Abernethy, the author of *Play Leadership*, R. Callois, the author of *Man, Play and Games* and Polly Hill, a Canadian who has taken a special interest in the "child's environment" and who has authored a CMHC study on *Children and Space*. The essence of the argument is that "play is not an unproductive activity but exists along a delicate continuum with experience and learning."[45] A child's environment is a great educator. It may serve to expand his horizons in the way Alice explored Wonderland, or it may constrict awareness and inhibit the child's proverbial curiosity.

Smith studied the "microspatial behaviour" of children at play in the west Annex area of Toronto, an area bounded by Bloor, Dupont, Bathurst and Spadina Road. Beginning in the late 'fifties, after the opening of the Bloor Street subway and some zoning changes, this area of comfortable middle-class single family homes became an area of active redevelopment – high-rise apartments, typically on a block basis. The children of one of these apartments, which was home for thirty-five kids under the age of thirteen, together with some children living in nearby low-rise homes were the subject of a comparative look at the play patterns in the area.

The concepts employed by the study were *home range:* the "linkages and settings" which constitute the familiar territory around the home; *nodes, paths and edges* which more specifically structure the home range, and as they imply represent the *lines of movement* through an urban space; the *boundaries*, for example, of a child's customary play area beyond which he may feel lost; and the *points of interaction* that occur along frequented pathways within the study area (Map 7.5) such as Kendal Park, a friend's house or a local store; and *mental mapping* which is a philosophy and technique for representing the perception and mental images a person has of his home range or other aspects of environment. The study's information was based on the mental maps and other behaviour specifics provided through interviews (friendly talks) with several sets of nine year old

336 CHANGING CANADIAN CITIES

Map 7.5. Study Area: Child in High-Rise, West Annex, Toronto

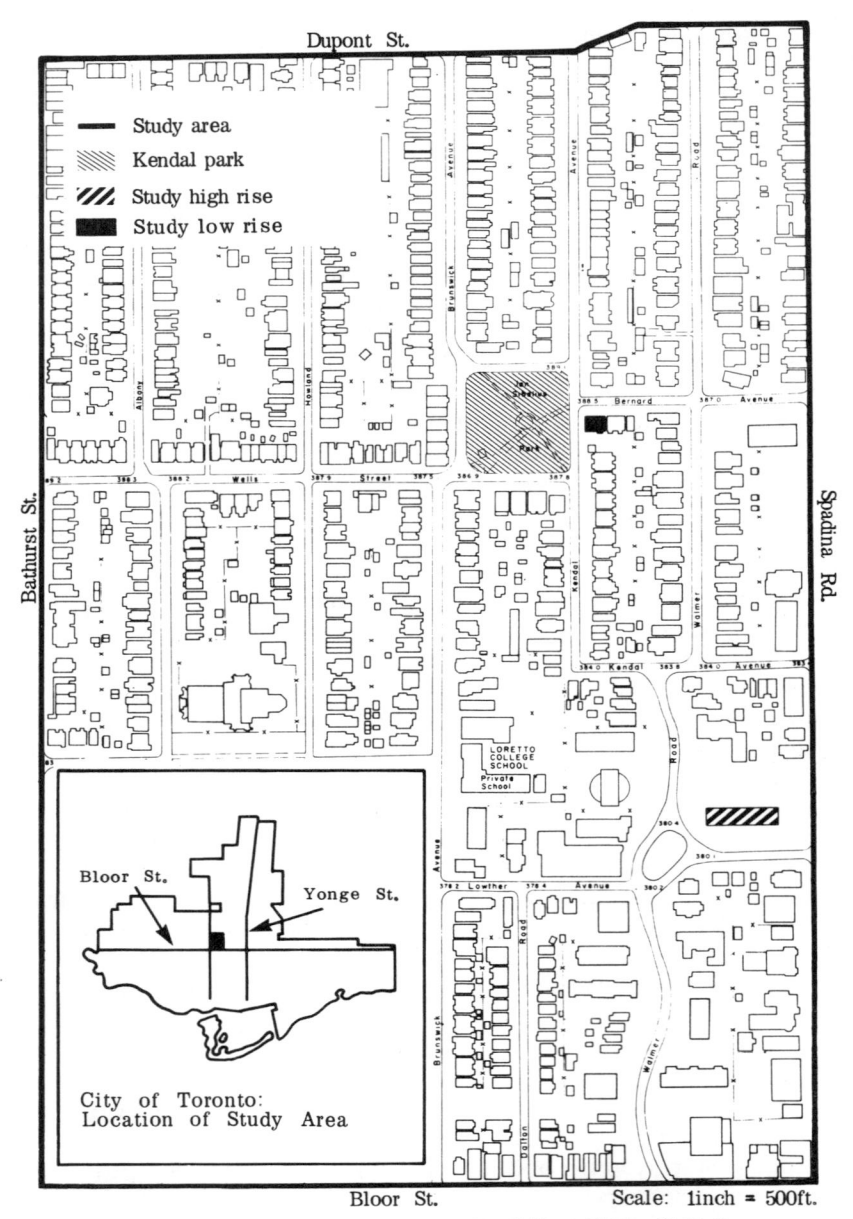

Source: City of Toronto Planning Board, drawing No. 21.and D. Smith, "Children in High Rises" in *The Toronto Geographical Expedition*, eds., R. Bordessa and W.W. Bunge (Ottawa: MSUA, 1974) (mimeographed).

THE URBAN HUMAN CONDITION   337

and twelve year old children – one from each housing form in each age group. Two of these are reproduced here: Map 7.6, the mental map drawn by a nine year old girl who at the time had lived in a low-level house for two years; and Map 7.7, which was drawn by a nine year old girl who had been living on the fourth floor of a high-rise apartment also for two years.[46]

The differences between these home ranges are striking. The horizontal and vertical forms of representation reflect dramatically contrasting experience and perception. The child in the home close to the ground explores a range, illustrated by the map and confirmed in discussion about where the child goes most often, which includes such nodes as the backyard and sidewalk, the playground across the

Map 7.6. Mental Map of Nine Year Old Girl, Low-Rise

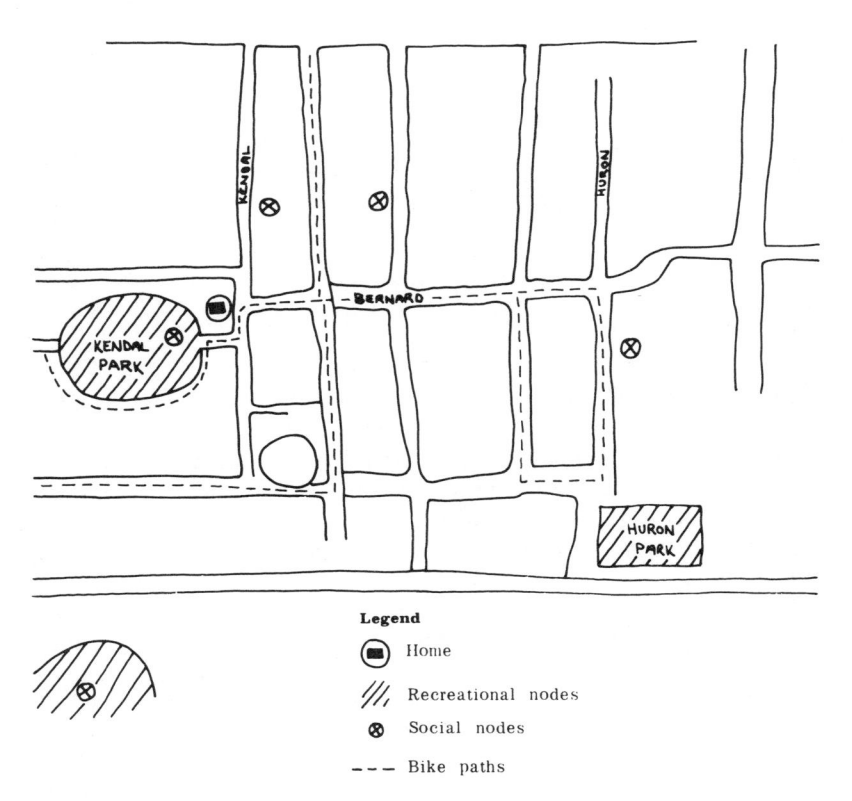

Legend
- ⬛ Home
- //// Recreational nodes
- ⊗ Social nodes
- --- Bike paths

Source: D. Smith, "Children in High Rises" in *The Toronto Geographical Expedition*, eds. R. Bordessa and W.W. Bunge (Ottawa: MSUA, 1974) (mimeographed).

Map 7.7. Mental Map of Nine Year Old Girl, High-Rise

Source: D. Smith, "Children in High Rises" in *The Toronto Geographical Expedition*, eds. R. Bordessa and W.W. Bunge (Ottawa: MSUA, 1974) (mimeographed).

street (Kendal Park), bike riding down the slope of Walmer Road in the next block, visiting two friends three and four blocks away, to the edge of the range where the schoolyard and an empty lot, five and six blocks from home, are visited one or two times a week. It is interesting to note that in the child's image of reality, "mentally bright" areas which she uses everyday, like Kendal Park, are exaggerated in size.

By contrast, the paths of the girl living in the high-rise are mainly back and forth between the apartment unit and the outside grounds. This vertical preoccupation shows up even in the representation of the parking lot, the scene of daily ball playing, which is depicted as a vertical element "standing" beside the apartment building. And there is no place in this "up and down" world to show the residences of two friends who live one and two blocks away. Most of the outside play is on the apartment property itself; and considerable time is spent indoors – in hallways, underground parking garage (note the stairway to the underground parking lot in the drawing), and in the home, watching television.[47]

Three interpretive points are important. One is that the physical *restraints* of the apartment, such as the noise factor and the inability to observe the child playing outside, produce human and institutional restraints, the parents' and managements' prohibitions – the "don'ts," which together constrict the child's spatial world. The second is the limitation imposed on the activities of the high-rise child. Boisterous, potentially creative but noisy play is discouraged in and around the apartment environment, and children as a result are pushed into more sedentary and passive recreation. And the third is the *caging effect* resulting from the inconveniences of moving in and out of an apartment, which involves a certain distance, waiting for the elevator, lugging bicycles through the "obstacle course" of elevator, stairways, doors, or the intercom system to get back in to the building. This is a critical difference from the low-rise case. "By the time the high-rise girl has reached her front door, the low-rise girl can already be playing in Kendal Park with her friends."[48] Figure 7.1 illustrates the caging effects in terms of time and space.

The researchers tend to view their findings with some alarm. The children are caged in their high-rise trap. "In a cognitive-developmental sense, the high-rise children's smaller home range reflects a restricted spatial experience within the environment and this shows in the restricted extent of environmental imagery." And if the advanced educators are right and experience can be equated with learning, the stifling of the child's play opportunities cannot be taken lightly. And one can sympathize with the researchers' heartfelt concern: "The nature of the problem cries out for immediate attention."[49]

The constructive thinking of the research report – "the what to do about it" part – takes a view of the role of high-density housing forms which is consistent with the broader appreciation afforded by Michelson's concept of the family mobility cycle, and of the findings of a Ministry study of Barry Wellman and Marilyn Whitaker which concludes that there is substantial satisfaction amongst high-rise residents of their chosen form of living.[50] The difficulty which is validly emphasized is that the apartment environment tends to be an adults only environment – more attention is given to cars than kids. The challenge is to overcome the poverty of the design and the tyranny of a housing market which will dictate the line of least resistance as long as the units move, i.e., are rented. The experience in the west Annex, with a sizeable child population in buildings where there were not supposed to be any, demonstrates the folly of urban design without *flexibility*; design that cannot respond to the inevitably

Figure 7.1. Caging Effects, the Child in High Rise

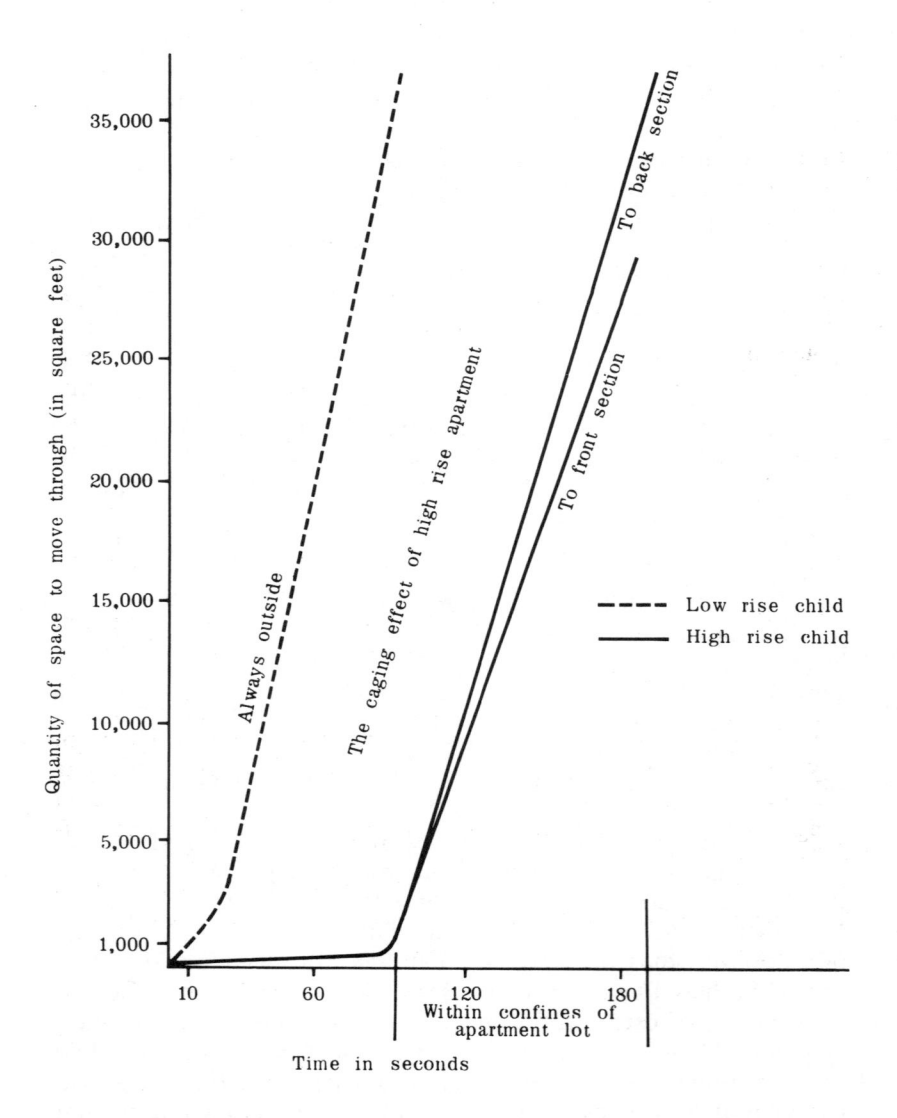

Y-axis: Quantity of space to move through (in square feet) — 1,000; 5,000; 10,000; 15,000; 20,000; 25,000; 30,000; 35,000

X-axis: Time in seconds — 10, 60, 120, 180

Labels on curves:
- Always outside
- The caging effect of high rise apartment
- To back section
- To front section
- Within confines of apartment lot

Legend:
- - - - Low rise child
——— High rise child

Source: D. Smith, "Children in High Rises" in *The Toronto Geographical Expedition*, eds. R. Bordessa and W.W. Bunge (Ottawa: MSUA, 1974) (mimeographed).

changing human condition. Whatever our views on high-rise and the city, this study has served to demonstrate that one of the conditions of the "good city," to facilitate access to the things required for "self-realization and self-fulfilment," is seriously limited in at least one, not untypical, massively redeveloped inner city area.

Policy Approaches

We have seen that it is not possible to speak realistically of *the* inner city. There are several. Each represents a different set of problems, potentials and peoples' needs. In areas of decline, physical and social problems interlock with poverty. Stable areas represent the continued existence of long-established residential communities which, though not by any means affluent, have within themselves the personal and social resources for decent survival as communities. Revitalizing areas were shown to be the "benefactors" of a family mobility cycle which would continue for some time to place such areas under pressure from new groups of people with different incomes and outlooks from the earlier blue collar inhabitants. And in those parts of the city where large-scale redevelopment is the rule, the plight of the child in a high-rise setting is a symptom of the inhumane environments that have proliferated since the mid-fifties.

Viewing the inner cities in this way should help in the formulation of suitable solutions and policies. Our perspective is broadened as well as refined. We can now see that the "urban renewal" programs, focused on redevelopment, that were pushed with such fanfare in the 'fifties and 'sixties were addressed mainly to the problems of physical deterioration in declining areas. And we should appreciate that the new generation of programs focused on the concept of Neighbourhood Improvement (NIP) through rehabilitation and self-help may only be effective in areas that enjoy considerable stability. The point has been made recently by Shirley Chan, whose deep involvement in the community issues of the Strathcona area in Vancouver gives her words a special interest:

> NIP and RRAP [Residential Rehabilitation Assistance Program] will not be successful in every declining inner city neighbourhood. There must be a sense of community in a NIP area. This is difficult to define but has to do with the residents' identification with the area and desire to continue living there. As a result, the community should exhibit characteristics of stability, high interdependence among residents (e.g. cultural minority groups), high degree of autonomy from exterior communities and high ratio of owner-occupancy.[51]

Inasmuch as the NIP program is to be applied, according to the terms of the National Housing Act, to "seriously deteriorated neighbourhoods," these criteria may not be met, and as a result we could be heading for a second serious misallocation of money and effort, of applying, in a sense, the "right programs to the wrong places."

But this need not happen. The varying conditions in the inner city suggest that policy wisdom lies in recognizing the different categories of needs and designing approaches that directly answer to those needs. Several guiding principles are suggested. One is that the repertoire of public/private action should be many-sided, having social, economic and environmental dimensions. The well-being of the inner city should not be sacrificed on the altar of the National Housing Act. Another is that policies and programs should make sense at the human level of the individual and the small group. In this connection, we can learn from the ongoing experience at the neighbourhood level, such as that of the Winnipeg Home Improvement Project which combines home repairs with training, economic institution building and the creation of jobs in depressed low-income neighbourhoods.[52] And finally, and of fundamental importance, we must aspire in the inner city to the attainment of those ultimate goals of the good city, notably the opportunity for self-fulfilment, a lively sense of community, and *controllability*, the feeling and the fact that people have a significant role in shaping the conditions of their lives.

Perspective

This chapter has presented four different ways of looking at the urban human condition. The first is based on *perception*: what images do we have of Canadian cities? The second view is *philosophical*: what aspirations do we have for Canadian cities? The third is *literary*: what aspects of urban life are reflected in creative literature? And the fourth, is the perspective of *policy research*: what have we discovered about urban conditions by scholarly investigation?

While each of these approaches highlight different facets of the urban experience and the urban reality, there are two themes that run through all of them. These are polarity and choice. There are cities with highly favourable images: large- and medium-sized metropolitan centres in Western Canada. And places with extremely negative images: centres of extractive and heavy industry in Ontario and Quebec. Morally, we are torn between regarding the city as a happy hunting ground for the pursuit of private interests, or as the place where social purposes, in terms of industry, art or environment, can be attained most abundantly. Heaven and hell are recur-

THE URBAN HUMAN CONDITION   343

rent motifs of our urban literature. And the inner city is shown to embody both forces of decline and renewal, emotions of despair and hope.

Looking at the same set of dichotomies from a slightly different angle, however, leads to a greater awareness of our urban choices. Canada's size and diversity provide many options by mixing the variables of regional setting, city size, culture, economic base and rate of growth. The conflicting forces within the city are rooted in our values, lifestyles and institutions; we can act on them to influence the balance between individual and communal objectives. Our literature warns us to choose the path of love and compassion, or face the city of the "concentration camp." And the painstaking study of people and their environments begins to provide some of the keys that will unlock the doors of human deprivation and suffering: protect the good, break the cycle of decline, build on the promising, develop more refined and flexible policy tools. These are some of the perspectives that we must build into the search for alternative forms of human settlement.[53]

Notes

1. Ellis Roberts, "The Residential Desirability of Canadian Cities" (Toronto and Ottawa: University of Toronto and Ministry of State for Urban Affairs, January 1974) (mimeographed).
   Study data were obtained by a sample survey, conducted by mail. A 70 per cent response was obtained, i.e. 157 of 232 response places. The response places were urban places over 10,000 in 1966, with smaller cities added to give regional coverage, e.g., Whitehorse and Yellowknife. Sampling was based on municipalities rather than metropolitan areas to allow for cultural and community types, pp. 35 and 36.
2. *Ibid.*, p. 11. The Toronto study was influenced by the work of Peter Gould, who has been "concerned with valued images and the preferential ordering of places shared by a group of people at one location." Note Peter Gould and Rodney White, *Mental Maps* (Middlesex, England: Penguin Books, 1974).
3. "Each object city is given a preference score by every response group. These scores when aggregated give a measure of the overall desirability of the object cities. The preference scores obtained from each response group may be standardized to allow comparison between patterns. This can best be done by transforming the scores to a distribution with mean of zero and variance of unity which preserves the directional content of the question. Cities are then identified by scores which are positive for desirable cities and negative for undesirable ones. When considering the total set of responses (9420 scores) the highest and lowest classes of preference may be defined by taking those scores

with a magnitude of greater than 1.5, which indicates the highest preference if positive and lowest if negative." *Ibid.*, pp. 61 and 62.
To facilitate visual comparisons in the form of preference maps, the preference scores were grouped into quintile divisions, as shown.
4. The preference returns were analysed by the method of principal component analysis to obtain for each response place, a single preference scale "accounting for as much as possible of the shared preference of the group." *Ibid.*, pp. 39 and 40.
5. The study's definitions of region, city size, growth, employment mix and income are given in *ibid.*, pp. 41-43.
6. *Ibid.*, p. 190.
7. *Ibid.*, p. 7.
8. Reference is to a seminar held in Toronto at the Park Plaza Hotel, March 26, 1974. Professor Lawrence Haworth of the Department of Philosophy, University of Waterloo, presented a paper on the subject of human needs in human settlements.
9. Lawrence Haworth, "Deprivation and the Good City," in *Power, Poverty and Urban Policy*, ed. Warner Bloomberg and Henry J. Schmandt (Beverly Hills, Calif.: Sage, 1968). The statement of Haworth's general position is based on this paper.
10. This aspect of Professor Haworth's statement is based on the manuscript of a book entitled *Decadence and Objectivity*, scheduled for publication by the University of Toronto Press. The material at this point draws from the chapter entitled "Work and Leisure," in particular pp. 60-68.
11. *Ibid.*, p. 77.
12. *Ibid.*, pp. 213 and 214.
13. Gail Stewart, "On Looking before Leaping," in *Social Indicators*, Proceedings of a Seminar, Co-ordinator Novia A. M. Carter (Ottawa: The Canadian Council on Social Development, April 1972).
14. Dr. G. Jones, *Butterfly on Rock* (Toronto: University of Toronto Press, 1970), pp. 166 and 167; and Elizabeth Waterston, *Survey: A Short History of Canadian Literature* (Agincourt, Ontario: Methuen, 1973), pp. 144, 151-153.
15. Louis Dudek, "The Poetry of the City," *The English Quarterly*, Vol. 1, No. 2, Summer 1969, p. 74.
16. *Ibid.*, pp. 74 and 75.
17. Harold Town, *Albert Franck, Keeper of the Lanes* (Toronto: McClelland and Stewart Limited, 1974), p. 24.
18. *Ibid.*, Foreword.
19. Reg McLemore, Carl Aass and Peter Keilhofer, *The changing Canadian inner city*, Urban Paper A.75.3 (Ottawa: Ministry of State for Urban Affairs, 1975), p. 5.
20. *Ibid.*, pp. 2 and 3.
21. R. Bordessa and W. W. Bunge, "The Toronto Geographical Expedition," Research Report (Ottawa: Ministry of State for Urban Affairs, 1974) (mimeographed), pp. 110 and 111.
22. McLemore, Aass and Keilhofer, *op. cit.*, Table 1, p. 6.
23. Gunter Gad, "'Crowding' and 'Pathologies': Some Critical Remarks," *Canadian Geographer*, XVII, 4, 1973, p. 380. Professor Gad's position is summed up in the cited phrase "crowding keys in with other deprivations." McLemore, Aass and Keilhofer, *op. cit.*, pp. 5-7.
24. *Ibid.*
25. George K. Jarvis and Harley B. Messinger, "Social and Economic Correlates of Juvenile Delinquency Rates: A Canadian Case," Discussion Paper B.74.13 (Ottawa: Ministry of State for Urban Affairs, May 1974), pp. 3-5. Delinquency rates were related to thirty-eight demographic variables, selected from the Census and other sources, by both factor and regression analysis.

26. *Ibid.*, pp. 4-10; the concepts and variables of these four factors are outlined in some detail.
27. *Ibid.*, pp. 11 and 12. This analogue is highly correlated with delinquency (0.746) and even more highly correlated with poverty (0.883).
28. David R. Johnson, Alan Booth and Donna Duvall, "Social Determinants of Human Crowding," Discussion Paper B.75.3 (Ottawa: Ministry of State for Urban Affairs, 1975). Using interview data from a probability sample of urban households the effects of occupational status, age, residential stability, ethnicity and household composition on human crowding are examined.
29. G. Frank Beer, "A Plea for City-Planning Organization," in *Report of the Fifth Annual Meeting*, Commission of Conservation, Canada (Toronto: Bryant Press Ltd., 1914), p. 113.
30. The most comprehensive Canadian treatment of the crowding phenomenon and its effects may be found in the following report: Peter Homenuck, James P. Morgenstern and Ronald Keeble, "An analysis of social and psychological effects of high rise," Discussion Paper B.75.9 (Ottawa: Ministry of State for Urban Affairs, 1975).
31. This account of the Booth studies is derived mainly from Alan Booth, "Preliminary Report Urban Crowding Project," Research Report (Ottawa: Ministry of State for Urban Affairs, August 1974) (mimeographed).
32. *Ibid.*, pp. 3 and 4.
33. *Ibid.*, pp. 7-10.
34. The screening out of related factors was by the procedure called multiple regression analysis. Booth, *ibid.*, p. 5. The reference to the introduction of stress factors is on page 12 of the Booth report.
35. *Ibid.*, p. 12. A study published concurrently with the Booth studies, and drawing on the same data, concluded that neighbourhood conditions rather than household crowding, are mainly accountable for adverse effects; at this stage, this remains an open, unresolved debate.

    William Michelson and Kevin Garland, *The Differential Role of Crowded Homes and Dense Residential Areas in the Incidence of Selected Symptoms of Human Pathology* (Toronto: University of Toronto, Centre for Urban and Community Studies, December 1974).
36. Alan Booth and John Cowell, "The Effects of Crowding Upon Health," Research Report (Ottawa: Ministry of State for Urban Affairs, April 1974) (mimeographed), p. 12.
37. Homenuck, Morgenstern and Keeble, *op. cit.*, p. 14.

    While in the conditions of our cities there is often a close association between crowding and high-rise buildings, the two phenomena are not always synonymous. Two recent studies examining the effects of *forms* of housing, are important: Linda Margaret Mary Hagerty, "The Family at Home, A Comparison of the Time – Budgets of Families in High-Rise Apartments and Detached Houses in Suburban Metropolitan Toronto," (Ph.D. Thesis, University of Toronto, School of Social Work, 1975); and Donna Duvall, "The Differential Effects of Housing Types on Women: Apartments and Single Dwellings," Research Report (Ottawa: Ministry of State for Urban Affairs, 1976).
38. Reg McLemore, Carl Aass and Peter Keilhofer, "Comparative Census Data on Inner City Areas in Four Canadian Cities," Research Report (Ottawa: Ministry of State for Urban Affairs, January 1975) (mimeographed). The statistical comparison is derived from Appendix B, Tables 14 and 16, pp. 41-42.

    The comparison of perceptions about Centre Sud and Hochelaga is based on Sorécom, "Les Notions de Voisinage, Quartier, Paroisse et Ville," Research Report (Ottawa: Ministry of State for Urban Affairs, 1974) (mimeographed), pp. 68-105 and 199-211.

    The introductory report of the study explains the design and selection of the sample for interviews, as follows: "L'échantillon que nous avons construit afin d'atteindre les objectifs de la CUM pour la présente étude, est un échantillon par air et grappes a plusieurs poliers avec sélection systematique des répondants.... Enfin, donc chacun des 214 bloc dispersés sur tout le territorie de chaque quartier, nous avons fait entre 10 et 15 sélections au hasard systematique pour arriver à un total approximatif de 3000 sélections."

39. Carl Aass and Peter Keilhofer, "Sandy Hill: A Neighbourhood Study," Research Report (Ottawa: Ministry of State for Urban Affairs, December 1974) (mimeographed), Section 2, "History of Sandy Hill."
40. William Michelson, David Belgue and John Stewart, "Intentions and expectations in differential residential selection," Discussion Paper B.72.5 (Ottawa: Ministry of State for Urban Affairs, 1972); and William Michelson, *Environmental Change* (Toronto: University of Toronto, Centre for Urban and Community Studies, October 1973).

    The sample was limited to "persons affluent enough to demonstrate some degree of choice when selecting housing, by the criterion of putting specific minima and maxima according to the month and year on the monthly costs of the housing rented or purchased. This procedure was successful in that median family income was about $13,000 with about 40 per cent over $15,000 (although only 16 per cent over $20,000); only about 12 per cent were under $9,000 [circa 1970]," Michelson, *Environmental Change*, p. 2.
41. *Ibid.*, pp. 6, 9, 20, 26 and 29.
42. *Ibid.*, pp. 55 and 56.
43. "Policies and Programs for Inner City Areas," (Ottawa: Ministry of State for Urban Affairs, July 1974 draft) (mimeographed), p. 16.
44. Douglas Smith, "Children in High Rises," in "The Geographical Expedition," ed. R. Bordessa and W. W. Bunge (Ottawa: Ministry of State for Urban Affairs, 1974) (mimeographed), pp. 135-213.
45. *Ibid.*, p. 139.
46. *Ibid.*, pp. 149 and 153. The researchers structure the home range in terms of the components, adapted for the purpose, which were presented by the American urbanist, Kevin Lynch, in his book, *The Image of the City* (Cambridge, Massachusetts: Massachusetts Institute of Technology Press, 1960).
47. Michelson, *op. cit.*, *Environmental Change*, pp. 156-160.
48. *Ibid.*, p. 160
49. *Ibid.*, pp. 173 and 143.
50. Barry Wellman and Marilyn Whitaker, "High-rise, low-rise: the effects of high density living," Discussion Paper B.74.29 (Ottawa: Ministry of State for Urban Affairs, 1974).
51. Shirley Chan, "The Social Aspects of Rehabilitation," *Habitat*, Vol. 17, Nos. 4 and 5, 1974, p. 30.
52. Eric J. Barker, Carl J. Blanchaer and Donald Epstein, "Limited House Rehabilitation and Job Training: The Winnipeg Home Improvement Project," in *Housing Innovation and Home Improvement*, ed. Donald Epstein (Winnipeg: Institute of Urban Studies, March 1974), pp. 7-62.
53. The viewpoint assumed by this and the following chapter reflects the influence of Professor K. Izumi. See, for example, Kiyo Izumi, "The (in)human(e) environment," External Research Paper C.73.3 (Ottawa: Ministry of State for Urban Affairs, June 1973).

CHAPTER 8

Forms of Urban Settlement: Towards the Open City

What is "Settlement"?

The term "settlement" is simply a convenient, but not wholly adequate way, of expressing how people relate – in the places where they have their homes and where they work – to their surrounding environment. The present Canadian settlement pattern was laid down in pioneer days. Ports were established; roads, canals, railways built. Over a period of not more than about a hundred and twenty-five years from the end of the eighteenth century, people moved, sometimes in vast waves of immigration, to occupy most of the country's arable land. Market and service centres sprang up; the original entrepôt cities like Montreal and Toronto – middle men exporters/importers, wholesalers and processors – provided the base for Canada's first metropolitan places.

During the period of original expansion when people were preoccupied with opening up the country, with establishing a survey grid, with constructing its elemental framework, and when they lived mainly in small dispersed rural and urban communities, settlement was taken for granted. It just happened. It wasn't much to think about. But today that has changed. The forces of population growth and concentration make the *form* of settlement a factor that influences, critically, the quality of life in cities. Whether people live in big places or small places; in concentrated, compact high-density towns and cities, or sprawling dispersed spread-out places; in places where the activities of the city are tightly organized and inter-related or just loosely connected; in places where people have easy access to the countryside or are trapped in the inner city – these are variables that increasingly affect the well-being of Canadians.

The Form and Structure of Cities

To speak of *settlement form* or *urban form* is to speak of certain broad aspects of the human environment that deeply affect the lives of individuals and groups. Form, in a sense, is the view from the air — say on a clear day at twenty thousand feet. From that height the on-the-ground commonplaces of houses, factories, office buildings, expressways and parks together, assume an over-riding shape. We may discover that the urban area we live in has the form of a ball, a star, an undulating serpent, a doughnut or, perhaps, a scrambled egg. Such forms may be expressed by the kind of descriptive terms illustrated in Figure 8.1 radial corridors, multi-towns, linear city, spread city, and so on.

If we fly around a city before landing, at five thousand feet, certain critical features come into focus. Groups of houses form areas bounded by main roads. Factories tend to concentrate along expressways and railways. High office buildings tend to cluster around points where main roads converge. If our flight takes place between about 4.30 and 5.00 in the afternoon, there will be a lot of

Figure 8.1. Four Urban Forms

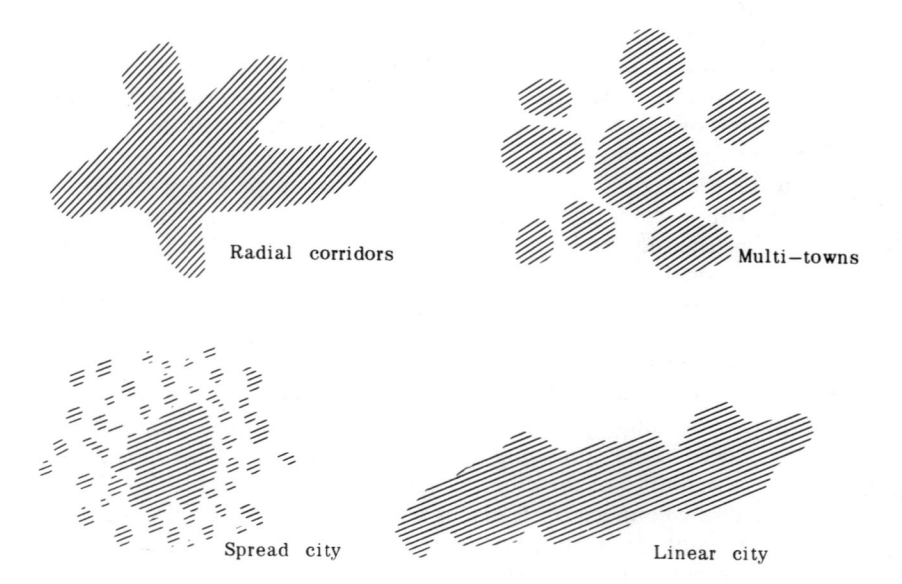

Radial corridors

Multi–towns

Spread city

Linear city

Source: D.E. Boyce, N.D. Day and C. McDonald, *Metropolitan Plan Making: An analysis of Alternative Land Use and Transportation Plans* (Philadelphia: Regional Science Research Institute, Monograph series No. 4, 1970), p 36.

FORMS OF URBAN SETTLEMENT 349

people and vehicles moving around. The parking lots of many manufacturing plants suddenly empty – the cars literally pouring out. Armies of people and cars and buses fan out from the office clusters, riding across town to dispersed residential areas. And in the midst of all this cross-traffic, trucks of every size and description are manoeuvring and "bulldozing" their way towards terminals, great sprawling low buildings and yards, on the edge of the city. These identifiable functionally distinct areas, residential, industrial and commercial – their location and distribution in the space of the urban area – and the inter-relationships that generate linkages between them, such as traffic and telephoning, illustrate the *structure* of settlement.

These two variables, form and structure, establish the framework of settlement. They may be viewed as two related co-ordinates (Figure 8.2). The form co-ordinate identifies a scale ranging from the

Figure 8.2. Form and Structure Co-ordinates

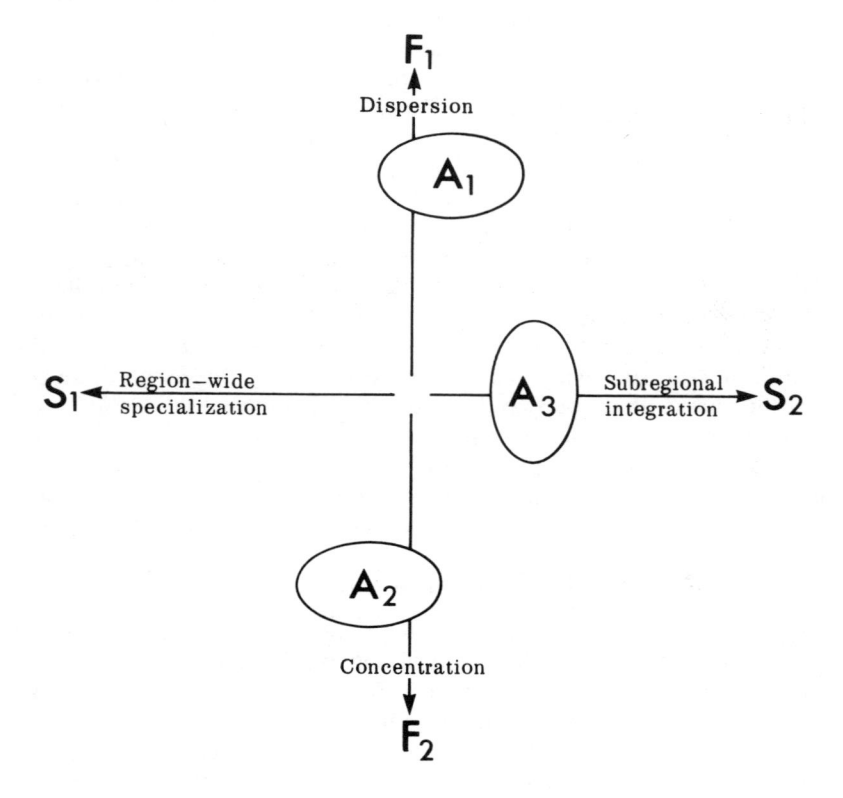

F_1 Dispersion

A_1

S_1 ← Region–wide specialization — A_3 — Subregional integration → S_2

A_2

Concentration F_2

extreme dispersion of an area's development (F1) to an extreme concentration (F2). And the structure co-ordinate indicates a scale which at one extremity (S1) represents region-wide specialization, for example, a single metropolis with specialized parts, and at the other (S2) sub-regional integration, for example, an urban area made up of a number of diversified communities, each with its own inner balance of urban functions.[1]

In the real world of urbanization there are a great variety of forces which will at any given time determine the place of a particular urban region on these key co-ordinates. Figure 8.2 for example, illustrates three alternatives; A1 which represents a "spread city" with its parts widely dispersed and biased toward integration, say a balance of jobs and homes, at the sub-regional level perhaps in quite small and scattered urban units; A2, a concentrated super city with a high degree of specialization at the regional level; and A3, an alternative that approximates "multi-towns," which combines some of the features of both integration at the town level and specialization of selected functions for the entire region.

Each of these alternatives represents a different set of living conditions. For example, if you live in a place like A1 you may have the advantage of living close to your work but you may have to make many long cross-city trips for other purposes: for major shopping items, for business contacts or for visiting friends and family. And because the city is so spread-out and low in density, most of these trips will have to be by car. By contrast, life in a place like A2 will be highly focused on its major business core where you most likely will have to travel every day for work; and, notwithstanding quite a highly developed public transit system, the main transportation routes, radiating towards the centre, will be chronically clogged and the journey to work will be increasingly a burden. But in A3 there is just the chance that you may have the best of both worlds. You may have access for both services and jobs to well-rounded town centres close to home; and for special things – a pro league hockey game, a ballet or a party at a fine hotel and sometimes a better job – you may be able to reach the centre of the region with comparative ease.

Canadian Regions: Big, Small, and Intermediate

Exploring the settlement form choices in Canada requires some clarification of the regional context. Do we speak of a place like Brandon, Manitoba or the Montreal Urban Community or what? In the earlier chapters on Population and Urban Patterns (Chapter 1) and Alternative Growth Forces: Towards Concentration and Decentralization (Chapter 3), a broad national picture of urban

FORMS OF URBAN SETTLEMENT 351

patterns was presented, with particular reference to variations in the size and type, environment and socio-economic characteristics of Canada's urban areas. At this stage, in considering urban form, it is important to recall that the places where the choice of form emerges most urgently as a public issue – big places and fast-growing places – are in each case expressions of a Canada-wide urbanization process.

This is illustrated in Figure 8.3, which shows the relative growth profile along the five thousand mile Trans-Canada Highway. The graph represents population growth rate, above and below the national growth rate, which is the straight line (1.0). Note that the peaks from west to east are in regions that have their focal points in Vancouver, Calgary, Regina, Winnipeg, Toronto, Montreal, Halifax and St. John's—all Census Metropolitan Areas including the three largest. There is a compelling case, as indicated in the earlier discussion of national urban patterns, that the Canadian urban growth profile is a highly structured one, dominated by Toronto, Montreal, and Vancouver and their associated sub-systems.[2]

Urban growth viewed from a national vantage point brings into focus several scales or geographical levels of urban form. These are the multi-metropolitan region (macro), the metropolitan region (meso or intermediate) and the city region (micro). The regions differ in population and areal size, in the number of major central

Figure 8.3. Population Growth Along the Trans-Canada Highway, 1911-71

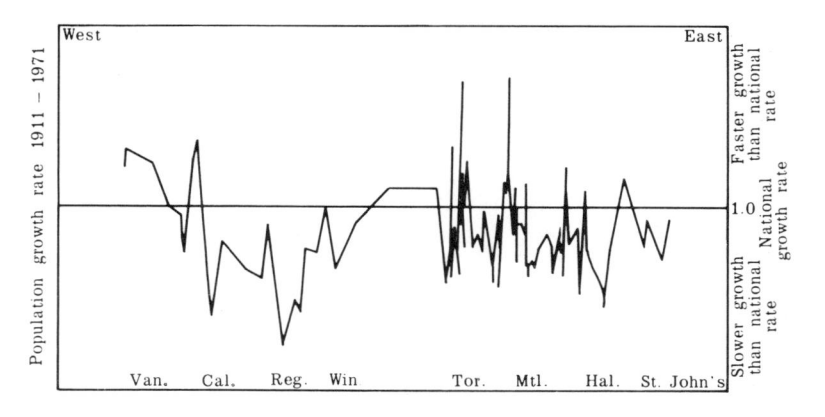

Note: The profile digresses from the Trans-Canada Highway between Montreal and Sudbury to follow Ontario Highways 400 and 401 in order to pass through Toronto.

Source: D.M. Ray and P.Y. Villeneuve, "Population Growth and Distribution in Canada: Problems, Process and Policies," *The Management of Land for Urban Development* (Ottawa: Canadian Council on Urban and Regional Research, 1974).

business districts they incorporate, and in numbers of constituent sub-systems — that is separate but related units with a comparatively comprehensive mix and balance of urban activities (Table 8.1).³

A macro-form is a large region made up of a number of interacting metropolitan and city regions. It is an area of predominant urban influence although the land use pattern will be a mix of urban, open space recreational, farm and other rural activities. The main examples in Canada are *the Canadian development axis*, which is sometimes called the "heartland" of the economic/settlement system, extending from Windsor to Quebec City; the *Georgia Strait urban region*, a complex, focused on Vancouver, which extends over the Strait to Victoria and flows outward over the lower mainland of British Columbia and into the mountains and along the plains of the Fraser River as far inland as Chilliwack; and the *Alberta Development Corridor*, which features the two rapidly growing metropoli of Edmonton and Calgary, and extends from the Peace River country and Fort McMurray waterways to the Lethbridge and Medicine Hat areas.

A metropolitan region may be a sub-system of a larger region, like Montreal in the Canadian development axis, or be on its own, or free-standing, like Winnipeg. It will usually include only one central

Table 8.1. Classification of Urban Forms by Scale, Canada

Trait \ Class	Macro-Form (or Multi-Metropolitan)	Meso-Form (or Metropolitan Region)	Micro-Form (or City-Region)
Number of Urban sub-systems	more than one, usually several	usually one	one
Number of central business districts	more than one	usually one	one
Population size range	over 1.5 million	500,000 to 2.5 million	less than 500,000

Source: Richard E. Preston, "*A Perspective on Alternative Settlement Forms*" (Waterloo: Department of Geography, University of Waterloo, July, 1975).

business-civic core and have quite strong region-wide integration and specialization of urban functions, although there are exceptions like Ottawa-Hull. In addition to the aforementioned, regions at this scale are Toronto, Vancouver, Edmonton, Hamilton, Calgary and Quebec City.

City region is defined as a single urban sub-system, with a dominant central business district, and less than 500,000 people within its daily commuting shed. This includes the smaller Census Metropolitan Areas like Halifax, Chicoutimi and Saskatoon, as well as important regional and provincial cities like Kingston and Fredericton.

While urban form can be considered at these three different scales, at this point attention is drawn to those regional settings—metropolitan and city—which people most directly experience. These should be seen in relation (1) to the treatment of the macro-region in the chapter on national urban patterns (Chapter 3); and (2) to the over-riding urban process, national and international, that works relentlessly on the "materials" of local and regional environments, affecting the rate and character of growth as well as the opportunities opened up and foreclosed.

Shapers of Urban Form

As indicated above in the illustrations of urban settlement options (A1, A2, A3) a great deal is at stake in the particular form and structure of our metropolitan and city regions. In one sense, this is what urban planning is all about. Can we take some comfort in the fact that such planning in Canada has become in the last two decades thoroughly institutionalized? In terms of planning legislation, numbers of planning staffs, the burgeoning membership of the Canadian Institute of Planners, the rise of Schools of Planning, and in terms of pounds of planning reports, the situation appears to be well in hand. What is critical to all this planning effort, however, is its basic philosophy: Is it primarily a "housekeeping" operation, content with making the impact of prevailing trends a little less disorderly? Or is it doing a more fundamental job—understanding and influencing the key elements that shape the character or our regions—and the satisfaction or stress that they yield?

If planning is to take this more searching, and ultimately more creative approach, the key elements that must be considered are (1) the needs, values, desires and lifestyles of Canadians; (2) certain policy variables that are likely to have the greatest impact on future urban form and structure; and (3) the possibilities and limitations ingrained in the varying conditions of Canadian metropolitan and city regions.

Shapers of Urban Form: Policy Variables

Notions of urban form and structure are associated with certain extremes—either towards dispersion or concentration in form, or towards integration of urban structure on a total regional basis or integration only within the parts or sectors of urban regions. Since the place of an urban region on these co-ordinates determines its basic character, for example, whether it is a low-density spread-out city or a compact highly centralized city, it is of some importance to understand the forces that push or pull urban development along these alternative paths.

And this leads to the concept of policy variable, which is an urban function, artefact and sub-system that significantly affects the present and future form and structure of the city. On the basis of an extensive survey of both the theory and experience of urban development, Richard Preston has identified four policy variables that together have the most far-reaching repercussions.[4] These are: (1) the distribution of employment and services; (2) housing density and distribution; (3) the transportation system; and (4) the distribution of open space and leisure amenities. Because these are high leverage variables—changes in these shake the whole system—they are of special interest to urban policy-makers and planners. To act on these variables intelligently and effectively, however, will require an understanding of the forces that shape them.

These forces can best be expressed in terms of their tendency towards concentration or dispersal, region-wide specialization (and integration) or sub-regional integration, or some position in-between in which a degree of balance is achieved between these sharply contrasting tendencies. Taking each of the policy variables in turn it is possible to distil from Canadian experience some of the shaping forces. These are presented in abbreviated form in a sequence of summary matrices, relating policy variables and shaping forces, or the expression of such forces. For example, the economic demand for large manufacturing sites to accommodate single-storey continuous production lines is the force. The expression or condition of that force which makes it necessary to disperse urban development is "space for modern industry." This abbreviated treatment of forces will be used in each of the four matrices that follow.

The different forces leading towards and away from the concentration of employment in city cores are in evidence in most Canadian urban areas. The elimination, in the national capital plan, of Ottawa's inner city railway tracks and their removal (along with station, factories, warehouses and terminals) to an outer loop, foreshadowed, as early as the late 'forties, a basic structural shift in Canadian cities. And in 1974 the Twenty-Ninth Parliament of Canada, by passing the Railway

Employment and Services

Towards Dispersal (D)	Balancing Forces (B)	Towards Concentration (C)
• Space for modern industry • Space for truck and rail terminals • Space (inexpensive) for large car parking areas • Routine and mechanical office operations • Shopping services for suburbs	*Away From D* • Costs and time of travel to work and to major services • Inner city labour supply: skilled, unskilled *Away from C* • Public reaction against large-scale development	• Offices as prestige symbols • Decision-making functions: face-to-face contact • Tourist attraction to the multi-purpose centre • Downtown as a setting for convention hotels and related services • Big investment, big catchment area facilities • Government offices at focal points

Relocation and Crossing Act *made this decentralizing trend "official," while providing the opportunity for public initiative to hasten the process—and cities like Regina and Winnipeg have picked up the challenge.*[5]

Suburban shopping centre development in Canada has been notoriously aggressive—clashes between downtown and shopping centre interests still provide perennial political sport—but outlying office development has been much less conspicuous. In the early 'sixties the master urban diagnostician, Jean Gottmann, declared before an international meeting in Toronto that the information and telecommunication revolutions would free routine and mechanical office operations from decision functions, and allow them to find less expensive and perhaps more agreeable locations in the suburbs and satellite communities.[6] Some of this has happened in places like Don Mills/Toronto and New Westminster/Vancouver, but more striking is the persistent attachment of offices to downtown areas.

Half a century after Louis Sullivan, one of the creators of the modern skyscraper, warned of its possible "social menace and danger," the Canadian skyscraper is alive—and apparently very well.[7] Since the mid-fifties, in particular, we have seen a remarkable expression of Manhattanism in Canada in the march of huge complexes across the Canadian urban-scape: Scotia Square in Halifax, Place Ville Marie and Place Bonaventure in Montreal, Place de Ville in Ottawa, Toronto

Dominion Centre and Commerce Court in Toronto, Lombard Place in Winnipeg, McCauley Plaza in Edmonton, and so on.[8] *These "contemporary cathedrals," as they have been so aptly called represent a powerful centripetal force, both physically and institutionally. McCauley Plaza, for example, accommodates 6,000 employees, or about 5 per cent of the work force of a city of some half million people. The physical dominance of these complexes is more or less an accurate expression of their economic and social dominance. In cities like Montreal and Toronto they are the focus for an intimate decision-making environment with national and international dimensions, solidified by various personal ties and associations, including certain clubs, part of the downtown scene, "where businessmen can entertain and make deals."*[9]

But even these prodigious forces produce counter-forces like the reaction of parts of the Vancouver public to two large-scale developments that have been stopped or drastically scaled down: Harbour Park and Project 200. The contentious issues in these cases were the preservation of public ownership, access and use of the waterfront; the protection of park land; the traffic repercussions; and the likely destruction of the city's historic Chinatown.[10]

Residential Density and Distribution

Towards Disperal (D)	Balancing Forces (B)	Towards Concentration (C)
	Away from D	
• Private space for home and garden	• Large-scale development: mixed housing types, population, higher density	• Cheap housing stock for the "poor"
• Attraction to natural amenities		• Attraction to the culture of the inner city, both low and high incomes
• Middle and upper class affluence and lifestyle	• High-density housing near jobs, core or mass transit stations	• Public programs for inner city renewal
• Escape from inner city conditions	• In-town apartment living, feature of second home life style	
• Expanding life space, e.g. second homes		• Preservation of historical and cultural values
• Developer's attraction to cheaper land	• High costs of scatteration	• High-density housing attracted to the facilities of the core on high cost land.
	Away from C	
	• High costs of inner city renewal	
	• Increased upward mobility of the poor	

The form of Canadian cities seems to reflect in full measure the operation of Michelson's "family mobility cycle" which is propelled by the ideal of the single family house with generous private outdoor space. Most cities have rings of suburbs inherited from the building binge of the 'fifties and early 'sixties which took the form of low-density development on farm and other rural land on the urban fringe. The predominance of the spacious spread out residential environment is indicated in the composition of our national housing stock (Table 8.2).

Table 8.2. National Housing Stock, by Type of Dwelling

Housing Forms	1951	1961	1971
		per cent	
Single detached	66.7	65.4	59.4
Single attached	7.0	8.9	11.3
Apartment or flat	26.0	25.3	28.2
Mobile home	0.3[1]	0.4	1.1
TOTALS	100.0	100.0	100.0

Note: 1) Percentage classified as "other"; there was no separate class for mobile home in the 1951 Census.

Source: Statistics Canada, *Perspective Canada: A Compendium of Social Statistics*, (Ottawa: Information Canada, 1974). Reproduced by permission of Minister of Supply and Services Canada.

At the last Census, over 70 per cent was in low-density types (split 59.4 per cent, single detached and 11.3 per cent, single attached). But this obscures the dramatic shift towards multiple forms since the mid-sixties – the cities have been building up as well as out. Within fifteen years single detached dwelling starts dropped from 70 per cent of the total to a little over 40 per cent (Figure 8.4).[11]

The impact of these trends on Canadian cities has varied because there has been a considerable difference in the mix of apartment building sizes from place to place. The contrasts, for example, between Toronto, Montreal and Vancouver are very great (Figure 8.5). The preponderance of buildings with over two hundred units in Toronto is expressed in the massive high-rise developments close to downtown, such as St. James Town that houses 15,000 people, and at transportation nodes. The quite different scale of multiple housing in Montreal, where buildings with under twenty units are the most common, reflects the city's long-established tradition of accommodation in low-rise structures like double duplexes and triplexes. Vancouver has had comparatively few

Figure 8.4. Dwelling Starts by Type of Unit, 1956-71

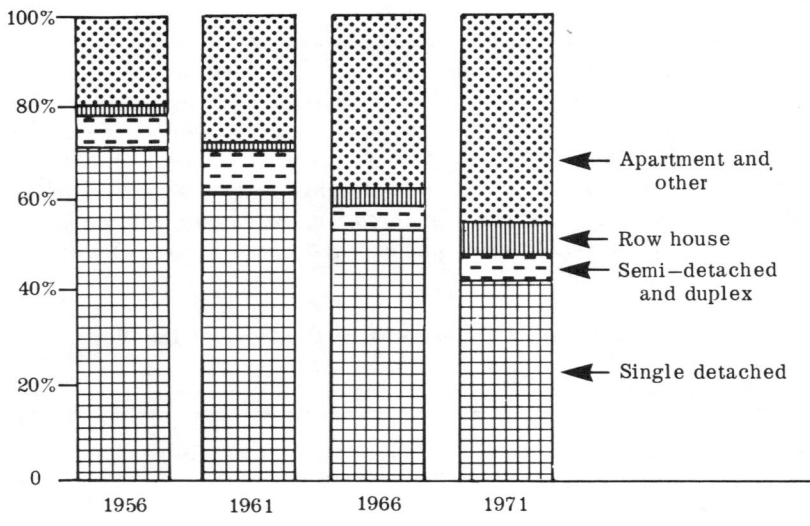

← Apartment and other
← Row house
← Semi–detached and duplex
← Single detached

Source: Statistics Canada, *Perspective Canada: A Compendium of Social Statistics* (Ottawa: Information Canada, 1974), p. 210.

Figure 8.5. Apartment Building Completions by Size of Building, for Selected Metropolitan Areas, 1970 and 1971

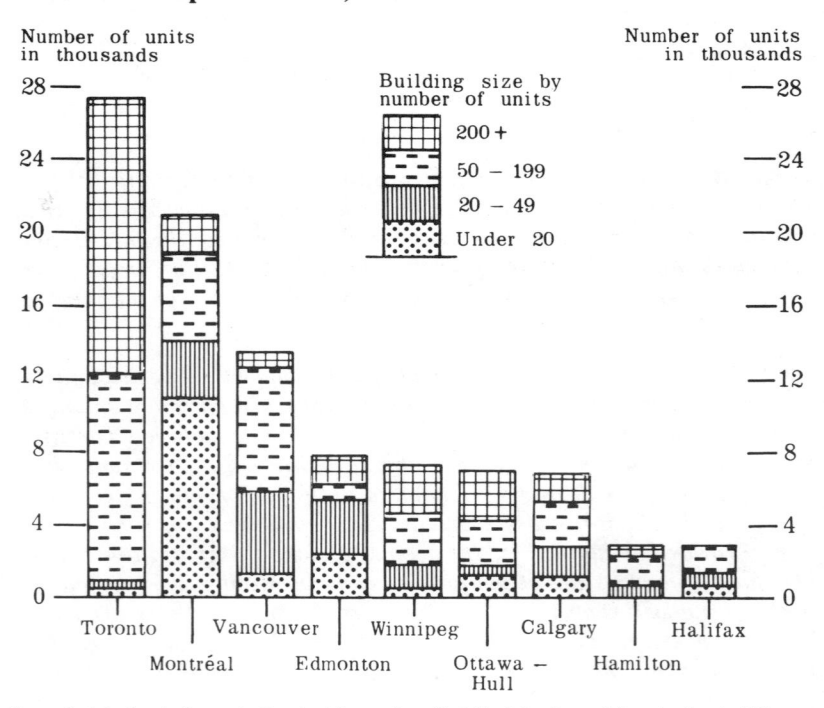

Number of units in thousands

Building size by number of units
200+
50 – 199
20 – 49
Under 20

Toronto Vancouver Winnipeg Calgary Halifax
Montréal Edmonton Ottawa – Hull Hamilton

Source: Statistics Canada, *Perspective Canada: A Compendium of Social Statistics* (Ottawa: Information Canada, 1974), p. 211.

large apartment buildings. The predominance of the 50 – 99 and 20 – 49 ranges is in keeping with the relatively modest scale of firms in the residential development industry in that city, as noted in the previous chapter.[12]

One of the important things about Canadian cities, which distinguishes them from most large American cities, is that the inner city as a place to live is not being abandoned. This is expressed in several ways. The middle-class housing ideal is between the suburb and the old city – many people want to live close to the centre. As one author has put it: "The car has made suburbia possible, and TV has made it bearable. But how much less trouble to be able to walk to the office, to leave for the theatre only ten minutes before curtain time, to let the children walk to their lessons and club meetings *and to maintain a single car that is needed only once or twice a week."*[13] *There is a sustained struggle to prevent crude encroachments on cherished older areas. The tenacity of the resistance is expressed in efforts to save particular districts (Chinatown, Vancouver; Kensington Market, Toronto), streets and buildings by volunteer groups. A recent Montreal study (1974) has identified twenty-seven such organizations, concerned with special landmarks, such as the* Society for the Preservation of Great Places, *with the protection of a local residential area, such as the* Esplanade Residents Association, *or with research and information, such as* Centre de reference et d'information sur l'environment *(CRISE). And attachment to the old city is expressed as well by the restoration for contemporary enjoyment of venerable city features, such as Lower Town in Quebec City or Bastion Square in Victoria.*[14]

The tendencies of the residential policy variable – one pulling towards the centre of cities and one away – have apparently not gone unnoticed by the Canadian development industry. In one sense the rise of the comprehensive project on the scale of a medium-sized city is an attempt to embrace and harmonize these polarities within a single new community. The developers of the largest example of this contemporary development form, Erin Mills (8000 acres, fifteen miles west of Toronto, target population 170,000) speak glowingly of a "large diversified community offering a superior range of urban experience to its inhabitants."[15] *And the major goals of this ambitious undertaking include: "a wide range of housing types for a broad cross-section of the population"; "a concentrated town-centre, with major commercial, cultural, civic and recreation functions"; and, "links to the central city and principal regional urban development centres by freeway and public transportation."*[16] *Is this the dawning of a new age, or merely a public relations mirage?*

Transportation System

Towards Dispersal (D)	Balancing Forces (B)	Towards Concentration(C)
• Automobility: dispersal of houses, business, services • Public subsidization or peripheral development, by expressways, etc. • Airport location in the urban fringe	*Away from C* • High capital/operating costs, mass transit • Communications as a substitute for transportation *Away from C or D* • High policy leverage of transportation facilities, as framework for development	• Mass transit focusing on multi-purpose older centres

The technology of transportation looms large in the contemporary city. It is inseparable from the functioning of the city as an economic machine and as a place for living. Transportation provides the accessibility required to attain a wide range of mutual choice between employers and job seekers, between buyers and sellers, as well as choice for individuals and groups in the location and type of homes, schools, shops, services and all kind of recreational and social opportunites.[17]

In theory, there is an expectation that the movement of people and goods should operate in a manner that achieves a certain stable balance between the extremes of dispersal and concentration. The benefits of increased mobility: wider choice and access to more space, cannot be enjoyed without limit because of the time, cost and inconvenience of travel. And there are some surprising consistencies in underlying human behaviour: the median time of the journey to work, in large cities, is about half an hour; and people are inclined to minimize the lengths of their work trips. These tendencies should, and to some extent do, result in a degree of sub-regional integration – materials suppliers attempt to locate close to manufacturers, and people move their residences close to work, shopping centres follow residents, and so on.[18]

But in practice, the centrifugal forces are strongest. This has much to do with the dominance of the car, which is the favoured mode for the journey to work for well over 70 per cent of Canadians. The impact of the car on the city is rooted in the culture of our times and is inseparable from general forces like consumerism, the obsession with gross production, residential privatism in the form of the free-standing bungalow, the "territorial division" of a city's population by social class, the proliferation of expressways and the "sport" of land speculation. Altogether there is a car culture which tends towards the fission of the city – the separation of major functions and activities and their dispersal over extensive areas.[19]

This basic bias of intra-urban transportation is reinforced by inter-urban air transportation. The most striking Canadian case is the new international airport at St. Scholastique, about thirty-four miles northwest of Montreal. The technology of the supersonic and jumbo jet dictates an airport site well buffered from existing dense development so that unencumbered flight paths and an adequate noise zone can be assured. In the Montreal case a site of approximately one hundred and thirty-eight square miles is required.[20]

Once established, the airport will become a major urbanizing force, shaping the form of metropolitan Montreal and of the macro-region extending eastward to Quebec City. A task force reporting on the location and impact of the airport brought into focus the following scenario of future events: direct employment for more than 25,000 people at full-scale operation (estimated, 1985); the attraction of airport-oriented activities such as industries with national or international markets making products with high value but low bulk, notably electronics, T.V. and radio, scientific instruments, optics and transport equipment; the generation of an additional 50,000 jobs by such attracted and auxiliary activities; the spread of the "urban fabric" to the airport, in the form of new development and the expansion of existing towns to accommodate 250,000 to 300,000 persons; and the stimulation of a development corridor (along a spine of "first-class road and rail networks") along the narrow plain of the north shore of the St. Lawrence. Thus Montreal, St. Jerome, Joliette, Trois-Rivières and Quebec City would be linked up in "a linear pattern of urbanization."

While the impact of the automobile is far-reaching, its very dominance sets in motion forces that work in the opposite direction: towards concentration in the region's core and towards transportation modes that favour a less sprawled urban structure. "People move to the 'suburbs'" Blumenfeld has noted, "in the expectation of being close to both 'the city' and 'the country'. But the more people who make this choice, the further they have to move away from the city and the further the country moves away from them. Viewed within this light, the general move to the low-density urban periphery is self-defeating."[21] Added to this argument are such considerations as (1) hazards to life and limb – the danger to persons is estimated at seventy-eight times greater in cars than buses; (2) air pollution from exhaust fumes *that precariously increase the risk of respiratory diseases, and (3) the squandering of fossil fuel energy – in terms of gallons per passenger mile, the efficiency of the car is only one-fifth that of the bus and one-twelfth, the train.*[22]

These effects are leading to a rising concern with the social costs of the automobile, and a search for a better balance between private and mass transportation. The prospect now arises in the larger Canadian cities in particular of the emergence of countervailing forces. These would be inclined to an urban form shaped towards the extension of public transportation: a form with a stronger articulation of centres and linear transportation/development paths. Considering the inertia of established habits and systems, however, the policies of public agencies, which as creators and investors hold the trump cards, will have to tip the balance in favour of the new alternatives.

Open Space and Leisure

Towards Dispersal (D)	Balancing Forces (B) *Away from D*	Towards Concentration (C)
• Desire for more spacious living • Attraction to open spaces in the urban fringe • Flight from unsatisfying city	• Public demand for preservation of public open space and natural amenities *Away from C* • Counter-attraction of conference retreats in calmer resort settings, or around airports	• Attraction of the centre for tourists • Attraction of the centre as a setting for large conferences • Attraction of the centre for cultural facilities

The call of the great outdoors is a well-established fact of Canadian life. Whether considering the choice of housing[23] *or the use of land,*[24] *the drive for living space is strong – both for private domestic use and in the general environment. This is best appreciated against the background of certain national symptoms. The massive urbanization of the country has been associated with a surge of interest in outdoor recreation – between 1966 and 1971 when Canada's population increased by 7 per cent, visitors to provincial parks increased by about 50 per cent. Parks are only one of several habitual recreational destinations of urban Canadians – next to Sweden we are (per capita) the greatest cottage owners in the world.*[25]

The lemming-like exodus from our cities, Friday night to Sunday night, at least raises the suspicion that some of this lust for the country is really a distaste for the city. As it becomes increasingly difficult to escape the city (congestion reigns in accessible lake country and on home-bound highways) there is a growing concern for the open space dimension of the urban environment. The major Canadian probe of the urban issues of the early 'seventies as perceived by the people of a metropolis, the Vancouver Urban Futures Project, reports an overwhelming bias towards land conservation. Respondents' land use priorities for the Fraser valley, the setting for Vancouver, were agriculture and recreation, with urban uses "a last resort."[26]

Leisure in the city turns two ways: towards open land and towards the centre. The major core still holds a fascination. This has its source in the centre as an expression of the common civic life (the centre as symbol): imagine Edmonton or Ottawa without their downtowns; in the appeal of variety and anonymity – a momentary release from social pressures; and in the location in our centres of certain unique facilities, drawing upon the broadest possible market, such as art galleries, museums, theatres for live drama, and concert halls for opera, ballet and classical music. Close to one-third of "adult" Canadians now frequent such places at least three or four times a year.[27]

The lifestyle of the late twentieth century ascribes another major role to city cores which intensifies their magnetic pull. This is the multi-purpose centre as the stage for tourists, the proverbial "visiting firemen," and for conferences and conventions. The persisting centre-orientation of the latter in particular provides a clue to the attributes of the Canadian "centre-ville." The clear importance of this factor can be seen in Montreal and Toronto[28] *where the convention business is most highly developed. In each case, the downtown is the sector which predominates in the number of rooms provided (50 per cent of the total in Montreal and 53 per cent, Toronto) with the airport sector following (17.5 per cent of the total, Montreal; 13.5 per cent, Toronto). In each case delegates appear annually in impressive numbers (1972, Montreal, 111,550; Toronto, 244,625) and account for substantial income. And in each city the scale of conferencing is reliably reported to be on the increase (to a 1976 level of about 358,000 delegates in Montreal and 410,000 in Toronto). Conference-going is recognized as a para-leisure activity: "Pour le congressiste le motif officiel du déplacement n'est pas le loisir mais, bien le travail. Cependant, l'existance de toute une organisation de divertissement qui occupe souvent une bonne partie du temps et des dépenses des congrès incite à definit cette activité comme étant bipolaire: travail et loisir."*[29] *As such the appeal of the city centre to the conference delegate resembles its attraction to the tourist. It is the appeal of the bazaar, the exhibition, the carnival and of the place where the human comedy, in its most vivid form, is to be found constantly on parade.*

The foregoing review of the forces working on each of the policy variables indicates that Canadian cities are buffeted between the two poles of concentration and dispersion. The first set of forces leads to one big city with a single overpowering centre. The second leads to a spread-out city with a weak core and many scattered loosely connected parts. The review also suggests that, balancing forces notwithstanding, the influences that work on the form and structure of the city can be capricious. They do not operate cybernetically. There are no reliable built-in self-regulating processes to maintain a stable balance between the extremes. That kind of adjustment requires deliberate action on the policy variables.

This now brings us to a first statement on the future form of the city. The question posed is this: what are the features of each of the policy variables that define an optimum form for the Canadian city of the future? "Optimum" at this point in the exploration of urban settlement alternatives is defined as that city form which has just the right amount of region-wide specialization (major centre dominance), and just the right amount of sub-regional integration (self-sufficiency and identity of component communities). In our view, it is the urban solution which is at the intersection of the form and structure co-ordinates – for example, A3 in Figure 8.1 moved a little to the left, to the centre of the diagram.

What would be the nature of the policy variables in such a first approximation of the ideal city? *Employment and services* would be distributed in such a way that parts of the urban region – districts or component towns depending on the size of the agglomeration – would enjoy a high degree of day-to-day self-sufficiency. This means that, within general constraints such as the attraction of truck terminals to main roads and the desirability of placing heavy industry down-wind, each district or town would offer diversified employment and service areas. These would take the form of centres or other multi-purpose districts. Whatever the form, employment would be mixed in terms of the distinctions that really matter, such as occupational categories: professional, managerial, skilled, unskilled; technology: advanced, such as scientific instruments and conventional as in shoe manufacturing; blue collar and white collar; manufacturing and service employment; for men and for women; and so on. The services available would be equally varied, covering many of the personal, professional, business, shopping and financial services required by urban communities.

This attempt to achieve a high degree of diversity, and hence integration within the sub-areas of the city or metropolitan region, has certain implications for the size and number of people in such sub-areas – be they called districts, communities, towns or, indeed, cities. The market thresholds for services and labour, associated with diversity and quality, would bias such constituent areas towards a certain adequacy of scale – more in the neighbourhood of fifty thousand and a hundred thousand than five and ten thousand – and a certain completeness and all-roundness in a social and human sense.

But there would be limits to this size, too, lest the objectives of sub-regional integration, related to residence, leisure and open space be seriously compromised. For certain highly specialized goods and services, and for certain working environments, such as the milieu for public or corporate decision-making, people would look to the core of the region. Head offices of national organizations; fine printing; a choice of convention-scale hotels; stores for rare books, stamps or gems; major hockey arenas and concert halls – these are the types of activity that would form the base of the city centre. To serve effectively in this way, such centres would have to be reachable from all parts of the region.

Because they would be highly accessible, people would use them and identify with them. Through common and almost universal usage such areas would begin to assume certain special symbolic qualities. As such, these esteemed places would enjoy new and as yet undefined potentials related to the urge for excellence and dramatic folk expression which still, on occasion, blossoms in the Canadian city of the late twentieth century.

The dual criteria of region-wide specialization and sub-regional integration might, sometimes in the future, require that some locales of specialized services be comparatively free-standing. "High order" functions and activities, such as major department stores or concert halls, serving an entire region are frequently inordinately space-consuming (consider off-street parking alone), and so their location at traditional focal points may not be practical. The geometry of the circle – the contraction of space towards the centre – might impose serious limits to such concentration. In those instances, cities of the future might contain at strategic points along transportation routes, a limited number of physically autonomous special places that would grace the landscape somewhat in the manner of Expo '67 or a boisterous country fair.

For the optimum solution, *the density and distribution of residential areas* would in some respects have to be drastically different from the present. In spite of our still exuberant celebration of democratic myths, Canadian cities are becoming more rather than less spatially differentiated by social class.[30] This kind of segregation works against sub-regional integration, which is an ideal requiring that each part of the metropolitan region contain all kinds of people. The monolithic residential area – all ranch houses or bungalows or mansions, or all high-rise apartments – spells exclusion. The optimum city would, by contrast, provide in each of its constituent districts or communities, accommodation for people who are different in age, income, family status, lifestyle and so on.

The three-dimensional form of the city, the density/height aspect, would be a by-product of meeting the needs of the various groups. One very welcome prospect is that the creation of substantial secondary centres would relieve some pressure on land near the regional core. Land prices, as a consequence of the market interplay between centres, would not be so swollen near the core, and apartment buildings would not be raised to such gargantuan proportions.

The *transportation system* would play a critical role in making the optimum city work. What is required is a finely tuned system which reinforces the over-riding form and structure objectives. The sub-regional centres will need good connections with the major regional centre, but not with a capacity, speed and frequency that would encourage massive daily commuting from the periphery to the centre. The types of sub-systems that link the regional centre to the sub-regional centres can either promote the mature development and stability of the outlying centres or contribute to the proliferation of competing centres. To attain the benefits of region-wide specialization for as many people as possible, form, structure and transportation would work together to maximize access to mass transit, and would avoid a settlement pattern too spread out to take advantage of such facilities.

For a metropolitan region with over a million people and an average radius from built-up edge to centre of about fifteen miles, it has been estimated on the basis of travel time and costs that the best sub-systems in order of preference are commuter rail, light rapid transit, bus rapid transit, full rapid transit and the transit expressway. These are for the radial corridors, leading to and from the major centre, under peak traffic conditions.[31]

Applying the principles appropriate to the optimum solution, as stated above, these sub-systems, together with automobiles, would be used as follows: commuter rail between centres and for the major region-wide movements; light rapid transit (a fixed guideway mode with about half the speed but substantially more capacity than commuter rail) for the journey to work in the inner city having a radius about seven miles; bus rapid transit (rating second for cities in the 100,000 to 250,000 range), which is a conventional bus using reserved lanes, for peak hour travel within component districts or communities; and conventional bus, dial-a-bus, shared taxis and private cars for feeder and local traffic throughout the system.

The car (or some equivalent) would continue to be used for all those trips characterized by dispersed origins and destinations, such as journeys to manufacturing plants along arterial roads, general business trips, curiosity and local shopping, and leisure and social travel of all kinds. The main road system developed for this purpose would also serve for the trucks transporting goods, which make up 20 per cent or so of the total road traffic. The creation of a number of strong sub-regional centres should minimize cross-region trucking.

To lend support to the optimum city form, the *open space and leisure* variable would perform a number of functions. First, by being planned and designed as a *network*, it would serve to give expression in the urban-scape to the basic character of the ideal city: a place with clearly defined physical limits and one major centre, consisting of separate, internally-integrated but related and interacting communities. The network has potential for giving emphasis in the visual landscape to both the linkage between the parts, and to their distinctiveness. Accordingly, such a system would be sensitive to opportunities in the environment: ravines, valleys, eskers to emphasize continuity; and scarps, small lakes, wooded areas and other land forms to dramatize individuality.

A second form-giving principle of this variable is *spatial specialization*: the distribution of open space and facilities in a way which would highlight those regional features of potential interest to residents in every part of the area. These features may be *physical* like a complex of hills for skiing. They may be *historically or culturally* determined like a community with a tradition of live theatre. Or they may have a *spatial/locational* basis, like the necessary placing of a major sports complex near a transportation node.

The evolution of an open space and leisure system combining aspects of all of these features would have some by-products that would be appreciated in and for themselves: imageability – the clear legibility of the environment; diversity – ecologically and in types of open spaces; conservation of unique natural areas; abundant and accessible recreational space, and strong landscape character.

Shapers of Urban Form: Lifestyles, Reality and Aspirations

SOME CONCEPTS

In examining the policy variables that influence Canadian cities, this account has maintained a tactical silence on the other shapers of urban forms. In particular, the lifestyles of people represent a factor which has been just below the surface. A phenomenon, like the search for the suburban ranch house or the attraction to the bright lights of city centres, is a force because it in some way satisfies the needs, desires and lifestyles of a lot of people.

We speak here of a fundamental consideration with far-reaching repercussions. "The heart's desire," writes Pierre Dansereau, "is a larger component to be fed into the economist's and the politician's computer, a social lever strong enough to burn cities, to take revenge upon the mighty, and to turn down the benefits of technological living."[32] While few would dispute this vigorous assertion, the difficulty in reckoning with this factor, as a basis for planning and design, is that "the heart's desire" is highly elusive. Its mysteries are unlocked and its operational meaning clarified to an important degree by the institutional theory of the city: the form of the city is grounded in its lifestyles, as conditioned by its basic institutions – of education, family life, work, or religion. There is a link between needs, values, desires and lifestyles. *Needs* are the physical, social and personal essentials for survival. *Desires* are the means preferred by different individuals and groups for meeting needs, in accordance with their *values*, which are their cherished beliefs. Some who value the family circle seek out a home where substantial seclusion and privacy can be enjoyed. Others place a high value on social relationships and the ideal of "fraternité" and so experiment with communal living. *Lifestyles* represent the fulfilment of desires; the behaviour patterns of individuals or groups resulting from acting out their desires. Altogether, lifestyles and institutions shape the form of the city and the substance of the experience it tolerates.[33]

Canadian cities display quite a wide range of lifestyles, reflecting differences in such factors as location, history, economic base, size, growth rate and ethnic and religious composition. This kind of diversity, particularly in its relationship to lifestyles and urban form, is difficult to grasp and communicate. The sequence of urban sketches that accompany this text were prepared as an attempt to reflect, in a way not possible by words alone, some of the differences that do exist in the "personalities" of our cities. In each instance, there is a subtle amalgam of influences that work on the urban-scape just as surely as the forces of wind, water and temperature work on the landscape. The eight cities that will be interpreted in this way are the same groups, reflecting every major regional setting except the north, which were looked at in terms of broad regional characteristics (Chapter 5). Here the emphasis is on the form of the city.

EIGHT CANADIAN CITIES

(1) *Vancouver*

The first city illustrated, *Vancouver*, is greatly affected by its natural setting. As the west coast writer, Eric Nicol, has noted:

> Vancouver lies at the exact junction of the inevitable with the impossible. From the shallow ridge of Burrard Peninsula the view to the south is placid, extrovert; the view to the north eruptive in barriers of mountains. Merely to turn around is to be reminded that though man may be infinitely perfectible, a certain humility is imposed by nature.[34]

Looking across Burrard Inlet, one is impressed by the way the mountains dwarf man's dwellings (Figure 8.6a). This is largely an area developed after Lion's Gate Bridge linked the north shore to downtown Vancouver in the late 1930s. It is inhabited predominantly by comfortable middle-class people who make a daily trek to jobs in the downtown core, and who behind their "moat" live out a characteristic Vancouver pattern: physical features reinforce segregation "on the basis of income and social class." Being on the sea Vancouverites are intrepid sailors. Some of their marina slips are close enough to downtown to encourage the switch, after office hours, from grey flannel suit to sails (Figure 8.6b). Planners are worried that the continued shoehorning of office towers within the physically constricted downtown peninsula (Figure 8.6c), will "dehumanize" the city and cause the tearing down of interesting older buildings which maintain continuity with the city's past[35] (Figure 8.6d). Mobility is highly prized in Vancouver. Private planes in one of its small boat harbours attest to links with coastal and hinterland areas not readily accessible by road (Figure 8.6e).

Figure 8.6a. North Vancouver

Figure 8.6b. Vancouver, Downtown Skyline

Figure 8.6c. Vancouver, Redevelopment

Figure 8.6d. Vancouver, Sun Tower

Figure 8.6e. Vancouver, Harbour

372   CHANGING CANADIAN CITIES

(2) Penticton
Inland from Vancouver, about a seven or eight hour drive along the Hope-Princeton Highway is the Okanagan valley, which is a distinctive Canadian region containing three small cities, Vernon, Kelowna and Penticton. *Penticton*, with about twenty thousand people, is the centre of an area of soft fruit production: one of the two regions in Canada (the other, Niagara) that grow peaches, cherries and apricots, on a commercial scale. The city is spread out between Okanagan Lake and Skaha Lake (Figure 8.7a), and seen with a bird's eye perspective it is, within a powerful alpine landscape, a city amidst an orchard (Figure 8.7b). Flumes run across and down the lower slopes to carry water by gravity from upland creeks and lakes to irrigate the fine silt loam terraces below (although there is a strong shift to sprinkler irrigation).[36] Penticton is an urban place that is deeply involved in agriculture, not only as a service centre but as an integral part of its environment and lifestyle. There are orchards within the city, and the municipality owns and operates an irrigation system, which is a necessity in an area with tropically hot summers that does not have in excess of 11 inches of precipitation per year. It is a city that has all the elements for fashioning a unique urban form, including a growth rate slow enough (2.5 per cent per annum, 1951-71) to comfortably accommodate physical expansion, but the character of the commercial centre suggests that the opportunity has not yet been seized with great imagination (Figure 8.7c). Two occurrences indicate certain local trends: the strong opposition registered in a public attitude survey (1974) against high-rise buildings; and the appearance in quite significant numbers of mobile homes, which are portable housing units, prefabricated and towable to "parks" where they are connected to utilities on leased sites.[37]

Figure 8.7a.   Penticton, Houses Around Lake

Figure 8.7b. Penticton, Alpine Landscape

Figure 8.7c. Penticton, Main Street

374   CHANGING CANADIAN CITIES

(3) *Edmonton*

Edmonton's mushrooming skyscraper skyline reflects a growth rate which has been sustained at 5 per cent per year (population doubling every twenty years) almost since oil blew in at the Leduc field in the late 'forties (Figure 8.8a). Behind this skyline, however, is a city of solid family virtues: about two-thirds of the population age fifteen and over is married (Census 1971). This percentage as well as that of the young people under nineteen considerably exceeds national averages – over 9 per cent (the part in the Census group 0 – 4) may be still in diapers. The city's private clubs seek out spacious surroundings in the North Saskatchewan valley (Figure 8.8b).[38]

The city in many respects has a split personality. Its traditional base is in agriculture – on Saturday afternoons the streets still throng with shopping-bagged, babushka'd farmers' wives. Edmonton's future is strongly linked with the petro-chemical industry that looms eastward, across the valley, downwind and almost discreetly out-of-sight (Figure 8.8c). Both of these bases join forces in the support of higher education (at a per capita level for the whole school system only slightly below Ontario's) – the new people, adventurers from all over the world, because education is part of "making it" in a new land, and farmers' sons and daughters, who believe education is perhaps insurance against their parents' still sour memories of the Great Depression.[39] Appropriately the University of Alberta dominates the skyline of the south bank (Figure 8.8d).

Figure 8.8a.   Edmonton, Downtown Skyline

Figure 6.6b. Edmonton, Recreation Space

Joseph Stewart

Figure 8.8c. Edmonton, North Saskatchewan Valley, East Towards Petro-chemical Industry

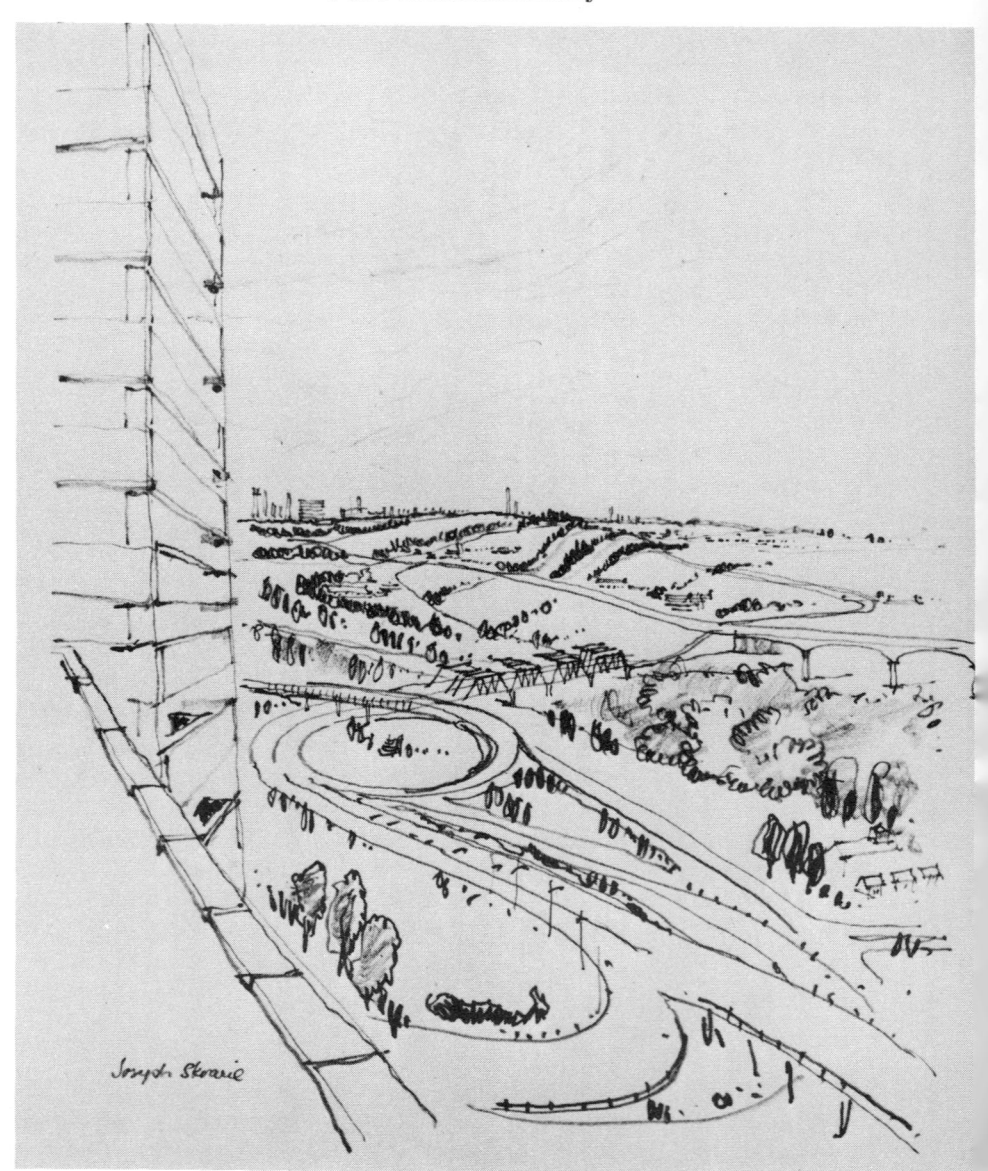

Figure 8.8d. Edmonton, High-Level Bridge and University

(4) Regina

Regina is the very image of the Prairie capital (Figure 8.9a). This is reflected in certain civil service characteristics of its working population: over 22 per cent of its labour force is clerical (Edmonton, by comparison, not quite 19) and 39 per cent of all people holding jobs are women (Edmonton, just over 36).[40] And it is reflected in the location close to the very heart of the city of a complex of provincial functions – the legislative and government buildings, the university, the Centre of the Arts, the Museum of Natural History, a major hospital (Figure 8.9b). These are sited in the spacious park/campus surrounding Wascana Lake, which is a monument to the stubborn prairie determination to turn a flat, treeless site into a place of civic beauty and appeal. Still the city, particularly in transitional seasons between snow and leaves, has a certain bare austerity (Figure 8.9c). A vigorous planning department, following a tradition that goes back to the comprehensive 1912 plan of T. H. Mawson (one of the first of its kind in Canada), has proposed concepts that give much attention to the future form, comfort and aesthetics of the city. These include a central business district with weather controlled corridors, malls to give the centre an intimacy and conviviality that it now lacks, and a Landscape Concept for future controlled growth westward along the wooded spine of Wascana Creek, preserved as a recreational amenity (Figure 8.9d).[41]

Figure 8.9a. Regina, Saskatchewan Legislature

Figure 8.9b. Regina, Wascana Lake, Centre of the Arts

Figure 8.9c. Regina, Skyline

Figure 8.9d. Regina, Proposed Downtown Mall

380 CHANGING CANADIAN CITIES

(5) *Sudbury*
Stompin' Tom Connors has probably given *Sudbury* some ill-deserved notoriety:

> The girls are out to bingo
> And the boys are getting stinko
> They think no more of *INCO*
> On a Sudbury Saturday night.

To be sure, on first encounter the city's open, rugged look with giant water tower ((Figure 8.10a) brazenly vying with church steeples bespeaks of its origins in the not too tender traditions of hard rock mining (Figure 8.10b). Its stark landscape is proof positive that the settlement was developed before the rise of Canada's environmental conscience (Figure 8.10c). Much of its original native wood cover fell victim to the air pollution, mainly sulphur dioxide fumes, that was common during turn-of-century nickel/copper mining and refining.[42]

Today Sudbury, a place of close to two hundred thousand people, at the hub of road and rail networks, has emerged as the predominant regional centre of northeastern Ontario. While employment is still weighted towards the mining industry, the city is becoming more diversified in both industries and social services, and there is a new sophistication in some of the more recent cultural and public buildings, like community centres and the city hall (Figures 8.10d and 8.10e). Amongst the influences that will shape the future form and character of the city are the following: its high annual growth rate (4.5 per cent, 1951–71); the establishment of the regional municipality of Sudbury; its ethnic diversity – Sudbury is the only Census Metropolitan Area outside Quebec in which people of British origin do not form the largest group; Laurentian University, notable among other things for being the first bilingual (English/French), non-denominational university in Canada; and, not least, the Superstack (1,250 feet high) which, according to reports, is beginning to clear the air for people and vegetation.[43]

**Figure 8.10a.
Sudbury,
View of the City,
Water Tower**

Figure 8.10b. Sudbury, View of the City, Church Steeples

Figure 8.10c. Sudbury, Urban-scape

Figure 8.10d. Sudbury, Social Centre

Figure 8.10e. Sudbury, City Hall

(6) Hamilton

Hamilton is strongly shaped by its heavy industrial character. Onefifth of its labour force is in manufacturing-related occupations, compared with about one-tenth in a metropolitan area of similar size (half a million) like Edmonton. And most of the factory workers are in steel and related industries. The metropolitan area is divided several ways: physically by the Niagara Escarpment – about 30 per cent of the population live on this upper level, increasingly in apartments taking advantage of the view (Figure 8.11a); and socially by the commuting patterns of day-time populations – most blue collar workers live in Hamilton, and many white collar workers escape the fumes of blast furnaces in Burlington, just across Hamilton Harbour (Figure 8.11b). The form of the city is increasingly shaped by planning policies, both by the direct involvement of residents in the planning of neighbourhoods and by such features as Jackson Square which brings together City Hall, art gallery, library, new concert/performing arts hall and other civic functions. The formality of this area provides a striking contrast to the casual disorder of the main business street (Figure 8.11c).[44]

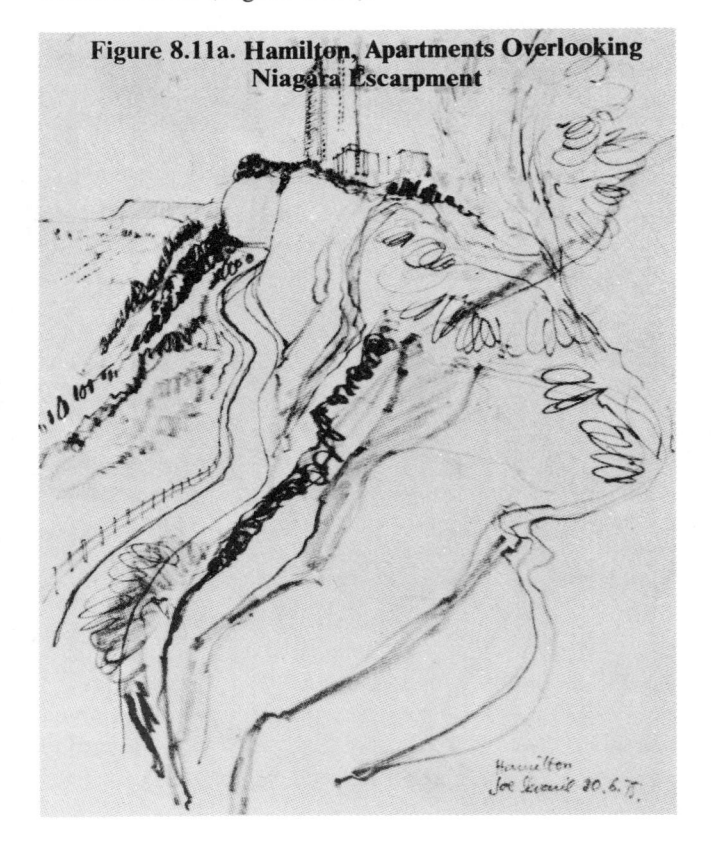

Figure 8.11a. Hamilton, Apartments Overlooking Niagara Escarpment

Figure 8.11b. Hamilton, Downtown and Across Harbour to Burlington

Figure 8.11c. Hamilton, Downtown Street

(7) Quebec

Five hundred miles east of Hamilton and inhabiting what some have called the same transportation and development axis is *Quebec City*. In terms of the atmosphere of the two cities (which are about the same size) they also seem five hundred years apart. In Canada's oldest metropolis the *dimension of time* is a tangible force (Figure 8.12a). It takes the form of Old Quebec, a seventeenth century city within a city, "clinging to Cap aux Diamants – a rocky promonotory 360 feet high – overlooking a narrows in the St. Lawrence River... a two-storeyed city with the Lower Town being the ground floor and the slopes and level part of the Upper Town inside the city walls forming the second storey" (Figure 8.12b).[45] History is also expressed in the architecture of the city, in the sedate stone of Place Royale (Figure 8.12d) or the ceremonial elegance of the Basilica (Figure 8.12c). It permeates the warm intimacy of its well loved little streets and squares (Figure 8.12e). And some feel that it is manifested in a certain surviving seventeenth century Cartesian order which is assumed by its urban form: the harbour and adjacent industry; the old French town with its mix of little shops, cafés, town houses and seminaries; the sector beyond which includes the House of Assembly, the provincial administration and the elegant nineteenth century *fin de siècle* residences of the Grande-Allée: and finally the spacious lawns and gardens of the middle and upper class suburbs.

But Quebec is also very much a contemporary city (Figure 8.12g). It is a power to be reckoned with, both in its strategic institutional and cultural role in French Canada, and in its more wordly attributes: a modern, containerized, year-round deep water port, a surprisingly diversified manufacturing sector, and a tourist industry of great depth and durability, which gives the city a large service sector (in

Figure 8.12a.   Quebec City, Historic Museum

terms of occupation groups, 1971, over 18 per cent compared to a national average of about 12 per cent).[46] The environmental relationship between the two Quebecs is not yet resolved. One model of the city is provided by the Château and the old world charm of Dufferin Terrace where visitors from Miami and Brussels mingle with boys and girls from Sainte-Foy and Sous-le-Cap. And another model by the streets sometimes clogged with cars, referred to ironically as "the last siege of Quebec," or by the high towers which, individual excellence and comfort notwithstanding, "do not blend," according to one observer, "with the old houses from before 1763, among which they are erected and whose harmony they disturb" (Figures 8.12f and 8.12h).[47]

Figure 8.12b. Quebec City, Steps to the Lower Town

Figure 8.12c.   Quebec City, Basilica

Figure 8.12d.   Quebec City, Place Royale

Figure 8.12e. Quebec City, Old Town Square

Figure 8.12f. Quebec City, Dufferin Terrace

Figure 8.12g. Quebec City, Harbour

Figure 8.12h. Quebec City, Hotel on Grande-Allée

(8) Saint John

Saint John, New Brunswick, shares with Quebec City the patrimony of Samuel de Champlain, whose heroic statue graces a central park (Figure 8.13a). One's first view of the inner city which comes panoramically into focus from the west side of the Saint John River estuary produces a moment of shock (Figure 8.13e). It is like an antique tapestry. It's as if time had stood still since the age of Victoria. The illusion is created by the too friendly, huddling together on hilly terrain of nineteenth century brick and stone business blocks and several tiers of mainly three-storey wooden flats coloured in brownish tones. While most of these go back no more than a century, to the period after the devastating fire of 1877, the city itself still reflects its late eighteenth century origins. The old Loyalist Burial Ground off King Square (Figure 8.13c) is a reminder that it was one of Canada's first "new cities," having been created almost overnight, in 1783, by three thousand refugees from the American Revolution.

The structure of the modern city is based on its position as an east coast port at the terminus of the CPR. Its Appalachian/Atlantic setting pervades both its economic life and urban form. The "break bulk" effect of the port leads to the processing of food and raw materials, and four pulp and paper mills in the region generate substantial cargo. The rough topography – dominant slopes as high as 25 per cent and thin soil punctuated by rocky outcroppings – has been a major constraint on the urban-scape. Saint John has been described as having an extremely compact inner city form, and the city can be traversed in about half an hour. It is at the focus of radiating development stretching out like "the tentacles of an octopus." Other influences are the search for cheap land and low real estate taxes, ineffective controls, and the yearning for a lifestyle that combines the virtues of both town and country. The city is still close to the sea and the land – fresh herring and vegetables (and other produce) can be obtained at the farmers' market every day except Saturday. The easy-going informality of the market hall (Figure 8.13d) may, when present downtown renewal plans materialize, contrast a little oddly with the new multi-purpose, multi-million dollar Market Square development on the site of the old market slip (Figure 8.13b).[48]

Figure 8.13a.   Saint John, Champlain's Statue

Figure 8.13b. Saint John, Redevelopment

Figure 8.13d. Saint John, Market Hall, Interior

Figure 8.13c. Saint John, King Square and Cemetery

Figure 8.13e. Saint John, Skyline

WHAT WE REACH FOR

Canadian cities, present a highly varied and paradoxical image as if seen through a kaleidoscope. It is well to bear in mind the "materials" with which we have to work in fashioning the city of the future. We do not start with a clean slate. Regional and historical factors provide both opportunities and limitations. In these circumstances, to think constructively about the future urban form, to work through and at the same time transcend existing circumstances, require an appeal to fundamentals. And this brings us to a definition of basic needs which underlie the range of discovered lifestyles. If these can be clarified then there is a good prospect that some useful guidelines can be formulated for the Canadian city. In a sense, we have to come down to earth before we can soar towards our aspirations.

The most basic things are sometimes the most complex. At this stage we are not seeking a catalogue of needs, but a way of thinking about needs which will provide a basis for deciding what is critical amongst a wide range of possibilities.

An approach which throws light on this matter, draws its inspiration from a general systems theory. As recently formulated by a group of Western Canadian social scientists (Westrede), the approach is based on the insight that all *living* or *self-maintaining* systems, from the most simple to the most complex, must if they are to survive meet a certain set of basic requirements or "fitness functions." For metropolitan regions the *three systems* that are of particular interest are those of the individual person, the group within the city, and the urban society or city as a whole.[49]

Each of these three urban-related systems are made up of different components, such as the young and old individual or city, and each system has certain characteristic areas of concern, which may vary from time to time in response to political and social change. In the most general terms such systems have six basic needs:

Resource throughput: the intake, use and discharge of raw materials and energy.

Protection: defense against built-in or accidental stresses in the system environment.

Communication: the gathering and dissemination of information enabling the system to anticipate stress and to mobilize resources to deal with them; and to sustain confidence in the capacity to do so.

Integration: the assimilation by the components of the system "through an internal co-ordinative network" of the required information, in a way that results in functional effectiveness.

Stored Collective Criteria: "Value system" or "culture" would be synonyms for this system need. It is the capacity to call upon an established value system or "a set of interacting principles," which, related to new information enables the system to cope with a wide range of situations.

Flexibility: Capacity to meet new challenges by restructuring existing criteria (values) or developing alternative criteria better adapted to changed conditions.

These needs must be met by all living systems, although the customary terms used to describe such needs may habitually vary from system to system. This is particularly so in the case of the individual in which requirements are often stated, in the style of certain social psychologists, in terms of the physiological and personal growth needs of the healthy individual.[50]

The basic elements: the system needs, system categories (breakdown into different kinds of groups) and areas of concern are presented with comments in a set of three-dimensional matrices, or sets of relationships.

Comments on this and the matrices that follow for intra-urban groups and city systems will not be exhaustive. The original work will have to be consulted for more detail. Attention will be focused illustratively on those aspects of the relationships between systems and needs that have implications for urban form.

The matrix (Figure 8.14) draws attention to the relationships between system needs (A) and types of individual by age (B) and areas of concern (C), for example the role of the family or school in meeting the individual's need for "belongingness." This kind of multi-dimensional model can only be considered a framework for thinking or an organizing device for relating a complex array of information on social and urban trends, and the findings of various disciplines to the question of how Canadian cities are (or are not), and ought to be shaped by the needs and lifestyles of their inhabitants. A few examples will make this point more concrete.[51]

Psychologists emphasize the importance of a person's early environment in emotional and intellectual development. By age nine, four-fifths of the lifetime developmental "learning" profile is complete. For the growing child, his immediate surroundings are a habitat in the literal sense of the word – nurture is provided in many ways. The more the opportunity to explore, and the greater variety of stimulation (of sight, sound and smell) the better. "The room, dwelling, yard, sidewalk,

FORMS OF URBAN SETTLEMENT 399

Figure 8.14. Individual Systems

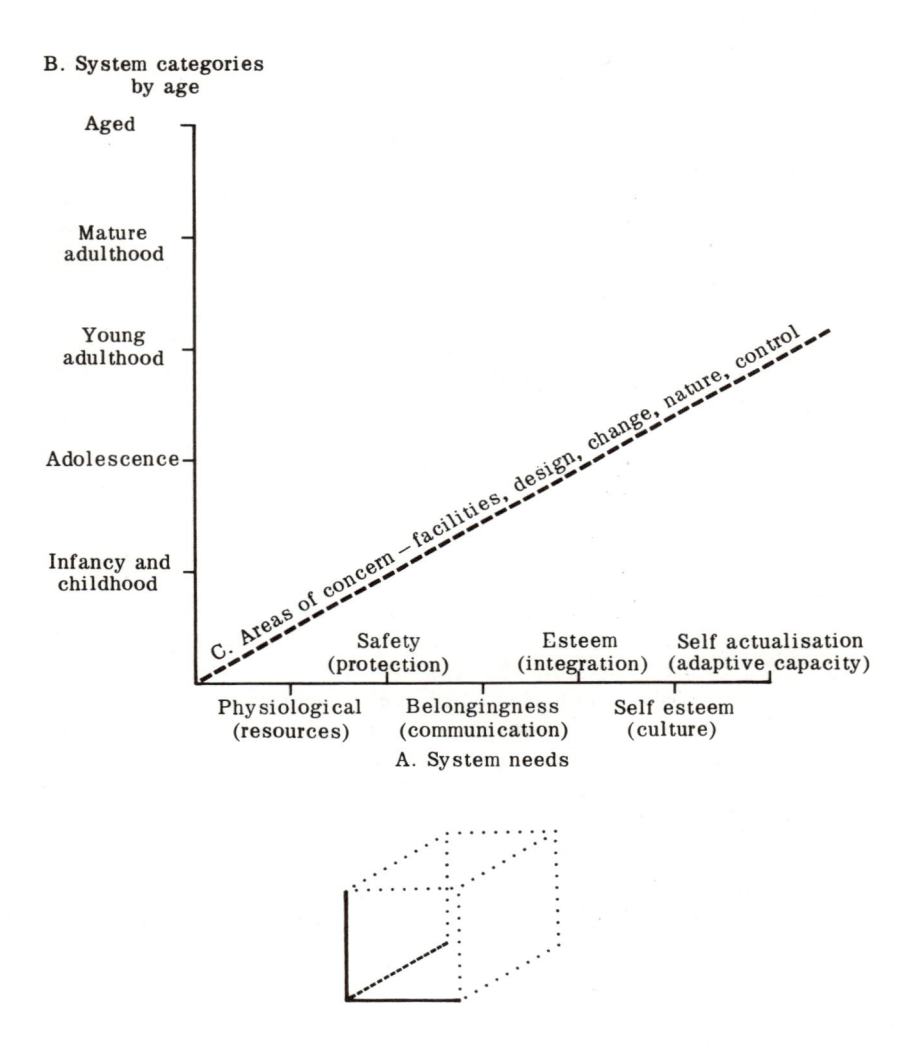

B. System categories by age

- Aged
- Mature adulthood
- Young adulthood
- Adolescence
- Infancy and childhood

C. Areas of concern — facilities, design, change, nature, control

Safety (protection) — Esteem (integration) — Self actualisation (adaptive capacity)

Physiological (resources) — Belongingness (communication) — Self esteem (culture)

A. System needs

Source: Westrede Institute, "Systems Needs and Urban Guidelines" (Ottawa: MSUA, 1974) (mimeographed), chart C.

street, corner store, playground and immediate neighbourhood are the fundamental sources of the stimuli needed for successful development and social functioning."[52]

The adolescent phase imposes a very special requirement on the urban environment: "the adolescent needs an anatomy of urbanism that provides from the most private to the most intensely communal."[53] In physical terms this means an opportunity for enjoying nature in the city: the natural park where solitude and peace can be found rather than the manicured turf. And it gives special importance to local community symbols and services with which the young person can actively identify. For example, it is suggested that multi-service community centres in which the adolescent has an opportunity to take initiative and responsibility, can assist in developing a sense of belonging, competence and self-esteem. The developmental needs of the young adult suggest that the built environment should help to break down a latent sense of social isolation. This might take many forms. One of the more important considerations in this time of preoccupation with the technology of communication, which fosters greater personal distance, is to build into our urban forms as many opportunities as possible for person-to-person contact. In a large metropolitan area in particular this gives priority to a policy of breaking down the urbanized region into a network of sub-regional communities, large enough to support a good level of services. If accompanied by a degree of responsibility for local functions, this kind of community can become an arena in which the young adult can begin to serve an apprenticeship in decision-making, which contributes to the adaptive capacity of the collective as well as the individual's self-fulfilment.[54]

Mature adulthood is a phase when a degree of stability has been attained, and the individual begins to play an important "generative" role. As parents and otherwise, the mature person provides the support for the developmental needs of younger people. "Family, place and work are all important networks for the mature adult.... Design principles should give recognition to sex, class, age and cultural variables. ... The role of teacher in handing information on to the new generation should be recognized in the urban form."[55] Those with grown-up children may have a preference for apartments, although apartments require two features that are unfortunately still not common to serve adequately. These are facilities that allow the individual to continue to be physically active and to enjoy casual social relationships. Examples of these would be nearby community spaces for outdoor cooking, repairing and making things and recreation; and garden plots in regional greenbelts.[56] Canadian population trends indicate a steady increase in the proportion of the population aged sixty-five and over for the last

FORMS OF URBAN SETTLEMENT   401

quarter of this century. Current projections indicate increases in the 1971–86 period of close to 50 per cent, which gives point to the special needs of this group. Of particular importance is the need to provide mobility by safe, regular transportation service, because most people in this age group do not drive cars (in a recent Toronto survey, less than one-quarter had drivers' licences). Another need is not to be shut out from the main stream of life, not to be segregated from children, not to live in ghettos for the old – "housing for the aged should avoid adding to the tendency towards isolation and loneliness."[57]

These matrices deal with systems formed by groups and cities. System needs (A) and areas of concern (B) are essentially the same for both types of system, although the system categories for each group and city, are different (Figure 8.15).

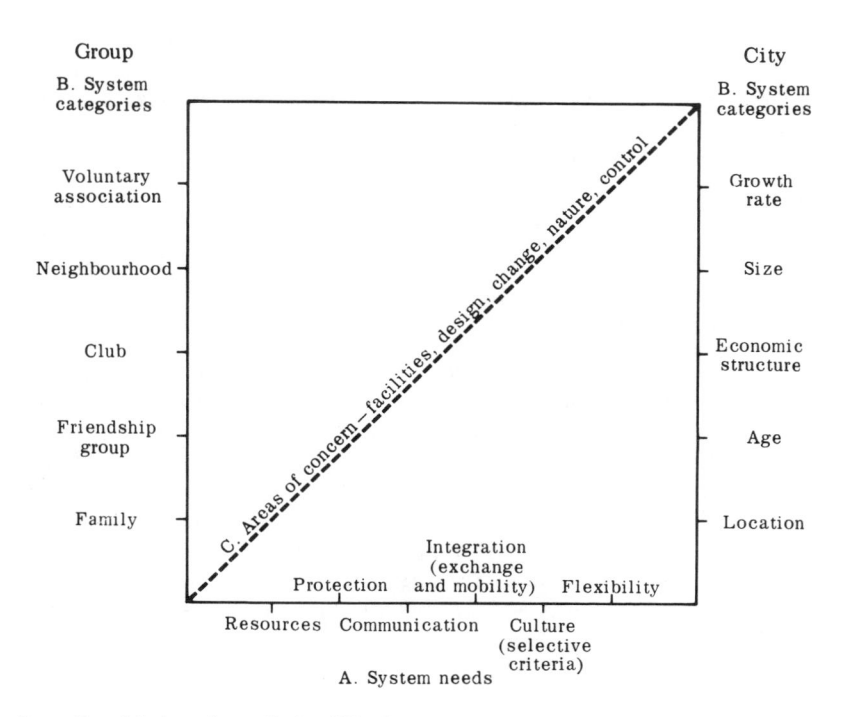

Figure 8.15. City and Group Systems

Group B. System categories		City B. System categories
Voluntary association		Growth rate
Neighbourhood		Size
Club		Economic structure
Friendship group		Age
Family		Location

C. Areas of concern – facilities, design, change, nature, control

A. System needs: Resources, Protection, Communication, Integration (exchange and mobility), Culture (selective criteria), Flexibility

Source: Westrede Institute, "Systems Needs and Urban Guidelines" (Ottawa: MSUA, 1974) (mimeographed), chart D.

Translating the system needs into specific terms for the various groups and cities for each of the main concerns – facilities, design and quality of environment, rate of change, relationship to the natural environment and means of control – depends on careful sustained observation, on dialogue with the people most directly concerned, and generally on a very broad knowledge base. This task, considered in a policy and action sense, is an ongoing one, and never finally completed. Needs evolve and change, as do our perceptions of needs. A few illustrations, will suffice to suggest the potentials of the adopted approach.

One motif that is identified in many groups and cities of different location and size is related to the cultivation among residents of the feeling and fact of neighbourhood and community – the presence, lack or degree of such communication. The general systems theory leans towards cities with component communities having the following characteristics: many, diverse, and convenient meeting places, a mix of functions at the neighbourhood level providing unprogrammed opportunities for encounter and acquaintance; facilities, design qualities and forms of interaction that cultivate a sense of common fate and common purpose; and governing institutions that give people significant control over their immediate environments. These qualities together are presumed to foster community interest, spirit, identity and distinctiveness; and in doing so contribute to the system needs of communication, integration and adaptive capacity. The key to systems endurance is the cultivation of a capacity for intelligent action, and this has to be ingrained in both the form and institution of the city.[58]

The Canadian reality expresses this ideal only ambiguously. The need to sort out myth and fact is very important. The segregation of people by social class was noted above in the case of Vancouver, Hamilton and Quebec City. And it emerges as a general feature of Canadian cities in an analysis of 1971 Census information.[59]

A recent study on the "urban situation" in Edmonton indicates two revealing trends. One was towards new growth in "the suburban towns at the expense of growth in the City of Edmonton" – particularly of single-family units, which increased from 15 per cent of the total units built in the region in 1962 – 66 on a steady upward curve to over half in 1972 – 73.[60] The second trend was towards the dominance of single functions, "monofunctionality," generally but to the greatest extent in the urban centres surrounding the city. This was reflected in the suburban bias towards the detached family unit (Edmonton proper in the last decade attracted from 93 per cent to 100 per cent of all multiple units), together with a relatively low attraction to the outlying areas of non-residential construction. In the period 1971 – 73 suburban areas accounted for 79 per cent of all metropolitan population growth, but only 5 to 10 per cent of all non-residential construction. What this appears to indicate is that people prefer the smaller places with stronger community identities: Sherwood Park, St. Albert, Spruce Grove and Fort Saskatchewan; together with the creation at such places of communities that are monolithic in housing type, family and social composition. Community at the local scale is being attained (or at least sought) at the expense of community, a sense of shared destiny, at the scale of the urban region. At the very least this question is raised: Does the division of the city into distinct but one-sided residential units – a network of solitudes – so strain the system requirements of "communication" and "integration" that the viability of the entire city system is threatened? The Edmonton study ventures its own tentative answer: the more we separate the people and functions of the city the more travel is required to satisfy a given need (whether shopping or visiting friends) and the lower the overall energy efficiency, and life quality – for some.

Alongside this preference for smaller places, there is evidence in Canada of value changes moving in the direction of system requirements. This is indicated in the new forms of living, such as the variety of communes that have been established, particularly since the early 'sixties.[61] And it is expressed in public issues and in the observations of informed people. In "conversations with Canadians about the future," arranged by the Advanced Concepts Centre, Environment Canada, it was discovered that next to international issues most people thought that "the most significant and complex problem in the immediate future would be in the area of urban forms and structures."[62] "Canadians" in this case were a group of some fifty or so concerned and well-informed people in various parts of the country who consented to searching conversations on Canada's future.[63] These have expressed certain worries and anxieties: "conversations were permeated with emotion – deep feeling, troubling conviction and even black despair"; and they have voiced a surprising degree of consensus on the necessary directions of Canadian society.

Some of what's wrong with Canada is summarized in the following terms:

> What is under question is the dehumanization inflicted by the competitive aggressive behaviour models according to which we organize and judge our public behaviour in the market place, at work, in our notions of social worth.

> The growth of large cities has given rise to expressions of alienation and isolation, of difficulties experienced in attempting to establish and maintain human relationships and human communities in large metropolitan areas.

> *For many in our institutions today, the work place has become a place to put in time, to conserve energies for the more personally fulfilling and frequently more socially productive work that is undertaken after hours.*
>
> *Economic well-being has become an end in itself, rather than a means to more humane ends.... As producers we have turned our world into a dehumanizing factory.*
>
> *Many expressed the view that the impersonal, fragmented world we have built for ourselves and the variety of narrow, specialized and often conflicting roles we are called upon to play is creating within persons a condition not unlike schizophrenia.*
>
> *The inroads of urban and industrial growth has prompted concern for conservation. Recently these concerns have been accompanied by heightened sensitivity about our dependency on remote large scale technology for even our most basic needs.*[64]

And some of what needs to be done *in Canada is stated, as follows:*

> *Our ability to shift directions and to find more adequate ways of facilitating human well-being will depend upon a restructuring of our patterns of knowledge and on our ability to discover more adequate images of ourselves as full persons....*
>
> *There's a felt need for more cooperative, more fully human behaviour modes, modes which would take account of the whole gamut of personal fulfilment.*
>
> *Impressions are accumulating that, in modern industrial societies, both very small and very large communities provide, for many of their inhabitants, little room for community.... Cities of intermediate size are seen to offer greater opportunities than do large metropolitan conglomerates for social cohesion...for Canadians to create together a sense of community, to find that lost ground of common consensus.*
>
> *If any consensus about what might be a more adequate image has emerged it lies in the call for an image which places persons rather than things as the central focus. The imagery of 'the Convivial Society' is perhaps closer to a more adequate symbol [than 'the Conserver Society'] capturing the notion of living together in community with self, with nature and with others.*[65]

These remarks on cities and groups within cities touch only briefly and without great depth on the implications of system needs. The discussion is intended to illustrate the relationship between such basic needs and *the form of settlement. The implications of such needs, together with the repercussions of the policy variables, provide a basis for a more fully-developed statement on the optimum form of the future Canadian city.*

The Open City Emerges

We now come to a point where the various perspectives on settlement form presented in this chapter, can be brought together in a summary but inclusive concept of the city. These – the discussions on form and structure and policy variables – as well as Haworth's moral criteria (Chapter 7), lead to a certain image of the city. This would be a city that would embrace some of the major features already identified (pp. 348ff.). It would be made up of a number of related, interacting communities, each with its own diversified employment and service base, but all relying on a regional core for certain highly specialized goods and services. Each community would be socially mixed and diversified in its housing types and forms, and the balanced distribution of multiple forms would temper the tendency towards apartment concentration near the regional core. The transportation system would be designed to make the whole set of communities and centres one effectively interacting system. To achieve this a mix of transportation modes will have to be developed in a highly integrated fashion, moving from region-wide to local requirements: commuter rail, light rapid transit, bus rapid transit, conventional bus, dial-a-bus, shared taxis, private cars (also to be used for feeder and general business purposes) and bicycles. These variables: employment and service; residential mix, density and distribution; and transportation would be given distinctive form by the open space and leisure system. Transportation would be designed to communicate both the continuity of the entire city system as well as to highlight the scenes and opportunities that are locationally unique, be they based on landscape, cultural history or accessibility.

To this concept of the city, pragmatically grounded in the key policy variables, other features must be added, based on the application of the six basic system needs. Here only some of these implications can be suggested.

First the "resources" criterion requires that man's settlement be in harmony with his surroundings – as a natural, production or lived-in environment. This must be visible in the form of the city, say in the manner that the buildings, roads and other facilities relate to good farmland (other things being equal the land of highest capability should remain in production); in the way outstanding hardwood forest is spared the power saw and the bulldozer, and allowed to

Figure 8.16. City Farming

CITY FARMING

**CPAC Planning Aid announces
'City Gardening Referral Service'**

In the Halifax-Dartmouth area there are:
-people who have property available for gardening but need a gardener
-gardeners who are looking for property to plant

We want to bring these two together.

Planning Aid offers a free referral service.

Interested people call 422-5564 weekdays 9-2:00

**Sponsored by:
Community Planning Association of Canada**

Source: Canadian Institute of Planners, *C.I.P. Forum* (July, 1975), p. 14.

The open city represents not only a new urban form but a new urban ethic. People may come again to understand the preciousness of land as a resource which is one of the basic requirements of life itself, rather than a property to be bought and sold like any other commodity.

penetrate settled areas; and in the scrupulous attention to effective waste disposal, allowing the rivers, for example, to retain (or recover) their sparkle and remain inviting to the fisherman, canoeist and family on a Sunday picnic. The city of the future, in a period of intensifying energy and food constraints, must embody basic changes in the use and management of natural resources. It must be open to dramatic changes in approach and to technological experimentation. Such changes might include the conversion of some of the private and public open spaces of the city to food production; the extension, for domestic and other heating, of solar energy, requiring a three-dimensional urban form that allows for maximum sunshine exposure of solar roof collectors tilted at an angle (about sixty to seventy degrees) perpendicular to the sun's rays; and lifestyles based on the eco-house principle along the lines of Canada's demonstration ark (a Habitat project) that combines under one household-sized roof the functions of generating energy, growing food, recycling wastes and providing shelter.[66]

The "protection" function in the city of the future cannot be based, fundamentally, on police power. As the urban experience of the last quarter century abundantly demonstrates, the punitive legal basis of society is not sufficient to remove violence and the threat of violence – the atmosphere of menace and the armed camp. This depends on more fundamental attributes like social justice and the absence of discrimination and a city form that expresses these civilizing qualities. Segregation, the ghettos of the poor and of the rich, conspicuous imbalances in the allocation of urban resources be they green space, housing, hockey rinks or schools – are conditions that violate the system's need for "protection." Where intrinsic, desirable differences exist, the city's well-being will depend on the attainment of some of the other systems requirements: communication, integration/co-ordination and flexibility.

Turning a physical concept into a human city, in Toynbee's sense of "an association of human beings who have a feeling that they constitute a community"[67] depends on meeting the systems' need of "communication." Indeed, the kind of physical form suggested: the articulation of a number of communities seeking their own identities and small-scale environments but enjoying the benefits of a wider association, will depend heavily on people's access to information. The media, as well as more direct opportunities for interaction like the many forms of recreation, can play a powerful role in building the self-image of the city – as either a *mélange* of bickering principalities, or as a brave association of free communities struggling for a common civic excellence. When the opportunities for communication are realized in a constructive manner then the requirements of "integration" are attained: the city is able to assimilate many individual and group differences while maintaining social cohesion.

The "culture" of the city, the values its people live by, will be crucial to the attainment of all other system needs. Certain cultures are life-asserting; others, life-denying. The qualities that the city must have for wholesome survival – conservation, social justice, unregimented choice, a sense of community – can be reinforced by its cultural life, say its graphic and performing arts, and by its larger-scale symbols: its buildings and public places, exhibitions, sculptures and landmarks.

A living city, however, must avoid the worship of static value systems. The Chamber of Commerce is not always right. In a society of some considerable turbulence, the city must have a capacity to take change in its stride – indeed to anticipate and meet new demands. This involves two special characteristics. One is to have built into its social fabric a great variety of lifestyles. And the other is to have a government in which the average citizen, through involvement in decision-making, develops the confidence and competence to cope with pressures for change. With this perspective in mind, the city's urban form and physical form will need to be aligned towards the principle of balance between region-wide specialization and integration within its component communities.

We chose to call the city that we have described – the open city – "open" in the way it relates to the countryside, in its rich array of opportunities, in its information and transportation channels, in its citizens' access to government, in its cultural and administrative flexibility, and in its hospitality to differences in lifestyles – ethnic background, social status and design.

Policy Approaches

While the open city has been portrayed in only general terms it is a concept with implications here and now for Canada's cities. In terms of the eight cities illustrated above, there are certain features which are not consistent with the open city: Vancouver's social segregation (in which it is not alone); Penticton's dubious use (e.g. ribbon development) of a magnificent site; Edmonton's facilities-straining growth rate; the lack of employment diversity in Regina; Sudbury's uncertain "conquest" of air pollution; the precarious integration of major communities within metropolitan Hamilton; old Quebec's excessive dependence on the car; and the persistence of the values, attitudes and symbols of the past in Saint John.

But the concept of the open city, developed as it has from the key policy variables and a general systems approach, also helps to identify those aspects of existing cities that contain the seeds of the good life. Briefly, these might be Vancouver's high recreation potential based on an extensive open space network; Penticton's embrace of both town and country; Edmonton's example of ethnic mix and compatibility; Regina's open value systems, receptive to environmental change and reconstruction; Sudbury's urge to overcome its environmental handicaps; Hamilton's neighbourhood movement; Quebec's genius for preserving the past and bringing it gracefully into the present; and the mix of lifestyles in Saint John's compact inner city.

With these examples in mind, attaining the open city in Canada becomes a matter of developing strategies that suppress the negative and enhance the positive elements of each city – and of building new cities that meet the open city specifications. The system needs are not merely convenient for analysis, but provide us as well with some clues concerning (1) the policy areas that are crucial to the life of the city; and (2) the criteria by which they should be evaluated. This leads to an approach in which policy-makers concerned with Canadian cities are confronted with the obligation to meet the basic system needs: Resources, Protection, Communication, Integration, Culture and Flexibility.

While the practical value of this approach can only be fully grasped by its rigorous application, there is a strong presumption that it would be fruitful, for three reasons primarily. One is that it draws attention to what is essential and salient to the form and quality of the city. Another is that it compels the consideration of the relationships between policy/program sectors. It asks not just, "What is the impact of a program of 'commuter service facilities' on the 'integration' function or of community cable television on the 'communication' function"? but, "What is the combined impact of transportation, communication, housing, health, etc. programs on the city system as a whole?" And finally, and by no means least, the suggested approach has the merit of being founded on the bedrock of basic human needs.

To move from where we are toward the open city requires that public policy also develop a strong sense of priority. The process may be regarded as having two related and concurrent phases: overcoming barriers and new city building. In the Canadian cities of the present there are four tendencies that are anathema to the open city. One is the profligate exploitation of land resources. Another in imbalance in housing production increasingly expressed as inequality in residential conditions. A third is the danger of transportation paralysis in the car culture city, both internally and on the roads to recreation. And finally there is the blind destruction of the city's history.

This is not to say that there are not deep counter-forces within Canadian cities, but each of the foregoing have a lot of push behind them and if they remain unchecked will make the open city increasingly unattainable.

Overcoming these barriers will require a high order of effort, imagination and social responsibility (1) in the substance of our planning – we must dare to innovate and to break away from abortive policies and practices, and (2) in the way we mobilize our creative private, social and government resources for decision-making.

Opportunities to build the open city are certain to arise in the Canadian development of the last quarter of this century. This is ingrained in such processes as the deconcentration of growth from the big cities, the struggle for better regional balance nationally, and the northward push of the development/settlement frontier. If Canadians are to meet the challenge of these processes, we must develop now, rapidly and with determination the necessary institutions and administrative skills. In this regard initiatives like Part VI.1 of the *National Housing Act* (New Communities), and their provincial counterparts, can be regarded as only the most tentative steps toward an effective new city building process. Otherwise, unprepared, we will surely as night follows day resort to pressured, expedient and discredited solutions.[68]

The chapter that follows will deal in more specific terms with the policies, programs and institutions that are required to formulate, initiate and sustain desired changes. If nothing else, one large conditioning conjecture emerges from this discussion – the city is an organism which to flourish must be healthy in all its system functions. Against this, there is another reality: the social resources that we can bring to bear to meet these needs work in another direction. Each of the basic human settlement needs depends on a mix of private and public sector actors, and the public sector is divided several ways. Each level of government is departmentalized – co-ordination between functions does not come easily. And the federal state in search of political virtue thrives on jurisdictional dispute. This dilemma poses a tough problem for the Canadian government system. But it is our conviction that by having a clear idea of our needs, the odds of discovering the right means are significantly improved.

Notes

1. For drawing the authors' attention to this formulation, based on a concept developed by Catherine Bauer Wurster, we are indebted to Professor Richard E. Preston, who prepared a background paper for this publication. Richard E. Preston, "A Perspective on Alternative Settlement Forms," (Waterloo: University of Waterloo, Department of Geography, July 1975), pp. 58-60; also to be published in L. G. R. Martin, R. E. Preston and L. H. Russwurm, *Essays on Urban Process and Form*, Geography Publications Series No. 7 (Waterloo: University of Waterloo, Department of Geography, forthcoming). Catherine Bauer Wurster, "The Form and Structure of the Future Urban Complex," in *Cities and Space*, ed. Lowdon Wingo Jr. (Baltimore, Maryland: The Johns Hopkins Press, 1963), pp 73 – 101.
2. D. Michael Ray and Paul Y. Villeneuve, "Population Growth and Distribution in Canada: Problems, Process and Policies," *The Management of Land for Urban Development* (Ottawa: Canadian Council on Urban and Regional Research, 1974), pp. 3 and 4. This work presents some of the results of the "urban growth" program in policy research of the Ministry of State for Urban Affairs, which for a number of years was co-ordinated by Dr. Ray.
3. Preston, *op. cit.*, pp. 3 – 5.
4. *Ibid.*, pp. 15, 21 – 34.
5. *The Railway Relocation and Crossing Act*, passed by the House of Commons of Canada, Second Session, Twenty-Ninth Parliament, 23 Elizabeth II, 30th April, 1974. See Part I, Joint Urban Development and Transportation Plans.
6. Jean C. Gottmann made this point in a paper distinguishing between quaternary and tertiary services, in an address to the Conference on Regional Development and Economic Change, February 15, 16 and 17, 1965, Toronto.
7. Louis Henri Sullivan, "The Chicago Period in Retrospect," *Roots of Contemporary American Architecture*, ed. Lewis Mumford (New York: Grove Press, Inc., 1959), p. 257.
8. Robert W. Collier, *Contemporary Cathedrals* (Montreal: Harvest House, 1975). This book presents an account of decision-making processes involved in each of the mentioned inner city schemes. Reference to employment in McCauley Plaza, Edmonton, is on page 89.
9. Wallace Clement, *The Canadian Corporate Elite* (Toronto: McClelland and Stewart Limited, 1975), p. 247.
10. Collier, *op. cit.*, pp. 45 – 83.
11. Statistics Canada, *Perspective Canada: A Compendium of Social Statistics* (Ottawa: Information Canada, 1974), p. 210.
12. *Ibid.*, p. 211, Chart 10.6.
13. Anne Falkner, *Without Our Past? A handbook for the preservation of Canada's architectural heritage* (Toronto: University of Toronto Press, forthcoming 1977), Chapter 6, p. 141.
14. Donna Gabeline, Dane Lanken and Gordon Pope, *Montreal at the Crossroads* (Montreal: Harvest House, 1975), pp. 187 – 192; and Falkner, Chapter 7, pp. 9 and 10.
15. Judy McLeod, "Decision-Making in Ontario New Communities" (M.A. Thesis in Regional Planning and Resource Development, University of Waterloo, July 1975), p. 166.
16. *Ibid.*, p. 163.
17. Hans Blumenfeld, *Criteria for Judging the Quality of the Urban Environment*, Occasional Paper No. 14 (Waterloo: University of Waterloo, Faculty of Environmental Studies, 1974), p. 3.
18. *Ibid.*, p. 4.
19. For data on modes of travel to work see Ian N. Dawson and Tom G. Burns, "The Use of Transit in the Atlantic Region," in *Transportation and the Atlantic*

Region, Challenge and Opportunities: Symposium Sponsored by the Road and Transportation Association of Canada, Moncton, April 22, 23, 1974 (Ottawa: Road and Transportation Association of Canada, 1974), Table 3, pp. 34–48.
20. Benjamin Higgins, "The Montreal Airport Site," *Growth and Change*, Vol. 2, No. 1 (January 1971), p. 115. The material on the Mirabel airport is based on this paper.
21. Blumenfeld, *op. cit.*, p. 5.
22. Kenneth P. Cantor, "Warning: The Automobile is Dangerous to Earth, Air, Fire, Water, Mind and Body," *The Environmental Handbook* (New York: Ballantine Books, 1970), p. 206.
23. William Michelson, "Environmental Choice," Discussion Paper B.72.9 (Ottawa: Ministry of State for Urban Affairs, 1972), pp. 80–85.
24. Glenda R. Lamont, *Land Use Policy—Population Growth*, Technical Report 8 (Edmonton: Alberta Land Use Forum, 1974).
25. Statistics Canada, *Perspective Canada*, p. 105.
26. " 'Profiling Urban Issues', an interview with John Collins, co-ordinator of the Vancouver Urban Futures Project," *Urban Forum*, Vol. 1, No. 2, Summer 1975, p. 29.
27. Carol Kirsh, Brian Dixon and Michael Bond, *A Leisure Study—Canada 1972* (Toronto: Canada, Department of the Secretary of State, Culturcan Publications, 1973), pp. 30, 34, 38, 48, 70, 71, 78 and 79.
28. Claude Ducharme and Serge Lavoie, "Le Tourisme de Congrès Dans Les Zones Métropolitaines de Montréal de Toronto," Rev. Géogr., Montr., Vol. XXVIII, 1974, pp. 254, 256 and 259.
29. *Ibid.*, p. 246.
30. Mario Polèse and Serge Carlos, "Le Canada Metropolitaine 1971: Une Ecologique Factorielle de Vingt-et-un Zones Metropolitaines du Canada," Research Report (Ottawa: Ministry of State for Urban Affairs, 1975).
31. Kates, Peat, Marwick and Co., "Comparison of Public Transportation Systems," report prepared for the Ministry of State for Urban Affairs, March 1974 (mimeographed), pp. II–1, II–2, IV–8, V–1.
32. *Cities for Tomorrow*, Report No. 14 (Ottawa: Science Council of Canada, September 1971), p. 5, from Dr. Dansereau's letter of transmittal to the then Chairman of the Council, Dr. O. M. Solandt.
33. Westrede Institute, "Systems, Needs and Urban Guidelines," Research Report (Ottawa: Ministry of State for Urban Affairs, 1974), pp. 11–14. The report is based on a study by the Institute undertaken by a group of participating sociologists, social psychologists and social workers, mainly associated with the University of Alberta. Members of the study group were Peter Boothroyd, Fulton Fisher, Charles Hobart, George Kupfer, Crick Schmidt and F. H. (Tim) Tyler.
34. Eric Nicol, *Vancouver* (Toronto: Doubleday and Company, 1970), p. 3.
35. Walter G. Hardwick, "The Georgia Strait," in *British Columbia: Studies in Canadian Geography*, ed. J. Lewis Robinson (Toronto: University of Toronto Press, 1972), p. 128; and *The Livable Region 1976/1986: Proposals to Manage the Growth of Greater Vancouver* (Vancouver: Greater Vancouver Regional District, 1975), p. 15.
36. A. L. Farley, ed., *Trans-Canada Field Excursions, Guide Book* (Vancouver: University of British Columbia, 1972), pp. 173-176.
37. Letter of J. P. Conelissen, Assistant Planner, Regional District of Okanagan-Similkameen to Angus Schaffenburg, graduate student, School of Urban and Regional Planning, University of Waterloo, August 25, 1975; "Building and License Department Report for the Year 1974," (Penticton: City of Penticton, 1975) (mimeographed); and G. Theodore Buel, "Alternative Housing in the Canadian Context: A Factory-Built Housing System Proposal" (Thesis, Master of Arts, Regional Planning and Resource Development, University of Waterloo, March 1975), p. 72.

38. Statistics Canada, *1971 Census of Canada, Census Tract—A Series: Edmonton*, Cat. 95-727 (Ottawa: Information Canada, 1973).
39. Statistics Canada, *Perspective Canada*, p. 92.
40. Statistics Canada, *1971 Census of Canada, Census Tract—B Series: Regina*, Cat. 95-754 (Ottawa: Information Canada, 1974); and Farley, *op. cit.*, p. 97.
41. Harry Heimark, "Regina," in *Urbanism and Environment*, ed. Georges Le Pape (Montreal: Federal Publications Service, 1974), pp. 230 and 240.
42. F. Wu, "Regional Economic Study of Sudbury" (Senior Honours Essay, School of Urban and Regional Planning, University of Waterloo, 1973); and Farley, *op. cit.*, p. 22.
43. Norman Webster, column, *Globe and Mail*, September 2, 1975.
44. Statistics Canada, *1971 Census of Canada, Census Tract—B Series: Hamilton*, Cat. 95-739 (Ottawa: Information Canada, 1974); and George A. Nader, *Cities of Canada*, Vol. 1 (Toronto: Macmillan of Canada, 1975), pp. 268 and 353-354.
45. Jean Cimon, "Old Quebec and Town Planning," in *Urbanism and Environment*, ed. Georges Le Pape (Montreal: Federal Publications Service, 1974), pp. 230 and 240.
46. Pierre Biays, "Southern Quebec," in *Canada: A Geographical Interpretation*, ed. J. Warkentin, Education Edition (Toronto: Methuen, 1968), p. 320; and Statistics Canada, *1971 Census of Canada, Census Tract – B Series: Quebec* Cat. 95-735 (Ottawa: Information Canada, 1974); and *Canada Year Book, 1973* (Ottawa: Information Canada, 1973), p. 356.
47. Warkentin, *op. cit.*, p. 326; and Cimon, *op. cit.*, p. 211.
48. C. N. Forward, "Cities: Function, Form and Future," in *The Atlantic Provinces: studies in Canadian geography*, ed. Louis Trotier (Toronto: University of Toronto Press, 1972), p. 147; John Porteous, "Why its new container terminal means so much to Saint John," *Financial Post*, February 8, 1975; *Comprehensive Community Plan, Saint John, N.B.* (Saint John: City of Saint John, Planning Department, 1972), pp. 4, 9, 10 and 88; and John Porteous, "Saint John approves new waterfront development," *Financial Post*, February 22, 1975.
49. Westrede Institute, "Systems, Needs, and Urban Guidelines," pp. 10-18.
50. *Ibid.*, pp. 27-30.
51. *Ibid.*, pp. 20 and 294.
52. *Ibid.*, p. 54.
53. *Ibid.*, p. 68.
54. *Ibid.*, pp. 36, 71 and 74.
55. *Ibid.*, p. 79.
56. *Ibid.*, p. 54.
57. Lorna R. Marsden, "Ageing and the 1980's," paper prepared for the Institute for Research on Public Policy, September 1975; Statistics Canada, *Population Projections for Canada and the Provinces, 1972-2001* (Ottawa: Information Canada, 1974), p. 88; and Westrede Institute, "Systems, Needs, and Urban Guidelines," *op. cit.*, pp. 84-86.
58. Westrede, *op. cit.*, pp. 158-159.
59. Polèse and Carlos, *op. cit.*
60. Peter Boothroyd, "Urban Situation Report, Edmonton, 1975," paper prepared for the Ministry of State for Urban Affairs, April 1975 (mimeographed), pp. 25, 26, 27, 37 and 38.
61. Novia Carter, *Something of Promise: The Canadian Communes* (Ottawa: The Canadian Council on Social Development funded by the Ministry of State for Urban Affairs, 1974).
62. Cathy Starrs, "Conversations With Canadians About The Future," An interim report on the Conserver Society Project of the Advanced Concepts Centre (Ottawa: Environment Canada, March 31, 1975) (mimeographed), p. 74.
63. *Ibid.*, pp. 7 and 9. The "data base" of the project was described as follows: "a) a small group (twenty or so) of persons from across Canada involved in what could be described as the first 'futures' exercise legitimated by the federal

government—an enquiry into the conceptual foundations underpinning social policy undertaken in 1970-71; "b) suggestions which came from federal officials whom the Director of the Centre approached for their comments and criticisms of the project, and for their suggestions as to who might be approached; and "c) suggestions elicited from each of the persons interviewed with respect to others whose views might add useful insights to the project." On the basis of the foregoing the authors estimate that about fifty "conversations" were held.

64. *Ibid.*, pp. 47, 30, 32, 44, 34, and 35.
65. *Ibid.*, pp. 79, 47, 76, 75 and 80.
66. "City Farming," *C.I.P. Forum*, Canadian Institute of Planners, July 1975, p. 14; Steve Jeffery, "Make energy while the sun shines," *Financial Post*, August 1975, p. 6; and "Canadian Urban Demonstration Program, Approved Project: An Ark for Prince Edward Island," News Release by the Honourable Barney Danson, Minister of State for Urban Affairs, Vancouver, April 15, 1975.
67. Arnold Toynbee, (ed.), *Cities of Destiny* (New York: McGraw-Hill Book Company, 1967). The quotation is from Toynbee's introduction on p. 26.
68. Norman E. P. Pressman, *Planning new communities in Canada*, Urban Paper A.75.4 (Ottawa: Ministry of State for Urban Affairs, 1975). This report contains a statement of new community concepts, as well as a critical interpretive view of Canadian experience and policies.

CHAPTER 9

Some Conclusions and Policy Notes

What the future holds for the cities and towns of Canada has become a question of general concern and speculation. All the evidence suggests that Canadians are worried about where this country's urban development is heading – about the national distribution of urban communities and about the form of regional growth. We have come to realize that there are critical choices to be made. We must weigh liabilities against advantages, identify realistic alternatives, and make the policy changes that will move us in the preferred directions.

Summary Perspectives

Canadian urban growth is dramatic in whatever context it is judged (Chapters 1 and 2). It has become commonplace to observe that 90 per cent of the Canadian population *will* be urban by the end of the century. And that is sometimes associated with the most dire consequences. But the past growth of urban Canada has not occurred in isolation nor without distinct advantages. The reciprocal relationship between economic growth and population growth has not gone unnoticed. Our technologies, our policies in support of economic endeavours, and our ideologies have all contributed to an acceptance of urbanization as a goal worthy of pursuit. Why otherwise would immigrants, or the sons and daughters of non-urban Canadians or indeed the urban born find city life so compelling? For some, cities have been seen to be the focus of the "good life." Perhaps, for significant others there has been no alternative.

What we have been trying to do in this book is to consider the implications of the trends that were identified in Chapter 2. Are these trends likely to result in an urban Canada which we collectively judge to be desirable? Are the forces which have been so compellingly urban likely to continue apace? Are they likely to be impervious to change over this "last quarter" of the century and in the future? Are our ideologies so fixed that cities are the only means to the "good life"? These are some of the not-easy-to-answer questions on our not-so-straight road to understanding.

The first place to look, we have thought, is in the diagnosis of the forces contributing to growth (Chapter 3) and in the diagnosis of the goods and ills of urban life (Chapters 5 to 8 inclusive). The Canadian urban pattern was not randomly imposed on the map – despite first appearances. The pattern reflects in a very real way the historical forces that have shaped our destiny – the ties to powerful neighbours and partners, the evolution of the Canadian economy through a succession of staples, and the various economic forces and technologies that have fostered urbanization. And once started, the growth of cities has had all of the appearances of being self-sustaining and perhaps self-generating.

But development has been far from monolithic. In fact, the Canadian urban scene is best described, as it is in Chapter 5, as a vast mosaic. Our cities are often widely different, not only physically, but also socially and economically – sometimes to the good and sometimes not. Too often, however, we have left the forces that be to take their own course. We have lost opportunities – perhaps not for all time, but at least in the past – to capitalize on the human and economic potential of large parts of this country. And the various "ties" to the land (Chapter 6) have been less than fully appreciated in the types of development which has taken place. Good housing and good farming and good recreation have tended to go together, usually to the detriment of those activities that may have high "human value," but low economic value – particularly in the short run.

Regardless of the many urban forms that comprise the Canadian mosaic (Chapter 8), after all is said and done, we are really talking about an external shell for people. Cities are places for people. Their structures may either accommodate and enhance, or constrict their lives (Chapter 7). But the types of people places we have are reflected in the forms of buildings we construct, in the nature of the recreation facilities we create, in the range of opportunities we collectively have for interaction and so on. Poets have been perhaps more perceptive than developers or politicians or social scientists in seeing the potential for good and ill in various urban forms (Chapter 7). We should be receptive to their message.

The challenge in all of this is to detect where we may have brought into play the negative factors and where we might bring into play the positive ones: where indeed the potential exists for realizing latent possibilities. The task requires perception of the underlying forces at work (Chapters 1 and 3), an understanding of the historical factors, the rich diversity that is Canada (Chapters 3, 6 and 8), and an appreciation of the criteria by which we can judge whether a city is "good" or "bad" (Chapters 2, 5 and 7). Finally it requires the imagination to discover new alternatives (Chapter 4.)

To summarize, what can we say about Canadian cities and the Canadian urban system? What forces are amenable to change and should be changed? It is dangerous to generalize answers to these questions when we are talking about the wide diversity of the Canadian scene. But some useful observations can and need to be made.

Canada is best viewed as a set of inter-related and highly interactive urban regions. The future of urban Canada will be determined by a number of interacting forces: the infrastructure and institutions that are our legacy from the past; the external forces that play such a large role in an economy as "open" as Canada's; and the internal balancing and centralizing forces that come into play every time a public or private decision is taken.[1] And, of course, one cannot forget the less systematic, perhaps chance, factors that can sometimes have far-reaching consequences. What results if immigration stops? Or Canada becomes energy self-sufficient? Or incomes and prices policies are imposed over long periods of time? Or severe restrictions are placed on foreign investment? Or?

Urban regions grow, decline or remain static as a result of many decisions and many factors. A key question is, which of these factors are, in fact, controllable? These factors include the productivity of the economic base, which in turn reflects foreign and domestic demand, tax structure, the degree of monopoly and a whole host of related factors. They include the locus of decision-making since, after all, besides government facilities, locational decisions (more or less constrained), are made by individuals or individual firms. They include judgements that are made on "equity" because behind all decisions is some notion of equity. They include the institutions that have been established, or might be established, to facilitate the resolution of conflicting points of view and the participation of communities. They include the commitment of our governments to providing services, to equalizing opportunities as far as possible, and to maintaining a diversity of urban systems or sub-systems in Canada.

The Imagined Future

We do have some understanding of the Canadian urban system – the forces that shape it, that trigger, accelerate or decelerate its growth, that create its distinctive patterns across the land and that distribute its benefits and generate its stresses. But we also have need for action on our problems, whether seen from the viewpoint of the housewife in one of our suburbs or in one of the hundreds of our resource towns; or of the child living on the twelfth floor of an apartment near the centre of a big city; of the miner in a remote coastal town in Newfoundland; or of the politician responsible for doing something about all of these concerns. There comes a time when analysis must lead to action if it is not to become an end in itself – and most likely, a dead end. The researcher, the scholar and the policy diagnostician must submit his (or her) ideas to the test of experience. We must dare to do the best we know how, and from the hard lessons of the struggle to improve our environment to attain, step-by-step, new levels of insight and policy wisdom.

It is in this spirit that we will offer a view of the Canadian urban future. This will be based mainly on our diagnosis of forces and conditions, and on our perception of the needs, values and lifestyles of Canadians. To convey a reasonably vivid image, we will first present our concepts without much consideration of the strategies that will be necessary to leap from the present to the imagined future. When the whole story has been unfolded we will turn back to the very real and inescapable task of thinking through the various means: political, legislative, administrative, technical and financial, required to move events in the direction indicated by our model.

NATIONAL URBAN PATTERNS

(1) *Cities: Big, Medium and Small*
In the last quarter of this century we will move towards a Canada which features a few predominant patterns. The biggest cities: Montreal, Toronto and Vancouver, will as a matter of public policy try to slow down their growth so that they can catch up with the backlog of unrelieved problems and unsatisfied needs. As a result, conditions in housing, transportation, recreation facilities and social services will gradually improve. The people of these places will be able to take stock of their growth and give their attention to the *form* of their development, considering such choices, and mixes of choices, as downtown *versus* regional town centres, inner city renewal and rebuilding *versus* development on fringe farm land, the extension of public transportation *versus* car-oriented systems, and so on. Provincial and federal policies will act to reinforce the preferred forms of development.

Parallel with this, the provinces and the federal government will give priority to encouraging the development of small and medium-sized cities, with a view to raising personal and community incomes, and extending job and life opportunities to a level that generally approximates the highest standards in the country. This will require attention to two different situations: the single city that stands very much on its own like Saskatoon or Sudbury, and the network of closely related cities like Alma, Jonquière, Chicoutimi and Port Alfred in the Saguenay valley of Quebec, or like Vernon, Kelowna and Penticton in the Okanagan valley of British Columbia.

This direction of change will be pushed along by a compulsive shift in peoples' values and lifestyles, which will move even more strongly than heretofore from an emphasis on making a living, to living more fully. People will not be content to suffer the denials in opportunities associated with living in small isolated communities. They will make choices about residence, work, and investment, and about government policies which will tend in each major region to create clusters of related and interacting communities. These complexes will be large enough to provide a wide array of services, from first class professional hockey to first class specialized hospitals; and to attain enough of a mix in economic activities to give not only a high level of employment choice but also greater economic stability.

Accordingly, in those regions which do not presently have such a mix of services, public policy will take initiatives that will foster their emergence. In some regions like the Atlantic provinces, this will involve encouragement to processes that are already under way, for example, in the central corridor extending from Saint John, New Brunswick to Halifax-Dartmouth, Nova Scotia.

(2) Canada's Developing Regions
In other parts of the country, the creation of such regional complexes will require a different approach. In mid-Canada, the present frontier of Canadian settlement, this will involve a development planning process, which will overcome the personal disadvantages of living in small, isolated, unstable communities located close to the mine or the source of the pulpwood. Each province concerned will evolve its own institutions and style for accomplishing this. But they will share the objective of creating in each of their resource development regions at least one highly accessible urban centre or closely-linked cluster of centres that will provide the basis for a fully-rounded social and economic life. This will be true, whether the area is the iron ore power complex in northern Quebec and Labrador, the base metals area of northern Manitoba, or the diversified resource region of Peace River in Alberta and British Columbia. In such areas, native peoples, in particular, will dramatize the importance of social conditions and ecological considerations, and insist on substantial benefits of development returning to the region.

This kind of positive regional development program will produce the welcome paradox of increased regional diversity with strengthened national integration. In each region, people will have a greater opportunity to create their own unique existence: a lifestyle of the anglophone north contrasted with the francophone north, for example. At the same time, because settlement patterns will assume the form of larger, more diversified and stable communities, these places will have greater interactions of all kinds with other like centres. In this country, the greatest number and most intense inter-place contacts are between metropolis and metropolis (places of 100,000 population and up). This is demonstrated in air and train travel as well as telephone calls, bank clearances, conferencing and the flow of all kinds of information (Chapter 3).

(3) *Growth Rates*
The experience of the late 'sixties and early 'seventies will make urban communities very cautious about allowing growth rates to get too high. Allowing for differences in local and regional variations in financial resources, the stock of serviced land, utility system capacities, and planning and administrative capabilities, it will become very clear that beyond a certain rate of growth – 4, 5, or 6 per cent – communities endure very heavy and seemingly inescapable social costs in land and housing, social capital and municipal services. Increasingly the places concerned, say Edmonton, Calgary, Kitchener-Waterloo or Sept-Iles, will make a strenuous effort to pull the reins on runaway growth, and they will call on provincial and federal reinforcement of that objective.

(4) *Prospects*
The overall effect of these tendencies operating across the entire country – the slowing of the growth of the biggest cities, the creation of large regional networks in slower growing and under-developed regions (for example, Maritimes and the mid-North), the greater integration and mobility between regions, and applying the brakes on excessive urban growth at particular places – all of these things acting together will tend gradually to reduce disparities between the Canadian heartland and the other regions of the country. Inter-regional gaps in living standards and opportunities will be narrowed, and the country as a consequence will be less divided, less fractious – and at once more viably diversified and unified.

THE REGIONS WHERE PEOPLE WILL LIVE

This Canada of the last quarter century will be a thoroughly urbanized Canada in the sense that most of the people will not work on farms. They will live in settlements which will exist because of their employment functions in manufacturing and services, and/or their qualities as pleasant places to live.

People will continue to talk of "city" and "country," but the form of settlement that will emerge will contain elements of both town and country and offer lifestyles that are increasingly a blend of each. This will be attained by development tending towards two alternate poles—either compact high-rise settlements that preserve relatively convenient access to the countryside, or forms that are quite spread out in which residential communities, recreational forests, work places and learning places, farm areas, and older villages and towns are all woven together.

(1) The Issue of Settlement Forms

A variety of forces will in fact bring the settlement form choices into focus as a major concern of individuals and families and governments. One such factor will be the growth and concentration of population—as numbers increase, comfortable living has to be planned for and designed with great care and forethought. Another is the regional, and increasingly in the background, national and global concern with conserving limited supplies of productive farm land.

A third factor will be certain inescapable transportation choices. As cities grow a number of critical decision points are reached: shall scarce capital resources go into the extension of expressways when the average journey to work by car begins to exceed tolerable limits? Or should a shift be made to higher speed and more efficient mass transit? These fateful choices will have consequences for the form of settlement.

The use of energy will increasingly affect the design and layout of settlements as well as the form and construction of buildings. The solar city cannot easily be a high-rise city. Research will discover significant differences in energy waste and consumption in different urban forms, generally indicating a bias towards minimizing travel distances, and towards transportation modes with low energy inputs per passenger mile.

(2) Settlements: Forces and Features

The forms that future settlement takes will be very much affected by the interplay of national forces, by certain needs and wants common to settlements anywhere, and by particular features of culture and landscape that are regionally distinctive. Generally, people will be attempting to push political forces towards equalizing opportunities for the good life. There will be increasing insistence that the kind of jobs a person can get, the housing available to families, the education and training choices open to young people, and the level of health and recreation services available, should be more or less equal in all parts of Canada. Accordingly, federal and provincial policies will become concerned, in a more rigorous and far-reaching way, with questions about the *allocation* of national resources between competing purposes, and the *distribution* of resources between regions and groups of people. And the outcome will be a set of strategies and actions which will be dramatically biased towards meeting social needs.

The future form of settlement will also be shaped by several very basic struggles of people in the localities and regions where they live. People will strive to maintain the sense and fact of community – a feeling of identity and shared purpose with a group of people in a particular place – in the face of the increasing size and impersonality of settlements. They will struggle to maintain control of the government of expanding regional settlement systems. And they will try to organize the form of such systems in a way that will maximize opportunities of component communities to share in the advantages of jobs and leisure and markets of the larger association. These strivings will tend to produce cities and towns and new city/country/town clusters that emphasize both community identity and a high degree of internal mobility, communication and integration. People will need to get around. They will need to know what's going on. And they will need to create and have access to services, facilities and institutions scaled to and benefiting the entire region.

In the last quarter of this century, the turbulence of the preceding quarter will impress on the urban Canadian that nothing is more certain than change itself. As a result there will be an attempt to build *flexibility* into the very form of settlement. In the physical environment, patterns of residence and transportation and services will be evolved that leave open options for shifting to meet unanticipated pressures. In political life such flexibility will be reflected in the awareness that there is no better preparation for meeting crises of change and urgent adaptation than the experience, day-by-day, of trying to run one's own affairs – the experience of governing. The form of settlement and its institutional expression in units of decision-making and administration will have to foster such opportunities for political engagement. We will have to think in terms of related spheres of political concern – from neighbourhood and towns, to metropolis and region. And each sphere will have a place in both communication and decision-making networks.

The increasingly multi-ethnic and multi-racial nature of Canadian society, together with the "awakening" of disadvantaged groups, including native peoples, will make us all more aware that civic serenity and order are based on social justice. And, conversely, we will learn, sometimes the hard way, that discrimination and inequality breed civic animosity and strife. Social reform will become more strongly linked with efforts to attain a more equitable and fair distribution of environmental goods.

(3) *Regional Diversity*
While these forces will operate and erupt wherever people live in Canada, the specific way in which they are expressed in the settlements of particular urban regions, say on the Prairies as compared to the Maritimes, will depend very much on the landscapes and lifestyles and unique histories and outlooks of the different places. Each city in Canada is remarkable for the way it expresses a certain individuality – "a spirit of place." This has come about and persisted in spite of powerful standardizing, metropolitanizing, homogenizing forces rooted in our technologies and economic systems – a bottling plant or a Holiday Inn looks the same everywhere and Coca Cola penetrates every nook and cranny of the country.

There are signs, however, that this spread of "sameness" has reached and passed its zenith. The resistance to standardization has very deep roots. People seem to express an innate sense that environmental diversity, which preserves their own identity, is a requirement for the decent survival of the human community. Resistance to the bulldozer of conformity will be expressed in an avalanche of concern, from Vancouver to St. John's, with preserving our history and unique landscapes. And it will be expressed in the city forms of the future in ways that are as different as Kennebecasis Bay is different from Wascana Creek, or the water towers of Sudbury from the basilica of Quebec.

(4) *The Quality of Environment*
The arousal of the Canadian "environmental conscience" which was a phenomenon of the 'sixties leaves ingrained certain strong and persisting attitudes. People will demand a cleaner biosphere – whether the worry is from fluorspar dust at the tip of the Burin Peninsula in Newfoundland, or from lead dust in the Niagara district of Toronto. All forms of urban/industrial pollution will be closely monitored, and more effective control systems established. Serious efforts to curb agriculturally-based pollution, which can affect the streams and watersheds of highly populated areas, will however only begin in this period.

The comparative economic austerity called for in the next decades can turn events either towards a retreat from social conscience and social investments, or towards a sober reappraisal of priorities, and a righting of the balance between private wealth and public poverty. In the short run, the first response will be favoured, but over the span of several decades, the basically populist and democratic nature of Canadian society will give an edge to the second approach. In the face of obviously limited resources we will find the mechanisms for more finely-tuned decisions on the allocation of resources. And we will be able to decide – as a deliberate choice of public policy – whether we want x-million dollars of available capital to go into non-profit, low-rental housing, or into another skyscraper temple of high finance.

The struggle for environmental quality will become merged with the struggle for redistributive justice. Most Canadians will want to move towards the West European model of social democracy rather than the traditional American model of economic privatism. The outcome of this contest will have far-reaching repercussions on the quality of our environment – particularly on the nature of our work lives and on the quality of housing and residential communities.

(5) *Housing and Community*
The period will see housing as a very important public policy issue. As a result, policy will move from its present preoccupation with coaxing and motivating the private sector to produce social housing, to the direct provision of housing for those who cannot get it on the open market. This housing will not take the form of ghetto-like projects, but will fit in with the regional strategies for shaping the character and mix of settlements. We will see a leap in creative energy and ingenuity in this area of public initiative, as the graduates from Canada's environmental and planning schools, established in a substantial way in the 'sixties, reach professional maturity. This factor, joined with the aforementioned forces shaping the form of settlements, will initiate a period of community building which will be national in scale, but highly regional in its character and impact.

(6) *Land Concerns*
Land, as outdoor recreational space, as farm land, or as the setting for residential communities – will figure prominently as a public issue. Conservation will be resurrected as a respectable public goal – particularly in the areas of interface between town and country. The preservation of the most productive farm land and choicest recreational landscapes in such fringe areas will make an impact on both urban and rural environments. It will influence the future development form of most metropolitan areas, and in some provinces, like Ontario, compel a drastic shift from established development corridors. Ribbon growth and sprawl, scattered very low-density building, which is costly to service, will fortunately be diminished. Farming areas near cities, for the first time in the country's history, will be able to contemplate a future of some stability. But the more open settlement patterns, with many living in the country and working in

the city, will make even more urgent than today the need to find some answers to the vexing problem of clashing rural and urban lifestyles.

(7) *The Inner City*
There will be a continuing concern with the quality of inner cities, those areas of residential and mixed uses on the immediate edge of the central core. Experience with the Neighbourhood Improvement Program (NIP) will, for the second time in two decades, impress on the minds of political leaders and administrators the facts of life about Canada's inner cities. It will re-emphasize the existence of several types of inner city, each with different conditions, problems and potentials, and each requiring a different policy/program emphasis. Objectives will be three-fold: to protect stable areas; to stop the decline of areas locked in a culture of poverty; and to adjust to change, whether in small or big doses, in a way that minimizes the disruption of existing inner city communities.

Strategies for the Imagined Future

To move from where we are in Canada to where we want to be, will require a very great effort. In its most direct terms the model that has been sketched is a recipe for "everyman's" good life: a comfortable dwelling in a pleasing, friendly neighbourhood, close to shopping and schools, not too far from work, with a choice of private or public transit travel to a city centre, offering a rich array of services and employment and some exciting beautiful places where people congregate, and with convenient access to the attractions of the region: a conference centre, a big park, a university or research centre, as well as the relief of the rural countryside with its refreshing green landscape, where you can enjoy a weekend ramble through the general stores, the country markets, the tea rooms and craft shops of its villages and small towns. Add to this a dash of clean air and water, and stir with a vigorous political life, and the recipe is complete.

While this image of the good life is not overly ambitious or unreasonable, it will become increasingly elusive in the Canada of the immediate future – unless we deliberately set out as individuals and as a society to use all the means at our disposal to make it happen. It has become necessary to think in these comprehensive terms, because it has become evident that what Canadians strive for locally is bound up with broad thinking and action at the level of the province and the nation. Given what we now know about the urban growth forces, there is a certain central and over-riding task that has to be faced. We have to somehow bring into alignment two aspects of Canadian life: one is the increasingly interlinked, interdependent nature of our urban places and regions; and the other is the divided and separated nature of political authority – our capacity to act for social ends within our federal state.

WHY A POLICY PROCESS?

To match up these two aspects we must give high priority to reshaping our policy and decision-making processes. This does not mean more bureaucracy. It does mean using our existing governmental system more effectively to attain the goals we may set for human settlements. The broad overall purpose is to make better use of limited resources to achieve those goals, which filter through our political systems as agreed and consensual ends. In the kind of complex, turbulent, intensely interwoven society we inhabit, this calls for some changes in the style of government.

We need mechanisms for clarifying goals and discovering the common ground between and within governments. Otherwise what a transportation policy might do to foster a commuter rail system for a big urban region, might be undone by what a utilities agency might do to foster land development along other corridors. We need mechanisms for relating agreed objectives to logical means. Otherwise a policy of urban decentralization declared by a minister on a Monday morning may be contradicted by a housing agency decision on the allocation of land assembly funds on a Thursday afternoon. And we must retain a sense of the total process in which we work – both of the key elements and actors involved – lest we attain consensus and link up ends and means, and forget that effective implementation depends on communication of purposes and legislation and necessary styles of operation to many private and public participants close to the scene of action.

ELEMENTS IN A POLICY PROCESS

For all of these reasons and more, we must begin by bringing into focus the requirements of a process through which public policies can be fulfilled. It will help to keep a simplified picture of such a process in mind (Figure 9.1). What is depicted is a number of interrelated elements which can function at any level of government.

Let us see how this process might operate in the case of the Maritime cities sub-system, identified in Chapter 4. The goal of encouraging the development of medium-sized and small cities is translated into the *objective* of increasing the growth rate of Maritime cities. *Trends* are examined to discover the forces operating,

SOME CONCLUSIONS AND POLICY NOTES   427

Figure 9.1. Elements of a Policy Process

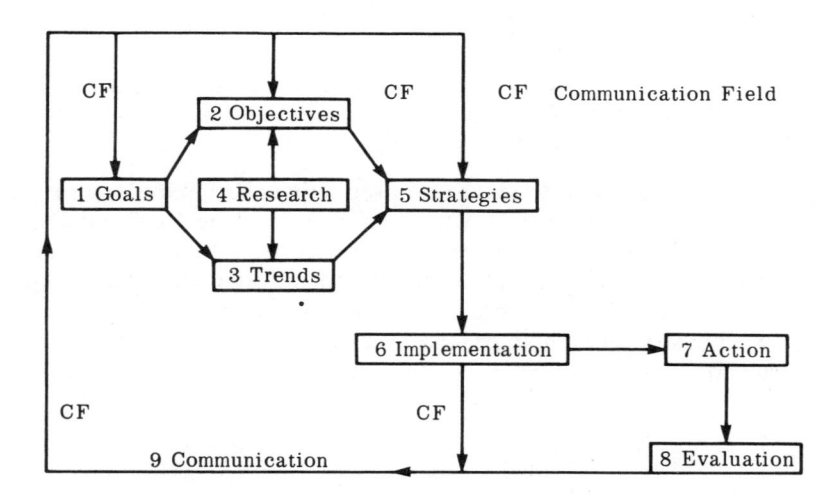

```
        CF              CF         CF  Communication Field
                 ┌─────────────┐
                 │ 2 Objectives│
                 └─────────────┘
   ┌───────┐  ┌────────────┐  ┌────────────┐
   │1 Goals│  │ 4 Research │  │ 5 Strategies│
   └───────┘  └────────────┘  └────────────┘
                 ┌─────────────┐
                 │  3 Trends   │
                 └─────────────┘

                     ┌──────────────────┐      ┌──────────┐
                     │ 6 Implementation │─────▶│ 7 Action │
                     └──────────────────┘      └──────────┘
     CF                   CF
              9 Communication                 ┌────────────┐
                                              │8 Evaluation│
                                              └────────────┘
```

either to facilitate or constrain the objective. *Research* on this question discovers the emergence of a central corridor of interacting cities in New Brunswick and Nova Scotia which have economic activities, employment mixes and levels, services and population features which are different from the rest of the Atlantic region, and which resemble the conditions of urban corridors in central Canada. There is potential for growth if certain constraints can be removed and opportunities seized. On this basis, a *strategy* is evolved which is designed to foster the development in a related and complementary manner of eight urban places, including Fredericton, Saint John, and Halifax-Dartmouth. The strategy outlines a sequence of private sector and public initiatives leading towards the improvement of regional communications and transportation; the strengthening of critical economic functions like deep water containerized ports and shipbuilding; and an expanded investment in human resources through extending opportunities for education and training, fostering a regional research capacity, improving health care and enriching cultural life through the support of performing arts and so on.

The strategy is *implemented* through the co-ordinated efforts of several public sectors (housing, transportation, etc.), and two or three government levels. It requires the elaboration of programs to enhance the roles of each urban centre, as well as programs affecting the entire central corridor. The following are examples of *region-wide* programs:

the improvement of regional air services, by the building and/or improvement of landing facilities and control equipment, with particular attention to the needs of a new STOL service planned by Eastern Provincial Airways;

the establishment of a regional computer software centre, undertaking software design and programming on a consulting basis, for business and government;

various measures to enhance productivity in manufacturing, such as an amendment to the regulations of the Regional Development Incentives Act (DREE), which would place modernization grants on the same basis as new industry grants; and the more thorough application of the Program for the Advancement of Industrial Technology (Industry, Trade and Commerce, Ottawa);

the sustaining of a major housing effort in places like Saint John and Halifax and others where demand is rising on a steep curve. This needs to be a many-sided approach which includes the allocation of funds to municipalities for servicing residential land; the financing and construction of a suitably mixed housing output, ranging from subsidized and limited dividend rental housing, through cooperative and non-profit schemes, to Assisted Home Ownership and conventionally mortgaged housing; the rehabilitation of old housing stock through Neighbourhood Improvement Programs; and the strengthening of the capability of the regional house building industry.[2]

The remaining elements in the process, *action, evaluation* and *communication* are closely related in concept and practice. Programs are delivered, industries and houses are built and various facilities extended and improved. The physical and socio-economic landscape begins, for better or worse, to change. There are secondary effects in employment, income, population migration, community patterns and the behaviour of investors and business men. It is important to know if the strategy is effectively meeting its objectives. Some system of keeping tabs on the situation, or monitoring, is necessary to provide basic information for the ongoing evaluation of conditions. Indeed the type of evaluation that is conducted will influence the type of information that is sought.

At least two kinds of evaluation can be anticipated. One is of a general nature, taking the form of various indices of social, economic and physical conditions (see Chapter 5). For the region in question some of the more important indicators would be educational achievement, income, occupational status, unemployment rates, and housing cost and choice. The other type of evaluation is in terms of specific programs, where the criteria of judgement will arise from the objectives of the individual programs. Thus the number of dwelling units produced for families earning less than $8,000 per year, as a result of programs designed to meet that requirement, will be compared to the estimated need for such housing; and the adequacy of the effort will be judged on that basis. There is also a need for a more personal response from the people on the receiving end of programs. The concern is to discover not only *what* was done, but *how* it was done. How do affected residents react to a Neighbourhood Improvement Program in Saint John? Do they feel that they have had a sufficient say in developing the program for their neighbourhood? Are they satisfied that the priority problems are getting attention? Has action been sufficiently timely, or have there been agonizing delays? How could the programs be improved?

The communication element pervades the entire process. It can best be viewed as a communication field, the yeast in the dough, that surrounds the actors in the process at every stage of their work. Communication activities may vary in intensity from time to time, as long as continuity is maintained. This is essential, both from the point of view of governments that want to be effective, and from the point of view of individuals, groups and the general public concerned with having a say about the substance of policy.

Unless there is almost continuous communication from the field of action and impact to responsible decision-makers, any development strategy will eventually lose its punch and its relevancy. Information must feed back along a variety of communication channels, from the daily press to special in-government arrangements, in a form that will make possible a regular, periodic review and adjustment of goals, objectives and strategies. In the case of the strategy for the Saint John-Halifax corridor, as for most urban-related strategies, much of this communication must be inter-governmental. All levels are involved directly or indirectly either in the support of programs or in experiencing their impact (Chapter 4). It becomes a very special challenge of urban and regional strategies to build the multi-governmental arrangements and institutions for attaining consensus on aims and means, as well as the capacity to respond, in a co-ordinated way, to feedback from the places and people affected.

A simplified picture of a policy process can help to sort out major phases and relationships, but it must not obscure the real complexities involved. Each step in the process, brings into play a new set of actors and forces, expressed in general form (Figure 9.2) but in the real world of urban policy-making and decision-making they represent such actors as the Minister of State for Urban Affairs, Ottawa,

Figure 9.2. Actors in a Policy Process

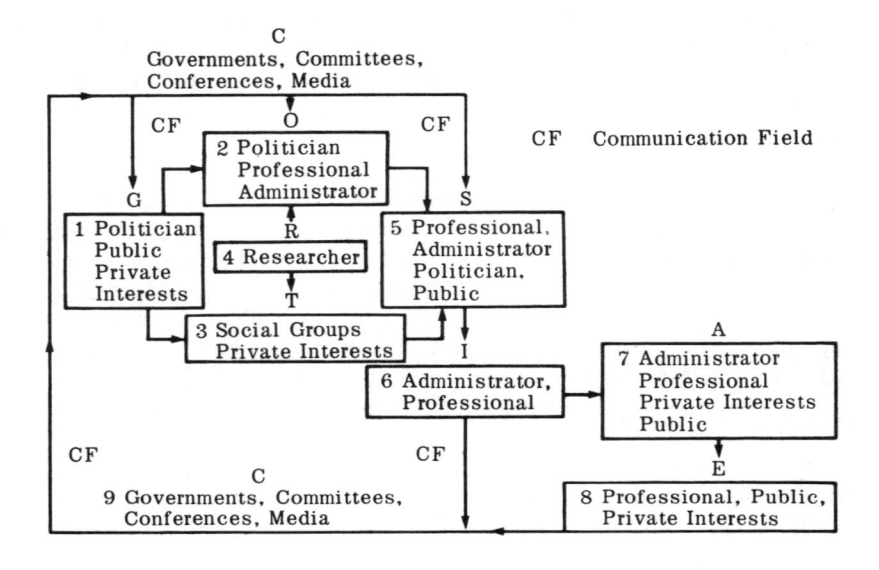

```
                    C
        Governments, Committees,
         Conferences, Media
         CF        O         CF           CF  Communication Field
              2 Politician
              Professional
              Administrator
      G                      S
1 Politician      R       5 Professional,
  Public     4 Researcher   Administrator
  Private          T         Politician,
  Interests                   Public
              3 Social Groups                  A
              Private Interests       7 Administrator
                          6 Administrator,    Professional
                            Professional      Private Interests
                                              Public
  CF                      CF                   E
              C                         8 Professional, Public,
     9 Governments, Committees,           Private Interests
       Conferences, Media
```

and the Minister of Treasury, Economics and Intergovernmental Affairs, Ontario, all kinds of professional people, organizations like the Urban Development Institutes and the Community Planning Association of Canada, as well as all forms of bilateral and tri-level meetings and conferences between federal, provincial and municipal governments. These meetings and negotiations (bilateral) and consultations (tri-level) may be seen, in terms of the policy process, as vital communication channels. That is the importance of the tri-level urban affairs process, which was launched nationally at a Tri-Level Conference in Toronto on November 21 and 22, 1972. The national (a second conference in Edmonton, October 22 and 23, 1973), provincial and metropolitan meetings that have followed are becoming essential to the conduct of government in a complex urban society. For they have two critical purposes: consultation across jurisdictional boundaries on shared urban problems and on possible solutions; and better co-ordination on urban policies among the three levels of government.

To understand the dynamics of the policy process, to grasp its potential realistically, we need to appreciate the play of forces operating both within and on government. Each participating jurisdiction has its own constitutional responsibilities and authority, and each is subject to the pressures of its own political environment. And Canada is a country in which the exercise of private power is a very real force, both directly in the land development and building industry, and in the strategic aspects of corporate planning and decision-making about capital investment and industrial development (Chapter 3).

URBAN POLICIES AND THE GOVERNMENT SYSTEM

In one important respect, however, the Canadian system of government is ideally arranged. Our diagnosis has pointed in two directions. One indicates that action on some of our conditions and problems, like putting the brakes on urban concentration nationally, requires a high degree of orchestration and co-ordination of effort between levels of government. And the other suggests that action on other concerns, like the struggle for a better environment, requires a high degree of autonomy and freedom of action, locally and regionally.

The first task involves the creation of a sound *national structure* for the good regional life. Large forces must be moved and shaped. A premium is placed in policy-making on attaining a goal consensus, on mobilizing limited resources across jurisdictional lines, and on precision in their application through the right levers, whether they be industrial incentives, housing, or direct public investments. Basic differences and conflicts between the actors concerned exact a very high price, and are counter-productive.

The second task places emphasis on quite different matters. The search for the right *form of settlement*, whether along the lines of the "open city" (Chapter 8), or otherwise, must be a search that is unique for each region, responding to its own history, needs, lifestyles, landscape and aspirations. Regional diversity is highly prized.

Viewed in this way, the Canadian government system, with its federal principle embodying the association of different levels of concern and action, has good potential for attaining the essential tasks of urban policy. Federal and provincial governments are well-equipped for the broad strategic role, and units of government and administration within provinces have the proximity to the conditions affecting settlement essential for sensitive planning. But the system is imperfect in a number of ways that will become apparent as we consider further some of the policy issues we have raised in the preceding chapters. These issues will be examined against the background of the policy process discussed here. By bearing in mind, in this way, the ultimate requirements of an effective process, some guidelines for helpful change will emerge.

432 CHANGING CANADIAN CITIES

NATIONAL AND BROAD REGIONAL ISSUES

(1) *Strategies for Cities of Different Size*
Growth, its distribution nationally between the major regions, Ontario *versus* the Prairies for example, and between cities of various sizes has emerged in our exposition as a major concern of Canadian people, and Canadian governments. At the same time, it has been established (Chapter 3) that the key to urban population distribution is urbanization: the process that increases the proportion of people who live in Canada in settlements of one thousand or more people, and the process which strongly influences the size, mix, and location of the entire set of settlements in the country.

If we as Canadians want to shape the size composition of Canadian cities along the lines envisaged in the imagined future, we must act directly on the urbanization process, fostering the growth of some places, restraining the growth of others and stabilizing the growth of a third group. A strategy highly integrated between sectors and governments is required, one bringing to bear a highly selective "battery of programs" that act on the most controllable factors. These are various aspects of the economic base affecting employment and income; particular services; and certain capacities for decision-making and for fostering innovative change. This approach may be illustrated by reference to three groups of cities spread along the urban growth continuum – small, medium to big. Each group responds to different objectives and requires a different policy/program approach (Table 9.1). Each combination of such programs represents a sub-strategy. Since there is a relationship between growth and environmental needs, these variations in "growth" objectives are reflected in the selected sub-strategies as variations in environmental objectives: to renew, maintain or enhance urban environments.

The accompanying table (9.1) demonstrates the deployment of federal programs. One could indicate also, for each province and many local and regional governments, programs that could play a role in the indicated strategies.

The essence of this approach is the formulation of sets of sub-strategies, for each city size group, as follows:

for big cities of 1,000,000 and over
- deflect employment and population
- support new regional forms
- improve the inner city

for medium-sized cities, 100,000 to 500,000+
- support good government

Table 9.1. Objectives, Strategies, Programs, by City Size Group

Objective by Size Group	I Restrain & Restructure Growth Renew Environment (Strategies and Programs)	II Stabilize Growth Maintain Environment (Strategies and Programs)	III Encourage Growth Enhance Environment (Strategies and Programs)
Urban Areas Size Group	*Big Cities* (1,000,000 +) Ex. Montreal Toronto Vancouver *deflect employment & population* Trade – Industrial Program Foreign Ownership Regulations Immigration Federal Decentralization *support new regional forms* Land Assembly New Communities Transportation, commuter *improve the inner city* Neighbourhood Improvement Residential Rehabilitation	*Medium Cities* (100,000 to 500,000 +) Ex. Regina Sudbury Quebec City *support good government* Research & Community Planning Urban Management *selectively improve growth-related facilities* Transportation Sewage Treatment Program Health Programs *strengthen and preserve environmental quality* Environmental Protection Historic restoration Neighbourhood Improvement	*Small Cities* (under 100,000) Ex. Lethbridge Brandon Fredericton *stimulate employment & population growth* Industrial Assistance Manpower Training Supply Program Advancement, Industrial Technology *provide for requirements of growth* Infrastructure Assistance Housing Sewage Treatment, Water *improve decision-making environment* National Telecommunications Devl. Computer Communications Research

- selectively improve growth-related facilities
- strengthen and preserve environmental quality

for small cities, under 100,000
- stimulate employment and population growth
- provide for the requirements of growth
- improve the decision-making environment and capacity

These sub-strategies become, in turn, the bases for the differentiated application of government policies and programs and hopefully for the private sector response. These are emphases and not to be interpreted as exclusive to each case. Nevertheless, by linking up broad policy objectives on urban growth with strategies and programs, a framework for greater effectiveness is created. The restraining of growth in Toronto and Vancouver and the encouragement of growth in Lethbridge and Fredericton become features of an urban strategy which is national in scope, although mainly provincial, regional and local in impact.[3]

(2) *Acting on the National Distribution of Population*[4]

While policies and programs that are sensitive to city size differences will help to attain the national urban patterns of "the imagined future," two inescapable questions remain: How big should a city grow? Or is there a population optimum? And which policy instruments (forms of intervention and programs) have the greatest potential for exerting significant influence on a nation's population distribution? There are likely to be a number of possible best or optimum sizes for cities. Current research does not suggest that product per person has declined as cities have grown; in fact, larger cities tend to have higher incomes than smaller ones. Even if certain costs are associated with size, there is a legitimate question whether a very large city may not serve an important role in the overall structure or hierarchy of cities and towns. Changes in the possibility of substituting telecommunications for transport, as well as in savings and economies associated with bigness, may dramatically affect the optimum population size. Moreover, these factors may change the optimum faster, and by magnitudes greater, than any policy can change actual population size. Hence, it is probably more appropriate to think of a range of population sizes within which a city can function best, with the range defined by environmental circumstances, available technology and institutional arrangements. In this context, the prime value of the concept of most appropriate size is that it provides a guide to asking certain questions which can in turn lead to solutions.

At any rate, regulations and incentives are based on the notion that there exists something (that is, a measure or function of well-being) which can be minimized or maximized, that it is advantageous to do so, and that a minimum or maximum position will not be reached automatically. Even setting aside the considerable difficulties of constructing a satisfactory index of well-being, it may be extremely difficult to correlate the index with variations in city size and type. Moreover, even if that were possible, it is not certain that the "peak" in question is the highest one, or that a distribution problem does not remain. The value for a well-being function is likely to vary not only with city size but also with a city's internal structure and with its position in an urban network or hierarchy.

Limits to increased efficiency occur because of constraints arising internally or externally. A city is a product of socio-economic as well as physical factors. Some of these factors change more rapidly than others, with the result that they differentially impose limits. A city might be regarded as one large input-output system, with "conduits" along which flow the inputs and outputs of human activities. Being limited in size, these conduits are subject to increasing congestion and rising costs. As well, there may be increasing costs to co-ordination. Similarly, the physical external environment of a city will set a limit to growth since, after a point, there are no substitutes for physical environment.

(3) *The Issue of City Size*

A tendency for a city to grow beyond some optimum size (or sizes) could reflect either a lack of built-in adjustment to problems and stresses, or the generation of substantial social costs falling primarily on the residential sector but generated by the commercial/industrial sector. For cities, balancing mechanisms which compensate for maladjustments are generally weak and moderate only slightly the forces working towards concentration.

Socio-economic systems are generally one of two types: (1) those subject to regulation through more or less centralized decision-making processes and sets of procedures; or (2) those given a degree of direction by non-centralized "cues" and dispersed sets of decisions in the *laissez-faire* tradition. A city is essentially a system of the latter sort. Unlike, say, a business firm, the index for maximization in a city is nebulous, badly defined and difficult to achieve. The methods that have been generally applied to "determine" optimum size (for example, survivorship and models of revealed preference) are clearly less effective as measures of size for cities than for firms.

Unquestionably, there are longer lags in the response of occupants of a city to excess size, and information processes at work are less efficient in throwing up the anomalies likely to lead to a response.

Moreover, the decision to move may not be as clearly associated with size or the index of well-being as one might expect. In fact, it is not size *per se* that stimulates out-migration, but rather correlates of size such as anomie and alienation, the absence of competitively priced inputs, and noxious environmental forces stemming from negative externalities, (e.g. congestion, noise, blight, pollution, lawlessness and lack of open space).[5] At least, these reasons appear to have been more dominant in the substantial exodus which took place from U.S. central cities during the 1960s.

With a variety of assumptions, it is not difficult to imagine a system with a capacity for self-adjustment, and sensitive to increasing divergences from optimality. Such a system would require that the individual and firms that generate social costs pay for them, that market competition be effective, and that the price system permit the shifting of costs among producers and consumers. This system might please economists, but the *economic* equilibrium implied may still not be at the level considered optimum since the economic indicator might not be highly enough correlated with the index of well-being.

It is useful to distinguish between direct and indirect "causes" for the divergence of actual from optimum distributions of population. Indirect causes are primarily associated with public policies: national transport policies, distribution of regulatory power, the establishment of regional jurisdictions, and most critically explicit or implicit policies concerning the size and distribution of a nation's population (Chapters 1, 2, and 3). Direct causes have seven principal sources: (1) an urban community may take a long time to become aware of problems created by the cumulative impact of a large number of separate decisions and actions (sometimes called a "high sensitivity threshold"); and therefore remedial action may not be timely; (2) public policy decisions may be irreversible or reversible only with long time lags; (3) a city may lack regulatory power, or the will to exercise it; (4) opportunity for generating and seizing excessive returns from urban land may stimulate speculators, due particularly to superior information; (5) the shifting of social costs from the private to the public sector may exacerbate growth trends because private sector decision-makers do not bear all costs of their decisions; (6) there may be a lack of information on alternatives and/or alternatives may be incorrectly evaluated; and (7) technological change may affect either actual or optimum sizes.

Of these seven causes of divergence of actual from optimum population distribution, land speculation, externalities, and the lack of information are most important because they probably result in an increasing divergence. High sensitivity thresholds and irreversible policy decisions work to reduce the degree of homeostatic response. Regulatory power and technological change are presumably institutionally determined and hence subject to discrete changes over the longer term.

These two sets of factors, the direct and the indirect, that cause maladjustment between actual and optimum populations, suggest two corresponding policy approaches. These are: (1) the establishment of *direct* countervaillants to particular sources of population maldistribution; and (2) the formation of policies with respect to transportation, regional growth, industrial incentives, and the like, so as to defuse the forces leading to concentration *indirectly* through influencing the decision to migrate. Considering these approaches it will be useful to keep in mind relevant Canadian, U.S. and West European experience.

(4) Direct Countervailants
The *direct* problems of the insensitivity of cities as systems and irreversible policy decisions may be treated jointly. It may be possible to utilize a number of distinct indicators differentially sensitive to different phenomena associated with variations in city size. Given the large number of possible indicators, those with which we are most concerned are those sensitive to changes, like air quality and housing costs (Chapter 5). Indeed, our view is that the promise of social and/or urban indicators lies not so much in establishing new general indicators as much as it does in establishing the utility of indicators for sub-components of the social and urban system.

In the case of *insufficient regulatory power* at the city level, the appropriate solution is a redistribution of jurisdictional powers, possibly including the restructuring of local government. Forms of taxation to publicly appropriate property values created by public investments (betterment taxation), though imperfect as the British experience demonstrates, could contribute towards a solution through taxation of excessive *urban land profits*. Likewise, financial "carrots or sticks" can be used to ameliorate the impact of shifted social costs once they have been identified and quantified. Public ownership of land around a city's boundaries, an option which has recently received attention, would permit more comprehensive planning of urban land use and direct public accountability for the size of urban agglomerations. The problem of lack of knowledge of alternatives would not be easily overcome, though presumably there is some scope through education and institutionalized exchange of information. Uncertainty among those who attempt to formulate policies is further exacerbated by the need to anticipate *technological change*, though this is easier said than done.

Notwithstanding the immense difficulties, many governments have attempted to implement some variant of direct controls with respect either to employment or to land use and building development. It is the latter which have been employed most frequently, though studies concerning the control of population distribution have concentrated almost exclusively on the former.

Controls over the location of employment have taken the form of licensing of industrial and office buildings in the United Kingdom, construction and occupancy permits in France, special construction/investment taxes in the Netherlands and Finland, and compulsory "consultations" in Sweden.[6] The rationale for such policies is reduction of employment demand, but the difficulty is that governments are seldom willing to compromise possible damages to economic growth or to the "status" of their largest cities. Generally, controls have been applied only as a reluctant last resort after incentives have proved inadequate, and they are inevitably the least popular of program measures, always resisted and attacked.[7]

The number of possible controls on land use and building development is extremely wide, ranging from classic zoning through specific tax and grant inducements, to sophisticated systems for transfers of development rights (TDRs). Although in operation throughout most Western countries, there is little evidence to suggest that such controls have a beneficial long run effect on shaping or restraining urban growth, and some evidence that they have contrary effects.[8] In Canada, one of the more edifying cases of land use planning has been in Alberta, where a regional system and a form of development control forestalled historic abuses during a period of very high urban growth rates in the 'fifties through to the 'seventies. In contrast the *ad hoc* and uneven application of rigid planning controls not surprisingly has perverse effects. Crude physical planning instruments intended to limit urban growth, such as the current "freeze" on buildings above a designated height in Toronto, are largely an inappropriate means of achieving what is, to a great extent, a social goal. The establishment of such limits has, for example, been assailed by one Toronto researcher for generally resulting in the redistribution of wealth and social opportunities, largely in socially regressive directions against those who can least afford it.[9] But a measure like height control may be useful as a short term tactic to buy time for a re-thinking of basic development policies.

A number of problems are posed by the direct implementation of controls on buildings, land and employment. First, regulations are sometimes exercised within geographical boundaries inappropriate to the task. If we are dealing with an urbanized region, the appropriate focus for regulating urban growth is at the metropolitan and not at the central city level. Secondly, an enthusiasm for controls must be tempered by the consideration that controls also provide greater scope for political chicanery. Thirdly, and most important, controls are often imposed on strong market forces, and when in conflict, are subverted by such forces. Nevertheless, they probably do have potential where developed and used in concert with a battery of policies which *indirectly* influence migration and population distribution.

(5) *Influencing the migration process*
Given the tendency of foreign immigrants to cluster in the largest urban areas, Canadian policy-makers concerned with the migration process have flirted with the idea of imposing restrictions on where newcomers may settle. According to the parliamentary Committee on Immigration Policy, future immigrants could be required to sign contracts specifying where they would live and work for a few years. If the contract were violated, the persons could be expelled or denied social services.

A more acceptable, and generally more viable alternative for decentralizing urban growth is a package of regional development policies. The issue of regional development is multi-faceted, and requires a full range of policy initiatives, some of which are listed on Table 9.2. To influence the distribution of the population, policies that affect the demand for labour (such as industrial incentive programs or foreign investment policies) or the supply of skills (such as manpower development/training programs) almost certainly have to be developed in concert. Programs to disseminate information on alternative employment opportunities, as well as programs to provide infrastructure – housing, transportation, utilities and so on – either within cities or between cities are also necessary. If regional development efforts are to result in the growth of alternative centres, governments cannot hedge on the provision of basic infrastructure.

Many of the countries of Western Europe – Britain, France, Italy, the Netherlands and Sweden – have attempted some form of comprehensive program for population dispersal and regional development. In each country, the original objective of the growth policy was to alleviate the plight of economically depressed areas. But as the ill effects of overcongestion in the metropolitan centres came to the fore, they adopted the broader goals of restraining growth in expanding areas, reducing inter-regional population flows and even, in some cases, specifying, in detail, the geographical distribution of jobs and population. Simultaneously the program of measures to achieve the ends broadened considerably. On the foundation of their first halting steps to improve physical infrastructure, provide industrial parks, and offer limited aid for new enterprise through loans

Table 9.2. Regional Development/Population Dispersal Policies

I. Policies to Affect the Demand for Labour Through the Location of Industry

(1) capital, labour and land subsidies to private sector locations (e.g. industrial incentives)

(2) provision of physical infrastructures to improve market operation (e.g. transportation, housing and utilities)

(3) government procurement policies

(4) decentralization of government offices and installation which directly provide as well as induce employment (e.g. defence bases, experimental farms, airports, hospitals, colleges and universities)

(5) foreign investment policies.

II Policies to Affect the Labour Supply

(1) mobility and retraining grants

(2) information on alternative employment opportunities

(3) contracts with landed immigrants to settle in designated locations.

III Comprehensive Alternatives Packages

(1) selective assistance to identified growth centres

(2) new community development

---

and tax concessions, the West European countries have erected complexes of mutually reinforcing policies. To stem the flow of migrants to the major urban centres, these nations have adopted, with varying degrees of emphasis, four approaches: (1) improvement in facilities and services to prepare areas of economic decline and out-migration for industrial growth; (2) industrial incentives, including cash grants, to encourage investors to locate in "development areas"; (3) disincentives and moral suasion to discourage investment in the major metropolitan areas; and (4) decentralization of government agencies, universities and state-controlled industries.[10] The co-ordination of such programs is generally assured through comprehensive regional development planning, which comprises a growth centre strategy in all five nations, and in Britain, Sweden and France, a new towns policy.

Although moving toward the same goals and gradually progressing in the same policy direction, regional development programs in the United States and Canada have not evolved to the same extent as have the European programs. As in the European case, Canadian development efforts began with improvements to the physical infrastructure, largely in rural areas (Prairie Farm Rehabilitation Act, 1935; Maritime Marshlands Rehabilitation Act, 1948; Agriculture Rural Development Act, 1961) and then proceeded to development of industrial parks and the provision of loans to prospective investors (Area Development Act, 1963). Priorities for the first initiatives were set according to the "worst first" rule and programs focused on small, chronically depressed, peripheral areas.[11] Hence welfare rather than development principles were stressed; equity considerations were accorded greater importance than efficiency. With the establishment of the Department of Regional Economic Expansion (1969), comprehensive regional development as a long term federal government priority came into its own. A multi-dimensional approach to the pursuit of developmental opportunities by means of the co-ordinated application of public policies and programs at both the federal and provincial level has been urged by the Department. In effect, a two-pronged effort has been mounted by DREE, including incentive grants (Regional Development Incentives Act) designed to stimulate private capital investment in manufacturing and processing facilities and the provision of physical as well as social infrastructure via its Special Area Program. Though essentially uncoordinated between departments, governmental activity has also involved mobility and retraining grants for labour and, more recently, a policy of decentralizing federal government employees and adapting procurement policies to regional development goals.

The full complement of programs and legislation necessary to support a national policy of population redistribution has not yet been developed in Canada. Although growth centre policy has been favoured in some circles, the strategy has never become a major plank in the nation's regional development program. The founding of "new communities" in Canada has been limited with some worthy exceptions in Alberta, Ontario and Quebec to northern single enterprise, resources towns. Unlike the European case, they have not been employed to any great extent as a technique for decentralizing growth.

With a substantial proportion of the manufacturing sector owned by foreign interests, and a heavy concentration of that industry in southwestern Ontario, foreign investment policy is probably critical for deflecting growth from the dense Windsor-Toronto corridor.[12] To the present time, however, the Foreign Investment Review Agency does not use "conformity with regional development policy" as a criterion for evaluating the acceptability of investment.

(6) *Population distribution: The Lesson of Experience*
In review, we note that a wide range of policies have been employed

to effect population redistribution, including improvement of community and regional facilities and services, financial incentives, government office dispersal, government procurement preferences, growth centre strategies and new town development. As individual measures these have had a mixed and uneven effectiveness, as may be illustrated by reference to the two most far-reaching of these measures: financial incentives and growth centre strategies.

Financial Incentives: Loans and loan guarantees, though popular in the United States and Canada, exert little influence on the locational decisions of strong, expanding companies with ample credit, although they may support marginal enterprises.

Tax concessions were once offered by most European countries, but direct subsidies in the form of cash grants are now preferred. To minimize subsidy budgets, most European countries, except Britain, have tried to employ rigorous eligibility tests. Generally, financial incentives, are thought to be effective in transferring new industry to designated areas.[13]

However, incentive grants have been, at best, marginal in affecting decisions on the location of tertiary activity (e.g. head offices). If the French experience is a reliable indicator, convincing the service sector to disperse is very difficult.[14]

Growth Centre Strategies and New Town Developments: Recognizing that lagging areas will rebound faster if investment is focused on a relatively few sites that exhibit potential for growth, many European countries have adopted growth centre strategies. Given the limited knowledge at hand and the political pressures involved, the selection of growth centres has, in practice, been somewhat arbitrary. As a comprehensive development package aimed at decentralizing growth, the British new towns' policy has met with a measure of success, particularly as it affects London.[15] However, the lesson of the British new town experience is that the success of a population dispersal policy depends on the co-ordinated implementation of a *battery* of policies over a reasonably *long-term* planning horizon.

Our assessment leads us to the conclusion that the achievement of objectives concerning population distribution depends on the formulation of a coherent, many-sided, policy package and its subsequent implementation over a long period of time. For example, the dual approach of subsidizing migration to help workers go where jobs are and regional development, to create jobs where idle workers live, is likely to meet with greater success than either approach by itself.

Secondly, although a federal form of government complicates the achievement of consensus on a national population policy, it may prove beneficial for the administration of regional development programs. A West European country like France, with a traditionally centralized form of government has been obliged, in response to severe political pressure, to "invent" regional organizations for development planning purposes.

(7) *A Strategy for Resource Frontier Regions*
In this book we have drawn attention to two sets of related conditions that are integral parts of the Canadian development pattern. One is the existence of quite a large number of small, isolated, unstable resource towns dispersed throughout the country's resource hinterland (Chapter 5). The other is the existence of a number of regions having a substantial, but largely unrealized potential for regional development, along with a settlement pattern that is relatively weak in terms of the number, size and facilities of centres (Chapter 4). An example of the first is provided by the mining communities of northern Saskatchewan and Manitoba; and of the second, by the Peace River region in Alberta. As indicated by these examples, the two sets of conditions often co-exist. Both are "resource frontier regions" – areas which are non-contiguous with Canada's main settlement corridor, and areas associated with investments in mineral, forest or power development, and less frequently, in agriculture.[16]

The co-existence of an unfulfilled community life and a large development potential suggests the main contours of a strategy for such regions. It is in essence straightforward. Concentrate instead of scatter population; foster a diversified pattern of economic development as opposed to an unrelated, lopsided dispersal of mine and forest-based projects. In so doing, create a stronger urban service system with at least one regional growth centre, having a sufficient range of business, personal and professional services to support development well beyond the level of extractive communities. And create an economic base of enough diversity, stability and strength to support a level of living that approximates the Canadian average.

In pursuit of these regional objectives, such a strategy would align with provincial and national strategies to attain a less centralized national pattern of settlement and economic growth. Indeed, if we view Canada's development broadly, the transformation of our so-called zone of resource exploitation (Figure 5.1), making it a more humanized, livable and productive environment, is one of the important tasks of the late twentieth century. If that can be achieved, then the Canadian urban pattern will not fulfil the calamitous forecasts of super-concentration of population and deepened inequality in the regional distribution of national wealth (Chapter 2).

It is this perspective, together with the very promising prospects of at least some of Canada's regions of the mid-north – as illustrated in the Peace River case study (Chapter 4) – that makes regional development planning the focus of a strategy for resource frontier regions. In this respect, Canada's development joins hands with the countries of the Third World. The development plan becomes a pivotal device, and for very much the same reasons. Investment capital for our zone of resource exploitation is comparatively scarce and must be allocated on the basis of well-considered priorities. "Planning is compelled by Poverty," as Galbraith has expressed it, meaning in such cases, capital poverty. The Plan, or more realistically, a development planning process, becomes the vehicle for breaking the established patterns of exploitation, and replacing it with a mechanism for development and desirable social change.

While there are no formulae for such plans, the experience of the Peace River region suggests that the development planning process will include comprehensive resource inventories and economic studies; social studies of the history, conditions and aspirations of the people; the formulation of policies related to resource development, growth, human settlement, services and environmental quality; and programs for the integrated stage-by-stage development of the region. The people of the region will be involved in the policy and decision-making process through local councils, regional planning commissions and various community groups. And planning at this scale will have to link up with policies and programs at the provincial and federal levels, both to assure reasonable concordance of objectives, and to benefit from the mobilization of larger capital resources – the indispensable requirement for the balanced development of resource frontier regions.

LAND STRATEGIES

Land – its use, cost, ownership and development – is a concern that has run through our book. The overview of land as a public policy issue in Canada (Chapter 6) leads to one over-riding conclusion: the land in the urban fringe of places with 10,000 and more people is the most critical 85,000 square miles in Canada. For this is the land which, in the last quarter of the twentieth century, will have to serve many of the vital needs of Canadians: it includes space for constructing communities; much of our "foodland," including most of the dairysheds of the country; the much-in-demand outdoor recreational land within a one day round trip distance from cities; and it includes many kinds of ecological resources, from rare plant species and wind shelter forests to major ground water storage areas. This land is truly a national resource.

We have also discovered that the future of this national resource is precarious. And it is made so by the very process of urbanization that is associated with the maturing of Canada's economic system, with the increase of national income and with the formation of our settlement patterns. As long as our national population was dispersed, the regional concentration of people not very great, and the various demands for land quite modest, then the impact of the urbanization process was no matter of great concern. But we are now in a period when the public issues related to land are becoming more sharply defined, and the consequences of our responses as individuals, groups and governments, are much more far-reaching. The issues concern cost and equity, preservation and use, and planning and control.

It is not necessary to demonstrate the existence of land speculation to observe that the steep rise in land prices in the fringe areas of most metropolitan regions since the mid-fifties contributed to the inflation of housing costs (Chapter 6), constituted a veiled tax on industry, and, redistributed income regressively. Wealth has moved from the poor and modestly comfortable to others, probably the immodestly rich, because land dealing and land development takes large capital resources. "Land speculation companies," argues Maurice Yeates, "own large tracts of land around major metropolitan areas, and in the Toronto sub-area, prices for agricultural land are now so high that it is difficult to believe that the entire area is not held for speculative purposes."[17]

The mischief of high land costs has been compounded, because it coincides with a time in the evolution of many of our metropolitan areas when the preservation of recreational land, and the responsible use of other land for urban growth involves public control on an unprecedented scale. Examples of this are the Niagara Escarpment, the Parkway Belt and sites for new communities in Ontario; sites for regional town centres in the Greater Vancouver district; and the provision of a bank of reasonably-priced land for housing along much of the "main street" from Windsor to Quebec City. Since the public control of strategic lands cannot be assured by the zoning power under provincial legislation, governments have no recourse but to obtain some form of title to the required land, either by outright purchase or easements, or by some other form of agreement with owners to acquire or constrain development rights. The escalation of land prices, however, is making the fulfilment of such programs increasingly difficult, if not prohibitive, and the public in general is the loser. This is particularly serious in the case of unique recreational land which if lost to urban or industrial purposes will be irretrievable.[18]

The third land issue concerns the vulnerability of Canada's most productive land. Over half of the country's first class agricultural land is in southern Ontario, in the path of heavy urbanization; much of the rest is within commuting distance of metropolitan centres in other provinces. Continuation of historic land use patterns will be more harmful than in the past, as many varieties of expanding demands compete for *a limited base* of quality land. The consequences are both regional and national, affecting both the quality and cost of living. For example, the next phase of farmland loss in Ontario will make the province a net importer of food, with repercussions on living costs, balance of payments, and so on.[19]

This overview suggests the need for a strategy that will moderate increases in the cost of land, allocate productive land to farming and comparatively unproductive areas to urban uses, and make possible the public control of lands that are strategic for growth management and recreational environments. Each of these needs will require a specific set of policy instruments, which will have greatest impact if they can be applied in a co-ordinated way – between problems and between levels of government.

While the conditions that surround the cost, use and control, of land are too complex to permit any neat blueprint solution, it is possible to sketch a policy scenario that may have some prospect of success. This is it:

A Federal-Provincial conference on urban fringe lands, would be held with the municipalities concerned invited to participate by their respective provinces.

The primary purpose of the conference would be to achieve some consensus on the *aims* of land use policy for the 85,000 square miles of urban fringe lands, and to set up a collaborative *mechanism* for producing a land use policy for such areas. This might be seen as an initial step towards a "national land-use policy" along the lines suggested by the Federal Environment Minister – "The several levels of government and the private sector will have to work together to develop an acceptable framework of land-use principles" (October 7, 1975).[20]

The immediate achievement of the conference would be an agreement on the *aims* of a land use policy which because of the nature of the issues, would present a philosophy for reconciling the competing demands for land: urban, agricultural, recreational, industrial, etc. It might, for example, adopt as a broad goal that Class 1, 2, 3 and Special Crop lands be reserved for agricultural purposes.

Task forces would be set up, by agreement at the conference, to explore *mechanisms* for obtaining consensual objectives, both those that can be applied by individual provinces and those requiring inter-governmental action. These task forces would be invited to report back to a second conference within say a period of one year.

SOME CONCLUSIONS AND POLICY NOTES   447

This in effect would be a conference that defined and launched a policy for Canada's urban fringe lands.

An important feature of this federal-provincial effort would be the lubrication of the information network on land policy in Canada. A process of information pooling and sharing, and critical comparative appraisal of different approaches to shared problems would be initiated. This pool of policy experience would, for example, include:

> the land freeze and designation of agricultural reserves in British Columbia;
>
> the comprehensive regional planning, and modified development control in Alberta;
>
> agricultural land banking in Saskatchewan, as well as urban land banking and management of the development process in Saskatoon;
>
> Manitoba's multi-faceted effort to offer a "stay option" for rural residents;
>
> The Niagara Escarpment Act, urban land banking, and tax on land speculation in Ontario;
>
> Quebec's interest in land conservation through a provincial plan;[21]
>
> Such concepts, in the Atlantic region, as Prince Edward Island's "minimum maintenance" approach – defining management levels for each major category of land capability.[22]

Out of this type of process there would gradually emerge a many-sided, multi-level strategy that might include the following: (1) provincial and municipal designation of the best agricultural, recreational and ecologically valuable lands through land use plans and zoning instruments; (2) the adjustment of land assessment policy to align valuations for tax purposes with land use policy, so that financial pressures on agricultural and other land would be eased; (3) the adoption of regional plans to direct housing, industry, other urban uses, and ex-urbanite homes to areas of relatively low productivity, and which establish regional gradients of population density and policies on residential in-fill, with a view to reducing the demand for fringe land; (4) long-term programs of strategic land banking, initiated and partly financed provincially, to be used flexibly either to salvage unique recreational resources, or to acquire and reserve development sites; (5) the co-ordination with the adopted land use plans of major provincial and federal facilities: highways, harbours, airports, hydro, water and sewage pipelines and treatment facilities, gas and oil pipelines, etc., for the purpose of reinforcing conservation and development objectives.

High on the agenda of the federal-provincial task force would be two basic concerns requiring joint study and action; (6) the relationship of broad policy areas – such as credit, tax, tariff, price support, trade, marketing – to the maintenance of a viable agricultural industry on Canada's best farm lands; and (7) the desirability and feasibility of the acquisition as "a national resource" of certain very important farming areas – the Niagara Fruit Belt, parts of the Lower Mainland in British Columbia, parts of the St. Lawrence Lowlands around Montreal – which are under such heavy competitive pressure from prospective urban uses that their total demise is predictable. Here the efficacy of the Saskatchewan technique of keeping the land productive by its lease back to *bona fide* farmers would have to be evaluated.[23]

Developing a sound land strategy is a very great challenge to the political leadership of this country. As our sketch of one approach indicates, all levels of government will have to get into the act. In the foregoing seven point strategy, all three levels of government are involved in numbers 1, 4, 5, 6 and 7; and provincial and municipal governments both have responsibilities for numbers 2 and 3.

Another observation that emerges from the scenario is the web of inter-relationships between problem and action areas. A land use policy would not only preserve good farm land, but by defining urban development constraints and potentials should – if the authorities demonstrate that they mean business – gradually restrain land prices. Selective lower assessments, regional plans, and land sensitive infrastructure corridors should work in the same direction. And, of course, any effort that moderates price level and public costs of acquisition will enhance public control for better growth management and the reservation of unique recreational/environmental resources and so on.

Perhaps this strategy has been explored sufficiently to demonstrate that the federal and provincial governments, if they have the public interest at heart, will establish an ongoing mechanism for monitoring the impact of their joint action, and for the periodic feedback and communication of results so that implementation problems can be identified and adjustments and improvements made in any part of the policy process that feels the strain. This will be difficult and demanding but surely worthwhile if it means the wise use of our precious but limited heritage of good land.

STRATEGIES FOR THE INNER CITY

We have projected a view of the future that embodies some quite definite values: opportunities for individual fulfilment, and for the choice and diversity of large integrated regions, as well as the joys of community identity and participation; a secluded neighbourhood life without loss of people control at the level of regional government; the expression of social justice in the distribution of housing, services and facilities between areas and groups; places of equality as well as diversity, of economic stability and flexibility; places where the air and water are not seriously polluted, where there is access to a beautiful countryside and where the older inner city experiences a process of renewal.

There is of course no way in which any person, group or government can guarantee the future. We shape our various utopias day-by-day in a multitude of personal and corporate decisions. Our ideals always appear to be within reach and at the same time devilishly elusive. Our experience, however, is cumulative. We can learn. The scale of contemporary urban development and the importance of certain large impersonal forces that operate on entire systems place a special obligation on governments to use the collective resources of society, to improve our understanding of problems, to try out solutions, to learn from mistakes, to create better solutions and services, and, step-by-step, to improve the delivery of services to people. We dignify these things with the words research, planning policies, strategies, programs, implementation and so on.

It is with this perspective in mind that we turn in conclusion to a policy area which, in the period immediately preceding the writing of this book, has been noted for perceptive diagnosis: the policy research on the inner city conducted at the Ministry of State for Urban Affairs (Chaper 7). While this work has not yet entered the policy stream, it will unquestionably make an impact. It provides a foundation for a broad and sensitive approach to the conditions of Canada's inner cities.

The key insight of the research has already been described (Chapter 7). There are at least four inner cities, four sets of conditions—each with its own potentials, problems and needs. Governments that presume to legislate, make policies and offer programs for such areas must be aware of these distinctions, if they are to avoid applying the wrong remedies and make matters worse. In all cases it is a *human condition* that is being considered, which is by its very nature many-sided. Strategies developed for such areas must accordingly be both broad and flexible, covering a wide range of economic, social and physical alternatives. These must be evolved within a general philosophy or image of the inner city. The attitudes and values of Canadians lean away from uniformity – consisting of only high-rise buildings or a single social class – towards the goal of a "diverse, multi-functional inner city, serving the needs of a variety of residents and users."[24]

Strategies have to be developed in direct response to the circumstances of the different inner cities, in the following way:[25]

The conditions	The strategy
Declining Areas steady loss of population particularly families and the economically mobile unemployment worsening houses and environment, including some crowding deepening social problems, poverty, family disruption lack of community organizations, capacity for self-help	*to stimulate* social change and economic improvement by channelling new capital, users, residents and functions into such areas, by • improving the delivery of social services • providing job opportunities • making rehabilitated housing available to low income groups • providing an alternative to rooming houses • introducing new functions and groups
Stable Areas stability in population, age, family/household mix, and income some unsteadiness in employment physical conditions decently maintained few serious social problems potential for effective community organization some external pressure for change	*to protect*, strengthen and improve the residential character, and its population and functional mix by • improving job security • strengthening the residential character of such areas • rehabilitating housing • developing and applying protective planning controls • assisting community organizations
Revitalizing Areas population disrupted by influx of upper and middle income households; mix of family and non-family units poorer households being pushed out physical conditions improving through private rehabilitation rapidly rising land and housing costs pressure for redevelopment	*to moderate* the rise of housing prices and the displacement of low income people, as well as strengthen residential character by • retaining low and medium income groups • increasing residential density to more economic levels • restraining rising land and housing costs • enforcing residential zoning

The conditions	The strategy
Massively Redeveloping Areas Population increasing overall, with loss in family units, and gain in single, young couples, the elderly Average income, educational and occupational levels increasing Housing conditions improving for newcomers, and declining for the displaced Environmental quality, selectively improving along with congestion and strain on services Housing and land costs increasing Striking shift to tenancy Strength of community organizations declining	*to control* more effectively, the process of large scale redevelopment through channelling high-density development into preferred locations, protection for certain lower-density uses, and provision for the needs of both the displaced and new populations, by • selectively locating community facilities for high-density redevelopment • introducing some medium-density, low-rise forms of development • retaining suitable housing for the resident population • fostering innovative design and construction for high-rise development, particularly for family living and special groups like the elderly • evolving and applying development standards

An important feature of the foregoing approach to inner city problems is that the framework of strategies provides a sound basis for the selective combination of programs to be applied by the governments concerned to each of the different cases. In this way, inner city policies can be carried out to a very significant degree by the packaging and application of existing programs. This requires a high degree of flexibility in the implementation stage. For example, housing, health and welfare, and economic development programs would be mixed in almost equal proportions in declining areas, while housing programs, particularly rehabilitation and neighbourhood improvement, would predominate in stable areas. The framework of selective strategies also provides guidelines for new programs that may be required, for example programs of community employment in declining areas, or of housing in-fill in revitalizing areas.

This view of inner city policies illustrates one of the dilemmas of urban program delivery: urban strategies are inherently multi-sectoral while delivery mechanisms are usually uni-sectoral. This calls for organizations near the scene of activity – the cities and regions – which are capable of a highly co-ordinated effort.

The complexity of inner city strategies and programs makes it imperative that the evaluation and communication stages of the policy process be emphasized not only as a kind of insurance against folly, but also as an integral part of sensitive policy-making. The linking of research/diagnosis, strategies and implementation should build a sound basis for action. But the many-sided nature of inner city problems, as well as solutions, gives extraordinary importance to keeping communication channels wide open.

Urban Settlement, Urban Policy and the Style of Governing

Issues of settlement form and the quality of environment are mainly regional in their impact. This is true for the human needs that have to be satisfied for the entire hierarchy of groups ranging from the family to the metropolis. It is true for the co-ordinates of form and structure that oscillate between the poles of concentration and dispersion, region-wide specialization and sub-regional integration. And it is true for the variables that shape the form of settlement: the location of employment and services, residential density and distribution, the urban transportation system, and open space and leisure (Chapter 8).

These are categories that intimately affect the lives of people, and as such they should be capable of being acted upon decisively by the units of government that are closest to where people have their homes. We have in fact seen this potential as one of the special virtues of the Canadian government system (see above, "urban policies and the government system").

While fully acknowledging the regional primacy of these issues in considering strategies for influencing the form of settlement and quality of environment, it becomes immediately apparent that provincial and federal governments are deeply involved. This is as true for housing, which perhaps among all urban functions, makes the predominant impact on the character of local and regional governments, as it is for employment and services, for transportation, and for major undertakings like planning and building new communities.

To illustrate this point and to trace its consequences we will again turn to an aspect of inner city policy, because that is an area where the implications of inter-governmental relationships are vividly demonstrated. On the face of it, the reasons for the involvement of federal and provincial governments in the development and renewal of inner cities are no mystery.

In a number of inner city areas, senior governments have office establishments and/or are big landlords. Each have responsibilities in policy areas that impinge on the inner city – the provinces, in the fields of welfare, education, housing, recreation, community planning and cultural matters; and the federal government, employment, industry, immigration, and housing as well. Such areas are highly conspicuous and sensitive to changing economic fortunes. They are the frames for the cores of the country's major urban regions. Concern for inner city conditions is in part a concern for the viability of these business and civic cores which establish the identity of a place, as demonstrated by Montreal, Winnipeg or Vancouver.

For all these reasons, since about 1955, municipalities all across the country have enjoyed the blessings of provincial and federal help with inner city problems. This help, in theory, has augmented financial resources, multiplied the potential for doing good. But it is an experience which has also been fraught with hazards. With the best of intentions each level of government adopts mechanisms to discharge their political and financial responsibilities, to see that funds are used legitimately and efficiently, to be sure that program objectives are carried out, that there is fair play, that programs are applied consistently – and, less magnanimously, to be noticed when political bouquets are being handed out. The difficulty arises when all these good intentions are translated into administrative processes.

The problem is illustrated by the Neighbourhood Improvement Program (NIP), introduced in an amendment to the National Housing Act in June, 1973. NIP (Part III.1), was heralded as a new, flexible approach to inner city improvement. Its key concept was a federal-provincial agreement which would define the rules of the game; the scope of programs, the criteria for eligible neighbourhoods, the annual funding available through Central Mortgage and Housing Corporation. Within this framework, each province would work out an acceptable arrangement with participating municipalities. The details of implementation would be left to the discretion of the city working with the communities designated as Neighbourhood Improvement Areas. The National Housing Act specifies that through the agreements, the province or municipality concerned is to provide, as a condition for approval of NIP projects, information on how "the participation of residents" is to be obtained.[26]

After two years of operation NIP has had a success of a kind. Agreements have been signed with the Provinces of Saskatchewan, Manitoba, Ontario, New Brunswick, Nova Scotia and Newfoundland. Some 252 NIP areas have been identified in 191 municipalities, involving a federal expenditure of close to $150,000,000, including amounts for such implementation items as social-recreational facilities (44 per cent), municipal services (23 per cent), land for social housing (15 per cent). Small as well as large municipalities are participating; 35 per cent of federal allocations have been in communities with less than 30,000 people.[27]

It is, of course, too early to offer a verdict on the overall effectiveness of the program. That must await further experience. But there are some symptoms of stress – early warning signals – which we would do well to heed. The difficulty appears to be not with the philosophy of the program, but with the way it is administered.

The disturbing bureaucratic fact that forces attention is that at the very end of 1975, no NIP funds had been expended in Toronto, a city which contains a substantial number of the neighbourhoods for which the program was intended. These are defined by CMHC eligibility criteria as areas having "a significant portion of the housing stock ... in need of rehabilitation," areas "inhabited for the most part by people with low or moderate incomes," and as neighbourhoods in which "amenities such as playgrounds, community centres, etc. are deficient. . . . "[28]

Behind this awkward Toronto statistic lies a tortuous tale of intergovernmental discussion, negotiation, conflict and impasse. Cutting through all of the detail to the essential trouble, we are led to this conclusion: the role of each level of government, and of neighbourhood groups, are confused – they are tripping over each other to the detriment of the public interest. The reasons for this are deep and complex. They range all the way from a sterile bureaucratic adherence to outmoded thinking, practices and legislation, to excessive paternalism, to lack of trust, to the confusion of the fundamental goal – the improvement of the human condition – with mere administrative criteria. The evidence and diagnosis that underlie these generalizations support a serious indictment of the urban government system.[29]

Our interest is not to establish blame – a fruitless endeavour in any case in view of the intermeshing of so many factors – but point to the necessity of change. The Toronto NIP experience has been cited because it demonstrates a fundamental dilemma in the delivery of complex programs in a federal state. On the one hand, provincial and federal governments assume responsibility for coping with some of the impact of Canada's avalanche of urbanization. On the other hand, the mechanisms and criteria they introduce render their policies and programs, however far-sighted, sterile and counter-productive. It therefore becomes an urgent necessity to find a new style of government, sensitive to the complexities of contemporary urban problems, to the pitfalls of long distance, telegraphic administration, to the capabilities of modern municipal administrations, and to the participatory requirements of our evolving democracy.

It is not possible to prescribe with any assurance what the new style should be. By juxtaposing experience to the policy process, though, what is suggested is an approach that would emphasize the following principles: agreement on objectives, general strategies and funding by the governments concerned; delivery and administration of programs within agreed financial limits, by relevant public bodies close to the scene of concern and activity: regional and local governments, or inter-governmental corporations; involvement of community groups, through arrangements varying with local circumstances, in the formulation and implementation of specific strategies; and monitoring, evaluation, feedback, periodic review and change of policies by the provincial and federal governments.

What we are asking for, in the interest of freeing the creative potential of government, is a major retreat from processes of heavy bureaucratic supervision of urban programs, involving two or more levels of government. Canadians as consumers of public services will have to recognize that there are many policy areas affecting the distribution, form and quality of settlement—policies related to such things as land, housing, transportation, utilities, neighbourhood improvement, or new communities—that will legitimately involve the interests of municipalities, the provinces and the federal government. Canadians as providers of public services will have to recognize that passing papers up and down the jurisdictional staircase, in a sequence of approvals and counter-approvals, is a costly soul-destroying process that can grind large parts of the system to a halt.

Changing the style of governing will take a new measure of maturity, but the trade-offs in the way of greater productivity and rationalization of roles should more than offset imagined losses of control. One of the by-products of the new style would be the releasing of provincial and federal governments to concentrate on public policy issues appropriate to their place in the total government system. In urban policy, these would be issues related to the broad development patterns: the structure of population and employment and services, and of the underlying financial allocations and industrial strategies, that reverberate on the entire urban system.

Looking at this matter of governing with some historical perspective brings us to a concept advanced by Humphrey Carver, the author who for all his genuinely modest disavowals was head of the CMHC brains trust for a dozen of its formative years, 1955 to 1967.[30] Looking back, Carver characterizes the evolution of government's concern with housing and urban affairs as a succession of three phases: the period of *Innocence and Authority*, immediately after World War II when "authoritative forms of management" were adopted to overcome monumental backlog needs resulting from the years of depression and war; a decade of *Expanding Horizons*, 1955 to 1967, when a "new intellectual-professional élite" had considerable success in deepening and broadening policy concepts, from a concern with house-building to the stresses and satisfactions of cities and regions: and then to the present, a time of *Turbulence*, in which a new generation has challenged the established top-down devices while searching for new forms of participatory government. In expressing appreciation for the current critical mood, Carver observes sagely that "somehow the new urban society must itself take over the organs of the state and make them work."[31]

Looking at the evolution of policy and government in this way, we cannot resist the observation that Canadian urban policies are unfulfilled – as a nation we are still attempting to carry over into the age of turbulence, the attitudes and styles of government from the old authoritarian days. The adjustment we make to the demands of our own time may determine whether the chronicler of 2000 A.D. will characterize our period as the age of *Wisdom and Mature Democracy*, or of *Mismanagement and Misguided Authority*.

Notes

1. James W. Simmons, *Canada: Choices in a National Urban Strategy*. Research Paper No. 70 (Toronto: University of Toronto, Centre for Urban and Community Studies, 1975), pp. 11 and 12.
2. C. D. Burke and D. J. Ireland, "An Urban/Economic Development Strategy for the Atlantic Region," draft of an Urban Prospects paper prepared for the Ministry of State for Urban Affairs, dated August 20, 1975, 7.1.1, 7.1.5, 7.1.6 and 7.1.18; the revised version has been published under the same title (Ottawa: Information Canada, 1976), Cat. No. SU32—3/1976—6.
3. Note the review of national settlement strategies by L. S. Bourne, which indicates a policy trend that "looks at all cities and regions as interdependent entities." L. S. Bourne, "Conceptual Issues in Designing and Evaluating Strategies for National Urban Settlement Systems," (Paper for a conference on National Settlement Strategies for East and West, IIASA, Schloss, Luxemburg, 1974), based on research for the Ministry of State for Urban Affairs and submitted in August 1973.
4. This section relies heavily on R. W. Crowley, "Population Distribution: Perspectives and Policies," *Internal Migration: A Comparative Perspective*, A. Brown and E. Neuberger (eds.), (New York: Academic Press, 1976); R. W. Crowley, "Reflections and Further Evidence on Population Size and Industrial Diversification," *Urban Studies*, Vol. 10, 1973, pp. 91 – 94; and J. J. Spengler, "On Regulating the Size of Cities," Discussion Paper B.73.29 (rev.) (Ottawa: Ministry of State for Urban Affairs, 1973).
5. J. Wolpert, "Migration as an Adjustment to Environmental Stress," *Journal of Social Issues*, Vol. 22, No. 4, 1966, pp. 92 – 102.
6. Gordon Cameron, "Constraining the Growth in Employment of London, Paris and Randstad—A Study of Methods" (Paris: OECD, Environment Directorate, 1973), U/CHG 73.4.72.
7. J. L. Sundquist, *Dispersing Population: What America Can Learn From Europe* (Washington: Brookings Institute, 1975).
8. R. W. Crowley, "A Case Study of the Effects of An Airport on Land Values," *Journal of Transport Economics and Policy*, Vol. 7 (1973), pp. 144 – 152.
9. L. S. Bourne, *Limits to Urban Growth: Who Benefits, Who Pays, Who Decides? A Commentary on the Current Planning Climate in Toronto*, Research Paper No. 68 (Toronto: University of Toronto, Centre for Urban and Community Studies, 1975).
10. Spengler, *op. cit.*
11. T. N. Brewis, *Regional Economic Policies in Canada* (Toronto: Macmillan Company of Canada Limited, 1969).
12. D. Michael Ray, *Dimensions of Canadian Regionalism* (Ottawa: Information Canada, 1969).
13. Cameron, *op. cit.*
14. Sundquist, *op. cit.*, pp. 143-144.
15. L. Rodwin, *Nations and Cities* (Boston: Houghton Mifflin Company, 1970).
16. John Friedmann, *Regional Development Policy* (Cambridge, Massachusetts: The Massachusetts Institute of Technology Press, 1966), p. XVI.
17. Maurice Yeates, *Main Street: Windsor to Quebec City* (Toronto: Macmillan Company of Canada Limited in association with the Ministry of State for Urban Affairs and Information Canada, 1975), p. 345.
18. Leonard O. Gertler, *Making Man's Environment: Urban Issues* (Toronto: Van Nostrand Reinhold, 1976).
19. "Canada needs a national land-use policy," statement by the Honourable Jeanne Sauvé, Minister of Environment Canada, on the occasion of National Environment Week, October 5—11, 1975; and Ontario Institute of Agrologists, *Foodland, Preservation or Starvation*, June 23, 1975, pp. 13 and 14.

20. News release on a statement by the Honourable Jeanne Sauvé, Minister of Environment Canada, October 7, 1975.
21. Douglas W. Hoffman, "The Disappearing Farmland of Ontario," *The Bulletin of the Conservation Council of Ontario*, October 1975, pp. 10 and 11; and Len Gertler, Ian Lord and Audrey Stewart, "Canadian Planning: The Regional Perspective," *Plan Canada*, 15/2 (September 1975), p. 76.
22. Hoffman, *op. cit.*, pp. 10 and 11.
23. Ontario Institute of Agrologists, *Foodland, Preservation or Starvation*, pp. 5, 24 and 25.
24. Reg McLemore, Carl Aass and Peter Keilhofer, *The changing Canadian inner city*, Urban Paper A.75.3 (Ottawa: Ministry of State for Urban Affairs, 1975), p. 10.
25. *Ibid.*, pp. 5–9 and 10–13.
26. Brad Hodgins, "Neighbourhood Improvement Program," briefing paper (Waterloo: University of Waterloo, School of Urban and Regional Planning, 1975), p. 2; and *National Housing Act*, Office Consolidation, R.S., c. N-10, amended by 1973, C.18, Part III.1.
27. Data assembled by Central Mortgage and Housing Corporation, Neighbourhood and Residential Improvement Division, and provided to the authors by the Ministry of State for Urban Affairs.
28. These are the criteria which were set up by Central Mortgage and Housing Corporation after the NIP legislation came into effect in the summer of 1973.
29. D'Arcy Goldrick, "Criteria for Federal/Provincial Aid to Municipalities for Neighbourhood Improvements," brief by the City of Toronto regarding NIP Procedures, adopted by the Committee on Urban Renewal, Housing, Fire and Legislation, City of Toronto (Toronto: September 18, 1974); and "South of Carlton NIP Saga," brief to the Honourable Barney Danson, former Minister of State for Urban Affairs, by the South of Carlton Working Committee, Toronto, April 1975.
30. Humphrey Carver, *Compassionate Landscape* (Toronto and Buffalo: University of Toronto Press, 1975), pp. 192–194.
31. *Ibid.*, p. 194.

Index

Absentee owners, 157, 290
Action Program (see also *GVRD*), 180-81
Advanced Concepts Centre, Environment Canada, 403
Age of migrants, 74
Agricultural land (see also *Farmland*), 99-100, 101, 278-79, 424
Agricultural Land Reserves, 295
Alberta Development Corridor, 352
Alberta Land Use Forum, 283
Alternatives to settlement, 350
American investment, 156
Amherst, N.B., 193
Apartment, 339, 340; caging effect, 339, 340
Arable land, 29
Atlantic region; Amherst, 193; Bridgewater, 193; development strategy, 193; Fredericton, 193; *Growth Centres in Atlantic Canada*, 213; Halifax-Dartmouth, 193; Moncton, 193; New Glasgow, 193; Saint John, 193; Truro, 193; urban-industrial core, 193
Automobile, social costs, 362

Birney, Earle, 319
Birth rate, 54
Blumenfeld, Hans, 361
Booth, Alan, 326, 327, 329
Boulding, Kenneth, 99
Brandon, Man., 285
Bridgewater, N.S., 193
British Columbia, Fraser Valley, 283
British Columbia Land Commission, 101

Bunge, W., 98
Burin Peninsula, Nfld., 259
Burrs, Mick, 311
Burton, T. L., 262

Caging effects (see also *Apartment*), 339, 340
Calgary, Alta., 90, 293, 303
Canada (see also *Canadian cities*); cities, 418, 423; Commission of Conservation (1911-21); 326; demographic characteristics, 51; development axis, 352; economic structure, 110; future, 403; government system, 410; growth centres, 185; heartland, 134; immigration to, 57-58; inner city, 359; mid-Canada, 419; migration from, 64, 66; multi-national corporations, 110; optimum city, 364, 366, 367; population, 84; spatial patterns, 51; style of governing, 455, 456; urban, 21-22, 24, 124, 160, 260, 415, 417, 418; urban development, 415; urban future, 418; urban growth, 351; urban systems, 124-31, 417; 2001, 84
Canada Land Inventory, 101
Canadian cities, biggest, 418; small and medium sized, 418; "a spirit of place," 423
Canadian Pacific Railway, 185
Car culture, 361
Careless, J. M., 139
Carver, Humphrey, 97, 455
Central Mortgage and Housing Corporation, 454
Central Ontario Lakeshore Urban Complex, 278
Centre for Settlement Studies, University of Manitoba, 254
Chan, Shirley, 341
Change, 408
Characteristics of demography, 51
Children and Space, 335
Cimon, Jean, 231
City; Canadian, 418, 423; city-forming activities, 133; Compact Highly Centralized, 31; contemporary, 386; core, 363; downtown, 363, 392; hinterland, 139; institutions, 308; large, 403; lifestyles, 308; Low Density Spread Out, 31; medium-sized, 90; metropolitan agglomerations, 51; metropolitan dominance, 308; open, 31, 32, 405, 406, 407, 408, 409; optimum form, 364, 366, 367; optimum population, 434; peripheral, 162; places for people, 416; preferences, 304; Primate, 48; quality of life, 347; region, 353; regional, 98; size, 97; system, 121
Colombo, John Robert, 317
Commercial elites, 152
Commercial projects, 159

Commission of Conservation (1911-21), 326
Communications, 31, 258, 397, 407, 428, 429
Community, 308, 402, 419, 422; clusters related and interacting, 419
Company town, 148
Connors, Stompin' Tom, 380
Controls, location of employment, land use, building, 438
Convivial society, 404
Core; city, 190, 363; Toronto, 149; urban, 179; urban-industrial, 193
Corporations; decision-making elites, 153; development conglomerates, 292, 293; elites, 112, 154; inertia, 150; job-providing organizations, 144; land development, 292; multi-functional, 143; multi-locational, 146; multi-national, 110, 146; New Brunswick Multiplex Corporation, 147, 188; post-industrial, 143; power, 144-45, 147; structures, 144
Countryside, 100, 278
Country residents, 287, 289; families, 289
Crombie, David, 319
Crowding; effects, 328; family relations, 328; household objective, 327; household subjective, 327; objective neighbourhood, 327; stress disease, 328; subjective neighbourhood, 327
Crowley, R. W., 136
Culture, 32, 408

Dansereau, Pierre, 368
Dawson Creek, 197
Death rate, 56
Decision-making elites, 153
Declining areas, 324
Demography; characteristics, 51; processes, 83; structure, 84
Department of Regional Economic Expansion (DREE), 151, 185, 188, 214, 441; General Development Agreement, 185
Desires, 368
Development; Alberta Development Corridor, 352; in Atlantic region, 193; Canadian development axis, 352; conglomerates, 293; corporations, 292; firm, 295; land, 290, 292; massive redevelopment, 334; models, 207, 214; package, 290; planning process, 419; regional, 26, 214, 419, 439; resource, 27; strategy, 193
Disparities; income, 117; regional, 25, 112, 117, 146
Downtown; city cores, 363; conferences and conventions, 363; renewal, 392
Doxiadis, C.A., 40
Dubos, René, 40, 219
Dudek, Louis, 313
Duvall, Donna, 326

Economy, 110, 140, 148, 153, 156-57, 351, 415; economic base, 140; economic growth, 415; economic power, 153; "economic shadow," 156-57; economic structure, 110; specialization, 140; urban, 148, 351; urbanization, 148

Edmonton, 27, 90, 224, 293, 303, 356, 374, 402; County of Parkland, 287; McCauley Plaza, 356; petrochemical industry, 374; University of Alberta, 374

Education of migrants, 74-75

Elites, 112, 152, 153, 154, 159

Employment, 31, 355, 438

Environment; early, 398; diversity, 423; quality of, 218, 424; sensitive, 295; urban, 27, 33, 218, 400

Erin Mills, Ont., 359

Evaluation, 428, 429

Exurbanites, 28-29, 268, 282, 296

Family; country residents, 287, 289; income, 116; mobility cycle, 30, 333; relations, 328

Farmland (see also *Agricultural land*), 278-79, 424; agroclimatically, 278; yields, 279

Fertility rate, 54

Flexibility, 32, 398, 422

Foreign initiatives, 157, 159

Forms; settlement, 33, 348, 421, 431; urban, 30, 354

Fort Nelson, 200

Fort St. John, 197

Franck, Albert, 319

Fraser valley, 283

Fredericton, N.B., 193, 234

Freidmann, John, 147, 150, 151

Frye, Northrop, 312

Fuller, Buckminster, 40

Genstar, 293

Georgia Strait urban region, 352

Glassco, John, 314

Gottman, Jean, 355

Government system, 410

Grande Prairie, Alta., 195, 197

Gras, N. S. B., 139

Greater Vancouver Regional District (GVRD), 174-75, 180-82; action program, 180-82

Groesbeck, Amy, 314

Growth; centres, 185, 213; economic, 415; population, 415; rates, 420; urban, 162, 351, 420

Growth Centres in Atlantic Canada, 213
Growth centre strategy, 440

Habitat conference, 308
Halifax-Dartmouth, N.S., 127, 193, 285
Hamilton, 27, 230, 283; Hamilton Regional Conservation Authority, 230; Jackson Square, 383; steel, 383
Hamilton Regional Conservation Authority, 230
Haworth, Lawrence, 308, 310
Heartland, 111, 112, 134, 157
High-rise, 30
Hill, Polly, 335
Hinterland, 111, 112, 139, 157
Home ranges, 337
Household; formation, 92-93, 95; objective, 327; subjective, 327
Housing, 31, 257, 357, 424; density, 31; multiple forms, 357
Human settlement, 27, 31

Imagined future, 432
Immigration, 51, 57-58
Income; disparities, 117; family, 116; per capita, 116
Inner city, 30, 322, 324, 329, 332, 334, 341, 359, 449, 451, 453; CMHC, 454; decline, 30; declining areas, 324; four basic types, 322; massive redevelopment, 30, 334; policies, 451; policy research, 449; revitalization, 30; revitalizing areas, 332; stable residential districts, 329; stability, 30; senior governments, 453; strategies, 449
Innis, Harold, 105-06
Innovation, 150-51
Institutions, 30, 308
Integration, 31-32, 397, 408
Inter-industry linkages, 140
International airport (St. Scholastique), 361
Inter-urban transportation, 360
Investment; American, 156; real estate, 159
Irrigation, 372
Izumi, Kiyo, 218, 346

Jarvis, George K., 325
Job-providing organizations, 144
Johnson, D. R., 326
Journey to work, 360
Juvenile delinquency, 325

Katz, Gertrude, 314

Labour force, 95
Lampard, E. E., 138
Land; absentee ownership, 290; acquisition, 299; agricultural, 99-100, 101; arable, 29; British Columbia Land Commission, 101; Canada Land Inventory, 101; as a commodity, 100; controls, 438; countryside, 101, 278; development, 290, 292; development corporations, 292; farmland, 278-79, 424; heartland, 111, 112, 134, 157; heartland-hinterland, 111, 112, 157; hinterland, 111, 112, 139, 157; land-use policy, 446; market, 296; monopoly, 295; multi-level strategy, 447; national land-use policy, 446; ownership and development, 293; policy experience, 447; prices, 290, 293, 295; public policy, 444; real estate market, 100, 293; as a resource, 100; tax delinquent, 293; use, 29, 438
Large cities, 403
Laurentian University, 380
Layton, Irving, 317-18
Lee, Dennis, 318
Leisure, 31, 309, 362, 367
Leyton, Elliott, 259
Lifestyle, 29-30, 308, 309, 368; communal, 309; individual, 309
Livingstone, Ken, 316
London, Ont., 325
Lower Fraser valley, 221
Lowry, I.S., 77
Lucas, Alex, 257

MacNeill, J. W., 41
Market, 142, 296; accessibility, 142; thresholds, 142
Marshall, J. V., 135
Massive redevelopment, 30, 334
Mathews, R. D., 316
Mawson, T. H., 378
Maxwell, J. W., 134
McLennan, Hugh, 312
Mental mapping, 335
Messinger, Harley B., 325
Metropolis, 148
Metropolitan; agglomeration, 51; areas, 37, 40, 48, 51, 72, 90, 305, 308, 352; dominance, 308; in-migrants, 72; metropolitan region, 352; migration, 72
Michelson, William, 333, 334
Mid-Canada, 419
Migrants (see also *Migration*); Age, 74; Education, 74-75; Occupation, 74-75; Occupational structure, 75; sex, 74

Migration (see also *Migrants*), 53, 64, 66, 67, 71, 72, 78, 439, 440; to metropolitan areas, 72; net population, 53; policies, 440; population, 53, 64, 66, 67, 71; process, 438; streams of, 71, 78
Miller, Malcolm, 315
Minister of State for Urban Affairs, Ottawa, 429
Minister of Treasury, Economics and Intergovernmental Affairs, Ontario, 430
Mobile homes, 372
Modes of transportation, 31
Moncton, N.B., 193, 234
Monopoly, 295
Montreal, 72, 90, 127, 293, 329-30, 332, 363; Centre Sud, 329-30, 332; Hochelaga, 329-30, 332; Montreal Urban Community, 332
Montreal Urban Community, 332
Multi-functional corporations, 143
Multi-level strategy, 447
Multi-locational corporations, 146
Multi-national corporations, 146
Mumford, Lewis, 98
Muncaster, R., 129

National Housing Act, 212, 295, 342, 410; New Communities, 410
National land-use policy, 446
National policy, 111
National structure, 431
National urban pattern, 33
Needs, 368
Neighbourhood, 190, 310, 327, 341, 402; Neighbourhood Improvement Programme, 341; objective neighbourhood, 327; subjective neighbourhood, 327
Neighbourhood Improvement Programme (NIP), 190, 341, 453, 454; in Toronto, 454
New Brunswick, Community Planning Act (1972), 185-86
New Brunswick Multiplex Corporation, 147, 188
New communities, 212
New Glasgow, N.S., 193
Newlove, John, 312
New towns' policy, 442
Niagara escarpment, 230
North Saskatchewan valley, 374
Nova Scotia, 163

Objective neighbourhood, 327
Objectives of policy, 25, 29, 102

Occupation of migrants, 74-75
Okanagan valley, 221, 372
Old Quebec, 386
Ontario Parkway Belt, 445
Open city, 31, 32, 405, 406, 407, 408, 409; anathema, 409; change, 408; communication, 407; culture, 408; integration, 408; protection, 407; resources, 405; urban ethic, 406
Open space, 31, 275, 362, 367
Open Space Conservancy, 276
Optimum city, 364, 366, 367
Optimum population, 434, 436
Optimum population distribution, 436
Ottawa, Sandy Hill, 332
Owner-builder, 293

Palmer, J. R., 163
Palys, T. S., 250
Parc des Laurentides, 231
Parson, G. F., 147
Patterns, urban, 24, 26, 33
Peace River District, 26-27, 193, 195, 197, 202, 206, 208, 210-11; Grande Prairie, 195, 197; *Patterns for the Future*, 206; Peace River-Liard Regional District, 202; Peace River Regional Planning Commission, 202; Regional Incentives Act, 210-11; regional plan, 206; resource development, 27; south-central bowl, 210; structural policy, 208
Peace River-Liard Regional District, 202, 210
Peace River Regional Planning Commission, 202
Penticton, B.C., 27, 221, 372; irrigation, 372; mobile homes, 372
Per capita income, 116
Peripheral city, 162
Planning; national scale, 298; process, 419; regional development, 444; urban, 353
Poetschke, L. E., 120
Policy; approaches, 298; countervaillants, 437; efficiency, 102; equity, 102; experience, 447; of the inner city, 451; intervention, 437; issues, 445, 455; land use, 446; migration, 440; national, 111; new towns' policy, 442; objectives, 25, 29, 102; process, 426, 428, 429, 430; public, 260, 444; research, 29, 261, 449; settlement, 211; variable, 354, 355, 356, 360, 362
Policy intervention, countervaillants, 437
Policy issues, 445, 455; cost and equity, planning and control, preservation and use, 445
Policy process, 426, 428, 429, 440; action, 428; communication, 428,

429; evaluation, 428, 429; of migration, 440
Policy variable, 354, 355, 356, 360, 362, 367; employment and services, 355; open space and leisure, 362, 367; residential density and distribution, 356; transportation system, 360
Pollution, 256
Population, 23, 28-29, 35-36, 41, 43, 51, 53, 54, 56, 57, 64, 66, 67, 71, 72, 78, 84, 85, 88, 90, 92-93, 95, 268, 282, 296, 400, 415, 434, 436; aged sixty-five and over, 400; ageing 57; birth rate, 54; of Canada, 84; death rate, 56; exurbanite, 28-29, 268, 282, 296; growth, 415; household formation, 92-93, 95; labour force, 95; metropolitan areas, 72, 90; migration, 64, 66, 67, 71; migration streams, 71, 78; in Montreal, 72, 90; natural increase, 51, 67; net migration, 53; optimum 434; optimum distributions, 436; projections, 85, 88, 90; rate of exponential increase, 35-36; in Toronto, 72, 90; urban, 41, 43; in Vancouver, 72, 90
Porter, John, 153
Post-industrial corporations, 143
Poverty, 326
Power, corporate, 144-45, 147
Prairie capital, 378
Pred, A. R., 146, 147, 160
Preston, Richard E., 123-24, 354
Primate city, 48
Process; of demography, 83; of migration, 438; of urbanization, 351, 430, 432
Professionalism, 309
Protection, 397, 407
Public intervention, 164
Public policy, 260, 444
Public Policy Issues, 445, 455
Purdy, Al, 312

Quality of environment, 218, 424
Quality of life, 218, 251, 254, 347
Quebec City, 27, 101, 163, 231, 386-87; contemporary city, 386; Grande-Allée, 386, Old Quebec, 386

Railway Relocation and Crossing Act (1974), 226, 354-55
Ray, D. M., 120, 142, 146, 156, 173
Reany, James, 316-17
Real estate; investment, 159; market, 100, 293
Recreation, 257, 424; landscapes, 424
Red Deer, Alta., 293
Regina, Sask., 27, 226, 378

Regional; city, 98; development, 26, 214, 419, 439, 444; development planning, 444; diagnosis, 261; disparities, 25, 112, 117, 146; diversity, 419; growth pole, 174; municipality, 380; plan for Peace River, 206; systems, 24; town centres, 26, 175, 176-79, 182-83
Regional development, 26, 214, 419, 439, 444; planning, 444; in Western Europe, 439
Regional development model, 214
Regional Incentives Act, 210-11
Residential; density and distribution, 356; desirability, 302; preference patterns, 303
Residential Rehabilitation Assistance Programme (RRAP), 190
Resources, development, 27; frontier, 443; frontier regions, 443; land, 100; open city, 405; system needs, 31; throughput, 397; towns, 28, 251, 254, 256-58, 263
Resource frontier, regions, strategy, 443
Resource towns, 28, 251, 254, 256-58, 263; communications, 258; housing, 257; pollution, 256; quality of life, 251, 254; recreation, 257; townsite planning, 256
Richler, Mordecai, 311
Riffel, Anthony, 254
Rural-urban movement, 71
Russwurm, L. H., 129
Russwurm, Lorne, 269

Safdie, Moshe, 217-18
Saint John, N.B., 26, 28, 184-86, 188, 190, 192, 193, 231, 234, 392; Canadian growth centre, 185; city core, 190; Comprehensive Community Plan, 186; containerization, 186; downtown renewal, 392; Multiplex Ltd., 188; in the nineteenth century, 392; Neighbourhood Improvement Programme (NIP), 190; regional development in, 26; regional growth pole, 184-85, 188; Residential Rehabilitation Assistance Programme (RRAP), 190; Rodney terminal, 188; Saint John River, 234; tri-level committee, 192
Saint John River, 234
Saskatoon, Sask., 293
Sensitive environments, 295
Services, 31, 355
Settlement, 27, 31, 33, 211, 347, 348, 349, 350; alternatives, 350; form of, 33, 348, 421, 431; human, 27, 31; policy, 211; structure, 349
Sex of migrants, 74
Simmons, J.W., 110, 121, 129
Single enterprise towns, 251
Small city, 148
Smith, Douglas, 335

INDEX 469

Social indicators, 235-36, 249
Social conflict and stress, 296
Society for the Preservation of Great Places, 359
Socio-economic status, 320, 326
Souster, Raymond, 313
Southern Ontario, 47, 136, 157, 282, 285; urban fringe-urban shadow landscape, 285
Spatial interdependencies, 149
Spengler, J., 161
Stable residential districts, 329
Statistics Canada Population Model, 85
Stewart, Gail, 311
Stored collective criteria, 398
Strategies, 193, 432, 434, 443, 447, 449; of big cities, 432; of development, 193; of inner city, 449; of medium-sized cities, 432; multilevel, 447; resource frontier, 443; of small cities, 434
Streams of migration, 71, 78
Structure; of demography, 84; of settlement, 349; urban, 30, 354
Style of governing, 455, 456
Subjective neighbourhood, 327
Sudbury, Ont., 27, 226, 380; landscape, Laurentian University, regional municipality, 380
System (see also *System needs*); in Canada, 417; cities, 121; living or self-maintaining, 397; regional, 24, 98; transportation, 31; urban, 25, 40, 120, 124-31, 417
System needs (see also *System*), 31-32, 397-98, 409; communication, 31, 397; culture, 32; flexibility, 32, 398; integration, 31-32, 397; protection, 31, 397; resources, 31; resource throughput, 397; stored collective criteria, 398

Tax delinquent, 293
Thetford Mines, Que., 303
Thompson, Wilbur R., 151, 152, 161
Thunder Bay, Ont., 285
Toronto, 72, 90, 127, 141, 149, 327, 335, 363; annex area, 335; central core, 149; Toronto Geographical Expedition, 335
Toronto Geographical Expedition, 335
Town, Harold, 319
Towns, 26, 28, 148, 175, 176-79, 182-83, 251, 254, 256, 257, 258, 263, 309, 442; company, 148; new towns' policy, 442; resource towns, 28, 251, 254, 256, 257, 258, 263; single enterprise towns, 251; town centres, 26, 175, 176-79, 182-83
Town centres, 26, 175, 176-79, 182-83
Townsite planning, 256

Toynbee, Arnold, 20
Transportation, 31, 141, 360, 361, 421; choices, 421; inter-urban 360; intra-urban, 360; modes, 31; St. Scholastique international airport, 361; systems, 31, 360
Tri-level, urban affairs process, 430
Tri-level Conference, 430
Truro, N.S., 193

University of Alberta, 374
University of Toronto, 333
Urban (see also *Urbanization, Urban system*); benefits, 149; Canada, 21-22, 24, 124, 160, 415, 417, 418; choices, 343; core, 179; development in Canada, 415; diseconomies, 149; economies, 148, 351; environment, 27, 33, 218, 400; ethic, 406; field, 267, 268, 289; forms, 31, 354; fringe, 28, 268, 269, 285; future, 418; Georgia Strait urban region, 352; growth, 162, 351; growth rates, 420; images, 29; indicators, 262; literature, 30; patterns, 24, 26, 33; planning, 353; population, 41, 43; poverty, 326; renewal, 341; social indicators, 235-36, 249; structures, 30, 354; surroundings, 28, 279; systems, 25, 40, 120, 124-31, 136-38, 417; urban affairs process, 351, 430, 432; urban-industrial core, 193; urban program delivery, 452
Urban Affairs, Ministry of State for, 21, 163
Urban Canada, 21-22, 24, 124, 260; three broad views, 260
Urban environments, 27, 33, 218, 400; adolescent phase, mature adult, population aged sixty-five and over, young adult, 400
Urban indicators, three dangers: elitism, mechanicalism, managerialism, 262
Urban surroundings; exurbanite, 296; farmer, 297; social conflict and stress, 296
Urban system, 25, 40, 120, 124-31, 136-38, 417; in Canada 124-31, 417; controllability, 128; diversification, 136-37; Halifax, 127; hierarchy and dominance, 129; independence, 129-30; Montreal, 127; openness, 130-31; specialization, 137-38; structure, 131; Toronto, 127; Vancouver, 127; Winnipeg, 127
Urbanization (see also Urban), 20, 21-22, 37, 43, 47, 67, 136, 148, 351, 432; in British Columbia, 43; in Central Canada, 47; economies, 148; in the Maritime provinces, 47; in Ontario, 43; process, 351, 432; on the Prairies, 47; in Quebec, 43; in Southern Ontario, 47, 136

Values, 368
Vancouver, B.C., 26, 27, 72, 90, 127, 174-75, 176-79, 180-82, 221, 276, 283, 293, 303, 341, 363, 369; Greater Vancouver Regional District

(GVRD), 174-75, 180-82; liveable region, 221; mountains, 369; *Open Space Conservancy*, 276; regional town centres in, 26, 175, 176-79; sea, 369; Strathcona area, 341; Vancouver Urban Futures Project, 363
Victoria, B.C., 90, 303
Village, 309

Ward, Barbara, 40
Wascana Lake, 378
Weaver, Edith, 320
Westrede, 397
Windsor, Ont., 101, 163
Windsor-Quebec City corridor, 101, 163
Winnipeg, Man., 127, 303, 342; Winnipeg Home Improvement Project, 342
Work, 309

Yeates, Maurice, 445

Zipf, G. K., 48

Credits

Every reasonable care has been taken to trace ownership of copyright material. Information will be welcome which will enable the publisher to rectify any reference or credit.

Table 1.2 Population of Urban Centres by Size Group, Canada, 1901-71, from *A Statistical Profile of Canadian Society* by Daniel Kubat and David Thornton. Copyright ©McGraw-Hill Ryerson Limited 1974. Reprinted by permission.

Figure 4.2 Citizens' Views Regarding Population Growth in the Peace River District, Alberta; **Figure 4.3** Citizens' Views Regarding Environmental Quality in the Peace River District, Alberta; **Map 4.7** The Peace River Region in the Context of Western North America; **Map 4.8** Watersheds of the Peace River Region; **Map 4.9** The Disposition of Agricultural Land in the Peace River District, Alberta; **Map 4.10** Recreation Facilities and Areas: Present and Prospective, Peace River District, Alberta; **Map 4.11** Major Transportation Facilities of the Peace River – Liard; Peace River Regional Districts and the "South-Central Bowl"; and **Map 4.12** Summary of Structural Policy; Peace River Regional Plan, Alberta, reproduced courtesy of the Peace River Regional Planning Commission, Grande Prairie, Alberta.

Map 4.3 Transit and Regional Town Centres; and **Figure 4.1** Illustrative Regional Town Centre Development Management Process, Vancouver, from *Regional Town Centres: A Policy Report*, Greater Vancouver Regional District, reproduced by permission of Douglas Spaeth.

Map 4.4 Planning Regions and Planning Districts in New Brunswick, 1974, from the *Canadian Geographer*, reproduced by permission of Ralph R. Krueger.

Figure 6.1 Land in the Urban Fringe, A National Estimate by City Size; and **Figure 6.2** Distribution of Urban Fringe Land, by Province, reproduced by permission of L. H. Russwurm. From "The Urban Fringe as a Regional Environment," In L. R. G. Martin, R. E. Preston, and L. H. Russwurm, *Essays on Canadian Urban Process and Form*, Publication Series No. 7, Waterloo: Department of Geography, University of Waterloo, 1977.

Map 6.6 Thunder Bay, Selected Fringe Features, from B. E. Tamminen, "The Rural-Urban Fringe of the City of Thunder Bay, 1972," B. A. Thesis (Thunder Bay: Lakehead University, 1973), p. 29. (Copyright Lakehead University Department of Geography.)

Figure 8.16 City Farming. Reproduced by permission of the Community Planning Association of Canada, Planning Aid, Nova Scotia Division.

Excerpt from "Roller Skate Man" from *Colour of the Times/Ten Elephants on Yonge Street* by Raymond Souster. Reprinted by permission of McGraw-Hill Ryerson Limited.

For permission to reprint excerpt from "Klaxon" from *Poems* (copyright 1972) by James Reaney thanks are due to the author and New Press, Toronto.

Excerpt from *Civil Elegies and Other Poems*, Dennis Lee, House of Anansi Press, 1972. Reproduced by permission.

Excerpt from "A City That Looks Like Punched Metal Strips" by John Robert Colombo, in *Abracadabra* (Toronto: McClelland and Stewart Limited, 1967). Reproduced by permission.

Figure 8.9d, definite design by Alex Hermann, MRAIC, visualized by Joseph Skvaril, MRAIC, MCIP, AIP, SAR.